Sidney Painter

THE JOHNS HOPKINS UNIVERSITY

A HISTORY OF THE MIDDLE AGES

284-1500

MACMILLAN

First Edition 1953
Reprinted 1954, 1956, 1958, 1960, 1961,
1963, 1965, 1968, 1970

Published by
MACMILLAN AND CO LTD
Little Essex Street London WC2
and also Bombay Calcutta and Madras
Macmillan South Africa (Publishers) Pty Ltd Johannesburg
The Macmillan Company of Australia Pty Ltd Melbourne
The Macmillan Company of Canada Ltd Toronto
Gill and Macmillan Ltd Dublin

Printed in Great Britain by
LOWE AND BRYDONE (PRINTERS) LTD
London

Preface

WHEN the first modern historians of Europe surveyed the past of their civilization, they saw three great historical periods—Ancient times, which were for them essentially the era of Greece and Rome; their own period, which they called Modern; and the years that lay between, the Middle Ages. As their interest centered primarily in Western Europe, they were inclined to begin the Middle Ages in A.D. 476, with the death of the last Roman emperor to rule in the West. These historians had been educated in the classical tradition and were deeply impressed by the achievements of science. Hence it seemed clear to them that the Modern era began with the Renaissance, when classical studies were revived and modern science seemed to have its beginnings. Thus the period from A.D. 476 to the Renaissance comprised the Middle Ages. Needless to say, a period marked out in so casual a fashion was unlikely to have much cohesion. Soon it was generally recognized that the year 476 had no significance, and most scholars began the Middle Ages either with the accession of the Emperor Diocletian in A.D. 284 or with the beginning of the Germanic invasions. But in broad outline tradition has by now sanctified the basic concept of the Middle Ages as the period between ancient and modern times. This book begins with the accession of Diocletian and ends with the first sparks of the Renaissance.

If one examines the historical content of this period, one finds that it falls into three natural divisions. In the tenth, eleventh, and twelfth centuries a distinct and extremely fascinating civilization took shape. This civilization that we call mediaeval reached its height in the thirteenth century. Thus these four centuries form the core of any history of the Middle Ages. The six centuries from 300 to 900 were a period of transition from Roman to mediaeval civilization, and the fourteenth and fifteenth centuries saw the mediaeval change into the modern world. The first three chapters of this book should be regarded as introductory. One treats those features of the history of the Late Roman Empire that were of prime importance in the development of mediaeval civilization. Another traces briefly the story of the Byzantine Empire and its Greek Catholic culture. The third describes the formation of the Christian Western Europe in which mediaeval civilization was to develop. Nine chapters cover mediaeval civilization from the tenth to the fourteenth centuries, and two describe the decline of mediaeval institutions.

The chapters are rather long, since each is intended to cover a broad and significant historical process. Chronological arrangement of events has been subordinated to the development of these major topics. Moreover, the various aspects of the history of states and individuals are sometimes scattered in different chapters. In order to minimize the disadvantages of this method of organization cross references are provided for the reader, and numbered subsections allow the teacher to rearrange the material to suit his own taste.

It is obviously impossible for the author of a general history to express specifically his gratitude to the scholars from whose works he has obtained his information or to the friends, colleagues, and students from whom he has drawn ideas and suggestions. He can, however, acknowledge his debt to the books that were used regularly for reference purposes during the actual preparation of the manuscript. William L. Langer's *Encyclopedia of World History* is a great boon to the writer who wants a fact in a hurry, and I used it continuously for this purpose. The *Cambridge Medieval History* was drawn upon heavily in areas where my knowledge was limited. Finally, the genealogies were taken largely from John L. La Monte, *The World of the Middle Ages*.

I also want to express my gratitude to Professor Peter Charanis of Rutgers University who read a large part of the manuscript, to Miss Lilly Lavarello, secretary to the Department of History of The Johns Hopkins University, who typed it, and to the entire staff of the College Department of Alfred A. Knopf, Inc., who have borne patiently with an author who always knows what he wants and wants it very decidedly.

SIDNEY PAINTER

Contents

Illustrations

Maps

BY THEODORE R. MILLER

A HISTORY OF THE MIDDLE AGES 284–1500

CHAPTER I

Roman and German

1. The Late Roman Empire
2. The Germanic Invasions

THE CIVILIZATION of Western Europe in the period generally known as the Middle Ages was a blend of the civilization of the Late Roman Empire and the civilizations of various peoples whom the Romans called barbarians. The term "Late Roman Empire" is used here to designate the state formed in the early fourth century by Diocletian and Constantine the Great. The institutions of the Roman Empire as founded by Augustus (31 B.C.–A.D. 14) had changed almost beyond recognition by the year 284, when Diocletian (A.D. 284–305) became emperor. He and his successor Constantine (A.D. 306–37) created a new empire that bore little resemblance to the old. It was the civilization of this new empire that merged with those of the barbarian peoples, chiefly Celts and Germans, to form mediaeval civilization. In this chapter we shall examine these civilizations, Roman, Celt, and German, as the background for the Middle Ages. No attempt will be made to describe them completely. We shall simply glance at those features that were to be of importance in the history of Western Europe during the Middle Ages.

1. The Late Roman Empire

IN GEOGRAPHICAL extent the empire ruled by Diocletian and Constantine differed but little from that of their predecessors. Its northernmost boundary was Hadrian's wall, which ran across Britain from the vicinity of Carlisle to that of Newcastle upon Tyne. From the North Sea to the Black Sea the line followed the rivers Rhine and Danube. From Trebizond on the south coast of the Black Sea to the Atlantic Ocean, the eastern and southern boundaries of the empire had no natural barriers. They enclosed the whole of Asia Minor and a strip of varying width along the eastern and southern coasts of the Mediterranean Sea, including what we now know as Syria, Palestine, Egypt, Tripoli, Tunis, Algeria, and Morocco. The empire was essentially a Mediterranean state—only in upper Egypt, northeastern Spain, northern Gaul, and Britain did any of its territory lie more than 250 miles from the shores of that great sea. Only Britain, northern Gaul, and the districts along the Danube lay outside what geographers describe as the Mediterranean region.

The political subdivision of the Late Roman Empire was extraordinarily complex. There were four great divisions called prefectures. The prefecture of Gaul included Britain, Gaul, Spain, and the district now known as Morocco. The prefecture of Italy covered the lands between the Danube and the Adriatic Sea, Italy, and the regions now known as Algeria, Tunis, and Tripoli. The prefecture of Illyria included Dacia, Macedonia, and Greece. The rest of the empire comprised the prefecture of the East. Below the prefectures were divisions called dioceses. Britain south of Hadrian's wall was the diocese of Britain. The diocese of Gaul was the territory of present-day France with its boundaries extended to the Rhine and the crest of the Alps. The diocese of Spain was modern Spain with Morocco. The diocese of Italy was modern Italy extended north to the upper Danube. North Africa from Morocco to Egypt comprised the diocese of Africa. As our chief interest lies in the western half of the empire, there is no need to list the dioceses of the prefecture of the East. The dioceses were divided into provinces. Thus there were four provinces in the diocese of Britain, fifteen in that of Gaul, and six in that of Spain. Finally there was the smallest political division: the *civitas*, or city, and the territory that depended on it. The Roman Empire was essentially an agglomeration of city-states; hence the city and its lands were its basic unit.

In theory, this great empire was ruled by two senior emperors called Augusti and two junior emperors called Caesars. Each Caesar was expected to act as the deputy of an Augustus, and to succeed him at his death. The imperial authority was not considered to be divided but rather to be enjoyed jointly by several persons. In practice, there

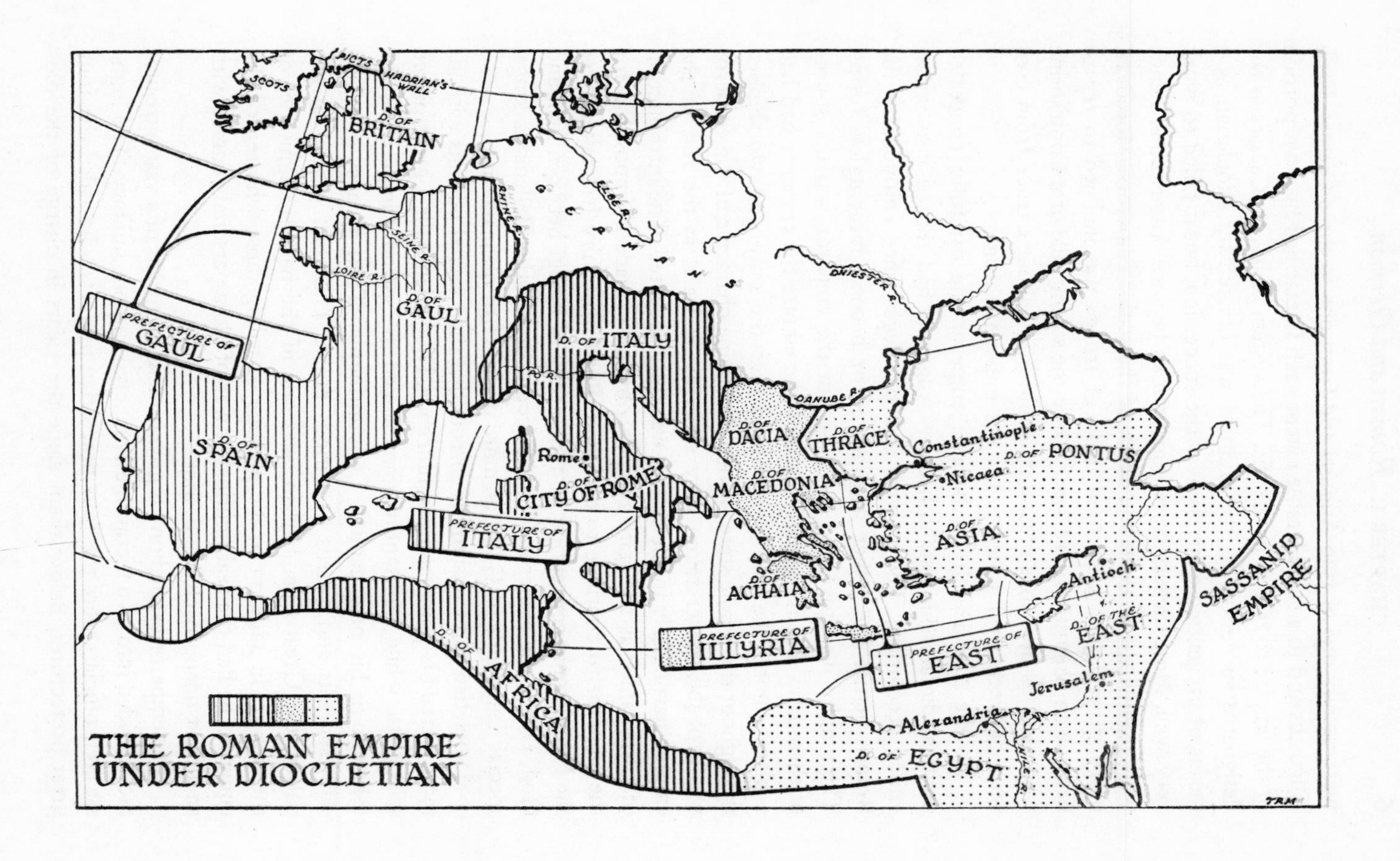
THE ROMAN EMPIRE
UNDER DIOCLETIAN
SCOTS
PICTS
HADRIAN'S WALL
D. OF BRITAIN
RHINE R.
ELBE R.
G E R M A N S
SEINE R.
LOIRE R.
D. OF GAUL
PREFECTURE OF GAUL
D. OF SPAIN
D. OF ITALY
PO R.
Rome
D. OF CITY OF ROME
PREFECTURE OF ITALY
D. OF AFRICA
DNIESTER R.
DANUBE R.
D. OF DACIA
D. OF MACEDONIA
D. OF ACHAIA
PREFECTURE OF ILLYRIA
D. OF THRACE
Constantinople
D. OF PONTUS
Nicaea
D. OF ASIA
Antioch
D. OF THE EAST
PREFECTURE OF EAST
Jerusalem
Alexandria
NILE R.
D. OF EGYPT
SASSANID EMPIRE
TRM

were usually one or two Augusti and from one to three Caesars. Each Augustus and to a considerable extent each Caesar had his own portion of the empire to rule as he saw fit. The system of having Caesars as the designated successors to the Augusti was created by Diocletian as a means of preventing quarrels over the succession, but it failed to work very well. Most Caesars were impatient to become Augusti and hence were disinclined to await the death of the senior emperors. Moreover, every general with a devoted body of troops was inclined to try to become an Augustus or a Caesar. Only the strong rule of a Constantine who used his own sons as Caesars could bring about a truce from civil wars between rival aspirants for the imperial throne.

By the time Diocletian became emperor the carefully concealed political dictatorship established by Augustus had turned into undisguised absolutism. The powers and privileges once enjoyed by the Roman Senate had either disappeared or become meaningless forms. The empire was governed by laws, but the emperor was the source of these laws. From the early days of the empire the emperor had had a place among the gods; he was in fact the only god worshipped throughout the whole state. While the divine character of the emperor was probably never taken very seriously in Italy, in the rest of the empire, particularly in the east, it was fully accepted. The introduction of Christianity as the state religion obviously made it impossible for the emperor to continue to be a god. But Christianity had taken over the Neoplatonic conception of a hierarchy of beings between man and God. Hence the emperors could become, as had the Hellenistic kings, special lieutenants of God, far more divine than ordinary men.

Diocletian and Constantine surrounded their sacred persons with almost incredible pomp and magnificence. Diocletian built a great palace at Spalato, while Constantine commenced the splendid imperial establishment in his new capital, Constantinople. Their palaces swarmed with servants and guards of various ranks. The chief official of the palace, the Great Chamberlain, was one of the highest dignitaries of the empire. In addition to the prestige of ruling those who served the emperor, he had the real political power of close personal contact with an almost unapproachable despot.

The emperor carried on his government by means of a vast bureaucracy divided into two hierarchies, one civil and one military. The highest civil officials were the four praetorian prefects who ruled the four great prefectures. Below them came the vicars in charge of the dioceses and the rectors or governors of the provinces. The central civil administration in Constantinople was divided into three departments each headed by a *magister* and combined under a *magister officiorum* who rivaled the praetorian prefects in dignity and power. These three departments had their local agents in the provinces. The military hierarchy was headed by two exalted officers: the master of the cavalry and the master of the infantry. The lower general officers who served as local commanders bore the title of *dux*, or duke. The legions were commanded by prefects.

Although the civil and military officials were the instruments for carrying out the commands of the emperor, the army was the basis of the imperial power. Whatever the theory may have been, in reality the man who had the loyalty of the army became emperor and could maintain his position as long as he kept the devotion of the troops. Moreover, the safety of the state from its external enemies depended on the army. The great emperors like Diocletian and Constantine were essentially good soldiers and able generals. *Imperator*, or emperor, a term that originally meant commander-in-chief, was the most important of the imperial titles. The army may be divided into three groups according to functions. There were two corps of imperial bodyguards whose duty it was to protect the person of the emperor. Then there was a mobile army ready to march to a threatened frontier or to combat a rebellion. Finally, there were the troops who watched the frontiers of the empire. The best estimate we have gives 250,000 infantry and 110,000 cavalry to the frontier troops, and 150,000 infantry and 46,000 cavalry to the mobile army; but it may be doubted that the army was actually so large. It is important to notice that a fair part of this army was composed of barbarians. Although the legions were still filled by drafts from the inhabitants of the empire, auxiliary forces, especially the cavalry, consisted largely of Germans. Sometimes these were bodies of German troops enlisted as individuals and commanded by Roman officers. But often a body of Germans was hired under its leader to defend the frontier of the empire. Germans also were enlisted in the imperial guard, and many rose to high rank as officers.

Relations between members of the bureaucracy, those between it and the people of the empire, and those among the people themselves were governed by the Roman Law. Since the earliest days of the Roman republic this law had been growing and changing to meet new conditions. It consisted of legislation by such bodies as the Senate, decisions made by judges, and decrees issued by the emperors. In the fourth century nearly all new legislation was by imperial edict. Thus over the centuries all the problems that arise when great multitudes of people live a civilized life together in a vast empire were settled by the Roman Law. It was to be many centuries later before questions arose for which it had no answer.

During the fourth and fifth centuries the law was modified in many respects to meet the demands of the new state religion, Christianity. Finally in the fifth and sixth centuries the Emperors Theodosius II (408–50) and Justinian (527–65) had this great mass of law drawn up in orderly form and published. The imperial legislation was collected into the Codes of Theodosius and Justinian. Then the mass of court decisions and opinions expressed by the writers of books on the law were collected in the Digest of Justinian. In both Code and Digest the law was organized into an orderly system. These careful descriptions of the legal institutions of the Roman Empire had great influence on the history of the Middle Ages.

The magnificent imperial palaces, the hordes of palace officials, servants, and guards, the vast bureaucracy, and the army were extremely expensive. Two Augusti and two Caesars burdened the state with four imperial establishments. Even if the officials had been honest, the cost of the empire to the people would have been very heavy. But it is clear that corruption was rampant and that even the most vigorous emperor could do little about it. The officials regularly extorted far more from the people under their rule than they passed on to their master the emperor. During the long period of almost continuous civil war between the death of Commodus and the accession of Diocletian, the coinage of the empire had been debased so often that the monetary system was in complete confusion. Hence Diocletian levied taxes in produce rather than in money. At the beginning of each year the emperor announced the rate of taxation for the year, and dates were commonly reckoned from these announcements. The taxes were collected by the chief citizens of the cities, the *curiales*, from whom the town officials were chosen. If these men were unable to collect the required amount from the people of the city and its dependent lands, they had to pay it themselves.

The weight of taxation and extortion might well have been bearable if the Empire had retained its early prosperity, but during the civil wars of the third century its economic condition had seriously deteriorated. The early empire had been an economic unit with an extensive flow of trade between the various parts. The civil wars had not only hampered trade directly but had also permitted the development of general disorder. Brigands menaced the roads and pirates the sea routes. By the time Diocletian ascended the throne, trade had declined and many provinces had little intercourse with the rest of the empire. All who lived by trade and industry were impoverished.

This situation created a serious problem for the imperial government, which had always relied heavily on services performed by various corporations or rather guilds. We have seen how the curiales, the upper classes in the towns, were held responsible for the collection of taxes. When the taxes could not be collected from the people, the curiales faced ruin. Their natural inclination was to desert their posts and try to make a living some other way. The government's answer was to make the position hereditary and forbid anyone to leave it. When shipowners found that they could not afford to carry out their duty of bearing grain to Rome and Constantinople for the government, they tried to enter other occupations, and they in turn were forbidden to do so. One by one the chief occupations of the empire were made hereditary and those engaged in them were forbidden to change.

Thus the government's attempts to solve its economic problems led to a rigid stratification of society. Many men were bound forever to the position held by their fathers. Another result was the gradual destruction of the middle class. As the demands of the government grew heavier and heavier, ruin overtook the groups on which the burden rested most heavily—the men with some property but with little political influence. But the same forces that impoverished the middle class elevated the aristocracy.

It is difficult to find a term that will describe accurately the upper classes of the Late Roman Empire. Though the aristocrats were not all senators, it is perhaps easiest to call them the senatorial class. It was essentially composed of high officials and their descendants. Its members were dignified by a marvelous array of honorary appellations such as *vir clarissimus*. A senator usually owned a vast estate that was outside the jurisdiction of the city governments. In theory he paid taxes directly to the imperial government; in practice he was probably able to avoid many of them. His lands were worked by men called *coloni*. Each *colonus* had a piece of land for which he paid rent in money, produce, or service. Imperial law forbade him to leave this land. Some of the coloni were the descendants of slaves who had been technically freed but kept as workers on their master's land. Others were small free farmers who had given up their land to avoid the burden of taxation. Finally many senators imported Germans from beyond the frontiers and settled them as coloni on their estates.

In short, the Late Roman Empire had a small upper class that had both wealth and political influence. The members of this class lived in beautiful houses in the midst of their vast estates. They were surrounded by servants and slaves. Many of them even had private bodyguards, often composed of Germans hired for the purpose. Below them the old middle class was rapidly disappearing and its members were falling to a status little better than that of the coloni who worked the senatorial estates. This lower class, in turn, which formed the largest part of the empire's population, was becoming mixed with recently imported barbarians.

When one leaves the political, economic, and social institutions of the Late Roman Empire and approaches those aspects of its civilization that are generally called cultural, the subject becomes extremely complex. The original Roman genius had been essentially military and political. It had developed an invincible army, an effective government, and a great body of law. But the ideas, inspirations, and models for most of its literature and art had come from the Hellenistic East. While in its golden age Latin literature had reached a high point, it had never been essentially Roman in its nature. The Roman army had conquered the Mediterranean world, but her language and culture had been far less successful. The eastern half of the Empire had remained basically Greek in all its cultural aspects. The Romans had supplied the Hellenistic world with new political institutions, but its general culture remained untouched. Thus Latin culture, which was in itself largely a development of the Greek, had little influence in the most advanced half of the Empire. It could disappear without seriously affecting the general cultural level.

In the West the peoples conquered by the Roman armies had little culture of their own. Latin became for them the language of literature and learning as well as of politics. What they obtained from the cultural heritage of the ancient world came to them through Latin. The extent to which Latin culture seeped into the mass of the population differed widely from region to region. In Gaul and Spain vernacular Latin—the language actually spoken by the Romans, which had in the course of time become quite different from the written form—supplanted the various native tongues. In Britain this transformation apparently did not take place. But even in the regions where Latin became the spoken language only a small part of the population can have had any real command of Latin culture. The pursuit of learning and the enjoyment of literature require education and leisure that only the upper classes can have had. Under the early Empire the prosperous middle class such as the curiales of the towns probably were in this educated group. Their destruction must have left Latin culture in the care of the senators and their households.

By the fourth century pagan Latin culture was no longer creative. The senators and members of their entourages read and studied the authors of the Golden Age and used them as models in their own writings. The writers of the fourth century were storehouses of classical culture, but they did little with their heritage beyond respecting it and preserving it. By the fifth century most of the men who were supposed to be educated could not easily understand the more difficult works of the ancients, and textbooks and simple guides were prepared for them by the few remaining men of real learning.

While in most respects the Late Roman Empire was a time of decline, in the field of religion it was a period of immense vitality. Perhaps there is truth in the generalization so frequently made that in times of political and economic confusion men's minds turn to things spiritual. Be that as it may, the third and fourth centuries saw the rapid spread not only of Christianity but of many pagan cults. The ancient Roman religion had had a very slight emotional content. A man performed the traditional proper services for the gods so that they would favor his own projects. Religion was largely a matter of scrupulously keeping a business bargain. The same was apparently true of the religions of the western peoples conquered by the Romans. The Roman religion had never been exclusive. The gods worshipped by Gauls and Britons were either identified with similar Roman gods or simply added to the heavenly galaxy. Rome itself was filled with gods of foreign origin. All these gods, general and local, were served with due formality but with little or no religious enthusiasm.

This enthusiasm that is for many men such an important element of religion was supplied by various cults imported from the East. The most important of these were the cults of Cybele from Asia Minor, of Mithras from Persia, and of Isis from Egypt. While these cults, commonly called mystery religions, differed greatly from one another, they all had certain general features in common. Each one initiated new members by an elaborate and impressive ceremony. Each had rites that were participated in by all initiates. These rites were dramatic and calculated to arouse a religious enthusiasm bordering sometimes on actual hysteria. Moreover, all the mystery religions promised their followers some sort of salvation by cleansing the soul of sin. Many of the ceremonies, such as being bathed in the hot blood as it flowed from a slaughtered bull, seem to us horrible and disgusting. Rites involving the enthusiastic use of a corps of temple prostitutes are immoral by Christian standards. But the general objects of these cults, cleansing from sin and the encouragement to lead a virtuous life, were eminently worthy. The mystery religions satisfied a need of the time and spread rapidly over the empire. They were no more exclusive than the traditional religion of Rome. One could continue to worship the gods as one's ancestors had and still become an initiate of several mystery cults. We read of noble Romans who had entered almost all of them.

What some men sought in the mystery cults, others hoped to find in various schools of philosophy. Stoicism and Epicureanism taught men to be sufficient unto themselves and to ignore as unimportant the world about them. Both these philosophies had strong followings in the educated classes. The third great philosophical school, Neoplatonism, was strongly tinged with mysticism. It was half philosophy and half religion. The Neoplatonists taught that truth, perfect knowledge, or as they called it the *logos*, was disseminated through the world in varying amounts. They conceived of an hierarchy of beings with rising proportions of the logos in them. By ignoring the things of the world and contemplating divine truth a man could rise in this scale toward complete knowledge or salvation. This mystical element, the offer of salvation, combined with a Platonic basic philosophy, made a strong appeal to the educated classes, especially in the East. It was particularly popular among Hellenized Jews; that is, Jews who had become essentially Greek in their thought and culture.

The great competitor of the mystery cults and philosophical schools was Christianity. The Christian preaching was tremendously appealing. There was one all-powerful God. His Son came to earth, lived among men, and died shamefully to obtain the salvation of mankind. He taught a way of life that would lead to salvation. The knowledge of the Christian life and various sacred and mystic powers were given by Jesus to his disciples, the apostles, to be passed on to their successors. In the chief Christian rite, the mass, the mystic powers of the priest changed bread and wine into the flesh and blood of Christ. In baptism the priest could wipe away man's sins. He could give absolution to truly penitent sinners who confessed. To those who believed that Jesus was the Son of God, Christianity offered the certainty of salvation. In addition to supplying the deeply moving story of Jesus' life on earth, awe-inspiring rites, and a sure path to salvation, Christianity had other appealing features. All men were equal before God; the lowest slave was as worthy as the greatest senator. Love, gentleness, humility were positive virtues.

Little is known either of the early history of the Christian Church or of the progress of its spread over the Empire. To the Romans of the first and second centuries the Christians were merely one of many heretical Jewish sects. Like the Jews they refused to worship the emperor as a god and hence seemed to threaten the unity of the state. Later, when the Christians emerged as a definitely recognized group, there were other reasons for considering them dangerous. They met in secret to perform their rites, and no government likes secret meetings, particularly of the poor and lowly. Moreover, they were opposed to violence and refused to serve in the Roman army. To a government beset by enemies the spread of such beliefs was indeed dangerous. At first the Christians were persecuted more or less accidentally together with the Jews. Later persecutions were definitely directed at the Christians. They were an illegal sect, and as such at the mercy of the government's policy.

It is clear that by the latter part of the third century the Christians were numerous enough to be politically important. They had begun to attract a number of members of the upper classes. Diocletian attempted to wipe them out in a particularly energetic series of persecutions, but he only succeeded in strengthening them. When Constantine as Caesar ruling Gaul was preparing for war against his imperial colleagues, he formed an alliance with the Christians. His first step was to decree toleration for Christians. Somewhat later he made Christianity the official religion of the state. Eventually, after several unsuccessful attempts, his successors made paganism illegal, and Christianity became at least nominally the religion of all the inhabitants of the Late Roman Empire. For this reason some scholars have called it the Christian Roman Empire.

The recognition of Christianity as the official religion of the Empire had profound effects on the Christian Church and its beliefs. The organization of the early church had been extremely simple; it was essentially an alliance of independent Christian communities. Each community was ruled by its bishop, who was assisted by priests and deacons. While some bishops undoubtedly had greater prestige than others because of the size, wealth, or antiquity of their churches, there was no real hierarchy. As soon as the Christian Church became the state church, however, it began to develop a hierarchy similar to that of the state. At its head were five patriarchs—the bishops of Rome, Constantinople, Jerusalem, Antioch, and Alexandria—who may be compared to the praetorian prefects. Then came the metropolitans, who would be parallel to the vicars of dioceses. Below them were the archbishops, who ruled individual provinces and were the ecclesiastical counterparts of the rectors. Finally, each civitas had its bishop. Although the patriarchates did not correspond territorially to the prefectures, the ecclesiastical and secular provinces were in general identical. Thus an ecclesiastical map of France in the Middle Ages shows accurately the Roman provinces and city territories. It is important to remember, however, that this church hierarchy was based on dignity and prestige rather than on authority. The generally accepted view was that all bishops as the successors of the apostles were essentially equal. Doubtful questions were settled by councils of bishops.

As the official church of the empire, the Christian Church received special privileges from the imperial government. It was given the right to receive legacies—an extremely important privilege for a perpetual corporation. Its clergy was exempt from taxation. Unfortunately this exemption proved to be a doubtful benefit. When the emperors found that the curiales were joining the clergy to escape taxation, they forbade them to do so without special permission. Soon imperial decrees prohibited all freemen from becoming members of the clergy without the emperor's leave. As a result the Christian clergy became divided into two sharp classes. Men of high position and influence could obtain the emperor's permission and were almost certain to reach the higher offices of the Church. The lower ecclesiastical grades were filled by coloni and freemen who only needed the permission of their patrons. When the Christians were a persecuted sect, they tried to keep out of the imperial courts and settled their disputes by arbitration of the bishops. After the recognition of Christianity, the law allowed bishops to act as judges in all civil disputes to which a Christian was a party. In addition the Church was given the rights of sanctuary that the more important temples had possessed. In short, the Church became a privileged corporation enjoying some governmental powers.

The fourth century saw not only the establishment of the Church's political organization but also the development of Christian theology. Jesus had taught a way of life and had made no attempt to construct a system of theology. As long as his followers preached chiefly to uneducated people, this was enough. The humble needed no more than the story of Christ's life and the knowledge of the Christian way of life. But educated men, men trained in classical thought, asked questions. They wanted to know the exact relationship between God and Jesus in precise terms. They asked the exact nature of angels. They wanted to know what happened in the mass—what did one mean by saying the bread and wine became the flesh and blood of Christ? The need for satisfactory answers to such questions became acute when Christianity became the official religion. The task of creating a Christian theology to satisfy the educated men of the Roman Empire was carried out by a group of scholars whom we call the Fathers. The most important of these were Clement of Alexandria, Origen, Jerome, Ambrose, and Augustine. These men were thoroughly imbued with the works of the classical philosophers and made full use of their concepts and terminology. They explained Christianity to the learned world in the language and ideas it was accustomed to. Since they also wanted to win over learned pagans, the Fathers quoted many passages from classical authors to show that their views were similar to those of the Christians. The concepts of Neoplatonism were in many ways like those of Christianity, and the Fathers made particularly extensive use of Plato and his later followers. Christianity was explained to the learned world largely in the terms of Platonic philosophy. At the same time the Fathers sought to make precise and definite the ideas and teachings of Christianity on all the important questions of their day.

Another task performed by the Fathers was to adjust the teachings of Christianity to the needs of the state church of the Roman Empire. A minority sect could oppose all violence and call the slaying of any human being a deadly sin. But a state must have judges, executioners, and soldiers. The Fathers gradually changed the Christian teaching on this subject until it reached its final form in the works of St. Augustine, who stated that it was not a sin to kill at the order of a legal government. While this was perhaps the major adjustment to be made, since the very existence of the state depended on it, many lesser ones were made by the Church Fathers as they constructed Christian theology.

It would be too much to expect that in this process of giving precise definition to Christian ideas and practices all theologians would arrive at the same conclusions. There were widely divergent views on all the most important questions. When this happened the only solution was to call a council of bishops together to decide the question. If the losers gave way, well and good. If they did not give way, and insisted that they were right, they became heretics. Unfortunately one council might not agree with a previous one and the heretics of one day might be the orthodox of the next. As one would expect, this period when Christian theology was being developed was the heyday of heresies.

Only one of these disputes, that between the groups called Arians and Athanasians, has any importance in the history of Western Europe in the Middle Ages. There were two divergent points of view among the theologians of the fourth century as to what class of people the church should particularly seek to win. One group was chiefly interested in convincing the men of learning—the other cared more for the masses. The first group was anxious to make Christian doctrine logical and reasonable. The other felt the emotional appeal to be more important. These two groups clashed over the definition of the relationship between God and Christ, Father and Son. The Arians maintained that a father must logically have existed before his son. God and Christ could not be exactly equal. The Athanasians refused to accept this view. Although they advanced many arguments, the basic issue seems clear. The most appealing feature of Christianity was the life and death of Jesus. Anything that lowered Christ's position would weaken the appeal of the Christian preaching. The Emperor Constantine called a council of all the bishops of the empire at Nicaea in western Asia Minor in the year 325 to settle this dispute. The Athanasians were victorious and the Arians became heretics. But Constantine's son and successor favored the Arians, and through his influence they were declared the orthodox party. Eventually the Athanasians were permanently victorious, but only after bitter struggles marked by fierce persecutions of the heretics of the moment.

The numerous disputes of the fourth century led to the calling of many councils. Most of these were local affairs summoned by a patriarch or metropolitan. But there were a considerable number of solemn councils of the whole church called by the emperor. These councils were usually summoned to settle some particularly serious dispute, but they discussed and decided other questions as well. When the council was over, a statement of the decisions made was handed to the emperor. If he approved them, he would issue them as the official law of the church. This was the beginning of the growth of canon law.

We have now seen how Christianity adjusted itself to its situation as the state religion of the Roman Empire. But this adjustment only heightened the contrast between the ideal Christian life as the more fervent Christians believed it had been preached by Christ and his apostles and the actual way of life of most Christians, even members of the clergy. Whether or not asceticism, or mortification of the body, was an essential feature of the teachings of Jesus is open to debate. It was clearly an important element of Christianity by the time of St. Paul. Perhaps the strong ascetic forces in Neoplatonism had something to do with this development. Certainly St. Paul taught the value of celibacy—the central feature of the ascetic life. Very early in the history of the church enthusiastic Christians began to leave their fellows and go off to lonely places to lead the lives of hermits. Alone, with the absolute minimum of clothes and food, they passed their time in prayer and contemplation. All lived a life of frugality and celibacy. Some mortified the body in more ingenious ways, as did the well-known St. Simon the Stylite, who sat upon a pillar. As the recognition of Christianity as the state religion moved most Christians to compromise to some extent with the demands of the Roman world, more and more enthusiasts turned to the extremely ascetic life of the hermit.

In the early fourth century two great leaders appeared among the exceptionally large number of hermits who lived in Egypt: St. Anthony and Pachomius. St. Anthony organized many of the hermits of northern Egypt into cooperative colonies. Each hermit had his own cell, but they worked together to produce the simple clothes and food that they needed. St. Anthony believed that the perfect Christian life was one of solitary prayer and contemplation. His hermits cooperated with one another only so that they could produce the necessities of life with as little diversion as possible from their chief occupation. Pachomius had a rather different idea. He believed that work was an essential element of the Christian life. His followers worked hard to produce as much as possible. Any surplus beyond their simple needs went to the poor. Although the followers of Pachomius lived in separate cells, they met together to perform their religious ceremonies.

About A.D. 360 St. Basil carried the ideas of Pachomius still farther. He believed that both work and fellowship were essentials of the perfect Christian life. His monks lived together, ate together, worked together, and worshipped together. By establishing this ideal of a simple, chaste, frugal life devoted to hard work and lived in common with others St. Basil became the true founder of Christian monasticism.

The contrast between the ideas of St. Anthony and those of Pachomius and St. Basil is an important one. St. Anthony believed that the best road to the perfect Christian life and to salvation lay in extreme asceticism. St. Basil, on the other hand, believed that useful work was more important. He wanted his monks to live as frugal a life as they could, but they were not expected to mortify their bodies so much as to hinder their work. Both these conceptions of the perfect Christian life played an important part in the Middle Ages.

As we have seen, monasticism began in a primitive form in Egypt under Pachomius, and was spread to the Greek world by St. Basil. It was carried to Italy and perhaps to Gaul as well by St. Athanasius, the great opponent of the Arians. He seems to have known nothing of Pachomius, and his ideas were basically those of St. Anthony. Thus it was the ideal of extreme asceticism that first spread to the western part of the empire. By the end of the fourth century there were monasteries in Italy, Africa, and Gaul. Three of the greatest of the church Fathers, Jerome, Ambrose, and Augustine, were deeply interested in the monastic life and encouraged its development.

2. *The Germanic Invasions*

Now that we have examined one of the basic elements of mediaeval civilization, the civilization of the Late Roman Empire, let us turn to the other two, the civilizations of the Germans and the Celts. It is important to remember that in doing this we are not crossing a clearly defined line. In the fourth century the frontiers of the Empire did not separate a purely Roman world from a purely barbarian one. Ever since the last century before Christ, Roman and barbarian had been influencing each other. By the fourth century there were hired bands of Germans in the Roman army, and German recruits were important in both legions and auxiliary units. Many high Roman officers were of German blood. Roman senators had brought in Germans both as servants and as coloni on their estates. Moreover, two great Roman provinces, Gaul and Britain, had been from the beginning combinations of Roman and Celtic civilization. Then, the civilization of Rome was bound to spread to some extent beyond its political frontiers. The barbarians outside these frontiers had been Romanized in varying degree, according to their receptivity and their proximity to the border. The influence of Rome might have affected her neighbors far more deeply if the Romans had had any interest in spreading their civilization outside the Empire. But the Roman mind was essentially political, and it had little interest in regions it could not rule. The first Romans to have an active desire to carry civilization to the barbarians were Christian missionaries.

In the fourth century the independent Celtic peoples were but a feeble remnant of a once mighty race. During the last five centuries before Christ the Celts had ruled a vast territory stretching from central Germany and the Balkans to the shores of the Atlantic. They had developed a fairly advanced civilization. They were experts at working metals and masters of graceful design in metal products. Their military capacity, however, was unequal to that of the Germans. By the time Caesar invaded Gaul the Germans had driven the Celts from the lands east of the Rhine, and were pressing across that river. It seems highly likely that only the Roman conquest of Gaul prevented that region from being overrun by the Germans. Then, in the first century A.D. the Romans conquered Britain, and Ireland became the only refuge of the independent Celts. The Romans called Ireland *Scotia.* Fierce Scots pirates and raiders were the terror of Roman Britain for several centuries.

The Celts apparently never developed an advanced political system. Their basic organization was in tribes or clans, consisting at least in theory of descendants of a common ancestor. Their religion was a rather primitive worship of the forces of nature with a complicated ceremonial presided over by priests called Druids. They were lovers of warfare, and the various tribes were in continual conflict with one another. The chief contributions of Celtic civilization to that of Western Europe in the Middle Ages was in the realm of the imagination—in song, in story, and in religious enthusiasm. Presumably these elements were strong in the civilization of the early Celts, but we do not know enough about that civilization to discover their manifestations. Only in their art such as the delicate decoration of brooches and mirrors can we see early evidence of the spirit that was to produce the Arthurian tales.

The earliest known homeland of the Germanic peoples was in the lands surrounding the western part of the Baltic Sea: the southern part of the Scandinavian peninsula, the peninsula of Jutland, and the north German coast as far east as the river Oder. From there they spread gradually over central Europe. By the time of Christ they had occupied the entire region now known as Germany. Their further migration to the west and south was checked by the heavily fortified frontiers of the Roman Empire, but to the southeast there were no such barriers. The eastern wing of the Germanic peoples passed through the regions now known as Poland and the Ukraine to occupy the steppes to the north of the Black Sea. In the fourth century the Germans faced the Roman borders from the mouth of the Rhine to the mouth of the Don. On the lower Rhine were the Franks, and the upper reaches of that river were occupied by the Alemans. The Marcomanni were in what is today Bohemia, and Vandals and Gepidae held the Hungarian plain. From there to the river Don stretched the land of the Goths. Behind the Franks in northwest Germany were the Saxons, while Angles and Jutes occupied the peninsula of Jutland. To the east of the Saxons were the Suevi, and beyond them the Lombards.

The names such as "Franks" and "Saxons" used in the last paragraph do not designate tribes, but rather groups of tribes similar in speech and customs. Presumably before they started their migrations the Germans differed little one from another in either language or customs, but individual groups became isolated from their fellows during their wanderings and developed linguistic and cultural peculiarities. Moreover, each group was obliged to adjust its way of life to the environment in which it found itself. Thus decided differences developed among the various Germanic peoples. In the fourth century the most striking differences were not between individual Germanic peoples, but rather between the western and eastern Germans. The Saxons, Suevi, Franks, and Alemans had simply moved south from their homeland into regions of essentially the same general nature, remaining in close touch with such peoples as the Angles and Jutes, who had not migrated. But the Lombards, Vandals, and Goths had moved into regions far different from northwestern Europe. The Hungarian plain and the steppes north of the Black Sea were essentially pastoral regions. Their German conquerors became horsemen and herdsmen. Moreover, the south Russian steppes had long been the frontier between Slavic farmers, Greek colonists of the Black Sea coast, and fierce nomads of the Asian grasslands. The region had been dominated for centuries by nomadic peoples who moved in as invaders, stayed as conquerors, and were in turn absorbed by new invaders. Here the Goths succeeded in defeating all rivals and setting themselves up as the dominant group. Like previous conquerors, they were a military minority ruling over a strange agglomeration of different subject peoples.

Throughout the fourth century the Germanic peoples pressed against the borders of the Empire. At times they would defeat the frontier guards and raid an imperial province, but eventually fresh troops would arrive and the Germans would be driven back. In the far northwest the Angles and Saxons took to their ships and raided the coasts of Britain. The imperial government appointed a special military officer, the count of the Saxon shore, to deal with them. Forts were built along the east coast, and a legion brought from Wales to hold them. On the lower Rhine the Franks occupied both sides of the frontier—those in Roman pay holding the border against the others. Frankish troops were heavily relied on to help control the Alemans on the upper Rhine. The same general policy was used along the upper Danube, bands of Germans being hired to reinforce the Roman border garrisons. By far the most formidable of the German neighbors of the Empire were the Goths. They were divided into two groups. The Visigoths lived along the lower reaches of the Danube, while the vast Ostrogoth state stretched from the Dniester to the Don. The Goths had developed a rather more advanced political organization than the other Germanic peoples: they were united under kings. During the fourth century the Goths were in close contact with the Empire. Periods of hostility were succeeded by times of peace. Gothic nobles visited Constantinople, and their people learned much of Roman ways. About the middle of the century a Christian Goth, St. Ulfila, began their conversion and before long the Goths had become Christians. But their conversion was made by Arian missionaries during the reign of the Arian emperor, Constantius (A.D. 337–61), and their Christianity remained Arian.

As I have suggested in an earlier paragraph, the Ostrogoths held three frontiers. To the south they faced the Roman Empire, to the north the Baltic and Slavic peoples, and to the east the wild nomads of central Asia. In the early fourth century the country to the east of the Ostrogoth state was occupied by a comparatively weak Asiatic people, the Alans. But about A.D. 370 a Mongolian people who were both fierce and numerous, the Huns, burst out of the Asiatic grasslands and fell upon the Alans. The Huns were lightly armed mounted archers—brave, hardy, ruthless and skillful. The Alans were almost immediately overwhelmed. Some small bands escaped to the west, but the majority of them joined the Huns. Thus, after 370 the Ostrogoths were left exposed to the Hunnish horde.

Although little is known of the political institutions of the western Germans in the fourth century, it is clear that they were extremely simple. Justice was administered in popular courts, assemblies of the people, presided over by the chief. Their law was primarily devoted to supplying alternatives to private vengeance. If one man injured another, the latter brought a complaint before the court. The accused was then summoned to appear. If he did not come, he was declared an outlaw. In short, private vengeance was given official sanction. If the accused appeared, he could establish his innocence by having a number of men swear that he had not committed the offense. If he could not prove his innocence, he had to pay the injured party according to a fixed tariff, which varied according to the nature of the crime and the persons involved.

In time of peace the chief probably had few duties beyond presiding over the popular courts. His primary function was as a leader in war. When a German chief was planning a military excursion, he issued a call to brave young men in search of adventure. They swore to serve the chief faithfully in the expedition in return for arms, food, clothes, and a share of the booty. These bodies of warriors had different names among the various peoples. The Romans called such a group a *comitatus*, or group of companions. The Franks seem to have called it a *truste* and its members *antrustiones*. In the case of a mere plundering raid the chief might take only his comitatus as his main fighting force. In larger expeditions it served as his bodyguard.

Many historians have described the early Germans as a democratic people. To some extent this represents recognition of genuine democratic elements in German society and to some extent confusion between two things—democratic government, and the idea that the individual has rights that no government can take away. Democracy means the rule of the people. A democratic government can restrict the liberty of the individual just as severely as can an autocracy. At the same time, a government that is not a democracy can believe that its rights over individuals are limited. The German system of dispensing justice in popular courts was undoubtedly democratic, but the distinctions made in the laws between men of different rank were not. It seems clear that election played some part in the choice of a chief. In all probability the chief was chosen by the warriors from among the members of one or two noble families. But there is no evidence of democratic control over the chief once he was elected. The democratic elements in German society must not be taken too seriously. On the other hand, it is clear that the functions of government among the Germans were extremely limited. Government provided leadership in war, and a means of settling quarrels without a bloody feud. For the rest it left the people to their own devices. Hence the Germans did have a tradition of personal freedom—of having a very small amount of government. They were wild fierce warriors, impatient of restraint of any kind. Their love of freedom, one may even say of license, was to play an important part in the development of Western civilization.

Some barbarian chieftains were given the title *rex,* or king, by the Romans. This was true of a number of the Frankish chiefs in Roman pay. Other German leaders undoubtedly took the title themselves. Hence among the Germans a king could be either the leader of a small Frankish war band or the master of the great Ostrogoth state. It is important to remember that the ancient world had two words that we translate as king: *rex* and *basileus*. The Romans used the title rex for almost any non-Roman to whom they gave some authority—such as Herod, king of Judea. It did not imply independent, sovereign authority. Basileus on the other hand was the term for the semidivine Hellenistic kings. No one in the Roman Empire except the emperor himself could have this title. In short, among the Germans the king was simply a chief whose primary function was to lead in war.

The Germans lived by agriculture and by fighting. The agricultural unit was the village community, the fighting unit the chief's war band. There is some reason for believing that there were two types of farming villages. In one type a chief would live supported by the labor of slaves. The other would be made up of ordinary freemen, without a chief. The arable land of the village was divided into two sections, one of which was planted every year, and the other allowed to lie fallow to recover its fertility. In the village community of freemen the arable was divided among the households, each one having the same amount of land in each section. The pasture land and woods were left undivided, for all to use. The people lived close together in the village, surrounded by their arable fields and pastures, and separated from the next village by deep forests. While this description of a German farming community is based on material of much later date than the fourth century, it seems probable that it represents the earlier way of life with fair accuracy.

The fourth century German turned easily to warfare as a means of making his living. It was far easier for a strong tribe to plunder the crops of a weak one than to grow food for themselves. A plundering raid over the Roman frontier was both enjoyable and profitable. Perhaps most pleasant of all was to be hired by the Romans as soldiers. As a soldier, one would be supported in time of peace by the people of the Empire. It seems likely that the Ostrogoths lived as a victorious army in their south-Russian state, and forced their subject peoples to supply them with what they needed.

In all probability it was a desire to live without working that made the Germans so anxious to cross the Roman borders. They led a simple agricultural life in the midst of deep forests. It was hard work for a meager living. Any day some stronger tribe might plunder them. Across the frontier they saw prosperous farm lands and flourishing towns. If one could cross the frontier, one could at least plunder something worth while, and there was always the hope of finding some way of living permanently at the expense of the peaceful peasants of the Roman provinces. The Germans did not want to overthrow the Roman Empire. They simply wanted to share its obvious wealth.

The gradual Germanization of the western provinces of the Empire, and the Romanization of the Germanic peoples that marked the third and fourth centuries were greatly accelerated in the fifth century by a new series of German migrations. While these movements were started soon after A.D. 370 by the Hunnish attacks on the Ostrogoths, they kept on for nearly two centuries under their own impetus. They represented a general southward and westward migration of the Germanic peoples. The Germans entered the empire under widely varying circumstances. In A.D. 376 the Visigoths begged the Emperor Valens (A.D. 364–78) to shelter them behind the imperial frontier from the advance of the Huns. It seems likely that the Emperor's chief reason for admitting them was a desire to secure their aid in holding the Danube frontier against the fierce Asiatic raiders. Remnants of the Ostrogoths who had fled west before the Huns were hired by the imperial government to garrison another section of the Danubian frontier. Those Franks already settled in northern Gaul as auxiliary troops simply took advantage of circumstances to make themselves masters of that province. Of all the German peoples who moved into the empire, only the Vandals and the Anglo-Saxons were real invaders who forced their way into the empire, ravaged its provinces without restraint, and ruled as purely military conquerors.

Throughout the fifth century most of the western provinces of the empire were dominated by barbarian generals commanding barbarian troops. Some of these, such as the Vandal and Anglo-Saxon leaders, were avowed enemies of the Roman government, others like the Visigoth and Ostrogoth chieftains considered themselves allies of Rome. The rest were barbarian officers in the imperial service. After the death of Theodosius I (A.D. 379–95), the emperors who ruled in the West were helpless figureheads under the control of barbarian generals. Thus, early in the fifth century a general named Stilicho hired German and even Hunnish troops in a vain attempt to crush the Vandals who were ravaging Gaul, and to prevent the Visigoths established at the head of the Adriatic sea from entering Italy. Stilicho was murdered. The Vandals crossed the Pyrenees to occupy northern Spain while the Visigoths passed through Italy to Gaul, plundering Rome on the way. After the Visigoths had moved on, other barbarian generals ruled in Italy until they were defeated by the Ostrogoths, who took possession of Italy. Meanwhile the Visigoths had driven the Vandals from Spain and the latter had taken control of North Africa. Thus by A.D. 490 the Ostrogoths held Italy, the Visigoths southern Gaul and Spain, and the Vandals the African coast.

These three Germanic peoples were comparatively few in number, and were destined to make no lasting impression on the regions they occupied. Both the Visigoths and the Ostrogoths were well acquainted with Roman civilization before they entered the Empire. While they rarely paid any attention to imperial commands and had no objection to fighting a Roman army that got in their way, they considered themselves military allies of the Empire, and occasionally functioned in that capacity. Thus in A.D. 378 the Visigoths destroyed a Roman army and slew its leader, the Emperor Valens, but in 451 the Visigoth king joined the Roman provincial troops of northern Gaul under the senator Aëtius and the Frankish war bands to defeat the Hunnish king, Attila (A.D. 445–53) who was invading Gaul.

The Goths were essentially armies living off the country. In both Gothic states the native landholder was required to give a portion of his produce to support a Gothic warrior and his family. The Gothic kings usually claimed to be agents of the emperor and delighted in such Roman titles as patrician. In common with other German peoples the Goths thought of law as personal rather than regional. The Goths were judged by Gothic law, but the Roman provincials continued to use Roman law. In general the Roman local administration was allowed to operate much as it had before. In fact the great Ostrogothic king, Theodoric (A.D. 489–526), employed Romans of senatorial rank in his administration, and furnished Italy with a far more effective government than it had had under Roman generals like Stilicho. The real source of conflict between the Goths and the people they ruled was in religion. As the Goths were Arians, they were considered heretics by the Catholic clergy. Most of the Gothic kings, however, were extremely tolerant. They established a few Arian bishops and left the major part of the Catholic clergy alone. Nevertheless, the Roman church could not be content under the rule of heretics, and occasional persecuting kings made the problem more acute.

The migrations of the Goths and Vandals and the establishment of their power over vast regions effectively destroyed the Roman Empire in the West. Although the Emperor Justinian, who ruled in Constantinople from A.D. 527 to 565, succeeded in overthrowing both the Vandal and Ostrogoth kingdoms and reconquering a strip of southern Spain from the Visigoths, his successors lacked the resources to hold these regions.* In 568 a new Germanic migration, that of the Lombards, engulfed Italy. By the end of the sixth century the emperor at Constantinople ruled Sicily, the toe of the Italian boot, Rome and its vicinity, and Ravenna and Venice on the Adriatic Sea. The rest of Italy was held by the Lombards.

It is difficult to estimate the other effects of the migration on the western provinces in the Mediterranean region. Before the Germans entered the empire in mass, the material prosperity and civilization of these provinces had declined. The Germans simply accelerated a process already started. But this acceleration must have been very decided.

* See pp. 33–4.

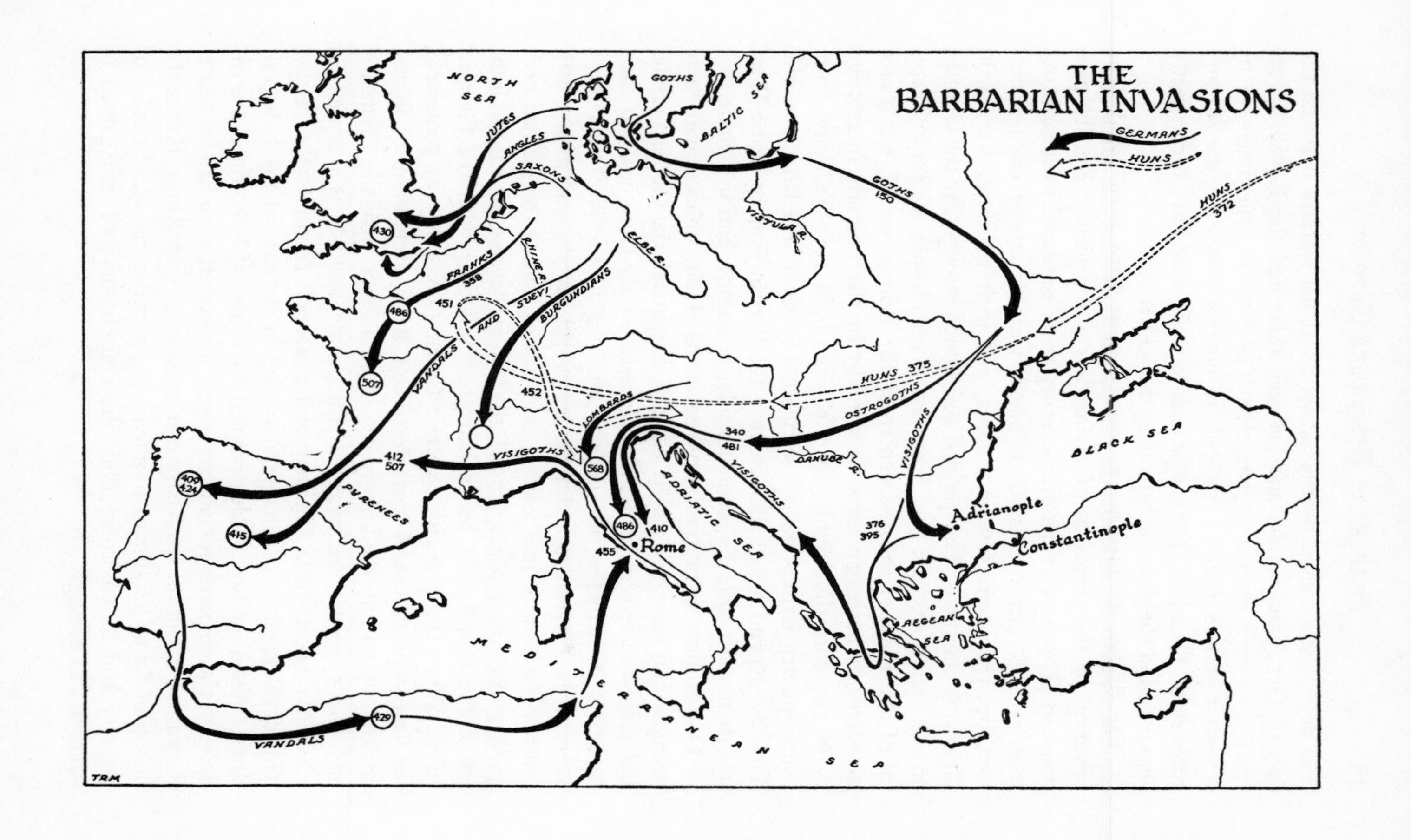
THE BARBARIAN INVASIONS
GERMANS
HUNS
NORTH SEA
BALTIC SEA
BLACK SEA
ADRIATIC SEA
AEGEAN SEA
MEDITERRANEAN SEA
JUTES
ANGLES
SAXONS
GOTHS
GOTHS 150
HUNS 372
HUNS 375
FRANKS 358
RHINE R.
ELBE R.
VISTULA R.
DANUBE R.
SUEVI AND VANDALS
BURGUNDIANS
LOMBARDS
OSTROGOTHS
VISIGOTHS
VANDALS
PYRENEES
Adrianople
Constantinople
Rome
430
486
507
451
452
568
340
481
376
395
410
455
412
507
409
424
415
429
TRM

The destruction caused by the almost continual warfare between the various Germanic peoples and between them and the Roman forces must have been extremely extensive. The Roman government in its strongest periods found it difficult to control piracy on the sea and robbery on the roads. These obstacles to trade must have been greatly aggravated in the disorder attending the migrations.

The decline in material prosperity must have been rapid. The lowering of the standards of civilization was probably equally pronounced. Throughout the fifth century there remained in these provinces great Roman nobles whose houses were centers of classical culture, but they were few in number, and their associates were wild Germanic chieftains. The spiritual destruction wrought by the German armies, moreover, must have been very severe. Rome, the ancient capital of the Empire, and the center of the Roman world, was twice plundered by barbarian hosts; once mildly by the Visigoths in 410, and again, far more thoroughly, by the Vandals in 455. We know from contemporary writers that these two events shook the Roman world. Thus by the end of the fifth century the Roman Empire in the West was shattered politically, economically, in culture, and in morale.

One Roman institution survived changed but imbued with new strength: this was the Catholic Church. In general, the German armies and their leaders respected the ecclesiastics, their churches, and their property. Nonetheless, the general lowering of the level of culture affected the Church as it did the lay world. By the end of the fifth century there were few learned ecclesiastics. But as the Roman civil government slowly distintegrated, the bishops became the natural leaders of the people, and hence had great influence with the German rulers. When the Frankish chieftain Clovis (A.D. 481–511) conquered the Roman provinces of northwest Gaul, Remi, archbishop of Reims, pointed out to him the importance of an alliance with the Church if he hoped to secure the loyalty of the people, and Clovis accepted his advice by becoming a Christian and a staunch friend of the clergy. This development is particularly striking in the case of the bishop of Rome. When the Lombards occupied the center of Italy, the representative of the emperor at Constantinople, the exarch, who had his seat at Ravenna, was cut off from easy communication with Rome. Hence the bishop of Rome became to all intents and purposes the secular ruler of the city and its environs. Thus the church survived and gained in strength and prestige.

In discussing the effects of the Germanic migrations on the central part of the Roman Empire in the West, the provinces that lay in the Mediterranean region, we have neglected several remote districts of the empire: the Rhine frontier, northern Gaul, and Britain. While from one point of view these districts were comparatively unimportant—their loss would have barely affected the Empire as a whole—they are extremely significant as cradles of mediaeval civilization. They were the crucibles in which the German and Roman civilizations really merged.

When the generals who were trying to defend the more advanced parts of the empire in the early fifth century found themselves facing the Vandals, Visigoths, and Ostrogoths, they called home the troops from the remote frontiers and largely abandoned these regions to their own devices. The Frankish war bands in Roman pay that had been defending the lower Rhine against their relatives beyond the frontier moved slowly farther into the empire. To the southward, the Alemans slipped across the Rhine and established themselves in east-central Gaul, while the Burgundians occupied the valley of the Rhone. Northwestern Gaul was held until 486 by a local senatorial family backed by the militia of the region. As we have already seen, it was this militia, supported by Frankish and Visigoth warriors, that defeated the Huns in 451.

In 486 Clovis, the commander of the Frankish war band at Tournay, who used the Roman title rex, conquered the northwestern region previously held by Aētius and his successors. Clovis was both a warrior and a statesman. He recognized at once the value of Archbishop Remi's advice that he form an alliance with the Church and thus secure the loyalty of the people of Gaul. His first step was to marry the only available Catholic princess, the daughter of a Burgundian king who had abandoned Arianism. Soon after Clovis and his warriors were solemnly baptized. He thus became the secular champion of the Catholic Church in a Gaul ruled by pagan and Arian chieftains. In 496 Clovis crushed the Alemans and absorbed them into his state. He also persuaded or forced the other Frankish bands to recognize him as their king.

Some ten years after his victory over the Alemans, Clovis announced that his conscience could not rest while Arian heretics ruled southern Gaul. He soon invaded the lands of the Visigoths. Deserted by the clergy and people of the region who favored the Catholic Clovis, the Visigoths were defeated and deprived of all their lands in

Gaul except for a narrow strip in the extreme south. Only the threatened intervention of the great Ostrogoth king, Theodoric, who had no desire to see the warlike Clovis installed on the frontier of Italy, saved the Burgundians from conquest. They were later overcome by Clovis' sons after the death of Theodoric.

The strength of the Franks lay in their homeland, lying on both banks of the lower Rhine. The number that entered Gaul itself was probably quite small. In the regions to the east and northeast of Paris Frankish immigrants seem to have occupied unused lands and formed a fair number of new villages. West of Paris such settlements were rare, and there were practically none south of the Loire. The Franks became the political and military rulers of Gaul. The officials and friends of the Frankish kings acquired estates and mingled with the Gallo-Roman aristocracy. But they had little effect on the basic civilization of the region. The peasants tilled their fields as they had in the past and spoke to one another in their vulgar Latin now on the way to become French. Frankish counts ruled in the cities beside the Christian bishops, but the ancient boundaries of civitates and provinces remained unchanged. In short, a vital difference between the Frankish state and the various states of the Visigoths, Ostrogoths, and Vandals was that the former contained the homeland of the conquerors. A Germanic monarchy rested on both Gallo-Roman and German foundations.

It is not clear when the last Roman troops were permanently withdrawn from Britain: A.D. 407 is the date usually given, and it is as likely as any other. From then until the late seventh century the history of the island is extremely obscure. There is good reason to believe that immediately after the withdrawal of the legions Scottish adventurers from Ireland overran Britain and established small kingdoms on its soil. One of these kings who apparently ruled in both Ireland and part of Britain was the semimythical Vortigern. But the German raiders who had been harrying the coasts of Britain for a century or more did not cease their raids. And before long they were coming not only as plunderers but as settlers. In general the people of Roman Britain had lived on the high country with light soils and had avoided the heavy soils of the river valleys. To the Germans, who were used to swamps and deep forest, these valleys were the ideal place to settle. Hence they ran their boats up the rivers of the south and east coasts, and settled along the banks of these rivers.

In some regions at least the Britons and Germans seem to have lived together in comparative peace for a long time, the Britons on the high ground and the Germans in the valleys. But as the Germans expanded their settlements conflict was inevitable. We know nothing of the struggle between the Britons and their German foes except that it was long and stubbornly fought. If there is a historical basis for the legendary King Arthur, he was one of the leaders of the Britons in their defense of their lands. Bit by bit the Germans triumphed. By A.D. 577 they had reached the Severn, thus cutting off the Britons of Devon and Cornwall—who were not to be conquered till the eighth century—from their allies in Wales and northwest England. In 613 these last two groups were separated by the German occupation of Chester. Thus by 615 the Germans held all of what is now England except for Devon and Cornwall; Wales; and Lancashire, Cumberland, and Westmoreland.

The German conquerors of England had come from the peninsula that is now Denmark and from the part of Germany just south of it. They called themselves Angles, Saxons, and Jutes. They were closely related in language, customs, and tradition. For the purposes of the historian there is little use in trying to distinguish between these three peoples, and the common practice of simply calling them Anglo-Saxons seems thoroughly justified. Their conquest of the major part of England was a far more thorough affair than the other Germanic conquests we have been discussing. While recent research makes it seem likely that some existing villages were left in the hands of their inhabitants and a certain number of Britons, particularly women, may well have been enslaved, in general the Anglo-Saxons slew or drove off the Britons and took over their land. The England occupied by the invaders before 615 became a land of German villages tilled by German farmers. This was not true of the regions conquered later. In Cornwall and part of Devon the Anglo-Saxons were military conquerors ruling a subject people, and this was even more true of the northeastern regions taken from the Celtic kingdom of Strathclyde. In no part of the island did Roman civilization survive, though traces of it may have lingered on. Britain was now divided between the Celts and the Germans.

We have examined briefly the Roman, Celtic, and German elements that formed the heritage of mediaeval civilization. We have also discussed the violent beginnings of the process by which these elements were merged. But it is important to remember that this process took several centuries. Many vital parts of this heritage lay dormant for a long time before they took their place in the final mixture that we call the civilization of the Middle Ages. Thus Roman law did not play a vital part in Western European thought before the eleventh century, and Celtic influence on Germanic culture began to be important only in the twelfth century. Hence the reader must be patient if he reads many pages before he sees the full relevance of subjects discussed in this first chapter.

Fully as significant as the merging of Roman and German civilizations was the geographic shift in the center of military and hence political power. While the Germans had conquered the western provinces of the Empire, they had not to any great extent occupied them. The Germanic peoples who established states in the Mediterranean region were comparatively small in numbers, and existed as armies of occupation. They maintained their positions only so long as they were faced by no serious enemies. The Ostrogoths and Vandals were overthrown by Justinian's armies, and a century and a half later the Visigoths were overwhelmed by the Moslems. Thus, although the Germans destroyed the military and political power of Rome in the western Mediterranean region, they were unable to replace it with any strong order of their own. The center of power shifted to the regions actually occupied by Germans, where their armies had a firm base on the soil. With the fall of the Ostrogoth kingdom in Italy, the Franks became the dominant military power of Western Europe; and as we have seen their strength lay in northeastern Gaul and the Rhine valley. Hence although mediaeval civilization grew from a union of Roman and German elements, it developed not in the Mediterranean region but in the Germanic homeland.

This removal of the center of power from the Mediterranean region to northern Europe brought a striking change in its geographical environment. In general the shores of the Mediterranean had a mild, dry climate and light, thin soils. Forests were few and sparse, and only in a few river valleys and some regions suitable for irrigation could the soil be described as fertile. Northern Europe was a land of cold winters and cool summers, with a comparatively heavy annual rainfall. It had once been entirely covered by vast forests of oak, beech, and ash. When settlers cleared a patch in the forest, they found heavy, deep, fertile soil. Compared to the Mediterranean country the Frankish homeland was cold, wild, and gloomy, but it held great potential wealth. Its rich soil was to be the economic base for the great mediaeval states of Western Europe.

CHAPTER II

Eastern Orthodox Civilization

3. The Byzantine Empire and Its Foes
4. The Beginnings of Russia

HE GREAT Germanic migrations that during the course of the fifth century brought the western provinces of the Roman Empire under the control of Anglo-Saxons, Franks, Burgundians, Visigoths, Ostrogoths, and Vandals had comparatively little effect on the eastern provinces. Although the provinces south of the Danube were fearfully ravaged, the Germans made no permanent settlements there; and Asia Minor, Syria, Palestine, and Egypt were essentially untouched. When Romulus Augustus (475–76) the last emperor resident in the West, was deposed, his colleague Zeno (474–91) continued to rule in Constantinople. Zeno and his successor were barely able to hold their own in the East and could do nothing to recover the western provinces; but in 518 control of the empire passed into the hands of a man of unusual ability, Justinian (527–65) who first as the deputy of his uncle, and later as Emperor, ruled for forty-seven years.

Justinian was fortunate to have in his service two great generals, Belisarius and Narses. At the head of armies that consisted almost entirely of hired barbarians, these two men defeated the foes of the Empire. A brief war against the Persians brought in 532 a peace that temporarily safeguarded the eastern frontier so that Justinian's armies could turn to the west. Then a ten-year campaign destroyed the Vandal kingdom and recovered North Africa. Nearly twenty years were required for the conquest of the Ostrogoths and the return of Italy to the empire. The southern fringe of the Spanish peninsula was wrested from the Visigoths. Although Britain, Gaul, and most of Spain lay outside his realm, Justinian held the heart of the Roman Empire in both East and West. But the long campaigns had used up the slender resources available to the empire, and Justinian's successors were unable to hold what he had gained. Three years after Justinian's death the Lombards entered Italy, and the Visigoths soon ejected the imperial forces from Spain. Soon Ravenna, southern Italy, Sicily, and North Africa were the only imperial possessions in the West.

3. The Byzantine Empire and Its Foes

JUSTINIAN has been called with good reason the last Roman Emperor. Although his successors continued to use the title, they had no control over the western and Latin part of the Empire, and little interest in it. Essentially rulers of the Hellenistic East, they are usually known as Byzantine emperors and their state as the Byzantine Empire. As a matter of fact, the Roman aspects of Justinian's empire were probably more apparent than real. Latin was the language of his court and government. His legists used Latin in writing the Code and the Digest, the great summaries of Roman law that were to have an immense influence on later civilizations.* But the fact that Constantinople was a Greek city and that Greek was the basic language of the major part of the empire is clearly demonstrated by the Greek abridgments of the Code and Digest that appeared almost immediately. And in his building Justinian turned to the styles of the East. His greatest monument, the magnificent church of Santa Sophia, was not a simple, flat-roofed Roman basilica but a vast domed structure designed by Greek architects with ideas developed in Syria. Although Justinian was essentially a Roman emperor, he was the founder of Byzantine architecture. Moreover, it is clear that within fifty years of his death the court and government of the empire had become Greek. When the future emperor Maurice wrote his famous treatise on military science about 580, he felt it necessary to supply Greek equivalents for any Latin terms he used.

The Byzantine Empire lasted for 888 years after the death of Jus-

* See pp. 7–8.

tinian. This long existence can be divided roughly into three periods. From 565 to 716 the empire struggled fiercely for survival. While it held off a series of terrible foes, it developed its economic resources, its political and military systems, and its version of European civilization. Then from 716 to 1057 came slightly more than three centuries of glory. The Byzantine Empire was the richest state of Europe, the strongest in military power, and by far the most cultivated. During these three centuries while Western Europe was a land of partly tamed barbarians, the Byzantine Empire was a highly civilized state where a most felicitous merger of Christianity and Hellenism produced a fascinating culture. The last four centuries of the empire's existence, from 1057 to 1453, was a period of gradual decadence in power. Enemies from both east and west cut her provinces away one by one until the great capital, Constantinople, was finally overwhelmed by the Ottoman Turks.

Few states have played as important a part in history as did the Byzantine Empire. In it was developed the civilization that can be called Eastern European, which still survives in Russia, the Balkans, and Greece. But of greater interest to us are the services Byzantium performed for Western Europe. For long centuries the empire served as a bulwark against the peoples of Asia and so protected the still weak states of the West. Moreover, bit by bit, directly or indirectly, the knowledge built up by the peoples of the ancient world and preserved in the Byzantine Empire found its way to the peoples of the West as they grew mature enough to receive it. Meager indeed would be our knowledge of the pre-Christian eras had the Byzantine Empire never existed.

During the first period of Byzantine history, 565–717, the empire almost succumbed to the foes who beset it on every side. In the north the most dangerous of these were the Avars, a fierce Turkish people much like the later Magyars. The center of the Avar power was in the Hungarian plain and the country west of the Danube and east of the Alps. Near them lived many Slavic tribes that were inclined to join them in their assaults on the empire. The Avars were essentially raiding plunderers who had no desire to settle in imperial territory and they cruelly devastated the lands south of the Danube. Several times their armies appeared at the walls of Constantinople, but they were never able to capture the strongly fortified city. As the emperors of this period were usually engaged in defending their Asian frontiers, the

Avars could raid much as they pleased. The Slavs, who were often the allies of the Avars in their invasions, were not, however, mere raiders. They wanted land to settle on. Bit by bit they occupied the European provinces of the empire. Some scholars believe that during the seventh century the population of this region, including that of Greece itself, became almost entirely Slavic. Although this seems improbable, there is no doubt that there was heavy settlement by Slavs everywhere, and that the nature of the population was essentially changed.

As far as the emperors were concerned, the European provinces of the empire already ravaged by German invaders were of comparatively little importance. The strong walls of Constantinople safeguarded their capital from Avars and Slavs, and they centered their attention on the protection of their rich Asiatic lands. Here they faced a truly formidable enemy—the great Persian state. A period of civil war and general confusion in the empire during the reign of the utterly incompetent Emperor Phocas, from 602 to 610, gave the Persians an excellent opportunity. In 611 they swept into Syria. In 613 Damascus fell, and in 614 Jerusalem. During the following year they overran Asia Minor and reached Chalcedon, just across the Sea of Marmora from Constantinople. In 619 their armies conquered Egypt while a great horde of Avars and Slavs besieged Constantinople. But Phocas' successor, Heraclius (610–41), was a determined and able soldier. In a series of campaigns he drove the Persians from the empire and invaded their country. In 627 a great victory near the site of ancient Nineveh crushed forever the Persian power.

While Heraclius was waging war against the Persians, events were taking place in the Arabian peninsula that were to create a new and even more dangerous foe to the Byzantine Empire, and profoundly influence the world's history. Five years before the battle of Nineveh Mohammed had moved from Mecca to Medina and began the establishment of his faith. Soon the fierce Bedouin tribes that occupied the oases of the Arabian desert and the grasslands that bordered it were bound together by a common religion. One of the basic tenets of this new faith was worthiness of war against the unbeliever. The Moslem who died fighting in the Holy War was guaranteed immediate entrance to a very concrete paradise where he would live a life of luxury, surrounded by beautiful women. But although the Moslem believed war against the unbeliever to be the most virtuous of enterprises, in the early days he was not intolerant of other faiths. The unbeliever should be conquered, but once subject he was allowed to follow any religion he pleased.

Ever since the fourth century the eastern provinces of the Roman Empire had been torn by religious strife. No sooner had the Arian heresy been suppressed than two more appeared. The followers of Nestorius insisted on a clear separation between the divine and human elements in Christ. The man Jesus became God, but Mary was the mother of a simple man, not the mother of God. The followers of this belief were condemned and suppressed. Many Nestorians left the Empire to settle in Persia, and eventually to spread out over Asia. The monophysites, who appeared at about the same time as the Nestorians, believed that Jesus was God and refused to give him human attributes. Although repeatedly condemned, this heresy persisted and was rampant in Egypt, Palestine, and Syria. Some emperors tried to wipe out the monophysites by persecution, while others attempted to concoct compromise formulas that would bring them back into the fold. The persecutions only made the heretics more determined, and the attempts at compromise annoyed the orthodox, and resulted in serious quarrels between the emperors and the popes. One of the reasons for the comparatively easy conquest of Syria and Egypt by the Persians in the early seventh century was the fact that the monophysites rather preferred them to the imperial government. This same situation was to aid the rapid advance of Arab hosts.

Mohammed died in 632. The next year his followers swept out of Arabia to invade the remnants of the Persian state, and the following year they moved into Palestine and routed a Byzantine army. The year 635 saw the capture of Damascus, and the following year the conquest of all Syria. In 637 Jerusalem fell. By the end of the year 642 the Arab armies had conquered Persia in the east and Egypt in the west.

In Egypt the Arabs built a fleet and prepared to struggle with the Byzantine navy for the control of the Mediterranean. In 655 this new fleet won a great victory and raided the waters about Constantinople. Some twenty years later the Moslems staged a full-scale naval assault on the capital of the empire, but were eventually repulsed. Meanwhile, their armies had been slowly gaining in a series of campaigns in Asia Minor and Africa. In 698 the capture of Carthage marked the end of the Byzantine power in North Africa. In the early years of the eighth century a series of incompetent emperors suffered defeat after defeat in Asia Minor. Finally in 717 an Arab army swept to the Sea of Marmora where it met the Arab fleet, and the combined forces laid siege to Constantinople.

While the Arabs were conquering the Asiatic and African provinces of the empire, a new enemy had appeared in the north. In 679 the Bulgarians, a Turkish people closely allied to the Avars, crossed the lower Danube and occupied the region between the river and the Balkan mountains. In the early eighth century they took advantage of the weak emperors of the period to ravage imperial territory, and the year 712 saw them at the walls of Constantinople. Thus in 717 the situation of the empire looked completely hopeless. While the Bulgars plundered the countryside, an Arab army and fleet besieged Constantinople. But in its hour of need the empire again found a savior in an imperial general, Leo, usually called the Isaurian, who ascended the imperial throne as Leo III (717–41). After a siege lasting over a year, the Arabs were repulsed, and peace was made with the Bulgarians. The accession of Leo marks the end of the first great period of Byzantine history.

Under the emperors of the dynasties of Justinian and Heraclius the institutions of the Byzantine Empire had developed rapidly. The rulers were fully aware that the empire's survival depended to a large extent on its economic resources. Most important of all was agriculture, for it not only supplied the food needed by the people, but manpower for the army as well. The emperors were extremely active in colonizing waste and uncultivated lands. Some of the Slavs who entered the European provinces came as invaders, but others were brought in as colonists. All of them when settled on the land increased the agricultural production. By the end of the period the provinces in Europe and Asia Minor were thickly populated and agriculture thrived. Although there were many great estates tilled by coloni, there were also villages of free farmers, and individual homesteads. Fields of grain, orchards, olive groves, and vineyards covered the land. In the reign of Justinian silkworms were introduced, and this valuable material was produced in considerable quantity.

The numerous cities of the empire were centers of industry and commerce. Constantinople held a population of 1 million people during this period, Thessalonica 500,000. While the other towns were smaller, there were many of them. The more important industries were carried on by guilds or corporations strictly controlled by the state. Each corporation had the monopoly of its particular manufacture. The state regulated its purchasing of raw materials, the marketing of the finished product, the methods of manufacturing, prices, and profits. Everything was carefully watched by government inspectors. Actually the craftsmen were employees of the state working under its direction. The result was a high degree of industrial stability, but little or no technological progress. Except for arms and armor the chief manufactures were of luxury goods: silks, fine woolens, tapestry, jewelry, and ornamental articles of enamel and ivory. Particular care was lavished on articles connected with religion such as chalices and reliquaries. The products of the Byzantine workshops were valued and copied throughout Europe.

Commerce was as closely controlled as industry. The two most profitable trades, those in grain and silk, were government monopolies, but all merchants were rigidly regulated. This tended to discourage initiative on the part of the Byzantine merchants. While they conducted the wholesale and retail trade within the empire, they were inclined to leave the importing and exporting of goods to foreigners. Constantinople was the greatest market of the world. To it came the products of the East: silks, cotton, sugar, and spices. To it also came many products of the West, carried in the ships of its Italian subject cities such as Venice, Ravenna, and Amalfi.* The merchants who came from distant lands to sell their goods in the markets of Constantinople bore back with them the products of the empire. The official imperial coin, the *bezant*, was carefully maintained in value, and became the standard coin of the western world. While few Byzantine merchants achieved great wealth, they and the artisans formed an active, vigorous middle class.

In a state surrounded with foes the most important institution is bound to be the army. The Byzantine army was well paid, carefully organized, diligently drilled, and thoroughly equipped. Its backbone was its heavy cavalry, which accounted for about half the total force. The Byzantine cavalryman wore a steel cap, a mail shirt reaching to his thighs, and metal gauntlets and shoes. His arms were the sword, lance, and bow. He was thus a heavily armed mounted archer, capable of harassing a foe with arrows and overwhelming him by a charge. The Byzantine cavalry was perfectly able to operate by itself without infantry support. In order that the soldiers should be able to devote all

* See p. 221.

their time and strength to drill and fighting, they were well supplied with servants who set up camp, procured supplies, did the cooking, and cared for the horses. The cavalry officers were always Byzantine nobles. The rank and file were small landholders, many of whom held state lands in consideration for their service. The infantry was of two sorts, light and heavy. The light infantry were archers who wore no protective armor but carried bows that could outrange those borne by horsemen. The heavy infantry wore helmet, shirt of mail, and often gauntlets. They also carried a shield and were armed with sword, lance, and battle-axe.

The empire was divided into districts called *themes*. In each theme a *strategos* or general was both military commander and civil governor. The number of troops at the disposal of the strategos depended on how exposed was the position of the theme, but he usually had from 8,000 to 10,000 men. The Byzantine emperors and their generals were deeply interested in military science and produced a number of treatises on the subject. We have already mentioned the *Strategicon* of the Emperor Maurice (582–602).* A similar work written in the ninth century by the Emperor Leo VI (886–912) shows that the military system had changed but little in the interval. In addition to describing the organization and equipment of the army, both writers discuss the tactics that should be used against various types of enemies. Thus there are detailed instructions for handling an Arab raid. When a strategos received word that an Arab force had invaded his theme, he should immediately send a small body of men to harass the enemy and reduce their plundering opportunities. Meanwhile the general should muster his cavalry to attack the foe. The mass of his infantry should be dispatched to occupy the roads out of the region, in order to block the enemy's retreat. The general would then try to force the invaders to retire without an actual battle, and would only attack them when they were already engaged with the infantry blocking the escape routes. Many an Arab raiding force was destroyed by these tactics. The Byzantine generals were professional soldiers, not dashing amateurs like the barons of Western Europe. They did not believe in taking unnecessary chances and never risked a battle unless they felt fairly certain of victory. They could not afford to waste their slender military resources by reckless encounters.

Both Maurice and Leo pointed out the value of various strategems.

* See p. 34.

When one saw that negotiations with an enemy were going to fail, the proper course was to lull him with fair words and prolong the discussion while the troops made ready for a surprise attack. Before a battle it was a good idea to write letters to some of the chief officers in the enemy camp and arrange to have them captured. Nothing could confuse a general more than to doubt the loyalty of his officers. As the Byzantine generals were continually fighting against superior enemy forces, they needed to be both skillful and wily, but it is easy to see why their ideas of how war should be conducted aroused the scorn of the knights of Western Europe. To the Byzantines war was a business, while to the western knights it was essentially a game. A few dashing generals of the western type would quickly have ruined the Byzantine Empire.

The government of the empire was a complex bureaucracy. Although it was large and extremely expensive, it was also comparatively efficient. Under weak emperors who neglected the business of state, it tended to grow corrupt, but the strong emperors carried out vigorous reforms. At the head of the government stood the emperor or, at times, emperors. During this first period of Byzantine history the imperial dignity was in theory elective. One became emperor by being proclaimed by the Senate, the people, or the army, or by any combination of these groups. Actually the son of the late emperor usually succeeded, but if he proved weak and incompetent he was likely to be overthrown and replaced by the leader of the revolt. As time went on the hereditary principle grew stronger. After the eighth century when an incompetent emperor was removed from power, he was likely to be left with the imperial title, and the leader of the revolt ruled as an associate emperor. By the eleventh century there was a strong feeling in the empire that only one who was *porphyrogenitus*, born in the building reserved for imperial accouchements, could properly occupy the imperial throne. The rather confused system of succession that marked the first centuries of the empire had both advantages and disadvantages. An incompetent ruler was likely to be deposed before he could do too much harm. But frequently the leader of the successful revolt was no better, and several times the empire was cursed by a series of incompetent rulers.

The Byzantine emperor was a sacred person appointed by God to rule over men. He was crowned and anointed in solemn ceremonies and everything connected with him was holy. Heraclius recognized that he was a ruler in the tradition of the semidivine Hellenistic kings by taking the title basileus. The emperor's subjects prostrated themselves before him as their ancestors had before the pagan god-kings. The emperor lived in magnificent state. His residence was a splendid palace that was actually a number of luxurious buildings surrounded by gardens, on the shore of the Bosporus. His life was a continuous solemn ceremony. At all times he was surrounded by a horde of officials, servants, and guards. This incredibly expensive and luxurious court was no mere extravagance. The traditions of the lands that composed the Byzantine Empire demanded that the king should be set apart from other men, and the court made this fact apparent. Its effect was often even greater on the empire's foes. When the envoys of the wild Mongol generals who were sweeping over Asia were received by the Byzantine emperor, they were so impressed by the richness and magnificence of the court that they reported to their masters that the empire was too strong to attack.

The emperor was an absolute monarch whose power was only limited by the danger of deposition or assassination. As long as he was in power the civil government and the army were absolutely at his disposal. He was also to a great extent the ruler of the Church. He controlled the appointment of the patriarch of Constantinople who was the head of the ecclesiastical organization. He summoned the councils of the Church and issued their decrees. While he might not actually claim the right to determine questions of dogma, by choosing the patriarch he could direct the course of orthodoxy. But the emperor's power over the Church was not absolute. The people of the empire were deeply religious and had a live interest in religious questions. The emperor could not with impunity attack a patriarch on an issue on which the latter had popular support. Thus we find strong emperors submitted to the patriarch, especially in questions involving the ruler's personal life.

During the second period of its history, 717–1057, the Byzantine Empire was ruled by two dynasties. The first of these was founded by Leo III, the Isaurian, and remained in power from 717 to 867. The second was established by Basil I, called the Macedonian, and ruled from 867 to 1057. In the north the Bulgars, who had intermarried with the Slavs to such an extent that they became essentially a Slavic people, established a strong state which was usually bitterly hostile to the empire. The Bulgar rulers went so far as to adopt the title Tsar, or Caesar,

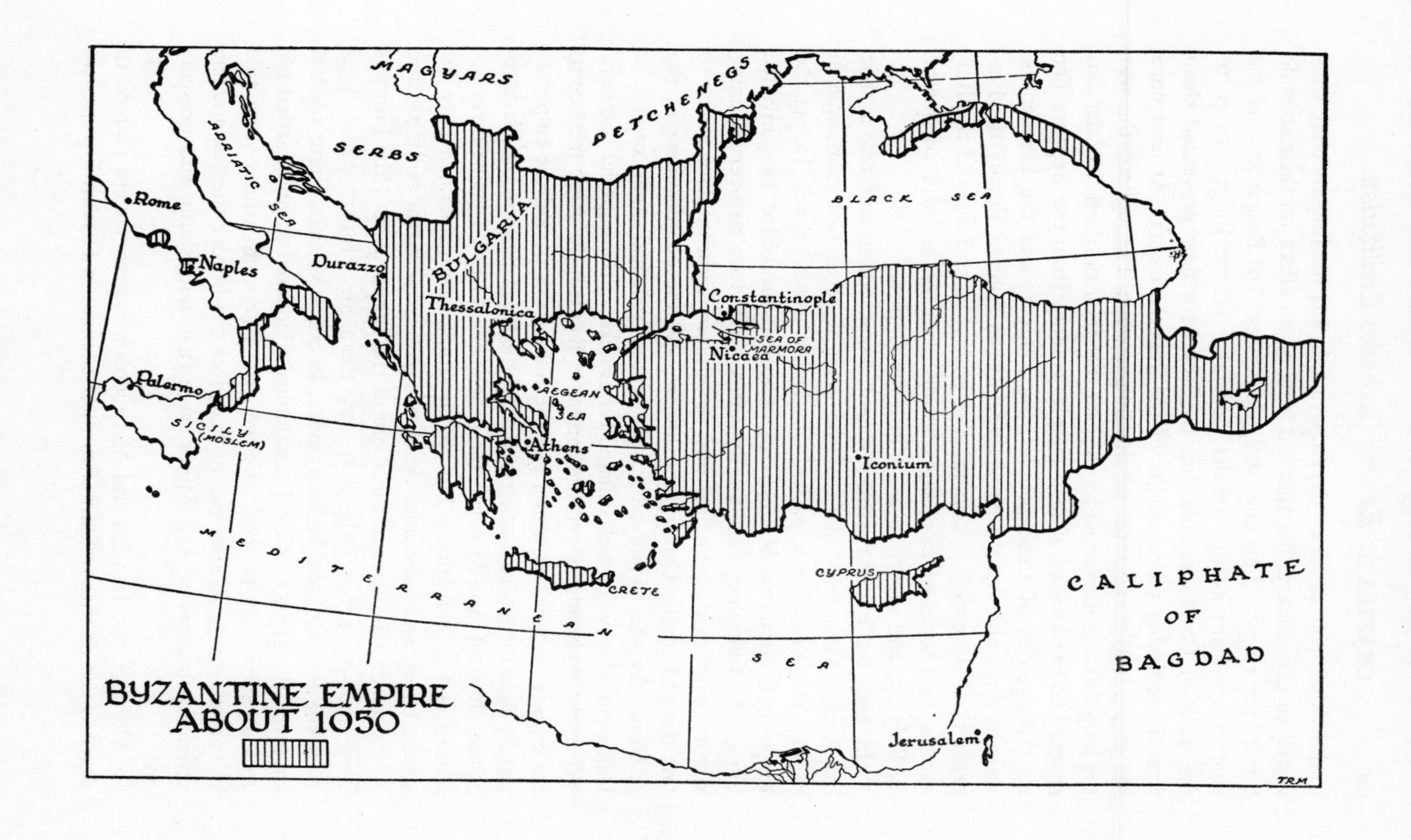
BYZANTINE EMPIRE
ABOUT 1050
MAGYARS
PETCHENEGS
SERBS
BULGARIA
ADRIATIC SEA
BLACK SEA
Rome
Naples
Durazzo
Thessalonica
Constantinople
SEA OF MARMORA
Nicaea
Palermo
SICILY (MOSLEM)
AEGEAN SEA
Athens
Iconium
MEDITERRANEAN SEA
CRETE
CYPRUS
CALIPHATE OF BAGDAD
Jerusalem
TRM

to show their equality with the emperors. In 864 the Bulgars were converted to Christianity, but this had little or no effect on their attitude toward the empire. This long struggle between the Bulgarians and the empire saw many bloody battles. Several times the Bulgars swept to the walls of Constantinople, but the lack of a fleet prevented them from undertaking serious sieges of the imperial capital. At least once the emperor reduced most of the Bulgar state. Throughout the war the Bulgars were hampered by the fact that their northern frontier was exposed to the attacks of new peoples coming from the steppes. The most dangerous of these peoples, the Magyars and the Petchenegs, were at times allies of the empire against the Bulgars. Finally the Emperor Basil II (976–1025), called *Bulgaroktonos* or Slayer of the Bulgarians, in a series of campaigns lasting from 996 to 1018 conquered all Bulgaria, and incorporated it into the empire.

In Asia, the imperial armies waged almost continuous war against the Arabs. After the failure of the great siege of Constantinople in 717–18, the Arabs were pushed slowly but steadily back. In 745 the Emperor Constantine V (741–75), who had succeeded Leo, invaded Syria. The following year the Byzantine navy won an overwhelming victory over a Moslem fleet and recaptured Cyprus. The year 750 saw the end of the Omayyad caliphate, and the establishment of the Abbasid. As the Omayyad caliphs (661–750) had their capital in Damascus, they were well situated for attacks on the imperial frontiers. When the Abbasids moved the capital to Bagdad, the Arab menace to the empire became less acute. For the rest of this period the emperors usually held the entire southern coast of the Black Sea and the Mediterranean shore of Asia Minor as far as Seleucia. At times their power extended as far as Antioch. But this position was maintained only by steady effort, and sometimes the Arabs won great victories. In 782 the Arabs once again reached the shore of the Bosporus, and the Empress Irene (780–802) was obliged to buy them off. Moslem pirate fleets were the terror of the Mediterranean. In 904 a Moslem pirate admiral captured the great city of Thessalonica, plundered it, and carried off 20,000 captives. In general, however, the Byzantine armies were able to confine the Arab activities to raids into the border themes, and the interior provinces of Asia Minor were rich, flourishing, and prosperous.

Although the Isaurian and Macedonian emperors were obliged to devote most of their attention to their enemies in Eastern Europe and

Asia, they could not neglect entirely their relations with Western Europe. Leo the Isaurian thought of himself as a Roman Emperor, and he held Venice, parts of southern Italy, Sicily, and Sardinia. Moreover, although the patriarch of Constantinople was independent for all practical purposes, he and the emperor usually recognized the pope as the head of the Christian church. As the pope was deeply involved in the politics of Western Europe, it was bound to have some effect on imperial policy.

The first crucial point in the relations between East and West came in 800 when Charlemagne (768–814), King of the Franks, assumed the title of Roman Emperor.* The Byzantine Empire was ruled for the first time in its history by an empress. Irene, mother of the Emperor Constantine VI (780–97) had deposed her son, had him blinded, and ascended the throne herself. Thus Charlemagne could argue with some justice that the imperial office was legally vacant, and that by assuming the crown he became the sole Roman Emperor. Irene at first refused to recognize her rival, but in 803 she came to terms with him.

When in the year 962 Otto I (936–73) of Germany revived the western empire of Charlemagne by assuming the imperial dignity, the Byzantine emperor was less alarmed by his new title than by his ambitions to absorb the emperor's Italian possessions.† For ten years the two emperors waged war upon each other in southern Italy without much success on either side. Otto found that he could not capture the strongly fortified towns garrisoned by Byzantine troops, and the latter were unable to cope with the German warriors in the open field. In 972 peace was made by a marriage between Theophano, daughter of the Emperor Romanus II (959–63), and the future Otto II. Otto II (973–83) continued his father's efforts to drive the Moslems from southern Italy, and to absorb the Byzantine cities, but he had no great success in either project. When he died, Otto III (983–1002) was a minor in the custody of his mother Theophano. He became essentially a Byzantine prince, and planned to make Rome the capital of his empire. The death of Otto III ended for some time close relations between the two empires. His successors as kings of Germany were far too busy at home to take much interest in Italy, and the Byzantine rulers confined their Italian activities to attempts to protect their lands from the Moslems.

The relations between the Byzantine emperors and the papacy were

* See p. 80. † See pp. 167–8.

gravely affected by the religious policies of the Isaurian emperors. For various reasons that will be discussed later, Leo the Isaurian issued a decree ordering the destruction of all images of Christ and the saints. This policy was vigorously opposed by the papacy, and relations between the pope and the emperor steadily deteriorated. In 781 Pope Adrian ceased to mention the emperor in his bulls. Although this marked an official break in political relations, no formal religious schism took place, and in 843 images were restored in the churches of the Empire. But the long period of disagreement over religious policy had weakened the bonds between the eastern and western churches. In 867 a quarrel over rival candidates for the office of patriarch of Constantinople led to an actual schism, and the eastern church formally renounced the pope's authority. Although several abortive attempts at peace were made, formal reunion of the two churches did not come until 920.

Then, in the middle of the eleventh century a new crisis arose. The Normans were gradually conquering the Byzantine possessions in southern Italy, and the pope claimed religious authority over the Norman lands.* This led to a bitter quarrel between the pope and the patriarch of Constantinople, in which each insulted the other. In 1054 the eastern church again renounced the pope, and the final schism between the two churches began. Despite various efforts to heal the breach, this schism still exists.

Leo the Isaurian fully realized that the survival of the Empire depended essentially on its internal strength. In his view there were two grave dangers to the welfare of the state—one religious, and the other social and economic. From very early times the Christian church had made extensive use of images, paintings, mosaics, and sculptures of Christ and the saints. They were of obvious value for the religious education of the illiterate, and supplied concrete inspiration to worship. But there was a strong inclination to worship the images instead of the saints they represented, especially in the regions where conversion from paganism had been recent. This had long been deplored by many earnest men, and in the Asiatic provinces especially there was a strong movement against images. Leo was extremely devout, and came from a district where this feeling ran strong.

The second problem that troubled Leo was the rapid development

* See pp. 197–8.

of large estates at the expense of the small freeholder. This was objectionable from several points of view. Small freeholders supplied the Byzantine government with its best soldiers, and the Empire could not afford to have them disappear. Then the growth of great estates decreased the imperial authority as the landholders almost always obtained some jurisdiction over their tenants. Sometimes a great landowner would usurp or obtain a grant of jurisdiction. In other cases an imperial official would obtain the ownership of land over which he had jurisdiction, and retain both as private property. The great landowners would use their political power to persuade small freeholders to sell their land and would take advantage of hard times to buy up small freeholds. Bit by bit the large estates were increasing and the small ones disappearing. Moreover, a seignorial system not unlike that of the West was rapidly developing.

Although the large lay estates seemed dangerous to Leo, those held by ecclesiastical corporations troubled him even more. The monasteries had vast estates and were rapidly increasing them. Moreover, the monasteries were exempt from taxation and had very extensive rights of jurisdiction. Thus large amounts of land were removed from the tax rolls with serious effects on the hard-pressed imperial treasury. As the monks were in general firm supporters of images, an attack on the latter would serve the purposes of both religious and land reform. Although it seems likely that the religious issue was the chief consideration in Leo's mind in attacking the images, he undoubtedly welcomed the double effect of his policy.

The first iconoclastic decree was issued in 726. It led to revolts in Greece and Italy which were suppressed with extreme difficulty, but Leo stuck to his purpose. His son, Constantine V, continued the policy vigorously. In 753 a church council held at Hieria gave approval to the iconoclastic decrees and prescribed severe punishment for those who opposed them. The destruction of images and the persecution of those who supported their use continued until 787, when the Empress Irene, who was ruling for her minor son Constantine VI, abandoned the iconoclastic policy. The question might not have arisen again had not the monks who had fought bitterly against the iconoclastic decrees abused their victory. They started anew to build up their estates and claimed almost complete exemption from the imperial authority. This moved the Emperor Leo V (813–20) in 815 to renew the controversy by ordering the destruction of all images. Not until 843, when the last Isaurian emperor, Michael III, finally restored the images, did the iconoclastic controversy come to an end.

During this controversy the emperors had deprived the monasteries of large amounts of land. Many monastic establishments were disbanded and their buildings used for secular purposes, such as barracks. Monks were imprisoned, humiliated in public exhibitions, and even executed. Many fled to Italy to escape persecution. While in the end the opponents of the iconoclasts won, and images retained an important place in Christian art, the political independence of the Byzantine church was greatly reduced and it became more completely subject to the imperial will.

Although the Isaurian and Macedonian emperors worked consistently to prevent the development of great estates, they met with no permanent success. During the iconoclastic controversy vast amounts of monastic property were seized, but once the struggle was over the monasteries flourished once more. Strong emperors issued decrees forbidding poor men to sell to rich men, punishing rich men who usurped small freeholds, and forbidding the transfer of military holdings. These strong emperors had some success in enforcing their orders. But as soon as a weak ruler appeared, the nobles once more began to increase their holdings.

Asia Minor was the chief center of the mighty land-holding nobles and the source of numerous fierce revolts against the emperor. Powerful families such as the Phocas, Ducas, Comnenus, and Palaeologus had enormous resources. The imperial dynasties that succeeded the Macedonian were drawn almost entirely from these noble houses. Early in the eleventh century something approaching feudalism developed around the heads of these families.* As the small freemen disappeared, the emperor was forced to seek his troops from the great estates, and the nobles gave lands to men who would enter their contingent in the army. No clear feudal hierarchy developed, and while the nobles held benefices from the emperor, they also had lands in full ownership. The nobles, however, did have vassals who served them in war. And by the eleventh century the political position of the Byzantine nobles was as strong as that of the barons in the states of Western Europe. Theoretically the emperor remained absolute, but actually he could rarely afford to oppose the nobles.

* See pp. 104–17.

The extinction of the Macedonian dynasty marked the end of the Byzantine Empire's era of glory. Although it was to survive for nearly 400 years, 1057–1453, it grew steadily weaker. During the last century of its existence, it consisted of no more than the city of Constantinople and the land just outside its walls. While internal conditions such as the destruction of the free peasantry and the increase in large estates undoubtedly weakened the empire to some extent, the Byzantine Empire did not essentially decline from internal decay: it was battered to pieces by formidable foes. In this last period of its existence the Empire faced enemies that were more potent militarily than any it had met before and who attacked from the west as well as from the north, east, and south.

By the eleventh century the Abbasid caliphate of Bagdad was in an advanced state of decay. Although Egypt and the Moslem lands in Asia recognized its spiritual sovereignty, the territory of the caliphate was divided into independent states ruled by local dynasties. The caliph himself was a puppet in the hands of whoever happened to command the troops in Bagdad. Late in the tenth century a band of Turks from Central Asia led by a chieftain named Seljuq ibn Takah and his sons entered the eastern part of the Moslem empire and took service under one of the local sultans. There they were converted and became enthusiastic, even fanatical Moslems. During the third decade of the eleventh century the Seljuq princes became masters of the eastern provinces of the caliphate, and in 1055 a grandson of Seljuq seized Bagdad and was solemnly proclaimed sultan by the caliph. Soon he was in complete control of the caliph and his capital. The first Seljuq sultan to rule in Bagdad died in 1063, and was succeeded by his nephew Alp Arslan (1063–73). The Turks had already been raiding the frontiers of the Byzantine Empire and had suffered several severe defeats. In 1071 the Emperor Romanus IV (1067–71) had the temerity to advance into Turkish territory. Alp Arslan met him at Manzikert in Armenia, wiped out the imperial army, and captured the Emperor. Alp Arslan himself then turned to a campaign in Turkestan, leaving his second cousin, Sulayman, to carry on the war with the Byzantines. Soon Sulayman had a sultanate embracing all Asia Minor with its capital at the great city of Nicaea. The Empire had lost all its Asiatic lands.

In 1081 Alexius Comnenus (1081–1118), one of the most powerful nobles of the Empire, seized the imperial throne. He found himself faced with a desperate situation. The Seljuq Turks held all the rich

Asiatic provinces of the empire. In the north another Turkish people, the Petchenegs, were raiding the European themes. Finally the Norman duke of Apulia, Robert Guiscard, and his son Bohemond had crossed the Adriatic Sea, routed an imperial army, and captured the city of Durazzo.* Alexius was an able and energetic general and a man of quick decisions. By offering the Venetians extensive commercial privileges, a quarter of their own in Constantinople, and freedom from customs throughout the empire, he persuaded them to cut Robert Guiscard's connections with Italy and so force him to abandon his invasion of the empire. Alexius then moved against the Petchenegs, but twice his armies were routed, and in 1091 the barbarian horde was at the very walls of the capital. In that same year, however, Alexius met them in battle and completely destroyed their host. Meanwhile he had been sending pleas to Western Europe for aid against the Turks. Alexius was not thinking of a crusade; he had little interest in Palestine, which had long been lost to the empire. Nor did he want a vast army headed by great barons. Alexius hoped the western princes would send him a few hardy and adventurous knights who would serve him for pay and aid him in driving back the Turks. His purpose was to save the Byzantine Empire.

The story of the First Crusade will be told in a later chapter.† Here it is sufficient to say that the crusading army aided Alexius to recover the city of Nicaea and dealt the Turks a crushing defeat in Asia Minor. Soon the Emperor had reconquered the southern shore of the Black Sea and the Mediterranean coast of Asia Minor as far as Seleucia. Driven from Nicaea, the sultan established his capital at Iconium. While his state comprised nearly half the area of Asia Minor, it had no outlet on the sea. Under the rule of Alexius' son, John II (1118–43), and his grandson Manuel I (1143–80), the Byzantine Empire became once more a great power. The princes of Antioch and even the king of Jerusalem were obliged to acknowledge themselves to be vassals of the Empire. The Emperor Manuel also tried to restore the imperial position in Italy. In 1151 he invaded the peninsula and took the city of Ancona. But the wily emperor got too involved in his own intrigues. He wanted to reach an understanding with Frederick Barbarossa, Holy Roman Emperor, and sought to attain this end by financing the Lombard cities in their revolt against him.‡ Apparently his idea was that if Frederick were in enough trouble he might seek a Byzantine alliance

* See p. 198. † See pp. 201–07. ‡ See pp. 279–80.

on terms profitable to Manuel. As one might expect, the result was that he won the hatred of all parties—the Norman kings of Sicily, the Emperor, and the Lombard towns. Even Venice, which had aided him against the Normans, was alarmed by his efforts to restore his authority in Italy. And in his ventures in Syria, Palestine, and Italy Manuel used up resources that his empire could ill spare.

In 1185 a great noble, Isaac Angelus (1185–95), overthrew the Emperor Andronicus Comnenus (1183–85) and ascended the imperial throne. He was weak and ineffective, and the Empire crumbled rapidly under his rule. Serbia had long been a semi-independent principality under Byzantine suzerainty. Taking advantage of Isaac's feebleness, the prince of Serbia broke away from the empire and extended his territory at the expense of other Slavic subjects of the emperor. At about the same time the Bulgarians rose in revolt and re-created their state. Isaac Angelus could not even control the territory that remained Byzantine. A relative of the previous emperor, Isaac Comnenus, became the ruler of Cyprus, and a great noble set up a state around Trebizond on the Black Sea. The empire was tottering and seemed to need only one good strong blow to end its existence.

The relations between the Latins and the Greeks had been growing steadily worse ever since the First Crusade. Godfrey of Bouillon and his companions had formed no very high opinion of the Byzantines. They considered them tricky, unreliable, and completely devoted to their own interests.* Although the Second Crusade failed because of the incompetence of its leaders, most Latins blamed its misfortunes on the Emperor.† Manuel Comnenus' activities in the west had increased the ill-feeling. Perhaps the most bitter western foe of the Empire was her former subject city Venice. When the Venetians aided Alexius Comnenus against Robert Guiscard, he had given them extensive commercial privileges, and before long most of the trade of the empire was in their hands. This alarmed Alexius, who tried to improve the situation by giving similar rights to the Pisans. His son took away the Venetian privileges, but was forced to restore them when he needed their aid against the Normans. He also added more commercial rivals by granting privileges to the Genoese. In 1182 a revolt in Constantinople led to a massacre of Latin merchants in the city. In short, by the end of the twelfth century the people of Western Europe in general disliked and distrusted the Byzantine emperor and his subjects, but the Vene-

* See pp. 203–04. † See pp. 212–13.

tians had a practical interest in their destruction. They wanted to have a monopoly of the rich trade of Constantinople.

In 1204 the Venetians found their opportunity. They persuaded the leaders of the Fourth Crusade to attack and capture Constantinople.* The victors then established the Latin Empire of Constantinople. Count Baldwin of Flanders became emperor with direct control over the capital, Adrianople, the lands between these two cities, and the adjacent coast of Asia Minor. The kingdom of Thessalonica, the duchy of Athens, the principality of Achaia, and several other states were formed for the benefit of crusading barons. While these states were in theory fiefs held of the emperor, they were in fact independent. The Venetians obtained a large section of Constantinople, all Euboea, Crete, Corfu, and a number of valuable ports such as Durazzo. In addition Venetian nobles were allowed to set up a number of island states that were held from the doge as fiefs. Meanwhile several Byzantine princes created states in regions not reached by the crusaders. Theodore Lascaris, whose wife was a daughter of the Emperor Alexius III Angelus, occupied the territory between the Asiatic lands of the Latin empire and the sultanate of Iconium, established his capital at Nicaea, and proclaimed himself emperor. In the wild mountains of Albania a bastard of the imperial house set up the despotat of Epirus. Finally, two Comneni princes founded the empire of Trebizond, which comprised the southern shore of the Black Sea.

The next fifty-seven years was a period of incredible confusion in the lands that had comprised the empire of the Angeli. The states that had been created in imperial territory were continually at war with one another. Then the Bulgarians from the north and the Seljuqs from the east entered into the conflict, sometimes acting independently, and sometimes as allies of one of the Greek or Latin states. The Latin empire had little chance of lasting very long. The people of the heart of the old Byzantine Empire, Constantinople and its environs, hated their conquerors and were always ready to revolt. The emperor could not muster enough European knights to resist successfully both the Bulgarians and the Byzantines of Nicaea. The other Latin states and the Venetians were highly unreliable allies at best and occasionally joined the emperor's foes. It soon became clear that the chief question was not the survival of the Latin empire, but whether it would be conquered from Nicaea or from Epirus. Finally the founder of a new Byzantine

* See p. 216.

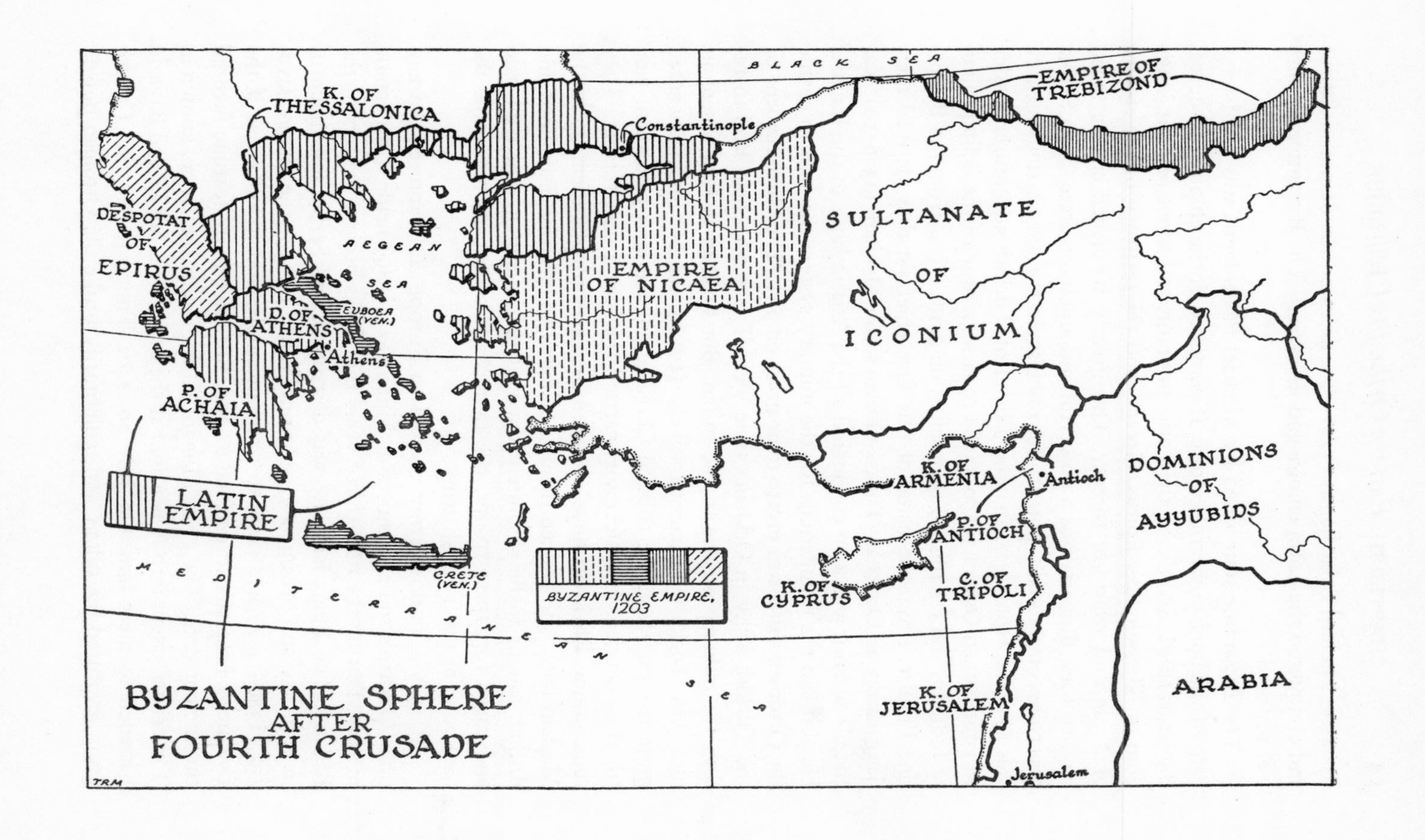
BYZANTINE SPHERE
AFTER
FOURTH CRUSADE
LATIN EMPIRE
BYZANTINE EMPIRE, 1203
DESPOTAT OF EPIRUS
K. OF THESSALONICA
Constantinople
D. OF ATHENS
Athens
EUBOEA (VEN.)
P. OF ACHAIA
AEGEAN SEA
CRETE (VEN.)
MEDITERRANEAN SEA
BLACK SEA
EMPIRE OF NICAEA
EMPIRE OF TREBIZOND
SULTANATE OF ICONIUM
K. OF ARMENIA
Antioch
P. OF ANTIOCH
K. OF CYPRUS
C. OF TRIPOLI
K. OF JERUSALEM
Jerusalem
DOMINIONS OF AYYUBIDS
ARABIA
TRM

dynasty, Michael Palaeologus (1261–82), defeated the despot of Epirus and conquered the Latin empire and its capital. The Byzantine Empire was restored.

The Byzantine state ruled by Michael Palaeologus was a sad remnant of the once powerful empire. It consisted of the empire of Nicaea, the lands ruled directly by the Latin emperor, and about half the kingdom of Thessalonica. Epirus, Greece, and the territory of the empire of Trebizond were lost forever. This greatly weakened empire faced mighty foes. Bulgaria was a powerful and ambitious state. Soon Serbia was to become equally potent. But once again the most serious menace was to come from Asia. In 1299 a band of Turkish adventurers under an emir named Osman (1290–1326) took service with the Seljuq sultan of Iconium and established themselves on lands taken from the Byzantine Empire. From the name of this first chieftain they derived their designation as Ottoman Turks. Osman's son Orkhan (1326–59) was an able warrior and soon conquered all the Asiatic lands of the Empire. He also laid the foundations for the military system that was to enable the Ottoman sultans to create their great empire. The chief element of the Turkish army in Orkhan's time were Turks who held land in return for military service to the sultan. But Orkhan had an ingenious idea. His Turks were comparatively few in number and he wanted more troops. Hence he enlisted Christian soldiers and paid them well for their service. His successors carried the idea a step further. They took young Christian boys captured in war, brought them up in the Moslem faith, and trained them as soldiers. Rigorously disciplined and drilled, taught to be absolutely devoted to the sultan, and well paid and cared for, these troops, the famous janissaries, soon became the backbone of the Turkish army.

In 1356 a Turkish army crossed to Europe and captured Adrianople. Orkhan's son and successor Murad (1359–89) made it his capital in 1365. During the next thirty years the Turks became masters of the Balkans. The Bulgarian state was destroyed, and Serbia lost much of its territory and became a vassal principality. In 1397 the Sultan Bayazid (1389–1402) laid siege to Constantinople, and it looked as if the Byzantine Empire had reached its end. But once more fortune favored the ancient state. The great Mongol Khan Timur the Lame, known as Tamerlane, swept into Asia Minor at the head of his horde, and Bayazid hastened to meet him. On July 20, 1402 Timur routed the Turkish army, captured the sultan, and temporarily broke the Ottoman power.

For the next fifty years the sultans were occupied with wars against the kings of Hungary and Poland on land and Venice on the sea. The helpless Byzantine emperor, who held only Constantinople and its immediate environs, could merely watch the struggle. By 1453 the Sultan Mohammed II (1451–81) at last found his hands free for a great attack on Constantinople. On May 29 of that year the city fell, and the Byzantine Empire was completely destroyed. Constantinople became the capital of the Ottoman empire.

The Byzantine Empire performed two important functions in the development of European civilization. It served as a vast storehouse of the knowledge accumulated by ancient civilizations that could be drawn on by rising cultures when they became ready to absorb it. Thus the wild Arabs who swept out of the desert to conquer a great empire found Byzantine civilization prepared to supply their avid thirst for knowledge. When the peoples of Western Europe reached the stage in their development that made them ready to use additional knowledge, the Arabs and the Byzantine Empire were there to open to them the civilization of the Hellenistic world. But the Byzantine Empire was more than a mere warehouse of learning for the use of barbarian peoples. It created a civilization of its own that continued to flourish in Eastern Europe. Many of the characteristics that mark the culture of the Balkan countries and Russia today have their roots in the Byzantine Empire.

Byzantine civilization showed its greatest originality in its art. In the Late Roman Empire two more or less distinct forms of Christian art had developed. One of these was essentially Greek in inspiration and was imbued with the earthly beauty and gaiety that marked Greek culture. For the artists of this school Christ was a handsome, beardless young man who was usually shown naked. The other type was developed in Palestine and Syria. Its basic feature was awesome dignity. Christ was a bearded figure in long, flowing Oriental robes. Both these schools had a profound effect on mediaeval art in Western and Eastern Europe.

In the Byzantine Empire these two trends were quickly merged to form the art we know as Byzantine. This art found expression in two ways—in mosaics and in the illumination of manuscripts. The Byzantine church was essentially built to house mosaics. Outside it was impressive with its great towering dome, but it was also plain and grim with no attempt at decoration. Inside it was a mass of marvelous mosaics. These depended for their effect almost entirely on the use of color—rich gold, blue, red, and purple. There was no attempt at what we call realism. The figures were not intended to look natural. They were essentially symbols that fitted into the design and spirit of the decoration. But the impressive dignity of these symbolic figures and the rich beauty of the color achieved a result unequaled by any other art.

These same characteristics appeared in the miniatures that illuminated the Byzantine manuscripts. There again the charm of symbolic figures carefully fitted into a design and rich color combine to produce rare beauty. But the love of beauty was not confined to makers of mosaics and illuminators of manuscripts. The Byzantine craftsman who made ornaments for both secular and religious use displayed the same skill in decorative art. Mosaics in enamel and beautiful carved ivories embellished such articles as reliquaries. In short, the Byzantine Empire developed a singularly effective and distinctive art that was an integral part of its civilization. Knowledge of it spread to Western Europe both through articles and through manuscripts. Western craftsmen used Byzantine models in their work, as did western illuminators of manuscripts. And the painters and sculptors who decorated the churches of Western Europe found their inspiration chiefly in illuminated manuscripts. Thus Byzantine art combined with early Christian art to mold the artistic forms of Western Europe.

In purely intellectual activity Byzantine civilization demonstrated originality in two directions: religious controversy and the practical application of learning. The scholars of the Byzantine Empire were profoundly religious and deeply interested in theological questions. Each of the heresies that have been discussed gave rise to a vast amount of controversial writing on both sides. In addition to these major disputes that shook the very fabric of the empire, there was continuous debate over minor theological questions. While it is difficult for a modern reader to get excited over many of the issues involved in these controversies, there can be no doubt of the subtlety and vigor of Byzantine religious thought. Byzantine writers also produced numerous practical works on subjects that were of importance to them. We have already mentioned their treatises on the art of war. There were in addition several important discussions of the Byzantine government and an extensive legal literature. Finally, the Byzantines were enthusiastic historians. Almost every period of Byzantine history is illuminated for us by the work of chroniclers.

In *belles-lettres*, philosophy, and science, Byzantine civilization was largely a passive preserver of the past. The literary works of the classical and Hellenistic periods were industriously copied, read, and studied. Commentaries, grammars, dictionaries, and encyclopaedias were made to increase the usefulness of accumulated learning, but little addition was made to it. While the Byzantines made various practical inventions such as the famous Greek fire, they did little to further basic scientific knowledge. What literature the empire did produce was largely antiquarian in nature. The writers used the Greek of classical times, or rather a somewhat florid literary version of it, while the spoken language changed with great rapidity. Before long there was little relation between literary and vernacular Greek. Such a situation is bound sooner or later to sap the vitality of a literature. Although Byzantine learning was not creative, it was solid, and in its influence widespread and respected. In the university of Constantinople and in schools throughout the land men and women were imbued with the ideas of the ancients. The members of the bureaucracy that governed the state were expected to have a thorough humanistic education; and both the noble and middle classes were highly literate, if not actually learned.

Except for some of its theological works, the creations of Byzantine civilization had little influence on Western Europe, but its copies of those of classical and Hellenistic times were extremely important. By the latter part of the twelfth century western scholars were translating works on philosophy and science from Greek into Latin. While the transmission to the West of the major part of Greek literature had to await the Renaissance, these philosophical and scientific manuscripts played a vital part in the earlier development of Western European learning.

Although Byzantine learning did have some direct influence on Western culture during the early Middle Ages, it had far more indirectly, through Arabian civilization. When the Arabs occupied the Asiatic and African provinces of the empire, they found many works of classical and Hellenistic times. The Arabs copied these works, studied them, and commented on them. The Arab philosophers, Avicenna and Averroes, translated Aristotle and wrote commentaries designed to adjust his ideas to Moslem culture. The geometry of Euclid, the astronomy of Ptolemy, and the medicine of Galen were all translated and used by Arab scholars. But the Arabs did more than simply absorb the Hellenistic knowledge they found in the Byzantine storehouse. In several fields they made important additions. The numbers that we call Arabic were apparently first used in India and adopted from there by the Arabs, who added the zero. Algebra was invented by a Moslem scholar. The Arabs also built observatories, studied astronomy, and created astronomical tables. In medicine the Arabs not only studied the established works but supplemented them by careful observation of diseases.

Arab learning was more accessible to Western Europe than was the Byzantine. Both in Spain and in Sicily western scholars could find the great Arab works and have them translated into Latin. As early as 1126 an Englishman, Adelard of Bath, went to Spain and obtained translations of Moslem astronomical tables and Euclid's *Elements*. In the last quarter of the twelfth century Gerard of Cremona translated at least seventy-one Arab works. The philosophy and science of the Hellenistic world with the additions made by the Arabs themselves formed the basis for Western European learning in the twelfth and thirteenth centuries.

4. The Beginnings of Russia

WE HAVE seen that during the sixth and seventh centuries the Slavs spread rapidly over the European provinces of the Byzantine Empire. Many of these were brought in by the emperors to colonize deserted lands, and many more came as invaders but remained as settlers. The Slavs who settled in Greece and Macedonia soon became Christians, but this faith spread more slowly to their relatives in the north. In the second half of the ninth century two Byzantine missionaries, Cyril and Methodius, invented a Slavic alphabet and created a Slavic liturgy. This was soon followed by the conversion of the Slavic peoples. There was, of course, fierce competition between the pope and the patriarch of Constantinople for these converts. The Croats and Slovenes became attached to Rome, but the Serbs accepted Greek Christianity. Then in 865 the Bulgars and their Slavic subjects were converted. Despite a few brief successes by Roman envoys Bulgaria too became firmly orthodox. During the tenth and eleventh centuries Byzantine culture became firmly established among the Balkan peoples.

In the ninth century the Slavic groups settled in the Balkans constituted the southern wing of the Slavic peoples. To the north their relatives occupied a wide band of territory stretching from the Gulf of Finland in the north to the Carpathian Mountains in the south, and from the Baltic Sea in the west to the headwaters of the rivers Dniester and Dnieper in the east. Between the northern and southern Slavs lay the lands of the Avars, who were masters of Hungary, and their close relatives the Magyars, who controlled the northwestern shore of the Black Sea. To the north and east of the Magyars lived another fierce nomadic people, the Khazars.

About the middle of the ninth century Swedish Vikings crossed the Baltic and invaded the Slavic lands. They established a post at Novgorod to the southeast of the Gulf of Finland. Soon these fierce adven-

RUSSIA UNDER THE VARANGIANS

turers had spread southward and established themselves at Kiev, on the Dnieper. The Vikings, or Varangians as they are often called, founded fortified posts throughout the Slavic lands. From these centers they conquered the rural Slavic population and made the people accept their rule. Like the Vikings of the west, the Varangians were merchants as well as warriors. At Kiev and other points on the rivers they loaded boats with the products of the Russian forests—furs and honey—and carried them down to the Black Sea and along its shores to Constantinople. Sometimes they visited the Byzantine capital as simple traders, but at other times they were invading enemies. Several times they launched large-scale attacks on the great city. Although they never succeeded in making much progress against its mighty walls, they did obtain commercial privileges from the emperor. Meanwhile they had driven back the Khazars and the Magyars had moved on into Hungary. The Varangians were the masters of what is now western Russia. Moreover, they had welded this vast territory into a state ruled by the prince of Kiev.

The relations between the Varangians and Constantinople were very close. The capital of the Byzantine Empire was their market and bazaar. There they sold the products of their forests and obtained rich ornaments, clothes, and weapons. Although they carried on trade with Bagdad as well, Constantinople was their chief emporium. Many Varangians took service with the emperor as soldiers. In 990 Vladimir (978–1015), prince of Kiev, was converted and established Orthodox Christianity as the religion of his state. Soon there was a Russian church, organized on the Byzantine model and housed in buildings of Byzantine architecture. The learning and culture of the Byzantine Empire spread rapidly to Kiev and other Russian cities. In the eleventh century the occupation of the steppes north of the Black Sea by the Petchenegs made communication between Kiev and Constantinople more difficult, but Russia remained an outpost of Byzantine civilization.

In the thirteenth century a great catastrophe definitely cut the links between Russia and the Byzantine Empire. In 1237 a great Mongol army usually known as the Golden Horde under the command of Batu (1224–56), grandson of Chingiz Khan (1206–27), swept over the steppes of southern Russia. The nomadic peoples of the steppes as well as the Russian princes were defeated and subjected. The Mongols moved on to overrun Hungary and Poland after destroying the armies of the king of Hungary and the combined forces of Poland and the

Teutonic knights. While his troops were plundering the eastern shores of the Adriatic Sea, Batu learned of the death of his uncle, the Great Khan, and immediately hastened to central Asia to take part in the contest for the succession. His army retired to the Russian steppes, where they established a Mongol state. Many historians have assumed that if Batu had not been interrupted he could easily have overrun the countries of Western Europe. But the Mongols were defeated several times by the Egyptian Mamelukes, and there is good reason to believe that they might have met the same fate before the knights of Western Europe. It was a fortunate accident that spared Europe the test.

For over two hundred years the Russians were vassals of the Mongol khans. Ruled by a number of petty local princes, they were completely subject to the khan who ruled from Sarai on the river Volga. In the fourteenth century one of the little Russian principalities began to outstrip the others. The princes of Moscow persuaded the Mongol khans to make them their agents in dealing with the other Russian princes. Then by 1380 they were leading an alliance of princes against the Mongols. Moreover, the prince of Moscow had succeeded in making his city the chief center of the Russian church. He was the Grand Prince, the chief of all the Russian princes. In the second half of the fifteenth century Ivan III, grand prince of Moscow, began the creation of the later Russian state. He not only conquered many of his rival princes and greatly increased the size and resources of his state, but he also cast off the Mongol yoke and became an independent sovereign. In 1472 Ivan married as his second wife a Byzantine princess, niece of the last emperor to rule in Constantinople. He then abandoned the title of grand prince and called himself Tsar, or Caesar. In Ivan's mind he was the successor of the Byzantine emperors, and Moscow had taken the place of Constantinople as the center of Orthodox Christian civilization.

CHAPTER III

The Germanic Kingdoms

5. The Frankish State
6. Anglo-Saxon England
7. The Vikings

THE YEARS between 500 and 900 in Western Europe can best be understood if they are regarded as a period of transition from the civilizations of the early Germans and the Romans to the civilization of the Middle Ages. During this period the Germanic peoples settled down and developed their institutions. The political and legal customs of roving tribes became the government and laws of organized states. The rather haphazard agricultural techniques of semi-nomadic peoples were fashioned into reasonably effective methods of exploiting the rich soil of northern Europe. These same years saw the evangelization of all the Germanic peoples except those of Scandinavia and the disappearance from their ranks of Arian heretics. By 800 Western Europe was firmly Christian and Roman Catholic. While the process of wiping out all traces of pagan beliefs and imposing the Christian system of ethics was to take several more centuries, by the end of this period it was well started. Here then are the two themes of this chapter: the development of the Germanic states and their institutions, and the gradually increasing influence of Christianity upon them. We shall see the creation of a Christian German civilization stretching from the Atlantic to the Elbe and from the Baltic to the Mediterranean. Finally we shall see that civilization shaken to its very foundations by a new wave of pagan invasions.

5. The Frankish State

FROM 500 to 900 the dominant form of government in Western Europe was what historians call Germanic monarchy. Although the states created by the Vandals in North Africa and by the Ostrogoths in Italy where comparatively short-lived, that of the Visigoths in Spain lasted some 300 years, and that of the Lombards in Italy about 200. The Anglo-Saxon and Frankish monarchies existed throughout the period. By the end of this period the same type of government had appeared in the Scandinavian countries * and had been established in Russia by Viking adventurers.† Recently Russian scholars have termed these states "barbarian monarchies" and pointed out many resemblances between them and the Mongol states of central Asia.

The most essential royal function in these Germanic kingdoms was leading the people in war. The king's basic privilege was the right to summon every able-bodied man to his army. In most of these states the kingship was elective, but eligibility was commonly confined to members of a single royal family. In the Frankish and many of the Anglo-Saxon states the special position of the royal family was derived from a legendary descent from one of the Germanic gods. As a rule the various royal houses considered the kingship a family property divisible among a king's sons. Except for the Gothic kings, who were deeply imbued with Roman ideas, the Germanic monarchs had an extremely limited view of the functions of government. They believed it was their duty to lead the people in war and to supervise the administration of the ancient customary law. Beyond this their chief preoccupations were hoarding gold, silver, jewels, and pretty women, and consuming vast quantities of meat and drink.

While Germanic monarchy in general is an interesting phenomenon, the historian of Western Europe is primarily concerned with the states established by the Franks and the Anglo-Saxons. When Clovis (481–511) occupied the Paris region in 486, he was already an officer in the Roman service, and his followers were Roman allied troops.‡ Hence he naturally thought of himself as a representative of the emperor. He assumed the title and costume of a Roman consul while his warriors bore him through Paris on their shields. For several generations Clovis and his successors placed the head of the Roman emperor on all their

* See p. 188. † See pp. 59–60. ‡ See p. 29.

coins. The Merovingian court swarmed with officials bearing Roman designations; his horses were cared for by a *comes stabuli,* or count of the stables. In every Roman civitas he placed a Frank with the title comes, and Franks replaced the Roman centurions in the subdivisions of the civitates. For a time at least the Frankish officials collected the Roman land tax. Thus from one point of view Clovis was simply a German successor to the Roman rulers of Gaul.

This apparent political continuity with the Roman past was, however, largely a pleasant illusion. The state ruled by Clovis and his successors was a Germanic monarchy that was little affected by Roman political tradition. The Merovingian family was believed to have been descended from a god, and the male members of the house let their hair grow down to their shoulders as a sign of their divine descent. The royal office was elective within the family. The chief feature of the ceremonies marking the accession of a new king was his elevation on the shields of his warriors as a symbol of election. The kingdom was treated as if it were the private property of the royal family. When Clovis died, the state was divided among his sons; and except for brief periods it was so divided during the entire Merovingian period. While the boundaries of the various realms were continually changing as a result of war and family arrangements, there were three generally accepted major divisions of the Frankish state. The ancient Frankish lands on both sides of the Rhine formed the kingdom of Austrasia, while northern Gaul was known as Neustria. The former kingdom of Burgundy in the valleys of the Rhone and Saône formed a third Merovingian state. Southwestern Gaul, usually called Aquitaine, where Frankish influence was slight, was at times independent and at others attached to one of the other states. Thus, while the territory ruled by the Merovingian house remained relatively stable throughout the sixth and seventh centuries, the actual states varied continually in composition.

Each Merovingian king had a body of men bound by oath to serve him faithfully. This group, which was clearly the Frankish version of the ancient German comitatus, was called the truste, and its members antrustiones. The antrustiones served the king as officials, bodyguards, and members of his household. From their number were probably chosen the counts who represented the king in the civitates, or counties. The actual functions of these counts must have varied greatly according to the region in which they ruled. In the land of Germanic villages they presided over and supervised the ancient popular courts. But in the districts where Frankish settlement was slight they probably sat as Roman judges enforcing the customary Roman law.

Clovis and his successors fully realized the value of their alliance with the Church and were determined to make the most of it. They were extremely generous in making gifts of property and privileges to both the secular and regular clergy. The bishops became great landholders, and rich monasteries sprang up. The special rights enjoyed by the church under the Roman government were greatly enlarged. The ecclesiastics who were accustomed to the sophisticated Roman judicial system had no enthusiasm for what seemed to them the very primitive German law. Hence they persuaded the kings to grant them jurisdiction over the clergy. Moreover, the great prelates did not want wild Frankish counts wandering over their lands and pleaded for "immunity." This privilege meant that no royal officer could enter the lands of the church. Officers of the church arrested criminals and turned them over to the count in cases where the church lacked the right to try the criminal itself. There were many areas of government in which the Frankish kings took no interest but which were serious matters for the church. German custom knew nothing of wills and testaments; regular rules governed the inheritance of property. But the church relied heavily on the bequests of the faithful. The result of these opposed points of view was a compromise. Land continued to be subject to Germanic custom, but movable property could be devised by will, and the jurisdiction over wills was given to the church.

Marriage and legitimacy also meant little to the Frankish kings. The Merovingians and their fierce warrior followers had become formal Christians, but it was to be a long time before Christian ethics made any great impression on their mores. The most the church could hope to achieve was to persuade a king to acknowledge one of the women who served his pleasures as his wife. He could not be expected to bother about which of his children were born in such lawful wedlock. The kings had no objection, however, to letting the church try to impose its rules on their people. Thus marriage and legitimacy became questions to be handled by the church and its courts. All the king insisted on was that he and his nobles be not unduly hampered in getting rid of an unwanted wife. Finally, the church felt that it had an obligation to protect the weak and helpless, like widows and orphans. Here again the kings had no objection, so the weak became the particular concern of the church. In short the church took over a number of functions that had been the concern of the Roman civil authorities but that were of no interest to the Frankish kings.

Although the monarchs of the Merovingian line endowed the church generously with lands and privileges, they were careful to keep it securely under their control. Archbishop Remi of Reims attempted to persuade Clovis to disavow any right to interfere in episcopal elections, but the king could not be moved. Later ecclesiastical efforts in the same direction were repulsed by Clovis's successors. The kings insisted that only clerks who met with their approval could fill the episcopal chairs. Under the more enlightened rulers, this meant a royal veto power over episcopal elections, and under other monarchs outright appointment by the king. Moreover, no Merovingian would permit a church council to meet except at his summons, and the decrees of the council had no force until they were issued by the king. Thus both the personnel and the legislation of the Frankish church were under rigid royal control.

This had important effects on the church. The Frankish church became divided in the same manner as the Frankish state. A bishop was the appointee of the king who controlled his diocese, and church councils included only the bishops of a single kingdom. Only for a brief period when the great Dagobert (623–38) for a time ruled the entire state were councils held that included all the Frankish bishops. The episcopate became largely Germanic. When the bishops who were in power at the time of the Frankish conquest died, they were largely replaced by Franks who were the king's servants and friends. This led to a rapid decline in both literacy and ecclesiastical discipline. It is true that after a few generations the distinction between Frank and Roman was forgotten, and the king's men might be of either origin; but by that time there was little if any difference in education or ideas between the descendants of Frankish warriors and the descendants of Roman senators. Finally, the late Merovingian kings were inclined to consider the bishops as part of their administration—as a different sort of count. When a throne changed hands, the bishops were replaced as casually as were the secular officials. In short the Frankish church became essentially part of the Frankish state, and its condition depended largely on the kings. As most of the kings were wild barbarians, the church was usually in a deplorable condition.

Below the level of high politics we know very little of the Merovingian state. The kings, nobles, and high ecclesiastics had great estates not unlike the villas of Roman times. These estates were cultivated by semi-free tenants, men who were not slaves but could not leave the estate. Each tenant had a hut and a little plot of ground for his own use, but most of his time was spent in working on his master's land. At first these estates were probably all Roman in origin, the property of senatorial families or part of the imperial domain. But as time went on some Frankish villages became much like them.

It seems clear that there were two types of Frankish village. One was a settlement of freemen who tilled the land together under the direction of a village council; the other type was composed of a noble and his followers. Although at the beginning the followers of the noble might be freemen, as time went on they tended to sink to the position of those who cultivated the old Roman estates. Nevertheless, despite the continuance of the Roman coloni and the assimilation of many Franks to a similar status, it is clear that there were many freemen of various economic and social levels. There were small free farmers working just enough land to support their families, and there were small landholders who had from five to twenty tenants working for them. Then there were men who although they did not own land were yet fairly substantial people. The church, and probably lay landowners as well, would give land to a man as a *beneficium*, or benefice. A benefice might be just enough to support a farmer and his family, or it might be a large piece of land with tenants on it. The holder of the benefice agreed to pay rent or perform some sort of service to the man who granted it. It seems likely that he often if not usually took an oath to be faithful to the grantor; that is, in the language of the time, he "commended" himself to the landholder and became his "man." By this system the landowner got his lands cultivated and obtained loyal followers, and the tenant obtained both a means of livelihood and protection. Various terms were used to designate the holders of benefices. One that was to become important in later times was that of *vassus*.

The gradual decline of civilization in Gaul, which had been in progress since the third century, became more rapid in the Merovingian period. The Franks were essentially warriors rather than traders, and they had no interest in urban life. Moreover their kings did not consider the encouragement of trade and commerce by keeping roads and bridges in repair, policing the trade routes, and protecting merchants and their goods, any part of their royal function. Although the ancient cities on the Mediterranean coast retained some sea-borne commerce, trade almost disappeared in the interior. By the end of the Merovingian era, Gaul was essentially an agricultural region with a localized agrarian economy. There was little money in circulation and few traders moved along the roads.

The decline in culture was equally marked. When Clovis conquered Gaul there were still a number of men, mostly prelates, senators, and members of their households, who had been educated in the Roman schools.* The poet Fortunatus was an intimate of several Merovingian kings and a decoration to their courts. Our knowledge of the Frankish state under Clovis and his sons comes chiefly from the *Ecclesiastical History of the Franks* written by Gregory, bishop of Tours. But after that generation disappeared, learning became extremely rare and literacy rather uncommon. If one is to call any period the "Dark Ages," the later Merovingian period is the one to choose. While here and there unusual men appeared such as King Dagobert, who had a taste for and some ability in theological studies, in general laymen were completely illiterate, and few clerks were much better educated.

One might well expect to find the great monasteries patches of light in this sea of darkness, but unfortunately the regular clergy failed to maintain standards higher than those of their secular colleagues. To some extent this was the result of the fact that the monastic rules were ill adapted to an uncivilized people. These rules had been developed among the sophisticated population of the Mediterranean regions, to whom a life of asceticism and contemplation had both meaning and appeal.† But the fierce Franks had little enthusiasm for asceticism and no conception of the contemplative life. Moreover, the extreme ascetic practices in regard to clothing, food, and drink that were reasonable in the mild Mediterranean climate were too rigorous for the northern lands. But entirely apart from the nature of the monastic rules, it is obviously difficult in the extreme for any group to embrace the contemplative life in wild and barbaric surroundings. The Frankish monasteries were primarily the refuge of those who were unfitted for the turbulent life of the time. When a royal prince failed to get a share of his father's kingdom, he was killed or put in a monastery. The same fate awaited princesses for whom no husbands could be found. In short, very few of the inhabitants of the monasteries were there for

* See p. 466. † See pp. 17–18.

religious reasons, and for the most part they cheerfully ignored the severe rules by which they should have lived.

There was a brief wave of reform in the Frankish monasteries late in the sixth century. When the Germanic conquerors engulfed Gaul, many learned monks had fled to Ireland, which seemed the last refuge of Catholic Christianity in the West. At a time when few people in Gaul could read, Irish scholars were reading some Greek and much Latin. The great monasteries of Ireland produced both scholars and saints. One of the latter, St. Columbanus, crossed to the continent and attempted to reform the Frankish monasteries. He founded the monastery of Luxeuil, and his influence spread to many other houses both new and old. But although St. Columbanus was imbued with a contagious religious enthusiasm, his rule was no more suited to the Frankish lands than those of earlier missionaries; and his influence did not long survive him. The seventh century saw the monasteries of the Frankish state rich and powerful but with little discipline, culture, or enthusiasm.

During the last century of the Merovingian period the effective power of the kings declined greatly. Historians have called the monarchs of this period the "do-nothing kings." Actually they seem to have been reasonably capable but remarkably short-lived. The result was that there were a series of minor kings; and the states were governed by the great nobles, who formed themselves into political cliques. The head of the group in power took the title of mayor of the palace or leader of the Franks, *dux Francorum*. The most successful of the noble houses that were contending for power was descended from Pepin of Landen, who had been mayor of the palace for the last strong Merovingian ruler, Dagobert I. Pepin's son and grandson in the male line attempted to become kings in place of the Merovingians and were defeated and slain, but his daughter's son, Pepin of Heristal, became mayor of the palace in both Austrasia and Neustria. When this second Pepin died his legitimate children were under age, and the Frankish states were plunged again into anarchy by the feuding nobles until his illegitimate son Charles (714–41), known to history as Martel or the Hammer, succeeded in defeating his rivals and becoming dux Francorum in the entire kingdom.

Although we know very little about Charles, he was clearly a man of unusual ability. When he came to power, he was faced with three problems: two essentially military, and one both military and political.

Moslem invaders from Africa had crushed the Visigoth power in Spain in 711, crossed the Pyrenees, and occupied southern France. At the opposite edge of the Frankish territory the Saxons were becoming extremely troublesome. The Merovingian military system was inadequate for defense against either of these foes. The Merovingian army consisted of the king and his nobles surrounded by their households and a general levy of all able-bodied men. But the royal and noble bodyguards were few in number, and the mass levy was untrained, poorly equipped, and completely undisciplined. A Merovingian army was a terror to its friends, as it plundered the countryside wherever it went; but it was no great danger to its enemies. If Charles was to cope with the Moslems and the Saxons, he needed an effective army. Moreover, if his house was to retain its power in the state and put an end to the continual revolts of rival families, it needed a strong and reliable military force. As long as the power of the duke of the Franks rested purely on his own military capacity and the support of a group of nobles, it could be overthrown fairly easily by any able warrior with his own alliance of landowners.

Although the Franks in general had remained foot soldiers, the Merovingian kings, their nobles, and their households usually fought on horseback. Naturally Charles would be inclined to model his new forces on these elite troops. The recent introduction of the stirrup into Western Europe had greatly increased the efficiency of cavalry. With the stirrup a mounted man could use his lance for striking as well as for throwing, and by rising in the stirrups he could strike highly effective strokes with his sword. Infantry were almost helpless against horsemen using the stirrup, protected by armor and a shield, and armed with sword and lance. But this equipment was extremely costly, and its effective use required continual practice. To handle a shield, sword, and lance while managing a horse was a feat that could only be achieved by long experience and rigid training. Soldiers of this type had to be rich enough to buy horse and arms and to be free from the need of working for their living. By the eighth century the Frankish state had little or no money revenue; the kings and nobles supported themselves, their families, and their households from the produce of their estates. If Charles was to have an army of mounted soldiers, he would have to supply each one with land and labor to cultivate it.

The system devised by Charles was the natural product of the customs and conditions of the time. He enlisted able warriors and had them swear absolute fidelity to him. They became his *vassi dominici*, vassals of the lord. To each one he gave a beneficium, an estate large enough to support him which he could hold as long as he served Charles well as a soldier. But it was difficult to find enough land to supply as many benefices as were needed. Charles undoubtedly used the royal estates for this purpose, but to do so too extensively would seriously weaken the resources of the government. Soon Charles was looking with a greedy eye on the vast lands of the church. The church was accustomed to grant out its land in benefices. Why should it not do so to his soldiers? Charles obliged the prelates to grant benefices to men on condition that they serve him as soldiers. Although in theory these benefices were held from the church and remained church land, they actually passed into the control of Charles. When the soldier to whom such a benefice had been given died, Charles gave it to another capable warrior. Thus Charles solved his military problems. He obtained a large force of mounted soldiers who were bound to him by oath and held their lands at his pleasure. With them he repulsed the Moslem northward march near Tours, and the Moslems retired to the fringes of southern France. These troops also enabled him to conquer a part of Saxony and free the Frankish state from the danger of Saxon attack. Moreover, they gave him a solid basis for his power as duke of the Franks. Rival nobles would hesitate a long time before risking an attack on Charles and his loyal, well-trained, and well-armed vassi.

When Charles Martel died in 741, he was succeeded in office by his two sons, Carloman and Pepin. Six years later Carloman, apparently quite voluntarily, retired to a monastery and left Pepin duke of all the Franks. Pepin (741–68) made good use of the military force his father had created. He drove the Moslems back over the Pyrennees and forced the duke of Bavaria to acknowledge him as overlord. Moreover, he twice marched into Italy to defend the pope from the Lombards.

Pepin's services to the Frankish state were not, however, primarily military. His chief achievement was the reform and reorganization of the Frankish church in cooperation with a great ecclesiastical statesman, St. Boniface. Boniface was an English monk who had become a missionary first in Frisia and then in Thuringia. About 722 the pope had consecrated him as a missionary bishop without a fixed see. Charles Martel, who was then ruling the Franks, was not noted as a friend of either the church or the papacy. He had used church lands to support his soldiers and had refused to aid the pope against the Lombards. He was, however, willing to aid Boniface. Supported by the power of the Frankish duke, Boniface made many converts in Saxony and Thuringia. In 732 the pope made him a missionary archbishop so that he could have other bishops to aid him in his work.

As long as Charles Martel lived Boniface was simply a missionary bishop under his protection. Charles had no interest whatever in reforming the Frankish church—in fact his government of it was particularly scandalous. The bishoprics were used to support his relatives and friends, and he had no objection to giving several sees to one man. But Pepin and particularly Carloman early came under the influence of Boniface. When Charles died, they were ready to undertake a general reform of the church in their lands. A series of church councils were held in both Austrasia and Neustria to provide the necessary legislation. In the hope of establishing discipline, archbishops were directed to hold provincial councils and bishops diocesan councils every year. All the prelates swore to obey the pope. As the papacy had had practically no influence in the Frankish church before this time, this was an important innovation. Then all ecclesiastics were commanded to wear distinctive dress. Before this the clergy wore special vestments when performing the services of the church, but at other times dressed as laymen. A regular clerical costume was bound to improve discipline. In addition, the monasteries of the Frankish state were ordered to adopt the rule of St. Benedict. This last was perhaps the most important reform of all. Not only did it establish reasonable uniformity and hence make discipline easier, but the Benedictine rule was far more effective than those previously used in northwestern Europe.

Benedict of Nursia was an Italian of noble birth who grew up under the rule of the great Ostrogoth king, Theodoric, saw the collapse of the Ostrogothic kingdom before the generals of the Emperor Justinian, and died a subject of this emperor. He thus lived in the twilight period of Roman civilization in Italy and was the contemporary of the last noted Roman scholars such as Cassiodorus and Boethius. While Boethius was reducing the learning of the ancient world to simple forms that could serve the people of the barbarized west, Benedict performed the same service for monasticism. About 520 St. Benedict founded the monastery of Monte Cassino, and soon after he composed his rule for the monastic life.

The central purpose of the Benedictine rule was the achievement of salvation by leading a perfect Christian life. The basic asceticism of the monastic tradition appeared in the three vows required of all Benedictines—celibacy, poverty, and obedience. The monk or nun must be absolutely celibate and could own no private property. Each individual abandoned his own will by becoming the absolute subject of the abbot. Although the abbot was expected to take counsel with his monks, his decision alone was final. Thus in becoming a Benedictine one abjured sexual pleasure, private property, and all personal independence. Perhaps the chief innovation of the Benedictine rule was the substitution of useful activity for contemplation. The monks were to spend long hours in performing the services of the church, were to do physical labor in the fields, and were to spend some time each day in reading and study. The monk's food was to be plain, but sufficient in quantity, and his clothing simple but adequate. The monastic life was to be led in common. The monks slept in a common dormitory, ate in a common refectory, and worked, studied, and performed the services of the church together. The Benedictine could not leave his monastery, but lived and died within its walls.

The advantages of the Benedictine rule are obvious. It provided a simple Christian life that could be followed by unsophisticated men and women. Although fundamentally ascetic, it did not impose extreme physical hardship. The absolute power of the abbot and the common life made discipline relatively easy to enforce. Thus St. Benedict effectively adapted the monastic tradition to the needs of the West. But in addition to providing for the salvation of its followers, the Benedictine rule increased the value of monasteries to society as a whole. The labor performed by the monks was economically productive, at a time when such production was gravely needed. The Benedictine monasteries became important centers for the practice of agriculture and industry. The hours spent by the monks in study did much to aid the survival of culture. The Benedictines copied the works of ancient Latin writers and so preserved them for posterity, and to some slight extent they kept alive the ancient learning. It is, however, important to realize that these services to society as a whole were by-products of the Benedictine rule and formed no part of St. Benedict's purpose. His object was to furnish enthusiastic Christians with a sane and practicable road to salvation in general accord with the monastic tradition.

The work commenced by the reforming councils was energetically carried forward by Boniface with the full support of Pepin and Carloman. The Frankish church was systematically organized and forced to acknowledge its obligations to the pope. Regular episcopal sees were set up in Bavaria, Thuringia, and the parts of Saxony ruled by the Franks. The Benedictine rule was imposed on most of the monasteries of the Frankish state, and new monastic foundations were established in the German lands. The joint efforts of Boniface and the Frankish dukes set a valuable precedent for future close cooperation between church and state.

This cooperation was soon made still closer by the mutual necessities of Pepin and the pope. We have seen in the previous chapter that the conquest of central Italy by the Lombards late in the sixth century had cut off communications between the imperial exarch at Ravenna and Rome and made the pope virtually the secular ruler of the ancient capital of the empire. The Lombards had established a kingdom in northern Italy and several independent duchies further south. As time went on they abandoned Arianism, became Catholics, and on the whole lived in amicable relations with the papacy. But in the early eighth century the Lombard kings began to expand their power, and showed their intention of making themselves true kings of Italy. They first absorbed the independent Lombard duchies and then commenced attacks on the remnants of Byzantine power. In 751 they conquered Ravenna and expelled the exarch. Rome was clearly next.

The Lombards would not have injured the see of St. Peter; they would in fact undoubtedly have made it the chief ecclesiastical seat of their realm. But the pope had no desire to give up his secular authority over Rome and its environs and become simply the chief ecclesiastic of the Lombard kingdom. The prelate who owed his independence in large measure to his distance from his imperial master in Constantinople did not want a king ruling in Rome. Hence the pope looked about for a military power that could protect him from the Lombards. When the Lombard king had absorbed the independent duchies, the alarmed pope had appealed to Charles Martel. As Charles believed he might some day need Lombard aid against the Moslems, he had refused to intervene. Nevertheless the Frankish state was the only power strong enough to aid the papacy, and the pope was anxious for its good will.

Pepin on his part faced a serious political problem. When King Theuderich IV (720–37) died, Charles Martel had not bothered to find a new king but had simply continued to rule as mayor of the palace and duke of the Franks. The illegality of this situation troubled Pepin, and he found a distant relative of the late king whom he placed on the throne. It seemed, however, essentially silly to have one man reigning while another ruled, and Pepin was inclined to declare himself king of the Franks. The only difficulty was that the Merovingian house was by tradition descended from a god and divinely appointed to rule. Hence Pepin felt that the transfer of the crown to a new line could be secure only if that line obtained divine sanction. In 751 two envoys of Pepin made their way to Rome to ask the Pope whether it was proper for one man to reign while another ruled. Here was the Pope's opportunity to gain a powerful friend, and he did not hesitate. In November 751 Pepin was crowned and anointed as king by St. Boniface acting as the Pope's representative. The new royal Frankish house had obtained its divine sanction.

The Pope soon had need of his new ally. In 753 the Lombard king moved his forces against Rome. But he dared not lay hands on the person of the Pope, and the latter was able to journey through Lombardy, over the Alpine passes, and into Pepin's domains. The Frankish king greeted the successor of St. Peter with appropriate enthusiasm, and he and his two sons were anointed as kings by the papal hands. Pepin on his side promised the Pope his aid against the Lombards. Here an interesting question arises. Throughout the Middle Ages the pope's claim to temporal sovereignty over what were later called the papal states were based on a rather clumsy forgery called the Donation of Constantine. According to this document the Emperor Constantine transferred to the pope all the imperial authority in Italy. While it is impossible to prove that the Donation of Constantine existed before the ninth century, most scholars believe that it was concocted in the eighth. It may well have been shown to Pepin to qualm any scruples he may have had about seizing for the pope lands claimed by both the Lombard king and the emperor at Constantinople. Be that as it may, Pepin invaded Italy in 755 and forced King Aistulf to beg for peace and to promise to surrender Ravenna and its hinterland to the pope. When Aistulf failed to keep his agreement and actually attacked Rome, Pepin returned with his Frankish army and defeated him once more. This time Pepin stayed in Italy until the pope was firmly in possession of the exarchate of Ravenna.

When Pepin died in 768, he was succeeded by his two sons, Charles (768–814) and Carloman (768–71). As the two brothers could not agree, it was fortunate for the state that Carloman died three years after his father. Charles ignored Carloman's infant son and promptly took possession of the entire Frankish state. Physically Charles was a moderately tall, powerfully built man with red hair, a bull neck, and a fine large belly. He loved both hunting and feasting well on the game brought in. His biographer, Einhard, assures us that he drank with great moderation, rarely taking more than three cups of wine with a meal. One who has seen the cups of the time will not worry too much over Charles's temperance.

In character Charles was aggressive, ambitious, determined, and utterly ruthless in attaining his ends. He had a keen, inquiring mind. He was soldier, statesman, and patron of scholars. But no process of adding up his known characteristics can give us an explanation of Charles's capacity. His achievements remain almost incredible, and to explain them one must resort to such vague phrases as force of character. He was the dominant figure of the western world in his own day, a legendary hero to the men of the Middle Ages, and historians still call him Charlemagne, or Charles the Great.*

Soon after Charlemagne ascended the throne it became clear that Pepin's settlement in Italy could not be permanent. As long as able and ambitious kings ruled the Lombard state, they were going to try to conquer all Italy. The papal state could never be safe while the Lombard kingdom existed. Hence in 773 Charlemagne led his Frankish army into Italy, besieged and captured the Lombard capital Pavia, put the Lombard king in a monastery, and himself assumed the Lombard crown. Although for administrative convenience he had his son Pepin crowned as king of Italy in 780, Charlemagne remained for the rest of his life the effective ruler of the Lombard state.

Even before he marched south to crush the Lombards, Charlemagne had set out to complete the work of his father and grandfather in northern Germany—the conquest of Saxony. In 772 he marched through southwest Saxony as far as the river Weser, receiving the submission of the local chiefs. But as soon as the King left for Italy the conquered Saxons rose and raided the Frankish frontier. In 775 Charlemagne returned to Saxony and subdued the same region once more. The Saxons were a stubborn, hardy, and warlike people. They fought bitterly until they were obliged to surrender and then rose in revolt as soon as the Frankish army had gone home. It was not until 780 that

* See pp. 452–3.

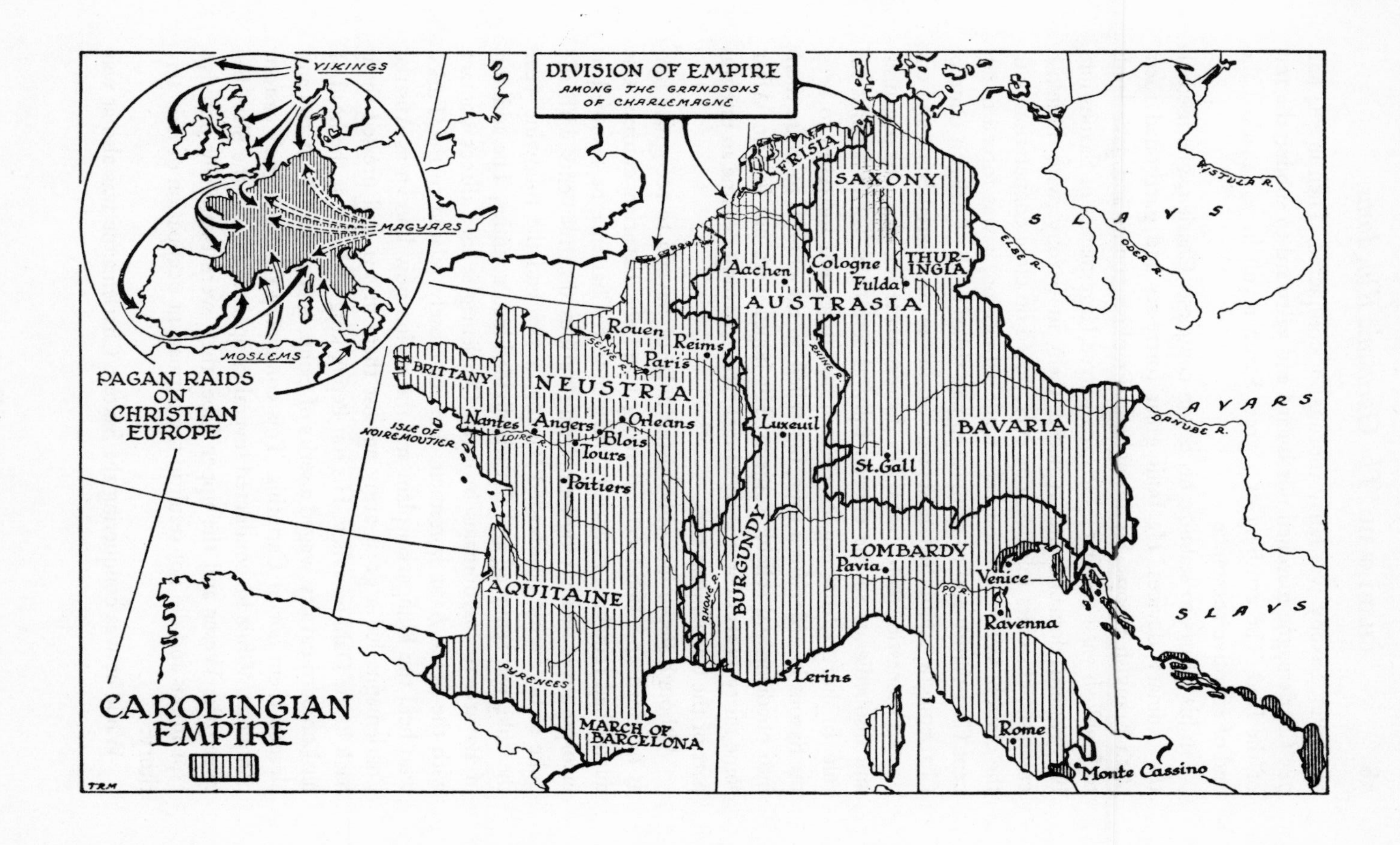

DIVISION OF EMPIRE
AMONG THE GRANDSONS OF CHARLEMAGNE
VIKINGS
MAGYARS
MOSLEMS
PAGAN RAIDS ON CHRISTIAN EUROPE
FRISIA
SAXONY
THURINGIA
AUSTRASIA
NEUSTRIA
BRITTANY
AQUITAINE
BURGUNDY
BAVARIA
LOMBARDY
MARCH OF BARCELONA
SLAVS
AVARS
SLAVS
Aachen
Cologne
Fulda
Rouen
Reims
Paris
Nantes
Angers
Orleans
Blois
Tours
Poitiers
Luxeuil
St. Gall
Pavia
Venice
Ravenna
Rome
Monte Cassino
Lerins
ISLE OF NOIREMOUTIER
SEINE R.
LOIRE R.
RHINE R.
RHONE R.
PO R.
DANUBE R.
ELBE R.
ODER R.
VISTULA R.
PYRENEES
CAROLINGIAN EMPIRE
TRM

southwest Saxony was fairly thoroughly conquered. Then in 784 and 785 Charlemagne marched northward and eastward to subdue the rest of the land. The crushing of a great Saxon revolt in 792 marked the end of effective resistance.

In his efforts to stabilize his Saxon conquests Charlemagne used all the ordinary devices. He built great fortresses and garrisoned them with Frankish troops. He brought in Frankish counts and gave lands to Frankish vassi dominici. He even moved large masses of Saxons into his western domains and replaced them in Saxony with Frankish colonists. His chief reliance, however, rested on close cooperation with the church. When a Saxon tribe made submission, it was forced to accept Christianity and to promise to pay tithes to the Christian church. Charlemagne established episcopal sees in the conquered lands and endowed monastic foundations. His decrees made relapses into paganism and disobedience to the church fully as serious as revolt against his rule. In short, Charlemagne expected his armies and fortresses to keep the Saxons in order for a time, but relied on the church to make them into obedient and reliable subjects. His hopes were not in vain. After some thirty years of war and evangelization, Saxony became an integral part of the Carolingian state.

Although Pepin had obliged the duke of Bavaria to recognize him as overlord and Boniface had reorganized the Bavarian church, this duchy had remained essentially independent. Charlemagne resolved to incorporate it in his kingdom. Using various disagreements with the duke as his excuse he invaded Bavaria in 787, and the following year the duke was removed and Bavaria divided into counties. The addition of Bavaria to his domains brought Charlemagne into direct contact with the fierce Avar horsemen, Asiatics closely related to the Turks, who held the Hungarian plain and the region now known as Austria. Charlemagne led a great army against them in 791 and pressed them back in the Danube valley. His son Pepin, king of Italy, at the head of his Lombard cavalry waged a series of campaigns against the Avars and cleaned them out of Carinthia. This completed Charlemagne's eastern conquests. While he conducted several campaigns against the Slavs between the Weser and the upper Elbe, they were essentially punitive expeditions and did not result in the permanent occupation of new territory.

While he was conquering the Saxons, Charlemagne was also at war with another foe at the opposite end of his kingdom. In 778 he led a large army into northern Spain. This expedition was not a great success. He spent most of his time fighting the Christian Basques, and as he returned home across the Pyrenees, they ambushed and destroyed his rear guard. This disaster was the original basis for the famous Song of Roland, one of the finest of the legends that grew up about Charlemagne.* The great king's persistence, however, eventually led to success. In a long series of campaigns he and his generals conquered a strip of northern Spain which was called the March of Barcelona, after its chief city. By granting benefices in this territory to many vassi dominici Charlemagne turned it into an effective buffer between the Frankish kingdom and the Moslems of Spain.

A mere systematic account of Charlemagne's conquests does not give a full picture of his astounding military achievements. This can only be gained by glancing briefly at the chronology of his campaigns. In 772 he invaded Saxony, in 773 and 774 he conquered the Lombard kingdom, in 775 and 776 he renewed his attacks on the Saxons, and in 778 he invaded Spain. The year 779 saw him back in Saxony. The mustering almost every year of the military resources of the Frankish kingdom and moving them to distant frontiers must have been a stupendous task. Even though his armies were probably comparatively small in numbers, the problem of supplying them must have been extremely hard to solve. The fact that Charlemagne was able to do this is all the evidence one should need of his unusual ability and unshakeable determination.

Fully as difficult as conquering new territory was the administration of so vast a realm. The peaceful interior parts of the kingdom were ruled by counts. In the border regions, where defense was important, larger territorial units were administered by margraves—from *mark graf*, *mark* meaning a border district and *graf*, count. Above these officials was a small group of lieutenants of the king who watched over his interests. Finally there were Charlemagne's sons, who were the titular kings of various parts of the state. The great difficulty was to be sure of the loyalty of these numerous officers, and Charlemagne had to suppress a number of dangerous plots. It was in the hope of securing adequate information about the behavior of his local officials that Charlemagne created the officials known as missi dominici. Two men, a

* See p. 453.

prelate and a lay noble, were sent out together to survey a section of the realm and bear the king's orders to the counts and margraves. Each year the pairs were shifted about so that the same men should not repeatedly visit the same region. This device was valuable as a means of supervision, but its actual effectiveness depended on the power and prestige of the monarch. As long as Charlemagne's sword loomed behind his missi, the administrative system worked fairly well. But Charlemagne did not succeed in devising any institutions that could make it possible for a weaker monarch to manage his vast state.

In the year 800 Charlemagne was called to Rome to rescue the pope from his enemies among the local aristocracy. On Christmas day the grateful pontiff approached the king as he was rising from prayer, placed a crown upon his head, and declared him Emperor. Our information is too scanty to allow us to know what lay behind this ceremony. Einhard assures us that Charlemagne was annoyed. Some scholars have deemed it unlikely that the pope would act without the king's consent and have supposed that Charlemagne had the affair carefully prearranged. Others have accepted Einhard's story and believed that the pope originated the idea. There are good arguments for both points of view. Charlemagne had been for some years patrician of Rome. As he ruled a fair part of the western provinces of the Empire, he may well have felt it fitting that he should bear the title. On the other hand the pope may have wanted to show his gratitude for Charlemagne's aid and at the same time free himself completely from dependence on Constantinople.* Charlemagne's annoyance may have come from a disinclination to offend the Byzantine ruler. Later in the Middle Ages the question as to whether initiative had come from king or pope was a matter of some importance, but in 800 it made little difference. Charlemagne was unquestioned master of his vast realm, and his new title could neither strengthen nor weaken him. The debate as to whether or not the later German kings would have thought of taking the imperial title if Charlemagne had not done so is essentially fruitless. No man who controlled Rome could help thinking of its past greatness and the position of its ancient rulers. Charlemagne's assumption of the imperial title was the most spectacular event of his career, but it did not increase his political authority.

One of Charlemagne's prime ambitions was to revive the light of

* See p. 45.

learning in his vast barbarous realm. To some extent he was probably moved by purely practical considerations; an effective government required some literate officials. But it seems clear that he had also a real curiosity and enthusiasm for the knowledge stored in books written by the scholars of previous ages. At any rate Charlemagne gathered about him in his palace some dozen learned men drawn from all Europe—some by quiet abduction, others by honest hiring. The chief of them was the Saxon Alcuin, who had been trained in the famous school at York.* From Italy he drew a grammarian, Peter of Pisa, and Paul the Deacon, who wrote a history of the Lombards. Einhard, the royal biographer, was a Frank. Other learned men were drawn from Spain and Germany. For fifteen years Alcuin conducted a school in Charlemagne's palace. The king himself studied industriously and is said to have mastered both Latin and Greek. Charlemagne also encouraged the establishment of schools in the cathedrals and monasteries of the realm for the education of the clergy and any laymen who should seek knowledge.†

These scholars brought together by Charlemagne began the long, slow task of making the learning of the past available for the men of the Middle Ages. The first steps were necessarily simple. The basic rules of Latin grammar were studied and taught. The elements of logic were slowly absorbed. The writings of the church fathers were culled for material that had meaning for the men of the day. The typical Carolingian scholarly work was a series of selections chosen and arranged to answer the problems that troubled them. It is important to remember that these scholars were very few in number—perhaps two dozen in all the kingdom. The light kindled by Charlemagne's efforts was not very bright, and it shone flickeringly in a vast sea of darkness; but it was never to go out completely.

Perhaps the most valuable work of the Carolingian scholars was the reproduction of manuscripts. When Alcuin retired from the court, he lived at the great abbey of St. Martin at Tours. There he established a "scriptorium" or publishing house. Under his direction copies were made of all available manuscripts and the handwriting known as the Carolingian miniscule was developed. The scholars of the Middle Ages were to owe much to the work of the monks of Tours and their successors at such centers as Reims, Cologne, and Fulda.

* See pp. 87–8. † See p. 467.

6. Anglo-Saxon England

THE ANGLO-SAXON invaders of Britain were led by many chieftains. The various groups must have combined to wage war on the Britons, but once the country was conquered they formed a score or so of petty states. Each state had a king and a council, or *witan*, composed of the most important nobles. The people were divided into a number of classes, which differed to some degree from state to state. At the top were the members of the royal family, the *aethelings*. Below them came the *gesiths* and the earls. The members of these three classes were warriors, but in all probability the gesiths and the earls were the soldiers who served the king and the aethelings. At the head of the classes that actually worked the land stood the ordinary freeman, or churl. Below the churl were several categories of men who were unfree. The witan elected the king from the ranks of the aethelings and advised him on all important questions. The ancient customary law was enforced by popular courts presided over by the king's representatives, who were members of the warrior classes. All freemen attended these courts, and the decisions were made by all those present. The king with the approval of the witan could issue decrees that modified or added to the mass of customary law.

The chief activity of the Anglo-Saxon kings was waging war on one another. When one king defeated another, he either absorbed the conquered state into his own or forced it to pay tribute to him. From time to time a king would succeed in defeating all his rivals and becoming the recognized overlord of England, or *Bretwealda*. This position was held by a South Saxon king late in the fifth century, by a West Saxon ruler a century later, by Ethelbert, king of Kent, from 584 to 616, and then by the king of the East Angles. These early Bretwealdas were apparently content to take tribute from their conquered enemies and made no effort to absorb the lesser states bordering on theirs.

This policy was changed with the rise to power of Edwin, king of Northumbria. Edwin (616–32) combined the two Northumbrian kingdoms—Bernicia, with its capital at Bamborough, and Deira, with its capital at York—and conquered the independent Celts to the west of these states. He then absorbed three petty Anglo-Saxon states to the south. Under Edwin's rule Northumbria extended from The Wash to the Firth of Forth on the east, and from the river Dee to the Solway on the west. He and his successors Oswald and Oswy were by far the most powerful rulers England had known.

Until the early seventh century the states of central England had been small and weak and hence easily dominated by the larger kingdoms on the coasts. The strongest of these midland states was the kingdom of Mercia, with its capital at Tamworth. Soon after 630 an able

and energetic monarch called Penda (632–54) became the ruler of Mercia. Penda waged a series of bitter wars with Oswald (633–41) and Oswy (654–70), kings of Northumbria, over the three minor states that lay between their realms. Although Penda's victories were only temporary, his successors were able to destroy the power of Northumbria and also to absorb all the minor states of the midlands. Wulfere (657–74), Aethelbald (716–57), and Offa (757–96), kings of Mercia, were Bretwealdas who ruled a Mercian kingdom extending from the Thames to the Humber and from the Ouse to the border of Wales. King Offa fortified or at least defined his frontier in Wales with a great ditch still known as Offa's Dyke.

While the kings of Northumbria and Mercia were struggling for control of the region comprising the present counties of Lincolnshire, Nottinghamshire, Derbyshire, and Cheshire, and the latter were extending their power over the whole midlands, the kings of the West Saxons were industriously enlarging their state at the expense of the Celts of Devon and Cornwall. By 802 the West Saxons were masters of all England south of the Thames and west of Kent and Sussex. In 825 Egbert (802–39), king of the West Saxons, defeated the king of Mercia and became Bretwealda. The two last Anglo-Saxon Bretwealdas, Offa of Mercia and Egbert of the West Saxons, were approximate contemporaries of Charlemagne. While England had not been really united, its separate kingdoms were reduced to seven: Northumbria, East Anglia, Essex, Kent, Sussex, Mercia, and Wessex.

The most important phase of the history of Anglo-Saxon England before 800, however, is the story of its conversion to Christianity. The third Bretwealda, Ethelbert, king of Kent, married a Frankish princess and through her became interested in Christianity. He may have invited Pope Gregory the Great to send him missionaries. According to legend Pope Gregory was so much attracted by Anglo-Saxon children he saw being sold as slaves in Rome that he decided to evangelize their homeland. An able and vigorous pontiff could hardly fail to see the great advantages to the Roman church in spreading its authority over England and re-establishing direct contact with Celtic Christianity. At any rate, Gregory dispatched a monk named Augustine with a small band of followers armed with letters of introduction to the rulers of the Frankish state.

The gentle Augustine took one look at the wild Franks who were theoretically Christians and decided not to go near their pagan relatives. Urged on by Gregory, he finally reached England in 597. He was enthusiastically received by Ethelbert, who became converted with all his subjects. Augustine built a monastery at Canterbury to serve as headquarters for the evangelization of England. He also sought to obtain the cooperation of the Celtic bishops, but here he met with complete failure. The Celtic church had been cut off from communication with Rome for over a century, and in that time the Roman church had changed its customs. Perhaps the chief practical difference was a change in the calendar that made the Celtic and Roman Easters come at different times. Other variations were in such minor matters as the form of the tonsure. But slight as the differences may seem to us, they were important to the Celtic bishops, and they refused to compromise. As a matter of fact, one cannot but suspect that the Welsh prelates who met with Augustine had no great enthusiasm for converting the bitter enemies of their people. Why should they want to save the Anglo-Saxons from the fires of hell? Augustine was more successful among the English. In 604 the East Saxons became converted and were given a bishop with his seat at London. When Augustine died in 605, Kent and Essex seemed securely Christian.

Unfortunately such rapid conversions as those achieved by Augustine were unlikely to be very deep. In his late years King Ethelbert married an attractive young wife, and when he died his son promptly made this lady his queen. When Augustine's successor pointed out that a Christian could not marry his stepmother, the king calmly returned to paganism. Somewhat later the king of Essex was reproved by the bishop of London for a casual homicide and replied by ejecting the bishop from his lands. In the view of these kings Christianity was all very fine, but it must not be allowed to interfere with the royal pleasures. For a time it looked as if the English mission was at an end. It was only saved by the new Bretwealda, Edwin of Northumbria, who had married a daughter of Ethelbert. He asked for Christian missionaries, and one named Paulinus went north to convert the Northumbrians. Paulinus was highly successful in converting the inhabitants of the kingdom of Deira before his work was cut short by the temporary conquest of Northumbria by the pagan Penda of Mercia. This conquest forced Paulinus and his fellow missionaries to flee to the south, thus ending the first attempt to evangelize Northumbria.

When King Edwin of Bernicia united all Northumbria by seizing the kingdom of Deira, the young heir to the latter state, Oswald, fled to the northwest and sought refuge among the Scots. Towards the end of the fifth century Scots from Ireland had driven the Picts from the region now known as Argyllshire and had founded the Christian Celtic kingdom of Dalriada. In 563 an Irish missionary monk, St. Columba, founded a monastery on the island of Iona to serve as a base for the conversion of the heathen Picts. It was to Iona or its vicinity that Oswald fled, and there he became converted to Christianity. Once he was secure on the Northumbrian throne after his defeat of the Mercians, Oswald sent for a Celtic monk, Aidan, to be bishop of his kingdom. Aidan founded as his seat a monastery on the island of Lindisfarne near Oswald's capital of Bamborough. Working under the protection of Oswald Aidan converted the Northumbrians to Celtic Christianity.

In 641 Oswald was defeated and slain by King Penda of Mercia. His brother Oswy soon expelled the Mercians, however, and became king of Northumbria. In the hope of ending the bitter rivalry between his house and that of Oswald's predecessor Edwin, Oswy married a daughter of Edwin who had been living in exile in Kent. This lady had been brought up in the Roman Christian tradition, and when she went north to marry Oswy, she took with her a chaplain. This brought confusion to Oswy's court because of the differences between the Celtic Christianity of Aidan and the Roman customs of the queen. What seems to have particularly annoyed Oswy was the fact that he and his queen celebrated Lent at different times. Meanwhile a devoted and enthusiastic but stubborn and turbulent Northumbrian named Wilfred who had also been trained in the Roman tradition had become abbot of Ripon.

Soon the rivalry between the Celtic and Roman clergy reached an acute stage, and Oswy determined to bring it to an end. In 664 he called a meeting at Whitby of the great men of Northumbria, both laymen and ecclesiastics, to decide between the two systems. The Celtic clergy were led by Aidan's successor, Colman, and Wilfred was the chief representative of the Roman view. For days the two groups argued learnedly before King Oswy, who probably had only the haziest idea of what they were talking about. Finally Wilfred made a remark that Oswy could understand; he said that the pope was the successor of St. Peter, who had been appointed by Christ to rule his church. The king immediately asked the Celtic clergy if this were true, and when they agreed that it was he gave the decision to the Roman party. Colman and most of his Celtic followers departed from

Northumbria and left the field clear for Wilfred and his allies. The English church was united in doctrine and practice.

Up to the time of the Synod of Whitby the English church was essentially a missionary organization. While the bishops usually had their seats in a monastery, they had no definitely marked dioceses and wandered about the country wherever the need for evangelization called them. Wilfred, who was well acquainted with the Frankish church, was anxious to increase the number of bishops and assign them to definite dioceses. In 669 his efforts were greatly reinforced by the arrival in England of a new archbishop of Canterbury, Theodore of Tarsus. Theodore immediately went to work to set up new dioceses and to persuade the kings to grant lands as endowments for both cathedral chapters and monasteries. It is interesting to notice that this involved a bitter controversy with Wilfred. Although Wilfred was anxious to establish a firm organization in the English church, to increase the number of bishops, and to draw clear borders of the dioceses, he resisted furiously when Theodore attempted to divide his vast Northumbrian diocese. When Theodore insisted on doing so, Wilfred departed for Rome to complain to the pope—the first English bishop to appeal to the papacy against the archbishop of Canterbury.

The last half of the seventh century saw the monasteries of Northumbria developing into centers of Christian culture superior to any other west of Italy. The victory of the Roman party at the Synod of Whitby was followed by the introduction of the rule of St. Benedict. Wilfred introduced this rule into the monasteries of Ripon and Hexham. When Theodore of Tarsus came to England he brought with him a Benedictine monk of English birth, Benedict Biscop. Biscop founded the famous monasteries of Wearmouth and Jarrow. But he was more than a religious enthusiast; he was a man of learning and a great teacher. He journeyed to Rome and returned with a supply of books to bolster the very meager resources of his monastic libraries.

Under his leadership Wearmouth and Jarrow became great centers of learning. Biscop's pupil, Bede, was probably the greatest scholar produced by Western Europe between the decline of Roman civilization and the Carolingian renaissance. He became the complete master of all the learning available to him and in his writings interpreted it and made it available to his contemporaries. Perhaps Bede's most valuable work is his *Ecclesiastical History of the English People*. Bede had a true historical sense, a realization of the distinction between knowledge and hearsay, fact and legend. Using some older sources now lost for the period before his own day, and his own knowledge for the events of his lifetime, he gives us our chief fund of information about Anglo-Saxon England before the Danish invasions. Bede was also a teacher and continued the work of Benedict Biscop. Their intellectual successor was Alcuin, whom we have seen as master of Charlemagne's palace school. The Northumbrian monasteries of the late seventh and early eighth centuries produced works of art as well as of learning. Very beautiful manuscripts, carefully written and brilliantly illuminated, such as the famous Lindisfarne gospels, were the products of their workshops. Finally, the same religious enthusiasm that inspired the missionaries, Benedict Biscop, and Bede, fired two writers of religious verse, Caedmon and Cynewulf, who produced a large number of devotional poems.

7. *The Vikings*

A BRIEF summary glance at Western Europe about A.D. 800 shows a Christian civilization surrounded by foes. The Emperor Charlemagne was king of the Franks and the Lombards. Except for the peninsula of Brittany he ruled the coast of the Atlantic Ocean and the North Sea from the Spanish March, below the Pyrenees, to the base of the Danish peninsula. The eastern frontier of his domains ran along the rivers Elbe and Saale and the Bohemian mountains. He was master of Italy north of Rome. In England the Anglo-Saxons under the vague overlordship of the Bretwealda Egbert of Wessex held the east coast as far north as the Forth, and the west coast except for Cornwall and Wales to the Solway. This was German Christian Europe. To its west lay a fringe of Christian Celtic lands: Brittany, Cornwall, Wales, Ireland, Scotland, and Strathclyde. Italy south of Rome and Sicily were still nominally under the rule of the Byzantine emperors. Around the borders of these Christian lands of Western Europe lay the non-Christian peoples. In Scandinavia lived Germanic pagans. East of the Elbe, the Saale, and the Bohemian mountains were the Slavs, and remnants of the Avars occupied the Hungarian plain. Spain and North Africa were held by the Moslems, whose fleets had taken command of the Mediterranean. Thus Christian Europe stood surrounded by foes—foes that were soon to strike with vigorous savageness.

In the closing years of the eighth century the peoples of Scandinavia started the last great wave of Germanic migration. The causes of this movement are far from clear. In all probability the basic explanation was a rapid increase of population in a land of very limited resources. Peasants who had no farms to till and nobles without lands to rule were inclined to take to the sea in search of adventure and a living. The era of migration also coincided with the period in which a semblance of orderly government was established in Scandinavia, and the numerous small groups that had been independent before the ninth century were gradually unified under the kings of Denmark, Norway, and Sweden. It has been suggested that as these kings began to establish internal order the more turbulent of their peoples migrated to other lands. Neither of these explanations seem completely satisfactory. The historian can only say that some combination of circumstances induced great numbers of Scandinavians, both nobles and peasants, to take to their ships and sail forth in search of booty. The Scandinavians called these warrior-seamen Vikings, and modern historians have adopted that term; but to the people of Christian Europe they were the Northmen. Although all three of the Scandinavian peoples took part in these migrations, only those of Norway and Denmark operated in Western Europe. The Swedish Vikings ruled the Baltic Sea and invaded the Slavic lands to the east.* With their bases in such fortified posts as Novgorod and Kiev they conquered the Slavs and established Viking states in what is now Russia. Although an occasional Swedish adventurer appeared in the North Sea and the Atlantic Ocean, in general these were the highways for the Vikings of Norway and Denmark.

The Viking raiders first struck England in the summer of 787, and within seven years the monasteries of Lindisfarne and Jarrow were plundered and burned. In 814 the Norsemen burned the monastery on the island of Noirmoutier, off the mouth of the Loire river. For about half a century almost every summer brought forth Viking bands ravaging the coasts and the lower parts of the river valleys of England and France. As a rule these bands were small and confined their activities to plundering isolated monasteries and the open countryside. But in

* See pp. 59–60.

841 a large fleet ran into the mouth of the Seine and plundered the city of Rouen. Two years later another strong Viking force sailed up the Loire to Nantes, took the town by storm, slaughtered the inhabitants, and plundered and burned the city. Then instead of returning home for the winter as they always had before, the Norsemen landed on the island of Noirmoutier and spent the winter there. In 851 a Danish fleet established its winter quarters on the isle of Thanet in the estuary of the Thames. Thus began a new phase of the Viking invasions. They were no longer mere summer raiders but permanent scourges with well-established bases.

From their base off the mouth of the Loire the Vikings intensified their operations in France. In 844 they ravaged the valley of the Garonne, moved on south to the coast of Spain, and eventually sacked Seville. The next year they plundered the valley of the Loire. By 857 Bordeaux, Tours, Blois, Orleans, Poitiers, and Paris had been sacked one or more times. Then in 859 a Viking fleet sailed south, plundered the coasts of Spain, passed through the straits of Gibraltar, raided Morocco and the Balearic Islands, and finally camped for the winter in the delta of the Rhone, in southern France. From there they ravaged the Rhone valley as far north as Valence. By 862 this fleet had returned to its base in the Loire. In 872 the Loire Vikings captured Angers and for some years used it as their headquarters. By 880 the western part of France had been thoroughly ravaged many times, and the Vikings were looking for fresh regions to plunder. In 885 a great fleet sailed up the Seine bound for eastern France. When it arrived before Paris, it offered to spare the city if the garrison would allow it free passage up the river. But the count of Paris refused the offer and the result was a two-year siege of the city that ended only with the arrival of the Emperor Charles the Fat (881–87) with a strong German army. Unfortunately the Emperor was at odds with the Burgundians and cheerfully allowed the Vikings to plunder that region.

Here we must pause to ask why the successors of Charlemagne had been unable to defend their lands against the Norse raiders. The most obvious answer is that they were too busy quarreling among themselves to pay adequate attention to the defense of the state. Charlemagne had been succeeded by his son Louis the Pious (814–40), a gentle, kindly monarch who was completely unable to rule his own family to say nothing of the wild Frankish nobles. Long before Louis' death his sons were waging bitter civil war over the division of the empire. Louis died in 840—the year before the first large Viking fleet appeared to sack Rouen. Three years later his sons made a treaty dividing the empire between them. Lothaire (840–55), the eldest, received the title of emperor, and rule over Italy and a strip of land running from Italy to the North Sea, comprising the Rhone valley, Alsace, Lorraine, and the Low Countries. The German lands to the east went to his brother Louis, and their half brother Charles the Bald (843–77) received what is now France. But the civil wars that had begun before Louis' death continued after the division. After the death of Lothaire's son, Lothaire II (855–69), his uncles promptly went to war over the division of his lands. Except for three years, 884–87, when Charles the Fat ruled the entire Frankish state, the successors of Charlemagne were continually at war with one another. On occasion they were not averse to using the Vikings to injure their enemies, as we have seen Charles the Fat doing in 887.

Even if the successors of Charlemagne had been united and had devoted all their energy and resources to the defense of the realm, it seems unlikely that they could have checked the Vikings effectively. The Norse bands were highly mobile, and one place was just as satisfactory to plunder as another. When they found a town well garrisoned they usually simply went around it, and they rarely risked battle with strong armed forces. An invader who seeks to conquer and hold a region can be met by defending key strategic points, but mere plunderers are almost impossible to cope with. Not until the early tenth century did the Franks discover an effective device—meeting Vikings with Vikings.

In 911 Charles the Simple, king of the West Franks, gave the Viking leader Rollo the land around the mouth of the Seine. Later this grant was enlarged until it included all the region since known as Normandy. The establishment of Rollo in Normandy effectively protected France from Viking raids along the Channel coast and gave the West Frankish kings valuable allies to help them in the Loire valley. Although raids on the Loire and southern France continued for some twenty years after 911, the Viking invasions then came to an end.

During the second half of the ninth century England had suffered even more severely than France. In 870 the Danes had conquered East Anglia. In 876 they occupied Northumbria, and in 877 most of Mercia. While the Vikings plundered and burned according to their custom, these were no mere raids, but serious attempts to conquer the country. The Anglo-Saxon resistance was organized and led by Alfred (871–99), king of Wessex. For a time it looked as if Alfred's cause was hopeless, but by 885 he had checked the Danes so successfully that they were willing to make peace. The lands south of the Thames remained directly under Alfred's rule, while western Mercia became an Anglo-Saxon duchy allied to Wessex. The Danes retained East Anglia, eastern Mercia, and the region now embraced in the counties of Lincolnshire, Yorkshire, and Lancashire. Alfred's son Edward (899–925) and his grandson Aethelstan (925–39) gradually reconquered the parts of England held by the Danes. The Danes were not driven from the country, but simply accepted the rule of the Anglo-Saxon kings. By the middle of the tenth century the house of Wessex ruled all England—an England half Anglo-Saxon and half Danish, in law and custom.

The Vikings did not confine their raids to England and France, but swept the northern seas from shore to shore. Early in the ninth century they attacked Ireland. For some years they were in control of most of the island, but eventually they were forced to retire to the eastern ports—Dublin, Wexford, and Waterford, which were essentially Norse settlements. The isles of the northern seas—the Orkneys, Hebrides, and Shetlands—and the Isle of Man, were occupied by Viking colonists. In 874 they made their first settlement on Iceland. Later, adventurers from Iceland went on to Greenland and even to the North American coast. Greenland is still ruled by the king of Denmark and Iceland was until 1944. Until the middle of the thirteenth century Viking kings ruled Man and the Scottish isles.

While the Vikings were raiding the Atlantic coasts of Europe, the Moslems were increasing their power in the Mediterranean. In 827 they invaded Sicily, and in four years had conquered the island. Soon they crossed to southern Italy. The year 843 saw the sack of Rome by the Moslems. They also occupied Corsica, Sardinia, and the delta of the Rhone in southern France. Although the Moslems made no regular settlement on the Italian mainland, they occupied bases there until 915, when they were finally expelled by a Byzantine army and fleet. During this entire period they ravaged the country brutally. Sicily remained in their hands for over a century more and was the seat of a flourishing Moslem culture.

In 895 a new Turkish people, the Magyars, arrived in the plains of Hungary, where they joined the remnants of the Avars. Five years later they swept up the Danube and ravaged Bavaria. In 906 they plundered Saxony, and two years later Thuringia. During the next twenty years they raided all Germany and the border regions such as Alsace and the Rhine valley. In 937 they reached Reims in France. Their ravages continued until they were crushingly defeated at the battle of the Lechfeld by Otto I, king of Germany, in 955.

The civilization that had been slowly and painfully developed in western Europe during the seventh and eighth centuries was almost wiped out in the great era of invasions. Organized monasticism completely disappeared from England, and the discipline and learning of the secular clergy reached a very low ebb. A conviction that but few of his clergy could read Latin moved Alfred the Great to translate the *Pastoral Care* of Pope Gregory the Great into Anglo-Saxon. In the West Frankish state few monasteries had escaped destruction, and most towns had been sacked and burned several times. Great numbers of people had been slaughtered, leaving much land untilled and rapidly turning to forest and waste. Although the Magyar raids in the East Frankish state had not been extended over so long a period as those of the Norsemen in the west, they had been extremely destructive. It was in the process of recovery from this deep slough that the mediaeval civilization of Western Europe was developed.

CHAPTER IV

Knights and Peasants

THE ERA of Norse, Moslem, and Magyar invasions brought to an end the period of transition between Roman and mediaeval civilization in Western Europe. The ruins of Charlemagne's empire served as the seedbed for mediaeval institutions. The purpose of the next three chapters is to trace the development of these institutions during the tenth, eleventh, and early twelfth centuries. We shall try to see how the men and women of this period cared for their souls, their bodies, and their minds—how they prayed, worked, played, and thought. We shall also examine the political institutions, both lay and ecclesiastical, that governed their lives. This first chapter will be devoted to a study of the basic economic and social institutions on which mediaeval civilization rested, and how men lived in the environment they created. It will be a tale of peasants and knights and their ways of life.

8. Rural Society

EARLY mediaeval society was almost entirely rural and agricultural. The urban life and extensive commerce that had marked the early Roman empire had been severely damaged by the civil wars of the third century and reduced still further by the Germanic invasions. The Germans had no interest in towns and no desire to live in them. Some towns were sacked and plundered in their raids, and overland commerce became difficult both because disorder was rampant and because there was no serious attempt to keep roads and bridges in repair. Then in the eighth century the Moslem supremacy in the western Mediterranean had destroyed the central artery of commerce in Western Europe. The Carolingian empire had little trade, and probably few if any real towns. While there were clusters of houses around cathedrals and royal palaces, the inhabitants lived from the produce of the adjacent fields rather than from industry or commerce. The same situation existed in an even more exaggerated form in Anglo-Saxon England. These groups of dwellings that were called towns and cities in the ninth century had suffered severely from the Viking raids.

Thus by the tenth century, Western Europe lacked all the essentials of a prosperous commerce. There was no urban population to engage in trade and industry, and communications were hopelessly bad. The Roman roads had fallen into decay, and the bridges on which they depended had largely disappeared. Moreover, there was a desperate shortage of money. Western Europe had no gold and was not exploiting its resources in silver. The disruption of trade with the East brought about the virtual disappearance of money. What little bullion there was ceased to circulate as trade declined, and it found its way into the treasuries of the churches. There never was a time when no money was in use, but it played an extremely small part in the economy of Western Europe in the tenth and eleventh centuries. Men lived directly from the land: food, clothes, and shelter had to be produced in the immediate neighborhood.

In order to understand an agricultural society it is necessary to know something of its fundamental features—the patterns of settlement and the ways in which the land was exploited. Western Europe knew two settlement patterns: hamlets and villages. In general, hamlets were found in regions of poor soils such as Scotland, Wales, Cornwall, Brittany, western Normandy, and the central highlands of France. The more fertile lands formed a country of villages.

In the poor regions, where hamlets predominated, the cultivation of the soil was extremely primitive. Each household would have a small plot of land close at hand that was cultivated continuously and fertilized to some extent by the manure from its stock. Then a section of open land would be cultivated for a year or two until it became exhausted and another plot was substituted for it. This type of agriculture is usually called "in-field" and "out-field" exploitation. It is suited to a sparsely populated region of poor soils.

The regions where people lived in villages fell into two great divisions. Most of England, France north of the river Loire and east of the mouth of the Seine, and the fertile parts of Germany, were cultivated by what we call the two- or three-field system. Each village was surrounded by a tract of arable land divided into two or three approximately equal parts. If there were two fields, one lay fallow and the other was planted. Where there were three fields, one lay fallow, one was planted with winter grain, and the third grew spring grain. Although our evidence is far from conclusive, it seems likely that in the tenth century few villages had three fields and that this system was developed later in the most fertile districts. As the three-field system used two thirds instead of one half of the arable land every year, it yielded a larger production if the land was sufficiently fertile. Each field was divided into long, narrow strips by "balks" made with the plow. In theory every house in the village had the same number of strips in each field. The division in long, narrow strips was probably dictated by the type of plow used—a great heavy affair drawn by from four to eight oxen. As it was extremely difficult to turn these cumbersome teams, the long strips were adopted to reduce such turns to a minimum.

South of the river Loire in France, and in the Mediterranean region in general, the lands of the village were divided into rectangular plots that were nearly square. Each house had several of these plots, and although there was a biennial rotation between fallow and crops there was no general division of the arable into fields for this purpose. Historians are inclined to associate this type of exploitation with the light plow used in Roman times, which could be drawn by small teams that were easy to turn.

The parts of Western Europe that use the two or three field system with long, narrow strips were the most fertile, the most heavily populated, and the centers of wealth and power during the Middle Ages. Hence most textbooks describe this type of exploitation as the typical one, and it will receive most of our attention here. But it is important to realize that other systems existed, covering large areas, and that social and economic institutions differed considerably according to the basic method of exploiting the soil.

The chief feature of mediaeval agriculture was its low yield per acre, per bushel of seed, and per agricultural laborer. By the thirteenth century, when methods of cultivation had improved somewhat over those of earlier times, only the best farmers could harvest ten bushels of wheat from an acre that had been planted with two bushels of seed. In 1850 England was producing twenty-six bushels per acre, and parts of France and Germany were obtaining even better yields.

The low yield of mediaeval times was particularly serious because the grain produced supplied not only the chief food, bread, but in many parts of Europe—such as England—the standard drink. It is estimated that bread and ale shared about equally the English grain crop. Hence it was necessary to put every possible acre under grain if the population was to be supported. But the growing of good hay requires land as fertile as that used for grain, and in all northern Europe the stock had to be fed during long winter months. As result, a perpetual problem of mediaeval agriculture was the shortage of hay. If the fields were to be cultivated, the plow teams had to be fed; and the teams of from four to eight oxen consumed a large amount of hay. By the eleventh century the invention of the horse collar, or more correctly its introduction into Western Europe, made it possible to use the horse as a draft animal; but this was no great gain. Although the horse was faster than the ox and could plow more land in the same time, he had to be fed grain and cost three or four times as much to feed. Only in a few very fertile regions, such as the Ile de France and the Loire valley, was the horse used extensively as a plow animal. The shortage of hay strictly limited the number of stock other than plow animals that could be kept over the winter, and this in turn kept down the amount of manure available. In general the fields got only the casual manuring that was the result of pasturing the village herds on the fallow. When one remembers that in addition to lack of fertilization of the land, all sowing was done broadcast to the great benefit of the birds, the low yields are easily understood.

Let us glance for a moment at the economic organization of a village in the region of the two- and three-field systems. Each house or tenement has its garden with a few fruit trees. It also has its strips in the fields and its share of the hay crop. The tenant can turn his stock loose to graze in the common pasture that occupies village lands unfit for the plow. In the village woods he can pasture his pigs and gather dead wood to burn. If there is a stream, he can fish in it. In short, the economic resources of the peasant were of two sorts: his own garden and his strips in the fields, and his share in the other resources of the village. The village was essentially an agricultural partnership. The villagers plowed together, reaped together, and threshed together. The narrow strips in the open fields made cultivation on an individual basis practically impossible. Pasture and woods were shared by all under rules established by common consent. The village herdsman looked after the stock of his neighbors as well as his own.

The peasant's life centered in his village, and he had few if any contacts with the world beyond its borders. The village church and its priest cared for his soul. His amusements were the village fetes, which were often survivals from pagan times carefully assigned to some day devoted to a Christian saint. The lands of the village supplied his food, clothing, and shelter. All these were extremely simple. He lived in a hut made largely of mud with a thatched roof. His clothes were the crude products of unskilled village women. His food was chiefly bread, and his drink ale or wine. The garden behind his hut produced some fruit and vegetables in season, and the woods occasionally supplied nuts and berries. If he was lucky, he had a few chickens. In the autumn when he slaughtered the animals that he could not keep over the winter, he got a little very tough beef. In general, however, the only meat regularly available to him was pork. Pigs could fend for themselves in the woods and pastures in winter and summer. They were thin and tough, but they were edible and cheap to keep. So important was the pig in the village economy that in the great Domesday survey of England in 1086 the size of a village's woods is expressed by saying how many pigs it could support.

The economic organization of the village was much the same in England, northern France, and most of Germany; but the political, legal, and social status of its inhabitants differed from region to region, from village to village, and even among individuals in the same village. In the tenth century the part of England that had been conquered and settled by the Danes was a land of free villages. The people worked their fields in common and enjoyed all their produce. The same situation existed in parts of Germany. But most villages were subject to a lord, and the inhabitants were his tenants who supported him in return for his protection.

The arrangements by which a lord exploited his tenants are usually called the seignorial system. Its origins and early development are far from clear. In France there had survived from Roman times some great estates worked by coloni. The land was divided into two parts: one cultivated by the tenants for the lord's benefit, and the other divided among the coloni. In England, the parts of France settled by the Franks, and in western Germany, villages founded by a chieftain and his followers probably had a similar organization. Then it seems clear that villages that originally had no lords were brought into subjection by powerful men. In the disorders that marked the ninth and tenth centuries no man was safe unless he had a soldier to protect him. Some villages probably made voluntary submission to a mounted warrior, while others were forced to do so.*

The villagers supported their lord by working for him, and by paying him rents in kind. A part of the arable land of the village, usually between a third and a half, was reserved for the lord. It usually consisted of strips in the fields and was called the *demesne.* The peasants worked the demesne for their lord. The lord also had a share of the meadow where his tenants harvested the lord's hay. The lord's stock grazed on the village pasture under the care of the village herdsmen. If the lord wanted a ditch dug or a barn built, the peasants supplied the labor. The amount of labor demanded from the tenants for the lord's benefit varied greatly; it could be as much as three days' work in a week. In addition to performing these services the tenants owed the lord a multitude of rents in kind. When they harvested the crop on their own strips, a part was due the lord. In return for grazing his cow in the common pasture, the tenant paid a rent in cheese. If he had pigs feeding in the woods, he paid the lord a rent in pork for the privilege. When the tenant fished in the stream or pond, he gave the lord part of the catch. In return for gathering dead wood in the woods, he kept the lord supplied with firewood. The list could be extended almost indefinitely. There were rents in chickens, in fruit, in vegetables, and in wool. The lord received a share of every type of produce raised by his tenants. These rents and services were due the lord as owner of the land.

In addition to the rents and services he received as possessor of the land, the lord had profitable rights that sprang from his control over the persons of his tenants. These rights varied greatly according to the position of the lord and the legal status of his tenants. The descendants of the Roman coloni on the great estates of the Frankish period were

* See pp. 104–05, 152.

what we call serfs. During the long era of disorder many peasants who had been freemen were slowly depressed in status by their lords until they too became serfs. By the tenth century most of the inhabitants of the villages of northern France and western Germany were serfs. The tenth and eleventh centuries saw a struggle between the church and the lords over the rights of these people. The lords wanted to deprive the serfs of all the rights of human beings, to say that they had no souls and to refuse to call their unions marriages. Although the church won the contest, the lords continued to refer to the family of a serf as his *sequela*, or brood. And although the serf could marry, he could not marry anyone outside his village without his lord's leave. The serf was bound to the land; he was the labor that went with it. He could not own property of any sort, for anything he possessed belonged to his lord. Whenever the lord felt that his serfs had accumulated more than they needed, he could take it away from them by an arbitrary *tallage*, or head tax. Economically the serf was completely at the mercy of his lord.

In the Frankish state political and judicial power in the countryside had been wielded by the counts and their deputies, the vicars. But the Frankish kings had granted what was called "immunity" to most ecclesiastical establishments, and probably to many laymen as well. It seems clear that this privilege was enjoyed by the Carolingian vassi dominici. The counts and their officers could not enter the lands of anyone who had immunity. At first in all probability this simply meant that the landholder arrested criminals and turned them over to the count, but by the ninth century most possessors of immunity were judging and punishing their own men. The counts naturally exercised full rights of jurisdiction over the inhabitants of their own estates. Then, as the feudal system developed, the counts often gave their vassals whole or part of their own judicial rights.* Finally, in the confusion of the ninth and tenth centuries, it was hard to prevent any powerful lord from usurping these powers whether he had any real right to them or not. By the end of the tenth century the rights of government were widely dispersed among the landholding class. An important lord would have full rights of jurisdiction over the men who lived on his lands; a less important one partial rights. The distinction lay in whether or not a lord could inflict capital punishment. If he could, he had what was later called "high justice." The possession

* See pp. 105–06.

of a gallows was considered an important symbol of rank and prestige.

The possession of rights of jurisdiction not only gave the lord a firm hold over his tenants but also permitted him to establish profitable monopolies. He could refuse to allow his peasants to own or operate hand mills to grind grain into flour, and so force them to bring their grain to his mill and pay a fee for having it ground. He could also oblige them to bake their bread in his ovens and pay a fee for that privilege. In short, the lord with rights of jurisdiction controlled both the persons and the property of his tenants; and all lords had at least some such rights.

Many historians have made a distinction between the status of the mass of the peasantry in France and western Germany and those of Normandy and England. They have tended to deny that the latter were serfs. Actually the position of the peasants of England and Normandy differed from that of the French serfs chiefly because the powers of government had been less widely scattered. In Normandy and England "high justice" was reserved to the duke and the king. The landholders had very limited judicial rights. In England most lords could hang one of their men caught on their land with stolen goods in his possession, but otherwise they could not inflict capital punishment. If a lord slew or maimed his unfree tenant, he could be haled into the king's court to answer for the offense.

A few general remarks seem in order in regard to the position of the unfree peasant. In theory he was economically at the complete mercy of his lord. The lord could demand any rents and services he saw fit. But there was obviously a practical limit to the use of this right. Dead peasants were of no use to the lord, and so he had to leave them enough to keep alive. Then, the Middle Ages was a period in which the authority of custom was very great, and men were inclined to do what their predecessors had done. A lord could increase the rents and services due from his tenants, and many undoubtedly did so; but there was always a presumption that change was evil, and this must have protected the peasants to some extent. Where the lord had full powers of jurisdiction the peasant's person was also at his lord's disposal; and even when a lord lacked the right to inflict capital punishment, his superior who did have the right would hardly quibble over hanging a peasant—if he got his clothes and personal property as fee.

In short, the lot of the unfree peasant was far from enviable. If his tenement was a full-sized one of about thirty acres, he and his family had just about enough to eat in good seasons. In bad seasons they starved. His only knowledge of the world of ideas came from the parish priest, whose learning was usually little greater than his own. His lord could usually hang him, mutilate him, or flog him at will. During the nineteenth century French scholars carried on a long debate as to whether or not the lords had possessed the privilege of enjoying every peasant bride before her husband did. This argument seems essentially unrealistic. There can be little doubt that if a lord desired a peasant girl he had no hesitation about taking her.

This discussion of the position of the peasantry of the early Middle Ages has been centered in the condition of the unfree inhabitants of the villages because in the tenth and eleventh centuries they formed the major part of the agricultural population of England, France, and western Germany. By the twelfth century the seignorial system had spread into central Germany. Later it moved on into eastern Germany and eventually into Russia. But it is important to remember that in the tenth and eleventh centuries there were many free peasants. Anglo-Saxon England held many small freemen, especially in the Danish districts; and although the Norman conquest reduced many of them to the status of unfree villeins, others kept their freedom. Throughout this period there were in eastern England "socmen" who were free and paid money rents for their lands. Certain parts of France, notably the region about Bordeaux, continued to have numerous small free farmers. And Saxony was a land of free farmers. The historian is obliged to concentrate on the dominant features of the society he is describing, but his readers should always remember that what is dominant is rarely universal.

During the eleventh and twelfth centuries the peasants of Western Europe laid the foundation for the future political and economic dominance of that region by enormously increasing its productivity, and hence its population. To some extent this was accomplished by improving agricultural technique. As we have seen, the introduction of the horse collar made it profitable to use this faster-moving animal in place of the ox in such very fertile regions as the Loire valley, and it seems likely that improved methods of harnessing oxen made it possible to plow with smaller teams. In some regions a shift from the two-field to the three-field system increased the productivity of the land. But the great increase in the total agricultural production of western Europe was chiefly the result of the extension of cultivated land at the expense of forest, marsh, and wasteland.

The earliest efforts at reclamation were directed toward the land that had been deserted during the period of confusion in the ninth and tenth centuries. Bit by bit, land that had grown up in brush and light woods was cleared and plowed. Then the peasants started nibbling at the edges of the great forests. As draining marshes was technically far more difficult than clearing forests, it was less common; but in some regions it was carried on with great energy and some success. Unfortunately this vast work of reclamation was of little interest to the contemporary writers, and we know little about it in detail. Some of our knowledge comes from place names. The word for a clearing was *assart*, and such names as *Assart-le-Roi*, the king's clearing, indicates a village founded on cleared land. *La Forêt-le-Roi* has a similar meaning. Perhaps the most common name for such villages in France was *Villeneuve*, new village. Then villages cut out of forests were usually laid out differently from the older settlements. Instead of being grouped close together, the houses were strung out along a street. Thus each tenement was enlarged as more land was cleared. The careful study of place names and of village maps gives us a fair idea of the extent of the reclamation.

The initiative in this process must have been taken by the lords; in general one could not occupy or clear land without the permission of its lord. Obviously the extension of the arable land in his property increased a lord's resources. During the twelfth century ten new villages were created along the road from Paris to Orléans in the demesne of the Capetian kings of France. The duke of Brittany and two of his chief vassals cleared and colonized a large part of the forest of Rennes. When Domesday book was compiled in 1086, almost all Yorkshire was waste, but within a century it was resettled and prosperous. Recent study has shown that the lands that recovered most quickly were those held by lords who had colonists available on their estates elsewhere in England. During the latter half of the twelfth century the lords of Knaresborough in Yorkshire enormously increased the value of their fief by clearing part of the forest of Knaresborough. One finds the English kings making gifts to great abbeys by allowing them to clear sections of royal forests. All over England, France, and western Germany, the lords were clearing forests and colonizing the reclaimed land. Sometimes it was a matter of clearing a large tract and founding new villages, but more often it was simply the extension of the arable land of villages bordering on a forest—the creation of little assarts along the edge of the woods.

Clearing new land and bringing it into cultivation was hard, grueling work, and peasants were unlikely to attempt it without encouragement. Hence the lord who wanted his resources increased in this way was usually obliged to offer special inducements. Peasants willing to become colonists were tempted by reduced rents and services. Thus to some extent at least the process of reclamation served to improve the lot of the peasants.

In England, France, and western Germany, the reclamation and colonization simply filled the waste spaces between the established settlements. A quite different process was underway in eastern Germany. During the twelfth century the great lords of Germany conquered wide regions to the east of their lands. The Slavs had never populated the country very thickly and many were slaughtered in the conquest. Hence the German lords sought settlers and offered them great inducements in the form of low rents and special privileges. From all western Germany and from the Netherlands peasants who wanted to be free from the tightening seignorial system went east as colonists. As these German settlers were good farmers by the standards of the day, they were sought by Slavic as well as by German lords. Thus the lands between the rivers Elbe and Oder became solidly German, and German settlements appeared in the predominantly Slavic regions farther east.*

9. The Feudal System

THE SAVAGE civil wars between Louis the Pious and his sons, continued after Louis' death between the brothers Lothaire, Louis the German, and Charles the Bald, were in themselves enough to create a period of anarchy in which armed force was the only effective law. The intensification of this internal confusion by Viking, Moslem, and Magyar raids produced an era that was the heyday of the soldier. No village, cathedral city, or monastic establishment was safe unless adequately protected by armed men. The peasant could not till his

* See p. 166.

fields nor the priest say mass in his church without the aid of the soldier.

As we have seen in an earlier chapter, the most effective soldier of the day, the backbone of the Carolingian armies, was the mounted warrior protected by shield, helmet, and body-armor, and armed with spear, sword, and battle-axe. While the armor of the ninth century was comparatively light—usually rings of metal sewn on a long shirt of leather or cloth—it could usually turn any strokes inflicted by an infantryman. And the tremendous striking power of the horseman rising in his stirrups placed the foot soldier almost completely at his mercy. When the mounted Frankish warriors met the Vikings in pitched battle they nearly always won, and no Frankish foot soldiers could possibly withstand them. In the Latin writings of the ninth century the mounted warrior was called simply *miles*, or soldier. Later in French he was designated *chevalier*, or horseman. We shall use the equivalent English term, knight.

The heavy cavalry used by Charles Martel, Pepin, and Charlemagne was made up of Frankish nobles and vassi dominici. While we have no clear idea of the number of horsemen Charlemagne could muster, it seems fairly certain that the ninth century saw a decided increase in the mounted warriors of the Frankish state. In the era of anarchy the ordinary freeman had two choices: he could become a soldier, or sink into the status of a serf. Except in a few districts there was no place for the free peasant with no lord to protect him. And there was an active demand for soldiers. The kings, their officials, great landowners, and even important vassi dominici, sought armed followers to aid them in war. In short, the only limit on the number of knights was the resources available to support them.

The sources for the history of the ninth century are extremely scanty, and hence the exact process of the development of feudalism must remain obscure. It is clear, however, that the acute need for soldiers moved every man who had more land than he needed to support himself and his family to give benefices to soldiers who became his vassi. The general anarchy forced small and even moderately important landowners to seek the protection of still more powerful men. When a vassus dominicus found that the king was no longer able to protect him and his benefice, he was inclined to shift his allegiance to some local potentate, perhaps to the local count. The biographer of St. Gerald makes a great point of his hero's refusal to give up his direct relationship to the crown at a time when all his fellow royal vassals were making submission to the counts. The small freeman, of course, had little choice if he wanted to become a soldier. Even if he had enough property to support him as a knight, he could not protect that property without aid. He was obliged to surrender his land to a powerful man, receive it from him as a benefice, and thus become his vassus.

Thus during the ninth century there developed a hierarchy of lords and vassals. The simple knight who had just enough land and peasant labor to support him and his family was the vassal of a larger landholder, who in turn would be the vassal of a still mightier man—perhaps of a count. The count might be the vassal of a greater count, of a duke, or of the king. In short, a great pyramid was formed with the king at the top and the ordinary knight at the bottom. Now in the ninth century this structure was not complete, nor did it cover all the Carolingian realm. It developed most rapidly in the West Frankish state—the France of today—and in Lorraine and Franconia. But even in these regions it was not all-embracing. Lands held in full ownership, called *allods* in contemporary records, were numerous until the twelfth century and persisted in some regions throughout the Middle Ages. Nevertheless, in France at least allods were rare by the end of the eleventh century, and the dictum dear to feudal lawyers, "no land without a lord," was in general accurate.

During the period in which this hierarchy was taking form the relationships between lords and vassals underwent profound changes. The most important of these was the transformation of the benefice from a revocable or at best a lifetime grant into an hereditary one. The basic reason for this development must have been the extreme difficulty of preventing an adult son of a vassal from taking over the family benefice. When Charles the Bald was about to set out for Rome to assume the imperial crown, he decreed that if a royal vassal died during his absence, the vassal's son should hold the benefice until his return. While lack of material makes it impossible to follow the process in detail, it is clear that by the tenth century most benefices were hereditary. It was probably customary for the son of a vassal to offer the lord a gift to persuade him to renew the benefice; such a practice would be the logical ancestor of the later feudal due known as relief. At about the time the benefice became hereditary there was also a change in contemporary terminology. The benefice became the *feudum*, or fief.

As long as the benefice was a revocable grant, the obligations of the vassal must have been essentially determined by the lord's will; but when the benefice became transformed into the hereditary fief these obligations were governed by a mutual contract. No longer could a lord take back a benefice whenever he saw fit; he could do so only if the vassal violated the contract. The terms of the contract, the mutual obligations of lord and vassals, were worked out more or less independently by each lord and his vassals. Moreover, the vassals were far stronger than the lord. The lord was utterly helpless if all or even a major part of his vassals combined against him, for they were his soldiers, his only available force. It became customary for the relationship between lord and vassals to be determined by the assembled vassals sitting under the presidency of the lord. As a result each fief had its own customs. While historians use the terms feudal law and feudal custom, there was really no such thing. There was the feudal custom of a particular fief; and rarely were the customs of two fiefs exactly alike. The description of feudal obligations in the next few paragraphs is simply a generalization. It will probably describe the exact situation in only a few fiefs.

The basic purpose of the feudal relationship was cooperation in war. The chief function of the lord was to protect his vassals and their lands, and theirs was to serve in his army. In the early days when Viking raids harassed the land and general anarchy reigned, there was probably no limit to the military service owed by the vassal to his lord. He joined his lord's army whenever he was summoned. But as time went on the vassals began to distinguish between two types of war—offensive and defensive. When the lord's fief was being invaded, his vassals were obliged to serve him until the enemy was driven off. On the other hand, when the lord was engaged in plundering his neighbors' lands or trying to add another castle or village to his possessions, the vassals were inclined to limit their obligations. As a rule forty days a year became the maximum time that a vassal had to serve in an offensive operation. It is interesting to notice that this period just about covers the time of pleasant summer weather between spring planting and the harvest. In some fiefs the vassal had to serve forty days at his own cost, and another forty if the lord fed him and his horse. In others the period of service was thirty days or even less. But everywhere there was the distinction between the defense of the fief and raids on neighbors.

Closely related to the obligation to serve in the lord's army in the field was the duty of acting as a member of the garrison of the lord's

CASTLE RISING, NORFOLK, ENGLAND

The village of Castle Rising lies at the very edge of the fens on the Norfolk side of the Wash. Its castle was the chief seat of the great barony which King William II gave to William de Albini, his pincerna, *or butler. It was held until the middle of the thirteenth century by his descendants, the earls of Arundel.*

Here we have a castle composed of a motte and two baileys. The large motte in the center of the picture is enclosed by massive earthworks and surrounded by a deep moat. The top of the earthworks is 30 feet above the enclosed area and 60 feet above the bottom of the moat. The principal bailey, in the foreground, is enclosed by earthworks 20 feet high and is surrounded by a moat. In the background behind the motte is another bailey with lesser earthworks and a shallower moat. It is probable that in the time of William de Albini, the butler, a wooden tower stood within the enclosure on the motte and the earthworks of both motte and baileys were crowned with wooden palisades. In the twelfth century the earls of Arundel replaced the wooden tower with the handsome hall-keep shown in this picture and built the stone gate tower. Courtesy of Aerofilms, Ltd.

WARKWORTH CASTLE, NORTHUMBERLAND, ENGLAND

Warkworth castle was one of the fortresses that guarded the Northumbrian plain from Scottish invasions. King Henry II gave it to a favorite knight, Roger fitz Richard. In 1330 King Edward III gave it to Henry Percy, grandfather of the first earl of Northumberland, who already possessed Alnwick castle a few miles to the north. Warkworth thus became one of the strongholds of the Percies.

In this illustration one can see clearly the outline of the original castle of earth and wood. At the right is the motte that once supported a wooden tower. To the left of the motte is the bailey. Except on the side where it is protected by the river, the castle is surrounded by a deep, wide moat. In the center of the picture one can see the vestiges of a moat between the motte and the bailey. The motte is now crowned with a magnificent fifteenth-century stone keep, and stone walls have replaced the wooden palisades that originally enclosed the bailey. At the extreme left there is a glimpse of the pier supporting the drawbridge over the moat which led into the massive gate tower. In the bailey one can see the foundations of a large church. Courtesy of Aerofilms, Ltd.

fortress. The early history of castles is extremely obscure, but there were probably few if any before the tenth century. Then there began to appear the "motte and bailey" fortresses. These were made by digging a ditch usually about ten feet deep and thirty feet wide, and piling the earth into an artificial mound. The edge of the ditch and the top of the mound were fortified with wooden palisades. On the summit of the mound inside the stockade stood a wooden tower. Usually shallower and narrower ditches with stockades would enclose one or two areas at the foot of the mound. The mound was the "motte," and the other inclosed areas the "baileys." The lord and his household lived in the tower on the motte. The baileys held the stables and other outbuildings, and served as a place of refuge for the peasants, their families, and stock, in case of danger. By the eleventh century every lord of any importance had at least one of these castles, and his vassals were expected to supply the garrison. This duty, called castle-guard, differed greatly from fief to fief. A petty lord with only a few vassals might arrange to have one of them always on duty in the castle to command the household knights and peasants in its defense. A great lord with many vassals could provide a strong permanent garrison. Thus the lord of the great barony of Richmond in England divided his 186 knights into six groups, each of which served two months in the castle. This was probably an unusually heavy castle-guard service. It seems likely that as a rule the vassal's garrison duty was limited to thirty or forty days.

Next to military service, the most important obligation of a vassal to his lord was to attend the latter's court when summoned. Such attendance could be for a number of purposes. The necessity of taking counsel before taking any significant step was deeply imbedded in the ideas of the Middle Ages. It is particularly noticeable in the monastic rules, where the abbot is directed to ask the advice of his monks before doing anything of interest to the congregation as a whole. It was also a basic feature of feudal custom. The lord and his vassals were partners in the fief, and what affected its welfare was of interest to all. Before the lord chose a wife for himself or his son or a husband for his daughter, he was expected to seek the counsel of his vassals. If he planned to go on a crusade or to wage war on a neighbor, he first asked his vassals' advice. In short, it was customary for a lord to seek counsel on any question of interest to the fief as a whole, and it was practically necessary if he had in mind a project that required his men's assistance.

Hence the obligation to give honest advice to his lord was an important duty of the vassal.

The assembled vassals in the lord's court decided any disputes that arose between lord and vassal, or between two vassals. If the lord charged a vassal with failing to fulfill his obligations to him, the question was heard in the lord's court. The same procedure applied when a vassal accused his lord of an offense against him. When such questions as who was the rightful heir to a fief arose, they came before this same court. It was the lord's court that gradually built up the feudal custom of the fief. But even if the lord needed no advice and had no cases to try, he could summon his vassals "to do him honor." The status of a member of the feudal hierarchy was determined chiefly by the number of men who were ready to follow him to battle. When the writers of romances wanted to indicate a man's importance, they told how many vassals stood behind him on a state occasion. It was the duty of vassals to bolster their lord's prestige by attending him when he summoned them.

Although military and court service were the two active obligations of vassals in general, a lord might grant a fief in return for other types of service. The chief officers of the lord's household, his seneschal, constable, marshal, and sometimes the chamberlain and butler, held fiefs as compensation. The constable of a castle might have a fief to support him. Such officers as foresters were usually holders of fiefs. The king of England granted a fief to a man as compensation for being "marshal of the prostitutes who follow the court." There are many cases of grants to a cook. In short, in the early days of feudalism a lord had but two means of paying his officials and servants. He could feed and clothe a man in his household or grant him a fief for his support. The feudal lawyers of the thirteenth century were inclined to make a distinction between these fiefs granted officials and servants and those given for the normal feudal services. The fief given to the official or servant was called a serjeanty. There is, however, no evidence that this distinction existed in the early times, and such fiefs were a vital part of feudal organization.

In addition to the basic feudal services the vassal had other obligations to his lord. One of these was called relief. In all probability relief originated in payments made to secure the renewal of the grant at the death of either lord or vassal, before benefices became hereditary. When the hereditary fief developed it became a feudal obligation.

There is evidence that originally relief was due when either lord or vassal died, but by the eleventh century it was usually demanded only when an heir succeeded to a fief. Apparently it was most often paid in military equipment—the arms and armor of the late vassal. By the twelfth century it was paid in money. No general rule laid down the amount that could be demanded, but there is evidence that a sum equal to the revenue of the fief for a year was commonly considered about right.

Another obligation of the vassal was known as aid. When a lord needed extra resources he naturally sought them from his vassals. If an heir found that he could not pay the relief for the fief, he expected his vassals to assist him. When the lord was captured by his foes, it was the duty of his vassals to raise his ransom. The knighting of the lord's eldest son and the wedding of his eldest daughter were occasions for expensive festivities. The vassals were expected to contribute to the cost of these affairs. At first perhaps the vassals simply supplied food and wine, but later a money payment was customary. Then if a lord planned to go on a crusade, build a new castle, or do anything that cost more than he could afford, he was inclined to ask his vassals to contribute. By the eleventh century aids were divided into two groups: those the lord could demand as his right, and those he had to ask for as a favor. As a rule in all fiefs the vassals recognized that they owed aid to ransom their lord, to knight his eldest son, and to marry his eldest daughter. In some fiefs the obligation to assist the lord in paying relief came in this compulsory category. But if the lord wanted aid for any other purpose he had to ask his vassals' consent, and they could refuse to give it.

Although relief and aid were the only economic services that were common to the vassals of all fiefs, the duty of offering hospitality to the lord was widely prevalent. At first this was probably unrestricted —the vassal was expected to entertain his lord and the lord's followers whenever the lord chose to visit him. But as time went on this obligation tended to be strictly limited. The lord could visit a vassal a certain number of times a year, for a certain length of time, with a fixed number of followers mounted on a fixed number of horses. In some cases the menus for both men and beasts were set by agreement, or by custom.

In addition to the feudal services the lord had certain rights over the vassal and his fief that grew out of the basic nature of the feudal relationship. When the daughter of a vassal married, she carried to her husband as her marriage portion some part of her father's fief, and thus gave him an interest and a foothold in the lord's lands. No lord could be expected to permit an enemy to secure such a position. Hence the vassal was bound to secure the lord's approval of his son-in-law to be. If a vassal died leaving a son too young to fight or an unmarried daughter, there was no one to perform the service due from the fief. The lord then had the right to demand that some male have custody of the fief and perform the service. Sometimes it was customary to have this function filled by a relative of the heir or heiress. Usually this duty fell on the eldest brother of the heir's mother, who could never inherit the fief and thus had no reason to want to remove the heir. If an uncle on the father's side were given custody, he might be tempted to get rid of the heir to secure his own succession.

In many fiefs, however, it was the rule for the lord himself to take custody of the heir and his lands. In the case of a male heir, he held the fief until the boy came of age. In the case of a female, it was the lord's duty to find her a husband who could perform the service owed him from the fief. This, as a matter of fact, was one of a feudal lord's most cherished privileges. He always had young knights in his household who were eager for fiefs, and from the lord's point of view the easiest way to satisfy such a desire was to grant his knight an heiress in marriage. This was almost the only means by which a landless knight could hope to become a man of importance.

When a lord rewarded a faithful follower with a fief from his own demesne, it was almost certain to be a small one, but he might give him the heiress to a barony. William Marshal, the fourth son of a petty English lord, was a favored servant of King Henry II of England. He was given an heiress so rich that he became at once one of the most powerful barons of England.

When a vassal died leaving no one whom the lord and his court would recognize as his heir, the fief passed into the lord's possession by what was called escheat. In theory any descendant of one who had held the fief was an heir to it, but in practice relatives more distant than first cousin were rarely considered. Only if a second cousin was a powerful man who could bring effective pressure on the lord did he have much chance of succeeding to the fief. Hence, although escheat was not a very common occurrence, it did take place. If a vassal were condemned in the lord's court for violating his obligations, the fief could be declared forfeit. This did not happen very frequently, for the assembled vassals were reluctant to condemn anyone to forfeit his fief. Each vassal realized that he might some day find himself in a similar difficulty.

So far we have been discussing the material obligations of a vassal to his lord, but it is important to remember that personal duties played a vital part in the feudal relationship. A vassal was bound to be completely loyal to his lord, to do everything possible for his benefit and nothing that might harm him. The most serious crime a vassal could commit was to wound or slay his lord. To seduce the lord's wife or eldest daughter was almost equally grave an offense. While younger daughters were rarely mentioned by feudal lawyers, it was probably considered bad taste for a vassal to seduce them. The vassal was expected to guard his lord and his lord's family as carefully as he did his own.

The relationship between a lord and his vassals was a mutual one; each had obligations to the other. On the material side the lord had one all-important duty to his vassal. He was obliged to protect the vassal and his fief from all foes outside the lord's own fief. The lord was also bound to "do justice" to his vassal in his court. If a vassal believed his lord was mistreating him and demanded a hearing before his fellow vassals, it was his lord's duty to grant it. The lord was also bound to respect the family and personal interests of his vassals. Thus when King John stole the fiancée of his vassal, Hugh de Lusignan, it was rightly considered a serious offense against the feudal relationship.* If a lord failed to fulfill his obligations to a vassal, the vassal could "defy" him—that is, declare that he was no longer his vassal. It was quite common for a vassal to renounce his lord because his lord had failed to protect him or his fief, and defiance for denial of justice was reasonably frequent. Needless to say the defiance of a lord by his vassal meant war, and as a rule a vassal made sure of the support of some enemy of his lord before he risked formal defiance.

The relationship between lord and vassal was inaugurated in a solemn ceremony known as swearing fidelity and doing homage. The vassal knelt before the lord, placed his hands between the lord's, and swore to be a faithful vassal and to perform the services due from the fief. Often the lord gave the vassal a clod of earth as a symbol of the granting of the fief. Historians have tried to distinguish between fi-

* See p. 253.

delity and homage, but without any great success. The most common hypothesis is that fidelity established the personal relationship, while homage was done for the fief and involved the promise to perform the customary services. This view is supported by the fact that prelates who could not with propriety do military service admitted their obligation to swear fidelity but usually refused to do homage. On the other hand it seems clear that homage was performed at times when no fief was involved. When a knight joined the household of a lord to serve him in return for food and clothing, he commonly swore fidelity and did homage. In short, swearing fidelity and doing homage ordinarily went together. When they were separated, I suspect the significance of each was interpreted according to the tastes of the parties involved and the custom of the fief in question.

Although it is conceivable that in the early days of the feudal system a vassal was expected to have only one lord, this situation cannot have endured very long. If a man received land as a marriage portion with his wife, he became the vassal of the head of his wife's family. A younger son might go forth, take service with a lord other than his father's, receive a fief from him, and eventually inherit the original family fief. Then a lord was inclined to buy the friendship and aid of powerful neighbors by granting them fiefs. Thus in England the Bigod earls of Norfolk were the dominant feudal power in East Anglia, and a number of lesser barons of the region were induced by persuasion or plain force to grant them fiefs. Open conquest was often politely covered by the performance of homage. Thus when the count of Anjou drove the count of Blois from Touraine, he did homage to the count of Blois for the conquered territory.

By the twelfth century most important landholders were vassals of several lords. The count of Champagne was vassal to the king of France, the duke of Burgundy, the Holy Roman Emperor, the archbishops of Reims and Sens, and the bishops of Langres, Châlons, Autun, and Auxerre. Among his vassals were men who held of the king and some eighty other lords. These complexities in the feudal system could obviously be a source of considerable confusion, especially when two of a man's lords were at war with each other. Hence as time went on a new conception was developed; that of "liege" homage. A man did liege homage to one lord and his personal services were due to him. To his other lords he simply rendered the services owed by his fief. Thus the count of Anjou was the liege vassal of the king of France. If the king and the count of Blois were at war, he was expected to serve the king in person and to send a suitable contingent to serve the count of Blois.

Before leaving the feudal system it seems well to glance at certain questions about how it actually functioned. The feudal system first appeared in France at a time when the country faced almost complete anarchy, and it was an alternative to that anarchy. The question naturally arises as to how effective it was as a means of keeping order. In theory the feudal system furnished means for the peaceful settlement of all disputes between a lord and his vassals, and between vassals of the same lord. All such disputes could be heard in the lord's court. There was no provision for quarrels between vassals of different lords, and these could only be settled by negotiation or war. Actually the practice did not follow theory very closely. If two vassals of the same lord had a dispute, their inclination was to go to war and fight as long as the lord allowed it, and the lord was unlikely to interfere unless one vassal seemed in danger of suffering so much harm that he could not perform his service. Moreover, no vassal of spirit who had a dispute with his lord was willing to accept an unfavorable decision of the lord's court. It had to be enforced by arms. Only as the great lords—kings and feudal princes—became overwhelmingly strong in the late twelfth and thirteenth centuries were they able to reduce materially the amount of feudal warfare by exercising their rights as suzerains.

Another interesting question concerns the location of the center of power in the feudal hierarchy. At what stage in this hierarchy was a man most independent of those above him and most fully able to do what he saw fit? Until the latter part of the twelfth century this situation was occupied by the lowest man in the scale able to build and garrison a strong castle. Even a motte and bailey castle was expensive in terms of labor and could only be built by a lord with adequate resources. Then only the lord of a fair number of knights could garrison a stronghold through the castle-guard obligations of his vassals. The lord who could have a strong and adequately garrisoned castle was in an excellent position. If such a stronghold was defended with any resolution, it was impossible to capture it during the forty days that a feudal host could ordinarily be kept in the field. Thus the holder of a castle who defied his lord could usually escape any serious consequences by shutting himself up in his fortress. At the same time his vassals who did not possess castles were largely at his mercy. In eleventh-century

France the term baron usually marked the owner of a castle, and high justice and the possession of a castle were likely to go together. Until the reappearance of a money economy gave new resources to the feudal princes, the possessor of a strong castle was practically independent.

In discussing the origins, development, and nature of feudal institutions our attention has been largely centered in France, where they first appeared. When William, duke of Normandy, conquered England in 1066, he brought to that kingdom the feudal institutions to which he was accustomed. In general, English feudal custom was similar to that of Normandy and hence of France. The Norman kings of England did, however, make certain innovations that greatly strengthened their power as suzerains.*

In France the king had no feudal relationship whatever with the vassals of his vassals: his only contact was with those who held from him directly. When the count of Champagne went to war with the king, it was the duty of the count's vassals to support him. In England the kings insisted that every freeman had to do them homage. No English knight could rightfully join his lord in war against the king. Moreover, the Norman kings claimed rights over their vassals that no other lord possessed. They insisted on their right to have custody over all the lands held by any one who was their direct vassal, even if most of his lands were rear-fiefs held from barons. The same applied to the right of marriage. In short, if an English knight had held twenty knights' fees from a baron since the Conquest and years later received a single fee from the king, the king had custody of all his lands and could marry his daughter to whom he pleased. When the vassal of a baron died, the baron was obliged to accept the homage of the heir and then collect his relief as best he could; but when a baron died, the king seized his lands and kept them until the heir had paid the relief. Finally, the English king maintained the competence of his courts to settle all disputes not cared for by the feudal courts and insisted that all disputes be brought to the appropriate court. No English king admitted the legality of feudal warfare.

The parts of the East Frankish state that had always been part of the Merovingian and Carolingian monarchies, Lorraine and Franconia, developed feudal institutions similar to those of the West Franks, at about the same time. As we shall see in another chapter, feudalism spread gradually to the rest of Germany, until by the twelfth century

* See p. 182.

Germany could be called a feudal state.* In general, German feudal custom was not unlike that of France and England, but it had one peculiar institution—the *ministeriales*. When the kings of Germany first demanded military service from the church lands, the prelates were faced with the necessity of providing fully armed men for that purpose. In England and France the prelates provided their service by granting fiefs to knights, but the German ecclesiastics were unwilling to do this. Once a fief was given to a knight it was almost impossible to prevent it from becoming hereditary, and the church lost all control of the land as long as the knight performed his services.

The German prelates solved this problem by taking men who were unfree, giving them the necessary equipment and land to support them, and sending them to the royal host. As these men were unfree, they had no rights against their lord. The prelate could take back the lands given them whenever he saw fit. Soon lay lords were adopting this device. They found ministeriales especially useful as officials. There was no danger that they could make their positions hereditary, and they could be removed at any time without question. Moreover, since they owed their positions entirely to their lord they could be relied on to be completely loyal to his interests.

It is obviously impossible to discuss all the variations in feudal custom found in the various parts of western Europe, but it seems well to indicate briefly the territory involved. The conceptions of vassals and benefices entered northern and central Italy in the wake of the Carolingian conquest, and feudal institutions in a more advanced form were carried to southern Italy and Sicily by the Norman adventurers who took possession of those regions in the eleventh century.† Except in Sicily, the southern part of the peninsula, and Savoy and Piedmont, feudalism was never of great importance in Italy because of the early rise to dominance of the towns. Comparatively little is known in detail about the feudal institutions of the Christian kingdoms of northern Spain. It seems clear that although feudal elements were important, they were never systematized as in France, England, and Germany. The same generalization seems applicable to the Scandinavian states. The most completely feudal states were those founded by the crusaders: the Latin kingdom of Jerusalem and the Latin empire of Constantinople. There feudal lawyers had full reign with no inconvenient traditions to hamper them. The king of Jerusalem and the emperor of

* See p. 277. † See pp. 197–8.

Constantinople were feudal suzerains with no power or authority from any other source. The great collections of the customs of these two states, the *Assizes of Jerusalem* and the *Assizes of Romanie*, picture ideal feudal states.*

Although the feudal relationship was probably the most important bond that united the members of the warrior class, there was another tie that requires mention. Family connections played a very vital part in mediaeval politics. When a lord went to war, he relied fully as much on his *lignage*, his relatives, as upon his vassals. Alliances among lords who had no feudal relations were commonly based on family connections. Members of a family often united to procure the advancement of the whole group. Thus the members of the house of Clare, high in favor with King Henry I, obtained a dominant position in England early in the twelfth century; and a hundred years later this same family formed the backbone of the resistance to King John. The baronial coalitions that plagued Blanche of Castile when she ruled as regent for young King Louis IX were essentially alliances of the members of the house of Dreux. In short a comparatively minor baron whose resources in demesnes and vassals were slight might be a man of great power through his relatives. Brothers and cousins might quarrel bitterly and wage war against one another enthusiastically, but they could usually be relied on to combine against the outside world. Close study of mediaeval politics leads to the conclusion that family ties were unusually strong in this period.

10. The Feudal Caste

LET us now pass from the institutions of feudal society to the men and women who composed it. It is difficult to find a satisfactory term to describe this class that dominated Western Europe in the early Middle Ages. The designations noble and knightly are adequate for the very early period, when every holder of a fief was a noble and a knight; but by the thirteenth century these two terms had become restricted in their use and did not ordinarily apply to all members of feudal society. The easiest course is to use the obvious term, feudal class or feudal caste, to describe those who participated in the feudal system and their immediate families.

* See pp. 208–10.

The feudal male had one primary function: fighting. His education and his way of life were aimed at fitting him for this occupation. At the age of seven or eight he was sent away from home lest the indulgence of his parents, especially his mother, might soften him. He received his education at some friendly feudal court, usually that of his father's lord or of a relative. For some years he was a page serving the lady of the castle. Any nonmilitary talent he acquired, such as playing a musical instrument or singing, was likely to be gained in these years. At fourteen or fifteen he became a squire and served the lord. He cared for the horses, polished armor, and served his lord at table. He was hardened to the wearing of armor and trained in the use of knightly equipment. When he was considered old enough and adequately prepared, usually when he was about twenty, he was given arms, armor, and horse of his own, and solemnly made a knight. In its simplest form, before the development of chivalric ideas, this ceremony consisted of putting on his new armor, kneeling before a knight—usually the lord who had trained him—and receiving a terrific blow from the knight's fist or the flat of his sword. Once the feudal male had been knighted he became of age. He could do homage and rule his fief.

The knight's principal occupation and favorite amusement was fighting. If he were a baron, he fought to keep his vassals in hand and to gain what he could from his neighbors. The simple knight who held a fief followed his lord to battle because it was his duty and in the hopes of sharing in the booty. The landless knight fought for his living. War could be extremely profitable. Although plundering peasant villages could rarely have yielded much booty, there was always the chance of capturing another knight and ransoming him. Gerard de Furnival, a simple knight who followed King John, captured a Breton noble and received enough money to buy for his son the heiress to an English barony. But entirely apart from the chance of profit it is important to remember that fighting was a delightful sport. And it was little more dangerous than football. The knight's armor protected him from the weapons of anyone who was not a knight and fairly well from the knightly sword and lance. Moreover no knight wanted to kill another, for a corpse was of no value. If a feudal lord went to war with a neighbor and killed him, he found the slain man's heir in his place ready to continue the struggle. But if he captured his foe, he could ransom him for a rich manor or even a strong castle. Even when kings and feudal princes fought supposedly serious wars in the early

Middle Ages, they were not bloody. In the great and decisive battle of Lincoln in 1217, where some 600 knights on one side fought 800 on the other, only one knight was killed, and everyone was horrified at the unfortunate accident.

When he was living peacefully at home the knight rose well before dawn, commonly as early as two or three o'clock, heard mass in his chapel, and got the business of the day out of the way. He consulted with his officials, judged cases, and generally saw to the business of his fief. By dawn he was ready for the really important occupation of the day—hunting. This could take many forms. The most highly esteemed—because it was most like war—was the pursuit on horseback of a stag or wild boar and the slaying of the quarry when the chase was over. Deer, wolves, and wildcats were hunted in the same manner. A more gentle form of hunting, considered peculiarly suitable for ladies but practiced avidly by their lords as well, was hawking. Here one rode through the green meadows beside a stream with a trained hawk on one's wrist and sent it in pursuit of any game bird that appeared. Hunting formed an extremely important part of a noble's life, and he kept great packs of hunting dogs and many trained hawks, or more properly falcons.

About two or three o'clock in the afternoon the knight settled down to a good solid meal consisting of course after course of meat and poultry well reinforced with bread and pastry, and washed down with incredible quantities of ale or wine, according to the custom of the country. When he finished this repast, he was in the mood to be entertained. Here tastes differed. King John of England considered a hanging a suitable after-dinner entertainment, but others preferred less gruesome forms. Wandering minstrels came by ready to display their varied talents. Some were merely storytellers, with a magnificent supply of the types of tale that have amused men of all epochs. Others had with them tumblers, dancing bears, or dancing girls. A few had learned long narrative poems that they recited.* As the only artificial light available was smoky torches, the knight was likely to go to bed soon after darkness set in.

Needless to say, the knight of the eleventh and early twelfth centuries was no model of gentleness and refinement. He drank himself into a stupor with considerable regularity. His castle was usually filled with prostitutes. If he got annoyed with his opponent during a chess

* See pp. 453–5.

game, he was inclined to brain him with one of the massive chessmen of the day. When a servant was slow in bringing his wine, he threw a javelin at him to speed his steps. If his wife annoyed him, he beat her savagely. In one contemporary tale there is a scene where a wife suggests to her husband that it is not quite the thing to murder a guest while he is taking a bath. She is promptly knocked down for her trouble. In the fourteenth century, when ways had grown gentler, the Knight of La Tour Landry wrote a book of advice for his daughters. He told them of a wife who was accustomed to contradict her husband. One day her husband lost patience, knocked her flat on the floor, and kicked her face until her looks were permanently destroyed. That was what happened to wives who contradicted their husbands.

There was little or no legal restraint on the personal behavior of a member of the feudal class. While he was bound not to injure his lord, his lord's immediate family, his vassal, or his vassal's family, and might have to answer in his lord's court for an offense against a fellow vassal, the feudal system left him entirely free in regard to all other persons. Before the thirteenth century only feudal custom had any vitality in France; public law was practically nonexistent in so far as nobles were concerned. In an attempt to reduce the disorder in Normandy in 1091, William Rufus and his brother Robert issued a decree directing that if a man wanted to slay his enemy, he should give him fair warning by blowing his horn before attacking him.

In England there was an effective public law before which all freemen were equal in theory. In practice, however, the royal officials ignored offenses committed by men of importance unless someone equally important complained. As a rule the nobleman's crime was blamed on his men. Thus we hear in the records of a band of armed men plundering a village and carrying off some of the inhabitants to the castle of a great baron, Roger de Clifford. Roger in person set the amount of their ransoms, but there is no suggestion that he should be accused of any crime. A girl is abducted on the highway, taken to a knight's house, and raped by the knight and his men. The court solemnly accepted the statement of the knight that he was horrified to hear that she had not been in his house of her own free will. In short, even in England if a member of the feudal class committed his crimes against anyone other than the king or a great lord, he was fairly safe from prosecution, or at least from punishment.

The knight was religious in the sense that he accepted without question the basic teachings of the church and followed the prescribed forms of observance. He heard mass and confessed regularly. According to his means he gave alms and made donations to religious corporations. He was careful always to have at hand a private chaplain dependent on him to hear his confession: he would go to great trouble to avoid having to confess to a comparatively independent parish priest. In general he was inclined to feel that repentance and atonement were far easier than virtue. He did much as he pleased and made generous gifts to the church. Perhaps he even went on a long pilgrimage or a crusade. There were few feudal families of any importance that did not found a religious house, and a great baron might have four or five such houses endowed by his family and its vassals. It is impossible to question the knightly zeal for religion and devotion to the church and its teachings, but faith does not seem to have interfered with personal conduct to any great extent.

The women of the feudal class shared the characteristics of the men. If we are to believe preachers and storytellers, they were far too fond of drink. In fact, a not uncommon description of a lady in contemporary tales is "the fairest woman who ever drained a bottle." They beat their maid servants, sometimes to the point of death. Of course their ordinary daily life was less violent. Their work was spinning, weaving, sewing, and supervision of their households. When they hunted, it was usually in the form of falconry.

The status of women in feudal society was extremely complex. Since a woman could not fight, she was always treated as a minor by early feudal custom. She was always in the custody of some man. Before she was married she was in the care of her father. Afterwards she passed under the authority of her husband. When her husband died, she was in the custody of his lord or her eldest son. She had no rights whatever against her husband, and her person and property were completely under his control. While the church tried to limit the brutality of husbands to their wives by restricting the size of the stick with which they beat them, its teachings did not improve woman's status. She was the source of all evil: Eve's sin had banished man from Paradise. She was in herself a weak vessel given to sin. Moreover, the church insisted on the wife's subordination to her husband. The husband was to the wife as God was to him. But before bemoaning too much the status of woman in the early feudal epoch one should compare it with her position in other contemporary societies. The Moslem women were confined in a harem under the supervision of servants, and the Byzantine noblewomen were little freer. The feudal lady was completely at the mercy of her husband, but against all others she enjoyed his rank. When a knight was away, his wife ruled his household and his fief. Despite their handicap women could and did play an important part in feudal society.

The life of the feudal class was simple and crude and its members enjoyed little more luxury than the peasants who tilled their fields. A knight had at his disposal a plentiful supply of whatever his lands produced. He could have all the bread and game he could eat and all the ale or wine he could drink. But although his food was unlimited in quantity, it was far from varied. He could also have all the woolen clothes he could wear, but they were fashioned by the comparatively unskilled hands of his wife and her maids. In short, he had more food and clothing than a peasant, but they were of the same general quality.

The knight's castle was extremely simple and must have been most uncomfortable. There were usually two rooms: the hall and the chamber. In the hall the knight did his business with his officials, his vassals, and his peasants. There he ate, on tables made of planks laid across sawhorses. The hall must have been a scene of wild confusion, filled with servants, men-at-arms, prostitutes, guests, and the lord and his family. At night the servants slept in the hall, either on the tables or the floor. The chamber was the private room of the lord and his family. There he entertained guests of high rank. At night the lord, his lady, and their children slept in beds, while their personal servants slept on the chamber floor. Sometimes a very great lord had a chapel in his castle. By the twelfth century a few were so luxurious as to have a dressing-room called a wardrobe attached to the chamber. The castles were cold and drafty. The windows were covered by boards, or open. If the castle was of wood—as most were before the thirteenth century—the knight could not have a fire. In a stone castle one could have fire, but as chimneys did not appear until the late twelfth century, the smoke must have been almost unbearable. It seems likely that if one of us were offered the choice between spending a winter night with the lord or his serf, he would choose the comparatively tight mud hut with the nice warm pigs on the floor.

CHAPTER V

The Unification of Western Christendom

THE TWO centuries following the era of invasions were probably the most significant in the whole history of the Roman Catholic Church. At no other stage in the development of Western European civilization has so large a part of man's ability, time, and energy been devoted to religious purposes. It was an age of faith and of faith that led to activity. During this period the theology and law of the church were systematized and clearly expressed. The political organization of the ecclesiastical hierarchy was definitely formulated and subjected to centralized control. In this same period monasticism reached full bloom and the major monastic orders were created. Closely connected with this flowering of monasticism was a widespread burst of religious enthusiasm that raised the church itself and with it society as a whole to a new and higher spiritual and moral level. This religious enthusiasm affected all men to some extent and produced such mass manifestations of faith as the great crusades.

But it is important to notice that while a very large part of man's spiritual, intellectual, and economic resources were devoted to the service of church and religion, the church and both the secular and regular clergy made vital contributions to the secular phases of civilization. The world of ideas was almost an ecclesiastical monopoly. Scientific and political thought were developed by churchmen.* New agricultural techniques were most likely to orginate in monastic estates. The administrative methods of the secular governments of Europe were to a large extent developed by ecclesiastics who used the papal government as a model. The best scholars in all fields, the best administrators, even the best military tacticians and strategists were ecclesiastics. Finally, as Mr. Toynbee has so clearly pointed out, in this era the church made its great and almost successful effort to turn all Catholic Christendom into one great state ruled by basically moral laws. The United States of Europe was nearly achieved by the popes of the eleventh century. The purpose of this chapter is to tell in so far as space permits the story of this very stimulating epoch in the history of Christendom.

11. The Church in the Tenth Century

THE CHURCH emerged from the era of invasions in an extremely weakened state. In England the monasteries had been almost completely wiped out, and the secular clergy reduced to a very low point in discipline and learning. In France many monasteries had survived, but they had suffered heavily, and with a few notable exceptions such as St. Benoît-sur-Loire they had little discipline and less learning. The prelates were little different in point of view and way of life from their knightly relatives. In Germany the picture was much the same. Moreover, throughout the Frankish state lay lords had taken advantage of the confusion to usurp church lands. The papacy was in a particularly sad plight. Rome and the papal states were continually threatened and frequently actually invaded by bands of Moslems from Sicily. The pope was chosen by the Roman nobles and was little more than the chief of a political faction—often not too reputable a chief at that. While such wild tales as that of the woman pope that were commonly believed in the Middle Ages clearly had no basis in fact, the papacy was at its lowest ebb in dignity and spiritual prestige.

In order to survive in France and Germany the Church had been obliged to enter into close relations with the lay nobles, the only power

* See pp. 430–8.

able to offer protection. The prelates became vassals of some great lord and hence obligated to perform the usual feudal services. With this status went seignorial authority over the people living on their lands. But as a prelate could not kill or sentence to death, he could not with propriety lead his contingent of knights to battle or carry out the functions of a secular judge. While there were warrior bishops—some used a mace in battle on the ground that dashing out a man's brains was not shedding blood—the majority sought some other solution. Usually a prelate chose a lay lord to act as his "advocate." The advocate led the prelate's knights in battle and performed his secular judicial duties, in return for a fief or some other consideration such as the chief share of the penalties imposed in the courts. Naturally the great lords whose vassals the prelates were expected to appoint whom they pleased as bishops and abbots without interference from any source. As a matter of fact these lords both appointed prelates and invested them with the symbols of their spiritual as well as their secular office. The high spiritual functions of the episcopacy became mere adjuncts to a secular fief. And the advocates were in an excellent position to usurp the lands and rights of the churches they served. During the tenth century the prelates of Germany succeeded in freeing themselves from local potentates like counts and dukes and from their advocates by a close alliance with the crown; but while one master was undoubtedly preferable to many, the secular control of the church was if anything more complete.

Although the internal history of the church during this era of confusion is extremely obscure, it is clear that several important developments took place. One of these was the rapid development of the parish clergy. Originally the bishop and his priests lived in the cathedral city and served the country about. But with the appearance of local lords, parish churches began to be founded. It seems likely that a lord wanted to control the religious side of his fief as well as the secular. He built a church, collected the tithes and the revenues from the land assigned to the church, appointed a priest, and paid him the minimum sum necessary to enable him to live. Thus the income from tithes and parish lands became an important source of revenue to the lords. Another result, however, was the creation of the network of parishes that was so important a part of the ecclesiastical structure.

A further interesting and important development was in the realm of ecclesiastical law. The accepted law of the church consisted of the canonical books of the Bible, the writings of the Church Fathers, and the decrees of popes and councils. As this law had been created in environments quite different from that of the ninth century, the prelates of that day found it inadequate for their needs. They wanted spiritual weapons to aid them in their struggle against their lay neighbors and to help them rule their own clergy.

The most convenient way to acquire such laws was to invent them. Hence there was created in France during the middle years of the ninth century the famous collection of forgeries usually known as the Pseudo-Isidorean Decretals. One or more ingenious clerks took genuine papal letters, changed them to say what they wanted said, and ascribed them to a legendary or imaginary pope. Then the whole collection was ascribed to that enthusiastic if somewhat confused scholar, St. Isidore of Seville. For good measure most collections of the Pseudo-Isidorean Decretals included an independent and probably earlier forgery, the well-known Donation of Constantine. In this document Constantine, having been cured of leprosy by Pope Sylvester, gave the entire western part of the Roman Empire to the pope. The Donation was probably created at some point in the debate over the proper relationship between the pope and the Carolingian emperor. It was until the fourteenth century a useful weapon in the papal arsenal. The Pseudo-Isidorean Decretals, combined with a collection of laws sent to Charlemagne by Pope Adrian I (772–95), became the foundation on which later canon law was built.

Before proceeding to discuss the development of the Church during the eleventh and early twelfth centuries let us glance briefly at its structure in the tenth century. The key figure in the ecclesiastical hierarchy was the bishop. The archbishop was more powerful than his suffragans only to the extent that his own episcopal see was larger and richer than theirs. He had no effective authority over them. The bishop possessed the full spiritual power of the church. He could perform all the sacraments and could by the sacrament of ordination pass on this power to others. He alone could perform the sacrament of confirmation. In theory at least he appointed all the lesser clergy in his diocese. He had control of the property of his church. In short he was the master of the personnel and property of the church in his diocese, and was practically independent of any higher spiritual authority. According to the canon law the bishop should be elected by the clergy and people of his diocese, but in practice only the clergy attached to the cathedral participated. As the clergy had little choice but to elect the man designated by the lay lord who was patron of the see, the method of election made no great practical difference.

The bishop was surrounded by a group of clergy of widely varying rank who aided him in administering the diocese and in serving the cathedral church. At the top of this group were his officials. The chancellor supervised the cathedral school and issued licenses to teach. The treasurer was responsible for financial administration. The archdeacon carried out the ordinary judicial business in the ecclesiastical courts. While these were the chief episcopal officers, there were a host of minor ones, and many priests, deacons, and sub-deacons who served the cathedral church. By the eleventh century an inner privileged group was forming within this cathedral clergy. The bishops themselves and generous lay lords endowed seats called canonries in the cathedral. The occupants of these endowed positions were called canons and formed a corporation headed by an elected dean. Before long the canons monopolized the powers of the cathedral clergy. All the officials of the diocese were canons, and the dean was the chief dignitary in the diocese after the bishop. The canons also became the body that represented the clergy in the election of the bishop.

Between the bishop and his officials and the parish clergy lies a region about which there is little information before the twelfth century. There were apparently for a time itinerant officers called archpriests who supervised the parish priests. Later these were replaced by rural deans. The rural dean was usually himself a parish priest. It was his duty to investigate the fitness of clerks nominated by the lords, report to the bishop, and install the clerk if the bishop accepted him. Priests were nominated by the lords. The bishop could reject a nomination, but he had no effective means of forcing the lord to suggest more suitable candidates. In general he could do little but accept a nomination, unless it was utterly and obviously scandalous. In addition to the parish priests there were the chaplains of the lords. Over them the bishop had no real control whatever.

It is important to remember that below the higher orders of the clergy—priests, deacons, and sub-deacons—were a host of men in minor orders. From them were drawn the clerks who served both lay and ecclesiastical lords as secretaries and in any other capacity in which literacy was required. Socially the clergy were divided as was secular society. The bishops, their officers, and the canons were usually members of the feudal class. The parish priests were ordinarily drawn from the ranks of the serfs. Although it was by no means impossible for a man of humble birth to rise to high office in the church, it was extremely difficult and happened most infrequently.

For the most part the monasteries of Western Europe subscribed to the Benedictine rule, but in comparatively few houses was it practiced effectively. They were more places of refuge for people who found the outside world too turbulent than centers of religious enthusiasm. Since each monastery was independent its discipline depended almost entirely on the abbot, and he was likely to be an appointee of a lay lord chosen for reasons that were essentially political. In fact, in tenth-century France it was common for the lord to be the titular abbot and enjoy his revenues while an ecclesiastical deputy cared for the spiritual function of the office. In theory the bishops were responsible for the monasteries in their dioceses and had the authority to inspect them, but this was not very effective. Most bishops of the day had little zeal and no desire to offend the lords by interfering in their monasteries. But the greater houses sought to escape even this meager control by obtaining papal letters freeing them from the supervision of the bishop and placing them directly under the pope. As the papacy was weak and a long way off, this meant complete independence.

12. The Cluniac Reform

DESPITE the general low level of religious zeal there were devoted churchmen who saw clearly the evils in the ecclesiastical organization and were anxious to ameliorate them. Early in the tenth century some of these men prevailed on William, duke of Aquitaine, to take an important step in that direction. In the year 910 Duke William founded the monastery of Cluny. Various provisions were made in the hope that Cluny could avoid the difficulties of other houses and act as a spearhead for general monastic reform. Cluny was never to hold land in return for feudal services. All gifts made to it were to be in free alms, that is, owing no service except masses and prayers for the donor. It is interesting to notice that Duke William did not allow his religious zeal to cloud his practical sense. The land with which he endowed Cluny was held by him from the duke of Burgundy, who lost the services due from it. Then an attempt was made to remove what was believed to be one of the chief sources of evil in monastic life: idleness.

According to the Benedictine rule the monks were to perform manual labor in the fields. But most gifts to monasteries were of land with its resident labor, and there was no need for the monks to work. Hence the rule was impossible to enforce. The founders of Cluny accepted this situation, but to keep the monks occupied they greatly increased the amount of time to be devoted to performing the services of the church. This was the chief modification made in the Benedictine rule. The founders of Cluny naturally hoped that other monasteries would be founded on the same bases, and that established houses would embrace the Cluniac rule. Here they planned to avoid another evil of contemporary monasticism—lack of effective supervision over the houses. The Cluniac order was to have only one abbot, the abbot of Cluny. All the other houses were to be ruled by priors. The abbot had general responsibility for the discipline of all the houses and was expected to make frequent inspections of them.

The Cluniac order spread with amazing rapidity under a succession of great abbots. Many daughter houses were founded, and a number of the proudest Benedictine monasteries of France and Germany accepted its rule. Moreover the order maintained a very high level of discipline and good order. But the influence of Cluny in the monastic world spread far beyond the Cluniac houses. Many monasteries in France were reformed on the pattern of Cluny without joining the order. In England monasticism, and in fact the English church as a whole, was revived in the late tenth century by a group of men with Cluniac ideas headed by the famous St. Dunstan. Within a century and a half after the foundation of Cluny its monks and those who absorbed their zeal and ideas had reformed a large part of the regular clergy of Western Europe.

By the eleventh century the zeal for reform that centered in Cluny had reached the secular clergy. Many priests and prelates were seeking means to improve the status and discipline of the church as a whole. The more intelligent of these men saw clearly that the first necessity was to unify the organization of the church under effective centralized control. An individual bishop was helpless before the feudal princes. Only combined action under strong leadership could bring about general reform. Naturally this leadership had to be sought in the papacy. Fortunately for the reformers the king of Germany and Holy Roman Emperor, Henry III (1039–56), was deeply interested in their plans and had actively aided the Cluniac reform in the German monasteries. He was ready to support an attempt to strengthen the papacy so that it could lead a similar movement in the church as a whole.

One of the first steps of the reformers was to attempt to put an end to secular influence in the selection of the pope. In theory the pope was elected by the clergy and people of Rome. This meant in practice that he was chosen by the strongest faction of the Roman nobility, unless the emperor was interested and had available force in Italy. The reformers sought to avoid pressure from either emperor or Roman nobles. Their device was to establish a permanent electoral body, the College of Cardinals. The six suffragan bishops of the archdiocese of Rome, the so-called suburban bishops, the priests of the chief churches of the diocese of Rome, and the more important deacons of that diocese were to compose the College of Cardinals. When a pope died, they were to meet and elect his successor. If any outside pressure was exerted upon them, the election was to be void. The College of Cardinals as it was founded in the eleventh century still exists. From a very early period non-Italian prelates were brought into the College by making them titular priests of Roman churches.

It is rather doubtful that the Emperor Henry III fully realized the significance of this reform. He was glad to see a system for the orderly election of the pope without interference from the Roman nobles, and he probably could not conceive of the possibility that a pope could be elected and installed without his approval. His successors were to discover that the reformers considered imperial influence fully as dangerous as that of the Roman aristocracy.

Any attempt of the papacy to intervene effectively in the affairs of the church outside Italy was made extremely difficult by the problem of distance. It was almost impossible for the pope to obtain adequate information about local conditions, and any action by him was likely to be both ill-informed and tardy. An obvious solution to this difficulty was the use of agents. The popes began to send officials called legates to carry out their commands throughout Christendom. Some legates had general commissions to reform any abuses they might find and were called legates *a latere* while others were sent to deal with a specific problem. The legates were to play a vital part in establishing papal control over the church.

In their effort to centralize the government of the church by increasing papal power the reformers used several devices. From very early times the popes had been accustomed to honor a particularly eminent archbishop by giving him a *pallium*, a band of white wool embroidered with four purple crosses. If it was at all possible, the archbishop was expected to journey to Rome to receive the pallium from the hands of the pope. By the eleventh century practically all archbishops received the pallium. While some made the journey to Rome, many more received it by messenger. In this custom the reformers saw an opportunity to give the pope a veto power over archepiscopal elections and an opportunity personally to instruct newly elected prelates. They declared that an archbishop could not perform his functions until he received the pallium and that only extremely strong reasons were to be allowed to free him from the necessity of visiting Rome for the purpose.

As we have seen in an earlier chapter, the ecclesiastical courts had a very extensive jurisdiction. They claimed the right to hear all disputes between ecclesiastical organizations and between individual members of the clergy. If any man in clerical orders was accused of a crime, the church courts claimed jurisdiction. All moral offenses such as fornication and adultery were in their care, as well as questions connected with marriage and legitimacy. They handled all disputes concerned with wills and legacies and with promises made under oath. Although by the twelfth century various royal governments were attempting to reduce the jurisdiction of the ecclesiastical courts, in the eleventh century their claims were rarely disputed. The lowest ecclesiastical court was that of the archdeacon. From its decision one could appeal to the bishop and from him to the archbishop. From the archbishop's court one could in theory appeal to the pope. But as this meant a journey to Rome and costly litigation there, only the very rich could consider it.

The reformers realized that the papal influence could be enormously increased if appeals to the pope could be facilitated. To secure this result they invented the system of judges delegate. One could write to the papal court appealing a decision and asking for the appointment of judges delegate to hear the appeal. The pope then directed a group of ecclesiastics in the country concerned to hear the case and render a decision. While this decision could be appealed to the papal court, in most cases it was accepted. This system of judges delegate hearing appeals from ecclesiastical courts did not reach full flower until the twelfth century, but it was started in the eleventh and greatly increased the papal power.

The reformers desired to correct all abuses in the church, but they naturally centered their attention on those that seemed most serious from the point of view of the welfare of the whole organization. By the eleventh century, ecclesiastical law definitely forbade the marriage of priests, deacons, and sub-deacons, and required them to live chastely. This law was not taken very seriously in western Europe. In Anglo-Saxon England it was common for parish priests and even higher church officers to be married and to pass their offices to their sons by inheritance. Although on the continent the female companions of clerks were rarely recognized as their wives, their existence was pretty much taken for granted. The issue was not purely a moral one. A clergyman who had a family was bound to have his interest diverted to some extent from his duty and was extremely likely to use church property to endow his children, whether or not they were considered legitimate by their neighbors. Hence one of the chief objects of the reformers was to enforce clerical celibacy. Another offense that particularly troubled them was simony—the buying of church offices. Here the issue was chiefly one of morality and decency. It shocked the devout to think of spiritual office being bought and sold. Moreover, as the money was usually paid to a lay lord, simony was closely connected with secular influence in the church.

Although the suppression of simony and the firm establishment of clerical celibacy were eminently worth-while objectives, these two questions were essentially peripheral. The central problem was lay control of the appointment of church personnel. The church needed devout, learned men imbued with genuine spiritual enthusiasm and completely devoted to its interests. The lay lords wanted the members of the ecclesiastical hierarchy within their lands to be primarily devoted to their interests. If the church was to be turned into a great spiritual organization serving God under papal leadership, the reformers had to win this controversy. At the same time this victory would ruin most kings and feudal princes. As the clergy were the only literate men, the princes needed their service as administrators. Even more important was the fact that the church controlled enormous resources in men and produce. The German monarchy under the Saxon and Salian kings rested almost entirely on control of the prelates and their lands.* The church was the chief mainstay of the much weaker Capetian monarchy.† In England control of the church was a vital royal prerogative. No monarch could allow anyone but himself to choose the prelates on whom he depended so heavily.

There was, of course, one obvious solution to the difficulty. The church could surrender all its possessions not actually needed to support its spiritual services and renounce any part in purely secular affairs. In the twelfth century this course was suggested by Abelard and others, and it even met with the approval of Pope Pascal II (1099–1118). The historian Toynbee has pointed out that if the church had taken this course, it might well have united all Christendom in a strong spiritual empire and thus changed the whole future of Western civilization. He seems to think that this might have been possible but for the towering ambition of the leader of the reformers, Hildebrand, who became Pope Gregory VII (1073–85). This seems to me most improbable. It is inconceivable that the prelates of Western Europe could have been persuaded to give up their temporal power—their positions as great barons with feudal and seignorial authority.

From 1045, when he first entered the papal curia, to 1073, when he was elected pope, Hildebrand had been one of the most vigorous of the reformers if not their actual inspirer and leader. He came to the papal throne determined not only to carry out the program of reform that was already under way but also to make the pope the acknowledged vice-regent of God. Pope Gregory believed that he was responsible to God for the rule of Christendom. Kings and feudal princes were essentially police chiefs who wielded their swords at his command. If a king was obdurate and absolutely refused to obey the papal mandates, the pope could remove him by absolving his subjects from their oaths of allegiance. In short, instead of freeing the church from lay control by withdrawing it from secular affairs, Gregory sought to establish ecclesiastical rule over the secular as well as the spiritual sphere.

The issue on which Gregory joined battle with the lay princes was, of course, the choosing of bishops. The bishops were not only the most important members of the ecclesiastical hierarchy, but they also were those most likely to hold high secular posts and to rule the greatest baronies. Gregory insisted that bishops were to be chosen according

* See pp. 165–6. † See pp. 155–6.

to canon law. The clergy of the diocese were to elect the bishop and notify the archbishop of their choice. If the archbishop approved the election, he would consecrate the new bishop and invest him with the symbols of his spiritual office. He would then direct the lay lord to invest the bishop with the insignia of his temporal power. Thus the feudal prince would merely give the barony to one chosen without his participation or approval. Needless to say the princes were inclined to ignore these dictates. The Emperor Henry IV (1056–1106), who had just come of age, proceeded to choose bishops and invest them with the symbols of both their spiritual and temporal office as had his predecessors. Gregory ordered him to stop under pain of excommunication, and Henry replied by summoning a council of his German prelates and declaring Gregory a false pope improperly elected. The pope then excommunicated the emperor. Fortunately for Gregory, Henry was deeply involved in troubles in his own kingdom, which will be discussed in another chapter.* He was obliged to humiliate himself before the pope and beg forgiveness and absolution. But Gregory's victory was only temporary. He spent his entire reign in a bitter struggle with Henry and died in exile with imperial troops in possession of Rome.

Pope Gregory centered his attention on the attempt to break the control of the German crown over the church for a number of reasons. For one, the emperor was by far the most powerful monarch in Western Europe. If he was obliged to surrender, other princes would be likely to follow suit. Moreover, as master of Lombardy and in theory at least ruler of most of Italy, the emperor was far closer to the papacy than other rulers. Although the struggle with the emperor absorbed most of Gregory's personal attention, he did not neglect France. He sent his legates into that kingdom to enforce his policy upon King Philip I (1060–1108). King Philip was a less satisfactory foe. He did not openly defy the papal commands but rather ignored them. Toward the English king, William I (1066–87), the Conqueror, Gregory showed far more mildness. William appointed his Norman and English bishops as he saw fit and refused to admit legates to England unless they had his permission to enter; but he appointed reasonably suitable prelates and was friendly toward the papacy. Hence when a legate sent to France wandered into Normandy, Gregory quickly called him off on the ground that the pope needed one friend among the princes.

* See p. 171.

And when the archbishop of Canterbury pointed out that if all married priests were deprived of office England would have no priests, Gregory gave him permission to enforce celibacy of the clergy gradually.

This great debate between Gregory VII and Henry IV over the appointment of bishops, commonly called the Investiture Controversy, was the *cause célèbre* of the age. It is important to realize that the church was not solidly behind the Pope. In Germany the clergy in general supported the Emperor, and it was the lay lords who for purely political reasons aided the Pope. When Gregory absolved Henry's subjects from their oaths of allegiance, many churchmen felt that he had exceeded his power. Although the Pope had a number of able writers who supported his cause, the opposition was also highly vocal. An unknown Yorkshireman wrote a fascinating work proving to his satisfaction that priests should be married and that kings were independent of the pope. Although the question at issue, the Investiture Controversy, was to be settled early in the twelfth century, the broader subject of the proper relation between lay and ecclesiastical power was to continue in very active dispute.

The Investiture Controversy was settled in the early twelfth century by a series of compromises, all essentially alike, between the papacy and individual monarchs. It was agreed that when a bishop died, the clergy of the diocese, in practice the cathedral chapter, should notify the prince and ask permission to elect a successor. The prince could then either order the chapter to send a delegation to hold the election in his presence, or he would send a representative to supervise the election. When the election took place the archbishop would invest the new bishop with the symbols of spiritual office, and the prince would present him with those of his temporal dignity. This compromise, of course, meant a complete victory for the princes. Few chapters dared go against a prince's will in his presence or that of his representative. In practice the representative sent to supervise the election was usually the prince's nominee for the office.

Gregory VII and his fellow reformers of the eleventh century started a process that was to go on for several centuries. They worked toward the standardization of the beliefs and practices of the church and the unification of its organization under the leadership of the pope. They strove to free the church from lay control and to subject secular lords to spiritual authority. They also vigorously attacked the more serious abuses in the church itself. All these lines of endeavor were continued by their successors with varying zeal and success. In this chapter we shall confine ourselves to the accomplishments of the period before 1150.

13. Theology and Canon Law

IF THE Church was to be fully effective in its work and truly unified, it was extremely important that the same beliefs and practices and the same ecclesiastical or canon law should be accepted throughout western Christendom. This was by no means true in the eleventh century. Since the collapse of the Roman Empire in the west the churches of the various regions had been left more or less to their own devices. The beliefs, practices, and laws of each church had been formulated in its own councils with little or no guidance. The Celtic church of Ireland, Wales, and the Scots Highlands continued to be very different from the churches of the rest of Western Europe; but even within the latter group there were striking divergences. The Anglo-Saxon church accepted married priests as a matter of course and had no ecclesiastical courts. Less violent differences marked the churches less remote from Rome. It was not simply a matter of divergence from an official standard; there was no such standard. Hence Gregory and his successors were faced with the necessity of creating one and procuring its general acceptance.

The relations between the members of the church organization and between the church and the secular world were governed by canon law. Its standardization was peculiarly important. Gregory VII fully realized this, and several of his colleagues produced collections of canon law that were accepted as official by the reform party. The enthusiasm for this work was greatly spurred by the revival of legal studies that marked the eleventh century in Italy.* An important part of the great legal works prepared under Justinian had lain forgotten during the early Middle Ages, but in the eleventh century they were rediscovered and studied with vigor. They gave the men of the day an example of something beyond their experience—a code of law to cover all the needs of a vast empire. This naturally encouraged the attempt to construct a system of canon law for the church as a whole. Throughout the late eleventh and early twelfth centuries a number of able canonists

* See p. 469.

produced collections of laws that aimed at this end. Although their eventual purpose was the same, in that all wanted a standardized code, not all by any means agreed as to what that code should be. Writers who supported the papacy chose from the mass of available material—the Bible, the Church Fathers, decrees of popes and councils, and such older collections as the Pseudo-Isidorean Decretals—whatever seemed best suited to strengthen the papal authority. Others chose what would support the independence of the individual bishops against their superiors. In short, each of these writers took what he pleased from the discordant mass and made no attempt to reconcile apparent inconsistencies.

The same sort of divergences existed, though probably to a lesser extent, in the realm of theology; and here it was a matter of differences between individuals rather than between regions. Just as there was no common code of canon law, there was no official point of view on many theological questions. There was continuous debate as to how many sacraments there were, and scholars held widely varying views on the subject. Minor points of theology were continually causing controversy. Thus Abelard, probably the greatest scholar of the early twelfth century, read the Greek philosophers and decided that their views were essentially Christian. He announced that the philosophers were Christians before Christ and that when Christ descended into Hell he brought up the philosophers as well as the Hebrew prophets. This view was, after long debate, declared to be an error; the point is that the debate was necessary. There was need for someone to produce a synthesis of theology that would reconcile the discordant views and serve as an official handbook.

Abelard seems to have been the first scholar to see clearly the confusion in the theological system. He noticed that the recognized authorities, the canonical books of the Bible, the Fathers, and decrees of popes and councils, were inconsistent in regard to many important questions. He wrote a book called *Sic et Non* which consisted of a list of questions and the divergent answers to them. Abelard clearly believed that these inspired writings could not in fact be inconsistent but were only apparently so, and that man's reason guided by faith could reconcile the differences. He did not, however, attempt to do this, but simply posed the problem and indicated the method by which it might be solved.

In the generation after Abelard, theology and canon law were standardized by two famous scholars: Peter Lombard and Gratian. Both followed the method indicated by Abelard. A question was posed. Then all the available answers were collected and commented on. Usually this comment tended to show that the views were not actually divergent. Finally the author wrote down his own decision. As has been suggested above, this reconciliation of apparently divergent authorities was a work of combined reason and faith. One who lacks the faith of these men may well feel that the inconsistencies were irreconcilable and that at times these authors performed feats of pure legerdemain. But to the men of the day, who were convinced of the close relationship between reason and faith, the two works were thoroughly acceptable and became the standard authorities in their respective fields. Obviously they soon needed interpretation and extension. New theological questions arose and had to be settled. Changing conditions called for additions to the canon law. But the works of Peter Lombard and Gratian remained the firm foundation on which later theologians and canonists were to build. And the method devised by Abelard and developed by Peter Lombard and Gratian was followed a century later by the great Thomas Aquinas.

Peter Lombard's chief service to the Church was the final clear definition of the sacramental system. Since it was through the sacraments that the church administered the spiritual powers given it by Christ, the sacramental system was the most vital feature of Christian theology. Peter Lombard described seven sacraments: the mass, baptism, confirmation, extreme unction, penance, marriage, and ordination. The mass was, of course, the supreme sacrament. To one who believed, as all men did, that the priest changed bread and wine into the flesh and blood of Christ, the mass was a majestic miracle and the true symbol of the spiritual powers of the church. Baptism, confirmation, and extreme unction were steps on the path of every Christian from birth to death. Ordination provided for the passing on from generation to generation of the spiritual authority given by Christ to his apostles. Penance permitted man to avoid the penalties for sins for which he was truly repentant. Marriage was the last of the sacraments to be generally recognized and was created to solve a serious dilemma. The church had consistently preached the superiority of the celibate life, in accord with its ascetic tradition. Yet if all men and women were celibate the race would quickly disappear: hence marriage was made a sacrament to dignify intercourse engaged in with the purpose of begetting children.

One of these sacraments, penance, requires rather detailed comment because of its prime importance and the fact that the methods of administering it were rapidly changing. The basic ideas behind the penitential system were relatively simple. The sacrifice of Christ had procured God's mercy for man. When one was sincerely penitent for sin and confessed to a priest, one was saved in the sense that one avoided hell. But a stain remained on the soul that had to be erased by a sojourn in purgatory. This could be shortened or even avoided altogether by doing some act or acts pleasing to God. These acts were called penance. Before the eleventh century confession and penance were reserved for the graver, so-called mortal sins. One could confess and do penance but once. Penance was usually severe, involving a long period of ascetic life. In the eleventh century this system was greatly modified. Confession was to be made at least once a year, preferably more often, and all sins whether grave or light were to be confessed. Penance was adjusted to the seriousness of the offense. For minor sins it was usually going for a short period without meat. Obviously this change enormously increased the influence of the church on men's lives. At every confession the ethical teachings of the church on every conceivable subject that was pertinent were brought to one's attention. Penitentials, or lists of sins and the penance suitable to them, had always been an important part of ecclesiastical literature. With the change in the conception of confession and penance these became far more complicated and detailed. They were, in fact, digests of the canon law as it applied to human ethics.

There was, however, another important development in the penitential system. Suppose a man was a rich and powerful lord who was truly penitent for his sins but was prevented by age and poor health from performing penance? What could be done for him? Obviously there were many worthy purposes to be served by gifts of money or property. To solve this problem the theory of the "treasury of good works" was developed. Christ had performed unlimited acts pleasing to God; and the saints, monks and nuns, and other Christians had done more such acts than were needed to save them from purgatory. When a penitent gave money to a worthy cause, he drew on this treasury. This doctrine played an extremely important part in all enterprises encouraged by the church. If a man gave property to a monastic house, he was usually made a participant in the grace earned by the virtues of the order. When a new cathedral was to be built, the pope could authorize the bishop to accept gifts as penance. Above all this system was used to finance the crusades. Those too old and sick to go in person could by contributing money earn the same plenary indulgence—full freedom from purgatory for all sins repented of and confessed—that the actual crusaders won. While this system was obviously open to abuse and was abused in later times, it was if properly administered an excellent way to obtain money for worthy purposes.* At the same time it undoubtedly gave many a baron the feeling that he need not worry about his sins so long as he confessed them and was sincerely penitent.

14. The Monastic Orders

THE GREAT wave of religious enthusiasm that marked the second half of the eleventh century and the first half of the twelfth is seen most clearly in the establishment of new religious orders and their rapid development. Thus in 1066 England contained forty-eight Benedictine houses—thirty-six of monks and twelve of nuns. By 1154 the realm possessed 245 houses of monks and seventy-two of nuns, distributed among six orders. These new orders were of different types and served varied purposes in religious life and in society as a whole. Eleventh century Italy saw a revival of the eremitical way of life that had played so important a part in the early church. Under the inspiration of the leaders of this movement—St. Romuald, St. John Gualbert, and St. Peter Damian—groups of hermits appeared throughout Western Europe. St. Romuald, St. John Gualbert, and St. Peter Damian supplied the rules for these groups of hermits living together. Similar establishments such as Grandmont and Grande Chartreuse appeared in France. These new orders were the product of extreme religious enthusiasm. Another order, that of Citeaux, was purely monastic in character and represented an attempt to observe the Benedictine rule with great strictness and severity. Then from very early times ecclesiastical reformers had attempted to improve the discipline of groups of secular priests serving collegiate churches by imposing on them a semi-

* See pp. 300–01.

monastic rule. Such reformers as St. Peter Damian and Pope Gregory VII were vigorous supporters of this policy, and these groups of "regular canons" as they were called became more and more numerous. By 1100 a majority of these groups had accepted a uniform rule—called the rule of St. Augustine because it was based on one of his letters—and they became essentially a new order. Several other orders of canons regular were established in this same period.

Although the rules followed by these canons were not unlike the regular monastic rules, there were essential differences. In an ordinary monastery many of the monks were not priests, but all canons had to be ordained to the priesthood. The canons were not so completely cloistered as the monks and hence could perform services that monks could not. The canons could serve as parish priests. They were particularly useful in conducting hospitals and almshouses. In short, regular monastic establishments sought to have their inmates lead the perfect Christian life. The regular canons were designed to lead as perfect a life as was consistent with the performance of certain services.

St. Stephen, the founder of the order of Grandmont, went with his father on a pilgrimage from his native Auvergne to Italy as a boy, and there became convinced that he wanted to be a hermit. When he returned to France in 1076, he settled in a cell near Limoges. Soon he was surrounded by a group of disciples for whom he set a way of life. After his death the congregation moved to a wild, deserted region called Grandmont. Following a custom developed in the Italian orders founded by hermits, the members of the order of Grandmont were divided into two classes: regular monks and *conversi*, or lay brothers. Although the regular monks lived together in common buildings, they lived as hermits in almost complete silence. They devoted all their time to contemplation and the services of the church. As Grandmont was a desert where little would grow and the rule forbade the order to own lands, stock, or rents of any sort, the monks lived in extreme poverty. The procurement of the bare necessities of life and the management of all the business affairs of the house were left to the lay brothers. So severe an order was unlikely to be very popular. Eventually daughter houses sprang up here and there that were all ruled by the prior of Grandmont, but it never became a numerous or powerful order. It had, however, a high reputation for sanctity.

Very similar to Grandmont was La Grande Chartreuse, mother house of the Carthusian order. Its founder, Bruno, master of the cathedral school at Reims, wandered into the diocese of Grenoble with a small group of followers after spending some years as a hermit, and settled in a barren mountain valley. Here too the division into regular monks and lay brothers applied. The monks spent almost their entire time in separate individual cells and gathered together only for certain church services and to eat in the refectory on Sundays and feast days. They never ate meat. Three days a week they fasted on bread and water, while on the other four they had vegetables, milk, or cheese, and wine mixed with water. Since the house refused to accept any property outside its wild valley, the poverty of monks was assured. The lay brothers grew the few vegetables and cared for the stock the desert valley could support. They were not, however, given control of the business affairs of the house. A monk was assigned to supervise their work and have full authority over them. In its early days the Carthusian order, like that of Grandmont, spread very slowly, as the severity of its rule appealed only to the extremely enthusiastic. Its great expansion and overwhelming importance in Christian monasticism was a comparatively late development.

Another order founded by a hermit deserves mention because of its special features. During the latter part of the eleventh century the status of woman was becoming more important in both religious and secular thought. The Virgin Mary was achieving her position as the kindly intercessor with her Son for sinful man. The cult of Mary Magdalene was spreading into Western Europe and she had become one of the patron saints of the great Cluniac abbey of Vézelay. The troubadour movement had begun in the person of William IX, duke of Aquitaine, and woman was becoming an important subject of secular literature. It was in this environment that Robert de Arbrissel, a priest who had become a hermit in the border lands of Brittany, Maine, and Anjou, founded the monastery of Fontevrault. Robert as a preacher and religious leader had appealed greatly to women and had a strong following among the great ladies of the countryside. At Fontevrault the chief element was a group of nuns who led a severely ascetic, contemplative life. Then there was a band of priests who served as chaplains to the nuns and lay sisters who acted as servants. The nuns included many women of noble birth. They were the dominant part of the house, and the abbess ruled over all the groups—nuns, monks, and lay sisters. While there were many nunneries in Western Europe, few if any were as large and rich as Fontevrault and carried as great prestige in both religious and secular society.

The order of Citeaux was closely related to Grandmont and Grande Chartreuse in the religious fervor that brought it into being, but far different in many essential respects. In 1098, Robert, abbot of Molesme, grew discouraged in his efforts to improve the observance of the Benedictine rule in that abbey. Followed by six of his monks, he migrated to a new site at Citeaux and there founded a monastery where the rule was to be strictly observed. Robert soon returned to Molesme, but Citeaux continued a rather tenuous existence until 1109 when a man of both energy and imagination, Stephen Harding, became abbot. Shortly after, in 1113, a young Burgundian nobleman named Bernard entered the monastery with some thirty companions. Three years later Bernard became abbot of the daughter house of Clairvaux. From then until his death in 1153, St. Bernard of Clairvaux was the dominant figure in the Roman church.

Bernard was a religious enthusiast, in many ways a true fanatic, who had no doubt that his views were right and no inclination to avoid combat with those who disagreed with him. He waged bitter verbal battle against the scholar and theologian Abelard, the monk and statesman Suger, abbot of St. Denis, and the whole order of Cluny. At the same time he showed flashes of tolerance and practical good sense. He was gentle and kindly toward his monks, even the erring ones. When the duke of Burgundy asked to be accepted as a monk, Bernard told him to stay where he was. There were plenty of virtuous monks, but few pious dukes. The chief feature of Bernard, however, was his capacity to lead and inspire. His preaching and influence brought about an incredibly rapid expansion of the Cistercian order. In 1115 there were five Cistercian houses, Citeaux, la Ferté, Pontigny, Clairvaux, and Morimond. When St. Bernard died in 1153 there were 343, and by the end of the thirteenth century this number was doubled. In their heyday the Cistercian houses were large as well as numerous. Rievaulx in England contained 650 monks in 1142, at a time when the largest of English Benedictine houses, Christ Church Canterbury, could muster no more than 150.

The basic purpose of the founders of the Cistercian order was implicit obedience to the Benedictine rule in its strictest interpretation. They insisted on the single simple garment and meager ascetic diet provided by the rule. The churches and other buildings were to be simple and undecorated. The accessories of the altar such as crucifixes and candelabra were to be simple and of cheap, plain materials. Banished was the profusion of gold and silver ornaments that embellished other monastic churches. Moreover, the Cistercians were not to be supported by the labor of a peasant population. Their monasteries were to be located on uninhabited land, and they were to refuse gifts of manors with their people. They were also forbidden to accept the patronage of churches.

When the Cluniac reformers of the eleventh century were attacking lay control of the church, they objected violently to the practice of lay lords of collecting the tithes of their lands and giving the parish priest only a part of them. Although many lords cheerfully ignored this assault, others solved the problem by giving the patronage of their churches to monasteries, and this became an important source of revenue for many houses. Eventually the Cistercians relaxed their rule and accepted churches, but in the early days such gifts were firmly refused. Thus the Cistercians were committed to supporting themselves on lands hitherto uncultivated, without additional sources of revenue.

The refusal of Cistercians to accept inhabited lands had important results. For one, it undoubtedly played a part in the rapid expansion of the order. To found a Benedictine monastery was a very expensive proposition demanding the donation of valuable manors. But a Cistercian abbey could be endowed with a tract of wasteland of no value to the lord. The spiritual prestige of the Cistercians and the spiritual benefits conferred by such endowment combined with the cheapness of a foundation to make a great appeal to any lord interested in his welfare in both this world and the next. Then, in making productive the wastelands they occupied, the Cistercians performed a great service to society at large. This was particularly noticeable in England where they turned the wild moors of Yorkshire into vast sheep pastures and made England into a great wool-growing center. In fact, so successful were the Cistercians at agriculture that they did not long remain in the poverty they so eagerly sought.

The Cistercians also restored the requirement of the Benedictine rule that the monks perform manual labor. They reduced the time assigned to study and worship in the contemporary monasteries and devoted the hours gained to work in the fields and in the shops. But if they were to use uninhabited lands and do all the work themselves the time available for labor was not sufficient for the necessary tasks. Hence the Cistercians adopted the device of lay brothers. The lay brothers took the monastic vows, but they spent little time in divine service and were forbidden to learn to read and write. Their function was to perform the bulk of the manual labor required to support the community.

The organization of the Cistercian order was an effective compromise between the completely autonomous Benedictine abbeys and the highly centralized Cluniac system. The Cluniac system was well suited to a small order well concentrated geographically, but it tended to break down as the houses grew numerous and so widely scattered that the abbot of Cluny could not effectively control them. The Cistercian system was essentially hierarchical and reminds one of the feudal political structure. When a new Cistercian house was founded, the nucleus of the new establishment was a band of monks from an older house. Thus Citeaux itself had daughter houses such as Clairvaux and Pontigny, they in turn had daughter houses of their own, and these could in turn colonize new monasteries. The mother house retained rights over its daughters. The abbot of the mother house was expected to visit the daughter houses regularly and oversee their compliance with the rule. Thus the responsibilities that in the Cluniac order rested solely on the abbot of Cluny were divided among many Cistercian abbots. Then, once a year all the Cistercian abbots gathered at Citeaux to consider the problems of the order as a whole. This assembly could remove abbots who seemed unworthy of their high office. Finally, the abbots of the four senior daughter houses—la Ferté, Pontigny, Clairvaux, and Morimond—were given the authority to visit Citeaux and remove the abbot if it seemed necessary. Thus the Cistercians provided for effective supervision and control while leaving a fair amount of independence to the individual houses and preventing the abbot of Citeaux from acquiring too much power.

One more significant feature of the Cistercian rule requires mention —one that was in fact contrary to the rule of St. Benedict. The Benedictine and Cluniac houses accepted young boys as *oblates* to be trained in the monastic life. While they were allowed when they reached maturity to choose between the monastic life and the secular world, most of them naturally remained in the career they had become accustomed to. As a result comparatively few monks in these houses were there because of genuine religious enthusiasm. The Cistercians, however, would accept no one under sixteen and rigidly enforced the rule that all newcomers had to serve a year as a novice before taking permanent vows. Thus most Cistercians had a real call to the monastic life.

The Cistercian was by far the most successful of the great monastic orders. Although as time went on it relaxed some of the provisions of its original rule, it retained a comparatively high standard of discipline. And while the passing of the wave of religious enthusiasm that brought it into being reduced the number of its monks, its houses remained well populated. For centuries it continued to serve society by keeping inhospitable lands productive, and the church by preserving an example of Christian life. Although the Cistercians had a high reputation for sanctity, and immense spiritual prestige, they were not beloved by their contemporaries. The other orders and the secular clergy resented the existence of men living more strictly than they were willing to. Moreover, the nobles and higher clergy were inclined to view the monasteries as convenient hotels, and from this point of view the Cistercian houses were most unsatisfactory. They refused to admit women guests, and all guests had to share the meager fare of the monks. To Walter Map, archdeacon of Oxford, the Cistercians appeared simply stingy. And, asked Walter, what must be the depravity of men who need such a strict life to keep them from sin?

The two most important groups of regular canons in this period were the Augustinian, often called the "black" canons, and the Premonstratensian, or "white" canons. As we have seen, the Augustinians came into being through the application of a common rule to many autonomous groups of canons who had been living according to local customs. While a number of small orders such as those of St. Victor of Paris and Arrouaise embraced some of the Augustinian houses, the group as a whole did not become an order until the thirteenth century. The Augustinians spread with remarkable rapidity during the twelfth and thirteenth centuries: in England they had more houses than any other group. One reason for this was their appeal to the feudal class. A monastic establishment conferred prestige as well as spiritual benefits on its founder and his successors, and hence every lord sought to have one on his lands. But only great barons could afford to endow a Benedictine abbey or Cluniac priory, and comparatively few lords possessed the wide expanses of wasteland sought by the Cistercians.

The men who followed William the Conqueror to England, and their contemporaries on the continent, usually solved this problem by founding cells or priories subordinate to some Benedictine house. But such establishments lacked the prestige of autonomous houses, and the lord's control over them was hampered by the power of the mother house. To the lord who wanted to have an autonomous establishment at low cost, the Augustinians were ideal. The house could be small. As the canons could serve parish churches, the endowment could consist almost entirely of the churches of the lord's demesne. And the relations between the lord and the house was governed by the charter of foundation. Thus the lord could reserve for himself a dominant part in the appointment of the abbot or prior. Actually the Augustinian houses differed widely. While some were small and the canons were expected to serve a group of parish churches, teach in a school, or run a hospital or almshouse, others were large monastic establishments that differed little in practice from the Benedictine houses.

The Premonstratensian canons were founded by Norbert, a friend of St. Bernard's, in 1120. They were clearly intended to bear the same relation to the Augustinian canons as the Cistercian monasteries did to the ordinary Benedictine houses. The Premonstratensians followed a strict rule based on the Cistercian and formed a definite order organized on Cistercian lines. In the early days of the order the white canons served parish churches and performed similar secular functions, but as time went on its houses tended to become more and more purely monastic. In England, where the development of the order came in the second half of the twelfth century, its houses were actually little different from the Cistercian and were likely to be in similar locations. On the continent one of the chief services performed by the Premonstratensians was the nurturing of able and enthusiastic candidates for high office in the secular clergy.

It would be difficult to overestimate the importance of monasticism in the development of Western European civilization during the tenth, eleventh, and twelfth centuries. While the primary purpose of the monasteries was to secure the salvation of their monks, they performed extremely valuable functions in both religious and lay society. Perhaps their chief service to religion was the intangible one of providing examples of Christian living closer to the apostolic ideal than that prevailing among the secular clergy or laymen and thus being a permanent inspiration to reform and improvement. Many of the spiritual leaders of the period received their inspiration and training in the monasteries. Some like St. Bernard and the great abbots of Cluny exercised their leadership from within the cloisters, while others like Lanfranc, Anselm, and St. Hugh of Avallon, quit the cloisters to become prelates. The re-creation of the English church after the Danish invasions was the work of monks who had become bishops under the leadership of St. Dunstan. The Cluniac reform grew and took form in the houses of that order.

Although the direct acquaintance of Gregory VII with Cluny was confined to a brief sojourn, his ideas came largely from there, and the Cluniac houses were his most energetic supporters. The great centralized orders like the Cluniac and Cistercian were potent factors in the development of papal monarchy. Then too in the tenth and eleventh centuries before the appearance of the universities the monasteries were the only reservoir of educated men on which the church could draw. The libraries that preserved the learning of the past were mostly in monasteries, and the copyists who made the libraries possible were monks. Finally, a very large proportion of the scholars of the period pursued their studies within the cloisters.

The monasteries also performed extremely valuable services for society as a whole. The preservation and transmission of knowledge was of benefit to all men. Historical studies in particular owe to monks a heavy debt. Almost every monastery kept an account of events that were important to the community. Although usually this account was little more than a series of brief notices of the election of a new abbot, the death of some neighboring lord or prelate, or some astounding natural phenomenon such as a severe frost or an earthquake, some houses maintained more extensive chronicles. King Alfred persuaded the monasteries of England to keep the historical accounts that we know as the Anglo-Saxon Chronicle; and Orderic Vitalis, a Norman monk, composed a disorderly but very extensive history of Normandy under the Conqueror and his sons. Almost all our knowledge of the events of the tenth and eleventh centuries comes from monastic chronicles. But the composition of chronicles did not end the monks' services to history. They insisted that all gifts to their houses be written in formal charters. Many houses composed registers of their possessions. These charters and registers are our chief source of knowledge about the economic and social history of the tenth and eleventh centuries.

The contributions of the monasteries to the economic life of the time were most important. As the monks were better educated and more thoughtful than the lay lords, their estates were usually better managed than others. Improved methods of cultivation were likely to be first developed on monastic lands. Although the Cistercians were probably the most effective at bringing wasteland into production, many monasteries played an important part in the great reclamation movement. There is also a good deal of evidence to indicate that the monks were progressive in regard to the invention of tools and industrial techniques. Certainly they were the best builders of the day. No one who studies such magnificent Romanesque churches as St. Denis, Vézelay, Notre Dame de Poitiers, or St. Sernin of Toulouse, can fail to be filled with admiration for the monastic craftsmen.

The social benefits derived by society as a whole from the monasteries are rather difficult to assess. The monks maintained schools where laymen could study if they wished, but since literacy was of little interest to the feudal class it seems unlikely that these educational facilities were used very much. All monasteries gave alms to the poor and cared for the sick of the neighborhood, but it is not clear whether either of these services was often performed on an extensive scale. The monasteries also served as hotels for traveling lords and prelates. Perhaps their chief social value in the early Middle Ages lay in their availability as refuges for the gentle, the thoughtful, and the scholarly men and women for whom there was little place in the turbulent world.

Many charges have been leveled against the monasteries by both contemporary and later writers. Most of these have to do with the morals and way of life of the monks. The monastic ideal was an extremely elevated one, and the monks were men living in their day. There were immoral monks, and many more who carefully avoided the more unpleasant features of their rules such as poverty and fasting. At wealthy Benedictine houses like Christ Church Canterbury, many monks managed to have private quarters and servants to attend them. Their health was likely to be so delicate that they ate in the infirmary, avoiding the rigid diet of the refectory. But it seems clear that the monks as a whole maintained a way of life far above the general level of those of the secular clergy and the lay world; and that is about all one could seriously hope for. Other charges concern the effect of the monasteries on society. It has been frequently said that it was undesirable to remove so many people from their natural place as propagators of the race. This argument seems to me essentially silly. In general the population of Western Europe was increasing as fast if not faster than its means of support. A far more serious question is whether or not the services of the monasteries to society justified the vast wealth dedicated to their support. If one refuses to accept spiritual services as valuable, with the possible exception of the Cistercians they most certainly did not.

But the men of the Middle Ages valued these spiritual services above all others. The man who believed that the prayers of the holy monks in the monastery he had founded would shorten his days in purgatory did not worry as to whether or not those monks gave a reasonable proportion of their income as alms to the poor. By purely materialistic standards the monasteries undoubtedly represented a prodigious waste of productive resources; but the Middle Ages was not a materialistic era.

CHAPTER VI

The Development of Feudal Monarchy

15. The Capetian Kings
16. The Saxon and Salian Emperors
17. Saxons and Normans in England

THE CLOSE of the era of invasions saw the major part of Western Europe divided into three states—those of the Anglo-Saxons, the West Franks, and the East Franks. To the north, in Scandinavia, the kingdoms of Norway, Sweden, and Denmark were beginning to take form. In the Celtic fringe only the kingdom of Scotland could be called a state; Ireland and Wales were ruled by petty kings who were little more than tribal chieftains. The hills of northern Spain sheltered the seeds of the kingdoms of Aragon, Castile, and León. The only well-populated and productive part of Western Europe that lay outside the boundaries of the three great states was the Italian peninsula. Sicily and southwest Italy were ruled by the Moslems. On the Adriatic lay the remnants of Byzantine possessions in Italy—a few actual Byzantine posts and some petty independent states under Byzantine influence. The rest of the peninsula, except for the papal lands, formed the Lombard kingdom and its semidependent duchies. There were kings of Italy, but they rarely ruled more than the valley of the Po.

The military and economic dominance of Western Europe lay in the lands ruled by the Anglo-Saxons and Franks. Hence the political history of the tenth, eleventh, and twelfth centuries is largely an account of these three states. During this period their political structures were vitally changed by the development and spread of feudal institutions and by the appearance of a rival power, the papal monarchy. In this chapter we shall see how the institutions already described, feudalism and papal monarchy, affected the political forms of Western Europe.

15. The Capetian Kings

THE TWO chief fragments of the Carolingian Empire, the West and East Frankish states, were essentially different in political structure and made different adjustments to the needs of the era of confusion. All of the territory of the West Franks had been part of the Roman Empire and had been ruled since the fifth century by the Merovingian and Carolingian dynasties. Except for Brittany and to some extent Aquitaine there were no groups who thought of themselves as a separate people with their own culture and traditions. The land was divided into counties based on the dioceses, which in turn, reflected the Roman civitates. Even in the regions thickly settled by Franks, the popular courts had disappeared and the count ruled as the king's agent. In short, when the royal power grew weak, there was nothing but the local potentates, counts and great landholders, to take its place. As we have seen, the feudal system developed with great rapidity.* By the beginning of the tenth century the ordinary free warriors had become the vassals of their more powerful neighbors, who in turn, were the vassals of the counts.

The counts were the key figures in the political structure of the West Frankish state. As delegates of the king they exercised the public powers of government, and as feudal lords they commanded the services of the knights living in their counties. Although the office of count was not yet fully hereditary in the sense that the succession was governed by generally accepted rules of inheritance, an able son could usually succeed his father. When the heir was weak, the king might assert his right to appoint someone else, or some rival might successfully usurp the office. Often a powerful noble would gain possession

* See pp. 105–06.

of a number of counties. One family in particular was extremely adept at the art of collecting counties. Charles the Bald appointed a very able warrior known as Robert the Strong as *missus* in the Loire valley to hold the region against the Vikings. Although Robert and his successors were only moderately successful at repelling Vikings, they were experts at extending their own power. Soon they were counts of Angers, Tours, Blois, Orleans, Chartres, Paris, and other places. The descendants of Robert the Strong were the post powerful nobles of the West Frankish state, but there were other similar dynasties well entrenched in several counties.

These great lords soon made the descendants of Charles the Bald mere figureheads. Historians have been inclined to deal unjustly with the Carolingian kings, describing them as feeble and incompetent. Actually they were reasonably able men who did their best to maintain their power; but they lacked adequate resources. The center of Charlemagne's power had been in the Rhine valley, and his demesnes in the western part of his empire had been comparatively few; hence the West Frankish kings had always been poor. Most of the crown lands they did have were given out as fiefs to obtain the support of the great nobles. By the tenth century all that remained was the city of Laon, and the last Carolingians were sometimes scornfully called "kings of Laon." Thus the king had nothing but the right to the obedience of his officers, the counts—a right he was utterly unable to enforce.

Although the early Carolingian kings had passed the crown from father to son, in theory the royal office had remained elective, and the great feudal lords were inclined to make this theory a reality. It was difficult for a monarch who gained the throne by election to act very strongly against those who chose him. In a purely elective system, moreover, each great lord felt that he himself might achieve the royal dignity. At first the nobles simply used the elective principle to choose among the various Carolingian claimants, but in 897 they elected as king Odo (888–98), marquis of Neustria, son of Robert the Strong. The next century was marked by bitter rivalry between the Carolingian princes and the descendants of Robert. At times a Carolingian would hold the crown, at other times a member of the rival house. Frequently the head of each family claimed to be king and waged fierce war on his opponent. From the point of view of the feudal lords, whose chief desire was freedom from effective control, this was an excellent situation. Each lord could sell his support to whoever offered the highest price in fiefs and offices. The noble class, bred and trained for warfare, thrived on continued anarchy.

One powerful group, however, longed for strong and effective government. The Church was by principle and tradition the foe of unnecessary warfare. Moreover, the general anarchy placed the bishops and abbots at the mercy of their fierce and greedy lay neighbors. In order to protect themselves, their clergy, and the property of the church, the prelates had been obliged to enter the feudal hierarchy by becoming vassals of the great lords. Even this did not prevent extensive usurpation of church property and privileges.* Although the prelates fully realized that a strong king could be a hard master, they preferred to have only one man to deal with, and that man one who was crowned and anointed by the church and hence under special obligation to protect it. For this reason the ecclesiastics steadily and consistently preached the sanctity of the royal office and strove to establish a monarchy strong enough to curb the great lords.

At the death of Louis V (986–87), the nobles and prelates of the West Frankish state were called upon to choose between two aspirants to the throne. The last surviving member of the Carolingian house, Charles, the uncle of the late king, had quarreled with his brother King Lothaire (954–86), entered the service of the king of Germany, and become duke of Lower Lorraine. His rival for the West Frankish throne was the head of the house founded by Robert the Strong, Hugh Capet, who bore the title duke of France. Hugh was count of Orleans, Paris, and Dreux, and direct overlord of the counts who ruled in Anjou, Maine, Touraine, Blois, Chartres, and some dozen other counties. His brother was duke of Burgundy. His candidacy was supported by the majority of the clergy headed by the archbishop of Reims, who was the primate of the West Frankish state and the anointer of its kings. The archbishop argued that Charles of Lorraine was unworthy to rule because of his desertion of his brother and general incompetence. Hugh's ability indicated that God intended him to become king. Hugh was elected and thus became the founder of the dynasty that was to rule France for centuries. His direct heir in the male line is the present claimant to the French throne, Henry, count of Paris.

The nobles who chose Hugh Capet to be their king had no intention of establishing a new dynasty on the throne. They fully expected

* See pp. 124–5.

to continue their established practice of giving the crown now to one family and now to another. But Hugh was determined to make the crown hereditary in his family. Hence shortly after his accession he announced that the royal duties were too heavy for one man and asked the nobles to elect his eldest son as his crowned and anointed associate. It was difficult to refuse such a request; the nobles grumbled but complied. This practice started by Hugh Capet was continued by his successors. Not until 1227 did a king of France die before he had seen his successor safely crowned. This scheme, combined with the Capetian ability to produce male heirs, succeeded in making the French crown hereditary.

In order to understand the position of Hugh Capet it is necessary to think of him in three distinct capacities. He was the crowned and anointed king of the West Frankish state, the successor to the Carolingian monarchs. He was also the feudal overlord or suzerain of the great lords of the realm. Finally, he was the ruler of his own duchy. Although for purposes of convenience the West Frankish kingdom after Hugh's accession to the throne will be referred to here as France, this term does not represent the contemporary usage. Hugh called himself king of the Franks, as had the Carolingians. France was the present Ile de France, i.e., Paris and the country around it. This region was the center of Hugh's power and comprised the bulk of his fief, the duchy of France.

As king, Hugh had in theory all the traditional authority of the Carolingian monarchs. He could issue decrees that had the force of law throughout his realm. He could summon every able-bodied man to follow him to battle. The counts were his officers, exercising jurisdiction as his agents. It was his duty to defend the country from outside foes, maintain internal order, and support and protect the church. His anointment gave him a special sanctity; he was almost as much priest as king. Most of these royal prerogatives were of little practical use to Hugh. If he issued decrees, his counts enforced them or not as they saw fit. The counts might be his officers, but they were hereditary officials whom he could not remove or control. And the warriors of the realm were all vassals of the feudal lords and bound to follow them to battle. Being an anointed monarch did have at least two decided advantages, however. The person of the monarch was sacred, and the wildest lord would hesitate long before violating it. Then he had the firm support of the Church. This support was by no means restricted to spiritual weapons. The prelates of France held vast lands and had enfeoffed many knights.

During the last years of the Carolingian period the great lords of France had striven to gain control of the bishops and abbots within their lands and had on the whole succeeded in doing so. The dukes of Normandy, Brittany, Aquitaine, Burgundy, and France were the lords of the prelates of their duchies. Only the prelates of the northeast, such as the archbishop of Reims, had remained in direct contact with the crown and owed their feudal service to the king. Fortunately for Hugh Capet and his successors, however, they controlled many prelates that

had not been dependent on their Carolingian predecessors. The ancestors of Hugh had at one time or another ruled many more counties than Hugh possessed when he ascended the throne. Some of these had been given to younger sons, and others had gone as fiefs to buy support. But in granting these lands the Capetians had carefully retained control of the episcopal sees. Thus, although Burgundy and the region we call Champagne were held by great lords, the bishops depended on the Capetian king. This control of bishoprics was of extreme importance. The lord or patron of a bishopric could in practice select the bishop. These bishops were great barons with many knightly vassals. The patron of a bishopric, therefore, was assured of a vassal he could trust and military support when he needed it.

As suzerain of the great lords of France, Hugh Capet stood at the apex of the feudal hierarchy. A small group of dukes, counts, archbishops, and bishops were his vassals, the men later called peers of France. Twelfth-century tradition set the number of the peers at twelve—six laymen and six prelates—but probably there was never a time when the group consisted of exactly that number. In theory at least, these great lords owed the king all the regular feudal services. Actually this did not mean very much. The duke of Aquitaine did not recognize the Capetian dynasty for several generations. Not until the twelfth century did either of the great potentates of southern France, the duke of Aquitaine and the count of Toulouse, bother to do homage to the Capetian king. The duke of Normandy admitted that it was his duty to do homage and attend the royal court, but he insisted that the king was obliged to come to the frontier of his duchy when these services were to be performed. The great lords of northern France also acknowledged their suzerain's right to demand military service. They had been skillful bargainers, however, and the contingents they owed to the royal host were ridiculously small compared to their actual resources in knightly vassals. Thus the count of Champagne, who had at his disposal some 2,000 knights, owed but ten to the royal host.

The real power of Hugh Capet rested on his duchy of France, which became the royal demesne at his accession to the throne. There, in his own counties, he exercised full powers of government and collected fines for criminal offenses, tolls at bridges, and other customary dues. There lay the demesne manors that supplied food and clothing for Hugh and his court. The men who held fiefs in the demesne, the vassals of the duke of France, owed him feudal services and were less able to ignore their obligations than were the great vassals of the crown. The power of the Capetian king depended chiefly on the size and resources of his demesne and the effectiveness of his control over it.

In reality the France of the late tenth century should not be thought of as a unified state but rather as a loose alliance of great feudal princes. These princes were bound together by their common vassalage to the Capetian king. In practical politics, however, they treated the king as one of themselves—as duke of France. When it suited a prince's purpose he allied with the king against other great lords, but he was just as willing to join a coalition against his suzerain when that seemed the most profitable course.

During the century following the accession of Hugh Capet to the French throne the feudal system had all the vitality of a growing institution, and it was impossible to check the further fragmentation of political authority. Not only were Hugh and his immediate successors completely unable to curb the independence of their great vassals but they could not retain their original power in the royal demesne. The greater vassals of the Paris region, like the lords of Puiset, Coucy, and Montmorency, built strong fortresses and cheerfully defied the authority of their duke and king. The successors of Hugh Capet could not travel in safety from Paris to Orleans without the leave of the lord of Puiset, whose great castle at Étampes dominated the road between the two cities. Moreover, feudal ideas of hereditary office were so strong that they were bound to affect the relations between the king and his agents in the demesne. Officials called provosts superintended the king's demesne manors and collected his dues. These positions were farmed; that is, the holders bargained with the king for a fixed amount to be rendered to him each year. In addition, the office of provost became hereditary, and its holders were almost as hard to control as the feudal vassals.

It would be difficult to exaggerate the simplicity of the court, household, and way of life of the early Capetian kings. The chaplain heard confessions and said mass in the chapel. The chamberlain looked after the bedchamber and watched over the king's valuables, were they jewels, clothes, or charters. The constable and the marshal saw to the horses. The steward was responsible for the provisioning of the household and was assisted by such officials as the butler, who procured the wines, and the dispenser, who supervised their issuance. These same officers who ministered to the domestic needs of the royal household conducted the business of the realm. The chaplain, who as a clerk was literate, wrote the king's letters. In time he was called a chancellor and had other clerks under him who served as chaplains. One of these clerks would be the almoner, who dispensed the royal charity. The constable and the marshal were the king's deputies in commanding his troops. By far the most powerful of these officers was the steward. As it was his duty to procure supplies, he was in charge of the provosts who held the manors that yielded the supplies, and hence, to all practical purposes he was the head of the administration. So powerful did the steward become that the kings left the office vacant after the twelfth century.

The monarch lived like any great noble. He had a number of residences consisting of a chamber, a hall, and probably a chapel. He and his household moved continuously from one to another, eating the produce of the royal estates, for it was far cheaper to move the court to where the supplies were than to transport the supplies to the court. What little money revenue the king had was easily handled by his household officers, and any surplus went into the treasure chest that stood at the foot of his bed.

Hugh Capet, his son, and his grandson were far from mighty figures. They wandered about among their estates in the vicinity of Paris and waged fierce wars against their vassals of the duchy of France. Occasionally they would become involved in warfare between the great lords, but as most of these lords had greater resources than they, the kings could not play a very vital part in such major affairs. One may well ask why, under such circumstances, the monarchy was able to survive. Probably the chief factor was the unflagging support of the Church. Moreover, the kings were so weak that they could not annoy the great lords seriously, and their demesne was too small to be an extremely tempting prize. To attempt to crush the anointed of God, the sacrosanct king of France, was a serious matter. The possible profits did not seem worth the risk. Finally, feudal theory required a suzerain; and what suzerain could be more harmless than the Capetian king?

The Capetian monarchy reached its lowest point in the reign of Philip I (1060–1108), great-grandson of Hugh Capet. By that time the great feudal states had become fairly stable, thus limiting the king's opportunities to take advantage of quarrels among the feudal princes. In the north, the county of Flanders covered what is now western

Belgium and extreme northern France. Next to it on the coast stood the duchy of Normandy, the fief of the descendants of Rollo the Viking. The Celtic inhabitants of the Breton peninsula and a band of French-speaking people along its eastern border from below Nantes to Mt.-St.-Michel formed the duchy of Brittany. East of Brittany and south of western Normandy lay the counties of Maine and Anjou. To the east of these feudal states, hemming in the royal demesne from two sides, lay the vast possessions of the house of Blois. After the Capetians ascended the throne, the viscount of their county of Blois made himself count of Blois, Chartres, and Tours. Somewhat later the family obtained the county of Sancerre to the southeast of their other lands. They also inherited the lands of another dynasty that held the counties of Meaux and Provins from the king and the county of Troyes from the duke of Burgundy. This mighty house thus came to control the country to the west and the east of the Ile de France. In the eleventh century they called themselves counts of Blois or of Troyes. Only in the twelfth century did they adopt the title of counts palatine of Champagne and Brie, but henceforth for convenience we shall call them counts of Champagne.

South of the county of Champagne, in the lands that had formed the extreme northern part of the kingdom of the Burgundians, lay the duchy of Burgundy. Then south of the river Loire, occupying the coast of the Bay of Biscay from a short distance south of Nantes to within sight of the Pyrenees, and stretching from the Bay of Biscay to the frontiers of the Empire just west of the river Rhone, was the vast duchy of Aquitaine. Finally, the Mediterranean coast of the kingdom and a broad belt of land running westward to Toulouse comprised the county of Toulouse.

The power of the masters of these great fiefs differed as did the political structure of the fiefs themselves. The count of Flanders ruled a well-organized feudal state, in which no vassal was powerful enough to dispute his authority seriously. This was even more true of the duchy of Normandy, where the duke had retained in his own hands the higher forms of jurisdiction and the most important fortresses. The house of Blois had effective control of its counties of Blois, Chartres, Sancerre, Meaux, Provins, and Troyes. The count of Anjou ruled his fief with a strong hand. While one must not think of these states as orderly in our sense of the word—for they were continually torn with feudal strife—in each of them the lord was powerful enough to be able to dominate his vassals and compel them to obey him when he was really determined.

The duchy of Brittany forms a striking contrast to these more organized fiefs. It was essentially a group of independent counties where one of the counts had the rather meaningless title of duke. The ducal title shifted from one count to another according to the fortunes of war. There was no ducal demesne. The duke of Burgundy was despite his title a rather unimportant figure. His richest lands were held from him by the far more powerful count of Champagne, and other great Burgundian lords were fully as powerful as the duke. The duke of Aquitaine had fairly effective control over Gascony and Guienne, with their centers of Bordeaux and Bayonne, and in the country immediately surrounding Poitiers; but the rest of his vast fief was in the hands of great vassals whom he was utterly unable to control. The counts of Toulouse were kept weak by the family practice of dividing the fief among all the sons, leaving the eldest only a hazy suzerainty.

While the feudal princes of France differed greatly in power, most of them were stronger and none of them much weaker than the ruler of the tiny duchy of France who was their king. It was the most powerful of these princes, the duke of Normandy and the counts of Flanders and Champagne, whose lands lay adjacent to the royal demesne. King Philip was completely hedged about by vassals far mightier than he. Early in his reign this situation was made still worse by the Norman conquest of England.* While England was a source of weakness rather than of strength to William the Conqueror, it increased very greatly the resources of his successors.

The reign of Philip I saw the fortunes of the Capetian house at their lowest level, but it also witnessed a turning point in those fortunes. Ever since the accession of Hugh Capet the royal demesne had been shrinking. Under Philip it was enlarged. When the viscount of Bourges wanted money to support him on the First Crusade, Philip bought his fief. Then, in return for recognizing a count of Anjou who had captured and imprisoned his elder brother, the King received some Angevin lands south of the royal forest of Fontainebleau. Philip's other contribution to the power of his family was negative rather than positive but was nevertheless of considerable importance. He resisted skillfully and vigorously the efforts of the great reforming pope, Gregory VII, to break the king's control over the choice of bishops.† In this struggle

* See pp. 175–7. † See p. 134.

Philip had advantages that he used to the full. Most of Gregory's attention was devoted to his bitter contest with the Emperor Henry IV, and he could not throw his full energy against Philip. Philip was a man who was never troubled by any flicker of conscience; he had no interest in principles, but only in facts. Unlike the Emperor he did not defy the Pope and argue the basic issues; he simply ignored the papal mandates.

A typical illustration of his methods is the story of the good abbot, a close friend of Philip's, who asked him to support his candidacy for a vacant bishopric. Philip replied that he loved the abbot and that he would make an excellent bishop. But the abbot had little money and would be unwilling to commit simony anyway. Moreover, Philip had already allowed the queen to sell the bishopric for money to buy jewels. The King, however, had a solution. The new bishop had promised to pay for his see within a year. Once the queen had her money, Philip would accuse the bishop of simony, have him removed, and see that the worthy abbot got the see. King Philip was equally casual in his other relationships. On a visit to the count of Anjou he took a fancy to the countess, whom the count had stolen from her first husband, and took her back to Paris as his queen, completely ignoring a shower of excommunications and interdicts. It is only fair to add that the count took the affair with good spirit and frequently visited Philip and his queen.

Philip was probably the most powerless king of the Capetian line, and suffered again and again humiliating defeats in the open field at the hands of his petty vassals of the Ile de France. He was also a man of entertaining but far from estimable character. But he did successfully resist the reforms of Pope Gregory and turned the fortunes of his house on their upward course by adding Bourges and the Angevin fief of Gatinais to the royal demesne.

The successor to King Philip, his son Louis VI (1108–37) was a great mountain of a man, imbued with incredible restless energy. He immediately set about the task of reducing to obedience the lords of the Ile de France. It was a long, slow, painful struggle, but Louis was determined, and he had the vigorous support of the Church, especially of the two great abbeys near Paris, St. Denis and St. Germain des Prés. The abbot of St. Denis, Suger, was to all practical purposes Louis' prime minister. Louis followed a regular procedure in his attacks on his vassals. He first summoned a lord to court to answer for some act of violence, giving him a safe-conduct to return to his castle after his hearing. Naturally, if the baron were condemned by the court, he defied the king as soon as he reached home and broke into open revolt. Louis would then have him excommunicated and march against him at the head of his own troops and those of the church lands. Several times Louis was defeated in the field, and often he failed to take a strong castle; but eventually he was successful. The two most troublesome of his vassals, Hugh de Puiset and Thomas de Marly, saw their castles torn down and their fiefs seized. The other lords hastened to submit to the king. From that time on the barons of the Ile de France headed by the lords of Montmorency were loyal servitors of the Capetian kings. It was among them that Louis' successors found their constables and marshals to lead their troops to battle.

King Louis' efforts to subdue the vassals of the royal demesne were hampered by the fact that he spent most of his reign in a series of bitter wars against a formidable coalition of feudal princes—Henry I (1100–35), duke of Normandy and king of England, and his nephew Thibaut, count of Blois. While Louis was able to hold his own by persuading the count of Anjou to attack his foes in the rear and by stirring up Henry's Norman vassals to revolt, the most he could achieve was a stalemate. He did, however, begin to make the royal authority felt in the great fiefs. When he learned that the count of Clermont, a vassal of the duke of Aquitaine, was besieging the bishop of Clermont in the episcopal city of Clermont-Ferrand, he gathered an army and hastened to raise the siege. This so astonished the Duke that he did homage to Louis and fully acknowledged his feudal obligations. Then, when the count of Flanders was murdered, Louis occupied the county, punished the criminals, and installed a count of his own choice. While his count was promptly rejected by the Flemings in favor of the man they considered the rightful heir, Louis had demonstrated his authority as suzerain. Perhaps the best sign of his prestige was that when the Duke of Aquitaine felt that his death was near, he entrusted his daughter and heiress, Eleanor, to King Louis.

At the death of Louis VI the foundations of the Capetian monarchy were firmly established. With no resources beyond those of his predecessors he had brought the royal demesne firmly under his control and had made his authority felt in at least two of the great fiefs. On these foundations his successors were to build a powerful state. But they lived in a different world than Louis, with new problems and new resources. Their activities will be told in a later chapter.

16. The Saxon and Salian Emperors

THE POLITICAL structure and traditions of the East Frankish state were quite different from those of its western neighbor. Except for Lorraine and western Franconia, none of its territory had formed part of the Roman Empire. Lorraine and Franconia were the only sections of the East Frankish state that had been an integral part of the Merovingian kingdom. While Bavaria had for a time been subject to the Merovingian kings, it had been little affected by that experience, and its actual incorporation in the Frankish state was the work of King Pepin. The conquest of Saxony was a purely Carolingian enterprise, started by Charles Martel and completed by Charlemagne. Although Charlemagne had established a few vassi dominici along the Slavic frontier, in general feudal institutions had not spread beyond Lorraine and Franconia. In most of the East Frankish state there were no organized counties. The counts were simply royal agents with powers of supervision over the local popular courts. Finally, the seignorial system had not penetrated far into the German lands and was practically unknown in Saxony. This was a land of noble and nonnoble free farmers.

When the power of the Carolingian kings began to crumble in the middle of the ninth century, the peoples of the East Frankish state had not had time to forget their independent past. In particular, the Saxons and Bavarians thought of themselves as distinct peoples. When their kings failed to defend the land from Vikings and Magyars, they sought local leadership that recalled their ancient traditions.* Thus in each of the chief districts of the kingdom—Saxony, Franconia, Swabia, and Bavaria—an important local landholder became the military leader of the people. These leaders took the title "duke," and historians have called them tribal, or stem dukes. The power of these dukes rested on their own landed possessions and on their personal influence over their peoples. They had no authority over the counts and no rights in respect to the bishoprics and abbeys in their duchies. Naturally, how-

* See pp. 91–3.

ever, each duke was ambitious to gain full power in his duchy by usurping the royal demesne, making the counts dependent on him, and obtaining the rights of patronage over the churches. During the feeble reign of the last Carolingian, Louis the Child (899–911), they made decided progress in this direction and were well on the way to becoming kings in their own duchies. They were inclined to leave the throne vacant and to consolidate their own power.

Two forces were chiefly responsible for the failure of the dukes to achieve their purpose—the Church and the Magyars. In Germany, as in France, the church wanted a strong monarchy. The prelates vastly preferred to deal with one king rather than with four dukes. But the church might not have been able to persuade the dukes to choose a king had it not been for the Magyars. Their raids were at their height, yet no duke could be convinced of the need for action against them until they entered his own duchy. It was clear even to the dukes that the Magyars could be curbed only by unified leadership. Hence they attempted a compromise. They chose as king the weakest of the dukes, Conrad of Franconia (911–18). This experiment was not successful. As Conrad was utterly unable to protect the church from the greed of his fellow dukes, he did not satisfy the prelates. And he was equally ineffective in his efforts to check the Magyars. Very reluctantly the great lords of Germany came to the conclusion that they would have to elect as king the most powerful of the dukes, Henry, called the Fowler, duke of Saxony. On his deathbed Conrad named Henry his successor, and he was elected without difficulty.

Henry (919–36) immediately set to work to solve the problem created by the dukes. His first step was to clarify their relation to the crown by requiring them to do homage and become his vassals for their offices. He then insisted on breaking their power over the counts and making those officers once again directly responsible to the king. He also aided the prelates to recover the lands that had been usurped during the reign of Louis the Child and gave them the authority of counts in their possessions. In this way the bishops and abbots became direct agents of the crown. On the military side, Henry made vigorous war on the Magyars and decidedly curbed their raids. Although the Magyar menace was not ended until his son Otto crushed them at the Lechfeld in 955, Henry laid the foundations for Otto's victory.

Henry's son and successor, Otto I (936–73), often called Otto the Great, was one of the dominant figures of the Middle Ages. In Germany he continued the policy of his father. When the duke of Franconia, the younger brother of King Conrad, died, Otto left the office vacant and ruled Franconia directly. While he gave extensive lands in Saxony to one of his favorites, Magnus Billung, he carefully withheld the ducal title. Thus he had complete control of two of the four stem duchies. Moreover, he carried still further his father's work in making the church the chief bulwark of the monarchy. The prelates were obliged to send strong bodies of soldiers to the royal army whenever they were needed. At the same time their privileges within their lands were steadily increased. In fact, they were frequently given the authority of counts over neighboring districts that did not belong to their churches. In this way Otto made sure of having a reliable army and established powerful supporters of the crown in all the duchies. If a duke rebelled, he found the forces of the church within his lands arrayed against him. Otto had no capital and no officials except the counts. His only army was his Saxon levy and the men supplied by the churches. But as long as his Saxons followed him and he retained his control of the church, his monarchy was strong and effective.

In addition to strengthening the internal structure of the monarchy, Otto strove successfully to extend its frontiers to the east. He inflicted a series of defeats on the Magyars, drove them back to the Hungarian plain, and established the March of Austria to hold the Danube valley against them. Farther north, with the active assistance of the lords and prelates of Saxony, he conquered the Slavs in the lands between the Elbe and the Oder. To hold this country he established fortified burghs garrisoned by German colonists, founded new bishoprics, and forced the conquered Slavs to pay tithes to the church. The archbishopric of Magdeburg was created with no eastern frontier so that it could include any later conquests at the expense of the Slavs. This expansion of northern Germany was not permanent. While Otto's successors were involved in Italy, the Slavs rose and wiped out the German colonists both lay and clerical in all except the extreme southern part of the conquered region, the March of Thuringia, where the burghs were particularly strong and numerous. But this later disaster should not detract from Otto's achievement.

In the early years of his reign Otto was essentially a northern potentate whose power lay in Saxony and Franconia. In southern Germany his influence was limited to control over the counts and the church. This situation was not alarming so long as there was no strong power in the south. But the dukes of Swabia and Bavaria were ambitious men, anxious to extend their authority. Both looked greedily at Lombardy, and the duke of Swabia had ambitions to secure the kingdom of Burgundy. Any such addition to one of the southern duchies would destroy the balance of power in Germany. Moreover, a combination of Italy and Burgundy under a strong ruler formed a menace to the German kingdom, as such a ruler was bound to want to regain the rest of the ancient realm of Lothaire.* Rudolf I, king of Burgundy, had conquered Italy and had attempted to take Lorraine from Henry the Fowler. While his son, Rudolf II, had not succeeded in gaining control of Italy, a new combination of the two kingdoms was always possible. When Rudolf II died in 937, this threat to Otto's position seemed imminent. Hugh of Arles, king of Italy, seized Burgundy. Otto acted quickly. He drove Hugh from Burgundy and placed the son of the late king on its throne under his protection. Fourteen years later he himself invaded Lombardy. In organizing this new province he followed the system that had been so successful in Germany. The bishops were given control of the secular as well as the ecclesiastical affairs in their dioceses and so were bound closely to Otto's interests.

Historians have accused Otto of allowing greed and love of conquest to divert his attention from Germany to Italy to the detriment of the German monarchy, but it seems clear that in his case at least expansion to the south was purely defensive. As long as there was no strong ruler in Lombardy, the region lay open to any adventurer, and Otto could not risk having it fall into the hands of a South German prince.

When Otto conquered Lombardy in 951, he planned to assume the imperial crown at once. The reasons that lay behind this intention were probably quite simple. The ancient Middle Kingdom ruled by the Emperor Lothaire had consisted of Italy, Burgundy, and Lorraine. All these regions were subject to Otto, and by becoming emperor he would secure the traditional title to them. But the Roman nobles who controlled the papacy were not anxious to have the imperial authority revived. Their opposition combined with troubles in Germany—a revolt of great nobles and fresh Hungarian raids—to delay Otto's plans, and it was not until 962 that he led an army to Rome and was solemnly crowned emperor.

Otto I built a vast territorial empire and revived the imperial title

* See p. 91.

in Western Europe, but his imperial authority rested on a slim basis. Even in Germany, outside Saxony where he could count on the loyalty of the nobles and people, his power rested on the ecclesiastical fiefs. In Italy he had a similar ecclesiastical organization in Lombardy. In the rest of the peninsula he was the master when he was present with an army but was otherwise powerless. Otto's son and grandson, Otto II (973–83) and Otto III (983–1002), concentrated their attention chiefly in Italy.* Had Otto III lived to a reasonably ripe age, the imperial power might have become firmly established in Tuscany and the Romagna. While Otto III was under age, his regents brought German officials into these regions and began to organize a strong and effective government. Otto continued their work, but he did not live long enough to establish his government firmly, and it collapsed after his death. He had no son and was succeeded by the head of a younger branch of the Saxon house, Henry II (1002–24). Although Henry belonged to the Saxon dynasty, his lands and interests were largely in Bavaria, and he could not command the loyalty of the Saxons. During his reign he was fully occupied maintaining his position in Germany.

At this point it seems well to pause for a moment to glance at a group that was to play a vital part in German politics: the great nobles called *Fürsten* by German historians, "princes" by English writers. Although the chief method used by the Saxon kings to curb the power of the stem dukes was to strengthen the ecclesiastical lords, they also employed the device of establishing favored laymen as rivals to the dukes. Thus, by the end of the Saxon period there were in Germany many powerful lords who were neither dukes nor prelates. The nature of their positions varied widely. A man might hold extensive lands in allodial tenure, be a count, and also hold fiefs granted him by the emperor or one of the dukes. Perhaps the most striking of the princely families of this period was the house of Billung. Magnus Billung, the first of the line, was an important Saxon landholder who was a favorite of Otto I and received extensive property as fiefs from the crown. Bit by bit the Billungs extended their holdings, until by the end of the Saxon period they considered themselves dukes of Saxony; it is not quite clear whether they were ever recognized as such by a Saxon king. But the Billungs were only one of many such families. Each was striving to build up its possessions and to obtain privileges and rights of jurisdiction. While these men represented the same social and political

* See p. 45.

group as the great feudal lords of France, they were not in this early period in so strong a position. Their allodial lands were theirs to pass on to whom they pleased; but offices such as that of count, which gave rights of jurisdiction, were not hereditary in Germany, and the hereditability of fiefs held from the crown was not fully recognized by the kings. In fact one of the chief aims of the princes was to make their offices and fiefs hereditary, if possible without giving the same rights to their subordinates.

When Henry II died in 1024, the nobles and prelates of Germany elected as their king Conrad (1024–39), called the Salian, duke of Franconia and the descendant of a daughter of Otto the Great. Conrad could do little more than attempt to recover the ground lost by the monarchy in Germany while the Saxon kings were absorbed in Italy and during the weak rule of Henry II; but his son Henry III (1039–56) began to build up the royal authority on a more secure basis. Henry realized that control of the ecclesiastical fiefs was too weak a foundation for a strong monarchy. There was need for a firm center of royal power such as Otto the Great had in Saxony. A truly effective government also needed loyal lay officials and an adequate money revenue. The Salian house were dukes of Franconia, and had extensive possessions in Swabia. If to these lands could be added southern Saxony and Thuringia, the crown would control the heart of Germany. Henry began to build castles in Thuringia and southern Saxony, and to garrison them with ministeriales from his Swabian lands. These men were completely dependent on him, devoted to his interests, and had no sympathy for the Saxon nobles who objected to this extension of the king's authority. With their aid Henry started to take into his own hands the ducal rights in southern Saxony. This naturally gravely annoyed the Billungs, who considered themselves dukes of Saxony, and troubled all the Saxon nobles who had for years been almost completely independent of royal control.

Henry III was an able monarch with a high conception of his function as king and emperor. While he thought of the Church as an important element in the political structure of his realm, he was also interested in its capacity to perform its spiritual obligations. He welcomed into his lands the representatives of the Cluniac reform movement and aided them to reform the German monasteries.* He also encouraged the members of the papal curia who were imbued with simi-

* See pp. 129–30.

lar ideas, and who wished to make the papacy the instrument for a reform of the Church as a whole. Henry apparently did not see the dangerous implications of his policy. From its very foundation one of the prime purposes of the monastery of Cluny had been to free the church from secular control. Sooner or later the followers of the Cluniac ideas were bound to object to the fact that the German prelates were practically royal officials chosen and even invested with the symbols of their office by the king. But it never seems to have occurred to Henry that the reform he was fostering could be aimed at the very foundation of his political system.

The reign of Henry III built up serious tensions in the political structure of the Empire. The reformers in the papal court were determined to break the control of the crown over the prelates. The Saxon nobles and freemen were annoyed by the building of royal castles in their territory, the revival of long-forgotten dues and obligations, and the presence of the Swabian ministeriales who were inclined to treat them as a conquered people. All the princes of Germany were restive under the heavy hand of Henry III, who was bent on reducing the independence they had gained in the previous two reigns. Moreover, when Henry died, his heir, Henry IV (1056–1106), was a minor, and while the realm was being ruled by regents the most fervid of the reformers, the German Hildebrand, became pope under the name of Gregory VII. Gregory was determined to end the appointment and investiture of ecclesiastical dignitaries by laymen, and he was also an exponent of a new conception of the royal dignity. For centuries the Church had preached that the king was God's vice-regent appointed to rule over men and that his anointment gave him a sacerdotal character: he was directly responsible to God. To Gregory a king was simply a sort of chief of police. It was his duty to maintain order and see that the commands of the Church were obeyed. If he was disobedient or contumacious, the pope had the right and even the duty to remove him from office.

As soon as Henry IV came of age, he proceeded to continue with vigor the policy of his father. He chose Goslar in the Harz mountains of southern Saxony as his capital. Henry III had built a castle there; his son added a palace. He also increased the number of royal castles in the vicinity, brought in additional ministeriales, and pressed still more firmly the demands for the ancient ducal dues. The exasperated Saxons rose in revolt, but the princes of Germany as a whole feared Henry's power and supported him. The revolt was suppressed, and the king's grip on southern Saxony seemed stronger than ever. If he succeeded in consolidating his position, he would have made a long step toward developing a strong monarchy. Franconia, Thuringia, and southern Saxony were the heart of Germany and an ideal base for royal power. Moreover, near Goslar lay the chief known silver mines of Germany. By exploiting them actively Henry could obtain a money revenue that would enable him to create an effective governmental organization.

Henry IV might well have succeeded in his plans for building a strong, centralized German monarchy had it not been for Pope Gregory VII. As we have seen in an earlier chapter, Gregory excommunicated Henry for refusing to heed his orders in respect to episcopal elections.* This gave the Saxons and the princes the opportunity they had been awaiting. They rose in revolt and announced that unless Henry became reconciled to the Church, they would elect a new king. To prevent such a reconciliation they carefully watched the Alpine passes. But Henry slipped through to Lombardy, rallied his partisans there, and obtained the Pope's forgiveness by humiliating himself at Canossa. While the princes of Germany were balked for the moment, Canossa really settled nothing. Henry had no intention of abandoning his control over the German church, and Gregory refused to compromise. And Henry's German enemies were bound to continue to take advantage of the quarrel between pope and emperor.

Henry defeated the Saxons in a series of long, bloody wars. But the contest against pope and Saxons gave him little time or energy to devote to the German princes. They made use of the general confusion to increase their power. Henry's son, Henry V (1106–25), did little to curb them in his short reign. In fact, he was inclined to grant them privileges in return for their support in his plans to continue his father's attempt to build a strong nucleus of power in Franconia and South Saxony. Henry V died without an heir. This gave the princes their great opportunity. Ignoring the most powerful of the dukes, Frederick of Hohenstaufen, duke of Swabia, son-in-law of Henry IV, they elected as king the heir to the house of Billung, Lothaire of Supplinburg (1125–37), duke of Saxony. Since he owed his throne to the princes and not to any hereditary claim, Lothaire was helpless before them. Moreover most of his reign was occupied in bitter civil war with Frederick of Swabia, who refused to recognize his election.

* See pp. 134–5.

Out of the fierce civil wars that marked the last quarter of the eleventh century and the first quarter of the twelfth emerged a new and quite different Germany. In every part of the realm the princes consolidated their power. They usurped offices and fiefs and passed them on from father to son. They strewed their lands with castles garrisoned by loyal ministeriales. This spirit of usurpation naturally spread downward in the political structure. Petty lords and knights forced the small freemen to become serfs, and the seignorial system became firmly saddled on most of Germany. The royal authority and the bases for it gradually disappeared. Even prelates tended to become dependent on neighboring princes who could offer protection. By the end of the period of confusion the countships and the jurisdiction that went with them had been swallowed up by the princes. Finally, feudal institutions spread over the land. The lesser lords became vassals of the princes, and the princes maintained that their offices and possessions were hereditary fiefs.

Henry IV had been well on the way to establishing a strong, centralized national monarchy. Lothaire of Supplinburg was as much a figurehead as had been Hugh Capet. As we shall see, the German monarchy was to have another century of apparent strength; but this strength was never very real. The rise of the princes had destroyed the German state.

17. *Saxons and Normans in England*

THE LONG struggle against the Danes that had marked the ninth and tenth centuries made England a unified state.* Although Alfred the Great (871–99) was never king of all England, he was the only English king. His son Edward the Elder (899–925) and his grandson Aethelstan (925–39) conquered the regions occupied by the Danes, and their successors were masters of the entire English realm. In fact, they ruled rather more than the England of today, for their kingdom included eastern Scotland as far as Edinburgh. But the unification of England under one king did not mean the wiping out of the difference between Anglo-Saxons and Danes. The Danish settlers remained on the land with their own laws, traditions, and customs. While the old Anglo-Saxon regions had long been largely organized in manors, the *Danelaw*

* See pp. 91–2.

as the Danish region was called was a land of independent farmers, and manors with their demesnes were almost unknown. Another mark of the Danish occupation was the reorganized political geography of a large part of central England. There each county had been given the name of its chief borough—Nottinghamshire and Nottingham, Cambridgeshire and Cambridge, Bedfordshire and Bedford, and many others. Only in East Anglia and the ancient kingdom of Wessex did the old counties remain intact.

The government of the Anglo-Saxon state was far more effectively organized than any other in western Europe. The monarchy was in theory elective, but it was generally assumed that eligibility for election was confined to the descendants of Alfred, the members of the ancient royal house of Wessex. The king had an extensive demesne consisting of estates scattered all over England. Every able-bodied Englishman owed him military service at his summons. He received two thirds of the penalties inflicted by the local courts for criminal offenses in general and probably the entire penalty in the case of certain serious crimes. He thus had an army, ample land to support himself and his court, and a regular if small money revenue. Moreover, in every county or shire he had an agent appointed by him, removable by him, and completely under his authority—the shire-reeve, or sheriff. In addition, he appointed bishops and abbots and considered them as a regular part of his administration.

The Anglo-Saxon state also had an assembly known as the *Witangemot.* Unfortunately we do not know very much about its powers and functions. It was an assembly of the great men of the realm—officials, landowners, and prelates. It went through the form of electing the king. He apparently was expected to seek its advice on important matters such as new legislation. King and Witan together chose the most important local officials, the *earldormen.* Apparently the earldormen were chosen from one or two important families in each county, and they received one third of the penalties imposed by the local courts.

It is important, however, to remember that only a small part of what we think of as the work of government was carried on by the king and Witan. The king was the military leader of his people. He probably set the penalty for certain serious crimes such as rape, murder, and arson. But the general enforcement of the law was left to the local courts. At set times the freemen of each shire met together in the shire court under the presidency of the earldorman, sheriff, and bishop. Each court had its own body of custom. This custom was carried out by the people themselves under the guidance of the presiding officials. If a man wanted to accuse another of a crime, he went before the shire court and made a formal complaint. Then the court summoned the accused. If he did not appear after being summoned in a certain number of sessions, he was declared an outlaw, and anyone could slay him without fear of punishment. If the accused appeared, the court decided how he should prove his innocence. Usually he was obliged to obtain a certain number of men who would swear to his innocence; a process known as compurgation. Sometimes he would have to undergo the ordeal, which usually meant being bound and thrown into the water. The ordeal was accompanied by complicated religious forms, and was in fact an attempt to obtain the judgment of God. Ancient Anglo-Saxon law provided only money penalties for offenses—payments to the injured or his family. By the tenth century, royal decrees had made certain crimes punishable at the king's pleasure, and he may well have used corporal punishments. By that time also when a man paid a money penalty to the injured he paid a sum to the court as well.

The social structure of Anglo-Saxon England in the tenth century was not much different from that of the period before the Danish invasions.* There was a noble class consisting of great landowners and officials. Lesser men commended themselves to these powerful dignitaries in order to receive their protection in the courts and in time of trouble. Then there was a group of men called *thanes*. They were usually fighting men who had been given land so that they could be ready at all times to serve the grantor. They were basically not unlike the vassi dominici of the Carolingian state. Below them came a large and varied class called socmen. *Soc* meant jurisdiction, and a socman was one over whom a great man had some form of jurisdiction. Then there were the ordinary peasants who lived on the organized manors. They were freemen, members of the popular courts, and had full rights before the law. They were, however, bound to the land and subject to manorial discipline. Finally, there were a few real slaves in England, mostly domestic servants.

Early in the eleventh century England was once more invaded by the Danes. This time it was not a matter of plundering raiders but a great fleet led by King Swein of Denmark and his son Canute. In the

* See p. 82.

summer of 1016 the Anglo-Saxon king, Edmund Ironside (1016), came to an agreement with Canute. England was to be divided between them, and if one died the survivor was to rule the whole realm. Edmund lived only a few months after this treaty, and Canute (1016–35) became king of all England. He proved to be a just and able ruler who maintained the laws and customs of his predecessors, and though a pagan himself he protected and even fostered the Church. He safeguarded his authority in England by maintaining a small standing army of Danish troops that he supported by collecting the *danegeld*, a tax originally levied to buy off Viking raiders—a bit of irony that may well have pleased him. When Canute died in 1035, his sons, who were quarreling fiercely over the Danish throne, were unable to maintain themselves in England. The Witan elected as king the younger brother of Edmund Ironside, Edward the Confessor.

Edward's mother was a sister of Richard II, duke of Normandy, and during Canute's reign Edward lived at the Norman court. When he returned to England a number of his Norman friends accompanied him and received lands and offices. Other Norman lords were frequent visitors at Edward's court. The king's favor to his foreign friends and relatives annoyed the most powerful family in England, Godwin, whom Canute had made *jarl* or earl of Wessex, and his sons. Godwin had played a large part in securing Edward's election by the Witan, and the King had married his daughter. As Edward had no children, Godwin dreamed of the day when he or one of his sons might be elected king. But there was another man with the same ambition. Edward's cousin, William, duke of Normandy, felt that he was the logical successor to his childless relative. In 1051 William found an opportunity to move toward his goal as the result of an open break between Godwin and Edward's Norman friends. The count of Boulogne and his followers were attacked in Dover by the inhabitants. Since Dover was part of Wessex, Edward ordered Godwin to punish his men, but as the earl sympathized with them he refused. As result, Godwin and his sons were exiled. The ablest of Godwin's sons, Harold, sailing from England was wrecked on the Norman coast and captured by a vassal of Duke William. As the price of his freedom Harold swore to aid William to become king of England when Edward died. He was to be the chief man of the realm and was to marry William's sister.

King Edward and the house of Godwin were soon reconciled, and at his father's death Harold became earl of Wessex. When Edward died in 1066, the Witan elected Harold king. But Duke William had no intention of abandoning his hopes. He promptly despatched messengers to the Pope accusing Harold of breaking his oath. Whether or not the Pope took this charge seriously, he had good reason to support William. The papacy was trying to unify the Church under its control and to enforce uniform laws and practices.* William had in general proved cooperative. The English church was but slightly under Roman influence. It was firmly controlled by the king and had its own peculiar customs such as allowing the marriage of priests. Hence the Pope blessed William's idea of enforcing his claim to the throne. The Duke summoned his vassals to follow him to England, but here he met a check. With some few exceptions the Norman lords refused to go, on the ground that they did not owe military service for adventures over the sea. William then issued a general invitation to adventurers who hoped to gain booty and fiefs. This was most successful. From Flanders, Brittany, Maine, Anjou, and Poitou, men flocked to his banner. A few great Norman lords who were William's close personal friends, and many younger sons of noble Norman houses also joined the host. A great fleet was collected, and William poised his invading force to await favorable winds.

King Harold was in an extremely difficult position. His elder brother Tostig, jealous of Harold's success, had formed an alliance with Harold, king of Norway, for an invasion of England. Edwin and Morcar, joint earls of Northumbria, had no great love for Harold. He was only sure of the earldoms ruled by his own brothers and his old earldom of Wessex. Harold gathered his army, consisting of his house carls or professional bodyguard and the pick of his Wessex fighting men, near the coast to wait for William. But suddenly he learned that Tostig and Harold of Norway had landed in the north and routed Edwin and Morcar. Harold hastened north, destroyed the invading army at Stamford Bridge in Lincolnshire, and turned south once more.

Meanwhile Duke William had landed. On October 14, 1066, Harold's exhausted army, reinforced by hasty levies from Wessex and East Anglia, met William's force near Hastings. Just what happened is far from clear. The raw levies broke fairly quickly, but the Norman cavalry could make no impression on the house carls and other regular fighting men drawn up in a solid line of spears on a rise of ground. In some way, perhaps by a feigned retreat, William got the Saxons to

* See pp. 133–5.

break ranks. Then his heavily armed knights plunged into the gaps and cut the Saxon infantry to pieces. Harold and his brothers died with their men. To all practical purposes England had been won by Duke William. Although it was some five years before the last stubborn Saxon rebels were routed out of their retreat in the fenland, the new king's position was never seriously threatened.

The conquest of England was a stroke of good luck. Had Harold not been called north to meet the Norwegian host and been able to oppose Duke William's landing with a fresh army, he might well have been successful. If instead of offering battle at Hastings he had retired to the midlands to await the reorganized musters of Northumbria under Edwin and Morcar, he would have had an excellent chance of victory. And if he had refused to offer battle and simply drawn William's army farther and farther into England, his eventual victory would have been almost certain. For the best Saxon troops were good fighting men, and no one realized it better than the Norman duke. As he moved through the country, he erected on the edge of each borough a motte and bailey castle to watch the burghers, the most renowned of English warriors. And one noticeable feature of his military arrangements in England was the care with which he assured himself of a safe retreat to the continent in case of need. At Dover he built a great castle, and all Kent was placed under his half brother, the bishop of Bayeux. Along the Sussex coast was built a line of fortresses: Bramber, Lewes, Hastings, Pevensea, and Arundel. Each was the seat of a compact fief granted to one of the Duke's most reliable followers. If the Saxons rose successfully, the Normans would have strong, well-garrisoned castles in which to take refuge until their fleet could take them off.

The military organization of his conquest was William's first concern, for it appeared to be menaced by foes on every side. To the north lay Scotland, whose king was a relative of the house of Wessex. To the west was Wales. It had not been many years since a Danish king had ruled England, and a Norwegian host had been defeated just before his arrival. To William the Scandinavian powers were a permanent threat. Finally, there was always the possibility of a Saxon rising. As William was the lord of a feudal state, the duchy of Normandy, he naturally conceived the new military organization in feudal terms, in terms of fiefs and knight service. The low, comparatively level country on the east coast just below the Scots border, the county of Northumberland, was given as a centralized fief to a great Norman lord, who bore the title of earl of Northumberland. The county of Durham was given as a block to the bishop of Durham. Northern Yorkshire was occupied by another compact fief, the castellany of Richmond, whose lord, a Breton count, was given extensive lands in England to aid him in supporting his frontier fief. Lancashire went to Roger of Poitou, son of Roger of Montgomery, one of the greatest of Norman barons. Then along the Welsh border William created three other centralized fiefs—the earldoms of Chester, Shrewsbury, and Hereford. Thus facing the Scots and the Welsh were a string of fiefs each under the unified command of a single lord.

No such localized security system was of any value against Viking invasions. They could only be met by the military strength of the country as a whole. Hence in dividing the rest of England into fiefs Duke William simply followed the most easy and natural course. Since he did not consider himself a conqueror in the usual sense but rather the rightful heir of Edward the Confessor, the Anglo-Saxon landholders who had not borne arms against him were left in the possession of their lands and simply became his vassals. Then each of the chief men of his army was given the lands of one or more Saxons who had resisted the conquest. As the Saxon landholders had not held compact blocks of territory but had had estates scattered over a wide territory, the fiefs of William's followers were similarly dispersed. Each holder of a fief, whether Saxon or Norman, was assigned a quota of knights that he was obliged to supply to the royal army. As William knew little of the size or productivity of the fiefs he was granting, these quotas were merely rough guesses as to how many knights the fiefs would support. William also assigned quotas of knights to the prelates, the bishops and abbots of the Benedictine monasteries. The total service provided for came to some 5,000 knights.

Fully as important as the knight in the defensive system of a feudal state was the castle. William himself built fortresses at the edge of each of the more important boroughs, and he encouraged his vassals to construct others. One can say in general that each direct vassal of the king and each rear-vassal of importance built a castle on his most valuable manor. Great lords with lands in a number of shires were likely to have a castle on the chief manor of every regional group. The density of castles depended largely on the region. In the interior, only men of considerable position felt able to afford the luxury of a stronghold, but along the Welsh border no knight felt comfortable without some sort of fortress.

The available evidence is insufficient to enable us to say how many castles were built during William's reign, but it is clear that by 1150 there were some 1,200 in England. Once this network of castles was constructed, another conquest of England became most unlikely. A strong castle adequately supplied and defended by a resolute garrison could withstand any mediaeval army for several months at least. And while besieging one castle the enemy was continually exposed to harassment by the garrisons of all the others in the neighborhood. Although it was obviously possible for an invader to ignore the castles and march through the open country, as soon as he had left a number of castles behind him their garrisons formed a potential field force threatening his rear. The garrisoning of the English castles was provided for by the feudal duty of castle-guard.* Each baron's vassals were bound to aid in defending his castle, and groups of baronies were formed to provide garrisons for the royal strongholds.

As we have seen, William considered himself the rightful heir to Edward the Confessor and hence bound to continue his government basically unchanged. He promised to maintain the ancient customs of England and to recognize the grants of the Anglo-Saxon kings. The popular courts continued to administer the customary law. The Anglo-Saxon sheriffs were replaced by Normans, usually the most powerful baron in the shire, but the office remained unchanged. On the other hand William did abolish the political functions of the earl. Under his rule the title remained an honor, and the holder received one third of the revenues from the popular courts; but he had no governmental function. William also separated the lay and ecclesiastical jurisdictions to conform with continental custom. The bishop no longer sat with the sheriff in the shire court but had his own court for ecclesiastical cases.

In addition to the changes in the English political structure that William made consciously there were bound to be unintentional modifications. William's feudal curia, the assembly of his vassals, took the place of the Witangemot. Then many English landowners had enjoyed the privilege of receiving the penalties imposed in one or more hundred courts, but this gave them no right to preside over the courts. In Normandy, however, the seignorial system was fully developed, and although the duke had retained high justice for himself and his officers, every lord had what we would call police jurisdiction over his tenants.† The idea of receiving the fees and not controlling the court was utterly foreign to Norman ideas. Hence these hundred courts became private courts in the hands of the Norman landlords.

Every Norman of any position was given *sac* and *soc*, or police court jurisdiction over his own men—essentially the privilege to which they were accustomed. More important men received the right of *infangentheof*, or the privilege of hanging one of their tenants caught on their land red-handed in theft. This was an important right from the point of view of the Norman lord; it enabled him to have a gallows, which was one of the chief symbols of rank in the seignorial world.

* See pp. 107–08. † See pp. 99–101.

Finally, the bishops and abbots of Anglo-Saxon England had possessed the right of immunity on at least part of their lands—the right of forbidding the entrance of royal officials. William extended this privilege to a few of the greatest of the lay lords.

The statement has frequently been made that the Norman conquest depressed the political, social, and economic status of the English people. This is unquestionably true to a certain extent. The few great Anglo-Saxon landowners who were not dispossessed were burdened with feudal services. Lesser Saxon landholders became vassals of the barons. But the chief effect was on the position of the socmen and the tenants on organized manors. The former had owed varied services to the lords to whom they were commended, while the latter had obligations resembling those of continental villeins. Yet in the Anglo-Saxon state both groups were regarded as freemen with full legal rights. Such a point of view was inconceivable to the Norman conquerors. To them the tenants on the manors were obviously villeins, and they gradually applied to them the customs of the seignorial system. In short, they became unfree. Moreover, the Normans knew of no middle group between the full freeman and the villein. Hence the socmen had various fates. Those whose obligations to their lords were slight retained the designation of socmen and were recognized as freemen, but many others were considered villeins and lost their free status.

There can be little doubt that the conquest added greatly to the number of people in England who did not work themselves but had to be supported by the working classes. Although there is no way of estimating the number of Anglo-Saxons rich enough so that they did not work the land, it seems most unlikely that they equaled the 5,000-odd knights established by King William. This change can be best grasped by considering the church estates. The abbey of Peterborough was an ancient, rich Benedictine house. The peasants on its vast estates supported the monks by their rents and services. Then King William imposed a quota of sixty knights on the abbey. This meant that in some manner or other these estates had to support sixty knights in addition to the monks. For a while some churches tried to hire the necessary knights, house them in a barracks, and feed and clothe them. But a troop of wild soldiers was not a suitable appendage to a monastic establishment. Moreover, hired knights were hard to find. Every man of knightly rank looked forward to a fief of his own and had no desire to live indefinitely as a mercenary. Hence the bishops and abbots like the lay lords soon granted fiefs to knights who would perform the service owed to the crown. Only a part of the lands of Peterborough could be used to support the monks; a much larger portion was divided into fiefs for the sixty knights. This large addition of unproductive mouths must have materially increased the burden on the productive classes.

Perhaps the most striking feature of the first two or three decades following the conquest was a modification of the relations between the king and his direct vassals, the barons. William and his barons had been partners in a great and hazardous adventure. They worked closely together to secure and hold the kingdom of England. They were strangers in a strange land surrounded by foes. But this situation soon changed. None of the things that William feared ever came to pass. Danish raiders killed several of his earls, but no serious invasion ever came from Scandinavia. The strong fiefs established on the frontiers were more than able to handle the Welsh and the Scots; in fact Norman lords were soon taking over the lowlands of South Wales and pressing their conquests up the river valleys into the hills. After the liquidation of the rebels in the fens, the Saxons gave no trouble. By the reign of Henry I, the Conqueror's youngest son, there were no longer Normans and Saxons but only Englishmen.

Although King William had been brought up in a feudal environment and hence held political ideas that were essentially feudal, he was also fully aware of the deficiencies in the structure of the ordinary feudal state. He himself had spent the early years of his rule as duke in a series of bitter struggles with his Norman vassals, and he well knew the weakness of the Capetian monarchy. He had no intention of allowing his English barons to become as independent as the great Norman lords, to say nothing of the great vassals of the French crown. He was resolved to maintain intact the powers of the Anglo-Saxon monarchy. The barons of England, on the other hand, wanted all the independence they could gain—certainly as much as their Norman peers enjoyed. Thus, while William strove to maintain and if possible increase the power of the crown and its agents the sheriffs, the barons tried to infringe on that power. The result was a baronial revolt that was quickly suppressed, but which only marked the beginning of a long series.

When King William died, he left the duchy of Normandy to his eldest son, Robert, and the English throne to his second son, William (1087–1100). His third and youngest son, Henry, got a few Norman estates to support him. William II, called Rufus, was a thoroughly unpleasant person, arbitrary, greedy, and probably sexually perverted. His greed led him to exploit every possible source of royal revenue to the utmost. This greed led him to complete and use the famous Domesday book, based on a survey ordered by his father. One of the most valuable rights of the Anglo-Saxon kings had been the privilege of levying danegeld; no other contemporary monarchy in Western Europe had at its disposal a regular land tax. Domesday book was essentially a tax roll. The Conqueror wanted to know how much he was owed, and by whom. He also was interested in the relation between the assessment and the real value of estates, and whether the tax could be made to yield more. In Domesday book all the lands of England were listed by counties and within the counties by baronies held of the crown. We have the name of the estate, the name of the baron who held it, and the name of the subtenant if there was one. Then we are told how many hides or assessment units the estate held. In addition we are given the arable land, the size of the labor force, the number of the plow teams, any extra item of value such as woods, mills, and fisheries, and finally the estimated annual value of the estate in King Edward's time and in 1086 when the survey was made. Obviously Domesday book is a mine of information for the historian, but King William wanted it for more practical purposes.

William Rufus' greed also led him to make the most of all the feudal rights that could produce cash. When a baron died, the king made the heir pay as high a relief as he could possibly raise. When a baron wanted permission to marry his daughter, he was obliged to pay a large fee. If a baron died leaving an unmarried daughter, the king sold her to the highest bidder. In one case at least Rufus collected an aid from the rear-vassals of a barony when the baron died. King William II was obliged to face several baronial revolts, but they were not, at least entirely, the result of his misuse of his rights as a suzerain. His brother Robert felt that he should have had England as well as Normandy and was continually stirring up trouble in England. William repaid this with interest by invading Normandy, which was already in a state of complete confusion under Robert's amiable but ineffective rule. Eventually Robert mortaged Normandy to Rufus and departed on the First Crusade.*

One day while King William was hunting in the New Forest one

* See p. 201.

of his noble companions mistook him for a deer and fatally wounded him with an arrow. The King's brother Henry, who was not far away, resisted his inclination to hasten to the scene and instead promptly secured the royal treasury in Winchester castle. Henry took no action against the man who had slain his brother—in fact the family of this man, the great house of Clare, became the most powerful in England during Henry's reign.

Henry obtained the English throne because he was on the spot; his claim was not so good or at least no better than that of his brother Robert. Under the circumstances, he felt obliged to conciliate the barons who accepted him as king. On the day of his coronation he issued a solemn charter in which he promised to put an end to the abuses established by his brother. This document is of great importance as an admission by Henry that he was bound by the law and as a definition of some points in that law. As a practical matter it was of little value, for Henry never allowed the promises contained in it to hamper his practices. He continued his brother's policy with even more enthusiasm.

King Henry (1100–35) was a vigorous and effective ruler and a competent captain. When the barons revolted, partly because of Robert's intrigues and partly out of resentment at Henry's firm rule, he crushed the risings and exiled the rebels. Then King Henry invaded Normandy and after a long struggle captured his brother and consigned him to an English castle. While the continuous interference of Louis VI (1108–37) of France in the affairs of Normandy kept Henry from giving the duchy anything that one might call peace and order, he ruled its turbulent lords far more effectively than had Duke Robert. England was a model of peace and quiet under his heavy hand.

Henry I increased the power of the royal government in England by developing devices used by his father and brother and by inventing some of his own. William I and William II had insisted that the pleas of the crown, the more serious criminal cases, be heard by special royal judges. At times they sent out judges for this purpose, but usually they simply ordered the local sheriff to hear them as a royal justice. Henry I established royal justices as a regular part of his administration and sent them through England to hear the pleas of the crown. William Rufus had begun replacing the barons who held office as sheriffs with men of lower rank who would be more dependent on the crown, and King Henry completed this process. His sheriffs and justices were for the most part men who owed whatever they had to his favor, instead of barons with ample independent resources.

An important part of the work of King Henry and his officials was the development of an effective financial administration. His predecessors had kept a reserve of money in a strong castle, but all current funds were kept in a chest in the king's chamber under the care of his chamberlains. Henry detached three chamberlains from his court and established them at Winchester as permanent financial officials. Before long one had taken the title of treasurer, and the other two were known as chamberlains of the exchequer.

Henry's treasurer worked out a system for keeping account of the royal revenue. Twice a year the sheriffs of England appeared before a body of royal officials called the barons of the exchequer to render their accounts. Each sheriff owed a definite rent or farm for his county from which he could subtract sums he paid out by royal command. The sheriff presented to the exchequer the orders authorizing him to pay out money, and the barons balanced his account. He also accounted for any special sources of revenue in his hands such as baronies in the king's custody because of minor heirs. The sheriff brought with him all the people in his county who owed the king money to answer for their debts. Thus when the accounting was complete the barons knew what the king's revenue had been and more important, what he was still owed. A record of this accounting called the Pipe Roll was drawn up. We have one such record from the reign of Henry I and a continuous series from the beginning of the reign of Henry II.

One of King Henry's contemporary biographers said with unconcealed admiration that he took seriously the divine command to populate the earth and was most successful at it. Unfortunately, however, only two of his extremely numerous offspring were legitimate—a son, William and a daughter, Matilda. While William was still a young man, he and a group of gay young nobles, all gloriously drunk, embarked on a ship with an equally drunken captain and crew. A storm came up and the ship was lost with all aboard. Thus Henry was left without a male heir. He compelled the prelates and barons of England to swear allegiance to his daughter Matilda, widow of the Holy Roman Emperor Henry V and wife of Geoffrey, count of Anjou.

Henry's only other living close relatives were Thibaut, count of Blois, and his brother Stephen, both sons of Henry's sister. When Henry died, Stephen, who was count of Boulogne by Henry's gift, hastened to England to claim the crown. The lords of England had sworn to accept Matilda, but they had no enthusiasm for her. No one believed that a woman could rule England effectively, and the barons had a strong suspicion that Geoffrey of Anjou, a feudal brigand of the first order, would rule it too effectively for their taste. Stephen was known as a gentle, kindly man, and the barons chose him as king. Count Thibaut made a few protests at having his younger brother placed ahead of him, but he was too busy with his enormous possessions in France to do anything about it. Matilda and Geoffrey, on the other hand, prepared for war. While Geoffrey invaded Normandy, Matilda crossed to England, rallied her supporters, and waged war on King Stephen.

The entire reign of Stephen (1135–54) was occupied by bitter civil war between the two parties. It was the perfect opportunity for the barons. Each lord could sell his allegiance at a high price in lands and privileges and then sell it again if the other side bid higher. Thus a powerful baron of Essex, Geoffrey de Mandeville, by shifting dexterously from one side to the other acquired the title earl of Essex, extensive royal demesnes as fiefs, the services of a number of minor tenants-in-chief, permission to build a number of castles and to tear down one belonging to the bishop of London that annoyed him, the hereditary command of the Tower of London, the hereditary office of sheriff and royal justice in London and Middlesex and Essex and Hertfordshire, and similar concessions for his relatives. In short, Geoffrey became to all practical purposes absolute master of four shires, including the city of London.

While few barons did quite so well as Geoffrey, most of them gained something. They became sheriffs of their counties and constables of the royal castles. They obtained for themselves royal demesnes and the services of minor tenants-in-chief. All over England new baronial strongholds sprang up. And while the great barons consolidated their power and became practically independent of the crown, lesser men gathered bodies of soldiers, seized some castle as a base, and unmercifully plundered the countryside. Thus, at the end of the period covered by this chapter England like Germany was in a state of confusion, with the king helpless before his vassals.

CHAPTER VII

The Expansion of Europe

HE LAST three chapters have described the political, economic, social, and religious development of mediaeval civilization in the central regions of Western Europe during the tenth and eleventh centuries. This same period saw the two basic groups of institutions, feudalism and the Church, that dominated these regions spread to other lands. The Scandinavian countries and their island possessions, the lowlands of Scotland, Ireland, Spain, various islands of the Mediterranean Sea, southern Italy, Greece, Syria, and Palestine were affected by this expansion of the civilization we have been discussing. The purpose of this chapter is to describe this movement that vastly increased the area that acknowledged the spiritual leadership of the papacy and knew in some form the institutions of feudalism.

The great wave of expansion that covers this period was the result of many circumstances. As we have seen, the period was one of vigor and vitality in many fields. The population, productivity, and wealth of the central regions of Western Europe increased with great rapidity. There was surplus manpower and wealth to be used for expansion. Moreover, the dominant groups in the population, the clergy, the knights, and the townsmen, felt the need for more room. The Church, led by the Cluniac reformers and the reformed papacy, desired to spread both its faith and its spiritual and political authority. Each generation saw younger sons of the feudal lords anxious to find fiefs as rich if not richer than those inherited by their elder brothers. The merchants of the rising towns wanted new markets.* In all the phases of this expansion of Western European civilization one sees clearly the guiding and encouraging influence of the Church and the papacy. Except in the case of the countries of Scandinavia the Church is found in close alliance with the feudal class, and in the Mediterranean the men of the Italian cities joined with them.

18. The Conversion of Scandinavia

DURING the major part of the great era of Viking activities, the ninth and tenth centuries, the Scandinavian countries had little political organization. There were local popular courts corresponding to the Anglo-Saxon hundred courts and regional assemblies called *things*. There were also regional chieftains who waged continual war against one another when they were not leading raids against the coasts of Christian Europe. Occasionally one of these chieftains would achieve a fairly wide dominance, but until the time of Harold Fairhair, who subdued all Norway in about the year 900, no one could be called the king of a Scandinavian state. Despite their lack of unity, however, the Scandinavian peoples occupied a vast empire in northern Europe. In addition to the Scandinavian peninsula and Denmark they held the Russian states of Novgorod and Kiev, Frisia, Normandy, eastern England, the west English kingdom of Strathclyde, a large part of Ireland, the Faroe, Hebrides, Orkney, and Shetland islands, Iceland, and some settlements in Greenland. This was at the height of their expansion. By the year 1000 Frisia had been recovered by the German kings, Normandy was a fief of the French crown, and the Anglo-Saxon kings had expelled the Northmen from their lands. In Ireland their power was confined to the towns they had founded—Wexford, Waterford, and Dublin. But they still held the vast scattered empire of the northern isles.

In the last half of the tenth and first half of the eleventh centuries three great kings, Harold Bluetooth of Denmark, Olaf, called the Tax-gatherer, of Sweden, and Olaf Trygvesson of Norway, firmly

* See pp. 221–3.

established the three Scandinavian kingdoms and made Christianity their official religion. In all probability the purpose of these monarchs in renouncing paganism was as much political as religious: they believed that the church organization was necessary to an orderly state. The change in religion was cheerfully accepted by the Scandinavian peoples, and by the end of the eleventh century there were eight dioceses in Denmark and four in Norway. For a century or more the archbishop of Bremen was considered the metropolitan of all the northern dioceses, but in 1104 Lund in Denmark, in 1152 Nidaros in Norway, and in 1164 Upsala in Sweden became seats of archbishops. Although there were at times fierce quarrels between the Scandinavian kings and the church, in general the ecclesiastical hierarchy supported the royal authority and aided in the unification of the three kingdoms.

Throughout the eleventh, twelfth, and most of the thirteenth centuries, the political history of the Scandinavian states was a tale of war and revolt. The three kingdoms fought one another, and rival families struggled for the throne in each state. Internally the period was marked by the rise to a dominant position of a landowning noble class. In the eleventh century there were large and small landowners, but all held the same general status and were required to answer the king's summons to war. By the thirteenth century, however, only the nobles were expected to perform military service and were exempted from taxation, while the ordinary free peasant paid taxes instead of serving. Naturally there was a tendency for the peasants to give up their land to the nobles and become their tenants. While the kings tried to prevent this conversion, the noble lands continually increased. The development of the noble class was hastened by the introduction of feudal ideas. Late in the twelfth century the kings of Denmark began to grant fiefs in return for military service, and later this custom spread to Norway and Sweden. Although the fiefs were not hereditary and the chief bases of the power of the nobles lay in their allodial lands, the fiefs added to the resources of favored individuals. The nobles in all three states met in great councils and worked to limit the authority of the kings. In 1282 the king of Denmark was forced to promise to call this body annually. By the fourteenth century the nobles were the dominant power in all three states, and the kings could do nothing without their approval.

On the whole it seems clear, however, that the feudal system never was dominant in the Scandinavian countries. There were nobles who held fiefs, but the noble class as a whole drew its power from allodial lands. The military service owed by the nobles and the use of imported titles such as baron, knight, and squire give a false feudal front to what was essentially a nonfeudal society. The seignorial system was even more strikingly absent. Fief holders and nobles had no rights of jurisdiction unless they happened, as was common in Norway, to hold a royal office as a fief; but the jurisdiction was recognized as a public function and did not go with the possession of the land. Although the church enjoyed with the nobles the right of exemption from taxation, the prelates did not hold their lands as fiefs.

The far-flung island empire of Norway shrank in size during the thirteenth, fourteenth, and fifteenth centuries. Iceland remained a Scandinavian land with its own culture and institutions. Although the Scandinavian hold on Greenland was weak, no one else wanted that bleak country. The Orkney and Shetland islands, however, passed into the hands of the kings of Scotland. In the thirteenth century Norwegian kings still ruled the Hebrides and the Isle of Man, but later the Hebrides went to Scots and Man to English noble families. Man is still in theory an independent state ruled by the English king.

We know little of the men through whom the Christian faith and the institutions of the Roman Catholic Church and feudalism were carried to the Scandinavian lands, but a vital part in the expansion of the civilization of Roman Christian Europe was played by a branch of the Scandinavian peoples—the Normans of Normandy. In fact, one can say that the greatest single force in the extension of the territory effectively controlled by the papacy was the Norman feudal class.

The Norman conquest of England brought the Anglo-Saxon church into the orbit of Rome. By the thirteenth century papal authority and feudal institutions were firmly established in the lowlands of Scotland. The Norman kings of England and their vassals conquered large sections of Wales and brought its bishops under the rule of the archbishop of Canterbury. The final conquest of Wales by Edward I (1272–1307) made that region a part of feudal Europe.* In the twelfth century Anglo-Norman adventurers from southern Wales conquered eastern Ireland. While feudal institutions were established in only a part of the island and the political authority of the English kings was never very great, the Irish church was made an integral part of Roman Christendom. Then it was during the period of Norman dominance

* See p. 275.

that French Brittany clearly won ascendancy over the Celtic section. As we discuss the campaigns of the European nobility against the Moslem rulers of the Mediterranean region we shall again and again encounter the Normans as soldiers and statesmen. They were, in truth, the sword-bearers of the papacy.

19. Christian and Moslem in Spain

ALTHOUGH the extension of feudal institutions and the authority of the papacy over the northern and western fringes of Europe was of great importance both to its contemporaries and to future generations, the chief interest of Christendom in this period was concentrated on the struggle against the Moslems. At the beginning of the eleventh century the Moslems held the southern two thirds of Spain, the Balearic Islands, Corsica, Sardinia, Sicily, the entire coast of North Africa, Palestine, and part of Syria. Religious enthusiasm and political and economic ambition moved the men of Western Europe to attack these Moslem lands. The feudal class, especially its cadets, or younger sons, saw unlimited opportunities to acquire both spiritual and temporal rewards, salvation and rich fiefs, through engaging in their favorite occupation. The papacy may have had more complicated motives. Certainly the popes desired to spread the Christian faith and their own authority, but it is quite possible that they thought it an excellent idea to turn the turbulent belligerency of the feudal class into worthy channels. Finally, the rising Italian towns, especially Genoa and Pisa, were anxious to free themselves from the continuous danger of Moslem naval raids and to conduct their trade peacefully along the shores of the western Mediterranean.*

The Moslem conquest of Spain had never been complete. When the Saracen hosts overran the country in the eighth century, the remnants of the Visigoth army retired to the northwestern corner, where they established the kingdom of Asturia. To the east of this state, along the southern fringes of the Pyrenees, Charlemagne created the Spanish March. Before the end of the ninth century the western portion of the Spanish March became the independent kingdom of Navarre, which included the land of the Basques with its capital at Pampeluna, and the region later known as Aragon. The eastern half of the

* See p. 221.

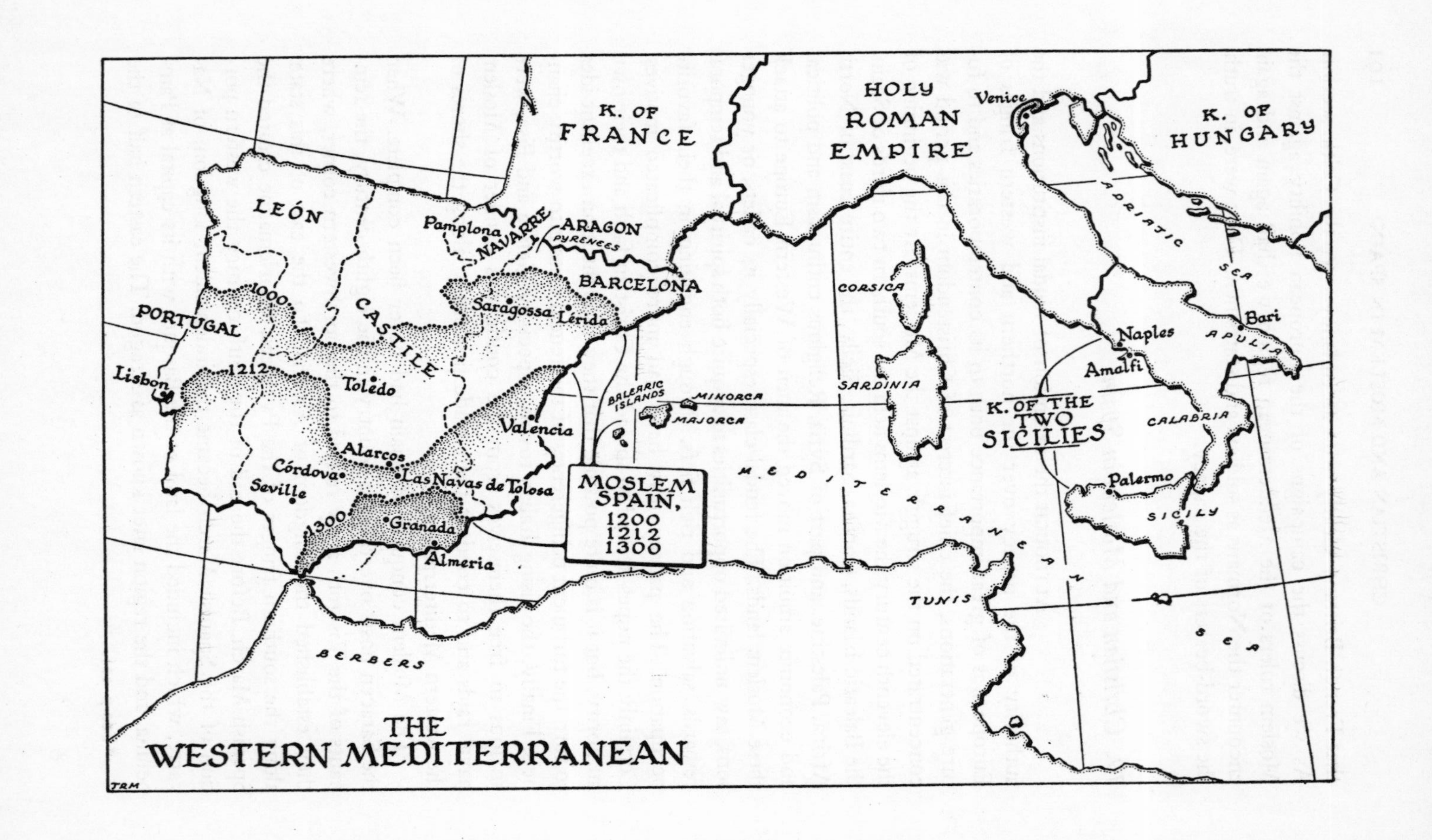
THE WESTERN MEDITERRANEAN
K. OF FRANCE
HOLY ROMAN EMPIRE
K. OF HUNGARY
Venice
ADRIATIC SEA
LEÓN
Pamplona
NAVARRE
ARAGON
PYRENEES
BARCELONA
PORTUGAL
1000
CASTILE
Saragossa
Lérida
Lisbon
1212
Toledo
Valencia
BALEARIC ISLANDS
MINORCA
MAJORCA
CORSICA
SARDINIA
Naples
Bari
APULIA
Amalfi
K. OF THE TWO SICILIES
CALABRIA
Palermo
SICILY
Alarcos
Córdova
Las Navas de Tolosa
Seville
1300
Granada
Almeria
MOSLEM SPAIN, 1200 1212 1300
MEDITERRANEAN SEA
TUNIS
BERBERS
TRM

March was known as the county of Barcelona. By the year 1000 the kingdom of Asturia had been divided into two states, León and Castile. With the kingdom of Navarre and the county of Barcelona, they comprised Christian Spain.

As long as the Moslem power remained reasonably united under the emirs and later the caliphs of Cordova, the Christian states could do little more than hold their own. That they succeeded in doing so was as much the result of dissension among the Moslems as of their own valor and military capacity. Then, in 1034 the quarrels among the Moslem chieftains came to a climax in the complete disruption of the caliphate of Cordova and the appearance of more than a score of independent Moslem kingdoms. This gave the Christian states their great opportunity, at a time when the forces of expansion were strong in Western Europe.

Very early in the eleventh century the idea of encouraging the nobles of France to undertake expeditions against the Spanish Moslems had occurred to the monks of Cluny. One can only guess at their motives. The Church was trying desperately to reduce feudal warfare by means of the Peace of God and the Truce of God: finding a new outlet for the military energy of the nobles might aid the good cause. Perhaps the monks foresaw the possibility of new foundations in Spain to spread the usefulness, wealth, and power of their order. And they may have been genuinely interested in driving back the Moslems. At any rate, they preached the crusade to Spain as a work well pleasing to God.

In 1018 Roger de Tony, a great Norman lord, led a force to Spain to war against the infidel. In 1033 a great army of Burgundian lords took the same path. The year 1063 saw an expedition led by Gui-Geoffrey, duke of Aquitaine and 1065 one under the command of the count of Châlon. In 1073 Eble, count of Rouci, marched against the Moors. The year 1085 saw what was probably the largest of these expeditions led by a group of Burgundian lords and Count Raymond of Toulouse. These were the major crusades under the command of men important enough to attract the attention of the chroniclers. In all probability there was a steady stream of smaller parties. Late in the eleventh century a Norman adventurer rose to high power in Portugal.

In the first two decades of the second half of the eleventh century most of Christian Spain came under the rule of two monarchs, Alfonso VI (1065–1109), king of León and Castile, and Sancho Ramirez (1063–

94), king of Aragon and Navarre. Aided by strong bodies of French knights, especially Normans and Burgundians, these two kings took the offensive against the Moslems. This was the era of the mighty warrior and semilegendary Spanish national hero Rodrigo Díaz de Vivar, usually called the Cid. While the French knights who came to Spain might be crusaders for the faith, that was not the attitude of the Spanish nobles. The Moslems were their neighbors—one day their enemies, and the next their friends. They had no objection to calling for Moslem aid in wars between two of the Christian states. The Cid fought valiantly and successfully for his lord, Alfonso VI, when the two were on good terms; but in their frequent quarrels he cheerfully served Moslem princes. Once, at the head of a Moslem army he defeated the Count of Barcelona, took him captive, and became the governor of the land in dispute, the region around Lerida; but he treated the Count so kindly that the latter married his son and heir to the Cid's daughter.

In 1085, with the aid of a large crusading force, Alfonso VI captured the important city of Toledo. While this was the most substantial permanent gain made during his reign, the long series of wars waged by him and his ally of Aragon and Navarre seriously weakened the Moslem states. This was particularly true of the campaigns of the Cid, who for some six years held the rich province of Valencia with its chief city. Alfonso married his illegitimate daughter to a crusading chieftain, Henry of Burgundy (1093–1112), and gave him the county of Portugal, comprising the northern third of the present state. Henry's son, Alfonso Henriques (1112–85), waged war against both the Moslems and his cousin and overlord the king of Castile. In 1149 the pope intervened in the latter quarrel and arranged a treaty of peace. Alfonso Henriques took the title king of Portugal, as a vassal of the papacy. Four years later a fortunate accident enabled the new king to make a great stroke against his Moslem foes. A fleet bearing English, Flemish, and North German crusaders on their way to join the Second Crusade to Palestine stopped at Oporto and listened to Alfonso Henriques' plea for aid. They captured Lisbon and turned it over to the king of Portugal before proceeding on their way.

The successful campaigns of Alfonso VI and Sancho Ramirez had quickly convinced the petty Moslem princes of Spain that they could not resist the Christian power without aid, and they appealed for help to the ruler of the Almoravides, a Berber people who were masters of northwestern Africa. The Almoravides arrived in Spain in 1086. It was their army that forced Alfonso to evacuate the extensive conquests made by the Cid in Lerida and Valencia. Fortunately for the Christians the Almoravides soon began to quarrel with the Spanish Moslem princes, and the Moorish power once more lost its unity. In 1118 Alfonso I (1104–34), king of Aragon and Navarre, captured Saragossa and thus almost doubled the area of Aragon. Meanwhile Raymond-Berenger III, count of Barcelona, had extended his power along the coast with the aid of a Pisan naval squadron and raided Majorca. Some thirty years later Alfonso VII (1126–57) of León and Castile swept far into Moslem territory to capture Cordova and, with the assistance of a Genoese fleet, the port of Almeria in Granada. Alfonso's contemporary, Raymond-Berenger IV of Barcelona, became king of Aragon by marrying its queen and so combined the two eastern states of Christian Spain.

The victories of Alfonso VII alarmed the Moslem princes as had those of his grandfather Alfonso VI. In 1125 another wild Berber tribe, the Almohades, had overthrown the Almoravides' power in North Africa, and the Moslems of Spain turned to them for aid. The Almohades arrived in Spain in 1146, but it took them nearly twenty years to consolidate their power over the Moslem states. They then began a vigorous campaign against the Christians that soon recovered most of the territory conquered by Alfonso VII.

Soon, however, they found themselves facing one of the ablest warrior kings in the history of Spain, Alfonso VIII (1158–1214), king of Castile. In alliance with his uncle, the king of León, he started an effective counteroffensive. The Almohades promptly brought reinforcements over from Africa and moved to meet the Castilian host. In a great battle fought at Alarcos in 1195 Alfonso was crushingly defeated and his army destroyed. His uncle of León and the king of Navarre, who had failed to send him the troops they had promised, took advantage of his defeat to invade Castile; but Alfonso soon drove them out of Castile and prepared once more to attack the Moslems. The next ten years were spent by both sides in preparing for a decisive campaign. The Almohades mustered all the forces of Moslem Spain and brought over fresh troops from Africa. The pope declared a crusade against the Moslems, and many knights of Europe led by the Spanish-born archbishop of Narbonne joined Alfonso's host, as did the forces of all the Christian states except León. On July 16, 1212 the two armies met at Las Navas de Tolosa. The result was an overwhelming victory for Christian arms and the end of the power of the Almohades.

The chief weakness of the Spanish kingdoms lay in the fact that whenever they won a victory over the Moslems, they heaved a sigh of relief and turned to fighting among themselves. This time the situation was aggravated by the involvement of the king of Aragon, who held important fiefs in southern France, in the struggle between his vassals and the Albigensian crusaders led by Simon de Montfort.* Thus it was not until 1230, when the grandson of Alfonso VIII, Ferdinand III (1217–52), became king of both León and Castile that the war against the Moslems was renewed with any vigor. In 1236 Ferdinand captured Cordova and in 1248 Seville. Meanwhile King James I (1213–76) of Aragon had conquered Majorca and Minorca. In 1238 James took Valencia. When Ferdinard III died in 1252 the Moslems had lost all the Spanish peninsula except the province of Granada, which they were to hold until it was wrested from them by Ferdinand the Catholic (1479–1516) in the fifteenth century.

The institutions of Christian Spain in the Middle Ages have been inadequately studied. Only a few general facts stand out clearly. The county of Barcelona had been part of the Spanish March, and its counts were deeply involved in the feudal politics of southern France. Hence this region had a fully developed feudal system on the French model. The same was true to a lesser extent of Aragon. There the nobles seem to have held their lands by feudal tenure, but there was no highly developed hierarchy, and a large proportion of the nobles were the king's direct vassals. The western states—Castile, León, and Portugal—can hardly be called feudal. There were men who held land in return for military service, but most nobles and churchmen seem to have had allodial holdings. There was no feudal hierarchy, and the fief holding vassals fought side by side with peasant warriors similarly armed and equipped. Serfdom of the European type was pretty well confined to the lands which had never been occupied by the Moors.

The reconquered territory was largely settled by free peasant farmers, with here and there a great estate worked by slaves. As time went on, the slaves grew fewer, and the peasants, while maintaining their technical freedom, were heavily burdened with dues to the king or some great lord. During the twelfth century the inhabitants of the

* See pp. 311–13.

towns began to acquire privileges by charter, and the bourgeoisie rapidly rose in importance. In 1188 representatives of the towns of Castile joined with the council of nobles to form the Cortes, and within a century similar bodies existed in all the states. The Cortes soon acquired extensive powers in legislation and the levying of taxes.

20. The Normans in the Mediterranean

OUTSIDE Spain the most direct contact between the Moslems and the peoples of Western Europe was in southern Italy. In the ninth century the Moslems had conquered Sicily and sent strong raiding parties to the mainland of Italy. They captured a number of towns, fearfully ravaged the countryside, and even plundered Rome itself. They were eventually expelled by a papal army aided by a Byzantine fleet. But southern Italy remained in a state of great political confusion. There were districts ruled by the officers of the Byzantine Empire, and others that were in the hands of Lombard chieftains. Between these groups there raged a continuous series of petty wars.

Early in the eleventh century a band of Norman knights returning from a pilgrimage to Jerusalem passed through southern Italy and immediately realized that there was an environment that would give full scope to their talents. Among these adventurers were three brothers—William, Drogo, and Humphrey—sons of a petty Norman lord named Tancred de Hauteville. At first the Norman knights were simply mercenary soldiers fighting for whoever offered the best pay, but soon they were seizing lands for themselves. When the eldest brother, William, died in 1046, he was master of Apulia. Meanwhile the brothers had apparently sent home enthusiastic reports of the opportunities open in southern Italy for good knights. Soon three younger sons of Tancred—Robert, called Guiscard, William, and Roger—came to join in the family adventure.

In 1057 Humphrey, the last of the first group of Hautevilles, died and was succeeded in the county of Apulia by Robert Guiscard (1057–85). In 1059 the pope recognized Robert as duke of Apulia and Calabria and took his homage for these fiefs. Robert then set to work to conquer the country held by the Byzantine emperor and sent his brother Roger (1061–1101) to invade Sicily. Both brothers were successful. In 1071 the fall of Bari gave Robert the last Byzantine possession in southern Italy, and in 1072 the two brothers combined their forces to take Palermo. Not content with driving the Byzantine forces from Italy, Robert invaded Greece; but the Venetian and Byzantine fleets cut his communications and forced him to retire. Meanwhile his brother Roger was slowly but steadily reducing Sicily. In 1091 Roger completed the conquest and began to organize his state, which was still a county held of the duke of Apulia, his nephew Roger (1085–1111), son of Robert Guiscard.

The next great figure of the Hauteville house was Roger of Sicily's younger son, Roger II (1103–54), who became count of Sicily in 1103. Roger turned his attention to the North African coast, and despatched expeditions to establish Norman posts there. By his death in 1154 he held the coast from Tripoli to Tunis. His fleets controlled the mouth of the Adriatic Sea and the straits between Sicily and Tunis, making him the master of the central Mediterranean. When William (1111–27), duke of Apulia, grandson of Robert Guiscard, died, Roger ignored the claims of William's cousin, Bohemond II (1126–30), prince of Antioch, and seized the duchy of Apulia. Three years later the pope gave him the title king of Sicily to hold as a vassal of the papacy. Roger's daughter Constance carried the kingdom of Sicily to Henry VI of Hohenstaufen after the death of her brother and nephew.*

Roger I and Roger II built a strong state with a highly centralized government. They tried to give equal treatment to the various peoples under their rule. Their chancery issued documents in Latin, Greek, and Arabic; and Norman feudal custom, Roman law, and Moslem law were enforced in their appropriate realms by professional judges appointed by the crown and supervised by itinerant justices. Financial affairs were handled by two bodies the names of which aptly illustrate the complex nature of this strange state: the *Duana de Secretis* saw to the ordinary royal revenues, while the *Duana Baronum* collected the feudal income. *Duana* derives from the Arabic *divan*, *secretis* was a common Greek term, and *baronum* was good feudal Latin. The barons and knights of the kingdom were organized in a regular feudal hierarchy, and their obligations to the crown were carefully registered in a *catalogus baronum*. The kings of Sicily had one great advantage over other monarchs of Western Europe. As vassals of the papacy and the conquerors of Sicily from the infidel they had been created by the

* See p. 282.

pope permanent papal legates. Hence they had absolute control over the prelates of the realm and could settle themselves all appeals from their ecclesiastical courts. Not even Norman England was a greater triumph of the political genius of the Norman race than this kingdom of Sicily.

The ambition of the Sicilian kings to rule the Mediterranean did not die with Roger II. While his possessions in Africa were lost to the conquering Almohades, later kings remembered their existence. Roger's son-in-law, the Emperor Henry VI (1190–97), had grandiose dreams of conquests in Greece and the Near East. While his son Frederick II (1211–50) was too deeply involved in his struggle with the papacy and the Lombard towns to conduct campaigns against the Moslems, he did lead one crusade and was for many years titular king of Jerusalem. When Charles of Anjou became king of Sicily he revived the dreams of Henry VI. The ill-fated crusade to Tunis in 1270 which was led by Charles and his brother King Louis IX (1226–70) of France was intended as the first step toward the creation of a Mediterranean empire. Although the attack on Tunis led to no permanent conquest, Charles was not discouraged and soon formed an alliance with Venice for an invasion of the Byzantine Empire. In 1282, however, his plans were frustrated by the loss of Sicily. King Peter III (1276–85) of Aragon had married the daughter of Manfred, king of Sicily, an illegitimate son of Frederick II, and hence claimed the Sicilian crown. His agents stirred up the Sicilians against their French masters. The result was the "Sicilian Vespers," a massacre of the three or four thousand French on the island. Peter moved promptly to support the rebels and assumed the title king of Sicily, which his descendants held for the rest of the Middle Ages. Charles of Anjou and his successors retained the continental lands under the title king of Naples.

The general offensive conducted during the eleventh, twelfth, and thirteenth centuries by the knights and townsmen of Western Europe against the Moslem masters of the Mediterranean had important and permanent results. All the Spanish peninsula except the province of Granada, the Balearic Islands, Corsica, Sardinia, and Sicily, were recovered from the infidel. We must now turn to the far more spectacular and for a time equally successful expeditions against the Moslems in the Near East. While these great crusades did not lead to any permanent expansion of the territory of western Christendom, they were an extremely important feature of the history of European civilization.

21. The Crusaders and Their States

IN THE last quarter of the eleventh century the idea of waging war against the Moslems for both spiritual and material benefits was widespread in Western Europe. In Spain Alfonso VI of León and Castile, supported by French crusaders, was pressing toward Toledo. Robert Guiscard and his brother Roger were engaged in the conquest of Sicily. The fleets of Genoa and Pisa were attacking the Moslems in Corsica and Sardinia and raiding their North African ports.* But while in the west the Christians were pressing back the Moslems, in the east the situation was far different. Since the middle of the ninth century the Abbasid caliphs in Bagdad had been mere puppets controlled by military chieftains. As we have seen in an earlier chapter, in the second half of the eleventh century the Seljuq Turks seized control of the caliphate and in 1071 defeated the Byzantine army and captured the Emperor Romanus IV at the battle of Manzikert. This victory quickly led to the Turkish conquest of all Asia Minor.†

After the battle of Manzikert the new Byzantine emperor, Michael VII (1071–78) asked Pope Gregory VII for aid against the Turks. The great pope was inclined to accede to this request. Only twenty years had passed since the Greek church had definitely renounced the papal authority, and effective assistance against the Turks might well heal the schism.‡ But at the time Gregory was in the midst of his bitter quarrel with the Emperor Henry IV and was in no position to embark on other ventures. In 1094 Emperor Alexius Comnenus (1081–1118), the founder of the Comneni dynasty, made a similar appeal to Gregory's successor Urban II (1088–99).

The idea of the papacy inspiring and directing a great expedition against the Turks appealed to Urban, but in his mind it took a form far different from that envisaged by Alexius.§ The Emperor wanted a body of knights to aid him in recovering his Asiatic provinces. This clearly did not greatly interest Pope Urban. He conceived the idea of an attack on the Turkish power in Syria and Palestine intended to recover for Christendom the holy places of the Faith. Despite the Moslem possession of Jerusalem, Christian pilgrims had been journeying there in considerable numbers. Perhaps their tales of ill treatment

* See p. 221.
† See p. 49.
‡ See p. 46.
§ See p. 50.

had some influence on the Pope. But there is no need to seek any particular source for Urban's idea. Toledo had just been taken by Alfonso VI, and Roger de Hauteville had completed his conquest of Sicily. What was more natural than for the head of Christendom to turn the eyes of the knights of Europe toward another Moslem land and one that was held sacred by all Christians?

On November 27, 1095, Pope Urban preached the crusade before a council assembled at Clermont in the hills of Auvergne. The Moslem victories were a disgrace to Christendom. The nobles of Europe should give up their continuous strife among themselves and turn their swords against the enemies of the Faith to aid the churches of the East and to recover the Holy Land. This would be a Holy War, and all who died in it would gain plenary indulgence. After the council was over Urban toured about France preaching the crusade. Other enthusiastic preachers moved through the various lands calling on men to undertake the holy enterprise.

While Urban II probably had no knowledge whatever about the topography and climate of Asia Minor, Syria, and Palestine and the military tactics of the Turks, he was no dreamy idealist who thought anyone could defeat the infidel with the aid of God. He was determined to send forth an army of the best troops he knew of—the heavily armed knights of Western Europe. As he fully realized that no one baron was inclined to obey another, he appointed a leader for the host, Adhemar, bishop of Le Puy. The baronial leaders formed a notable group. There were the brothers of the kings of England and France—Robert, duke of Normandy, and Hugh, count of Vermandois. With Duke Robert went his brother-in-law Stephen, count of Blois and Chartres. The Flemings and the men of the northwestern fiefs of the Empire were led by Count Robert of Flanders and Godfrey de Bouillon, duke of Lower Lorraine. Although Godfrey's fief of Bouillon was held of the Empire and the Emperor Henry IV had given him the almost empty title of duke of Lorraine, he was by birth a Frenchman, a younger son of the count of Boulogne. The men of southern France followed the banner of Raymond de St. Gilles, count of Toulouse, a veteran of the wars against the Spanish Moslems. Finally Bohemond, son of Robert Guiscard, gave up his fierce war with his brother Roger over their Apulian inheritance to take part in the crusade.

Unfortunately Pope Urban conveyed to those who preached the

crusade throughout the countryside his enthusiasm but not his good sense. Although Urban had contemplated the enlistment of no one but responsible lords who could equip and finance their bands, the preachers gave the cross to penniless knights and adventurous peasants. As these men had no preparations to make, they started for the Holy Land in the spring of 1096. They marched in a number of bands. The first two were led by Peter the Hermit, the most successful of the preachers, and a poor French knight named Walter Sansavoir. In southern Germany Peter was joined by a mass of German crusaders that included a few nobles. As neither of these parties carried either supplies or money, they could only support themselves by receiving gifts or by plundering. The king of Hungary was well disposed toward the crusade and kept them so well supplied that there was comparatively little trouble in his lands, but in Bulgaria they were less well received and took to wholesale plundering. After suffering severely from the aroused Bulgarians, these two bands finally reached Constantinople. After one look at the half-armed and completely undisciplined mob that had come to his aid, Alexius hastily shipped them across the straits to Asia Minor. There the Turks quickly cut them to pieces. A few managed to find refuge with Byzantine garrisons and awaited the arrival of the baronial host.

The other bands that formed part of the so-called Peasants' Crusade never reached Constantinople. Two of them commenced their plundering in Hungary and were destroyed by the Hungarians. A third led by a noted robber baron was met and routed by the king of Hungary at the frontier of his kingdom. These three bands started a most unpleasant custom that was to blemish future crusades—wholesale massacres of Jews before the expeditions left Germany. To some extent these pogroms were the result of the excessive religious fervor connected with the crusade. The Jews had slain Christ. Should men bound to deliver Christ's birthplace leave his murderers alive at home? It seems likely, however, that the wealth of the Jews and their profession of moneylending was more important than their religion. Robber barons and penniless knights were tempted by rich houses, especially if they happened to owe money to the owners. Certainly later pogroms, notably that at York before the Third Crusade, were essentially attempts to clear up debts by murdering the creditors.

The Peasants' Crusade was a completely harebrained affair. It is astounding that as many as two of its bands reached Constantinople.

Even if the entire force had reached Asia Minor intact, it is certain that it would have been easily wiped out by the Turks. Undoubtedly many disreputable men whose chief hope lay in plunder joined the crusaders. But when all this has been said, the Peasants' Crusade remains a magnificent manifestation of faith. Thousands of sincere men faced with confidence the terrors of a long journey and a savage foe. They believed very literally that God willed it and that he would nourish them on the journey and give them victory over the Turks.

The crusading barons and their followers who started in the late summer of 1096 followed three different routes to Constantinople. Godfrey de Bouillon took the most obvious all-land route—that down the Danube through Hungary and Bulgaria. The count of Toulouse invented a route of his own that no one else was silly enough to use. He marched across Italy, through the territory of Venice, and down the Adriatic coast to Durazzo. Passing through this land of wild mountains and still wilder peoples cost him many men. The Normans and North French, Robert of Normandy, Stephen of Blois, Robert of Flanders, and Hugh of Vermandois, went down the Italian peninsula to Apulia and from there crossed to Durazzo. In Apulia they were joined by Bohemond, his nephew Tancred, and several other members of the house of Hauteville. While many of the crusaders were genuinely moved by religious zeal, it seems fairly clear that Bohemond was not one of them. His sole purpose was to win in Palestine or Syria the fief that he had failed to acquire in Italy.

The Emperor Alexius was considerably perturbed when he learned of the composition of the crusading host. He had hoped for a body of knights who would serve under him for pay. Instead of that he was getting an army well if not over-well supplied with baronial leaders whose primary purpose was to recover the Holy Land and only incidentally to aid him. Moreover, one of the leaders, Bohemond, was his bitter foe who had led his father Robert Guiscard's troops in an invasion of Greece. The policy Alexius adopted was both simple and wise: he would supply the crusaders with food and transportation and exact in return an oath of allegiance from the leaders. But nothing Alexius could do was likely to avoid all trouble with his dangerous allies. To the western barons and their men the Greeks were degenerate, soft, luxury loving, and completely untrustworthy. At the same time the Emperor and his subjects could only think of the westerners as wild barbarians.

The first baron to arrive in Constantinople was Hugh of Vermandois, who was quickly persuaded to take the oath of allegiance. The western accounts say that Hugh was imprisoned until he agreed to take the oath, but it seems likely that this was just a rumor that reached Godfrey's forces. At any rate Godfrey believed the story and started to ravage the countryside. He did not desist until Hugh came to him in person. Even then Godfrey was suspicious and apparently demanded that the Emperor give him hostages. Alexius refused, but offered Godfrey and his troops shelter in a suburb of Constantinople. Somewhat later something angered the crusaders. They burned the suburb and began plundering once more. The Emperor then came to terms with Godfrey and gave him hostages, while Godfrey took the oath of allegiance. Soon Godfrey and Hugh crossed to Asia Minor with their troops.

His troubles with Godfrey made Alexius even more careful with the other crusading bands. They were met on the Adriatic coast by high Byzantine officials who were to see that they had ample supplies, and on their march through Greece they were accompanied by Byzantine troops who were ordered to prevent them from plundering. Except for a few skirmishes with the escorting troops, these contingents passed peacefully through the empire and crossed to Asia Minor. Their chieftains after some argument took the required oath of allegiance. Once all the crusaders were safely in Asia Minor, the Emperor must have breathed a sigh of relief. Considering all the circumstances, he had scored a great triumph by tact and diplomacy. In May 1097 the crusading host laid siege to Nicaea, once the Turkish capital and a fortress dangerously near to Constantinople. When it fell about a month later, the crusaders turned it over to the Emperor. Alexius then set to work to clear the Turks out of the vicinity, while the crusading host began its long march to Palestine.

By good luck rather than by calculation, the crusaders had chosen an excellent time to attack the western fringes of the Abbasid empire. The Moslem chieftains of the region had broken away from the control of the sultan in Bagdad and were quarreling fiercely among themselves. Most of Asia Minor belonged to the sultan of Roum, and petty princes ruled in Aleppo, Antioch, and Damascus. As soon as he learned that his capital of Nicaea was under siege, the sultan of Roum began to muster his troops; but he was not ready for battle until the crusaders had captured the city and commenced their march across his realm. Considering that they were in hostile territory the crusaders marched in a magnificently casual fashion. The army split into two columns, the northern one commanded by Robert of Normandy and Bohemond, while the southern was headed by Godfrey of Bouillon and Raymond of Toulouse. According to some accounts this division was accidental, but others say it was made because of a shortage of forage for the horses. Be that as it may, the two columns made no serious effort to keep in touch with each other, and neither had more than a faint idea where the other was.

Unfortunately there is little evidence that can be used to determine the size of the crusading host. Contemporary figures that set it at 100,000 knights and 600,000 infantry are utterly fantastic. It seems likely that there were 2–3,000 knights and 8–12,000 infantry. In addition the army was followed by a horde of noncombatants, both men and women. Many pilgrims went along with the crusaders, and no mediaeval army could be expected to get along without its servants and prostitutes. The countryside had been severely ravaged in the wars between the Turks and the Greeks, and the Turks carefully destroyed whatever lay in the path of the crusaders. Hence the army was soon suffering severely from lack of food for both men and horses.

On July 1 Bohemond, who was in command of the northern column, learned from his scouts that a strong body of Turks was approaching. He immediately placed his baggage and noncombatants by a small swamp and ordered his infantry to guard them. He then despatched messengers to notify the other column and drew up his knights in line of battle. The Turkish host was composed entirely of mounted archers and was greatly superior to the crusaders in numbers. The Turks quickly surrounded the knights and rode around their position showering them with arrows without coming within reach of their weapons. A few groups of knights tried charging the Turks, but the lightly armed horsemen kept out of their reach until they were far from the main body of the crusaders and then cut them to pieces. Seeing that such attacks were useless, Bohemond ordered his men to stand together on the defensive. But knights were never intended to sit passively under a rain of arrows, and the line began to waver. Meanwhile the Turks had charged the ill-armed infantry and were plundering the camp and slaughtering the noncombatants. Although the Turkish arrows had little effect on the heavily armored knights except to annoy and exasperate them, many of the horses were killed, and their riders left helpless. The situation of the crusaders looked completely hopeless when suddenly Godfrey de Bouillon and his knights appeared at the top of a nearby ridge and immediately charged the Turks. This completely disrupted the Turkish tactics. Caught between two bodies of knights, they were helpless before the swords and lances of the heavy horsemen. Many were killed, and the rest fled in disorder.

This great victory, called the battle of Dorylaeum, broke the spirit of the Turks for the time being, and they dared not attack the crusaders again on their march to Antioch. The crusaders' success was, of course, the result of pure good luck. The camp of Godfrey de Bouillon had been only six miles from the scene of the battle, yet it took Bohemond's messengers five hours to find it. Obviously they had no notion where to look and could easily have failed to find it in time.

After their victory the only peril that faced the crusaders was an acute shortage of supplies. Many of the infantry died of want, and the army lost a large proportion of its horses. Fortunately the army reached the friendly Christian Armenian states before it was completely destroyed by the rigors of the journey. Then Godfrey's brother Baldwin left the host with a small band of followers to establish a fief for himself around Edessa. The rest of the army marched south to Antioch. There they settled down to what the Middle Ages called a siege. The army was nowhere nearly large enough to invest the city, and it had no siege engines. All it could do was camp near the walls and keep scouting parties out to make it difficult for the garrison to communicate with the outside country. Obviously the city could stand such a siege indefinitely. But after the crusaders had defeated two Turkish forces that sought to relieve Antioch, some of the garrison got discouraged. Bohemond succeeded in bribing the commander of a tower to surrender it to him. He then proposed to his fellow barons that they should make an assault. The first one to get inside the city should have it for his own. Thus Antioch was taken. Within a few days fresh Turkish troops arrived and besieged the crusaders in the city. On June 28, 1098 the crusaders sallied out to offer battle. This time the Turks made a mistake. They allowed the crusaders to catch them in a confined space with water behind them, and were thus forced to fight at close quarters. The result was another Christian victory.

Leaving Bohemond in his dubiously won stronghold to carve out a fief for himself in northern Syria, the crusading host marched on down the coast, ignoring the Turkish garrisons in the coastal cities. In June 1099 the army reached Jerusalem and laid siege to it. On July 13 they succeeded in entering the city. There followed a frightful massacre of the inhabitants. According to contemporary accounts 10,000 were slain in the Temple of Solomon, and the floor was ankle-deep in blood. Even granting room for enthusiastic exaggeration, the "judgment of God" hailed by the chroniclers was a horrible one.

As soon as they were firmly established in Jerusalem the crusaders proceeded to elect a king to govern the state they were founding. During the siege of Antioch and the march to Jerusalem, Raymond of Toulouse had quarreled continually with Bohemond and Robert of Normandy. There was no chance that either of these parties would allow the other to hold the crown. The only important leader who was neutral was Godfrey de Bouillon; he was promptly elected. Shortly afterward Godfrey did homage to Daimbert, archbishop of Pisa and patriarch of Jerusalem, thus admitting that his kingdom was held from the Church.

Within a month of their capture of Jerusalem the crusaders were forced to defend their conquest. Jerusalem had not been a part of the Turkish lands when it fell to the crusaders but had been under the rule of an officer of the Fatimid caliph of Egypt, who promptly despatched an army to recover it. Godfrey mustered his men and met the Egyptians near Ascalon in the extreme south of Palestine. The caliph's forces consisted largely of lightly armed cavalry without bows, and they were no match for the European knights. Godfrey easily won a complete victory, and the First Crusade was over.

Godfrey de Bouillon lived less than a year after the capture of Jerusalem. He was succeeded by his brother Baldwin, count of Edessa, who became the real founder of the Latin kingdom of Jerusalem. With the assistance of Italian naval squadrons Baldwin (1100–18) conquered all the coastal towns except Tyre and Ascalon. He also crossed the Jordan and established fortresses there. Meanwhile Bohemond and his nephew Tancred expanded the principality of Antioch at the expense of the Moslem lords of Aleppo. On the coast between the southern boundary of Bohemond's lands and Beirut, the most northern fortress of the kingdom of Jerusalem, Count Raymond of Toulouse and his son

Bertram established the county of Tripoli. When Baldwin II, cousin of Baldwin I, captured Tyre, the entire coast of Syria and Palestine was held by the crusaders' states.

Godfrey had distributed the conquered lands, and many of those still to be conquered as fiefs. Baldwin continued the process. There were four great baronies—Jaffa, Karak, Galilee, and Sidon—and about a dozen lesser fiefs held in chief. Jerusalem and the ports of Tyre and Acre formed the royal demesne. The barons in turn gave fiefs to their men, and a fully developed feudal hierarchy was established. In the two most completely feudal states of Europe, England and France, the monarchs retained in theory at least the powers of the Anglo-Saxon and Frankish kings in addition to the prerogatives of a feudal suzerain. In Jerusalem, however, there had been no kingdom, and there was no royal tradition. Hence the king was simply a feudal suzerain. The real power in the realm lay in the High Court, the assembly of the tenants-in-chief. This body chose the king, and he could do nothing without its approval. It acted as the chief court of justice in all matters involving the barons, as executive council, and as the legislative body. Each baron had his own feudal court that performed the same functions within his fief. The barons owed feudal services to the king, but the nature and extent of these services were determined by the High Court.

In 1162 the most powerful of the kings of Jerusalem, Amaury I (1162–74), materially changed the nature of the High Court. With the court's approval, he decreed that all fief holders, whether they were tenants-in-chief or rear-vassals, had to do liege homage to the king and owed their primary obligation to him. If a baron defied the king, it was the duty of his vassals to persuade him to obey or to join the king against him. All the fief holders were made members of the High Court and could bring their disputes with their lords before it. When a strong and efficient man held the crown, this innovation greatly strengthened the kingdom; but when the king was weak, it only added to the confusion by weakening the great barons. In a land always threatened by war, the local baron needed complete control over his vassals. Even the English kings recognized the value of the palatinate powers of the earl of Chester, the bishop of Durham, and the lords of the Welsh Marches. In summary, one can say that the Latin kingdom of Jerusalem was the perfect feudal state, where the king enjoyed no powers except those given the suzerain by feudal custom.

The High Court and the feudal courts of the barons dispensed justice to the noble fief holders. Another set of courts, called courts of the bourgeoisie, had jurisdiction over the non-noble population. Each lord had a court of the bourgeoisie for his own demesne. The lord's

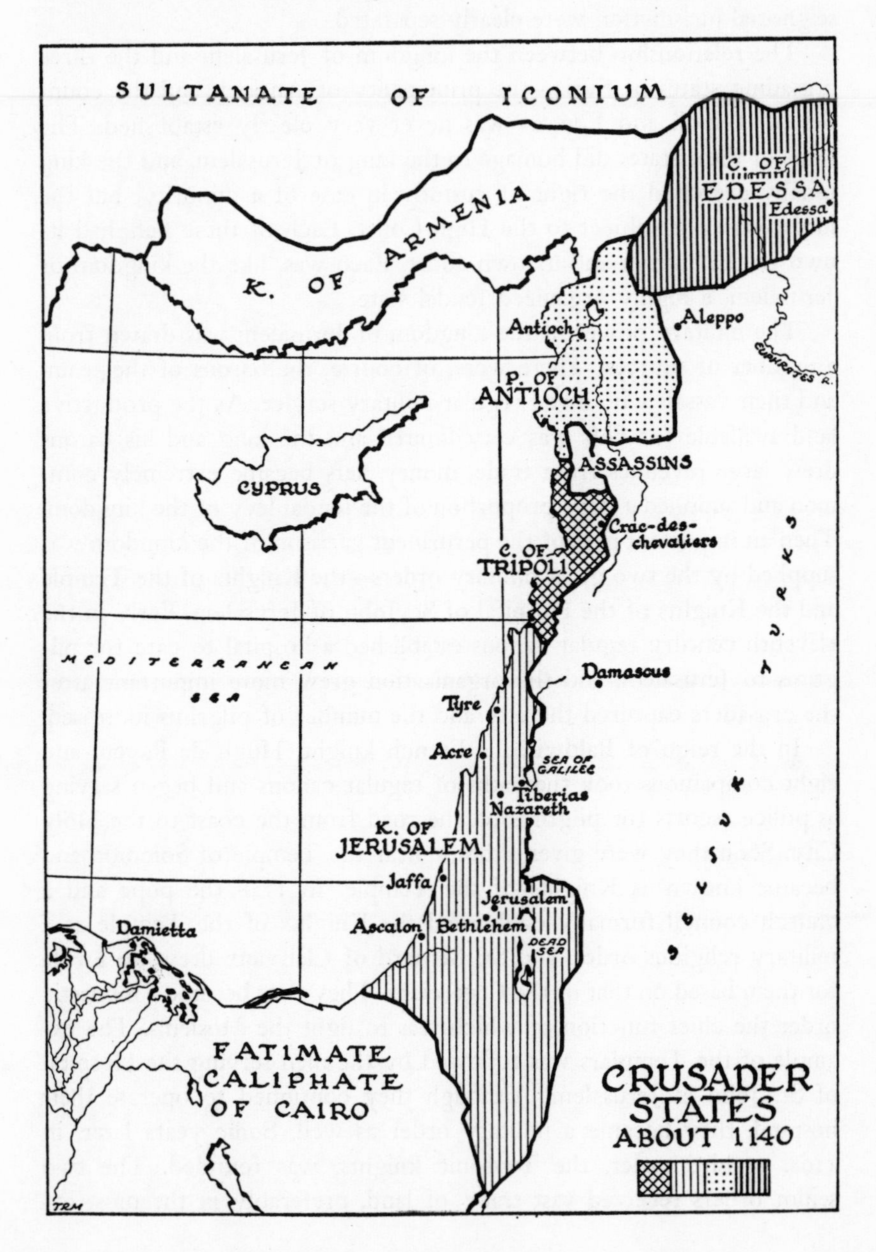

agent, the viscount, presided over the court, but its decisions were rendered by twelve jurors appointed by the lord from the bourgeoisie of his lands. Subordinate courts under native judges cared for the needs of the native population. Thus, in the kingdom of Jerusalem feudal and seignorial jurisdiction were clearly separated.

The relationship between the kingdom of Jerusalem and the three crusading states of Syria—the principality of Antioch and the counties of Tripoli and Edessa—was never very clearly established. The lords of these states did homage to the king of Jerusalem, and the king usually exercised the right of custody in case of a minority, but the lords were not subject to the High Court. Each of these fiefs had its own feudal custom and its own court. Each was, like the kingdom of Jerusalem, a highly organized feudal state.

The military power of the kingdom of Jerusalem was drawn from a number of sources. There were, of course, the barons of the realm and their vassals who owed regular military service. As the productive land available for fiefs was very limited and the king and his barons drew large revenues from trade, money fiefs became extremely common and supplied a large proportion of the feudal levy of the kingdom. Then an important part of the permanent garrison of the kingdom was supplied by the two great military orders—the Knights of the Temple and the Knights of the Hospital of St. John of Jerusalem. Early in the eleventh century regular canons established a hospital to care for pilgrims to Jerusalem, and the organization grew more important after the crusaders captured the city and the number of pilgrims increased.

In the reign of Baldwin I a French knight, Hugh de Payen, and eight companions took the oaths of regular canons and began serving as police escorts for pilgrims on the road from the coast to the Holy City. Soon they were given a house near the Temple of Solomon and became known as Knights of the Temple. In 1128 the pope and a church council formally established the Knights of the Temple as a military religious order, and St. Bernard of Clairvaux drew up a rule for them based on that of the Cistercians. They thus became a monastic order the chief function of which was to fight the Moslems. The example of the Templars was followed by the men serving the Hospital of St. John in Jerusalem. Although they continued to operate their hospital, they became a military order as well. Some years later, in 1198, a third order, the Teutonic knights, was founded. The two senior orders received vast tracts of land, preferably in the most exposed regions, from the kings of Jerusalem. These lands they protected with great fortresses supplied with strong permanent garrisons. Perhaps the most famous of these was Crac des Chevaliers, which held the frontier between the Turks and the county of Tripoli.

At their height the Hospitalers could supply 500 knights for service in the field and the Templars 300. These enormous military establishments were only to a slight degree supported by local resources. Throughout Europe the two orders acquired extensive and valuable properties to support their activities in the Holy Land. They thus furnished the kingdom of Jerusalem with a permanent military force maintained by endowments beyond the reach of Turkish arms. While the usefulness of the two orders would have been greater if they had not quarreled fiercely with each other, together they were one of the chief mainstays of the Latin kingdom.

The permanent military forces of the Latin kingdom were reinforced by widely varying numbers of temporary visitors—crusaders and armed pilgrims. A special emergency in the Holy Land might bring to its aid a large crusading army. In between such major expeditions there was a steady flow of crusaders coming as individuals or in small bands. There was probably never a time when there were not in the Holy Land some knights who planned to fight the Moslem for a year or so, visit the tomb of Christ, and then return home. Some of these men stayed to become vassals of the king of Jerusalem, but most of them went back to Europe or died on the crusade. Thus when Henry the young king, eldest son of Henry II of England, lay on his deathbed, he asked his friend and mentor, William Marshal, to bear his cross to Jerusalem. William went to Palestine, did some fighting, and returned with a rich silk cloth to be used to cover his coffin. When Amaury and Guy de Lusignan were believed by King Henry II to be responsible for the death of his governor of Aquitaine and found that duchy too hot for them, they went to the Holy Land on crusade and remained there. Both became kings of Jerusalem, and Guy was the first Latin king of Cyprus.

Finally, it is extremely important to remember that the Latin kingdom could not have come into existence, much less survived, without the fleets of the Italian cities. They maintained control of the sea and kept the Moslem fleet at bay. The army of the First Crusade was furnished the supplies needed for the march on Jerusalem by an Italian fleet, and troops from the fleet participated in the capture of the Holy

City. Baldwin I could not have reduced the coastal towns without naval aid. It was the ships of the Italian towns that carried supplies and pilgrims to the Holy Land throughout the existence of the Latin kingdom. At best the crusaders' states were frontier posts that needed continuous aid from Europe, and the communications vital to their existence were supplied by the Italian towns.

Between the foundation of the kingdom of Jerusalem in 1099 and its final destruction in 1291, some eight major expeditions departed from Europe to aid in its defense. The first of these started in 1101 under the leadership of the archbishop of Milan; William IX, duke of Aquitaine; Odo, duke of Burgundy; and Count Stephen of Blois. The Duke of Burgundy was a veteran of the wars against the Spanish Moslems. Stephen of Blois had disgracefully deserted the First Crusade during its time of travail at Antioch and hoped to recover his lost reputation. The crusaders could not even agree on a route across Asia Minor but traveled in three bands, by different roads. All suffered fearfully from lack of food and water, and all were cut to pieces by the Turks. The Duke of Aquitaine and a few knights reached Antioch; the others perished on the way.

In 1144 the sultan of Aleppo conquered the county of Edessa. This Moslem victory horrified Christendom and moved the pope to preach a crusade to recover the lost territory. The success of this plea was largely the result of the unusual persuasive powers of St. Bernard of Clairvaux, who devoted all his enthusiasm, energy, and oratorical capacity to encouraging the nobles of Europe to take the cross. The two chief potentates of Western Europe, Louis VII of France and Conrad III of Germany, took the cross; but of the great lords of France only the count of Flanders joined the King, and Conrad was at bitter feud with most of the German princes. Hence, though the rank of the leaders was imposing, their armies were probably not very large. King Roger of Sicily offered them passage to the Holy Land aboard his fleet, but they preferred to proceed by land.

Ten days after leaving Nicaea Conrad's army was attacked by the Turks and almost destroyed. Conrad himself and about a tenth of his men managed to retreat to Nicaea and there take ship for Palestine. Louis, who reached Nicaea just as the defeated Conrad returned to it, marched on through Asia Minor. In a mountain defile he was attacked by the Turks and lost his baggage, many of his horses, and most of his camp followers. This persuaded the King that he did not like the land route. He marched to the coast and took ship for Antioch with all his knights and part of his infantry. As there were not enough ships for all, the rest of the infantry were ordered to proceed by land and were promptly massacred by the Turks. Once arrived at Antioch, Louis was urged by its prince to aid him in recovering Edessa, but the King insisted that he was going to go to Jerusalem. One cannot say whether his motive was a burning desire to visit the Holy Sepulchre or determination to get his queen away from her too-affectionate uncle, Raymond of Aquitaine, prince of Antioch. At Jerusalem he met Conrad, and the two monarchs consulted with the local barons as to what they should do. The lords of the kingdom of Jerusalem had little interest in distant Edessa and persuaded the two kings to attack Damascus. It was a completely harebrained scheme. The army was not large enough to invest the city and could simply camp on one side for a while, then move to the other, and finally give up in disgust. The crusade had accomplished exactly nothing.

At the beginning of the third quarter of the twelfth century the kingdom of Jerusalem fell on evil days. The last of its strong kings, Amaury I, died in 1174, leaving the throne to his son Baldwin IV (1174–85), who suffered fearfully from leprosy. When Baldwin became utterly incapable of ruling, in 1184, the High Court crowned his nephew king as Baldwin V (1185–86), who died within a year. Then the mother of Baldwin V and his stepfather Guy de Lusignan (1186–92) seized the throne. Baldwin V was the last resident king of Jerusalem to rule in his own right. From 1186 to 1243 the kingdom was held by queens or by kings ruling in the right of their wives. From 1243 to 1291 the kings were absentees—Frederick II (1225–43), his son and grandson, and Hugh III (1268–84) and Henry II (1285–1324), kings of Cyprus. During the period 1186–1243 the crown was usually in dispute between sisters. Unfortunately for the kingdom the accession of Guy de Lusignan, who was generally disliked by the barons, came at a time when the strength of the Moslems had greatly increased. The great Turkish general known to history as Saladin had made himself master of Egypt in 1169 and in 1174 had taken over Damascus. By 1186 Saladin was master of both Egypt and Moslem Syria, and the crusading states were faced by the same power on two frontiers.

In June, 1187, Saladin mustered all the forces of his extensive lands for an invasion of the kingdom of Jerusalem, marched up the western shore of the Sea of Galilee, and laid siege to Tiberias. The town fell easily, but its lady—wife of Raymond, count of Tripoli—retired into the castle with her troops and was besieged there by a detachment of Saladin's army. Guy de Lusignan, king of Jerusalem, decided to throw all his resources into a supreme effort to defeat Saladin's host. He summoned his feudal levy and the troops of the military orders. The garrisons of the fortresses of the kingdom were drained of almost all their men. It is possible that Guy collected as many as 1,200 knights and 15,000 footmen.

The army mustered at Saffaria, a village lying in a well-watered valley some sixteen miles from Tiberias. But the sixteen miles between Saffaria and Tiberias ran through wild desert country almost totally devoid of water. Despite the fact that his wife and children were being besieged in Tiberias, Raymond of Tripoli advised the king to wait for Saladin at Saffaria, where there was plenty of water and fodder for the horses. The other lords, however, insisted on going to seek the Moslem host. It was a fatal mistake. No sooner had the army entered the desert country than it was surrounded by Turkish mounted bowmen. Finally, in a state of almost complete exhaustion the army reached a point six miles from Tiberias and halted to take counsel. It was faced by a range of high hills covered with Turks. Raymond insisted that the only course was to push on at any cost in order to reach water, but once more Guy spurned his advice and ordered the army to pitch camp. All night the Turks harassed the camp, and in the morning King Guy drew his troops up in line of battle. It was, however, a hopeless situation. Neither men nor horses had had water since the day before, and they were completely surrounded by a superior Turkish force. Count Raymond and a small body of followers cut their way through the Moslem host and escaped. The rest of the army was killed or captured. Saladin treated King Guy and the other lay prisoners with great courtesy, but he slaughtered every Templar or Hospitaler who fell into his hands. The battle of Tiberias completely destroyed the military power of the Latin kingdom, and Saladin had little difficulty in conquering the whole interior of Palestine and Syria including the city of Jerusalem.

When the news of the disaster at Tiberias reached Europe, the pope preached a crusade to rescue the Holy Land from Saladin. Henry II (1154–89) of England, Philip Augustus (1180–1223) of France, and the Emperor Frederick I (1152–90) took the cross, but the kings of France and England were too intent on their own quarrels to get started promptly, and Frederick departed without them in 1189. He followed the well-worn land route through the Balkans and Asia Minor, where so many armies had met their end. Frederick, however, was an extremely able captain. He had mastered the art of using infantry bowmen whose bows could outrange those of the Turkish mounted archers to hold the enemy at a distance, and he knew when to use his cavalry to best advantage. Again and again the Turks attacked the crusading host, but they were always beaten off with heavy losses. When he reached Iconium, the capital of the sultanate of Roum, he took the town by storm, and found it full of provisions as well as plunder. This capture of his capital so discouraged the sultan that he offered Frederick free passage through his lands if he would move on quickly. Unfortunately, the great emperor was drowned while bathing in the Calycadnus river. While his army arrived in safety at Antioch, many of its members went home from there.

Henry II died before his crusading preparations were complete, but his successor, Richard I (1189–99), known as the Lionhearted, started with Philip Augustus from Vézelay in central France in the summer of 1190. After quarreling furiously all winter in Sicily, the two kings sailed from Messina in the spring of 1191. Philip went directly to the Holy Land, but Richard was delayed by a diversion. A storm carried some of his ships, including the one bearing his financée, onto the coast of Cyprus, and the Greek ruler of the island attempted to make her prisoner.* This was too much for Richard's fiery temper. He landed on Cyprus, captured and imprisoned its ruler, and took the island into his own hands. Richard first planned to sell the island to the Templars, but instead in 1192 he gave it to Guy de Lusignan to compensate him for the loss of the kingdom of Jerusalem, of which he had been deprived at his wife's death. Guy was succeeded as king of Cyprus by his brother Amaury, and Amaury's descendants ruled the island until the fifteenth century, when it became a Venetian colony. Guy de Lusignan organized the kingdom of Cyprus as a feudal state with the same laws and customs as the Latin kingdom of Jerusalem.

During the summer of 1189 the forces of the kingdom of Jerusalem laid siege to Acre. A year later they were joined by the remnants of the army of Frederick I, and in the early summer of 1191 Philip Augustus and Richard arrived. As Richard and Philip continued to quarrel, it was difficult to arrange a general assault on the city, but

* See p. 51.

eventually the garrison ran short of food and surrendered. King Philip then went home. Richard marched to within sight of Jerusalem, but did not feel strong enough to start a siege. He marched to southern Palestine and built a strong castle at Ascalon. Then he made a truce with Saladin. Christian pilgrims were to be allowed free access to Jerusalem, and Jaffa and several other coastal towns were returned to their Latin lords. It was a rather meager accomplishment for a great crusade led by the rulers of the three chief states of Western Europe.

If the early crusades after the first accomplished little, the later ones achieved even less. The great Pope Innocent III (1198–1216) had as one of his chief ambitions the launching of a crusade that would restore the Latin kingdom to its former glory.* After much effort he succeeded in getting an army under way aboard a Venetian fleet. But the Venetians were far more interested in their own commercial enterprises than in the recovery of the Holy Land. They persuaded the crusaders to turn their arms against their chief commercial rival, Constantinople.† The city was assaulted, captured, and thoroughly plundered. The crusading leaders then established the Latin empire of Constantinople. These western lords ruled the magnificent city and its environs until it was recaptured by the Byzantine emperor in 1261. Various vassal states of the Latin empire that had been established in Greece lasted longer. A French nobleman, Geoffrey de Villehardouin, became lord of Achaia, which included most of the Peloponnesus. This state passed into the hands of the Angevin lords of Naples after the death of William de Villehardouin in 1278. The duchy of Athens remained in the possession of its French lords until 1311, when it was conquered by a company of freebooters from Catalonia. Thus for about a century Greece was occupied by feudal states where French barons lived in their castles as their fellows did in France.

Innocent III was not unduly discouraged by the diversion of the crusade of 1204. He forgave the crusaders and accepted the addition of another realm to Latin Christendom. But he continued to preach a crusade to Palestine; and though he died before it started, his preaching was successful. The crusading army arrived in Palestine in 1218. The then king of Jerusalem, John de Brienne, doubted that even with the aid of the crusading army he was strong enough to attack Jerusalem, and he thought of an ingenious alternative. With the support of the Italian fleet they could attack the important Egyptian port of Damietta

* See p. 295. † See p. 52.

and perhaps exchange it for Jerusalem. Soon after the siege started, the sultan of Egypt offered the crusaders just what they sought—all the land of the Latin kingdom to the Jordan if they would leave Egypt. But the papal legate who accompanied the expedition refused to accept these terms. Damietta was taken, and the army marched inland against the sultan's capital. Soon they found themselves hopelessly entangled in the various branches of the Nile and were obliged to accept the sultan's greatly reduced offer—safe passage home to Acre. Thus another crusade came to an inglorious end.

The next crusade was a weird affair. As early as 1215 the Emperor Frederick II had promised to lead a crusade, but he never seemed to find time to carry out his promise.* Despite the continuous urging of three popes he delayed and delayed. In 1225 he married Isabelle, daughter of John de Brienne, and assumed the title of king of Jerusalem, but still he failed to start for the Holy Land. In 1227 the exasperated pope excommunicated Frederick. Then, without waiting to be reconciled to the church, the Emperor set out for Palestine. When he arrived in Jerusalem, he was fiercely denounced by the patriarch as an excommunicate. This did not, however, trouble Frederick. He marched his army about Palestine, all the while carrying on negotiations with the sultan of Egypt, who held Jerusalem. Eventually the sultan got tired of the proceedings and came to terms. Frederick was to receive Jerusalem, Bethlehem, Nazareth, and a few other towns—in short, the Holy City and a wide corridor leading to it. Both Christians and Moslems were to have freedom of religion in Jerusalem, and Frederick promised not to aid any crusade against the sultan or his lands. This treaty horrified the patriarch. No sooner had Frederick entered Jerusalem than it was placed under an interdict. Soon Frederick learned that his father-in-law, John de Brienne, was invading his Italian lands at the head of a papal army. Frederick hurried home, and the magnificent comedy came to an end. It must be pointed out, however, that Frederick had gained more than any other recent crusader. He had recovered Jerusalem.

Frederick's treaty with the sultan was to last for ten years. When the end of this truce approached, the pope preached another crusade. In 1239 Thibaut, king of Navarre and count of Champagne, arrived in Palestine accompanied by his old crony Peter Mauclerk, former duke of Brittany. After a pleasant winter at Acre and a few skirmishes

* See p. 285.

with the Moslems, they made an even more advantageous truce than had Frederick and went home content. Shortly after they left, the younger brother of King Henry III of England, Richard, earl of Cornwall, arrived with a crusading army. As Thibaut and Peter had been in too much of a hurry to put their agreement with the sultan into effect, Richard was able to complete the proceedings and feel that he too had accomplished something. But all this was of little avail. In 1244 the Egyptians swept over Palestine and captured Jerusalem once more.

The fall of Jerusalem led to the last great crusade. King Louis IX of France took the cross and collected a great host. His plan was to strike at Egypt as the center of the Moslem power. The story is much the same as that of the earlier effort to attack Egypt. Damietta was captured, and the army started its march through the delta of the Nile, soon becoming hopelessly confused among the many branches of the river. They were attacked and completely defeated by the Egyptian troops. Louis was captured, with most of his noble followers. The King eventually obtained his freedom by paying a large ransom and spent four years in Palestine, but all he accomplished was to build a few fortresses.

Confined to a few fortress cities on the coast, the kingdom of Jerusalem could not long endure. That it lasted as long as it did was largely the result of the coming of the Mongols, who took Bagdad in 1258. The Mongols were pagans who on the whole preferred Christians to Moslems and were willing to negotiate with the Latin states. Except for the prince of Antioch, however, the Latins considered the more civilized Egyptians less dangerous. For a few years the Mongols kept the Egyptians occupied. Then in 1260 the sultan of Egypt routed the Mongols and was ready to turn against the Latin states. One by one the fortresses fell until in 1291 the last strongholds of the Latin kingdom were reduced.

The long and valiant defense of Acre in 1291 had given most of the Christians time to escape to Cyprus. The Templar forces in Palestine died in defending their castle in Acre, but a strong body of Hospitalers withdrew to Cyprus. Some years later they transferred their headquarters to Rhodes, where they remained as a vigorous and belligerent outpost of western Christendom until they were overwhelmed by the Ottoman Turks under Sulayman the Magnificent in 1522 and forced to retreat to Malta. Long before the fall of the Latin kingdom the Teutonic knights had transferred their base of operations to Prussia.

There they fought heathen Prussians, extended the German territory, and obtained for themselves a rich principality.

A great deal of good printer's ink has been used in discussing the effects of the Crusades on Western Europe. Actually these effects seem to have been very slight—insignificant, indeed, when one considers the enormous cost of the expeditions in both material and human resources. The capture of naval control of the Mediterranean by the Italian cities was hastened by the demands of the crusaders. The returning warriors undoubtedly brought home some knowledge of the East and a taste for its products. But one cannot claim that without the Crusades the Italian cities would not have sought the markets of the East or that they could not have taught the peoples of Europe to like sugar and spices. While no one can say what might have been the result if the enthusiasm, energy, man power, and wealth that was expended on the Crusades had been devoted to the development of Western Europe itself, it is an interesting subject for speculation by those pondering the "results of the Crusades."

The Crusades remain, however, of extreme interest to the historian of the Middle Ages. They are at once the chief proof of the tremendous vitality and expansive power of mediaeval civilization and the most concrete illustration of the meaning of the common expression "an Age of Faith." Although some men undoubtedly went crusading in search of fiefs and plunder, because they found their native land too hot for them, or simply from love of adventure, it seems clear that the majority were moved by genuine religious enthusiasm and complete confidence that the crusade was the path to salvation. Innumerable men mortgaged or even sold their lands, left their wives and families, and faced all the terrors of a long journey through inhospitable lands or over fearsome seas to serve God against His foes. The general assumption was that a crusader would never return home. Although many did return, usually worn and bankrupt, far more found their graves in distant lands. To all who question the faith of the men of the Middle Ages the Crusades stand as a crushing refutation.

CHAPTER VIII

The Revival of Urban Life

22. Merchants and Fairs
23. The Rise of Towns
24. A Changed Society

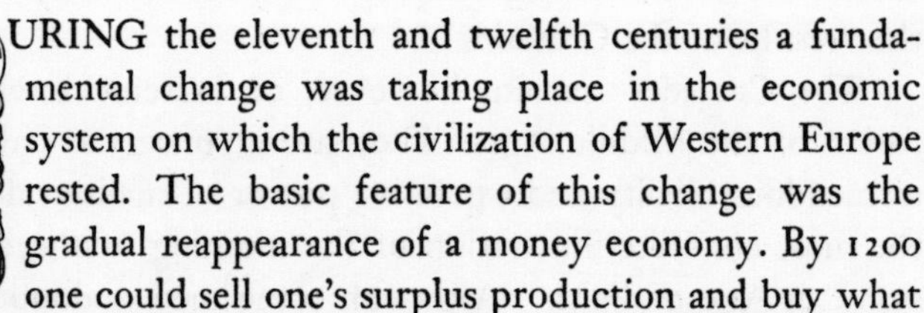

DURING the eleventh and twelfth centuries a fundamental change was taking place in the economic system on which the civilization of Western Europe rested. The basic feature of this change was the gradual reappearance of a money economy. By 1200 one could sell one's surplus production and buy what one could not produce. Closely related causally to this rise of a money economy, and simultaneous with it, were an increase in trade and commerce, a revival of specialized craftsmanship, and the development of towns. Into a society of priests, knights, and peasants were introduced merchants, tradesmen, and artisans. These new phenomena had a profound effect on every phase of mediaeval civilization—political, cultural, social, and economic. This chapter will trace the revival of trade and commerce, the growth of towns, and the reappearance of a money economy, and show the general effect of these developments on mediaeval society.

22. *Merchants and Fairs*

THE GENERAL decline of trade in Western Europe, which began with the civil wars of the second and third centuries and was aggravated by the Germanic invasions, reached its climax in the ninth century. The Mediterranean routes that had served as the chief arteries of commerce for the Roman Empire were for the most part dominated by the Moslems, who held the coasts of Africa and Spain and the islands of the western Mediterranean and whose fleets controlled the sea lanes. The Byzantine navy kept open the route up the Adriatic to Venice, and a few Jewish merchants operated between the Moslem and Christian lands, but large-scale commerce disappeared. In the north, the Viking raiders destroyed the few merchant settlements that existed on the coasts of Europe. Although the Vikings themselves did some trading along with their plundering, the total commercial activity in northern Europe became extremely slight.

The commercial revival that was to have profound effects on all Western Europe first appeared in Italy. Throughout the ninth century Venice shipped grain, wine, and lumber to Constantinople and received in return the manufactured products that she sold to her north Italian neighbors. By the tenth century Venetian trade was flourishing, and its influence was being felt on the Italian mainland. The inland towns of northern Italy began to have some industry of their own, notably the weaving of cloth. But as long as the only available trade-route led to Constantinople, which was itself highly industrialized, the markets for this cloth were quite limited. The opening of new routes to new markets was largely the work of the coastal settlements of western Italy. In the tenth century the men of Genoa and Pisa began to sail along the coast toward France on trading ventures, despite the ever-present threat of Moslem raiders. As late as the early years of the eleventh century Genoa and Pisa were periodically plundered by Moslem squadrons, but in 1016 their combined fleets drove the Moslems from Sardinia. While Genoa and Pisa conquered Corsica and Sardinia and raided the Moslem ports in Africa, Norman adventurers from southern Italy occupied Sicily.* When the Norman conquest was completed in 1091, the western Mediterranean was essentially free for Christian commerce.

The development of Genoa and Pisa was greatly accelerated by the Crusades. Although the princes, barons, and knights who composed the army of the First Crusade in 1096 marched through the Balkans to Constantinople and proceeded from there through Asia Minor to Palestine, they expected to be supplied and reinforced by sea. In 1097 a Genoese fleet made its way to Antioch. Soon Genoese and Pisan ves-

* See pp. 197–8.

sels were sailing regularly to the newly established Latin kingdom of Jerusalem with crusaders, pilgrims, and supplies, while the war fleets of the two cities gradually wrested from the Moslems the control of the eastern Mediterranean. The kings of Jerusalem and their barons were duly grateful to their allies. Genoa and Pisa received free access to the markets of the Latin kingdom and made highly profitable use of it. From Bagdad, probably the world's greatest emporium, the goods of the East flowed to Damascus and from there to the Italian merchants in the ports of Syria and Palestine. Silks, sugar, and spices that had trickled into Western Europe from Venice and other Adriatic ports began to flow in large quantities along the new routes. From Genoa and Pisa these products of the East were carried along the coast to Marseilles, Narbonne, and Barcelona.

While northern Italy was becoming the center of a revived Mediterranean commerce, Flanders was playing the same part in northern Europe. From before the Roman conquest of Gaul the country along the coast of what is now Belgium and northwestern France had been famous for its woolen cloth. In the Carolingian period this cloth had been one of the few products in which there was an active trade. Flanders suffered severely from the Viking raids, but by the second half of the tenth century strong counts had established order in the region. Soon it was producing cloth more vigorously than ever. The location of Flanders gave it easy access to markets for what it produced. When Scandinavian merchants came down from the north with the valuable products of their homelands—furs and hunting hawks —Flanders was close at hand and could supply cloth in exchange for their wares. Then the Flemings had at their disposal the Rhine with its tributaries to serve as convenient routes into France and Germany.

By the middle of the eleventh century the Flemings were selling their cloth throughout northern Europe, and their chief towns, Bruges, Ghent, Lille, Ypres, and Arras, were flourishing centers of both trade and production. Before long, the salt marshes of Flanders could not produce enough raw wool for the spinners and weavers. Flemish merchants carried cloth to wool-producing regions and returned with raw wool. Southern England was one of their chief sources of supply in the eleventh century; and in the twelfth, when the Cistercians began raising sheep on the moors of northern England and in Wales, England became the chief wool-producing region of western Europe. Thus Flanders became a great center of commerce. Merchants carried raw wool and all the products of the north to Flanders and returned home with cloth.

Although the trade in cloth was the chief impetus to the revival of commerce in northern Europe, at least one other such impetus deserves mention. The Anglo-Saxons drank ale made from the grain they grew themselves. But when Edward the Confessor became king, his Norman friends could not become accustomed to so rude a drink and wanted the wine they were used to. Boatmen who lived along the Seine in Paris went up the river, loaded their boats with wine in Gatinais, and carried it down the Seine to Rouen. Merchants of Rouen transported it to London. The Norman conquest greatly stimulated this trade by placing in England many more wine-craving gullets. Soon the wine trade between Rouen and England was flourishing. When Henry II, count of Anjou and duke of Aquitaine, became king of England in 1154, the valley of the Loire and the region around Bordeaux became the chief sources of wine for England.

By the end of the eleventh century Flanders and northern Italy were active centers of commerce, but trade between these centers was comparatively slight. This was primarily the result of the difficulty of transportation. The sea route from Italy to Flanders was extremely dangerous. The Straits of Gibraltar and its vicinity was still dominated by Moslem pirates, and the Bay of Biscay was noted for its storms. Only strong war fleets such as that which carried the army of Richard I of England to the Third Crusade could risk the journey. Not until the fourteenth century did Italian merchants use this route and then only in the great galley fleets sent out by Venice. The easiest and most practicable route from Italy to Flanders was to sail to Marseilles, cross Provence to the Rhone valley, and follow the valleys of the Rhone and Saône to east-central France. From there a short journey would bring one to the Rhine, the Moselle, the Seine and its tributaries, or to the Loire. But such overland trade was both dangerous and costly. Entirely apart from the actual costs of transportation was the expense of satisfying the feudal lords along the way. Every baron claimed the right to charge tolls to merchants passing through his lands. If he wanted a lot of money in a hurry, he rarely had any objection to plundering the merchants of all their goods.

Early in the twelfth century a powerful feudal dynasty saw in this situation a chance to obtain a large revenue. The key region, the lands between the upper Saone and the tributaries of the Rhine, Seine, and

Loire, was dominated by the counts of Champagne. These counts set to work to turn their lands into a vast market place. At a number of their chief towns, such as Troyes, Provins, and Lagny-sur-Marne, they founded fairs. The counts set aside a place for the fair, erected booths, provided police to keep order and judges to settle disputes, and set up money-changers to handle the wide variety of coins brought in by merchants from many lands. The fairs were spaced so that there was usually one being held somewhere in their lands. Moreover, the fairs were carefully organized. Each day was set aside for trade in a different product or group of products. During the days of trade no money changed hands, but careful accounts were kept. Then, on the last day all the merchants took their money to the exchange, secured the official money of the fair, the pound of Troyes, and settled their accounts. The count collected a sales tax on all goods sold at the fair, rented the booths at good prices, received the money penalties paid for offenses against the rules of the fair, and, finally, enjoyed the profits of the exchange. This revenue he used to extend his own power and to develop the business of the fairs. The barons who lived along the chief routes by which merchants traveled on the way to the fairs were offered money fiefs—annual incomes in return for homage and service. Their chief function was to protect the merchants bound for the count's fairs.

The fairs of Champagne became the meeting place of the merchants from Italy and those of the north. There the Italians brought products of Italy such as cloth, fine swords, and magnificent Lombard war horses. They also bore the silks, sugar, and spices they had obtained in Syria. The men of the far North brought furs, honey, and other products of the great forests. From Flanders came Flemish cloth, and from England its invaluable tin. For about two hundred years these fairs were the most important market places in Western Europe. But they were by no means the only fairs. In fact during the twelfth century a network of fairs appeared in Western Europe. Every great lord, both lay and ecclesiastical, wanted a fair at his chief town or manor. Many of these were, of course, little more than annual cattle markets where a few peddlers appeared with goods from afar. Some, however, were extremely important. The bishop of Winchester had the fair of St. Gilles just outside his cathedral city. While the fair was in progress, all business was stopped in Winchester, so that all buying and selling had to be done at the fair. Merchants who landed at

Southampton just before the fair had to take their goods to Winchester or wait until the fair was over before selling them. In eastern England, Boston fair was a great wool market. There the Flemish merchants came with the products of the East bought from the Italians, and sold them to obtain money for purchasing raw wool. In fact, by the late twelfth century there were Italian merchants in England seeking raw wool for Italian spinners and weavers.

The great fairs were essentially what we call wholesale markets. Foreign merchants would bring their goods and sell them to local merchants who would distribute them through the country around. But princes and great lords did much of their buying at these fairs. When William Marshal, then a young knight-errant, wanted a new war horse, he went to the fair of Lagny-sur-Marne to buy it. When Boston fair was about to open, the sheriff of Lincolnshire would receive a long shopping list from the king's steward of the household. In the early thirteenth century Robert Grosseteste, bishop of Lincoln, wrote a letter advising a young noblewoman how to manage her affairs. He told her that she and her steward once a year should figure out what she and her household would need for the year and at what fairs the goods could best be bought.

The fourteenth century saw the decline of the fairs of Champagne and the development of other routes between Italy and the Northwest. This was partly a result of the fact that Champagne came into the possession of the kings of France, who charged higher booth rents and sales taxes than the traffic would bear. There were, however, rival routes appearing. The Venetians began to send galleys by sea to England and Flanders. These were great heavily armed ships, owned and equipped by the Venetian government, in which the merchants rented space. Then in the middle of the fourteenth century a group of north German towns formed a trading alliance known as the Hanseatic League. They formed alliances with towns throughout Germany and developed the overland route from Italy. From Venice and Genoa merchants carried their goods over the Alpine passes to Ulm and Augsburg and on to the north. The Hanseatic towns then distributed them along the coasts of the northern seas. The League maintained trading posts in all the commercial centers of the North, such as London and Bruges. The route up the Rhone was not entirely deserted, but it terminated at Lyons. There was held a great fair that to some extent replaced those once held in Champagne.

23. *The Rise of Towns*

WHILE the revival of commerce played an important part in the development of towns, it was but one of several circumstances favoring urban growth. Towns in the economic sense, places where merchants and artisans supported themselves by plying their trades and buying their food with their profits, largely disappeared from western Europe with the Germanic invasions. There were, however, places where a fairly large number of people lived together. In France the ancient Roman civitates were still the seats of bishops and usually of counts, and they were likely to be the sites of important monasteries. Thus in Rouen there stood the Tower of Rouen belonging to the Norman duke, the cathedral, and the great monastery of St. Ouen. Each of these was the center of a manor that embraced agricultural lands outside the town. In the tower were ducal officials and a garrison. Around the cathedral, in addition to the clergy who served it, were always some specialized artisans who cared for the fabric of the church, fashioned its ornaments, and performed other necessary functions. In Paris the *Ile de la cité* held the cathedral, the bishop's palace, the dwellings of the clergy, and a royal residence. Across the river on the left bank were the monasteries of St. Geneviève and St. Germain des Prés. On the other side of the Seine some distance to the north was the abbey of St. Denis. In short, although the ancient towns lacked real urban life they were centers of both lay and ecclesiastical administration.

Kings, counts, bishops, and other great lords were very likely to encourage their tenants to become specialized craftsmen. They needed many things that could only be produced effectively by men who had acquired skill by training and practice. Thus, by the eleventh century we find villeins who were craftsmen paying their rents in the products of their craft. While these men were probably originally intended to produce solely for the use of their lord, one would expect that they would soon be selling what they might make beyond the lord's needs. It seems probable that every manor where a lord resided had a few specialized craftsmen such as a blacksmith and armorer. When the manor was the chief seat of a great baron or prelate, there might be many such men. Where several such seats were in close juxtaposition, as in Rouen, there could be a fairly large settlement of craftsmen.

As long as the artisans were villeins, their production was likely to be limited. Since everything possessed by a villein was the property of his lord, an unfree craftsman had no reason for producing more than he required to pay his rent. This disability resulting from unfree status was even more serious for one who wanted to live as a merchant. In order to trade one had to move from place to place, and a villein had no right to leave his lord's land. While it seems probable that many of the early merchants in northwestern Europe were runaway serfs, such a man would make no great progress at his business unless in some way he obtained the status of a freeman. Moreover, even though the trader was essentially a wanderer, he wanted a safe place to keep his family and his stock of goods. He was naturally attracted to the settlements of craftsmen that lay near a castle or church.

By the end of the eleventh century these groups of artisans, merchants, and prospective merchants were obtaining from their lords the privileges needed for the effective conduct of their businesses. At first the initiative probably came from the artisans and merchants. They approached the lord and offered to supply him with a tempting money revenue if he would grant them the privileges they wanted. Often they were able to produce a large lump sum to whet his appetite. Later the initiative often came from the lord. When a baron saw his neighbor profiting from the revenues of a flourishing town, he wanted one himself. Sometimes a lord would grant privileges to a few people living near his castle in the hope that others would be attracted there.

The basic privileges required by a settlement of merchants and craftsmen were extremely simple. They had to be freemen who could own property and go where they willed. Usually the charter granted by the lord provided that everyone living in the town created by the charter should be free and that anyone who lived there for a year and a day should become free. Thus if a runaway serf went to a town and escaped capture for a year and a day, he was a freeman. Often the lord stipulated that his own serfs could not take advantage of this right, but he was always delighted to receive the serfs of other lords. Ingenious lords, in fact, chartered towns along the borders of their territory to draw off their neighbors' serfs. Then a merchant or artisan had to be able to pay the rent for his house or warehouse in the product of his business—money. He could not be effective in his trade if he had to perform labor services for his lord. The charter usually stated that the inhabitants of the town should hold their lands and buildings by "burgage tenure"; that is, for a money rent. The rent for a tenement was often fixed in the charter. Finally, the townsman had to be secured from arbitrary seizure of his property. No one was likely to strive hard to make money if the lord could take it at will. This security was difficult to arrange because of the numerous ways a lord could extort money from his tenants. The charter usually provided that tallage could not exceed a certain sum.* Often the money penalties for crimes were also fixed. In some cases the lord's right to debase his money was limited. In short, the lord's opportunities to raise money at will were restricted as much as possible.

The three basic privileges discussed in the last paragraph were found in practically all town charters, but further than this it is almost impossible to generalize. Sometimes the lord retained, sometimes he gave up such seignorial monopolies as his oven and his mill. Often he granted the townsmen freedom from all kinds of tolls on bridges and sales taxes in his lands. It was quite common to provide that a burgher could not be tried for a crime committed in the town nor sued for property located in the town except in the town courts. Traders needed quick decisions in commercial disputes, and many lords gave the townsmen jurisdiction over such cases—the right to hold a piedpowder, dusty-foot, or merchants' court. The grant of such a privilege automatically involved the right to some sort of political organization. When such an organization existed, the lord commonly gave it low justice, or the right to handle what we would call police-court cases. Town government was likely to take the form of a provost or mayor and a council of aldermen. In England a town frequently bought from the king the right to have their own government represent him within the town. The burghers' officers collected the king's dues and performed the sheriff's functions within the town. Sometimes the chief official of the town was appointed by the lord, sometimes he was elected by the burghers.

Many town charters stated specifically that the inhabitants could form a "guild." In others it was taken for granted that a guild already existed. Among the Germanic peoples the term "guild" had long been used to designate a social and especially a drinking club, but it is clear that the guilds of the town charters were something different. They were, in fact, organizations created by the burghers to serve their

* See p. 100.

common interests. They were on one hand organized for security of all sorts. When a merchant lost his stock in a wreck or at the hands of a robber baron, his fellows aided him to start again. If a man in another town refused to pay his debts to a guildsman, the guild would seize the next inhabitant of the same town who came its way. When a member died, his fellows would bury him and care for his widow and children. Often the guild maintained a school to train the members' sons. The guild usually also acted as a religious fraternity to sponsor religious festivals and to aid the local church. On the economic side, the guild secured a monopoly of the town's business for its members. No one not a member could sell at retail in the town. If a foreign merchant brought goods to the town, he had to sell them to a member of the guild or at least pay a very heavy sales tax. Often the guild was the agent for its members in dealing with the lord. In fact, as a rule the officers of the guild and the officials of the town were the same men operating in the two capacities.

At first in most towns there was just one guild to which both artisans and merchants belonged. But as time went on these two groups were likely to draw apart. The merchant could make far more money than the artisan and become much richer. Then there was likely to be a conflict of interest. The merchants who brought goods of all sorts into the town wanted high prices to enhance their profits, while the artisans who consumed the goods wanted lower prices. The common result was for the craftsmen to leave the guild and form their own craft guilds. Thus the original guild became the merchant guild. There were craft guilds in the more important industries of most towns by the end of the twelfth century, and they grew with astonishing rapidity in the thirteenth. Every conceivable occupation had its guild—there were even guilds of prostitutes. In a complex industry a different guild represented each process of manufacture. In cloth making there were guilds of spinners, weavers, fullers, and dyers. As a rule the members of a guild lived together on the same street.

The basic functions of the craft guilds were the same as those of the merchant guild. The guild buried its members and cared for widows and orphans. It formed a religious fraternity to conduct the religious side of guild life. The marvelous stained-glass windows in the nave of Chartres Cathedral were contributed by the guilds of the town. The guild also rigidly controlled the economic activities of its members. It prescribed the price and the quality that had to be maintained and also the methods of manufacture. The object was to prevent competition. No member was allowed to make goods cheaper or faster than the others. Even the hours of labor were regulated to prevent anyone getting ahead by harder work. Then, to make sure that the supply of goods did not exceed the demand, the guild controlled the number of men that could enter the trade. An artisan started his career by becoming an apprentice and serving as such until he learned the trade. The number of apprentices and their length of service were settled by the guild. When an apprentice had finished his service, he showed his ability by producing a "masterpiece"; that is, a product that proved him worthy to be accepted as a master and a guildsman. Then he could open his own shop and have his own apprentices.

In the early days of the craft guilds every apprentice could feel pretty certain that he would become a master. Each shop was small, and a master had few apprentices. But as the time went on the masters were inclined to take advantage of their position. Fewer and larger shops meant far more profit for the masters, and the masters ran the guild. The first step was to introduce a new stage, that of journeyman or hired worker, between the apprentice and the master. When an apprentice finished his service, he had to spend a certain number of years as a journeyman working for a master before he could become a master himself. Then the masters began to make it more and more difficult to join their ranks. By the late fourteenth century in many guilds only the sons of masters or the husbands of master's daughters had much hope of becoming masters themselves. Many men spent their lives as journeymen. The guild cared for them after a fashion. In most guilds the masters were forced to hire the journeymen whether or not they had work for them. But the journeymen were at the mercy of the masters and resented their position. They made attempts to form organizations of their own to defend their interests, but as the town government supported the masters, they were not very successful.

As we have seen, the government of the merchant guild was often hardly distinguishable from that of the town. When the craft guilds were formed, they objected to the political monopoly maintained by the merchants and demanded a share in the government. In some cases this was arranged peacefully, but in others there were revolts and civil war within the towns. In the fourteenth century the craft guilds of the Flemish towns rose in revolt and routed an army sent against them by the ally of the rich merchants—the king of France. Eventually in most towns representatives of all the guilds were admitted to the governing council.

The guilds protected their members from many of the ordinary hazards of life and from competition both from other members and from outside the guild. They undoubtedly did much to attract men into industry and to maintain standards of quality. They played an extremely important part in the development of urban life, industry, and commerce. Yet it is necessary to realize that they had certain disadvantages from the point of view of society. As each guild had a monopoly of its craft in a town, it was always tempted to raise prices and lower its standards of quality. In England, where the royal government was strong, the quality, measure, and price of necessities such as bread and ale were strictly regulated. Government inspectors also watched over the quality of cloth manufactured by the English guilds. But where the only government consisted of town officials controlled by the guilds, they were able to abuse their monopoly. Then guild regulations prevented any improvements in manufacturing techniques unless they were available to and desired by all members. Thus, in the thirteenth century it became clear that a water mill could perform the operation of fulling far more effectively than it could be done by hand. But water power was not available to all the fullers' guilds, and they violently resisted the innovation and persuaded other guilds to refuse to accept cloth fulled in mills. The early fulling mills were usually established on lands controlled by lords who were so powerful that no one dared protest or decline to accept the product.

So far we have been discussing towns as economic and social organizations and assuming that the essential political powers such as high justice were retained by the lord. As a matter of fact many, perhaps most, towns never achieved extensive political authority. In Paris, for instance, the burghers had an elected head, the provost of the merchants, who held commercial courts and exercised low justice; but high justice remained in the hands of the royal provost of Paris. Feudal princes and great barons could fairly easily be persuaded to grant economic privileges and low justice, but they were likely to be most unwilling to abandon more of their authority. When a town gained extensive political powers, it usually did so by force rather than by persuasion. This force was commonly exercised by means of a sworn alliance of the townsmen—by what was called a "commune."

Communes first appeared in Italy, where urban life had never declined to the same extent as in the north. In Lombardy and Tuscany in particular the basic conception of the city state—that is, of the essential unity of the town and the country around it—had been preserved. The town was usually ruled by its bishop, and the nobles whose lands lay about it were his vassals. Whether they lived in the town or on their rural estates, the nobles were bound to be interested in the affairs of the town. The political authority of the bishops was strengthened by the Holy Roman Emperors, who relied on them as the bulwark of the imperial authority. But towards the end of the eleventh century the chief inhabitants of the towns grew restive under episcopal rule. The merchants and artisans formed sworn alliances or communes with the bishops' noble vassals to destroy their authority. When the commune of a town rose in armed rebellion, the bishop was essentially helpless and could only give way to their demands. The bishops lost their political powers, and the communes set up their own governments. This led in the twelfth and thirteenth centuries to long and bitter struggles with the emperors that will be discussed in a later chapter, but in the end the communes were victorious, and the towns achieved practically complete independence.*

The intense civic pride of these Italian townsmen led to rapid political, economic, and cultural progress. The men of the communes first attacked the rural nobles who had not joined them and forced them to submit to the communal authority. Then the larger towns attempted to bring under their rule their smaller neighbors. Finally the great communes waged ceaseless war on one another as each sought to extend its territory. At first the men of the communes did their own fighting, but as time went on the citizens preferred to devote their energies to business and internal politics, while they hired professional soldiers to do their fighting for them. Soon Italy swarmed with bands of professional fighting men led by experienced captains called *condottieri* who were ready to serve whoever offered the best pay. While the towns struggled to increase their political power, they also made rapid progress in commerce and industry. Craftsmanship of all sorts but particularly in the metal and textile industries flourished in Lombardy and Tuscany. And the inland towns as well as the sea ports saw the development of great merchant families whose trading ventures extended from Syria to England. The people of the towns were ex-

* See pp. 279–80, 285.

tremely proud of their political and economic success and were determined that their towns should show to all men their wealth and prosperity. The magnificent leaning tower of Pisa celebrated a victory won by the Pisans. Throughout the towns appeared splendid cathedrals, town halls, and private residences. Often the town hall was decorated with paintings depicting the victories of the commune over its foes.

The same enthusiasm and energy that led to progress in so many directions brought bitter party strife to the internal politics of the Italian towns. No sooner had the communes achieved independence than rival parties appeared, and these parties could rarely resist the temptation to form alliances with outside powers. Thus in most towns one party, called *Ghibellines*, supported the emperor while another, known as *Guelfs*, was allied with the papacy. So bitter were the rivalries of these parties and so violent their methods of expressing them that orderly city government was almost impossible. Many towns attempted with considerable success to solve this problem by importing a neutral chief magistrate or *podesta* who could keep the parties in some sort of order. But eventually most of the cities of Lombardy and Tuscany came under the rule of "despots," or as we should say of dictators. These despots were of widely different origins. Thus Ferrara came into the possession of an ancient noble house, the Este family, who ruled as hereditary dukes. In other towns condottieri who served the citizens used their troops to seize control of the government. In Florence the despots were essentially political bosses. The famous mercantile and banking family of Medici left the republican and democratic government apparently intact, but actually they ruled absolutely through personal influence and economic power. Not all Italian cities fell under the control of despots. Venice was ruled by an oligarchy of nobles and rich merchants throughout the entire mediaeval period.

In the late eleventh century, communes began to appear in France and Flanders. When these sworn associations rose in armed revolt against a lay lord, they had little chance of success, for the lord could usually muster sufficient force to suppress them; but the bishops could rarely do so. The success of the risings against the bishops was aided by the fact that kings and feudal princes liked to see the episcopal political power decreased and were inclined to aid the communes. By the early twelfth century St. Quentin, Beauvais, Noyon, Laon, and other towns were ruled by communes. Although in the strictest sense the term commune should probably be confined to towns where sworn associations achieved political independence by armed revolt, historians have generally applied it to all towns that acquired extensive political authority, and many towns persuaded their lords to give them powers much like those gained by the communes. All attempts to define commune in this wider sense—that of an independent town—have failed, because conditions varied widely from town to town; but certain generalizations can be made. A commune elected its own officials, and no agent of the lord had authority within its territory. Its obligations to the lord were definitely fixed—usually a definite annual payment and a certain amount of military service. The town officers had high justice and full rights of government in the town. While it is extremely difficult to say whether a specific town such as London should be classified as a commune, the difference between the essentially independent towns and a town like Paris, where the royal provost had high justice, is fairly clear.

It is important to remember that the geographical area of an urban settlement and the territory controlled by the town government rarely coincided. Usually the merchants and artisans had settled outside the walls of a baronial castle or an episcopal city in what was called the *faubourg*. As this settlement grew, the inhabitants built walls for its defense. When the space within the walls was filled, a new faubourg developed that would in its turn eventually be enclosed with walls. Then physically the settlement might spread onto the lands of lords who refused to give up their political authority. In Paris the merchant settlement occupied the right bank of the Seine; there lay the district ruled by the provost of the merchants. The Ile de la cité remained divided between the bishop of Paris and the royal provost. Then on the left bank the abbots of St. Geneviève and St. Germain des Prés and later the rector of the university each ruled his own territory. Narbonne was divided into three parts; one ruled by the archbishop, another by the viscount, and the third by the town government. Even where communes had violently freed themselves from a bishop, as at Beauvais, the ancient episcopal city that had formed the original nucleus of the settlement was left in the bishop's hands.

Before leaving the discussion of mediaeval towns something should he said about their general physical appearance. Since walls were extremely expensive to build, the space within them was always used to the utmost. This meant extremely narrow streets with the second stories of the houses built out over them. In fact, the houses were often crowded so close against the wall of the town that many had to be destroyed in case of a siege. Before the fourteenth century almost all the houses were built of wood, and hence a town could burn with great ease and rapidity—and be rebuilt rather quickly as well. The chief architectural feature of a town was its churches of which there were an incredible number, London in 1200 having as many as 120. When the town adjoined an episcopal city, the cathedral towered far above the other buildings and was the pride and glory of the citizens. In addition to the cathedral there would be a number of collegiate and monastic churches and a crowd of parish churches. Church towers and spires were the chief feature of the town as seen from a distance.

Next to the churches in prominence would be one or more castles. In Italian towns numerous fortified towers marked the residences of the nobles who lived there. In the north the nobles did not live in towns, and fortified residences were less numerous. Paris held two great royal castles, the Louvre and the Bastille, and a smaller fortress that served as the seat of the king's provost. In London in addition to the royal castle, the Tower of London, there were two baronial strongholds. In Winchester both the king and bishop had castles. As a rule the castle belonging to the lord of the town straddled the walls, so that it could be supplied and reinforced from outside. This was desirable because the castle was intended as much to keep the citizens in order as to aid in their defense. Other than churches and castles the chief buildings in the towns were the guild halls that showed to all the wealth and prosperity of the community. By the fourteenth and fifteenth centuries a few rich merchants were building palatial stone houses such as the house of Jacques Coeur at Bourges. That magnificent mansion was erected on sloping ground so that one side looked like a large and ornamental merchant's house while the other had the appearance of a baronial stronghold.

The revival of commerce naturally increased the need for coined money very greatly. Western Europe had no gold mines, and this precious metal was not available for coinage until the fourteenth century. Except for a few Italian gold coins, the money of Western Europe in the early Middle Ages was of silver. The basic coin was the silver *denarius*, or penny. Twelve of them made a *solidus*, or shilling; and twenty solidi a *livrum*, or pound. There was also a *mark*, worth thirteen shillings and four pence. But shillings, pounds, and marks were merely used for accounting and were not represented by actual coins. Every lord who coined money established his own standards of weight and purity and changed those standards as he saw fit. To mention only the more important moneys of northern France and England in the twelfth and thirteenth centuries, there was the English pound sterling and the pounds of Paris, Tours, Anjou, and Provins. In England there was only one money, the pound sterling, but on the continent every lord of any importance had the right to coin. In the thirteenth century King Louis IX decreed that his money, the pound of Paris, should be accepted everywhere in his lands, but that did not end the local circulation of other coinages. And the temptation was always strong for a lord, or for that matter a king, who was deeply in debt to depreciate his coinage in order to pay off his obligations more cheaply.

In the twelfth and early thirteenth centuries the chief instruments of foreign exchange were the two great military orders, the Templars and the Hospitalers. They held large properties in every part of Western Europe and the fact that they combined religious sanctity with military power made anything in their possession peculiarly safe. They would accept money in one country and pay it out in another. King John kept large balances with both orders to use in ransoming his men who were captured in war and in paying subsidies to his continental allies. But by the thirteenth century there were merchants whose activities were widespread enough to enable them to take part in foreign exchange operations. When a western monarch sent an embassy to the papal court, he gave the members letters stating that any sum up to a certain amount furnished them would be repaid by him at his treasury. Thus Italian merchants would advance money to English envoys, and their agents would collect the debts in London.

The development of banking operations was a slow process because of the Church's prohibition against receiving interest for loans—against the sin of usury. As a matter of fact the church of the ninth and tenth centuries was suspicious of all commercial activity, and penitents were forbidden to engage in it. For a long time the church maintained that it was sinful to sell a product for a profit unless one had changed it in some way by one's own labor. While by the eleventh century it was generally recognized that the merchant who transported goods from one place to another should be recompensed, what we call speculation was never countenanced. It was sinful to buy anything to hold for a higher price. In general the church maintained the theory that there was a "just price" for everything. An artisan or merchant sold for a just price if he made just enough profit to live as his father had. As time went on this doctrine was made more liberal. Thomas Aquinas stated that a just price was one determined by the seller's needs and not by greed.

But although the church adjusted its doctrines in some respects, it never in this period gave way on the question of usury. In the eleventh, twelfth, and thirteenth centuries the moneylending business was in the hands of the Jews, who were not bound by Christian law. They were, however, completely at the mercy of the feudal prince or great lord who protected their persons and aided them to collect their debts. To a baron a colony of Jews could be a valuable asset. They loaned money to barons, knights, and even to ecclesiastical organizations at a high rate of interest and made large profits. As they had no rights against the lord, he could seize their capital whenever he felt in need of money. Thus the Jews of England were there by the king's permission and were under his protection. Whenever a Jew made a loan, it was registered with royal officials. The king collected ten per cent for aiding the Jew to recover the money loaned, and when a Jew died he took one third of his capital. If at any time the king was in great need of funds, he could tallage his Jews to any extent that he pleased. As moneylenders are always unpopular and the Jews' religion made them doubly so, they were tolerated only while they were necessary. By the thirteenth century merchants were inventing ways to avoid the usury laws. An Italian merchant would lend money to an English baron. The loan was to be repaid in wool priced low enough to give the lender his interest. The availability of Christian moneylenders made the Jews unnecessary, and they were banished from both England and France in the thirteenth century.

By the fourteenth century many merchants had more capital than they could use effectively in their business and were searching for ways to use it. Some bought land. In Venice it was possible to buy government bonds. As a rule, the merchant who put money into land or bonds soon gave up mercantile activity to live on his income. But a few mercantile houses, or rather partnerships, used their money in what we would call banking operations. Probably the most successful as well as the best known of these partnerships was the house of Medici. The Medici family started as Florentine merchants dealing in anything that might show a profit but particularly in textiles. They bought raw wool, distributed it to Florentine spinners, bought the thread from the spinners to pass on to the weavers, and finally bought the finished cloth and sold it on the world markets. They thus employed what we call the "putting-out system." The Medicis financed large-scale production of cloth and sold the product. In order to carry on efficiently their widespread commercial activities they had agencies or branch houses scattered over Europe. When possible they used their capital in regular commercial ventures, but they had other resources. One of the most profitable was extensive dealings in foreign exchange. Far more speculative were loans to princes. As usury was unlawful, these loans were not formally made at interest, but there was some consideration involved. As a rule what was bought with the loans was privileges and good-will.

The wool trade with England was extremely profitable. But no foreign merchant could trade in England without the king's good-will and hence when he asked for a loan, it was hard to refuse. As the loans were rarely repaid, the merchant had to calculate whether the right to trade was worth the money loaned. In general, loans to princes were exceedingly risky business and the great mercantile houses avoided them as much as possible.

In the fourteenth century the English wool trade gave rise to one of the first mercantile "companies." In the first half of the century the Italian merchant houses came to the conclusion that the wool business was not worth the cost of keeping the English king supplied with loans. Then for a while it was taken over by German merchants, but they too found it unprofitable. Finally the English government organized the trade. It decreed that all English wool had to be shipped to a designated continental port, called the "staple" port, and that this shipping could only be done by merchants who were members of the "Company of the Staple." Thus the king secured the monopoly of the export of wool for a group of his subjects. When he wanted to borrow money, he borrowed from them. The staple was first located at Bruges. Later, when the English captured Calais, it was moved to that port.*
The merchants of the staple formed a company only in the sense that they were organized to monopolize the export of wool. Each merchant conducted his business as an individual under company rules.

* See p. 336.

24. A Changed Society

The revival of commerce and the reappearance of a money economy had profound effects on mediaeval society. One of the most striking of these was the creation of the middle class—the bourgeoisie, or men of the towns. Within this class there were, of course, wide differences. The rich merchant in his magnificent town house was far removed both socially and economically from the struggling journeyman. But all had common characteristics. They were all legally freemen. All measured their wealth in movable goods—money or stock in trade. All lived together in the towns under the town governments. As a rule, there was no love lost between the townsmen and the nobles of the countryside. The merchant considered the noble an idle waster who was ready to plunder him if an opportunity arose, while the nobles saw in the merchants rivals for their exclusive position at the head of society. The merchant was likely to have more ready money than the noble. He could often dress as well and live as luxuriously. Yet he was inclined to be careful with his money, as it was his sole wealth. The nobles considered the merchants incredibly stingy because they spent with care. The noble's wealth was in land, and his money represented income. Hence he could and did spend it recklessly.

What particularly annoyed the nobles was the inclination of merchants to buy land and compete with them directly. In France, royal decrees forbade anyone whose father and grandfather were not nobles to buy land held by military service, but this ruling was never very effective. The nobles also persuaded the government to issue what we call "sumptuary laws," which forbade people to live in too luxurious a style. Certain rich furs and other luxurious garments could under these laws be worn only by nobles. None of these devices were very successful. Merchants continued to live in style and to buy land with their surplus funds. And if the funds were great enough, it was not impossible to buy a royal patent making one a noble. There was, in fact, a continuous seepage from the merchant into the noble class, often, perhaps usually, through service to the crown.

It is important to notice that the middle class was not the only one that appeared with the development of towns, for the same movement brought into being the urban proletariat. While the journeyman was far below the rich merchant, he was far above the unskilled worker. When the towns were developing rapidly, it seems likely that most immigrants could be absorbed into the guilds and became full citizens. But soon the guilds wanted few new members, and peasants who fled to the town became simply ordinary laborers. Their condition was miserable. Wages were low, and they had no political rights and no one to protect their economic interests.

The growth of the towns and the consequent development of a market for agricultural produce fundamentally changed the organization of rural society. As this change was extremely gradual, with many of its phases going on simultaneously, it is difficult to describe it in orderly fashion. One aspect was a great increase in the number of serfs being freed. The Church had always preached that it was a pious act for a lay lord to free a serf—it was mortal sin for a prelate to do so, since this dissipated church property. Piety and gratitude for good service moved many lords to free individual serfs, but large scale enfranchisement had to await the appearance of stronger motives. This came with the growth of towns. This made it possible for a peasant to sell his surplus if he cared to work hard enough to have one. The serfs of a village could offer their lord a tempting money revenue in return for freedom. Moreover, the existence of towns made freedom more attractive. In them lay opportunities of which a freeman could take advantage. At the same time, by offering temptation to serfs to run away, the towns increased the lords' problems.

In the twelfth and thirteenth centuries mass freeing of serfs became fairly common. The lord would issue a charter declaring the men who lived in a certain village to be free. Then he would list the obligations they were to owe him. Ordinarily this list included everything they had owed when they were serfs. The only exceptions would be a few dues that were considered special marks of serfdom, and they were often little changed. Thus, a serf could not marry without his lord's consent. The free villein could marry as he chose, but he had to pay his lord a fee when he did. The serf could not leave the manor. The free villein could leave, but it was usually provided that he leave dressed only in his undershirt. All the personal property of the villein on the manor was left to the lord. In short, from an economic point of view the villein gained nothing from being freed and might actually lose because of higher rents promised the lord to make him grant the enfranchisement.

Once the lord had freed his serfs by charter he could not increase the services, however; these were fixed forever by the grant. Hence, in addition to the prestige and dignity of a freeman the free villein had definite and fixed obligations. Heavy as these obligations might be, he was no longer subject to the arbitrary will of his lord. Although serfdom was to exist in England until the fifteenth century, in France until the eighteenth, and in parts of eastern Europe still longer, the enfranchisements of the twelfth and thirteenth centuries were widespread and important.

Whether a man remained a serf or became a free villein, the development of a market for agricultural produce modified his position. As soon as it was possible for the peasant to sell part of his produce and pay the lord a rent in money there was an inclination on both sides to make this change. As a rule the first rents to be commuted were the payments in kind for the land the peasant tilled and for the use of the facilities of the manor. These were a nuisance to both parties and were soon largely changed to money rents. Then came the commutation of labor services. These were heartily disliked by the peasants. When the weather was just right for planting, harvesting, or cutting hay, they were obliged to work in the lord's land and let their own wait. These services were also unattractive from the lord's point of view. Unwilling labor is inefficient labor. Contemporary books on estate management devote a large amount of space to describing methods for supervising the peasant workers and making them do an adequate amount of labor each day. If the lord took money instead of service, he could hire labor to work his demesne and pay it what it earned. As a matter of fact, most lords must have hired their own peasants, since they were the supply of labor most easily available. As hired labor, they could be controlled. Commutation of rents and services progressed very rapidly in Western Europe. By the end of the thirteenth century most peasants in France and England paid money rents.

When commutation of rents first took place, it was simply a convenience for both parties, lord and tenants. But once a tenant held his land for a fixed rent in money, any increase in prices or depreciation in the value of money improved his situation. Most lords had little idea of economics, and it never occurred to them that what seemed at the time to be good rents would some day be very low. Here and there a cautious lord protected himself. When the monks of the monastery of Christ Church at Canterbury commuted their tenants' labor services, they reserved the right to demand the services if they saw fit; but few lords took such precautions. Prices rose slowly but steadily during the thirteenth century under the stimulus of an expanding market. In the fourteenth century the Black Death cut down the number of workers and so boosted both prices and wages. In the same century many continental lords, notably the kings of France, gravely depreciated their currencies. As a result, the real value of fixed rents declined, to the profit of the peasants and the loss of the lords.

After they had commuted into money rents the services owed by their tenants, the lords cultivated their demesnes with hired labor. Soon, however, many of them came to the conclusion that this was more trouble than it was worth. The agents who supervised the demesnes and sold the produce had excellent opportunities to cheat their masters and could only be restrained by a complicated system of accounts carefully audited by other officials. It was much easier to divide the demesne into farms and rent them out to tenants. Then all the lord needed was a rent collector. During the thirteenth and fourteenth centuries more and more lords followed this course, until very few nobles were actually engaged in agriculture. They were simply landholders who lived on rents. This, of course, increased the effect on them of rising prices and the fall in the real value of rents. Many peasants who rented fair-sized farms from their lord's demesne became extremely prosperous.

The first effects on the knightly class of the development of a money economy were thoroughly pleasant and greatly changed its mode of living. The knight could sell the surplus from the production of his demesne and the rents received from his tenants. With the money he got he could buy luxuries that he had never before enjoyed. He no longer had to be satisfied with rough clothes made from his own wool by unskilled peasant women, but could buy high quality woolens from the looms of Flanders. Sugar and spices became a regular part of his diet. For state occasions he had a gown of silk from the East. His armor was made by skilled artisans. Soon he was living far more luxuriously than had his ancestors. The change was even more striking for the baron with many manors. No longer need he journey from demesne manor to demesne manor, eating the supplies from each one. He could fix his residence in one place, sell the produce of the other manors, and use the money to live on. Instead of four or five wooden castles on earthen mounds he could build a fine stone castle at his chief seat, and he could make it more comfortable. He moved out of the grim donjon and built a pleasant house surrounded by high stone walls flanked with massive towers. The walls of the rooms were at first decorated with mural paintings and, later, hung with tapestries.* Bright jewels adorned his wife, and masses of plate his table. And if his desire for luxury was too costly for his income, there were moneylenders who would help him get in debt.

The revival of commerce greatly widened the gap between the mass of the nobles—the knights and petty barons—and the feudal princes. While the former might receive some income from small fairs or by charging passing merchants tolls at bridges, the bulk of their revenue came from agriculture. But the big profits lay in controlling the great fairs and in owning large and prosperous towns; and these were in the hands of the princes. While the fairs of Champagne were at their height, the counts of Champagne were among the richest lords in France, and the count of Flanders drew immense revenues from his flourishing towns. While all the nobles benefited from the revival of trade, the greater ones gained far more than the lesser.

The availability of money altered greatly the relationship between lord and vassal. With a money revenue a lord could hire soldiers to fight for him and officials to administer his affairs. Instead of a feudal levy that went home at the end of forty days, a lord could have troops who would serve as long as they were paid. Moreover, by engaging as officers men of the middle class, a lord could procure agents who would put his interests first. A seneschal who was a vassal always had in mind the point of view of his fellow vassals; a middle-class seneschal had no such sympathies. There was also a tendency to commute feudal services into money payments. The lord would accept a sum of money from a vassal instead of requiring his service in the host, and with the money he would hire a soldier. Bit by bit the relations between lord and vassals became less personal and more purely financial. By the end of the thirteenth century tenure by knight service was largely a rather expensive way to hold land.

During the twelfth and thirteenth centuries a number of forces combined to civilize to some extent at least the knights and their way of life. The reappearance of a money economy certainly played some part in this change by allowing the knights to live a more easy and luxurious life and by strengthening the power of the feudal princes.

* See p. 464.

Greater ease of living is likely to make a man less savage and to give him interests other than fighting; and as the feudal princes increased in power they succeeded in decreasing the feudal warfare in their lands. But fully as important as these circumstances was the gradual civilizing influence of the Church. From the time of the conversion of the Germanic warriors the church had been trying patiently and consistently to impose its ethics upon them. While as we have seen the attitude of the church toward women was ambiguous, it steadily preached respect for them and gentleness towards them. Moreover the increasing importance of the cult of the Virgin and those of such female saints as Mary Magdalene increased the prestige of women in general.*

The Church had always opposed and tried to curb feudal warfare. It had preached the sinfulness of fighting for booty. In the eleventh century, church councils had proclaimed the Truce and Peace of God. The Truce of God provided that there should be no fighting on holy days—Sundays and the chief feasts of the church. The Peace of God forbade attacks on noncombatants such as women, merchants, peasants, and priests. While neither of these could be effectively enforced, they played a part in reducing and ameliorating feudal warfare. And while it is impossible to measure the effects of sermons and the personal influence of prelates, priests and chaplains, there is no reason to doubt that they were extremely influential. Finally, the noblewomen themselves played a part in the process. As their status in society improved, they used their increased influence to civilize the wild warriors with whom they had to live. The chief vehicle for spreading the ideas of the ladies, and one used freely by ecclesiastics, was the vernacular literature of the day. This literature and the ideas it conveyed will be discussed in another chapter: here we are interested simply in the changes in knightly behavior.†

The earliest signs of the new and more civilized knightly ethics—what we usually call chivalry—appeared, as one would expect, in connection with warfare and seem to have been primarily calculated to make it more pleasant for the participants. When one knight captured another, he no longer put him in chains and threw him in a dungeon until his family and vassals ransomed him. Instead the captive was treated as an honored guest. In fact, it soon became the custom to let him go free to seek his ransom on his promise to return if he could not raise it. Then, knightly armor was extremely hot, heavy, and generally

* See p. 142. † See pp. 447–58.

uncomfortable. To travel in it on a warm day must have been pure misery. Yet a knight never knew when he might meet a foe and dared not ride unarmed. By the middle of the twelfth century it became improper, in fact disgraceful, to attack an unarmed knight. Any decent knight would give his foe a chance to put on his armor before he attacked him. This permitted a knight to travel in comfort, with his armor loaded on a pack-horse to be put on in case of need. The insistence of the church on the sinfulness of fighting for profit also affected the knights' consciences. By the end of the twelfth century many knights would no longer admit that this was their motive. They fought merely for glory—for prestige among their fellows and for reputation with future generations.

As the feudal princes succeeded in reducing the warfare among their vassals and began to impose comparative peace in their fiefs, the knights grew bored. Fighting was not only their function in life but also their chief amusement. Hence they began to arrange semi-friendly battles called tournaments. Some great lord would send messengers through the countryside announcing that on a certain day at a certain place the knights of Normandy would tourney with those of the Ile de France. On the appointed day the knights would form two parties, and these groups would charge each other as in a regular battle. In fact, these early tournaments differed but little from battles. Usually two places were roped off as safety zones where knights could put on or repair their armor, and men who were captured were always allowed to go free to collect their ransoms. For the rest, the tourney differed from the battle only in that there was no purpose beyond amusement and personal profit.

As time went on the tournament grew gentler. By the late twelfth century the mass attack of the two parties, the *melée*, was often preceded by a series of single combats. Soon these combats, called jousts, became the chief part of the tournament. Then ladies began to attend the tournaments as spectators, and after the tourney there would be a great banquet and the ranking lady present would give a prize to the knight who had fought best. Thus tournaments became great social affairs where knights fought for glory and the praise of the ladies—in theory at least. In practice, most knights retained a keen interest in possible profits. The biographer of William Marshal continually insists that his hero fought only for glory, yet his story shows clearly that William kept his eye very closely on all chances to take prisoners or horses. And the author himself quotes with pride an estimate of William's profits during a season of tourneys. In short, if knights had to fight, tournaments were better than war. At least they only injured other knights. But tournaments were dangerous and were largely fought for private gain. The church rigidly forbade them, without having any great effect on their popularity.

The influence of the Church on the knightly class is shown most clearly in the crusades. While many motives moved men to go against the foes of Christendom, religious enthusiasm was clearly a most important element. The Church found it extremely difficult to persuade knights not to fight, but comparatively easy to direct their warlike energy toward her enemies.

Although I am personally convinced that the steady pressure of the clergy wrought during these two centuries, the twelfth and thirteenth, a vast improvement in the general level of family life and the status of women in society, I can see no way of proving it. The only definite evidence is in the field of matrimony. In the early twelfth century no member of the feudal class had any compunctions about abandoning a wife of whom he was tired and marrying another. By the end of that century it was generally recognized that this act required the approval of the ecclesiastical courts. While the church was still obliged to be lenient toward powerful lords and not enforce its laws too rigidly, matrimony was securely established under the rule of canon law. If both parties were willing, a fairly feeble pretext could bring annulment; but if the lady protested, the church stood ready to protect her interests, and its right to do so was generally accepted.

The influence wielded by the ladies either directly or through the literature imbued with their ideas is even harder to estimate. While the knights were willing to devote long evenings to listening to romantic tales of courtly love, it is difficult to discover how much their actual conduct was affected. There was certainly some improvement, at least superficially. Most knights tried to acquire some art pleasing to ladies such as singing, playing a musical instrument, or reciting lyric love poems. Women were treated with greater consideration. There seems little doubt that the seduction of a noble woman in the thirteenth century was a far more delicate and refined process than it was in the eleventh century. Evidence of the general improvement in the status of women is fairly extensive. Thus, in the eleventh century a woman could not do homage for her lands and rule them; if she had no husband she had to be in some male's custody. But early in the thirteenth century it was common for a lord to accept the homage of a widow for the lands of her own inheritance.

One must be careful not to exaggerate this change in the status of women and the morality and manners of knights: the Victorian age was not born in the thirteenth century, and few knights would recognize themselves in the *Idylls of the King*. Wives were still brutally beaten by their husbands. A woman's testimony was unacceptable in court except in regard to the rape of herself or the murder of her husband in her presence. The mode of living in a crowded castle made what we consider female modesty out of the question. If a noble lady who lacked a spouse heard of rumors that she was pregnant, she thought nothing of calling her vassals together and letting them view her entirely naked. In the fourteenth century the knight of La Tour Landry, a very rigid moralist, suggests to his daughters that they should not undress in the hall if many strangers are present. Prostitutes still swarmed in the castles, and no noble blushed because of his bastards. In short, the change in both morals and manners was important but still only comparative.

CHAPTER IX

The Feudal Monarchies

25. France
26. England
27. The Holy Roman Empire

THE TWELFTH and thirteenth centuries were an extremely important era in the political history of Western Europe. The effects of the revival of trade, the development of towns, and the reappearance of a money economy began to influence governmental institutions. Kings had money revenues obtained in part at least by taxation, and hence they could hire officials and soldiers. No longer did their activities depend on the services rendered by their feudal vassals. The political scene was complicated by the appearance of the middle class with its own desires, ambitions, and social and economic interests. The comparatively simple world of kings, nobles, and peasants, all of whom lived from the produce of the land, was no more.

During this period the three great states of Western Europe—England, France, and the Holy Roman Empire—took on the general political complexion and developed the political institutions that were to mark them for at least half a millennium. A student of eighteenth-century Europe who glanced at the institutions of the region in the eleventh century would see little that was familiar, but a similar survey in 1300 would reveal the seeds of the institutions of his own day. The course of development in these three states during these two centuries was not consistent. The monarchy that had been strongest in the eleventh century, the Empire, became far the weakest; while the weakest, Capetian France, grew into the most powerful and centralized. It is a period of growth, of change, and of great political activity. One would be hard pressed to find two centuries of greater significance in the development of the political ideas and institutions of the Western world.

At the close of a previous chapter we left England and the Empire in political confusion. In England, King Stephen (1135–54) barely held his crown against his rival Matilda and was completely unable to control his barons who were adding to their feudal power in lands and vassals, securing their military positions by building castles, and extorting hereditary offices from the two contestants for the throne.* In Germany, the princes were developing their power under the mild sway of Lothaire of Supplinburg (1125–37). Each prince was sowing castles over his lands and usurping imperial privileges.† Only in France was the monarchy making progress. There the sturdy Louis VI (1108–37) had reduced to obedience the vassals of the duchy of France and had at least called the monarchy to the attention of the great feudal princes.‡ Unfortunately Louis VI was succeeded by Louis VII (1137–80), who could barely hold the position his father had achieved; and although on Lothaire's death the German princes had elected as king a member of the mighty house of Hohenstaufen in whom ran the blood of the Saxon and Salian monarchs, they carefully chose not the head of the house but his feeble and powerless brother Conrad. But the latter half of the twelfth century saw a new political age ushered in by three kings of unusual ability and force of character. In 1152, Conrad died and was succeeded by his nephew Frederick (1152–90), duke of Swabia, known to history as Barbarossa. Two years later Henry, duke of Normandy, count of Anjou, and by right of his wife duke of Aquitaine, became king of England. Finally, in 1180 Louis VII was succeeded by Philip Augustus (1180–1223) on the throne of France. These three men were to set Western Europe on its course.

25. *France*

THE LAST act of King Louis VI of France had been to arrange the marriage of his eldest son Louis to Eleanor, duchess of Aquitaine. At first glance, this vast duchy extending from the southern

* See p. 186. † See pp. 162–3. ‡ See pp. 171–2.

borders of Brittany, Anjou, and Touraine to the Pyrenees, and from the shores of the Bay of Biscay to the frontier of the kingdom of Arles, would seem to be an immensely valuable acquisition. Actually, however, it was more a source of weakness than of strength to the Capetian monarchy. The dukes of Aquitaine effectively controlled only a few small districts around their chief towns such as Poitiers, Bordeaux, and Bayonne. The rest of the duchy was held by powerful and turbulent barons who paid little heed to their duke. Eleanor's son, Richard Plantagenet, was to show that an able warrior willing to live in the saddle at the head of his troops and permanently resident in the duchy could curb the barons to some extent and exercise real authority in the great fief, but a gentle, pious duke residing in Paris was utterly helpless. King Louis' rule of Aquitaine was never more than a formality. The Capetian house would have profited far more from a small barony with one or two strong castles in the vicinity of Paris.

Eleanor and Louis were personally incompatible. Louis was a gentle, serious, devout prince whose chief interest lay in protecting the Church. Eleanor's grandfather had been the troubadour William IX of Aquitaine, and she was thoroughly imbued with the gay ideas of the cult of courtly love. Even if one discounts most of the contemporary tales about her way of life, one is still forced to the conclusion that she was far from prudish. According to the rumor of the day Eleanor had intimate relations with her uncle Raymond, prince of Antioch, and with the seneschal of France, Geoffrey Plantagenet, count of Anjou. The first of these affairs was considered especially shocking as it took place during a crusade.* But although Eleanor's frivolity probably troubled her husband, there was a far more serious reason for a breach between them. Eleanor bore Louis two daughters but no son, and the future of the Capetian house depended on a male heir. Whatever the exact reasons may have been, Louis and Eleanor agreed to separate, and early in 1152 an assembly of French bishops declared the marriage annulled on the ground of consanguinity. A few months later Eleanor became the bride of Henry, duke of Normandy and count of Anjou.

Although the loss of the nominal rule over Aquitaine was not a serious blow to the Capetian house, the possession of that duchy by the master of Normandy and Anjou was extremely dangerous, and the menace became more acute two years later when Henry became king of England. Louis fully realized this, but there was little he could do.

* See p. 213.

He declared the marriage illegal, since it had been arranged without his consent as feudal suzerain, and waged war against Henry, but this did not trouble the young Duke unduly.

The second marriage of Louis VII, with a princess of Castile, produced only daughters, and in 1164 he took a third wife, Adèle of Blois, sister of Henry the Liberal, count of Champagne; of Thibaut, count of Blois; and of William of Blois, archbishop of Reims. As Louis's two daughters by Eleanor of Aquitaine, Marie and Alix, married at about this same time the counts of Champagne and Blois, a firm alliance was formed between the king and the house of Blois, which had formerly been bitterly hostile to him and his father. To gain the support of this mighty feudal dynasty against the even more powerful Henry Plantagenet was clearly sound politics, but the weak king was soon being governed by his strong-willed brothers-in-law. For a time it looked as if France would be divided between the dukes of Normandy and the counts of Champagne.

Despite his essential weakness Louis struggled manfully to maintain the position of his dynasty. He followed his father's policy of increasing the prestige of the monarchy by defending the church against predatory lords. Although he was no match for Henry II on the field of battle, he injured him when he could by intrigue. Thus, he supported Henry's foe, Archbishop Thomas Becket, and lent both aid and encouragement to a great baronial revolt led by Henry's three eldest sons.* But Louis could make little progress. Henry suppressed the revolt and tightened his grip even more firmly on his vast lands—England, Normandy, Brittany, Maine, Anjou, and Aquitaine. King Louis slipped quietly into his dotage under the rule of the house of Blois.

By Adèle of Blois Louis VII had a son whom he named Philip. When he reached the age of fifteen, Philip decided to break the hold of the house of Blois on his aged father and his kingdom. To gain support for removing his uncles from power he married the niece of Philip of Alsace, count of Flanders, and sought an understanding with Henry II. Successful in these ventures, he obtained effective control of the realm a year before his father's death in 1180 made him king in name as well as in fact.

Despite the fact that he had come into power with the aid of Henry II, Philip realized that his chief aim had to be the defeat of the Plantagenet power. The French monarchy could never be very strong

* See p. 266.

CHURCH OF NOTRE DAME LA GRANDE, POITIERS, FRANCE

This picture shows the intricately carved façade of this lovely Romanesque church. The sculpture dates from about 1150. It was created in the favorite city of Eleanor, duchess of Aquitaine, at about the time of her marriage to Henry, count of Anjou and duke of Normandy. The carvings just above the portals depict scenes from a mystery play. Above in two rows are the twelve apostles and two bishops, probably St. Hilary and St. Martin. At the top above the central window is Christ in glory with the symbols of the Four Evangelists. Courtesy of the Archives Photographiques d'Art et d'Histoire, Paris.

CHURCH OF NOTRE DAME LA GRANDE, POITIERS, FRANCE

This view of the interior of the nave shows the barrel vault that marked the Romanesque style. It has the majestic, solid simplicity characteristic of the churches of its period. This nave was built about 1100, in the time of Duke William IX of Aquitaine, the troubadour and crusader. Courtesy of the Archives Photographiques d'Art et d'Histoire, Paris.

while the kings of England held Normandy, Maine, Anjou, and Aquitaine. Moreover, Henry was not satisfied with what he had; he made several attempts to absorb the county of Toulouse and conducted negotiations with the counts of Maurrienne in Savoy. At first Philip could only follow his father's policy of intrigue. He stirred up Henry's sons against him and aided them in their revolts. When Henry died in 1189, both his surviving sons, Richard and John, were in alliance with Philip. But once on the throne of England, Richard proved fully as formidable a foe as his father, and Philip could only wait hopefully. Early in 1190 Richard and Philip departed together on the Third Crusade. They fought a brief war in Sicily and quarreled continually throughout the expedition until in July 1191 Philip announced his decision to leave Palestine and return home.* His excuse was poor health, but his motive was probably political. The count of Flanders had died, and Philip was anxious to secure his wife's share of the inheritance. Moreover, with Richard in Palestine there might well be an opportunity to seize some of his lands.

Shortly after Philip arrived in France he presented to the seneschal of Normandy a document that purported to be a treaty agreed to by Richard in Sicily that gave Philip a large slice of Normandy. When the seneschal refused to recognize the treaty without direct orders from Richard, Philip summoned his barons to attack Normandy. But as a crusader Richard and his lands were under papal protection, and the barons refused to move. Philip then turned to intrigue once more—an alliance with Richard's brother John. Philip would aid John to become king of England in return for John's surrender of the continental fiefs of his house. Richard soon heard rumors of this plot and hastened back from Palestine. He landed at the head of the Adriatic Sea and tried to make his way in disguise through the territory of his foe, the Duke of Austria, but he was recognized and captured. The impecunious duke soon sold him to the Emperor Henry VI. Philip immediately offered Henry a large sum to keep his prisoner in confinement, and Henry, who hated Richard, was inclined to comply. Richard, however, was well served. His emissaries bribed the princes of Germany to demand his release, and in 1194 he was freed for an enormous ransom. Once more Philip was foiled and could only try to hold his own in a long, drawn-out war with his doughty antagonist—by far the ablest soldier of the day. When in 1199 Richard was

* See pp. 215–16.

slain in a quarrel with a petty Poitevin baron, Philip had made no headway whatever in his attempt to reduce the Plantagenet power.

King Philip found Richard's successor, John, a less difficult opponent. While John was a competent captain and able administrator, he lacked the personal qualities of Richard and could not hold the confidence and loyalty of his barons. Moreover, there was a rival claimant to the English crown—John's nephew Arthur, duke of Brittany and count of Anjou, son of his elder brother Geoffrey. Philip made his preparations carefully. He courted the friendship of Arthur and built up a reserve of money for a war chest while he waited for John to give him a good opportunity. This John soon supplied by marrying the fiancée of one of his vassals, Hugh de Lusignan, count of La Marche in Poitou. The outraged count of La Marche appealed to Philip's court. As John refused to appear when summoned, he was condemned to lose his fiefs held of the French crown. Philip then formed an alliance with Arthur, loaned him some troops, and attacked Normandy while Arthur invaded Poitou. Arthur laid siege to the castle of Mirabeau where his grandmother, the aged Queen Eleanor, was living; and there he was surprised and captured by John. Arthur promptly disappeared into John's castle of Falaise and was never seen again. While it seems likely that John had him murdered, there is no absolute proof that he did. But Arthur's Breton and Angevin vassals immediately demanded the release of their lord, and when it was refused they went over to King Philip.

Philip had a reserve of money and no scruples about how he used it. When he could buy the constable of a castle, he did so. When he could not use bribery, he brought up his mercenary troops. John lacked both money and the confidence of his men.* Philip captured the royal fortresses and great towns of Normandy one by one. Then he went into Touraine and successfully besieged the strongholds of Chinon and Loches. By the end of 1205 he was master of Normandy, Maine, Anjou, and Touraine, and had received the submission of most of the barons of Poitou. John refused to accept his defeat as final. He went to work in England to raise funds for the recovery of his lands in France and built up a series of alliances with his nephew Otto (1208–15), the Holy Roman Emperor; the princes of the Rhine valley; and any French vassals who were open to bribes. In 1214 this great coalition struck. John invaded Anjou while Otto and his army marched

* See pp. 267–8.

on Paris from the north. Philip met Otto at Bouvines, in northern France, and completely crushed him. This great battle ended for over a century any danger that the English would recover Normandy, Maine, or Anjou. Poitou remained a border region. Its turbulent barons were in time of war the friends of anyone in Poitou with an army and in time of peace, with whatever lord was farthest away and least likely to trouble them. Only in the coastal region of Aquitaine, in Gascony and Guienne, did the English king retain a firm hold.

The conquest of Normandy, Maine, Anjou, and Touraine was a major step in the development of the Capetian monarchy. Normandy alone yielded a revenue as large as that of the entire royal demesne before the conquest. And about half Philip's revenue before the acquisition of these lands came from the county of Artois, which he had obtained as his first wife's share of the possessions of her uncle, the Count of Flanders. Thus King Philip quadrupled the revenue of the French crown and made the monarchy far more powerful than any of its great vassals.

These additions to the royal demesne made the rather primitive organization of the Capetian monarchy entirely inadequate. King Philip created two new classes of administrative officials—*baillis* and seneschals. Each of these officers was entrusted with the government of a fairly large district; Normandy was divided into five bailiwicks. The baillis administered justice and collected the king's revenues, in return for a regular salary. They also acted as royal agents in handling the king's relations with the vassals of the demesne. As a rule they were moved frequently from district to district, in order that they might not develop a community of interests with the people they governed. Moreover, the baillis were drawn from the middle class, owed their position to the king's favor, and hence were devoted to his interests. The seneschals ruled bailiwicks that lay near hostile territory and so required a strong military force. They were barons or knights who could command the king's troops and conduct the necessary local campaigns. Otherwise their functions were the same as those of the baillis. Both baillis and seneschals had agents who aided them in governing their bailiwicks, and these rapidly increased in number to form a rather formidable bureaucracy.

King Philip Augustus laid firm foundations for the development of a strong monarchy, and the next four generations of Capetian kings completed the structure. The royal demesne was steadily expanded.

Philip's grandson, King Louis IX (1226–70), usually known as St. Louis, gave the heiress of the last count of Toulouse of the ancient line to his brother Alphonse, and when Alphonse died without heirs the county of Toulouse entered the royal demesne. St. Louis' son, Philip III (1270–85), arranged the marriage of his eldest son with the heiress of Champagne and so brought that great fief into the hands of the crown. If the kings had kept possession of all the lands that came into their hands, the royal demesne in 1328 would have embraced more than half of France, but this result did not take place because of a policy revived by Philip Augustus' son, Louis VIII (1223–26); that of giving *appanages* to the king's younger sons.

The problem of how to provide for the king's younger sons was a perplexing one in all feudal monarchies. Even if the royal revenue permitted the payment of allowances in money, no high-spirited prince would be satisfied with such a solution. He wanted his own manors and vassals and the independence that came with the possession of a fief. The early Capetians had been fortunate in having small families. King Robert II (996–1031), son of Hugh Capet, gave his second son the duchy of Burgundy, which had escheated to the crown. Henry I (1031–60) made his second son, Hugh, count of Vermandois. Louis VI was the only son of Philip I who survived him, but he had several sons in addition to his heir, Louis VII. To Robert he gave the royal county of Dreux, while Peter was married to the heiress of a minor barony. Philip Augustus and Louis VIII were only sons. Thus the early Capetians had regularly endowed their younger sons from the royal demesne, and only the lack of sons had limited the results of this policy. Louis VIII simply followed the customs of his line when he provided for his three cadets. Robert was given the county of Artois, Alphonse the county of Poitou, and Charles received Anjou and Maine. Thus Louis' own inheritance from his mother and about half the land taken from King John by Philip Augustus passed out of the direct control of the crown. Later kings gave the counties of Clermont, Valois, Evreux, Alençon, Mortain, and Angoulême to their younger sons.

At first glance this policy of creating appanages appears most unwise, and many historians have so regarded it. Actually it was probably both wise and necessary. The royal demesne of Philip Augustus and Louis VIII was too large to handle through the available administrative organization. When Louis IX, an extremely conscientious monarch, came to the throne, the land was ringing with the complaints of the people of the demesne against the extortion and tyranny of the king's officers. Louis conducted a series of inquests that revealed shocking conditions. If the baillis were to control the turbulent nobility, they needed extensive powers, but only careful supervision could prevent them from outrageous abuse of those powers. By granting lands in appanage the king supplied a lord who could govern effectively. But this policy did weaken the crown. A king's brothers would usually be loyal to him, their sons might feel equally bound to his son, but the tie between second cousins was too vague to have much force. The appanages created a new group of feudal princes. By 1328 only four of the great ancient fiefs survived—Flanders, Brittany, Burgundy, and Aquitaine—but there were a number of important appanages. Had Alphonse of Poitiers produced an heir to enjoy his counties of Poitou and Toulouse, that prince would have held almost as much land as the king had in his demesne. A custom once established has great force, and long after there was no longer any sound reason for creating appanages new ones continued to be formed.

As we have seen in an earlier chapter, the development of towns, the revival of commerce, and the reappearance of a money economy had greatly increased the power of the feudal princes.* The master of rich towns and flourishing fairs enjoyed a revenue in money with which he could hire officials devoted to his interests and soldiers ready to obey his commands. The lesser nobles were essentially helpless. No longer could a strong castle guarantee the independence of a turbulent lord. If a feudal prince cared enough, he could use mercenary troops to besiege the castle as long as was necessary. Philip Augustus and his successors made use of their revenues in money to hire middle-class officials and mercenary soldiers: no longer could a petty baron of the demesne hope to defy the king.

But the other feudal princes were developing their power in the same manner. Hence it was extremely fortunate for the Capetian kings that so many great fiefs came into the hands of the crown during this period. Those that remained in the possession of their princes—Brittany, Burgundy, Flanders, and Gascony—continued to be practically independent states vaguely subordinate to the French crown. The same can be said of the appanages, except that as most of these were far smaller than the ancient great fiefs they were less able to maintain their independence. In general, however, when one speaks of the increase

* See p. 243.

of the royal power at the expense of the nobles, one refers only to the royal demesne. Although infringements on the independence of the princes were frequently attempted, they nearly always ended in failure. No royal officer could enter Brittany without the duke's leave. No appeals could be made from his court to the king's. He nominated the bishops of Brittany. Only homage and fidelity bound the duke to the French crown.

Louis IX was a devout and conscientious monarch with a high conception of the royal office. He was as anxious to give other men their rights as he was to insist on his own. Instead of attempting to drive the English from Gascony, he made peace with King Henry III. Henry was to surrender all claim to Normandy, Maine, Anjou, and Poitou in return for Louis' recognition of his right to hold Gascony as a vassal of the French crown. When a man who had been enfeoffed by Louis' father was asked to prove his right to his fief and presented a badly torn charter, Louis was urged by his officers to refuse to accept the damaged document; but the King said he could recognize his father's seal and insisted on honoring it. Louis was firm in demanding what he conceived to be the rights of the crown, however. He insisted that appeals could be taken from the courts of his vassals to his court. His officers supervised the baronial administrations and interfered in them continually. As a pious and devout man Louis detested feudal warfare. He first hedged it about with restrictions. Before starting a war a noble had to defy his enemy well in advance. He also had to notify his foe's relatives and ask them if they planned to take part in the war. If one party asked for a truce, the other had to grant it. In short the waging of private war was made so complicated that it was very little fun. Later in his reign Louis forbade private war entirely and even prohibited his nobles from riding around the country at the head of armed bands. Under his rule and that of his son and grandson France was more orderly than it was to be again for several centuries.

Philip III (1270–85) and Philip IV (1285–1314) continued the policy of St. Louis. Their officers continued to infringe on the jurisdictions of the nobles and private war was sternly repressed. Under the sons of Philip IV a reaction appeared. In a number of regions the nobles banded together and threatened revolt unless they were promised that their rights would be respected. The result was a series of charters guaranteeing certain privileges to the nobles of the various provinces. The ban against bearing arms was to be repealed. No bailli could try a case involving a nobleman but was to be obliged to send it to the king's court. Nobles were to be allowed their customary rights of jurisdiction. While these charters differed from the English Magna Carta in that they were regional and did not apply to the country as a whole, they were the product of a similar movement and had the same purpose.*

The royal administration developed very rapidly under St. Louis and his successors. The central financial administration of Philip Augustus had consisted of an annual audit of the accounts of the baillis and provosts held in the house of the Templars in Paris by members of that order acting as royal agents. The Temple also served as a storehouse for the king's reserve treasure. When Philip conquered John's fiefs, he took over intact the complicated and efficient financial system established by the Angevin kings.† In all probability he and his successors used this system as a model for the improvement of their own administration. The first step was to appoint a group of household officers and royal clerks to conduct the annual audit. Philip IV, however, found that there was too much business for a group of dignitaries who could only devote a short time to the task and created a permanent financial body, the *chambre des comptes*. Philip also moved the treasury from the Temple to his castle of the Louvre and appointed officials to receive and pay out his moneys.

The administration of justice followed much the same course as that of finance. In the reigns of Louis VII and Philip Augustus, cases were heard by members of the royal household, barons, prelates, and knights, aided by a few clerks with special knowledge of the law. This court wandered about with the king and was in fact simply part of his household. By St. Louis' reign the business of the king's court had increased so much that it had to stay in one place and sit fairly continually. The barons and prelates only took part in the proceedings when the importance of the litigants required their presence. Thus if a case involved a great vassal, a "peer," at least one other peer had to sit on the court. In cases involving ordinary barons or prelates, men of equal rank had to be present. But most cases were heard entirely by a body of professional jurists that soon came to be called the *parlement* of Paris. By the time of Philip IV the parlement was divided into three sections. The *chambre des plaids* actually heard and decided cases. The *chambre des requêts* received complaints and determined whether or

* See pp. 268–9. † See p. 185.

not they should be heard, while the *chambre des enquêtes* conducted judicial investigations.

In addition to the men who managed his finances and dealt out justice in his court, the king had a group of councilors to give him advice. These men took a special oath to give the best advice they could. Thus the functions that had been performed by the king's household under the early Capetians became divided among three bodies—the council, the chambre des comptes, and parlement. This does not mean that the personnel of these groups was completely distinct; an important servant of the crown might have a place on several of them. But in general, the royal administration was carried on by specialists who were professionals as well. It is important to notice that the growth of the central administration added to the bureaucracy. When one considers the members of the central administration and the baillis and seneschals with their numerous subordinates, it is clear that a large number of men were living on the king's pay.

Every feudal lord had his curia, the assembly of all his vassals, and the Capetian kings were no exception to this rule.* This body met at certain times such as Christmas and Easter and whenever the king needed advice on an important question. When a case arose involving a great vassal, such as the plea of the count of La Marche against King John, it was usually heard by the full curia. Legislation that affected the interests of the king's vassals was issued only with the advice of this assembly. Legally this was the king's court and the groups of household officers and clerks that conducted the routine business of the government can be thought of as permanent committees of the full curia. The obligations of a lord to seek advice and of his vassals to give it was deeply embedded in feudal custom; the court was the instrument through which this counsel was sought and supplied. Before the reign of Philip Augustus this court was usually only an assembly of the prelates dependent on the crown and the barons of the demesne, but as the monarchy grew in power, prestige, and dignity the attendance of the great vassals became more frequent. In 1216 a decree of this court deciding a disputed claim to the county of Champagne was subscribed to by five ecclesiastical peers—the archbishop of Reims and the bishops of Châlons, Langres, Beauvais, and Noyon—one lay peer, the duke of Burgundy, four bishops, and eight important barons.

As long as the king of France was essentially only a feudal suzerain,

* See pp. 108–09.

the assembly of his vassals could give him whatever advice he needed. But as the Capetians developed their functions as kings, as distinct from those they exercised as feudal overlords, they felt the need of contact with other groups of their subjects. Thus the towns supplied an important part of the financial and military resources of the realm, and the good will of their inhabitants was extremely important to the king. Moreover, as general taxation began to take the place of purely feudal revenues, the lesser nobles who might not be direct vassals of the king acquired an interest in royal policy. The kings soon found that it was easier to collect taxes and enforce legislation that had been agreed to by those whom it involved. Hence the crown sought from time to time the advice of various groups that were not represented in the curia. Then in 1302 King Philip IV found himself engaged in a life and death struggle with the papacy and felt the need for the support of his people as a whole. He therefore summoned the church, the nobility, and the towns to send representatives to meet in the first Estates General.

This body vigorously supported the king's policy and enabled him to face his foes at the head of a united people. Philip and his successors continued to summon this new body when any emergency arose. It was found particularly useful when the king needed money or when he desired legislation that went against established custom. In short, the power of a feudal monarch was limited by custom and tradition. Only when supported by his people through their representatives could he change or transgress custom in important matters without meeting at least passive resistance. Thus the Estates General was established because it was useful to the king and strengthened his power. With its approval, he could do things that he could not do otherwise. It was only later that the idea appeared that the Estates General could also control the king by refusing its approval.

Philip Augustus, St. Louis, and the men who served them worked to increase the royal power, but they operated within the limits set by custom. They aspired to make the Capetian state a strong feudal monarchy. Philip IV, on the other hand, had at his court a group of men who thought of the royal power in quite different terms. Trained in Roman law, they were inclined to think of the king as God's agent on earth appointed to rule the realm with absolute power. It was his duty to rule for the benefit of the country as a whole, but only he could decide what was beneficial. These ideas were absorbed to a considerable extent by the bureaucracy as a whole. This body of royal servants developed very exalted ideas of the power not so much of the king as an individual as of the crown as an institution. Moreover they were inclined to think of themselves as the crown—that is, as the royal government. Before the end of the fourteenth century this bureaucracy was attempting to prevent the king from dissipating the power of the crown. Thus under Philip IV one finds both the seeds of absolute monarchy and of an all-powerful bureaucracy.

26. England

WHEN Henry, duke of Normandy and Aquitaine and count of Anjou, ascended the English throne in 1154, he found the royal power at its lowest point since the Conquest. The barons had extorted from Stephen and Matilda lands from the royal demesne, the homage and service of minor barons, and numerous hereditary offices. They had taken advantage of the civil war to fill their lands with strong castles. Moreover, Henry himself when he was waging war against Stephen bought baronial support with reckless promises of lands and privileges. If the barons had retained what they gained under Stephen and Matilda, and if Henry had kept his promises, the English monarchy would have been seriously weakened for a long time. Fortunately for his dynasty, Henry was not troubled by many scruples. He made almost no pretense of keeping his own promises. Moreover, he calmly ignored many of the grants of his immediate predecessor. He and Stephen had agreed that illegal castles, those built without the king's leave, should be destroyed. Henry was inclined to consider any castle that seemed dangerous to be illegal and either razed it or took it into his own hands. In the case of hereditary offices, Henry usually ignored the claimants and appointed his own men. Within a few years of his accession he had recovered most of the ground lost by the monarchy during the troubled reign of King Stephen.

King Henry promptly set to work to increase the royal power in every possible direction. Like the Norman kings he was determined to make the most of his rights as feudal suzerain of the English barons. Feudal custom required a vassal to seek his lord's leave before giving his daughter in marriage, and the Norman kings had always sold their permission at a good price—a very dubious procedure that Henry I had solemnly promised to abandon. Henry II improved on his grandfather's abuse of his rights. He obliged the barons to obtain his permission to marry their sons and charged a fee for granting it. When a baron whose title to his lands was not open to question was succeeded by his son, Henry usually felt obliged to accept what was considered the correct relief, £100, but if there was any cloud on the title or the heir was not a son, he demanded all he thought he could collect. He also devoted particular attention to increasing the value of the military service owed him by his vassals.

William the Conqueror had established the English military system in the belief that the 5,000-odd knights his vassals owed him were barely enough to defend the realm from Saxon revolts, raids by Welsh and Scots, and Viking invasions. All this had changed by the time of Henry II. No one was quite sure who was a Saxon and who a Norman, and certainly there was no question of a Saxon revolt. The Scandinavian kingdoms were no longer dangerous, and the Welsh and the Scots could be handled effectively by the barons of the border shires. It was on the continent that King Henry needed troops. There he was engaged in a long series of wars with Louis VII of France and his allies of the house of Blois.

The feudal levy of England, however, was of little use in Normandy. It was impossible to transport and supply 5,000 knights. Moreover, the feudal levy was bound to serve only for a limited term, and it could barely cross the channel before its term expired. Henry tried several devices to solve this. He asked for part of the service due for a longer term. But the most convenient solution was to allow his vassals to pay a sum of money for every knight owed and to use this money to hire troops. The only objection to this system was that it often enabled the barons to profit more than the king from a call to service. Most barons had enfeoffed more knights than they owed the king. Thus when Henry took a *scutage*, a payment by shields, the baron collected more than he paid. The earl of Norfolk owed sixty knights to the host, but he had enfeoffed 162. If the king levied scutage at one mark per fee, the earl paid sixty marks and kept 102 for himself. In 1166 Henry held a great inquest to discover how many knights his barons had enfeoffed and used the results to demand that they pay scutage on the entire number. The barons objected, and eventually the question was compromised: they were to pay on all fees created before the death of Henry I but not on later enfeoffments. This resulted in a large gain for the crown.

The chief contribution of Henry II to the development of the English monarchy was to extend the jurisdiction of the royal courts. Henry I had sent his judges through his realm to hear the pleas of the crown. Henry II set to work to increase their business. The only way a criminal case could be brought into court was by an "appeal," or formal accusation by the injured party or one of his friends or relatives. Under this system many criminals went unpunished. If a man who was slain had no friends or relatives, no one would bring an appeal. If the suspected criminal was a powerful man, it might be indiscreet to accuse him. Henry inaugurated the idea of having prosecution initiated by the government. He ordered that twelve men from every hundred and four from each township should appear before either his justices or the sheriff and state on oath whether anyone in their district was suspected of committing murder, robbery, or theft since the beginning of his reign. If they said someone was suspected, he was to be arrested and brought before the king's justices. There he was to be tried by the ordeal of water—that is, after certain religious formalities he was bound hand and foot and thrown into a pool, on the theory that water duly blessed would reject a guilty man and he would float. The innocent man would be accepted by the water and sink. Henry seems not to have had too much faith in the efficacy of this test. If a man was proved innocent but the twelve jurors still said they suspected him, he was to go into exile. This device of King Henry's was the ancestor of our jury of presentment or grand jury. It brought many more criminal cases into court and improved public order. Moreover, as the crown confiscated all the property of convicted criminals, it materially increased the royal revenue.

In the realm of civil law King Henry had equally ingenious ideas. His first step was to place possession of property under the protection of his courts. By the law of the day, the rightful owner of land could forcibly eject an occupant without fear of punishment. Hence, if a powerful lord claimed a piece of land and ejected its occupant, he could enjoy the property while his opponent attempted to establish ownership. King Henry decreed that if anyone ejected the occupant of land by force and without a court order, the injured party could complain to the chancellor. That official would issue an order to the sheriff to collect twelve men to appear before the king's justices to swear whether or not the dispossessed man had been ejected by force and without legal sanction. If the jury said he had been so ejected, he was replaced in possession, and the man who had seized the land was heavily fined. If the jury said he had not been so ejected, the complainant was fined for bringing a false charge. Thus possession was protected, and the king collected a fine no matter how the case came out. Cases of this kind were called "possessory assizes," the assize being the twelve men who gave the decision.

The invention of the grand jury and the possessory assize greatly increased the business of the royal courts without infringing on the jurisdictions of the barons. They were new procedures that had never existed before. But another of his devices was not so innocuous. Disputes regarding the ownership of land were heard in a feudal court if both parties were vassals of the same lord and in the county court if they held of different lords. The only method of trial was by battle. The plaintiff could not fight himself; he had to supply a vassal who believed his claim to be just. Presumably, however, he could choose the best warrior available. Trial by battle was obviously a hazardous affair and was unlikely to appeal to a man in possession who felt sure that his cause was just. King Henry provided for him an alternate procedure. The defendant could decline to accept the challenge to battle and could seek an order or "writ" from the chancery ordering the sheriff to gather twenty-four knights who would state on oath which party had the better right to the land. This procedure was called the "grand assize." Through it the royal courts took business away from both the feudal and popular courts.

In addition to taking cases from the feudal courts by means of the grand assize, King Henry interfered even more directly in their business. A litigant in a feudal court who felt that he had been treated unjustly could procure a writ transferring his case to a royal court. Thus if a widow believed that her husband's heir had not given her an adequate dower and the lord's court did not support her position, she could obtain a writ commanding the heir to assign her the dower she claimed or explain to the king's judges why he was unwilling to do so. Such writs could be used in almost any case to bring it before the royal justices.

These legal innovations of Henry II were the essential beginning of the common law. Common law meant law that was applied throughout the realm—that was common to all men and all regions. Each popular and feudal court had its own customary law, but the royal justices enforced the king's law wherever they went. Under Henry I the royal judges had used common law to decide the pleas of the crown, but this was only a small fragment of the total judicial business of the realm. As the jurisdiction of the royal courts was expanded by Henry II, however, more and more cases came or could be brought before his justices. A feudal court that knew that a case could be removed from it by a royal court was likely to try to decide the case by the common law. Thus gradually this law supplanted its rivals. And for about a century the common law expanded with great rapidity. Whenever a royal judge heard of an injury that seemed to need redress, he was inclined to invent a writ that would bring it into his court. This process was only stopped in the thirteenth century, when the barons insisted that the king and his judges stop making new law in this way. From that time on the common law could only be changed or added to by a "statute" issued by the king in parliament.*

Before leaving the subject of the beginnings of the common law, it seems worth while to discuss briefly the origins of the petty or trial jury. There was a long tradition in Anglo-Norman government of using a body of sworn men to testify as to facts; Domesday Book was based on information obtained by this means. Henry's judges began to use a jury of twelve men in a special way. When a jury of presentment said that it suspected a man of committing a crime, but he felt certain that he was innocent and that his neighbors knew him to be so, he could ask the judges to call a "jury of life and member" to state whether or not he was guilty instead of subjecting him to the ordeal. This device was particularly valuable to a man who had been accused by a private individual out of spite. But the defendant had to ask for this method of trial: he could not be compelled to place his fate in the hands of a jury. The ordeal by water was still the only legal means of trial.

In 1215, however, the Fourth Lateran Council condemned the ordeal and forbade the clergy to participate in it. As the ordeal was a "judgment of God," it was senseless without the aid of a priest. Thus the judges of England suddenly found themselves without any way of trying criminals. They did their best to persuade every accused man to ask for a jury trial. For a while they simply had to release those who refused. Then they invented an ingenious scheme. If a man refused to ask for a jury trial, he could not be convicted, but he was stripped, tied to a stone floor with a board on his body, and

* See p. 274.

heavy stones were placed on the board until he was crushed to death. The threat of this "*peine fort et dur*" was enough to persuade most defendants to ask for a jury trial. Hence the petty jury became the normal means of trying criminal cases.

The government of Henry II was not popular with his barons. They resented his efforts to increase their feudal services and to take cases away from their courts. They looked back longingly to their independence under King Stephen. At the same time Henry had alienated his eldest son Henry. King Henry could not help remembering the confusion brought to England by the disputed succession at the death of Henry I, and he wanted to be sure that there was no question about his successor. Hence he used the Capetian device of having his eldest son crowned as associate king. But while he gave young Henry a royal title, he did not give him lands or castles or even a regular revenue. This displeased the prince, and he entered into a conspiracy with his father-in-law, King Louis VII of France, and the dissident barons of England and Normandy. The result was a great baronial revolt combined with invasions of Normandy by Louis and of England by the king of Scotland. This was the supreme test of the administration King Henry had built, and that administration stood it well. Supported by a few loyal barons, the king's servants defended his realm successfully, and the revolt was suppressed. Henry forgave his son, but several barons spent long years in prison, and all the rebels saw their castles razed to the ground. The English crown was to have no more trouble with its barons until a new generation faced King John.

The sons of Henry II, Richard (1189–99) and John (1199–1216), continued their father's policy. They demanded heavy reliefs, made as much money as possible out of the military service due them, and sold heiresses to the highest bidder. They continued to extend the jurisdiction of the royal courts and the common law. Richard was an attractive man and a thoroughly bad king. He was handsome, gay, frank, open, and generous. A patron of poets, he wrote passable poetry himself. As the leader of a crusade he was usually in favor with the church. Moreover, he was by far the ablest soldier of his day. But during a reign of ten years he spent less than a year in England. War was his one delight, and his only interest in England was as a source of funds for his crusade and his bitter wars with Philip Augustus. Except for a few who plotted with John and Philip while Richard was in prison in Germany, Richard had no trouble with his barons. They liked him personally and feared wholeheartedly the weight of his sword.

John was a striking contrast to his brother: he was an able and conscientious king and a thoroughly unpleasant man. He worked hard at the business of government, sitting in person in his courts and at the exchequer, and devising ways to improve his administration. He saw a problem that had not greatly troubled his casual brother. The towns of England were growing, trade was flourishing, and the market for agricultural products was increasing rapidly. The merchants of the towns and the members of the feudal class who drew their income from agriculture were rapidly increasing in wealth. But the revenues of the crown were largely fixed and increased very little. John was determined to have his share of the new wealth. To some extent he could do this by demanding scutage more frequently, insisting on high reliefs, and charging enormous sums for favors granted by the crown. But he also tried novel devices. Henry II had levied an income and property tax to finance a crusade, and Richard had done the same to pay his ransom. John levied such a tax to raise a war chest. He also tried collecting customs duties. Convinced that the fixed sums paid by the sheriffs for the counties were grossly inadequate, he removed the sheriffs and replaced them with custodians who received a salary and paid into the exchequer all the money they collected. In short, John was an efficient monarch who strove to increase his power and revenue. As this increase was bound to be at the expense of his barons, his policy was deeply resented.

John lacked the one thing most necessary to the prestige of a mediaeval king, a reputation as a valiant fighter. Only once in his reign did he personally lead his troops in battle, in the surprise attack in which Arthur was captured. While he conducted successful campaigns in Scotland, Wales, and Ireland, his continental ventures were complete failures. He lost Normandy to Philip Augustus, and his great effort to crush the French king with the aid of the Emperor Otto ended in humiliating defeat.* Justly or not his people called him John "Softsword." He had at the same time a quality that no mediaeval king could afford—an inability to forgive. The best baron was turbulent and unruly. A king had to expect that during his reign he would quarrel at least once with every baron. Richard either crushed his foe completely or forgave him equally completely. John pretended

* See pp. 253–4.

to forgive but never again trusted the man he forgave. As result, by the end of his reign he trusted no baron and no baron trusted him.

This mutual distrust was made more acute by John's love of devious methods. Thus when John believed that a baron would soon ask him for a castle he thought he had a right to, the king would tell his constables not to deliver the castle to anyone unless the order to do so contained a countersign such as "I take you by your big toe." Then when the baron asked for a castle, John would cheerfully give him letters ordering its delivery to him and would even commiserate with him on the obstinacy of the constable who refused to obey. Finally, John was extremely lustful and cruel. He seduced the wives and daughters of his vassals. He pretty certainly ordered the murder of his nephew Arthur, and the wife and son of a baron who was out of favor were starved to death in a royal castle.

Throughout John's reign individual barons or small groups with personal grievances against the king had plotted against him. When he returned defeated from his continental campaign in the autumn of 1214, all his baronial foes joined together against him and held a great meeting to organize a revolt. With them met Stephen Langton, archbishop of Canterbury. Stephen had no reason to love John. The King had refused to accept him as archbishop and had kept him in exile for seven years.* He had driven his relatives from the realm. But Stephen was one of the great men of his age. He had been professor of Theology at Paris and a cardinal in the papal court. An expert in both theology and canon law, he had labored to explain the works of Peter Lombard and Gratian and apply their principles throughout Christendom. He believed that just as the church was ruled by canon law there should be a law to govern lay society—a law that king, barons, and people had to obey. He persuaded the barons to relegate their private grievances to the background and to draw up a general plan of reform that would appeal to all the barons of the land.

Early in the spring of 1215 the barons rose in armed revolt. John could not decide what to do. At one moment he was offering to negotiate, and at the next summoning troops from Gascony. Finally, with the aid of the citizens, who thoroughly hated John, the rebels occupied London. Protected by its walls they were in a very strong military position, and John gave way. The barons met the king in the Thames River meadows near Windsor at a place called Runnymede,

* See pp. 293–5.

and presented a written schedule of reforms—the so-called "Articles of the barons." John agreed to accept the demands and had his seal affixed to the schedule. Then the expert royal clerks went to work to draw up the formal charter that would embody these reforms. This document we know as *Magna Carta.*

The provisions of Magna Carta fall naturally into four groups. One of these comprises only one article, dealing with the relations between church and state. John promised the Church her full rights. Then fifteen chapters concern the feudal relations between the king and his vassals. John promised not to demand more than £100 for the relief for a barony, or £5 for a knight's fee. He also agreed not to levy a scutage or a special aid without the consent of an assembly of all tenants-in-chief of the crown. Thirty-five chapters deal with the procedures and practices of the royal government. For instance, John promised not to try to get more revenue from the sheriffs but to accept the customary "farms" or rents for the counties. Another chapter provided that civil cases between subjects of the king in which he had no interest would not be tried before the court that wandered about with him, but in regular sessions held at Westminster. These three divisions of Magna Carta comprise the reform program of the barons. The fourth was intended to satisfy their personal desires. The barons were promised their just rights, and a committee of twenty-five elected by them was to see that they got them.

Most of the provisions of Magna Carta were of purely temporary significance. Few had any real meaning a century later. There were, however, two notable exceptions. The promise by John that except for the three recognized occasions—the knighting of the king's eldest son, the marriage of his eldest daughter, or paying his ransom if he were captured—he would not levy an aid without the consent of a council composed of all his tenants-in-chief was not included in later reissues of the charter. The kings observed it in practice, however, and it became the basis for parliamentary control of taxation. Then, chapter thirty-nine states: "No free man shall be arrested, or imprisoned, or deprived of his property, or outlawed, or exiled, or in any way destroyed nor shall we go against him or send against him unless by legal judgment of his peers or by the law of the land." This famous passage forms the basis of the Anglo-American conception of personal freedom. The government can take no action against an individual without going through the proper legal procedures—what we call by "due process of law." And this promise was not limited to barons or knights, but applied to every freeman. Now it is true that in 1215 well under half the population of England was free, but as time went on and freedom spread, these rights spread with it.

Despite the importance of this clause protecting all freemen from arbitrary actions of the government, the significance of Magna Carta does not lie in its precise provisions. By issuing Magna Carta John admitted that he was subject to the law. This was of extreme importance. While one can argue that the feudal relationship was essentially a mutual contract and that all feudal suzerains were subject to feudal custom, the charter of liberties of Henry I and Magna Carta are the earliest explicit recognitions of this fact.* The generations that followed John fully realized this. Whenever the barons of England felt that the king was getting too autocratic but had difficulty in finding specific abuses to accuse him of, they simply demanded that he confirm Magna Carta. By so doing he recognized the supremacy of the law of the land. Thus Magna Carta served as a perpetual reminder to English kings that they were "limited monarchs."

John's son, Henry III (1216–72), was an exceedingly weak monarch. Throughout his reign he was governed by friends and favorites whom he chose with little discretion. For the most part they were foreign adventurers—relatives of him and his wife. After John's death, Queen Isabelle of Angoulême had married Hugh de Lusignan, count of La Marche, the son of the fiancé from whom John had stolen her. Her younger sons came over to seek their fortunes at the court of their half brother. Henry married Eleanor, daughter of the count of Provence, and her impecunious uncles sought soft berths in England. These relatives obtained offices and lands from King Henry and also tempted him into costly foreign ventures. Then Henry was a pious man who could not resist the pleas of the Pope, who was engaged in a bitter struggle with the Emperor Frederick II of Hohenstaufen.† The Pope persuaded Henry to allow him to raise large sums of money in England, and he involved the foolish king in a wild scheme to conquer Sicily for his second son. Hence, throughout his reign Henry needed money, and when he got it he had neither the will power nor the wisdom to spend it well. The barons resented his favor to his foreign relatives, his subservience to the pope, and his careless extravagance. Moreover, like many weak men Henry could be hasty,

* See p. 184. † See pp. 285–6.

capricious, and arbitrary when aroused, and he frequently violated what his barons considered their rights.

The chief political interest of Henry's reign lies in the efforts of the barons to control the king for the benefit of the realm and themselves. Although most of the baronial movements against Henry III were not basically selfish in their conception but were rather honest attempts to improve the government for the common good, the great lords were rarely able to resist the temptation to use any power they acquired to increase their own wealth and independence. Early in the reign the barons confined their opposition to attempts to get the king to spend his money wisely and efficiently. When this appeared to be hopeless, they started to refuse to grant him special aids. Finally under the leadership of Simon de Montfort, earl of Leicester, they took stronger measures. They forced the king to accept a baronial justiciar to head his government and baronial control of the royal administration. This was too much for Henry, and he attempted to crush his foes. This effort ended in his defeat and capture. For several years Simon de Montfort and his allies ruled England in Henry's name. Simon dreamed of an England governed by the feudal class working as a whole for the good of the realm, but once the victory was won he could not hold his baronial allies together. They quarreled fiercely over the spoils and resented every attempt to limit their rapacity. Henry's son, Edward, took advantage of this situation to negotiate with Simon's foes, escape from custody, and gather an army about him. Edward was a man of first-rate capacity both as a soldier and as a statesman. Moving with incredible rapidity, he surprised Simon's sons, who were marching to his aid, and dispersed their army. He then met and crushed Simon's forces at the great battle of Evesham. Simon was killed and his party completely destroyed.

One of the first tasks that faced Edward (1272–1307) was to recover the ground that the crown had lost during the civil wars of his father's reign. The barons had used this period of confusion to usurp privileges of all sorts—especially rights of jurisdiction. They had forbidden the sheriffs to enter their lands and had taken over their functions. They had stopped their tenants from attending the hundred courts and obliged them to carry their cases to their private courts. Edward decided to recover the royal rights usurped during the civil war and to prevent future usurpations. He ordered every lord who claimed any privilege that was legally a "franchise," or grant from the crown, to appear before his judges and prove his right to it. The lord must either show a royal charter or prove that he had enjoyed the privilege in King Richard's reign. Actually Edward did not deprive many lords of their franchises; he usually took a round sum of money for confirming a usurpation. But once a lord had listed the franchises he claimed, he could not claim new ones without a royal grant to support his position. Thus the usurpation of public rights by private individuals was stopped.

Another measure of Edward's stopped the growth of the feudal hierarchy and started its slow decline. By the second half of the thirteenth century continued sub-infeudation had made the feudal system incredibly complex. There could be six or seven lords between the man who actually held a piece of land in demesne and the king. This made it almost impossible to enforce feudal obligations. The scutage paid by the actual holder of the land got lost among his lords before it ever reached the king. Edward solved this by ignoring the intermediate lords to a large extent and collecting from the man in physical possession, but he also decided to stop the increase in sub-infeudation. This was done by a statute called "*quia emptores*." Before this time land could not legally be sold; it could only be given as a fief. If a man wanted to buy a piece of land, he offered its holder money to give it to him as a fief. Edward's statute allowed land to be bought and sold, but provided that the buyer should hold of the seller's lord. This effectively stopped the progress of sub-infeudation. While there were lords and vassals until the actual abolition of the feudal system in 1660, more and more men came to hold directly of the crown.

By Edward's reign the English administration had become definitely divided into specialized bodies. We have seen how the exchequer was established under Henry I and how the royal courts became important under Henry II. Although the exchequer and the *curia regis* had different functions, they shared the same personnel. The king was surrounded by a group of household officers and servants who acted as barons of the exchequer, as judges, and as councilors as the occasion might require. As time went on, however, each of these branches became specialized. There were four barons of the exchequer who supervised accounts and decided cases dealing with the king's revenue. The deputy of the chancellor who had sealed the orders summoning debtors to pay in the money they owed became an independent officer, the chancellor of the exchequer. Then two distinct royal courts appeared. The court of common pleas, consisting of four judges, heard all civil cases between subjects. The court of king's bench heard all cases, whether civil or criminal, that were of interest to the king. Finally, there was a group of sworn councilors who advised the king. Thus the functions of the ancient curia regis in England as in France became divided among specialized bodies.

Perhaps the most important development of the reign of Edward I was the appearance of an assembly that closely resembled later parliaments in form and purpose. The Norman and early Angevin kings had been accustomed to summon their great council, the assembly of all their prelates and barons, on certain formal occasions and whenever there was particular need. Their legislation was issued after consultation with this body. Thus the decree of Henry II that established the jury of presentment was made "with the counsel of all his barons." When John announced that he would levy an income and property tax in 1207 he specified that it was being done "with the common counsel and assent of our council at Oxford." No one knows just what the composition of this body was, but it probably did not include minor tenants-in-chief, men who held one or two fees directly of the crown. The council provided for in Magna Carta included all tenants-in-chief, but actually attendance at councils would have been too great an expense for the lesser men, and it is doubtful that they would have come even if summoned. At any rate, that clause was not included in reissues of the charter. Under Henry III the body that was asked to give its assent to special aids and that frequently declined to do so was the old great council of prelates and barons. In the reigns of Henry III and Edward I the meetings of this council were commonly designated as parliaments, that is, talkings or discussions. Thus, in the period under discussion most parliaments were simply assemblies of prelates and barons.

During the reign of Henry III knights elected in the county courts were several times summoned to meet with the great council as representatives of the lower feudal class—the rear-vassals. In 1265 Simon de Montfort summoned two knights from every shire and two burgesses from each borough to meet with the prelates and barons. Simon's purpose was to gain the support of the knights and the townsmen at a time when his baronial supporters were inclined to desert him. But the appearance of representatives of shires and towns as regular members of parliament seems to have grown out of fiscal needs. Taxation in mediaeval England was of two general types. Aids based on the knight's fee or on income were levied on the rural population, and tallage was collected from the royal demesne, which included most towns. As the prelates and barons were the lords of the countryside, it was felt that their consent was adequate authority for an aid. But by Edward's reign the government decided that such aids might be easier to collect if the consent of a wider group was sought. Hence it became customary to summon knights elected for this purpose in the shire courts to agree to a tax. Sometimes they met with the barons; sometimes they met separately. Meanwhile, since the time of Henry II, tallage had been levied on the towns by means of bargains with the taxpayers. The king's agents would go to a town and negotiate for a grant of tallage. At times the process was simplified by summoning representatives of the towns to a general meeting to agree to a tallage. Finally, if the king wanted to tax the clergy, he consulted a gathering of prelates and representatives of the lower clergy.

In 1295 King Edward I decided to gather all these elements together in one body. The members of the great council, the prelates and barons of the realm, were summoned individually, according to custom. Then, each bishop was ordered to bring with him the dean of his chapter, his archdeacons, one representative of the chapter, and two representatives of the parish clergy of his diocese. Finally, the sheriffs were directed to send two knights elected in the county court and two burgesses from each borough. Because this assembly contained all the ingredients of later parliaments, it has usually been known as the "Model Parliament."

By the end of the reign of Edward I it was generally recognized that only parliament could change or add to the common law and that its assent was needed before a tax could be levied. Parliament was also the highest court of the land, where the most important cases were decided. Parliament was considered the manifestation of the realm as a whole—king and people assembled together. But it would be a mistake to overemphasize the importance of the representative element. Many parliaments continued to be meetings of the prelates and barons alone. Sometimes when the commons were summoned, all the important business was finished before they arrived, and they were simply informed of the result. Even when they were present throughout the proceedings, they were completely dominated by the prelates and barons. Although the presence of the commons was important in theory and for the future, in the practice of the time it had little significance.

During the reign of Edward two steps were taken toward uniting all Britain in one realm. One of these was abortive, but the other was completely successful. Ever since the Norman conquest the barons and knights of England had been waging war against the Welsh and extending their lands at the latter's expense. As early as the reign of Henry I the lowlands of southern Wales and the rich river valleys running westward from England into Wales had been held by Norman lords. But the Welsh had held their own in their mountain fastnesses and from time to time they broke out to attack their foes. Again and again English kings led armies of knights into Wales. These armies marched along the valleys while the Welsh sat calmly on the hills out of their reach. During the civil wars of the reign of Henry III the Welsh had aided the Montfortian party. When he came to the throne, Edward was determined to crush them once and for all. He called out the feudal levy of England to move into Wales from the south and the east to drive the Welsh into their most remote hills. Then he summoned bands of infantry collected in the western shires to blockade them there. All around the central mass of mountains he constructed a line of great castles strongly garrisoned. Before long the Welsh were forced to submit, and Wales was divided into shires. While there were to be many Welsh risings, never again were they for long free from English rule.

In 1290 the death of Margaret the last of the elder line of the Scots royal house gave Edward an opportunity to extend his influence to the north. There were some dozen claimants to the Scots throne, and Edward I was asked to decide who was the rightful heir. His legal experts debated long and earnestly and finally awarded the throne to John Balliol, an English noble who was descended through a female line from the brother of a Scots king. John was obliged to do homage to Edward for the kingdom of Scotland. But when the English king attempted to make his suzerainty a reality by interfering in the government of Scotland, the Scots rose and drove Balliol out. Edward invaded Scotland and soon occupied the country. A revolt led by Sir William Wallace, a Scots patriot, was crushed and Wallace hanged. Soon, however, the Scots found another leader in Robert Bruce, also an English noble, whose grandfather had been Balliol's chief rival for the crown. While Edward was busy elsewhere, Bruce made considerable headway against his troops. Edward learned of the rising and moved north to suppress it, but he died on the Scots border. This gave Robert Bruce a breathing spell. By the time Edward II (1307–27) was ready to act against him, he had reduced all but one of the English fortresses in Scotland. Edward marched with a great army to relieve this stronghold, Stirling castle. By a small brook called Bannockburn he was met and utterly defeated by Bruce and his army. Scotland became once more an independent state under the rule of Robert Bruce.

27. *The Holy Roman Empire*

BEFORE his death in 1125 the last monarch of the Salian line, the Emperor Henry V (1106–25), had turned over his personal lands to his nephew Frederick of Hohenstaufen, duke of Swabia, and had designated him as his heir. But Frederick and his father had been firm supporters of the Salian kings against the princes and the papacy. Under the leadership of the archbishop of Mainz these two parties had combined to pass over Frederick and to elect as king Lothaire of Supplinburg, duke of Saxony.* Being essentially the creature of the papacy and the princes, Lothaire (1125–37) was a mere figurehead as king and emperor. Moreover, throughout his reign he was obliged to wage a bitter war with Frederick of Hohenstaufen, who had refused to recognize his election. Lothaire married his daughter and heiress to the head of another mighty princely house, Henry the Proud, duke of Bavaria, who thus became his apparent heir. The papacy and the princes, however, considered the master of both Saxony and Bavaria fully as dangerous as the duke of Swabia. They wanted a weak king. Hence they turned their eyes toward the rival house of Hohenstaufen. They chose not its chief but his younger brother, who was elected king as Conrad III (1137–52). This, of course, simply increased the tempo of the civil war between the houses of Welf and Hohenstaufen, and Conrad's reign was a period of almost complete anarchy.

The princes of Germany preferred a weak king, but they did not want continual internal confusion. For one thing, they needed a period of peace to consolidate the gains they had made at the expense of the Salian house. Then anarchy favored the mass of petty lords whose

* See p. 171.

castles now covered the land and who had become a serious menace to princely authority. Hence when Conrad died in 1152, the princes were ready for a king who could maintain order. They chose Frederick of Hohenstaufen, called Barbarossa, duke of Swabia, the son of Lothaire's bitter foe. It seemed an ideal choice. Frederick was head of the house of Hohenstaufen, nephew of Conrad, and great-grandson of Henry IV. He was also the first cousin of the new chief of the house of Welf, Henry the Lion, duke of Saxony and Bavaria. And whether or not the princes knew it, Frederick was in addition a statesman of the first rank who was fully the peer of Henry II of England and Philip Augustus of France.

When Frederick (1152–90) came to the throne the royal demesne of the Salian kings was sadly depleted. Moreover, during the reigns of Lothaire and Conrad the princes of Germany had made great progress in establishing themselves as semi-independent rulers. The only firm basis of power that Frederick possessed in Germany was his own duchy of Swabia. The new king had two obvious choices. He could set to work to recover the Salian demesnes, especially those in Franconia and southern Saxony, and attempt to reduce the power of the princes. That would certainly involve war with his cousin Henry the Lion, who coveted Goslar and the district dependent on it. The other was to adopt the policy that had always tempted Swabian dukes—expansion into the kingdom of Burgundy and Italy. If he could build a firm power and collect an ample revenue in these regions, he could have a strong state even though his authority in Germany was limited. And once well established in the south he might be strong enough to reconstitute the German monarchy along the lines planned by Henry IV. It was this second alternative that Frederick chose. He gave Swabia itself to Conrad's son Frederick, and Goslar to Henry the Lion. At the same time he made Austria into a duchy to balance Henry's power in Bavaria and strengthened the hands of Henry's rival in the north, Albrecht, called the Bear, another scion of the house of Billung. Thus, having pacified and created competition for Henry the Lion, Frederick left Germany to the princes. He took their homage and insisted on their recognizing their feudal obligations to him as their suzerain, but he also gave them a free hand in curbing the lesser lords, who were obliged to become their vassals. Germany had at last become a feudal state.

In 1156 Frederick married Beatrice of Burgundy and in her name took possession of that kingdom. The next step in his program was the

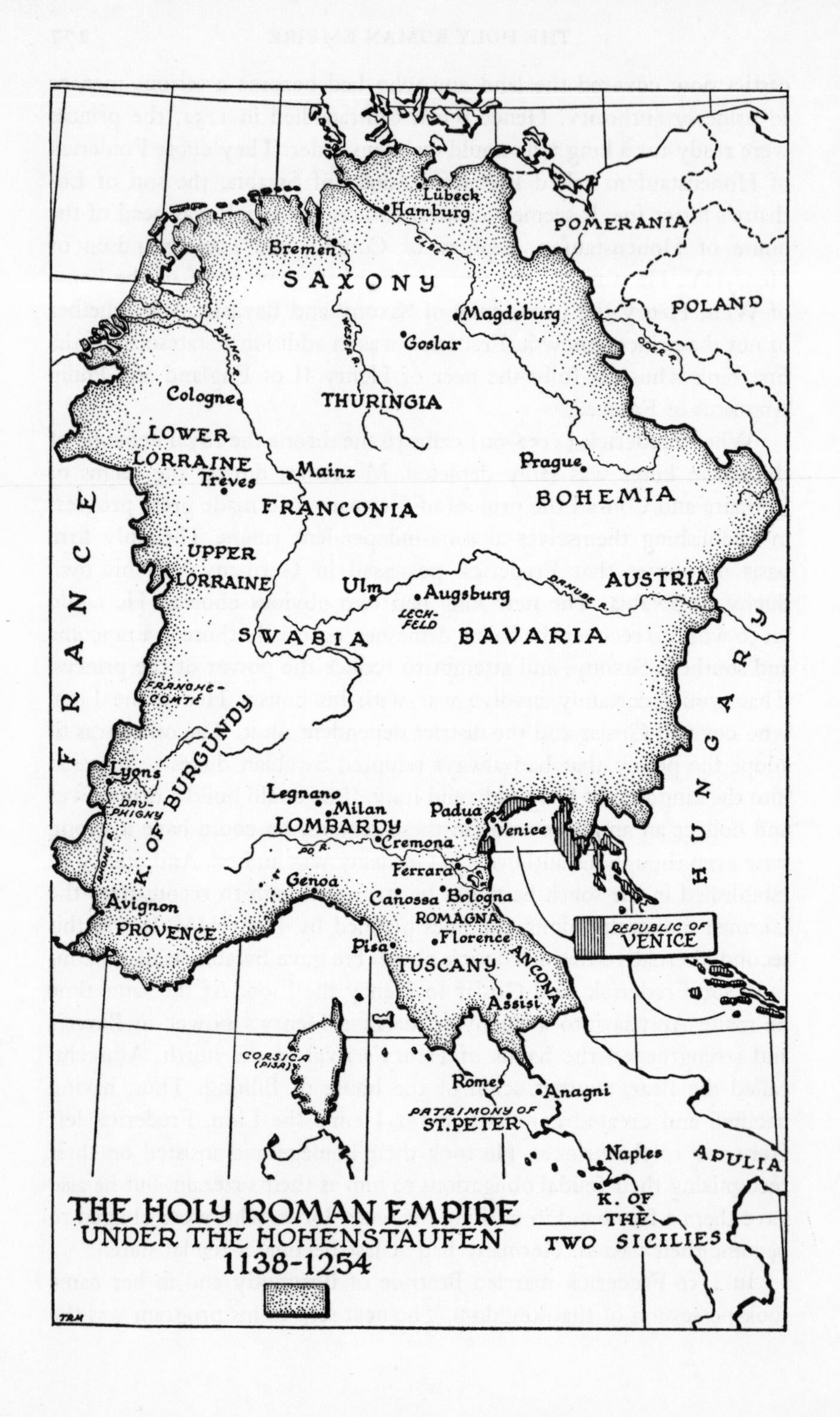
Lübeck
Hamburg
POMERANIA
Bremen
SAXONY
POLAND
Magdeburg
Goslar
Cologne
THURINGIA
LOWER
LORRAINE
Trèves
Mainz
Prague
BOHEMIA
FRANCONIA
UPPER
LORRAINE
Ulm
Augsburg
AUSTRIA
LECH-
FELD
SWABIA
BAVARIA
FRANCHE-
COMTÉ
FRANCE
HUNGARY
Lyons
K. OF BURGUNDY
DAU-
PHIGNY
Legnano
Milan
Padua
LOMBARDY
Venice
Cremona
Ferrara
Genoa
Canossa
Bologna
Avignon
ROMAGNA
REPUBLIC OF
VENICE
PROVENCE
Pisa
Florence
TUSCANY
ANCONA
Assisi
CORSICA
(PISA)
Rome
Anagni
PATRIMONY OF
ST. PETER
Naples
APULIA
K. OF
THE
TWO SICILIES
THE HOLY ROMAN EMPIRE
UNDER THE HOHENSTAUFEN
1138-1254

restoration of the imperial authority in Lombardy. Since the reign of Henry IV a great political revolution had taken place in that district. The nobles and merchants of the cities had deprived the bishops of their political authority and had established self-governing communes.* As the bishops had also been counts and in that capacity the emperor's agents, many of the powers taken over by the communes were imperial ones. The Lombard communes were engaged in bitter rivalries among themselves, and the country was burdened with continual wars. Milan, the most powerful of the cities, had established an extensive hegemony, but her position was being fiercely contested by a group of cities led by Cremona. Hence the cities were in no position to resist the imperial authority effectively. Frederick marched into Lombardy and claimed the rights of the Lombard crown. He had no desire to restore the bishops, but he insisted that he have a voice in choosing the officials of the communes, that these officials recognize that they were his agents, and that he receive a regular revenue. Moreover, he insisted that the authority of these town officials be confined within the city walls and that imperial officials exercise the emperor's rights in the countryside.

Outside of Lombardy three men dominated Italy—Frederick's uncle, Welf VI, lord of Tuscany and Spoleto; the pope; and William I, king of Sicily. William's grandfather Roger I had built the Norman kingdom of Sicily into a strong feudal state comprising the island of Sicily and the Italian peninsula south of Rome.† Roger had been a staunch ally of Gregory VII against Henry IV, and the kingdom of Sicily was held by its rulers in theory at least as a fief from the papacy. Neither the pope nor the king of Sicily wanted to see a restoration of imperial authority in Italy. Hence, when Milan rose in revolt, they formed an alliance with her against Frederick. But for the moment the Emperor was too strong and enjoyed the support of Welf VI. In 1162 Milan was captured and largely destroyed. Frederick filled Lombardy with wild German knights, who ruled with a heavy hand. Soon these imperial agents had roused all the communes to desperation. They put aside their quarrels and combined in a general federation, the Lombard League. When Frederick moved to suppress them, in 1176, they routed his army at the great battle of Legnano.

Frederick's defeat at Legnano was to a great extent the result of troubles in Germany. Henry the Lion and his princely allies had re-

* See pp. 232–3. † See p. 198.

fused to send their troops to his aid. Shortly after Frederick's defeat of Milan in 1162, Welf VI of Tuscany had gone over to the papal party, and this naturally did not improve the relations between the houses of Welf and Hohenstaufen. In 1167 Frederick of Swabia died without heirs, and the duchy reverted to the Emperor, giving him a firm base in Germany once more. He then moved to recover the old Salian demesnes in the north and deprived Henry the Lion of Goslar. When Frederick asked Henry's aid against the Lombard League, the Duke offered to give it in return for Goslar, but Frederick refused to agree. After Legnano the Emperor returned to Germany determined to crush his foe. Soon he had his opportunity. Henry the Lion was ambitious and arrogant. He seized church property and engaged in a fierce quarrel with a group of bishops. Frederick summoned him to court as his vassal and deprived him of all his fiefs. Henry the Lion retired to the court of his father-in-law, Henry II of England, and Frederick was master of Germany. The duchy of Saxony was split in half and the western part, Westphalia, given to the archbishop of Cologne, while the eastern section went to Bernard of Anhalt. Bavaria was given to Otto of Wittelsbach, ancestor of the present claimants to its throne.

Having secured his position in Germany, Frederick returned to Italy, but this time he used diplomacy rather than war. In 1183 he made peace with the Lombard League. The communes were left independent, but their officials recognized that they were imperial agents and the cities paid a large annual sum for the exercise of imperial jurisdiction. Moreover, the League promised to aid Frederick in establishing his power in Tuscany and Spoleto. The Emperor's next step was to deprive the papacy of its chief ally by coming to an agreement with Sicily. Frederick's son and heir, Henry, was married to Constance, sister of King William I and aunt of the then king, William II. This alliance enabled him to ignore the papacy. Tuscany, Spoleto, and Ancona were divided into administrative districts and placed in the charge of German counts. These officials exercised jurisdiction and collected extensive revenues. Since the few large cities of Tuscany, such as Florence, were left outside this system as free communes, Frederick's policy met with little resistance except from the helpless pope, who insisted that most of these lands belonged to him.

Frederick Barbarossa had established a new empire, and one essentially different from the one that had been ruled by the Saxon and Salian emperors. They had aimed at a strong, centralized German kingdom with imperial appendages in Burgundy and Italy. Under Frederick, Germany was a feudal monarchy where outside his own duchy of Swabia and a few royal demesnes such as Goslar he was simply a suzerain of the princes. The bulk of Frederick's revenues came from outside Germany—from Burgundy, Lombardy, Tuscany, Spoleto, and Ancona. The centers of his political authority were Swabia and central Italy. In addition to laying the material foundations for his imperial regime, Frederick had attempted to give it a sound theoretical basis. After the fall of the Salian line the triumphant popes had continually asserted that the imperial title was a benefice granted by the papacy. The emperor was chosen by the pope and could not exert imperial authority until he had been crowned in Rome. The revival of the study of Roman law enabled Frederick and his advisers to see very clearly that the Roman emperors had been themselves vice-regents of God on earth and independent of any other authority. Frederick announced that Charlemagne and Otto I had been emperors by right of conquest and as such had enjoyed the full privileges of the Roman emperors. He was Otto's rightful successor. He also took steps to emphasize the sacred character of the imperial office. Charlemagne was canonized in 1165; unfortunately by an anti-pope, so that he did not for long enjoy that status. Frederick was the first monarch to use the term "holy empire." While for convenience we have followed the usual custom of calling the empire of the Saxons and Salians the Holy Roman Empire, the term becomes strictly appropriate only in the time of Frederick I.

It is impossible to judge the soundness of Frederick's conception of the Empire, because we do not know what his plans for the future were. An imperial authority resting on bases as far apart as Swabia and Tuscany could not be very solid. There were, however, forces in Germany that would have supported an attempt to revive the royal power there. The towns were growing rapidly in wealth and size, and they were openly hostile to the princes and in favor of a strong monarchy. If Frederick's successors had used the resources drawn from Central Italy to build their power in Germany, the future history of that land might have been quite different.

Frederick Barbarossa was drowned in 1190 crossing a river in Asia

Minor while leading the vanguard of the Third Crusade to recover Jerusalem from the Seljuq Turks.* He was succeeded by his son, Henry VI (1190–97), who was already king of Germany and hence assured of the succession. The new emperor was faced with several major problems. The dispossessed chief of the house of Welf, Henry the Lion, had found a firm ally in the new English king, his brother-in-law Richard I. Well supplied with English money, he was stirring up trouble in Germany. In Italy the papacy was still bitterly hostile to the house that had deprived it of a large part of its estates. The opposition of the pope was particularly serious because a great temptation lay before Henry—the crown of Sicily. King William II (1166–89) had died without children to succeed him, and the throne had gone to his cousin Tancred (1190–94), count of Lecce. Tancred was illegitimate, and his aunt Constance, wife of Henry VI, had a much better claim to the throne; but the Sicilians had no enthusiasm for being ruled by a German prince. There was, however, a strong party favoring Constance, and it seemed most unlikely that Tancred could withstand the power of Henry VI if he chose to assert his wife's claim.

Henry VI paid little attention to his German kingdom. He visited it long enough to take the captive King Richard of England from the duke of Austria and to arrange for and collect the first installments of his ransom.† He also obliged Richard to do homage to him and gave him the purely titular dignity of king of Burgundy. Perhaps he hoped that these arrangements would put an end to English support of the house of Welf. If such was the case, he was disappointed. Richard returned to England more hostile than ever to the house of Hohenstaufen. Then, in 1194, Henry moved south and invaded Sicily. Soon he was completely in possession of the Norman kingdom and had placed German officials in its key administrative posts. He was then at the height of his power; master of a truly impressive empire comprising Germany, Burgundy, all Italy, and Sicily.

With the Norman kingdom Henry took over the dreams of extensive Mediterranean conquests that had long possessed its kings.‡ No sooner was the Emperor secure on the Sicilian throne than he began to plan a conquest of Greece and a crusade to Palestine. But before embarking on these adventures he needed to come to an agreement with the pope and the German princes. The future integrity of the vast

* See p. 215. † See p. 252. ‡ See pp. 198–9.

state he had constructed depended on the election as king of Germany of the heir to the Sicilian crown, Henry's young son Frederick. Moreover, Henry fully realized the importance of making the German crown hereditary and thus removing the succession to it from the control of the princes. He offered the princes a bargain. If they would agree to declare the German monarchy hereditary, he would recognize the full hereditability of their fiefs. As at the time no king had admitted that the fiefs were hereditary except in the case of the succession of a son to his father, this was a decided concession. But the great ecclesiastical princes, who largely controlled the election and coronation of the German king and who had no interest in the inheritance of fiefs, kept the other princes from accepting. They agreed to crown Frederick, but would go no further. Forced to be satisfied with what he could get, Henry next turned to the pope. He offered him a large annual income from all the churches of the empire in return for the lands claimed by the papacy. But the specter of one man ruling all Italy except Rome and its immediate vicinity was too terrifying for the pope, and he declined to accept the terms. The negotiations were interrupted by a fierce Sicilian revolt. Henry suppressed it savagely, but died almost immediately afterwards.

It looked at first as if Henry's untimely death would do no great harm to his empire. The German officials who ruled in Sicily and Italy held their places with firm hands. Henry's younger brother Philip of Hohenstaufen hurried to Germany and was accepted as regent for his young nephew Frederick. But this opportunity was too good to be passed over by the house of Welf. Henry the Lion was dead, but his second son Otto was living at the English court. King Richard supplied him with plenty of money and sent him into Germany to seek his fortune. By generous use of pounds sterling Otto rapidly gathered a party of princes and was elected king of Germany in 1198. This moved the supporters of Philip of Hohenstaufen to urge him to take the crown—advice which he promptly followed. Thus Germany had rival kings and another civil war. That same year saw an even more serious blow to the house of Hohenstaufen. Innocent III (1198–1216), a man of high ambition, invincible determination, and great capacity, was elected to the papal throne. Innocent was absolutely determined to prevent the combination of Sicily and the Empire. As long as those two states were in separate hands, the papacy could hope to play one against the other. When they were under one ruler, the pope could do little. Hence Innocent III lent his support to Otto.*

Unfortunately Otto was not very bright and had almost no real support in Germany. Philip of Hohenstaufen was able and generally liked and trusted. Soon Otto had retired to England once more, and Innocent was sadly contemplating the necessity of making terms with Philip. Suddenly in 1208 the whole situation changed. Philip was murdered by a private enemy, and Otto quickly obtained control of Germany. In 1209 he was solemnly crowned emperor by the pope. But Innocent was soon disillusioned about his ally. While he had promised to give the papacy the lands it claimed, he made no move to do so. Worse yet he gathered his forces for an invasion of Sicily. Innocent promptly excommunicated him and declared him deprived of the imperial title. Rarely can a great pontiff have been in as unpleasant position as was Innocent at this time. In all the Empire there was but one man who could hope to defeat the excommunicate Otto—Frederick of Hohenstaufen, king of Sicily. Innocent hesitated a long time. It seems likely that Frederick's cause was urged by King Philip Augustus, who had no desire to see John's ally Otto master of Germany.† At any rate, Innocent finally swallowed his extremely well-grounded fears and crowned young Frederick as emperor.

In 1212 Frederick entered Germany. On the way there he had met and formed an alliance with Philip Augustus, and it was King Philip who solved his immediate problems in his German realm. The battle of Bouvines in 1214 broke the power of Otto and made Frederick master of Germany. But Frederick was half Sicilian in blood and more so in taste. He found Germany a cold, damp, gloomy country with altogether too many swamps and forests. While he stayed in his northern kingdom until 1220, he did so only to organize it so that it would need the least possible attention, and after his departure he returned only for brief visits. In his organization of his German realm Frederick followed his grandfather's general policy with much more consistency—one might say with abandon. He gave the princes practically everything they asked for. Their fiefs were made fully hereditary, and they were given complete powers of jurisdiction. The king promised not to build fortresses or levy taxes in the lands of the princes without their consent. He even delivered over to the princes the last firm bulwark of the royal power, the German towns. Some years later, when his

* See pp. 290–1. † See pp. 253–4.

eldest son Henry as king of Germany tried to modify this policy and prevent the complete disintegration of the royal authority, Frederick sided with the princes against him, and Henry died in his father's prison. Needless to say, this method of handling the princes was successful only in one sense; it kept them quiet. Once they had gained everything they wanted from Frederick, they took no interest in his fortunes and cheerfully refused to aid him in his Italian campaigns.

Frederick was a remarkable man who captured the imagination of his own contemporaries and has exercised the same charm over later writers. He was highly educated and highly intelligent, a poet and a patron of poets. He had been brought up in the Sicilian court, which was deeply imbued with Moslem culture. He was rumored to have a harem filled with Moslem beauties. While his antagonism to the church has often been exaggerated, he was certainly far less devout than most monarchs of his day. The priestly, even the papal, office filled him with little awe, and he had not the slightest objection to entering into friendly relations with Moslem princes. When he went on a crusade, he did no fighting whatever, but concluded a treaty that gave him far more than he could ever have won by arms.* In short, he was exactly the type of monarch that would not be thought well of by the papacy no matter what realm he ruled. When in 1220 he left Germany, determined to build Italy into a centralized state dominated by the Norman kingdom of Sicily, he became almost at once a deadly foe to the papacy.

There is no need to trace Frederick's activities in detail. For some sixteen years he labored to consolidate his power in his Sicilian kingdom and in central Italy. In the latter region the German officials of his father and grandfather were replaced by Sicilians, who were even less popular. During this period Frederick strove earnestly to come to terms with the Pope. He even offered to restore a fair part of the lands claimed by the see of Peter. But the Pope could not accept his share in such a bargain: permitting Frederick a free hand in the rest of Italy. Moreover, Frederick was determined to reduce Lombardy to submission and filled it too with his Sicilian agents. Soon the Lombard League had revived under papal encouragement and was waging war against the Emperor. The Pope contributed money collected from the churches of all Christendom to aid the war against Frederick and did his best to persuade the princes of Europe to intervene. As Henry III of England

* See p. 217.

had nothing to intervene with and St. Louis of France, though a pious and devout monarch, had little sympathy with the more extreme claims of the papacy, this last effort came to nothing. But Frederick could not defeat his foes. Deserted by the German princes, his resources in men and money were not sufficient to defeat the forces of the League in the field and then reduce their walled towns. His reign is a long and involved tale of excommunications, temporary reconciliations with the church, battles, and sieges. When he died in 1250, Lombardy was still unsubdued.

The death of Frederick II marked for all practical purposes the end of the house of Hohenstaufen. In 1251 his son Conrad (1250–54), who had been ruling as a helpless figurehead in Germany, came to Italy, but he died in 1254 without accomplishing much. His half brother Manfred, an illegitimate son of Frederick, became king of Sicily. But the Pope, who had excommunicated Conrad and preached a crusade against him, was equally hostile to Manfred. He approached Henry III and offered him the Sicilian throne for his second son, Edmund of Lancaster. Then, when it became clear that the English barons were not going to supply Henry with the means to invade Sicily, the Pope called in Charles, count of Anjou and Provence, brother of Louis IX of France. In 1266 Charles conquered Sicily and established the Angevin dynasty there. Meanwhile the German princes had made sure that no strong king would appear to trouble them by electing two rival foreign princes, neither of whom had any real support in Germany. Then in 1273 they chose as king Rudolf, count of Hapsburg, a petty lord who was not even a prince. Although Rudolf (1273–92) used his position very effectively to lay the foundation for the future greatness of his house by marrying his son to the heiress of Austria, he did nothing to increase the authority of the German crown. In fact there was but little that could be done. The princes of Germany had become masters of the realm, and they had no intention of permitting a revival of effective royal authority. Essentially Germany was no longer a single state but a loose alliance of princes under the vague suzerainty of an elected king.

In closing the discussion of the political history of the three great states of Western Europe during the twelfth and thirteenth centuries, it seems well to recapitulate briefly. By the early fourteenth century both France and England had developed strong royal governments based on similar institutions. While the English parliament and the

French estates general, the English exchequer and the French chambre des comptes, and the English central courts and the French parlement were not exactly alike, the differences between them were not essential. Both were feudal monarchies with the same general conception of the nature and limits of the royal power, and in both the king exercised authority and commanded resources that were not feudal. The provincial charters of liberties issued by the sons of Philip IV were similar in purpose and general nature to Magna Carta. There were, however, several important differences between the two countries.

Except for the palatinates of Durham and Chester, all England was fully subject to the royal government, while in France the large areas ruled by the feudal princes remained outside its authority. Moreover, the English common law had spread both widely and deeply over the realm, largely replacing local custom. In France the law of the parlement of Paris dealt only with the pleas brought before it. Even in the royal demesne there was a wide variety of local customary law. Perhaps this was the fundamental reason why the nobles of France acted by provinces instead of combining together, as had the knights and barons of England on several important occasions. Finally, the personnel of government in the two countries was basically different. The members of the English central government in London were paid professional royal servants, but the local government was largely in the hands of unpaid local landholders. The sheriff had become an office limited to one year and hence essentially powerless. It and other local offices were held by knights and squires chosen by the king but deeply rooted in their localities and not financially dependent on the crown. In France, on the other hand, both central and local officials formed a closely integrated bureaucracy of professional royal servants. In France the government was already becoming something separate from the people, both noble and common; while in England the local government was an integral part of the ruling class.

The Empire had moved in a far different direction than its sister states. After the death of Frederick II the imperial government largely disappeared. The Norman kingdom of Sicily became once more independent under the house of Anjou, while the pope regained the papal states. In the rest of Italy the communes and local lords were left without a master and turned once more to bitter warfare among themselves. Burgundy split into smaller divisions such as Provence, Dauphigny, and the Free County of Burgundy, all of which were soon to be absorbed by the growing power of France. Germany itself became a loose federation of princes headed by an elected king. A powerful prince might use the resources of his own estates to exercise some real authority, but when he did so it was usually to increase the strength of his own dynasty rather than that of the crown. Under a purely elective monarchy no prince who might hold the throne was likely to be much interested in the institution of monarchy. His interests were bound to be personal and dynastic. In short, the popes had won their struggle with the emperors. The Empire had been completely destroyed and the German monarchy rendered impotent.

CHAPTER X

Mediaeval Theocracy at its Height

28. Papal Monarchy in Full Flower
29. Albigensians and Waldensians
30. The Friars

N THE thirteenth century the mediaeval Church reached the apex of its spiritual, intellectual, and temporal power. The papal monarchy perfected its organization and expanded its authority over both ecclesiastical and secular affairs. The integration, development, and application of canon law was continued steadily, culminating in the *Decretals* of Pope Gregory IX. The theological system enunciated by Peter Lombard was interpreted, broadened in scope, and explained in terms of the new knowledge acquired during the period. The result of this process is seen in the monumental *Summa Theologica* of St. Thomas Aquinas. As the ardor of the monastic orders cooled with the passage of time, their place as leaders of the spiritual world was taken by the new mendicant or begging orders.

This same century saw bitter rebellion against both the spiritual and temporal authority of the Church and the papacy. It was an age of heresy, of well-organized heresy powerfully rooted in popular favor. Never since the beginning of the Middle Ages had the spiritual authority of the Church been so effectively challenged. Moreover, as the power of the lay monarchs grew, their impatience with papal dictation became more dangerous. The century was marked by the long, fierce struggle between the papacy and the emperors and by bitter skirmishes with other monarchs. Fortunately for the Church the close alliance between spiritual and political opposition, between heretics and lay princes, that was to mark the Reformation never became more than a vague threat in the thirteenth century. The Church triumphed over its foes. While heresy was not wiped out, it was driven underground and ceased to be a danger to the Church's spiritual monopoly. The Empire was completely destroyed and with it the German monarchy. Italy and Germany fell into the state of mild anarchy that was to last until the nineteenth century. Yet in the very victory of the Church lay the seeds of future defeat. The sword that had been taken up by Gregory VII was far too tempting an instrument. It served to crush the heretics and to destroy the Empire, but its very effectiveness alarmed the secular world.

28. Papal Monarchy in Full Flower

In 1198 the College of Cardinals elevated to the papal throne Lothar Conti, who took office as Innocent III (1198–1216). This thirty-seven year old scion of a powerful noble house was well prepared for high office in the church. After studying theology at Paris and law at Bologna, he had served in the curia under five popes. He had a thorough command of both theology and canon law and a clear, incisive, orderly mind. Although he was imbued with the most exalted ideas of the function of the papal office and was extremely ambitious to increase its power and prestige, he was in no respect a fanatic. Although he always aimed high, he was willing to accept the best he could obtain and attempt to make the most of it. Unfortunately, he was more interested in the political authority of the church than in its spiritual welfare and was too prone to use the secular sword to further both political and spiritual ends. He was the greatest of mediaeval popes both in ability and in achievement, but he laid the foundation for the later rapid decline of the papacy.

When Innocent ascended the papal throne, he found himself immediately involved in the political affairs of two great states, the Empire and France. The late Emperor Henry VI (1190–97) had died in possession of a large part of the patrimony of St. Peter and of the kingdom of Sicily, which was a papal fief. Innocent was determined to recover the papal lands and to separate Sicily from the empire. The Pope took young Frederick II under his protection and supported his right to the kingdom of Sicily while he supported Otto of Brunswick against Philip of Hohenstaufen in the empire. But when an assassin removed Philip and enabled Otto to triumph, Innocent found that he had been over optimistic. Otto showed no intention of restoring the papal lands and made clear his intention of conquering Sicily. The Pope then threw his support behind Frederick II, who was able to secure the imperial throne.* Innocent had exerted enormous influence in this struggle for the empire. He had kept Philip of Hohenstaufen from an easy victory and had obtained the imperial title for Otto. Unfortunately the eventual result was exactly what he had been trying to avoid—the union of Sicily and the Empire. And instead of the mild, gentle, and rather pious Philip the imperial throne was occupied by the ambitious, cruel, and almost totally irreligious Frederick II.

Innocent's participation in the contest for the imperial crown was bound to affect his relations with other states. Otto was the nephew of the English kings Richard and John. Richard had financed the beginning of his struggle against Philip of Hohenstaufen and had left him a large sum of money in his testament. While John was not sufficiently interested in Otto to give him the entire legacy, he did furnish considerable financial support. Thus as long as Innocent favored Otto, he was anxious to keep on good terms with John. Philip Augustus, on the other hand, had always been friendly to the house of Hohenstaufen. Hence Innocent was inclined to distrust him, until the papal policy changed to match his.

In addition to the disagreement with Philip Augustus over the rival claimants to the empire, Innocent III inherited a controversy over the domestic affairs of the French king. In 1193 King Philip had married a Danish princess, Ingeborg, partly for a large marriage portion in cash, and partly in the hope that the Danish fleet might aid him in an attack on England. But he had barely seen his new queen when he felt an overwhelming personal distaste for her. Two years later he persuaded a group of French prelates to annul the marriage on the usual ground of consanguinity. As there was no blood relationship between them, the decision was a triumph of political power rather than of ecclesiastical justice. Ingeborg and her Danish relatives appealed to

* See p. 284.

Rome, and the aged Pope Celestine III (1191–98) declared the annulment void. King Philip cheerfully ignored the Pope's pronouncement and in 1196 married Agnes, daughter of the Duke of Meran, a south Bavarian lord. Innocent III was not the man to allow a king to defy the papacy in a matter so clearly in its sphere. A legate was sent to persuade Philip to give way and if he refused to lay an interdict on France. As the King refused to yield, the interdict was imposed, in January 1200. Philip was not anxious to risk the weakening of his influence in France through the resentment caused by an interdict. Moreover, in July Agnes died, and the King's interest in the question became less acute. He submitted, and the interdict was removed in September. But Philip had simply agreed that his annulment was void; he had reserved the right to reopen the case, and he promptly did so. Not until 1213, when Philip had sound political reasons for an accord with Innocent, was Ingeborg formally restored to her position as queen of France.

From the very beginning of his reign King John of England was a source of trouble for the Pope. As the supporter of Otto of Brunswick, Innocent was anxious to get John to pay Otto Richard's legacy. John loaned Otto money and paid some of his debts, but he showed no inclination to turn over the whole legacy. Then the pope was the natural protector of widows, and John made no move to provide a dowry for his brother's widow, Berengaria of Navarre. Innocent wrote letters that were usually ignored. When he grew insistent, John promised to provide for Berengaria, but never actually did so. It was, in fact, King Philip who finally cared for her. When he conquered the Angevin lands, he gave Berengaria the city of Le Mans as a dowry.

Another source of friction was John's illegitimate brother Geoffrey Plantagenet, archbishop of York. Geoffrey was both haughty and cantankerous. He quarreled continually with his chapter and with his royal brother. Whenever John grew sufficiently annoyed, he expelled Geoffrey from his see. Each time Innocent managed to patch up the quarrel, only to have another break out soon after. Another archbishop unpopular with John was John Cumin of Dublin. The King had driven him into exile and absolutely refused to allow him to return to his see. This matter too led to endless papal letters that had little or no effect until King John felt the need to clear up old quarrels to prepare for new and better ones. In 1204 the see of Winchester, one of the richest in England, fell vacant, and John secured the election of his favored servant, Peter des Roches, by the simple expedient of putting the rival candidate and his supporters in chains in a royal prison. Peter was a shrewd and able diplomat who was able to persuade the Pope to confirm his election, but Innocent spent several years and many letters trying to get the defeated party out of John's prison. In short, it seems clear that only Innocent's desire to keep on good terms with Otto's uncle gave him the patience to suffer John for so long a time.

The death in July, 1205, of Hubert Walter, archbishop of Canterbury, started a long, bitter quarrel between the English king and the pope. Hubert had been an independent prelate whom John feared and respected but never liked. When he died, the King was determined to replace him with one of his favorites, John de Grey, bishop of Norwich. As soon as he heard of Hubert's death, the King hastened to Canterbury and made the monks who formed the cathedral chapter agree not to take any action toward electing an archbishop until December. Presumably John wanted this time to prepare the way for his favorite. But at least part of the chapter met secretly, elected their own sub-prior, and sent him off to Rome to seek confirmation of his election from the pope. He was instructed not to reveal his election until he reached Rome. Unfortunately the sub-prior could not keep a secret, and soon John learned that he was calling himself archbishop-elect. The King went to Canterbury in a fine fury, and the terrified monks denied the earlier election and obediently chose John de Grey, who in turn set out for Rome to seek confirmation of his election. Thus Innocent was faced with a double election. He heard both stories and annulled both elections. The election of the sub-prior was obviously dubious as it was held by only part of the chapter, in secret, and without the King's permission. But once any election was appealed to Rome, no other could be held until the pope made a decision; and hence John de Grey's election was invalid. Innocent then directed all the interested parties to send delegates to Rome with power to act.

When the delegation from the chapter arrived, it was called into the Pope's presence and ordered to elect an archbishop. The delegation split evenly between John de Grey and the sub-prior. Innocent then suggested the election of Stephen Langton, a canon of York, a noted theologian, and a cardinal. The monks accepted this idea and unanimously chose Stephen. Then John's representatives were asked to give the royal assent, but they stated that they had been authorized to give it only to John de Grey. The Pope then wrote to John announcing the election and asking him to accept Stephen. To this the King replied in violent terms that Stephen was personally objectionable and chosen without his assent. He also sent agents to Canterbury who expelled the monks and seized the property of the Christ Church abbey into the king's hands.

In June 1207 Innocent consecrated Stephen Langton as archbishop of Canterbury and gave him the pallium. He thus challenged King John directly. The result was a long and complicated struggle which can only be outlined here. In March, 1208, England was placed under interdict and in November, 1209, John was excommunicated. It seems likely, though it cannot be proved, that late in 1212 Innocent issued letters deposing John and ordering Philip Augustus of France to drive him from his realm. During all this time there were continual negotiations between the two parties. At first John insisted he would never accept Stephen, but by 1208 he had weakened a little. He would accept Stephen if the Pope would agree that the affair would not constitute a precedent and that in the future no election of an archbishop of Canterbury would be valid without the king's assent. This was John's avowed position during the rest of the controversy. Innocent was unwilling to grant John's demands in full, and the King was in no hurry to have the quarrel settled. When the interdict was declared, he seized all the property of the church and the clergy, and as long as the struggle lasted vast revenues streamed into his coffers. Neither interdict nor excommunication bothered him in the slightest degree, however much they might trouble his people. Finally in 1213, when Philip Augustus was mustering a host to invade England, John gave way in style. He accepted Langton and promised to repay the money extorted from the church. Then he surrendered his kingdom to the pope and received it back as a fief to be held from the papacy.

On the central issue in this famous controversy both Innocent and John were right. It was the pope's duty to see that worthy men received high church offices. Stephen Langton was fully qualified for the post of archbishop of Canterbury. He was an Englishman, a distinguished scholar, and an able and devoted ecclesiastical statesman. His rival John de Grey was a pure courtier and civil servant. On the other hand, no king could agree that he had no control over the choice of the primate of his realm. The archbishop of Canterbury was an important political personage and the holder of a very large barony. The King had to insist that he be acceptable to him. On the basis on which the quarrel started Innocent won a resounding victory: John accepted Stephen without conditions. Moreover, he greatly added to the prestige of the papacy by becoming its vassal. But by 1213 John's needs had changed. His barons were restive, and he felt the need of support against them.* Here John came out ahead. Innocent firmly supported him against the barons, and when Langton, who sympathized with the barons, hesitated to enforce the Pope's orders against them, he was suspended from office. And John never repaid any major part of the money he had taken from the church. In short, this quarrel had an unusually happy ending; both sides won.

These three great controversies show clearly the power wielded by Innocent III. He twice chose an emperor, he forced Philip Augustus to receive Ingeborg as queen, and he obliged King John to submit. Thus he won major struggles involving the heads of the three chief states of Western Europe. There were similar victories in lesser states. The king of Aragon became a papal vassal, and the pope obliged the king of Portugal to recognize his predecessor's homage to the Holy See. The king of Castile was forced to give up his wife because of too close blood relationship, and he too became Innocent's vassal. While this vassalage to the papacy had little practical effect, it increased the prestige of the pope, and to some extent his revenues, as each vassal monarch was expected to pay an annual tribute. Innocent's influence over the secular world is further demonstrated by the fact that he was able to launch three crusades—two against the infidel, and one against the heretics of southern France.† While the crusade of 1204 was diverted to the conquest of Constantinople, its organization was almost entirely the result of the Pope's preaching. Here again Innocent got things done; though not what he had originally planned. In short, throughout his reign Innocent III was the leader of Christendom in a sense that no previous pontiff had been.

The exércise of authority over powerful secular princes was possible only to strong popes, and the activities of Innocent III supply the best illustration of the process. The general development of the organization, resources, and power of the papal monarchy, however, was a continuous affair and cannot be effectively discussed in terms of individual pontiffs. Great popes made important innovations, but lesser ones with able servants did equally well. Hence we must turn from the intriguing personality of Pope Innocent to follow topically some of

* See p. 268. † See pp. 216–17, 310–13.

the broad features of the development of the Church and the papacy during this period.

Throughout the twelfth and thirteenth centuries the activities of the papal curia and its agents expanded enormously. The system of papal delegates was used more and more extensively. If one wished to carry an appeal to the papal court, all that was absolutely necessary was to send a letter to the pope outlining the case and suggesting suitable delegates. While the pope could, of course, select his own judges delegate, he seems usually to have followed the suggestions made in the appeal. Usually the appellor sent an agent to Rome; and if the agent were not himself an expert in canon law, he hired local legal talent to press his case. Gifts to members of the papal court were considered as very useful, if not necessary. By the thirteenth century the volume of cases carried to Rome and heard by judges delegate was extremely large. They ranged from the attempt of a petty knight to get rid of his wife to the resounding quarrels between Duke Peter of Dreux and the bishops of Brittany. It was this system of comparatively easy appeal to Rome that made the canon law truly universal. It also kept the pope in close touch with the problems involved in the internal organization of the church and in its relations with the lay world. All major controversies and many minor ones eventually found their way to Rome.

During this same period the use of papal legates was greatly increased. Wherever the pope felt the need of an agent with wide powers, he despatched a legate. A legate was sent to England to accept John's submission and another to lift the interdict and reconcile the English king with his clergy. When John died, leaving young Henry III under age, the Pope ordered his legate to safeguard the interests of his youthful vassal. Actually the legate and the regent, William Marshal, earl of Pembroke, ruled England jointly for several years. When Blanche of Castile was regent of France for her minor son, Louis IX, the Pope sent a legate to support her. Then legates were appointed to guide such major papal enterprises as the suppression of the Albigensian heretics and the crusade. While legates entrusted with particular missions were usually members of the papal court, legatine commissions were sometimes given to local prelates. Thus when Richard I of England went on the crusade, his justiciar who was to rule England in his absence was granted legatine authority. In fact, the continuous rivalry of the archbishops of York and Canterbury made it impossible for anyone but a legate to hold a council of the whole English church. But legatine commissions to local prelates were simply a means of granting extra authority where it seemed needed. It was the members of the papal court acting as legates who carried the pope's influence into every corner of Europe. Through them he could lessen the effect of the chief hindrance to his government—the vast extent of Christendom.

This tremendous extension of papal activity required corresponding development of the central administration at Rome. Perhaps the most important branch of the papal court was the chancery. Except for the comparatively rare occasions when a legate or *nuncio* was sent from Rome, the pope's commands, decisions, pleas and exhortations had to be conveyed in writing. While important letters must have been dictated by the pope himself, routine letters were probably composed by his officials. As precision of statement was of enormous importance, this work required a skilled staff. It was necessary to develop set forms and formulas to make successful forgery more difficult. Forgery of documents was a favorite mediaeval pastime. Every king, even most barons, had established forms for important documents, and every charter carried a list of those who witnessed its issuance. Forging charters of local magnates was rather hazardous, as these witnesses could be consulted, and many men knew the proper forms. But the cardinals who witnessed papal letters were a long way off, and the forms of the papal chancery were less widely known. Hence forging papal letters was a very common practice. One obvious way to discourage forgery and also to give the pope a record of his and his predecessor's actions was to keep a register of all letters sent. These registers became very full and highly developed under Innocent III and his successors. The papal chancery developed earlier and more rapidly than those of the lay monarchies of Western Europe, and the monarchies used it for a model to a great extent.

The enlarged personnel and increased activity of the papal administration raised its cost, and the popes were continually trying to find new sources of revenue and to improve the yield of the old. As lord of the Patrimony of St. Peter, the states of the Church, the pope had revenues similar to those of other temporal lords. Demesne manors and towns paid annual rents. There were tolls on bridges, sales taxes at fairs, and the profits of justice. Most of the feudal vassals of the pope paid an annual rent in addition to other services. When Innocent III recovered the papal lands that had been usurped by Frederick I and Henry VI, he reorganized the entire Patrimony and greatly increased the revenue drawn from it.*

The early popes had several sources of income outside their own lands. Beginning in the ninth century, various monastic foundations asked for and received papal protection against lay or ecclesiastical lords. These houses were taken under the permanent protection of the pope and paid an annual sum for the privilege. As these rents were usually small, the total income from this source was not great. Certain countries paid the papacy an annual tax called Peter's Pence. In theory every hearth in these lands paid a penny a year. This tax was established in England by the tenth century and is supposed to have been extended to Denmark by King Canute. An English cardinal serving as legate in Norway and Sweden in the twelfth century probably established it in those countries. It was also paid in Poland. In England, at least, most of the tax was pocketed by the local collectors, and the pope received the very modest sum of £200. Innocent III tried vigorously to remedy this situation but was unable to make any progress. Another resource was the tribute paid by kings and princes who became vassals of the papacy. By the end of the thirteenth century, Portugal, Castile, Aragon, Sicily, and England owed annual tribute. The English tribute was a thousand marks—a very substantial sum. The kings did not pay their tribute very regularly, however, and this source of revenue was essentially unreliable.

From at least the eleventh century, the popes occasionally asked gifts from the prelates of Christendom as a whole or of a particular region. These levies were called subsidies and consisted in theory of voluntary grants of lump sums. Actually, of course, they were no more purely voluntary than the "gracious aids" collected by secular princes from their vassals. Although subsidies were sought only when there was some special need for funds, almost any papal requirement was considered an adequate excuse for such a levy.

In addition, popes began in the thirteenth century to collect income taxes from the clergy. These had their origin as did several other sources of papal revenue in measures taken to finance crusades. Before the Third Crusade both Henry II and Philip Augustus levied income taxes in their kingdoms on both clergy and laity, with the pope's consent, to pay the costs of the expedition to recapture Jerusalem from

* See p. 283.

Saladin. In 1199 Innocent III levied an income tax to finance his crusading plans. In 1228 the pope demanded a tenth of the income of the clergy to pay the costs of his war against Frederick II. From that time on such taxes were levied whenever the pope needed large sums for any purpose that he could claim was of importance to the Church. Actually he did not succeed in getting any very large proportion of the money collected. Kings did not like to have the resources of their realms drained off by the pope, and he usually had to give the local ruler a large share of the proceeds in order to secure permission for the levy.

One of the most important types of papal revenue was closely connected with the pope's efforts to control appointments to church offices. When the investiture controversy was ended by compromises that were on the whole favorable to the secular princes, the papacy resorted to another line of attack.* By the end of the twelfth century the pope maintained that if any prelate died while in Rome, he had the right to appoint his successor. Soon this claim was extended to any prelate who died within two days journey of Rome. The pope also insisted that in the case of a disputed election he had the power of appointment. As he was inclined to call any failure by a chapter to reach a unanimous decision a dispute, this would give him wide powers of appointment. Innocent III went so far as to declare that the pope had the right, whether or not he cared to exercise it, to dispose of all ecclesiastical benefices. The result of these various claims was that by the end of the thirteenth century the pope appointed most of the prelates of Christendom. This was not actually a victory over the secular princes, as the pope practically always appointed the king's nominee in return for such other favors as minor benefices for non-resident Italian clerks. As a rule king and pope cooperated effectively for their mutual benefit.

From very early times the pope had received gifts when he made or confirmed an appointment. As time went on, these gifts were made regular obligations called "services," and their payment was enforced by excommunication if necessary. Before the thirteenth century papal appointments and confirmations were on the whole confined to archbishops and the abbots of the great monasteries that depended directly on the pope. But as Innocent III and his successors extended the appointing power, more and more prelates owed the services. The serv-

* See p. 135.

ices proper seem to have been set at a third of the annual revenue of the benefice, but additional fees of various sorts brought the total to nearly a whole year's income. This yielded an extremely large revenue to the papacy, and was a considerable hardship on the Church. A series of short episcopal reigns could ruin the finances of a diocese. Closely related to the services were the "first fruits," also a part of the first year's revenue of a benefice. Before the thirteenth century these had been collected by lay and ecclesiastical lords from men they appointed to church offices. Bit by bit the papacy established a monopoly for itself in collecting first fruits. They were paid by prelates who did not pay services.

A highly lucrative and extremely controversial source of papal income was the sale of indulgences. According to the doctrine of the church a truly repentant sinner who confessed and was absolved was relieved of the menace of hell; but a blemish remained on his soul that had to be removed either by a stay in purgatory or by performing an act pleasing to God—by penance.* Penance could take a wide variety of forms, such as prayers, fasts, and pilgrimages. The number of days of purgatory that the sinner was relieved of varied with the severity of the penance. Rather early the church began to accept gifts for pious purposes from penitents physically unable to perform penance, and later penance in the form of money given to the church became common. But except in a few cases involving kings and great lords, such gifts in lieu of penance were local affairs and had nothing to do with the papacy.

At the head of the list of good works available to the men of the Middle Ages stood a crusade. The crusader received a "plenary indulgence," that is, complete relief from purgatory for sins duly repented of and confessed. Many men took the cross who were for one reason or other unable to go. Some were too old or too sick. Others could not leave their responsibilities at home. These people were allowed to receive the crusaders' indulgences for contributing money to the crusade. By the middle of the thirteenth century the collection of this money was highly organized. Local prelates collected the money and gave it to the actual crusaders to help cover their expenses. But while the fall of Acre practically ended the crusades, it did not end plans for crusades and the selling of crusading indulgences. While

* See pp. 139–40.

part of the money went to prospective crusaders, much went to the papal treasury.

Indulgences were frequently offered for other purposes than the support of the crusades. If money was needed to repair a church or for some other worthy local purpose, the pope could declare indulgences for all who contributed. Sometimes all the money was used for the designated purpose, but usually the pope took a third or a half. Early in the fourteenth century the papacy began the practice of issuing indulgences in connection with jubilees or Holy Years. In 1300 Pope Boniface VIII (1294–1303) offered a plenary indulgence to all who visited the churches of St. Peter and St. Paul in Rome a certain number of times during the year. No money was asked for these indulgences, but the papacy drew large sums from the voluntary gifts made by the pilgrims. In 1350 another jubilee was held, under similar arrangements.

In 1390 the system was improved. People who did not make the journey to Rome could obtain the indulgences by paying amounts equal to the gifts they would have made and the cost of the journey. Finally the papacy began to sell indulgences "as of the jubilee." For several years after 1390 people could buy indulgences as if it had been the jubilee year. The jubilee indulgences were extremely profitable to the papacy. While the bulls authorizing them made clear that they were of benefit only to those who were truly penitent and had confessed their sins, there is reason to believe that not all local collectors were sufficiently careful to explain this to their customers. Certainly, popular opinion in much of Europe thought of jubilee indulgences as all that was necessary to obtain salvation.

The chief financial officer of the papacy was the chamberlain who ruled over the *camera*, or financial branch of the administration. He was assisted by a treasurer and a group of highly trained clerks. They kept careful records of all the sources of papal revenue and audited the accounts of the local collectors. Before the fourteenth century these local collectors were usually either prelates of the region or legates sent to collect a particular levy. Later, permanent collectors were appointed to handle all the various types of revenue in their districts. The collectors turned the money over to the representatives of organizations that were able to transfer it to Rome. Before the middle of the thirteenth century this function was a monopoly of the

Knights Templar. Thus they would receive papal revenues in their houses in London or Paris and pay it to the pope's treasury in Rome. By 1250 Italian merchant houses had enough scattered agencies so that they could engage in this business, and soon they were doing it all. The collectors paid their money to the agents of the merchants, and the merchants turned it over to the papal treasury. It was a highly profitable business. While the money was in their possession, the merchants could use it for their own purposes. Moreover, the mere fact that they were the pope's agents and hence under his special protection facilitated their general business. A fair part of the banking activities of such houses as the Medici consisted of the transfer and safekeeping of papal funds.

29. Albigensians and Waldensians

THE SAME era that saw the papacy and the Church at the apex of their power brought serious threats to their position from two directions. In the twelfth century Peter Lombard and Gratian had placed theology and canon law on firm bases by reconciling all divergent views that could be found in the mass of knowledge available in their day. The *Sentences* and the *Decretals* became the standard authoritative textbooks, on which all study and instruction in these subjects were based.* Men like Stephen Langton interpreted these works and applied them, but they made no change in their essential nature. Peter Lombard and Gratian, however, were to suffer from one of those strange ironies so common in history: their supposedly final statements were obsolete almost as soon as they were written.

The contemporaries of these two scholars knew little or nothing of the thought of Aristotle, but within a generation his complete works were to be available in Western Europe. The Arab conquerors of a large part of the Hellenistic world had absorbed its learning and added to it in many ways. The Arab philosopher Avicenna, who lived in the late tenth and early eleventh centuries, had made extensive commentaries on the works of Aristotle and made it an integral part of Arabic thought.† In the second half of the twelfth century Avicenna's work was taken up by Averroes, a scholar of Moslem Spain who made his own commentaries on the writings of the famous Greek philosopher.

* See p. 138. † See pp. 57–8.

At that time many scholars of Europe were becoming aware of Arabic learning, and men like John of Salisbury had agents in Spain procuring Arabic manuscripts and translating them into Latin. Soon the commentaries of Averroes were so well known in Europe that he was called "the Commentator," as Aristotle was called "the Philosopher."

The theological system of the Christian Church had been founded on Neoplatonism, and centuries had been devoted to molding it into the form it held in the twelfth century. The mere fact that Aristotle's thought was different from Plato's would have made it a disturbing influence. But in the form in which his works first reached Western Europe they were the writings of a pagan philosopher commented on by Moslem scholars and translated into Latin by men whose grasp of both Arabic and Latin had distinct limitations. Needless to say this "new knowledge" gravely threatened the theology established by Peter Lombard and with it, the intellectual supremacy of the Church. By the beginning of the thirteenth century certain enthusiastic followers of Averroes were condemned as heretics.

The new learning came from outside Christian Europe and affected only a few scholars. While its long-range threat to the bases of Christian theology was grave, its immediate effects were not very dangerous. Far more menacing were ideas that were deeply rooted in the ideals and teachings of Christianity itself. Christ had preached absolute poverty. A camel could go through the eye of a needle, as easily as a rich man could enter heaven. The apostles were commanded to take no thought for the morrow. In the early, enthusiastic, and persecuted Christian community all property had been held in common. The idea that poverty was absolutely necessary to the ideal Christian life was a fundamental concept in monasticism. No monk or nun could own anything; all property belonged to the community as a whole. And this was no merely technical theory of ownership. The religious was forbidden the exclusive use of property of any sort. While the regular clergy had maintained the importance of poverty, the secular clergy had allowed this ideal to trouble them very little. The wealth of the church had steadily increased, and the way of life of the higher clergy had grown more and more luxurious. As we have seen, their property not only drew them away from apostolic poverty but also involved them deeply in temporal affairs. Abelard had seen the problem clearly and had advocated the abandonment of all church property not absolutely necessary for the support of the clergy and the cult. In the twelfth century many earnest Christians were profoundly disturbed at the striking contrast between the wealth and luxury of the secular clergy and the apostolic ideal of poverty. Some of these men became convinced that poverty was necessary for salvation and formed groups devoted to its practice.

The enthusiastic devotees of poverty were a continual source of embarrassment to the secular clergy. They could not deny that a life of poverty was pleasing to God; the Church had approved the monastic rules embodying this principle. But neither could they fail to realize that those who practiced poverty created a contrast with their own way of life. The bishops were the successors of the apostles, but it was the regular clergy that avowed the full apostolic ideal. The monastic orders in general were not very disturbing in this respect. While no monk could own property, the order could, and most monks lived in considerable comfort. The layman was unlikely to feel that the way of life of a Benedictine or Cluniac monk differed very strikingly from that of the secular clergy. The Cistercians, especially in their early days, had been a different matter. They had practiced poverty and simplicity as an order.* As result, they were cordially disliked by the more luxurious orders and by the secular clergy. Although the way of life of the Cistercians created an embarrassing contrast, they did not attack the wealth of the secular clergy or the clergy themselves for owning property. Hence they could be resented, but no attack could be made on their position. There were, however, groups that were more aggressive and constituted a direct threat to the church. These groups were of two sorts. Some were simple devotees of poverty who believed poverty to be necessary to salvation and wanted to preach their belief. Others were heretics whose fundamental beliefs differed from those of the church, and who gained popular favor because of their practice of poverty.

Among the many sects that competed with Christianity in the Roman Empire was that of the Manichaeans. As its doctrine contained elements that savored of Zoroastrianism, scholars have been inclined to believe that it originated in Persia. During the fourth and fifth centuries this sect was strong in the eastern part of the empire and in North Africa. After the sixth century, one hears nothing of the Manichaeans in the West, but a few probably continued to operate in secret. In the eleventh century, reinforced by missionaries from the

* See pp. 143–5.

Balkans, they reappeared as Cathari, or "the pure," and began actively to spread their faith. Although their chief strength lay in Lombardy, Tuscany, and southern France, scattered communities were established throughout France and Germany. Their one attempt to enter England discouraged further efforts. King Henry II seized the entire group of missionaries, flogged them, branded them, and turned them out to freeze and starve to death in the wintry countryside.

The original Manichaeans were not heretics but pagans. While their doctrine contained elements similar to certain Christian beliefs, they were essentially followers of an independent religion. The Cathari are hard to classify. Close association with Christians and centuries of competition with Christianity had increased the resemblance between their faith and Christianity. The situation is further confused by the fact that many groups of heretics, such as the Waldensians, adopted some of the beliefs and practices of the Cathari. In short, it seems clear that the true Cathari were Manichaeans rather than Christians, but they were enough like Christians to be called heretics in Western Europe.

The basic feature of Catharan doctrine was belief in a dual supreme deity—God and Satan, good and evil. God created and ruled the spiritual world, and Satan the material. This doctrine was essentially Manichaean and non-Christian. As all material things were produced by Satan, the perfect life according to the teachings of the Cathari was extremely ascetic. Its devotees had to be absolutely celibate and could eat no animal food. They could not possess property of any sort. The problem as to how a sect with these principles could survive was solved by having two classes—the *Perfecti* and the *Credentes*. The Perfecti were bound to lead the ideal life of rigid asceticism. They constituted the priestly class. They were inducted into this grade in a ceremony called the *Consolamentum*, which was conducted by two Perfecti. The Credentes could live much as they liked; they could marry, eat meat, hold property, and follow any career. Their only obligations were to renounce their obedience to the Christian Church and to receive the Consolamentum before they died. This ceremony wiped away all previous sins, but it could not be repeated and hence was usually performed when a Credentis was about to die. In fact, there was a feeling that the proper course was to commit suicide after the ceremony to avoid the danger of sinning. The Cathari did not believe in eternal damnation. A soul was obliged to live again and again in human bodies until it achieved salvation.

As a large part of our knowledge of the beliefs of the Cathari come from the writings of their Christian enemies, the best known features of their doctrine are those that directly opposed the teachings of the Church. The Cathari maintained that as Christ disapproved of sacrifices, it was wrong to speak of the mass as a sacrifice, and they believed that the doctrine of transubstantiation was blasphemous. They rejected infant baptism on the ground that only the mature could understand what was involved in such a ceremony. They denied the power of saints to aid men. Any sexual intercourse, even that sanctified by a marriage ceremony, was mortal sin. It was wrong to kill any living creature. The Cathari absolutely refused to take an oath of any sort. The rejection of important articles of the Christian faith was enough to make them the foes of the Church and of all devout laymen. Their refusal to take oaths made them particularly dangerous in an age when the cohesion of society depended so largely on the oaths binding one man to another.

The chief appeal of the Cathari lay in the ascetic life led by the Perfecti. While some of their foes charged the Perfecti with carrying their asceticism to absurd lengths such as testing their devotion to celibacy by sleeping naked with women, in general even their persecutors admitted that they adhered rigidly to their strict way of life. Thus they offered a striking contrast to the Catholic clergy who lived in luxury and whose moral conduct was not always above reproach. In fact, it is fairly clear that the regions in which the Cathari flourished most were those in which the Catholic clergy were especially negligent of their obligations. Pious Christians, especially the poor and lowly, observed this contrast between the two priestly classes and were strongly drawn toward the Cathari. It is also likely that the extreme freedom allowed the Credentes was attractive to many people. Especially in the gay land of southern France the idea of living as one pleased without worrying about sin and then achieving salvation through a deathbed ceremony was most alluring.

During the course of the twelfth century there appeared in various parts of Western Europe little bands of men who preached and practiced apostolic poverty. Some of their beliefs were similar to those of the Cathari, but they do not seem to have actually been members of that sect. The most noted of their leaders were Peter of Bruys and Henry of Lausanne. Peter was a priest in southern France who became a wandering preacher in that region and gathered a band of followers.

Henry covered more ground. He is first heard of preaching in Le Mans in 1116, and he later visited Tours, Reims, Bordeaux, Albi, and Perigeux. At first Henry was simply an enthusiastic preacher of reform who attacked the luxury of the clergy, but in southern France he met Peter and adopted from him various Catharan ideas. In general, this seems to have been the pattern followed by these leaders and their groups. They started as devotees of poverty and critics of the Church's wealth and later adopted definitely heretical ideas. This was certainly the course followed by the most important chief of an heretical movement—Peter Waldo.

Peter Waldo was a prosperous merchant of Lyons who added to his profits by the practice of usury. In 1173 he happened to hear a wandering minstrel recount the story of St. Alexis, the son of a wealthy Roman noble who gave up his position and his inheritance to live in poverty and celibacy as a wandering beggar supported by alms. The tale made a profound impression on Peter Waldo and that night he decided to emulate St. Alexis. He told his wife to choose between his personal and real property to keep for her support. When she chose the real estate, Peter began to give away his personal property. First he repaid all the usury he had taken. Then he made generous gifts to several worthy causes. The remainder of his money he simply distributed to the poor of Lyons. Once rid of his property, he proceeded to beg his bread from door to door. This hurt his wife's pride, and she appealed to the archbishop of Lyons. Peter was ordered not to beg from anyone but his wife. Still, he had begun his life of poverty.

As soon as he began to follow the apostolic way of life, Peter Waldo wanted to learn its precise nature from the original source—the Bible. Since he could not read Latin, he persuaded two priests to translate parts of the New Testament for him. Armed with these, he began to preach his conception of the way of life taught by Christ. Soon others joined him and went about the countryside preaching. Now the church's interpretation of the Bible had been slowly constructed over many centuries. Naturally unlettered men who read the text might reach rather different results. In 1178 word reached the archbishop of Lyons that Peter and his followers were making grave mistakes in their preaching. According to canon law no one could preach without a license from his bishop, but this rule had not been enforced very vigorously. The archbishop, however, used it to silence Peter and his followers: they were to stop preaching in public. Peter

Waldo was puzzled. He and his followers were repeating memorized passages from the New Testament and preaching the Christian life as they found it there. How could this be wrong? Gathering a small group of followers, he journeyed to Rome to appeal to the pope. He found the pontiff presiding over the Third Lateran Council, which had been summoned to deal with the Cathari. Peter and his followers were examined by learned clerics. It soon became clear that they had no intention of attacking the doctrines or practices of the Church but that through ignorance they made interpretations of the Bible that were heretical. The pope approved their plan of living in poverty, but he forbade them to preach without the permission of their bishop.

As their study of the New Testament had convinced them that preaching was a necessary part of the apostolic life, Peter Waldo and his followers ignored the pope's prohibition. They preached with new vigor over a steadily widening area. In 1181 the pope condemned them as heretics along with the Cathari, and in the same year a new archbishop of Lyons expelled them from his diocese. They then spread over the neighboring regions and became especially strong in southern France where they competed for converts with the local Cathari, who were called Albigensians because their center was in the town of Albi.

The basic purpose of the followers of Peter Waldo, who were called variously the Poor Men of Lyons and Waldensians, was to live the perfect Christian life as taught by Christ. Had they been willing to give up preaching, no one would have troubled them. But they regarded this as a vital part of the apostolic life and refused to cease. Thus they committed two offenses: preaching without license and refusing to obey the authorities of the Church. Yet for some years they went no further and made no attacks on the church or its doctrine. Only when they were finally condemned as heretics and persecution began did they take the offensive against their enemies. They then declared that Christ had taught the way of life that led to salvation and that his teachings could be read in the New Testament. All that men needed to achieve salvation was to learn what Christ commanded and live accordingly. The church and its sacraments were completely useless. As their ideas developed further, they were inclined to state that they were the true successors of the apostles because they lived the apostolic life. The Catholic prelates who did not strictly follow Christ's teachings were no true successors to his apostles. It seems likely that their condemnation as heretics in 1181 was basically unjust;

they were at that time simply disobedient enthusiasts. But soon they became actual heretics and attackers of the very foundations of Catholic doctrine.

There were obviously a number of ways by which the church could combat the heretics. The simplest and most direct was the use of force. The heretics could be condemned by the ecclesiastical authorities and executed by the secular government. This method was used sporadically throughout the twelfth century. Henry II flogged and branded a group of heretics, forbade anyone to aid them, and left them to freeze and starve to death in the wintry countryside. Many heretics were burned to death by the princes of Europe. On one occasion the count of Champagne burned a fair-sized band. In regions where the heretics were few in number and lacked the sympathy of the secular princes, they could easily be exterminated by force. But in Southern France, where they were strongest, this method was of little use. Although comparatively few nobles actually joined the heretic sects, the majority of them, headed by the count of Toulouse, were extremely sympathetic towards them. Moreover, the heretics were so numerous that their extermination would mean the depopulation of the land. Hence the feudal lords of southern France turned a deaf ear to the church's pleas. A somewhat similar situation existed in parts of Lombardy and Tuscany. In some towns the Cathari were the dominant power; and in others they were far too numerous to be destroyed by their fellow townsmen, even if the latter had not sympathized with them, as they frequently did.

Another possibility was to convince the heretics of the error of their ways by argument. In the latter part of the twelfth century many optimistic clerks tried to do this by holding disputations with the heretics, but needless to say they had little success. Men who have consciously defied the clergy and denied the validity of their teachings were not likely to be won over by arguments, no matter how logically or eloquently they might be presented. A more promising method would have been to remove the abuses criticized by the heretics by reforming the clergy. This too was attempted, but not even the great Innocent III could make much progress. Given time and determination, the papacy might have reformed the church in the affected regions by careful supervision of ecclesiastical appointments, but it was extremely difficult to remove a man once he was in office. It took Innocent III long years of bitter struggle to remove an archbishop of Narbonne who did not even bother to reside in his diocese and completely neglected its affairs. Any rapid reform of the personnel of the church was out of the question. There was one other possible device. The church could not remove the unworthy clergy, but it could add to its organization men who would compete in their asceticism with the Perfecti. In effect the Church could say, "We cannot have all the clergy lead apostolic lives, but we cherish and appreciate those who do." It was this idea that lay behind the foundation of the Dominican Order and probably influenced Innocent III to recognize the Franciscans.

When Innocent III ascended the papal throne, he was determined to take effective action against the heretics of southern France. At first he tried peaceful means. Preachers were sent into the region under the leadership of the abbot of Citeaux, several prelates, and a legate, Peter de Castelnau. The preachers made no progress, and the legate could not persuade the great lords to take an interest in the problem. The chief potentate of the land, Raymond VI, count of Toulouse, was a luxury-loving, gay prince who was well supplied with concubines and almost totally indifferent to religion. While he went through the forms required of a good Catholic and was generous to monastic foundations, he was well disposed toward the heretics and absolutely refused to take any action against them. His vassal, Raymond Roger, viscount of Béziers and Carcassone, had the same point of view. The count of Foix was even more impartial. He too was a formal Catholic, but his wife and one of his sisters were Waldensians, while another sister was an Albigensian.

By 1204 Innocent III was discouraged and listened to the advice of those who believed that only force could crush the heretics. As the count of Toulouse refused to supply this force, it had to come from elsewhere. Innocent appealed to Philip Augustus to lead an army against the heretics, but the French king was much too completely occupied with his war against King John to consider other ventures. The appeal was repeated in 1205 and 1207, with equal lack of success. Meanwhile, a crisis had arisen in the south. In 1207 the legate Peter de Castelnau excommunicated the count of Toulouse. In the following year the legate was murdered by one of the count's squires. While there was no evidence that Count Raymond had ordered the slaying, the church was naturally inclined to hold him responsible. Innocent III immediately confirmed the Count's excommunication, and released his subjects from their oaths of fealty to him. The Pope also renewed his appeal to King Philip.

Philip Augustus was faced with a difficult decision. He was at the moment not actively fighting King John and could spare troops. But to attack the lands of a vassal without adequate provocation was a clear violation of feudal custom and might well alarm the other great lords of France. And Philip had no desire to see the principle that excommunication was sufficient cause for dispossession established. In short, the French king was no devotee of the church who was willing to take risks for her sake, and a crusade against the count of Toulouse seemed an unwise enterprise politically. Philip did make an offer that he knew was safe. If the church would condemn Count Raymond as a heretic, Philip as suzerain would take over the custody of the county of Toulouse. But Raymond was not a heretic, and no one could prove that he was. King Philip, however, had no objection if his vassals wanted to attack Toulouse as crusaders. Innocent had to be satisfied with what he could get. He preached the crusade, and an army of knights gathered in northern France. There were the archbishops of Reims, Sens, and Rouen; six bishops; the duke of Burgundy; the counts of Nevers and St. Pol; and Simon de Montfort, lord of Montfort l'Amaury and titular earl of Leicester in England. Under the general command of the new legate, Arnold Amalric, the crusading army moved south in the early summer of 1209.

In July the crusaders appeared before the town of Béziers, a rich, gay place that contained many heretics. On July 21 the town was taken by assault and the entire population massacred. As the crusaders were carrying the walls, someone suggested to the legate that many good Catholics lived in Béziers, but his only reply was "Kill all! Kill all, for God will know his own." Seven thousand people were slaughtered in a single church in which they had taken refuge. The frightful fate of Béziers had the intended effect; it struck terror into the hearts of the people of the region. Raymond Roger surrendered Carcassone, an almost impregnable stronghold, and himself became a prisoner on the promise of good treatment.

The legate soon left the host. He was elevated to the archepiscopal seat of Narbonne and soon was quarreling fiercely with the crusaders over his temporal authority in that city and its vicinity. His place as leader was taken by Simon de Montfort. The ancestral lands of the house of Montfort lay on both sides of the border between the royal demesne of the Capetian kings and the duchy of Normandy. The elder line, counts of Evreux, lost almost all their possessions by making bad guesses as to which side to support in the struggle between the Capetians and the Plantagenets. Simon had supported King Philip and hence had kept his barony of Montfort l'Amaury, but he had never been able to get possession of his rich English earldom of Leicester. He was thus a minor baron. But he was a man of boundless ambition, blind devotion to the church, and great military capacity. Soon after the surrender of Carcassone, its lord, the Viscount Raymond Roger, disappeared in the crusaders' prison. The leaders of the host promptly elected Simon viscount of Béziers and Carcassone. He then proceeded to reduce one by one the strongholds of the county of Toulouse. These conquests were, of course, accompanied by an enthusiastic slaughter of heretics or at least of those suspected of being heretics. By 1212 Simon had conquered all the county except for the towns of Toulouse and Montauban. This conquest was made with extremely modest forces. The main crusading army had gone home after the first victories, leaving Simon a few paid troops and some adventurers in search of fiefs taken from the heretics. These were occasionally reinforced by small bands of fresh crusaders.

The success of Simon de Montfort seriously disturbed Peter II (1196–1213), king of Aragon and count of Barcelona. Peter was lord of Montpellier and suzerain of the county of Provence. In addition, he claimed suzerainty over the part of the county of Toulouse known as the duchy of Narbonne, which included the viscounty of Béziers, and over the counties of Foix and Commines. In 1213 he appealed to the pope to aid him in protecting his vassals from Simon's attacks. When he found that he could do nothing by peaceful means, he gathered an army and marched into southern France. There he pitched camp before the fortress of Muret that was held by a garrison of Simon's troops. Simon promptly collected what troops he could, 240 knights and some 500 mounted sergeants, hastened to Muret, and threw his men into the castle to reinforce the garrison. He had no high opinion of his opponent. King Peter was known as a gay, reckless knight who loved tournaments and pretty women. Simon had captured one of his couriers bearing a letter to a lady of the region, saying that the king's expedition was undertaken solely for love of her. Simon asked his men what need could there be to fear a man who declared war on God to please a wanton. The counts of Toulouse, Foix, and Commines, who were with King Peter, had always shown a strong disinclination to fight pitched battles.

Simon decided on a bold maneuver. He ordered the gate of Muret that faced the hostile camp to be thrown open and his infantry to mass inside it. He gathered his cavalry near another gate on the opposite side of the stronghold. As he had hoped, the king of Aragon immediately sent a force under the count of Foix to force its way through the open gate. The rest of the army sat in their camp watching this assault. Meanwhile, Simon and his cavalry sallied out of Muret by the other gate and rode straight for the Aragonese camp. The king and his followers had held high revel the night before and were still none too sober—Peter himself could hardly ride his horse. Moreover, they were not in line of battle and were completely absorbed in watching the count of Foix's attack on Muret. Simon's horsemen took the enemy completely by surprise and routed them easily. The king of Aragon died on the field; the counts of Toulouse, Foix, and Commines tactfully departed at full speed before their situation grew too dangerous. After the battle, Simon and his men spent a pleasant few hours slaughtering the citizens of Toulouse who had come to aid their count and were helpless when their cavalry support was driven off.

The victory of Muret gave Simon de Montfort effective possession of the county of Toulouse with the exception of Toulouse itself. In 1215 a crusade led by Louis, eldest son of Philip Augustus, captured Toulouse and turned it over to him. In that same year the Fourth Lateran Council disposed of the legal possession of the county. Raymond VI lost all his lands. His young son was placed in possession of his imperial fief, the Marquisate of Provence. Apparently this action of the council was not in accord with the wishes of Innocent III, who would have preferred to grant Raymond easier terms. The Pope implied that some day young Raymond VII should have the family lands if he proved worthy. But for the time being Simon was count of Toulouse. His success was short-lived. Three years later the city of Toulouse rose in revolt, and Simon was killed in attempting to recapture it. His son Amaury took over the county, but he was unable to hold his own and surrendered the fief to the French crown. Eventually Raymond VII recovered the county of Toulouse at the price of marrying his daughter and heiress to Alphonse, count of Poitou, younger brother of Louis IX. At Alphonse's death both Poitou and Toulouse were added to the royal demesne.

The Albigensian crusade served the purpose it had been intended for. The power of the nobles of southern France who had protected the heretics was destroyed, and the heretics were left at the mercy of the church. All that was needed for their extermination was an effective ecclesiastical organization to discover them and bring them to trial. This was supplied by the gradual development of the Inquisition.

Under the canon law of the twelfth century there were two ways of bringing a case into the ecclesiastical court: accusation by the head of the court, usually the archdeacon, or accusation by a private individual. This system did not work very well where heretics were numerous. The archdeacons were too busy to do much heretic-hunting, and private individuals either sympathized with the heretics or feared their vengeance. In 1184 the Council of Verona ordered bishops to go through their dioceses to inquire about heresy and try all those found to be generally suspected, but the bishops were also too busy to do this task well. Soon special groups of men were established to hunt out heretics and present them before the ecclesiastical courts. Apparently, however, the clergy of Southern France lacked either the courage or the enthusiasm to proceed effectively against the heretics, and Innocent III sent in such legates as Peter de Castelnau. While their original purpose was to win over heretics by argument, they had the power to arrest them and try them. This was the system used to exterminate the heretics after the Albigensian crusade removed their secular protectors. In 1233 Pope Gregory IX (1227–41) replaced these special papal delegates with a regular permanent organization to combat heretics. Friars, both Franciscans and Dominicans, were sent into the dioceses with orders to discover and try heretics. These inquisitors were to all practical purposes exempt from local ecclesiastical authority and depended directly on the papacy. Thus a special investigative organization and special courts were set up to combat heresy.

The purpose of the Inquisition was twofold—to save the soul of the heretic, and to prevent him from corrupting others. In so worthy a cause any means were considered proper. Every good Catholic was urged to denounce heretics. When a man was accused, he was arrested and questioned. If he could explain away the charges, he was, of course, released. It was rather difficult to do this, however, as he was not allowed to face his accuser, nor was he even told who his accuser was. This policy was considered necessary in order to protect informers. The chief object of the questioning was to obtain a voluntary confession of guilt. If this confession was obtained, the accused became subject to penance. This might consist of a pilgrimage; public flogging—often in church; the wearing of a badge of some sort, such as a cross; or imprisonment. A confessed heretic was also deprived of all his property. Usually it was divided between the king or other prince and the church, but in France the royal government was soon taking it all. This greatly increased the crown's enthusiasm for the Inquisition.

If a man or woman accused of heresy could not explain away the charge and yet refused to confess, torture was freely used to encourage confession. According to law, torture could be applied but once, and the confession had to be voluntary. These difficulties were surmounted by "continuing" instead of "repeating" the torture and by having anyone who confessed under torture confirm the confession later. If the accused absolutely refused to confess and successfully resisted both arguments and torture, he was surrendered to the secular government —with the request that he suffer neither death nor mutilation. It was, however, generally understood that the secular government would ignore this request and burn the offender at the stake. Anyone who confessed, did penance, and then once more relapsed into heresy was immediately turned over to the secular government.

From the point of view of modern ideas of justice and humanity the Inquisition was fiendishly cruel and decidedly unjust. But it is important to remember that we live in an age when the belief that there is but one clear and certain path to salvation is not generally accepted. Many people do not consider heresy either a crime or a danger to society. To the men of the Middle Ages heresy was the most frightful of all crimes—treason against God himself. Moreover, it was a communicable disease that destroyed men's souls. We should have little sympathy with a doctor who allowed a man whom he suspected of having smallpox to mingle with his fellows, even if the diagnosis was far from certain. The Middle Ages felt even more strongly about people suspected of heresy. It was far better to punish some innocent people than to permit the fearful disease to spread. While there is little doubt that some inquisitors allowed greed and vengefulness, or even politics, to influence their actions, the purpose of the Inquisition was honest, and its leaders usually devout, if rather fanatical. What makes the Inquisition hard to defend is its hypocrisy—its violations of its own rules and principles in regard to torture, voluntary confession, and surrender to the secular government. The Church was not adhering to its own conception of right. In short, the honest historian can only call the Inquisition evil; but he must make clear that it was an understandable evil in the light of its environment.

30. The Friars

THE SAME basic religious impulse that turned men into heretics brought into being the two religious orders that were to play a large part in suppressing the heretics and in strengthening the fabric of the Church. In fact, the origin and early development of the Franciscans are almost exactly parallel to those of the Waldensians. Francis was the son of a prosperous merchant of Assisi. He was a gay young man who liked to sing the songs of courtly love and fight in the perpetual local wars between Assisi and her neighbors. Captured in one of these affairs, he was put in prison and became ill. This seems to have turned his mind to more serious matters, for shortly thereafter he received what he believed to be a command from God to repair the local churches. He took some goods from his father's shop, sold them, and gave the money to a priest to repair his church. When his father showed a lack of appreciation for this idea, Francis left home. For a while he went around repairing churches with his own hands. Then one day in 1208, as he prayed in a church, he believed that he received a command to lead and preach the apostolic life. Francis was a man of attractive personality—gay, simple, friendly, sympathetic. He wandered about preaching repentance and the virtue of the apostolic life. Each day he tried to earn by labor enough food to keep him alive. If work could not be found, he accepted gifts. He did not take money and refused more food than he needed for the day. He enjoyed this life and believed others should. He felt a rare affinity for nature in all its forms, birds, animals, flowers, fire. Men loved him and were inspired by him. Soon he had a group of followers, and he drew up a simple set of rules for them. The chief distinction between this rule and ordinary monastic ones was the absolute poverty insisted on by Francis and the fact that his followers were wanderers.

In 1210 Francis went to Rome to ask Innocent III to approve his rule. This was a critical point in the history of the Franciscans. They were in much the same position as were the Waldensians when Peter Waldo approached the Pope. The Franciscans practiced their conception of the apostolic life and preached without license. Innocent III was gravely troubled. He considered Francis' rule impossibly severe and hesitated to approve it. Why could not Francis and his followers quietly join a monastic order? But one of the cardinals pointed out that the Church could hardly in logic refuse to approve the way of life preached by Christ. Innocent himself may have remembered the case of the Waldensians and feared to create a new band of heretics. He gave verbal approval to the rule and the permission to preach.

The Franciscans increased very rapidly. While their headquarters was a group of huts clustered about the church of the Portiuncula in Assisi, they wandered all over Italy. In 1217, missions were sent out across the Alps and to Tunis and Syria. In 1219 larger groups departed for France, Germany, Hungary, and Spain. These first Franciscan missionaries had a difficult time as they were generally taken to be heretics because of their way of life. Francis himself accompanied the crusading host to Damietta, made his way to the court of the sultan of Egypt, and preached before him. Then he went on to Palestine. In 1220, however, disturbing news called him back to Italy; his followers were showing inclinations towards changing the rule.

Innocent III had been basically right when he hesitated to approve Francis' rule: it was both too severe and too simple. Only rare enthusiasts were willing to live the life of absolute poverty, and only a small group can exist without organization. Francis was opposed to property of any sort, and he distrusted organization. Moreover, he was determined that his followers should not have privileges and spiritual authority. He did not want papal letters protecting them from the local clergy, and they were to convert by preaching and example not by excommunication. When he returned from Palestine he found his friars established in a comfortable house and quickly drove them out of it. But the majority of his followers wanted change. Already a rule had been made forcing new recruits to serve a year before being finally admitted to the order and forbidding a friar to leave it. In 1224 Francis retired from the leadership, and he died two years later.

As soon as Francis retired, there began a general change in the rules of the order. The friars were permitted to have furniture, books, and other personal belongings. They could have the use of houses, but the title to them remained with the donor. If the donor was unwilling to do this, ownership went to the papacy. In 1257 Bonaventura was elected head or general of the order and set about to wipe out what he considered unfortunate traditions. He wrote a life of St. Francis and ordered the earlier biographies destroyed. He believed the friars should have large houses in the chief cities and should be protected by papal privileges. In 1322 the papacy took the final step in this direction: it declared Francis' doctrine of apostolic poverty heretical.

From the beginning of these modifications in Francis' rule, some friars had opposed all change. This group, called the Spiritual Franciscans, vigorously attacked the acquisition of houses and papal privileges. They stood firmly by the original ideas of the founder. These friars were enthusiastically persecuted by their fellows. Many were imprisoned, and a few were actually burned at the stake as heretics. Thus, while Francis himself was duly canonized, his stubborn followers were declared heretics. Illogical as it may seem to us, this was perfectly right according to the laws of the Church. Francis had never defied his ecclesiastical superiors, and his followers did. In 1215, when the heretics were a major menace, Innocent III and his cardinals saw the value of a religious order that lived the apostolic life that made the heretics so respected, but to have such an order in existence indefinitely was a nuisance. The secular clergy did not want the contradiction between the life of the apostles and their successors pointed out too persistently. Hence the rules of the order were gradually modified to fit it into the framework of the church.

St. Dominic, the founder of the other great mendicant order, was born in Castile and became a priest. His bishop took him with him on a trip through the region dominated by the Albigensians. At Toulouse Dominic argued with a heretic. The bishop believed that the best way to combat heresy was to have learned men who led the apostolic life convince the heretics that they were wrong. Dominic determined to found an order that would carry out this idea. He went to the Fourth Lateran Council in 1215 and asked the pope's permission to organize an order of friars dedicated to preaching. As the council had just passed legislation forbidding the establishment of new orders, the pope suggested that Dominic adopt the rule of St. Augustine, which was so vague that it could be used for almost any type of ecclesiastical organization. Thus was founded the order of Dominican friars, called

Black Friars in contrast to the Franciscans, who were known as the Grey Friars.

Although the Dominican rule required its followers to live in poverty, this virtue was not stressed as it was by St. Francis. The latter's emphasis on manual labor and such services as caring for lepers had no place in St. Dominic's plan. The primary function of his order was to preach, and for this purpose his friars had to be well trained in theology. The Dominicans established schools at different levels to educate their members. After two years in a *studium artium*, or school of arts, the friar passed to a *studium naturalium*, or school of nature, where he stayed for three years before going to the highest school, the *studium theologiae*. The most important of the schools of theology were called "general" because they drew students from the whole order and were usually connected with a university.

In addition to the Dominicans and Franciscans, the thirteenth century saw the creation of a number of other mendicant orders most of which were both small and short-lived. Only two of these became of lasting importance. In 1155 a French priest founded an order of hermits on Mount Carmel. About 1238 they migrated from Palestine to Cyprus, Sicily, and southern France. In 1241 they appeared in England. In 1247 this rule was revised with the aid of two Dominicans. They ceased to be hermits and began to live in communities, were permitted to have their houses in towns, could beg, preach, and hear confessions. The Council of Lyons in 1274 recognized them as a regular mendicant order. They were called Carmelite or White Friars, and their purpose and functions were similar to those of the Dominicans. The other order, called the Friars Hermits of the Order of St. Augustine, or Austin friars, was a combination of several groups of Italian hermits and friars into one order. In 1274 the Council of Lyons recognized the Austin friars as a mendicant order.

The mendicant friars were an extremely important element in the church. Perhaps their most important service during the thirteenth century was the defense of the spiritual and intellectual supremacy of the Church from the heretics and the new learning. While the apostolic lives and effective preaching of the friars may have won over some heretics, and it seems likely that many religious enthusiasts who might have turned heretic became friars instead, their chief work against heresy was the conduct of the Inquisition. From the very beginning of that organization its agents were friars. For a time Dominicans and

Franciscans attempted to work together, but they quarreled so fiercely that at one time it was necessary for the pope to forbid them to persecute each other. Eventually they divided the field so that in some lands the Inquisitors were Dominicans and in others Franciscans. Although the Inquisition did not succeed in wiping out heresy, it reduced it to very slight proportions.

The friars also played a dominant part in the adjustment of the doctrine of the church to the new learning. Alexander of Hales, a Franciscan who taught at Oxford, was the first to make a large scale attempt to reconcile Aristotle with theology and his *Summa* laid the foundation for the work of later scholars. The chief of these were the Dominicans, Albertus Magnus and Thomas Aquinas. Albertus Magnus was an incredibly prolific writer who among many other works produced a commentary on Aristotle that carried forward the task of bringing his ideas into line with those of the church. The task was completed by his pupil Thomas Aquinas, whose vast *Summa Theologica* covered every conceivable phase of theology and ethics. In it the teachings of Aristotle became an integral part of Christian doctrine, and the theological system of the mediaeval church reached its final form. Although St. Thomas was bitterly criticized by the Franciscan scholars Duns Scotus and William of Ockham, who maintained that logic and religion were irreconcilable, that one was based on reason and the other on faith, the merger of the two made by Thomas has survived as the basis of Catholic thought.

While Alexander of Hales, Albertus Magnus, and Thomas Aquinas were engaged in making Aristotle a part of Christian theology, other friars were using his works as a basis for progress in pure learning. The most important among these men were three scholars who taught at Oxford: Robert Grosseteste, Adam Marsh, and Roger Bacon. They were what we call scientists. Grosseteste learned Greek so that he could read Aristotle in the original and thus avoid the errors of the very bad texts that were the result of mistranslation. Bacon compiled grammars of both Greek and Hebrew. Bacon saw the vital importance of mathematics to the study of physics. He also emphasized the value of observation and experimentation. Results arrived at by logic should if possible be confirmed by experimentation. Some of Bacon's contemporaries believed that he gave reason too much scope and was too critical of reliance on the authority of accepted works such as the writings of the Church Fathers, but he also had many vigorous supporters, headed by the pope himself. While Robert Grosseteste and Roger Bacon may have threatened to some extent the complete domination of intellectual life by accepted dogma, they greatly increased the prestige of the clergy as scholars.

Perhaps the most fascinating activities of the friars were their missions to distant lands. When the Mongols conquered Babylonia and threatened Syria, Palestine, and Egypt, it occurred to both the Pope and King Louis IX of France that the Mongols might be persuaded to ally with the Christians against the Moslems. Each of these potentates sent a Franciscan to the court of the Great Khan at Karakorum. They were well received by the Khan, a broadminded pagan who was inclined to prefer Christianity to Mohammedanism. As the Mongols were routed in a series of battles by the sultans of Egypt, the plans for an alliance never bore fruit, but the friars acquired a firm base in the Mongol Empire. A group of Franciscans penetrated to China, and their mission was active there until the overthrow of the Mongol emperors in 1368. John of Monte Corvino labored in China from 1289 to 1328 and became archbishop of Pekin. The Dominicans were also active in Asia. In 1318 the pope divided that vast region between them, entrusting all missionary activities in northern Asia to the Franciscans, and in Armenia, Persia, and India to the Dominicans.

Less spectacular, but fully as important as the special functions performed by the friars was their day by day work throughout Western Europe. The Fourth Lateran Council had decreed that every Christian should confess at least once a year, but the parish priests were inadequate both in numbers and learning to carry out this legislation. The friars wandered about the countryside hearing confessions and preaching. They also performed other priestly functions such as the burying of the dead. While there is little doubt that they served a useful purpose in this way, they naturally incurred the jealousy of the local clergy. There were continuous undignified quarrels about donations and fees. Moreover, the position of the friars was obviously open to abuse. A sinner naturally was inclined to confess to a wandering friar who knew nothing of his past and would be gone the next day, rather than to his parish priest who was all too well informed about him. And the friars were tempted to give light penance in return for fat donations. While the friars still begged from door to door in their wanderings, they lived in comfort, even in luxury, in their houses. One has only to read Chaucer's *Canterbury Tales* to get a vivid account of the charges aimed at the friars in the late fourteenth century. In the universities the friars quarreled with the secular clergy just as enthusiastically as they did in the countryside, and only the steady support of the papacy enabled them to hold their own in these institutions. Everywhere the secular clergy felt that the gifts and fees of the faithful were inadequate to support both them and the friars. At the same time the rapid development of the penitential system was very largely the work of the friars. The official handbook for confessors that was approved by the papacy in the middle of the thirteenth century was the work of Raymond de Penafort, a Dominican. And any survey of the intellectual history of the time will show the important part played in the universities by the friars.

The partiality of the papacy for the friars is not difficult to understand. Despite the vast increase of the pope's authority over the Church as a whole, his control of the local clergy was still limited, but the friars formed a large, highly organized army directly subject to his command. While each order held representative general chapters, the executive authority in each rested in a single man, and he was immediately responsible to the pope. Thus the mendicant orders added significantly to the strength of the papal monarchy.

CHAPTER XI

The Hundred Years' War

FROM 1066 to 1904 the relations between England and France were generally hostile. Although during these eight and a half centuries there were many periods when the two states were at peace and a number of times when they were allied by treaty, the occasions on which French and English troops fought side by side were extremely few: the alliance between Queen Elizabeth and Henry IV, the Dutch War of 1672–78, and the Crimean War, are all that come immediately to mind. The longest period of formal war unbroken by a peace treaty stretched from 1201 to 1259. Thus the era between 1337 and 1450, which historians have chosen to designate as the Hundred Years' War, was by no means unique. Moreover, it was not one war but several, being broken in theory at least by a number of peace treaties. These wars did, however, have certain similarities that justify dealing with them as a unit. Throughout the whole period military equipment and tactics remained essentially unchanged, as did the formal objectives of the two parties. Hence it seems well to abide by tradition and continue to speak of the Hundred Years' War. While it was going on, this contest monopolized a major part of the human and material resources of the two states and was deeply intertwined in the general politics of Western Europe. A knowledge of it forms a necessary background for the comprehension of the political, social, and economic history of this region during the fourteenth and fifteenth centuries. Moreover, in itself the Hundred Years' War is a fascinating fragment of the history of military institutions.

31. Background of the War

BY THE Treaty of Paris in 1259, King Henry III (1216–72) had abandoned his claims to Normandy, Maine, Anjou, Touraine, and Poitou, while Louis IX (1226–70) of France recognized his right to hold as a fief from the French crown the fragment of the duchy of Aquitaine that was still in the English king's possession. This consisted of a strip of land varying from sixty to a hundred miles in width along the shore of the Bay of Biscay between the island of Oléron and the Pyrenees. Another hundred square miles of Aquitaine including Perigord and the Limousin was to be added to the fief of the English king if Alphonse, count of Poitou and Toulouse, should die childless. The effective authority of the king of England as exercised by his seneschal of Gascony was largely confined to the districts surrounding Bordeaux and Bayonne. In the rest of the fief that we shall call the duchy of Gascony the local lords did much as they pleased. The loyalty of these lords to their duke was largely based on the fact that being rarely in residence in the duchy he could give them little trouble.

In the days when the Capetian kings had no authority within the great fiefs held of the crown, there had been no basic difficulty involved in having a foreign sovereign hold one of those fiefs. But by the second half of the thirteenth century the French kings had reduced the independence of their great vassals. Their most effective weapon in this process was the accepting of appeals from the courts of the vassals to the king's court in Paris—that is, to the Parlement of Paris. The hearing of such appeals involved sending royal officials into the fiefs to sequester goods under litigation and to enforce decisions. This annoyed all the great vassals, but it was peculiarly exasperating to the English king, who was the peer of the Capetian monarch. Bitter quarrels burst out between the seneschal of Gascony and the royal officials, and often these quarrels involved their royal masters. In 1294 and again in 1324 the French king seized the duchy of Gascony on the ground that its duke was a contumacious vassal. While each of these disputes was finally settled by negotiation and the duchy restored to the king of England, they left angry memories. Moreover, the king of France began to feel certain that he could confiscate the duchy whenever it seemed convenient, and his English rival continually suspected him of planning to do so. Finally, the Capetians never kept their promise of 1259. Alphonse of Poitou died childless, but the English king never obtained the promised lands. In short, the French and English monarchs were always quarreling over questions concerning Gascony, and at any time this could lead to open war.

While the duchy of Gascony was the major cause of friction between the two kings, there were other irritants. In the thirteenth and fourteenth centuries the terms pirate and seaman were synonymous. No shipmaster could resist the temptation to plunder a vessel weaker than his own. Year in and year out the seamen of France and England preyed on each other with rare enthusiasm. This piracy was more or less legalized by "letters of reprisal." When an English seaman was robbed by a French mariner, he could go to the chancery and obtain royal letters authorizing him to take the same amount of property from the next Frenchman he met. The same process was used in France. Obviously before long most shipmasters would be equipped with letters of reprisal. When they wanted to be at peace, the two kings calmly ignored the continual bickering of their seamen even when it resulted in large-scale naval engagements, but when they were contemplating hostilities the complaints of the seamen were a very convenient excuse.

Another fruitful source of discord between France and England was the complicated political situation in the county of Flanders. In the early fourteenth century the artisans of the towns grew restive under the political and economic domination of the rich merchants. This led to frequent riots and revolts.* As the count of Flanders was unable to handle the situation, the French king was inclined to intervene. Flanders was the chief market for English wool, and the export duties on wool formed an important part of the revenue of the king of England. Hence the latter was most unwilling to have the king of France in effective control of Flanders so that he could at will disrupt the wool trade. Since the king of France was inclined to support the rich merchants, the English king sympathized with the artisans.

The relationship between the kings of France and England were

* See p. 230.

further complicated in 1328, when Edward III became a potential claimant to the French throne. In 1316 Louis X (1314–16) of France threw his realm into consternation by dying, leaving a daughter and a pregnant widow. While the country eagerly waited to see if the Capetians still kept their ability to produce male heirs, the late king's brother Philip took over the government as regent. In due time the queen bore a son, but he died almost immediately. Thus France was faced with a question that had never before plagued her—could a woman succeed to the throne? According to the general feudal custom of the time, a daughter could succeed to her father's fief; and many argued that the same rule should apply to the crown. Others maintained that kingship was a peculiarly sacred dignity to which no woman could aspire. The quarrel was bitter and fiercely argued, but as one might expect the claimant in actual control won, and Philip (1316–22) was crowned king of France. Louis' daughter Jeanne married her cousin Philip, count of Evreux, received the kingdom of Navarre, which her grandfather had acquired by marriage, and bore a son who was to plague her rival's successors for many years. For there was a question left unsettled. Even if a woman could not wear the crown, might she not transmit it to her son?

When King Philip V died in 1322, leaving only daughters, there was no serious debate, and his brother Charles (1322–28) succeeded him without question. Charles too failed to produce a son, and at his death in 1328 the senior branch of the Capetian house was extinct in the male line. If one believed that the French crown could neither be worn nor transmitted by a female, the heir to the vacant throne was Philip, count of Valois, son of Charles, count of Valois, the younger brother of King Philip IV. But if a woman could transmit the crown to her son, there was a closer relative with a better claim. King Edward II of England had married Isabelle, daughter of Philip IV and sister of the last three kings; and her son was Edward III of England. In 1328 Isabelle and her paramour Roger Mortimer had arranged the murder of Edward II and were ruling England in the name of young Edward III.* Isabelle protested the accession of Philip of Valois to the French throne, but she could do nothing more, and young Edward felt unable even to protest. In 1329 he went to France and did homage to Philip VI for his duchy of Gascony and thus seemed to recognize him as king of France.

* See p. 367.

In 1330, at the age of eighteen, Edward III (1327–77) arrested his mother and Roger Mortimer and took the government of England into his own hands. Mortimer was executed with peculiarly ingenious cruelty, and the queen was confined in one of the manors of her dowry. Edward was quite unlike any of his recent predecessors; perhaps he resembled most closely his great-granduncle Richard I. He was a strong-willed and firm-handed ruler who could handle the turbulent baronage of the realm. While he knew how to choose able men to conduct his administration, he had little personal interest in the details of government. He loved luxurious living and pretty ladies. He also had a burning desire for glory and prestige, and like most nobles of his day he believed that these were to be gained chiefly by military exploits. Fortunately, under the circumstances, he was an excellent captain and tactician who could inspire his men and handle them ably on the field of battle. He had too little grasp of reality to be a competent strategist. Here one finds him in striking contrast to his grandfather, Edward I. When Edward I went to war, he had a practical aim that he felt sure he could accomplish, and he carefully planned and carried out the necessary operations. Edward III was always aiming at something that was far beyond his capacities and resources. Although he was usually practical in details and did not allow the whimsies of chivalry to carry him too far, he was essentially a crowned knight and a thoroughly chivalrous monarch. As such he had no slightest objection to squandering the human and financial resources of England to seek honor and glory for himself.

King Philip VI (1328–50) of France had his rival's weaknesses in even more exaggerated form, a few extra ones of his own, and no good qualities to compensate for them. Before he ascended the throne Philip's love of pomp, luxurious living, and such knightly sports as tournaments had kept him continually deep in debt. As king he indulged his expensive tastes to his heart's content. Like Edward he sought prestige and glory as a warrior, but unlike the English king he had no ability to lead men and no comprehension of tactics. He was proud, easily offended, and almost pathologically suspicious of everyone. Philip was the ideal chivalrous monarch, and not very bright.

Clearly enough almost any provocation could bring two such monarchs as Edward III and Philip VI to war. This provocation was supplied by that perennial bone of contention, the duchy of Gascony. The lawyers of Philip's court, the men who had invented the Salic Law to get him the throne, decided in 1330 that the homage performed by Edward III in 1329 had been improper; it had been simple and not liege homage. As Edward refused to remedy this defect, a pleasant diplomatic controversy developed. Meanwhile there was a new burst of appeals to the Parlement of Paris from Gascony. Edward was at war with the Scots, and Philip encouraged French knights to aid the Scots against him. The English king's protests were blandly ignored. Finally Philip decided that the time had come to drive the English from Gascony, and in 1337 he declared the duchy confiscated. Edward's answer was prompt. He declared war on Philip, "so-called king of France." While Edward did not immediately assume himself the title of king of England and France, he had clearly shown his intention to do so. He was no man to play around with limited objectives.

From the point of view of total resources there was no comparison between France and England; any contest between them would be a struggle of a pigmy against a giant. England had about 2.2 million inhabitants, while the lands that recognized the rule of Philip VI contained some 16 million people, of whom about 12 million lived in the royal demesne. France was also a highly productive and prosperous land with a high standard of living. But in the fourteenth century total resources had little bearing on the military power of a country: the question was who controlled the resources, and whether they could be used effectively. In an age when transportation was costly and difficult an efficient system of supply was almost out of the question, and armies in general expected to live off the country. Thus they could not be very large, no matter how many men were theoretically available. Then, warfare required men who were trained and equipped, and obviously their ratio to the total population could vary greatly. France still relied on its mounted nobility supported by town militia and a few mercenary crossbowmen, while England had developed an effective peasant or at least yeoman infantry. It seems likely that the total number of men capable of effective military service was not utterly different in the two countries. Finally, wars cost money; and here it seems fairly clear that the resources of the two kings were about equal. In fact, it is quite possible that the revenue of Edward III was a little larger than that of his enemy.

The French army of 1337 differed little from those of the twelfth and thirteenth centuries. Its basic element was the levy of heavily armed noble horsemen who followed their lords to battle. The armor of the knight was somewhat heavier than it had been in the past. Visored helmets were usual, pieces of plate metal protected exposed spots, and the horses wore armor as well as their riders. As this equipment was extremely expensive, only the richer lords possessed it, and other nobles served in lighter armor. They were as a rule called squires or mounted sergeants. The only essential difference between the heavy cavalry of 1337 and the feudal levy of the thirteenth century was that it was paid for its services; but as each great lord received the money to pay the vassals who followed him, the discipline of the army was little improved. In addition to the cavalry there was the militia of the towns, consisting of infantry armed with pikes. When the cavalry was patient enough to allow the infantry to arrive on the field, something that happened but rarely, these troops were reasonably useful in battle. The only troops in the French army equipped with missile weapons were mercenary crossbowmen, who were usually foreigners. The Genoese were particularly noted for their skill with this weapon and were frequently employed, but as such regular professional soldiers were expensive their numbers were usually very small.

The English army had come a long way since the days of John and Henry III. When Edward I was planning the conquest of Wales, he realized that he needed infantry to follow the Welsh into their mountain fastnesses.* For this purpose he levied large numbers of men from the western shires and paid them for their service. Later when he conquered Scotland he used the same device. Thus there was built up in England a body of men who had military experience and who were willing to fight for pay. At the beginning almost all these infantrymen were armed with the pike, but as time went on many of them adopted a new and highly effective weapon—the longbow. The longbow was apparently invented by the Southern Welsh. During the Welsh wars it was taken over by some of the English infantry, and soon every shire was well supplied with men who were adept in its use. Some six feet long, this great bow had rather better range and striking power than the crossbow. If the range were not too great it could pierce chain mail. But its great advantage was its speed of fire. A good longbowman could shoot ten or twelve arrows a minute as against the two bolts of the most expert crossbowman.

* See p. 275.

Edward I had little enthusiasm for the clumsy, undisciplined feudal levy with its short term of service, and he called it only when he needed a large body of heavy cavalry for a special purpose. As a rule he relied on paid companies. An experienced and able soldier, usually a knight, was given a sum of money to raise a company. He hired a few other knights or squires to serve as officers. Then he sent men out to recruit archers and pikemen. A company thus consisted of a few mounted men and a fair-sized body of infantry—perhaps a hundred men in all. Then, the very great lords, earls and powerful barons, were expected to serve without pay for as long as they were needed, and each of these brought with him a small retinue of horsemen. This supplied a small body of heavy cavalry. In addition to these troops when war was being conducted in France the English king relied heavily on his Gascons. The nobility of the duchy furnished a body of heavy cavalry similar to that of the French army, and Gascony could always supply a fair number of crossbowmen.

In addition to developing a new weapon, the English had learned how to use it tactically. John Giffard of Brimpsfield marching to relieve a castle besieged by the Welsh had found a strong body of enemy spearmen ensconced on a rise of ground blocking his path. Giffard put his bowmen between his horsemen so that the Welsh could not attack them. Then the archers rained arrows on the Welsh formation until it wavered and gaps appeared in its ranks. At that point his cavalry charged and cut the enemy to pieces. Similar tactics were later used to defeat the spearmen of the Scots Highlands who followed William Wallace. On another occasion a fairly small force of knights accompanied by a strong body of pikemen and archers found themselves faced by the entire feudal levy of Scotland. The knights dismounted and fought with the pikemen. The archers were thrown in front and on the flanks of this line of pikes. The whole formation took its position on the top of a hill. The Scots horsemen also dismounted and with their pikemen formed a solid mass that marched slowly up the hill. But from both in front and on the flank English arrows rained on their ranks. When they reached the English infantry, the archers drew off to one side and continued to shoot at the Scots, who eventually broke and fled. These two tactical devices, one offensive and one defensive, were to be the English army's chief reliance throughout the Hundred Years' War.

32. *The Conquests of Edward III*

KING EDWARD made his preparations carefully. While he gathered his army, his agents, well supplied with money, were active among the princes of Germany building up a coalition against France. Louis of Wittelsbach (1314–47), duke of Bavaria and Holy Roman Emperor, was persuaded to create Edward vicar of the empire in the lower Rhine valley and thus give him theoretical authority over the princes he subsidized. The English king crossed in 1338, too late to do

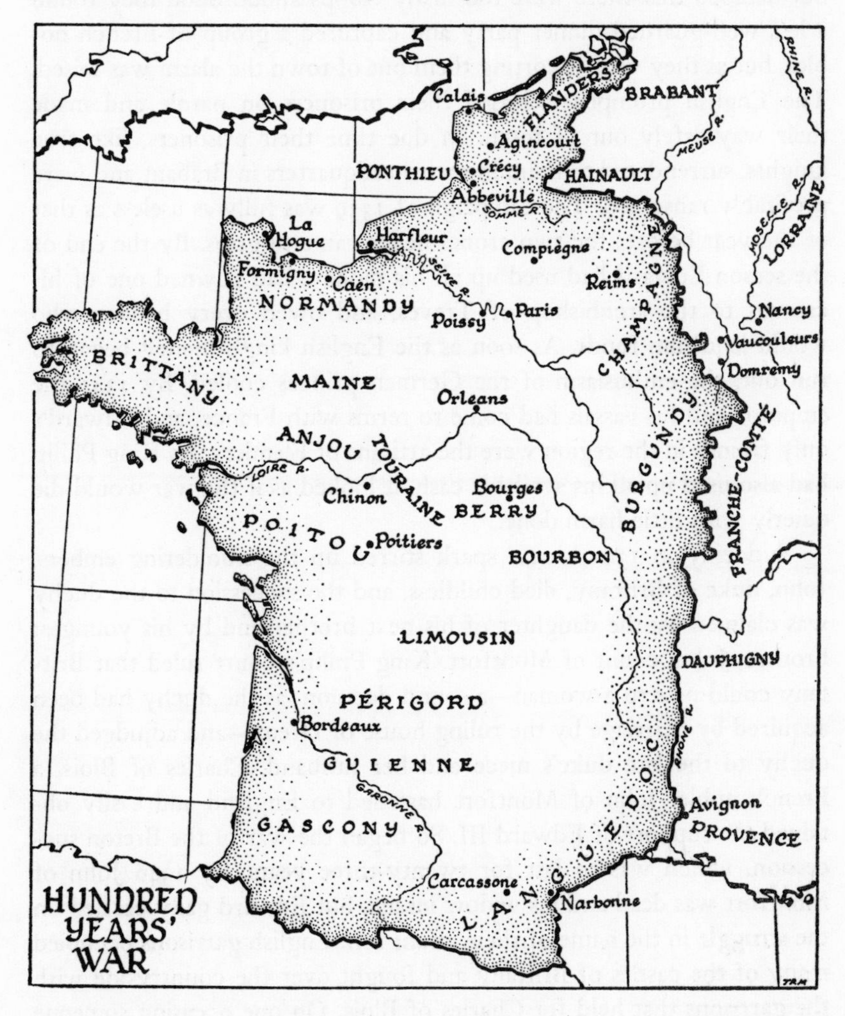

anything but hold love-fests with his allies. In 1339 he was back again with his army, and Philip mustered his host. The two kings moved back and forth around the country, but neither felt strong enough to risk a pitched battle, and each satisfied his pride by offering the other battle under impossible conditions. There were a few marvelous adventures. One day a small group of English knights rode gaily in the early evening into the town where the heir to the French throne, John, duke of Normandy, was comfortably camped. Their modest purpose was to kidnap the Duke. They got into the room where he was dining, but decided that there were too many troops about. Soon they found a less well-guarded dinner party and captured a group of French nobles, but as they were escorting them out of town the alarm was raised. The English promptly released their prisoners on parole and made their way safely out of town. In due time their prisoners, like true knights, surrendered to them in their headquarters in Brabant and were profitably ransomed. The campaign of 1339 was fully as useless as that of the year before; the two armies never came to grips. By the end of the season Edward had used up all his money, had pawned one of his crowns to the archbishop of Treves, and owed every banker who would lend him funds. As soon as the English king's money began to run out, the enthusiasm of the German princes cooled. By 1341 the emperor and his vassals had come to terms with France, and Edward's only friends in the region were the artisans of Flanders. As King Philip had also used up all his available cash, it looked as if the war would die quietly with little harm done.

Suddenly in 1341 a new spark stirred up the smoldering embers. John, duke of Brittany, died childless, and the succession to the duchy was claimed by the daughter of his next brother and by his youngest brother, John, count of Montfort. King Philip's court ruled that Brittany could pass to a woman—a sound decision, as the duchy had been acquired by marriage by the ruling house of Dreux—and adjudged the duchy to the late duke's niece and her husband, Charles of Blois, a French noble. John of Montfort hastened to England and easily obtained the support of Edward III. So began the war of the Breton succession, which was to last for twenty-three years. By 1346 John of Montfort was dead and his widow insane, but Edward gaily carried on the struggle in the name of their infant son. English garrisons occupied many of the castles of Brittany and fought over the countryside with the garrisons that held for Charles of Blois. On one occasion someone had the idea of settling the matter by a battle of thirty champions. The champions met and dutifully carved each other up, but as no one could agree as to which side won, the war went merrily on.

While English and French captains were fighting in Brittany, King Philip's forces were attempting without much success to conquer the duchy of Gascony. Early in the summer of 1346 King Edward mustered an army to go to the assistance of his troops in the duchy. But when he set sail, contrary winds blew him back on the coast of Cornwall, to his great annoyance. He then announced that he would go where the wind wanted him to and on July 11 landed at La Hogue in Normandy. On July 20 he took and plundered the prosperous city of Caen, but soon after he heard that King Philip was mustering all the forces of France at Paris in order to crush him. As Edward had only about 9,000 men, he decided to go home. In this plan, however, he reckoned without his seamen. They had gotten bored waiting for him, and when Edward arrived on the coast he found that the fleet had gone home and that he was stranded in France. He had only one hope—to get to Flanders and find refuge with his allies there until a new fleet could be mustered to take his army home. The English army promptly marched to the Seine and tried to find a crossing, but Philip had moved all boats to the north bank and the bridges were either destroyed or strongly held. Finally they found a weak force holding the bridge at Poissy and succeeded in crossing the river. The next obstacle was the Somme. Here Edward by good luck found a ford that was usable at low tide and got across just before the advance guard of the French army came up. But the king knew that the chase was over. His army was tired, and his infantry could not move as fast as the French cavalry that was pursuing them. On August 26 he halted near the little village of Crécy in the county of Ponthieu and drew up his army in battle array.

King Edward chose a fairly strong position on a hill just to the north of the forest of Crécy. His right flank was protected by a stream that ran along the edge of the forest, but his left was covered only by the rising ground and a tiny village. The army was drawn up in three divisions or "battles," each of which consisted of a solid core of dismounted knights and pikemen with archers on each flank. Two of these battles formed the front line, while the third was held in reserve to the rear. Edward himself climbed to the top of a windmill just to the rear of his right flank, from which he could watch the whole battlefield. While Edward was arraying his host, the French army left Abbeville on the Somme and started north on the road that passed to the west of the forest of Crécy. King Philip had no idea where the English were, but he assumed that they were still hastening toward Flanders. As he rode north, however, he received word that his enemies were north of the forest near the road that passed to the east of it, and he immediately ordered his forces to move across to the other road. He also sent scouts out to discover what Edward was doing. The scouts soon found the English position and returned to inform King Philip of the situation. The leader of the scouting party was a soldier of experience and intelligence. He pointed out to the king that the French army was scattered in utter disorder along the road from Abbeville, that the day was rapidly passing, and that the only sensible course was to halt some distance from the English position and wait until the next day to attack it. Amazingly enough this sound idea penetrated the chivalrous haze that shrouded the king's mind, and he sent orders to his vanguard under his brother the count of Alençon to halt where it was.

When the order to halt reached Alençon, it was late in the afternoon and he had just come in sight of the enemy. He obeyed his royal brother's command and stopped his advance, but the divisions behind him all tried to press as far forward as possible and so threw the situation into incredible confusion. When Philip himself arrived on the scene, the sight of the enemy and the eagerness of his knights quickly overcame his judgment, and he ordered Alençon to attack. Alençon had with him the only troops in the French army who were armed with missile weapons—a strong band of Genoese crossbowmen. He sent them forward to drive off the English archers covering Edward's left flank, while he followed close behind with his heavy cavalry. Unfortunately the English longbows slightly outranged the crossbows, and the English had the additional advantage of shooting downhill. The Genoese wavered under the rain of arrows. This deeply annoyed the impatient Alençon, and he ordered his cavalry to charge, despite the fact that the Genoese were between them and the enemy. The result was, of course, complete confusion. The horsemen and crossbowmen became hopelessly entangled on the lower slopes of the hill, while the English archers gaily poured their arrows into the struggling mass of men. Soon Alençon's whole division was destroyed.

While Alençon's attack was in progress, the other French troops who had arrived on the field managed to form a line and prepare for a charge. As soon as they were ready, they pressed forward against the enemy. Among them rode John of Luxembourg, king of Bohemia, who despite his royal title was actually a mercenary captain in King Philip's pay. King John was blind, and his knights took the bridle of his horse to lead him into battle. As the French rode up the hill, the English archers poured arrows upon them, killing many horses and wounding some knights. The few horsemen who reached the line of English spears were easily killed or captured. John of Luxembourg died in the midst of his faithful knights. This was the last attack that was made with any semblance of order. After its failure every French division as it arrived on the field charged up the hill at the English position, and each was routed in the same way. The English archers firing from the flanks always reduced the charging force to a number that the pikemen could handle without too much difficulty. There were some fifteen or sixteen separate assaults, of which the last was made about midnight. Then the exhausted English lay down on their arms where they stood, while the remnants of the French host fled towards the south. Early the next morning the earl of Salisbury marched out with an English force and cut to pieces the infantry of the French towns that was marching toward the battlefield, apparently unaware that the battle was over.

King Philip had used no tactics whatever at Crécy: his men had simply charged at the enemy as soon as they reached the field. Usually the historian has no hesitation in saying what a commander should have done, but in the case of Crécy this is extremely difficult because we have only the vaguest notion as to the size of the French army. The figures given by mediaeval chroniclers are notoriously unreliable. While the size of the English army can be established from documents, no such material exists for the French forces. Sir Charles Oman believed the French army to be at least three times the size of the English. Ferdinand Lot, while following Oman's account of the battle, argues that the French army was no larger and perhaps even smaller than the English. If one accepts Lot's theory, the actions of both Edward and Philip become utterly incomprehensible. The English king flees madly toward Flanders before an inferior force, and Philip attacks an enemy superior in numbers in a strong position. Certainly both Edward and Philip must have believed the French army to have been overwhelmingly superior. Philip could probably have won in either of two ways.

He could have moved his army to the north, cutting Edward off from Flanders and forcing him to take the offensive. This was, however, too much to expect of a royal knight yearning for glory. He could also have waited, as he apparently at first intended, until his whole army was in battle array and then throw all the weight of his heavy cavalry against the English position. If he really had a superiority of three to one, he could hardly have failed to win. The English archers would have dismounted some of his knights and even killed a few, but enough would have gotten by to crush the small bodies of pikemen.

As he counted his prisoners and the bodies on the field of Crécy, King Edward realized that he had won a great victory; but it was difficult to think of any way to exploit it. Although northern France lay open before him, he dared not attempt an invasion with his small and extremely tired army. The most useful course seemed to be to capture a port on the coast that could serve as a permanent beachhead for future invasions. With this in mind, he laid siege to the port of Calais. Edward built a complete string of fortifications around the landward side of the town facing both toward Calais and toward the inland roads by which a relieving army would have to approach. As many as 30,000 troops were used in these works at one time or another, but it seems most unlikely that more than 10–15,000 were ever there at one time. After some months it occurred to Edward that he was doing little more than annoy the garrison of Calais. Although he had blocked all entrance from the land, the town was being adequately supplied by sea. The English king then brought up a fleet and blockaded the sea side as well. Once this was done the garrison was lost if it was not relieved in a reasonable time. Late in July, 1347, King Philip mustered an army and marched to Calais, but he dared not attack Edward's force behind its strong fortifications. On August 2 he called on the English king to behave like a true knight and come out to fight in the open. But the practical side of Edward's mind was able to resist his chivalrous inclinations, and he refused. Philip retired in disgust, and Calais surrendered on August 4. At first Edward was determined to slaughter all the inhabitants, but he agreed to be content with hanging the mayor and a few prominent citizens and eventually was persuaded by his queen to spare them as well. He did, however, deport a fair part of the population and replaced them with English colonists. He then strengthened the fortifications of the town and placed in it a powerful garrison. Calais was to remain an impregnable English fortress until 1558.

King Philip VI died in 1350 and was succeeded by his son John (1350–64), who was called for no reason any historian has been able to fathom "the Good." John was more stupid than his father and even more thoroughly imbued with chivalric ideas. He was incurably suspicious and saw treason in everything. While he was usually weak and vacillating, he was capable of bursts of decisive energy in which he was likely to be brutal and savage. His only redeeming features were his reckless personal courage and his rather quixotic conception of knightly honor. As a man he was thoroughly unpleasant, and as a king he was utterly worthless. Soon after he came to the throne one of his blind fits of rage raised a new and terrible enemy to plague his house. King John had a favorite, a Spanish prince called Charles of Spain, whom he had made constable of France. Charles of Spain was heartily detested by the French nobles. A prince of the royal blood, Charles, count of Evreux and king of Navarre, grandson of King Louis X, lured the constable into an ambush and murdered him.* Charles of Navarre, usually called Charles the Bad, was a close friend and boon companion of the king's eldest son. One day shortly after the constable's murder, King John heard that his son and Charles were enjoying themselves in Rouen. He gathered some troops, hastened to Rouen, invaded the hall where his son and Charles were dining, and had all Charles' companions slaughtered before his eyes. Charles himself was cast into prison. But the king's resolution soon weakened, and he released Charles the Bad, who promptly formed an alliance with Edward III. Charles' kingdom of Navarre was a long way off and could give little trouble, but his Norman lands bristled with strong castles that were thrown open to English troops.

A series of truces interspersed with small-scale hostilities followed the capture of Calais, and major operations were not undertaken until 1355. In that year the English conducted two invasions of French territory. Edward III landed at Calais and marched inland while King John mustered his forces to meet him. The two kings exchanged challenges to pitched battles and at least one was accepted, but no combat actually took place. Meanwhile Edward, prince of Wales, known from the color of his armor as the Black Prince, marched from Gascony into southern France at the head of a small but highly mobile army. His archers were supplied with horses so that they could keep up with the English knights and the Gascon nobles. Young Edward plundered and

* See p. 326.

burned the entire length of the county of Toulouse; he boasted that he had burned 500 places including the suburbs of Carcassonne and Narbonne. The French commander in the region saw his own lands ravaged without daring to offer battle or even come near enough to annoy the English army. Early in December the Black Prince returned to Bordeaux laden with booty. This was the sort of expedition the English were particularly fond of. The army marched through the open country stealing everything of value and burning the unfortified towns and villages. No attempt was made to attack fortified places, and every effort was made to avoid battle with anything like an equal force. It was great fun and highly profitable.

There is some reason for thinking that during the spring of 1356 the English conceived what was for them an astonishingly complex idea, two coordinated invasions of France. The most powerful of the English barons, Edward's second cousin Henry, duke of Lancaster, was to cross to Brittany with a small force, gather the English companies that were already in that duchy, invade Normandy, and eventually move south toward the Loire. The Black Prince would march north from Gascony to meet Henry near the Loire. If there really was such a comprehensive strategic plan, it was carried out with characteristic incompetence. Duke Henry landed in Brittany in mid-June and invaded Normandy, but early in July he learned that King John was approaching at the head of his army. As Lancaster had but a tiny force, he hastily withdrew into Brittany while John vainly besieged one of the four Norman fortresses he had captured. The Black Prince on his side did not start from Gascony until the middle of August. He marched in leisurely fashion through Périgord, the Limousin, and Berry, plundering and burning as he moved. About the first of September he reached the Loire, but since the river was in flood and the French had removed all the boats to the northern bank, he could not cross the stream. While this mischance prevented him from joining Duke Henry in Brittany, it probably did not worry the Black Prince. The Loire valley was rich and prosperous, and it had never been really thoroughly plundered. Young Edward did a good, complete job and then on September 11 started back toward Bordeaux with a long train of wagons loaded with plunder.

When King John learned of the Black Prince's expedition, he determined to march against him. As most of the French host had gone home after Lancaster's retirement, it took some time to reassemble, but shortly before the English left the Loire valley for the south the French crossed the river and moved to cut them off. The Black Prince had no desire for battle. His army was small and tired from a long campaign, besides being heavily laden with booty. In full accord with the casual methods of the day, neither army made the slightest serious attempt to find out where the other was. As result, on September 17 the French marched across the English line of march and only discovered their presence when the English advance guard suddenly collided with the rear of the French column. After a brief engagement in which two valuable French counts were captured, the Black Prince hastily turned southeastward in the hope of getting away without further fighting. Unfortunately the wagon train of plunder moved very slowly, and Edward soon realized that he must either abandon it or fight. He therefore drew his army up in battle array, prepared to give battle if the French attacked promptly or to take up his retreat again if they delayed. This time, however, it was not the French king but a cardinal who delayed the action. Talleyrand, cardinal of Périgord, had been following the two armies in the hope of arranging a peace or at least a truce. The Black Prince was anxious to make terms, as his position seemed close to desperate. But King John felt that he had the English at his mercy and was unwilling to offer anything the Black Prince would consider. Hence the only result of the cardinal's effort was to give the English a day's rest. On the night of the eighteenth the Black Prince laid his plans. He started his wagons on the road to Bordeaux. At dawn his troops would follow if the French delayed their attack long enough.

Prince Edward had taken up his position on slightly rising ground southeast of the town of Poitiers. His left flank was protected by a deep ravine containing a small river, while his right was covered to some extent by the outskirts of a thick wood. The front of the position was guarded by hedges and thickets except where a small road crossed it. The army was formed in the usual three battles of dismounted cavalry, pikemen, and archers. Early in the morning of the day of battle one of the three divisions fell back to begin the retreat and was hastily recalled when the Prince saw that the French were going to attack before he could retire.

King John and his advisers had been thinking deeply. They saw that the battleground was strewn with thickets and hedges and hence far from ideal for a cavalry charge. They also remembered that at

Crécy the English knights had fought on foot and had won. The obvious answer seemed to be to dismount his knights. What the king forgot was that a march of a mile or so across rough country would be incredibly exhausting for heavily armed men used to fighting on horseback. The English knights who had fought on foot at Crécy had stayed in one place on the defensive. The French knights dismounted and arrayed themselves in three massive divisions. The crossbowmen were carefully placed behind the men-at-arms so that there would be no danger of their getting into action and depriving the gentlemen of the glory of victory. But John did have one ingenious idea—to send a body of cavalry down the road to punch a gap in the English line for the main divisions to exploit. This force of 300 picked knights was commanded by the marshal of France, John of Clermont, who incidentally had advised against an attack on the English position, had been called a coward for his pains, and was determined to show his courage.

The idea was a good one, and a large mass of cavalry charging down the road might well have broken the English line, but 300 were far too few for the purpose. Fired on from both sides by the English archers, most of the knights never reached the line, and those who did were easily captured. Then the first French division under the command of the king's eldest son, the Dauphin Charles, advanced against the English. This was a powerful body, and despite their exhaustion after their long march the knights fought vigorously. Prince Edward was forced to throw in his reserve division in order to rout them. But routed they were, and the remnants fled in disorder. The second division of the French host was under the command of John's younger brother, Philip, duke of Orleans. Orleans and his captains took a long look at the fleeing remnants of his nephew's troops and decided they preferred some other neighborhood. Without striking a blow, the whole division fled from the field. This left only the third division, commanded by the king in person. With two thirds of his army dispersed, the day was obviously lost. Any sensible monarch would have saved himself and the men he led. But John was a knight who would not flinch before the enemy, and he led his division against the English line. Once more the battle was sharp and furious, but the English soon gained the day. King John's household knights were killed around him, and he and his youngest son Philip were captured. The battle was over. In addition to the booty loaded on his wagons the

Black Prince now had the King of France, his son, an archbishop, thirteen counts, five viscounts, sixteen men of baronial rank, and many lesser captives. Well pleased with his success, he marched back to Bordeaux.

The battle of Poitiers brought to an end the first phase of the Hundred Years' War. The next step was to make a peace treaty by which the French king would be released. Meanwhile the Dauphin, who took over the government in his father's absence, was kept occupied by a rising of the bourgeoisie of Paris, a revolt of the peasants in the country north of Paris, and a war with Charles the Bad of Navarre.* Eventually the Dauphin and Charles the Bad united their forces to suppress the revolts, which seemed to menace the whole noble caste. Some Gascon captains, notably the Captal of Buch, were so bored with the era of quiet that they went off to help the Teutonic knights fight the Prussians. On the way home from his expedition to Prussia the Captal had an opportunity to show his knightly courtesy by rescuing the wife of the Dauphin and a number of other noble women who were besieged by a large force of rebellious peasants. The Captal and his troops slaughtered every peasant in sight and escorted the ladies to safety.

King John was treated with extreme courtesy by the Black Prince in Bordeaux and by his father in London. Edward allowed his captive to live in royal state—at his own expense. The other noble prisoners were allowed to go where they pleased within the island realm to the considerable perturbation of English noblemen with handsome wives. In 1359 a treaty of peace was agreed to by King John. He was to pay a ransom of 4 million crowns. Gascony was to be extended to include the entire ancient duchy of Aquitaine, and Edward was to have in addition Touraine, Anjou, Maine, Normandy, the suzerainty over Brittany, and a block of territory surrounding Calais. He was to surrender his claim to be king of France, and John was to renounce all rights over Edward's French lands. It is doubtful that anyone expected this treaty to go into force. The Dauphin treated it as a pleasant joke, and he and the Black Prince began serious negotiations. The result was the treaty of Brétigny, later confirmed by the two monarchs at Calais. The ransom was reduced to 3 million crowns. Edward was to have the ancient lands of the duchy of Aquitaine, the county of Ponthieu, and a small territory surrounding Calais. When all the territorial changes had

* See pp. 386–8.

been carried out and the ransom paid, Edward and John were at the same moment to renounce their respective claims to the throne of France and the suzerainty over the English lands in France. This masterpiece of an arrangement was probably concocted in the subtle brain of the very keen young man who was soon to be king of France. He had no desire to see the French crown renounce its right to valuable lands in return for Edward giving up a vague claim, and he felt fairly certain it would never happen under this treaty.

33. The French Recovery

THERE was never the slightest chance that the treaty of Brétigny would be carried out. The French government could not possibly raise 3 million crowns. Moreover, the territorial adjustments were highly difficult. No two people agreed exactly on the boundaries of the districts mentioned in the treaty, and this could lead to years of pleasant negotiation. Many castles in Normandy and Maine were held by English captains, while the parts of Aquitaine to be given Edward were in the hands of French nobles. The French lords had no desire to become vassals of Edward and made as many delays as possible, but the real difficulty lay with the English captains. They were comfortably seated in strong fortresses ruling the countryside, and they had no intention of giving up their positions just because they were ordered to.

Although only 400,000 crowns of the 3 million crown ransom had been paid when the treaty of Brétigny was ratified at Calais, Edward accepted it as a first installment and released his royal captive. The King's brother, two of his sons, and many of the greatest nobles of France remained in England as hostages for the payment of the ransom. The Dauphin had been making heroic efforts to raise the money for the ransom and had sold his sister to the duke of Milan for a fine round sum, but when the amiable and chivalrous king arrived in Paris, he promptly spent the money in a series of festivities to celebrate his liberation. As France could not at once support King John and collect money for his ransom, the gathering of the ransom made slow progress. Then came a stroke of good fortune for France. John's second son, Louis, duke of Anjou, was a hostage for his father. He was living in Calais and had full freedom to wander about the countryside at will. Just before Poitiers he had married a charming wife, and she was living in one of his castles not far from Calais. Temptation was too strong for young Louis' honor. One day he simply left Calais and went to join his bride. To the shocked protests of his father and brother he turned a deaf ear. King John, a thoroughly chivalrous gentleman, saw only one possible course; he surrendered himself once more as a prisoner. In 1364 he died in London.

The new king of France, Charles V (1364–80), was a far different man from his father and grandfather. They had been large, handsome, and stupid; he was small, homely, and highly intelligent. He had no love for battles; his experience at Poitiers was enough to satisfy him for the rest of his life. Instead he worked diligently with his ministers and spent his spare time reading Latin. But he knew how to choose men, both soldiers and civilians, and how to use them to the limits of their talents. In the sixteen years of his reign he recovered what his father and grandfather had lost.

During the years 1364–67 three important events took place; two of which ended sources of trouble that had long harassed the French crown, and one that was to bring serious difficulties to plague it in the future. In 1364 the young John of Montfort utterly defeated the forces of Charles of Blois, and Charles himself was left dead on the field. Thus the question of Brittany was finally settled. In the same year Charles the Bad was crushed by a royal army at the battle of Cocherel. He was obliged to give up a large part of his Norman lands and to accept in exchange the distant lordship of Montpellier. While he continued to intrigue, he was no longer a serious menace to the government. But more significant than the closing of old quarrels was the rise to power of the new house of Burgundy. The last of the ancient line of dukes of Burgundy died in 1361, leaving as heirs the descendants of his two great-aunts, King John and Charles the Bad. As Charles was descended from the elder aunt, he believed his claim was the better, and it was John's seizure of the duchy that led to the rebellion broken at Cocherel.

John kept Burgundy in the royal demesne, but turned the government over to his youngest son Philip. Charles made his brother duke of Burgundy. The young duke was ambitious and grasping, and soon his eye was on the richest heiress of the day, Margaret, daughter of Louis III, count of Flanders. As her father's only child she would in time inherit his lands, the counties of Flanders, Rethel, and Nevers. Flanders was one of the most valuable fiefs in Europe, and Nevers was the chief county of the duchy of Burgundy. In addition, Margaret would receive in time the possessions of her grandmother: the county of Artois and the imperial county of Burgundy, later known as Franche-Comté. But Margaret's father had strong inclinations toward an English alliance and had affianced her to Edmund of Langley, earl of Cambridge, the fourth son of Edward III. Charles had no intention of allowing the vital county of Flanders to fall into English hands. He promptly persuaded the pope, a firm ally of the French crown, to declare that Margaret and Edmund were too closely related. Then in 1367 the well-trained pontiff granted a dispensation for her marriage to Duke Philip of Burgundy. While it took several more years to persuade the count of Flanders to agree, the marriage finally took place. Philip, known as the Bold for his conduct at Poitiers, was master of Burgundy, Flanders, and the Franche-Comté.

Charles V fully recognized his obligation to go through the forms of carrying out the treaty of Brétigny. The negotiations about the territorial settlements went on, although at a leisurely pace, and he continued to collect money for the ransom. In 1366 a new agreement was reached under which Charles promised to maintain a regular schedule of payments. In return Edward released the hostages of royal blood. As a matter of fact Charles actually paid 400,000 crowns. In short, Charles was a man who wanted his position to be absolutely correct. He fully intended to recommence the war and regain what had been lost, but he was resolved to do so with complete propriety. Fortunately he had little trouble finding an excuse. The Black Prince, who was ruling Aquitaine for his father, was an efficient, strict, and severe administrator. His taxes were high, he collected them firmly, and he insisted on prompt obedience to his commands. The people of the provinces added to Gascony by the treaty of Brétigny were used to the heavy-handed agents of the French crown and were not troubled by the Black Prince and his officers, but the nobles of Gascony were accustomed to easygoing and powerless officers whom they could defy with impunity. Soon two of the chief barons of Gascony, John I of Armagnac and Arnaud Amanieu, lord of Albret, had lodged appeals with the Parlement of Paris. In 1369 the Black Prince was declared contumacious and condemned to forfeit Aquitaine. The war was on once more.

The war that raged for the next five years was a weird affair. The English used their favorite device of large-scale plundering expeditions. Thus in 1373 the third son of Edward III, John of Ghent, landed with an army at Calais marched down through Champagne and on to Bordeaux. He ravaged the open country and burned any unfortified places he passed. When he reached a castle or walled town, he paused to have a few pleasant, chivalrous little skirmishes with the knights of the garrison but made no attempt to take the stronghold. As he moved through the hills of central France, food grew scarce for both men and horses, and by the time the army reached Bordeaux, it was completely exhausted. Under the direction of the canny Charles V the French carefully kept out of battles. A few French knights would place themselves in the fortresses along the English route to participate in the entertaining little skirmishes. Sometimes, if the expedition showed signs of exhaustion while still in French territory, small French forces would move in to harass its march, but no attempt was made to stop these excursions by pitched battles.

While the English were proudly and futilely marching across the land, Charles' captains were systematically reducing their fortresses by any means that came to hand. The general direction of this campaign against English Aquitaine was in the hands of Charles' younger brother Louis, duke of Anjou, governor of Languedoc; but the actual work was done by a varied group of captains. The most noted of these both in his own day and in the pages of history was Bertran Duguesclin. This petty Breton nobleman took his name from a barren island off the coast of Brittany near St. Malo. Bertran was a man of courage, personal prowess, and considerable competence as the leader of small bands. He was hopelessly ineffective as a tactician and could nearly always manage to lose a pitched battle, but he was a genius at ambushes, surprises, and sudden unexpected assaults on castles.

As a young man he had entered the service of Charles of Blois and taken part in such chivalrous affrays as the battle of the thirty champions. Bit by bit he acquired a reputation as a stubborn fighter and bold captain. When the war was renewed, King Charles made Duguesclin constable of France and turned him loose on the English. His first exploit was to harass an English force that had marched from Calais through the Ile de France on its way to Brittany. So skillfully did Duguesclin operate that he succeeded in cutting off and destroying a fair part of the English army. But his true forte was the taking of castles. If possible he would bribe someone within to open a gate late at night. He was not above sending fair ladies of easy virtue into a castle to seduce the garrison and when the time came, let him in. Often he would simply rush suddenly on the castle in the dead of night, and his men would have scaled the walls before the garrison knew what was happening.

Duguesclin was not the only captain engaged in this good work. One of the most successful was Louis, duke of Bourbon, a prince of the blood royal and one of the greatest lords of France. One of Duke Louis' exploits shows particularly clearly the nature of much of this warfare. He was operating on the borders of Poitou at the head of a strong company, almost a small army, consisting largely of his own retainers and vassals. He decided to attack a castle that was held for the Black Prince by an English garrison commanded by a squire. The Duke first attempted to take the place by assault, but it was too strong and too well defended. He then settled down to mining. The garrison soon guessed what was going on and started a countermine. One day as the Duke was sitting in his tent, one of his men came to tell him that the two mines had met. He immediately ordered his herald to inquire whether any noble knight in the castle would like to meet a noble French knight in the mine. The captain replied that the garrison lacked knights, but a noble squire would be delighted to fight in the mine.

This satisfied the Duke, and arming himself from head to foot he descended into the mine to meet the English captain. The mine was so low and narrow that one could neither raise a weapon nor move one's arms far from one's sides. Fighting consisted of the two men poking swords at one another. As it was impossible for knights in armor to hurt each other in this way, it was a thoroughly enjoyable affair. The Duke got so excited that he shouted his war cry, and the squire recognized it and asked if he were really fighting the Duke of Bourbon. When he learned what a great honor had been done him by being allowed to fight so noble a prince, he offered to surrender the castle if Bourbon would dub him a knight. The Duke agreed, but asked that the surrender be put off till the next day. It would be selfish of them to deny their followers the pleasure of fighting in the mine. So all that day, two by two, French and English poked at each other joyfully in the mine. Next morning the castle surrendered, the duke dubbed the squire, they exchanged gifts, and everyone went his way. The biographer of Duke Louis assures us that everyone who heard of this affair was filled with admiration for the courtesy of the two participants. The Duke of Bourbon was a chivalrous gentleman, beloved by both knights and ladies. His biographer suggests that Edward III released him from captivity in England at the earnest request of his nobles who feared for the virtue of their wives. It is worth noticing, however, that he got the castle.

The French armies were quickly successful. Edward III was growing old, the Black Prince was in wretched health and had few more years to live, and their captains seemed no match for Duguesclin and his colleagues. One by one the English fortresses fell, until the capture of La Réole in 1374 reduced the duchy of Gascony to the coastal region between the mouth of the Garonne and the Pyrenees. By avoiding battles and systematically taking the enemy strongholds—and thus the land dependent on them—Charles V had recovered rather more than his ancestors had lost.

Unfortunately the defeat of the English did not free France from the horrors of war. When a mediaeval monarch no longer had need of his hired troops, he stopped paying them. He felt no responsibility whatever for seeing that they got home. Moreover, many of the captains and men who served Edward and his sons were not Englishmen but adventurers from many lands who fought for pay and booty. When their pay stopped, they proceeded to live off the countryside, wandering about and plundering at will. Freed from what little discipline their noble generals had been able to impose on them, they became fiendishly cruel marauders. These "Free Companies," as they were called at first, became a serious menace in the interval of peace after the treaty of Brétigny. The renewal of the war kept them busy for a while, but when hostilities slackened after 1374 they became unemployed once more. While they ordinarily avoided fortified places, they would at times storm a small castle or town and were not above holding noble ladies for ransom. Attempts were made to send them off into other lands, but France was good plundering, and they usually refused to move. When the nobles of a region grew desperate and marched against them, the Companies usually won. Several times they defeated royal armies in pitched battles. Duguesclin's last battle was fought against them. He won the battle but was killed in it. These companies were to be the bane of France for over a century.

The Black Prince died in 1376, Edward III in 1377, and Charles V in 1380. There was no formal peace between the two hostile states until a twenty-year truce was concluded in 1396, when King Richard II (1377–99) of England married Isabelle, daughter of Charles VI (1380–1422) of France; but in this period internal troubles in the two kingdoms kept their rulers busy at home. The reign of Richard II saw a series of baronial revolts and a serious popular rising. It ended in the deposition of the King and his replacement by his cousin Henry, duke of Lancaster, son of John of Ghent; who took the crown as Henry IV (1399–1413).* Henry was a competent soldier and a firm and able statesman, but his seat on the throne was never very secure. John of Ghent had been the third son of Edward III; and if the crown was to pass in the male line, Henry IV was the rightful heir of Richard II. But few Englishmen, in fact not even Henry himself, believed that the English succession was restricted to males. He claimed to be king by hereditary right on the fantastic argument that his mother's great-grandfather, Edmund, earl of Lancaster, son of Henry III, had in reality been older than his brother Edward I. Actually Henry IV was king by Parliamentary election; and the barons who gave him the throne never let him forget that they could take it away equally easily. Standing ready to supplant him was Edmund, earl of March, great-grandson of Lionel duke of Clarence, second son of Edward III. Throughout his reign baronial risings and threats of rising kept Henry busy in England.

The political situation in France was even more confused. When Charles V died, his son Charles VI was a minor, and the government was taken over by a group of royal princes: Louis, duke of Anjou; John, duke of Berry; Philip, duke of Burgundy; and Louis, duke of Bourbon. As each of these princes was primarily interested in increasing his own power, they quarreled continuously. When Louis of Anjou died in 1384, Philip of Burgundy became practically the master of the realm, until the young king grew tired of his tutelage and took over the government himself. King Charles restored his father's ministers who had been removed by the princes and showered lands and offices on his younger brother Louis, duke of Orleans. Unfortunately Charles VI was highly unstable mentally and inclined to a life of luxury and dissipation that increased the difficulty. In 1392 he became insane, and the Duke of Burgundy was made regent. Charles had brief periods of sanity in which he took over his royal duties to some extent but actually simply followed the advice of his brother Orleans. Thus, when Charles was insane, Burgundy ruled, and when he was sane Orleans was in power. Needless to say, the government was in perpetual chaos while these two princes struggled for power, and Berry and Bourbon tried more or less ineffectually to mediate between them. In 1404

* See pp. 377–8.

Philip of Burgundy died and was succeeded by his son John, an able, ambitious, and completely ruthless prince.

Duke John soon decided to get rid of his rival. One evening in 1407 as Louis of Orleans was on his way home through the streets of Paris he was set upon and murdered by a band in the employ of the Duke of Burgundy. This act of violence split France into two hostile parties. The young duke of Orleans, Charles, and his father-in-law the count of Armagnac became bitter and implacable foes of the Burgundian duke. Duke John boasted of his crime and maintained that he had simply rid France of a dangerous tyrant. He obliged the poor mad king, his family, and the court to listen to a long sermon on the virtue of tyranicide delivered by one of his clerical partisans. In general, the nobles favored the Orleanist party while the towns, especially Paris, preferred the Burgundian. For some years Duke John was master of Paris and the government, but in 1413 the Armagnacs—as the Orleans party were called—captured the city, and the Duke retired to his own lands.

34. Henry V and Jeanne d'Arc

KING HENRY IV of England died in 1413 and was succeeded by his son Henry V (1413–22). The new king was an able captain and brave soldier whose name has gone down in history wreathed in martial glory. Away from the battlefield he was a thoroughly unpleasant person. He was so avid for power that he had tried to depose his father so that he could take his place. He was a cold, heartless bigot with no interest except his own welfare. Henry's love of war, combined with his lust for power and a belief that if he kept the English barons busy in France they would be less likely to revolt at home, led him to reopen the long-suspended war. He had no difficulty finding good excuses. He still claimed the crown of France. Moreover, both parties in that kingdom had asked his aid in their quarrels, but Henry's demands were heavier than either Burgundians or Armagnacs felt able to meet. Henry wanted all Aquitaine, Anjou, Maine, Touraine, and Normandy, with suzerainty over Brittany and Flanders. In August 1415 the English king landed in Normandy with some 2,000 men-at-arms and about 6,000 archers, and immediately laid siege to the town of Harfleur. The place fell on September 22, but an epidemic of dysentery had gravely reduced both the size and efficiency of his army. Henry decided to go home, but in order to show his contempt for his enemy, he planned to go by way of Calais. Meanwhile the host of France had been slowly assembling. The duke of Burgundy refused to answer the summons, but many of his nobles headed by one of his brothers joined the army.

King Henry's idea of marching to Calais was an extremely reckless one. Disease and the casualties incurred at the siege of Harfleur had reduced his army to some 6,000 men. He was so short of supplies that his men were almost starving, and heavy rains had turned the countryside into a sea of mud. When he learned that the French army was marching against him, his men were too weak and exhausted to attempt to flee further, and he was obliged to prepare to fight. Choosing a position where his flanks were covered by the gardens and orchards of two villages, Tramecourt and Agincourt, Henry arrayed his men in the usual three divisions with the knights and pikemen forming solid blocks flanked by the archers.

The French had learned from Poitiers not to risk either their king or his heir in battle. The nominal commander of the army was the constable, the lord of Albret, but as he was a comparatively insignificant lord he could do little with the royal princes such as Orleans and Bourbon. The constable was an old soldier who remembered the methods of Duguesclin. He saw no point in attacking the English position. If the French army placed itself between Henry and Calais, Henry would have to take the offensive. But once more the noble knights had their way. The only course for gentlemen was to fight at once. The tactics of Poitiers were followed almost exactly. A small body of horse was to charge first. Then the chivalry of France were to attack on foot, ranged in three divisions. The crossbowmen were apparently once more placed behind the men-at-arms, so that they were utterly unable to use their weapons.

The plan of battle that made some slight sense at Poitiers was utterly insane at Agincourt. For one thing, armor had been steadily increasing in weight. In the hope of protecting themselves completely from missile weapons, the knights of France and England had adopted massive plate armor. It was extremely difficult for them to walk any distance, and if they fell down it was almost impossible for them to get up without help. Moreover, the rains had reduced the countryside to a quagmire. As at Poitiers, the French cavalry charge was largely stopped by the English archers. While their arrows could not pierce the armor of the knights, they killed the knights' horses and so broke up the charge. Then the French dismounted divisions advanced. By the time these knights had struggled through the mud to the English line, they were much too exhausted to fight. Seeing their plight, Henry ordered his archers to drop their bows and go out to fight the French hand to hand. As the tired French knights could hardly raise their arms to use their weapons, they were easily captured or slain. By the time the third French division was ready to attack King Henry had almost as many prisoners as troops.

Then, just as the last French battle moved toward his line, Henry received word that another enemy force was in his rear attacking his camp. Actually it was only a country squire, the lord of Agincourt, at the head of a group of peasants who had decided to see what plunder he could find in the unguarded camp, but Henry was thoroughly alarmed and ordered his men to kill all their prisoners. No one paid the slightest attention to this command. Most of the prisoners were great nobles whose ransoms meant incredible fortunes to the archers who had captured them, and they had no intention of killing them. Finally Henry ordered his household knights to conduct the slaughter, and many noble Frenchmen were murdered before the King learned that his fears had been groundless. The lord of Agincourt was not dangerous, and the French third division discreetly retired without attacking. The French losses had been extremely severe—some 1,500 nobles, and 3,000 ordinary men-at-arms. Despite the killing of many prisoners, Henry still had over a thousand captives, including the dukes of Orleans and Bourbon. The English losses were fantastically small—less than a hundred. Their most important casualty was the King's cousin, Edward, duke of York. Edward had lived well and easily. The weight of his armor in the hot summer day and the excitement of battle were too much for him, and he died of apoplexy.

The defeat of Agincourt had practically wiped out the Armagnac party, and the Duke of Burgundy once more became master of the realm. The remnants of his foes were led by the heir to the throne, the Dauphin Charles. In an attempt to restore peace in the kingdom in the face of the English menace, the Dauphin and Duke John had a series of conferences. At one of these conferences, held in the middle of a bridge, an old Orleanist captain finally avenged his duke's death by slaying the Duke of Burgundy. The new duke, Philip, called "the Good," promptly made an alliance with Henry V, who was engaged in methodically reducing the strongholds of Normandy. As the Burgundians were masters of Paris and the King, this led in May 1420 to the Treaty of Troyes with Henry V. This treaty declared the Dauphin Charles disinherited for his "horrible and enormous crimes." In fact, as the queen had obligingly stated that he was not really the son of Charles VI, he was referred to as the "so-called Dauphin." Henry V was to marry the King's daughter Catherine and become heir to the French throne. While his father-in-law lived, Henry was to hold Normandy as well as Aquitaine. The Duke of Burgundy was guaranteed all the rights and privileges he claimed in his own lands—something very close to complete sovereignty.

During the year 1422 both Charles VI and Henry V died, and in accordance with the Treaty of Troyes the crowns of France and England passed to the latter's son Henry, who was only a few months old. The infant king's uncles, John, duke of Bedford, and Humphrey, duke of Gloucester, became regents in France and England respectively. Actually, France was divided into three separate states. The Duke of Bedford ruled in the name of his nephew over Normandy, Maine, the Ile de France, and Champagne. Paris and the region to the west were actually held by English garrisons, while Champagne was occupied by Burgundian troops acting as Bedford's allies. The near-independence granted the Duke of Burgundy by the Treaty of Troyes was made virtually complete by the minority of the King. Bedford was obliged to treat him as a sovereign ally. In theory, the Duke of Brittany acknowledged Henry VI, and hence his territory formed part of the English domains; but he was always ready to do what seemed most profitable to him and was a most unreliable vassal. The Loire valley and all France to the south of Loire river outside of the duchy of Gascony recognized as king the Dauphin Charles, who made his capital at Bourges. A large proportion of the civil servants of the French crown moved to Bourges and from there governed the southern two thirds of the realm.

The Dauphin's position was essentially strong. The English upper classes had little interest in their child monarch's French kingdom and no intention whatever of paying for its maintenance. Bedford had very few English troops and found it extremely difficult to raise the money needed to support them. His efforts to increase taxes in the region he controlled made him less popular and failed to obtain enough money. The Duke of Burgundy was interested solely in schemes for increasing his own power in eastern France and the Low Countries. He would cheerfully promise Bedford troops, but they rarely arrived. Most of the nobles of the lands ruled by Bedford had stayed loyal to the Dauphin and followed him to the south. Moreover, most of the captains of the French army had accepted the Dauphin. All through Bedford's territory, especially to the east of Paris, were fortresses held by these captains in the name of the Dauphin. Thus, along the frontier between Champagne and Lorraine, Robert de Baudricourt, captain of the castle of Vaucouleurs, dominated the countryside. The Dauphin's chief disadvantages were his own character and the selfish cupidity of his chief advisers.

Charles was a sickly, homely, weak-willed, and timid young man whose oversensitive feelings had been deeply wounded by the Treaty of Troyes—especially by his mother's statement that he was a bastard. He was surrounded by greedy and ambitious men of strong character. For a long time the most potent of these was George, duke of La Trémoille. La Trémoille's landed power was centered in northern Poitou, and he persuaded Charles to reside at Chinon, where his retainers were close at hand. The Duke calmly stole the money raised by taxes in southern France and when he felt generous loaned it to the Dauphin at interest. On one occasion, when a French baron came to visit the Dauphin, La Trémoille and his men abducted him as he left the royal chamber and tortured him till he made a will in the Duke's favor. La Trémoille and his friends had no desire to see Charles recover the throne of France, as this would increase the competition for his favor. They were very happy wasting the revenues of two thirds of the kingdom. The only serious obstacle to La Trémoille's power at court came from a woman, Yolande of Aragon, duchess of Anjou, whose daughter became Charles' wife. Yolande was a strong personality and an able politician who knew how to build up court parties. La Trémoille was to end his career under the daggers of Yolande's friends.

In the year 1428 Bedford found himself faced with a perplexing problem. He wanted to extend his nephew's territories south of the Loire, but the valley of the river was controlled by two great princes, the dukes of Orleans and Anjou, whom he hoped to win over to the cause of Henry VI. Charles, duke of Orleans, had been captured at Agincourt and was a prisoner in England, but the duchy was being vigorously defended by the duchess and the duke's illegitimate half brother, the count of Dunois, known as the bastard of Orleans. After long consideration Bedford decided that it was better to offend Orleans than Anjou, and his troops moved into the duchy and laid siege to its fortresses, including the city of Orleans. The English built works to blockade the city and conducted the siege as energetically as their very small numbers would permit. The local militia and a few professional soldiers conducted a rather lackadaisical defense. As time went on it looked more and more as if the English army would capture the key to the Loire valley. The supporters of the Dauphin seemed to lack all spirit and cohesion. They would cheerfully ravage Bedford's territory and surprise isolated castles, but they showed no desire to meet English troops in battle. The long succession of defeats suffered by the armies of France seems to have hopelessly destroyed their confidence.

Meanwhile, on the eastern border of Champagne Robert de Baudricourt, captain of Vaucouleurs, was as perplexed as the Duke of Bedford but for a quite different reason: a young and very determined peasant girl from the village of Domrémy was bothering him to death. For a century after the county of Champagne had come into the possession of the crown, Domrémy had been part of the royal demesne. Then it had belonged to Louis of Orleans, who had been a kindly prince well loved by his people. The affections of the peasants were with the Dauphin and his cause. While they knew little about the English except that they were in some way responsible for the wars, their villages had recently been plundered by the Burgundians, and they longed for the peaceful days of Duke Louis. In Domrémy lived a simple, completely uneducated, and deeply religious peasant girl named Jeanne d'Arc. Her mind was filled with stories of the saints and with the wrongs done by the English and Burgundians to France and her rightful king. She believed that several of her favorite saints appeared to her and commanded her to raise the siege of Orleans and have the Dauphin crowned at Reims. Jeanne made her way to Vaucouleurs to tell Robert de Baudricourt of her visions and to urge him to send her to the Dauphin. Robert was a tough, rather brutal professional soldier and a man of the world. He knew that this was no new phenomenon. There had been a regular epidemic of women with visions, and all had been declared either insane or witches. He had no desire to annoy the court with another, and he may have been kindly enough to hate to see a foolish girl get into trouble. But Jeanne was determined. She won the faith of some of Robert's men, and the captain finally told them that they might take her to Chinon if they were foolish enough to want to.

On February 23, 1429, after safely crossing a countryside held by the English and Burgundians, Jeanne and her slender escort arrived at Chinon. She is said to have told Charles something that gave him new hope and courage—perhaps she assured him that he was legitimate. But the Dauphin was suspicious of women with visions, and he ordered his clerks to examine Jeanne. They found her to be what she was, an ignorant young girl filled with belief in her mission and fully confident that she was obeying the commands of God. There was a rough and ready test for witchcraft, and the examiners decided to use it and abide by the result. As witches have regular intercourse with the devil, a virgin could not be a witch. Hence, when a committee of noble matrons certified to Jeanne's virginity, the clerks assured Charles that she was not a witch. Since nothing could make his troops fight worse, Charles saw no reason for refusing Jeanne a chance, especially as she had quickly won the confidence of several of his captains including a prince of the blood, John II, duke of Alençon. Alençon was about to lead a force to carry supplies into Orleans, and Jeanne went along with him.

The captains who served the Dauphin were a mixed crew. There were two great nobles, the Duke of Alençon and Arthur, count of Richmont, constable of France, and brother of the Duke of Brittany. Then there were gay and reckless young lords such as Gilles de Rais, later to win immortal ill fame as Bluebeard, and Dunois, the bastard of Orleans. Finally there were the fierce, brutal, rapacious mercenary captains who served Charles when he paid them and plundered the countryside for their own profit when they were unemployed. All these varied types seem to have been impressed by Jeanne's simple faith. Still more important, her confidence inspired the soldiers themselves and made them believe that perhaps Frenchmen could beat Englishmen. This restoration of confidence was the miracle wrought by Jeanne d'Arc. The garrison of Orleans sallied out, destroyed the English works, and drove off the besieging army. The same fate quickly overtook the English forces besieging the other fortresses of the duchy, and an English army hastening to their assistance was crushed in a pitched battle. In the space of a few weeks the Loire valley was cleared of the enemy and Bedford's military resources temporarily crippled.

By raising the siege of Orleans Jeanne had fulfilled one of the tasks imposed upon her by her visions. The second, the consecration of the Dauphin at Reims, was even closer to her heart. Although here and there signs were appearing of what we call national feeling, a belief that there was such a thing as the French people, in the minds of most men France was still simply the land ruled by the king of France. Hence until the Dauphin was crowned, there could be no true France. Jeanne, with the strong support of the king's chief ecclesiastical counsellor, the archbishop of Reims, urged an immediate expedition to the primate's seat. Late in June Charles started the long march, at the head of some 12,000 men. What had appeared to the timid as a dangerous expedition across hostile territory, was in fact a pleasant parade. Bedford was frantically mustering his forces to defend Paris and Normandy, while the Burgundians were completely unprepared for effective action. As Charles moved through the country, the towns opened their gates to him. On July 16 he occupied Reims, and the next day he was duly consecrated in its cathedral. Although the crown and sceptre were in the possession of the English and no lay peer of France was present, the sacred oil that created a king was the prime essence of a coronation. The Dauphin Charles had become Charles VII (1422–61) of France.

Her success in her two chief objects did not quench Jeanne's enthusiasm, and her burning zeal carried the armies of France to the very walls of Paris. But the English garrisons held firm in the great city and a ring of subsidiary fortresses. Meanwhile the king and court were slipping back into their customary apathy. The campaign in the Loire valley, the march to Reims, and the campaign that followed had drained the treasury. The courtiers hated to see money that could be used for pleasant living wasted in military campaigns. Now that Charles was king, diplomacy seemed to them a more suitable weapon than the sword. If Brittany and Burgundy could be won over, the English cause would be lost. Even the captains were a little tired of Jeanne's zeal for fighting. To them war was a business, and plundering its most profitable element. One had to fight battles occasionally, but they were not to be sought too avidly. Hence the campaign ground slowly to a halt. Worse yet, the Burgundians had now mustered their forces and were beginning a counterattack by attempting to reduce the strongholds north of Paris that had long been held by captains in Charles' pay. One of Duke Philip's captains, John of Luxembourg, laid siege to the town of Compiègne. Burning to be in battle once more, Jeanne hastened there with a few troops to reinforce the garrison. Some days later she led a sortie against the besieging forces. Although they were taken by surprise, the Burgundians rallied quickly and routed Jeanne's force, which retired toward the gate. Jeanne, however, refusing to admit defeat, continued to fight at the head of a few devoted followers. The commander of the town, who feared that if he left the gate open too long the Burgundians would rush in, ordered it closed, and Jeanne and her followers were captured.

It was but natural that the English and Burgundians should have considered Jeanne the source of all their recent troubles. Her presence had inspired an army that had been able to do no more than defend rather feebly a few strongholds and make occasional plundering raids to win victory after victory. Her fiery enthusiasm had deprived Bedford of several of his best captains and nearly half his territory in France. The modern historian, little given to belief in divine intervention, finds himself inclined to call this accomplishment by a simple peasant girl a miracle. To the ordinary man in that age of faith Jeanne's success was clearly supernatural, and whether he believed that it sprang from God or the Devil depended largely on which side he was on. The learned doctors of the university of Paris, whose sympathies were overwhelmingly Burgundian, demanded that Jeanne be turned over to the Inquisition for prosecution for witchcraft; and it is likely that they fairly represented English and Burgundian opinion. Whether Bedford believed Jeanne to be a witch or simply an intolerable nuisance is a matter of small moment except to his own conscience. He promptly bought her from the impecunious John of Luxembourg, placed her safely in Rouen castle, and assigned Peter Cauchon, bishop of Beauvais, to conduct her trial.

According to the customs of the time the trial was not unfair. The Church had the power to judge whether a person had genuine visions or mere delusions of the devil. By refusing to accept Cauchon's pronouncement that her visions were delusions, she became a heretic. She had also worn men's clothes in defiance of canon law and refused to admit that this was wrong. In short, Jeanne defied the church and was condemned. The university of Paris, perhaps the greatest authority in Christendom on such questions, fully supported the court's decision.* At the same time it is important to remember that Cauchon was a

* See p. 475.

political bishop completely under Bedford's thumb. The Duke never allowed him to forget that his task was to send Jeanne to the stake, and whenever he seemed to waver or delay he was vigorously prodded by his master. I do not believe an Edward III would have burned Jeanne. She was essentially the victim of the cold, savage bigotry of the house of Lancaster. Her death will always be a stain on the honor of English soldiers.

Fortunately for Bedford's reputation, his calculating cruelty has been overshadowed in the pages of history by Charles' pusillanimity. Despite his heavy obligations to Jeanne, Charles did nothing whatever to save her. And there were a number of things he might have done. John of Luxembourg was a thoroughly decent soldier who would have preferred to sell Jeanne to her friends, but no one made him an adequate offer. Charles had noble English prisoners who could be used to negotiate for exchange. While rescue of Jeanne by force was probably impossible, a major military effort against the weak English positions might well have obliged Bedford to release Jeanne in return for a truce. Only when some years later he realized that it was not dignified to owe his crown to a condemned heretic did Charles make any move in Jeanne's favor. Then a carefully packed ecclesiastical court declared that she had been a good girl. While this may seem a sensible conclusion to the skeptical mind, to a man steeped in mediaeval religion it was, as Bernard Shaw has so keenly seen, utterly ridiculous. Jeanne had claimed divine inspiration. If it was genuine, she was a saint; if it was not, she was a heretic. Only the complete reversal of Cauchon's decision, Jeanne's sanctification in the twentieth century, makes her story complete and acceptable.

After Jeanne's death the war went on in much the same desultory fashion as before her appearance. Charles lacked the energy and the resources to do anything decisive, and Bedford could merely hold his own against the petty operations of the French captains. It soon became clear that the only course for Charles was to make peace with Burgundy. Duke Philip still remembered bitterly the murder of his father and was too completely the noble knight to turn suddenly against his English allies, but his affection for the latter had for some years been growing cooler. This was the result to a considerable extent of the exploits of one of the most amazing men of the day, Humphrey, duke of Gloucester, youngest brother of Henry V. Duke Humphrey was a gay, luxury-loving prince who was a patron of learning and a collector of books. His library was the foundation of the great Bodleian library at Oxford. He was also ambitious and reckless. The valuable counties of Hainaut, Holland, and Zeeland, lying near Philip of Burgundy's county of Flanders, were held by a young woman who was Duke Philip's cousin. If she died without heirs, the counties were his. He carefully married her to a young man who he felt sure would serve his purpose. But the young countess was gay and vigorous and had no use for her colorless spouse. She ran away to England, and enlisted the sympathies of the dashing Humphrey of Gloucester. By diligent canvassing of rival popes she obtained the annulment of her marriage and became the wife of Gloucester. Philip of Burgundy promptly marched into her lands, drove out Gloucester, imprisoned her, and took over her inheritance, but the whole affair gravely injured his relations with Bedford, who had made no great effort to control his impetuous brother. The only bond that held the two dukes together was Bedford's wife, who was Philip's sister. When she died in 1434, peace between Charles and Philip became possible. After long negotiations conducted by the count of Richmont, who was also Philip's brother-in-law, the Duke of Burgundy agreed to discuss terms of peace, but he insisted that the conference should include his English allies.

In August 1435 the three parties met at the town of Arras. It soon became clear that peace with England was impossible. Bedford insisted that Henry VI be recognized as king of France and that Charles hold the lands in his possession as Henry's vassal. The English quit the conference on September 1. Then Duke Philip, whose conscience was now at rest, began serious negotiations, and on September 20 the Treaty of Arras was concluded. Philip obtained two counties bordering his Burgundian lands, Macon and Auxerre, and two adjoining Flanders. While Charles lived, he would not do homage for his fiefs held of the French crown. Charles would make public amends for his part in the murder of Duke John.

Bedford died shortly after the conclusion of the Treaty of Arras. While the men who commanded in France for Henry VI held out for another fifteen years, it must have been fairly clear that their cause was hopeless. One by one the towns and castles held by the English surrendered to Charles' captains. The last battle in the north was fought at Formigny in Normandy, in 1450. A small English force sent to relieve the garrisons being besieged met a French army under the Constable of

Richmont. The battle had a novel feature. The English took up their favorite position on a hill, but instead of attacking directly, Richmont mounted cannon and bombarded them until they broke their formation. Then he easily cut them to pieces. Two years later the crushing defeat of the earl of Shrewsbury near Bordeaux ended the English rule in Gascony. All that was left to Henry VI of his kingdom of France was the town of Calais and its environs. While all English kings until George III continued to bear the title king of France, it was an entirely empty dignity.

35. The Art of War in the Late Middle Ages

THE FINAL capitulation of Bordeaux in 1452 ended the Hundred Years' War, but before closing this chapter it seems well to glance briefly at the important changes in military institutions that marked the late Middle Ages. One of the most interesting of these was the gradual increase in the use of gunpowder. Cannon were known in Europe as early as 1324. Edward III possessed a fair number. While the statement of some chroniclers that he used cannon at Crécy is dubious, he certainly had them at the siege of Calais. From that time on, cannon formed a regular part of the military equipment of the states of Western Europe. This early artillery was not, however, very effective. The balls of stone and metal were too light and were thrown with too little force to do much harm to stone walls. As the cannon lacked movable mounts, they were of little use in the field except when an army on the defensive wanted to forbid the enemy the use of some narrow passage. The noise of cannon created a certain amount of confusion and consternation, but there is little evidence that during the fourteenth century they did anyone much harm. Captains besieging castles usually found it more effective to use the powder intended for their cannon to make explosions in mines. The smaller firearms, commonly called *ribaulds*, were not much more effective. These were mounted on wheels, usually two or three barrels to a carriage, or a number of them were placed on a cart. They were intended to kill or wound troops, but they took so long to load and fire that they were not much use in battle.

In the fifteenth century, artillery began to be important in the siege and defense of castles and towns. Professional artillerymen appeared who acquired great skill in handling their weapons. While the cannon were still not very effective against the massive stone walls of fortresses, they could batter down gates and thus gain entrance for the besieging troops. A common device in the early fifteenth century was to place a number of cannon in a semicircle so that all bore on a town gate and gradually battered it to pieces. As soon as cannon became common as siege weapons, the owners of castles felt the need of them for defense, but this created serious problems. The recoil of the cannon quickly shook to pieces the walls on which they were mounted. The usual solution was to cut down the outer wall to about a third of its height and increase its thickness so it could support the cannon. Artillery was still of little value in the field except under unusual circumstances. If an army was operating on the defensive, cannon could make the ground directly in front of them untenable, but they could be moved only with great difficulty. Occasionally they could be used against an army drawn up in a defensive position, as at Formigny. But in a battle where the troops had freedom of movement, they could easily get out of the way of the enemy cannon.

The ribaulds became more numerous in the fifteenth century, but as a rule were not very valuable. Their chief use was from the walls of fortresses against besieging troops. When the Emperor Sigismund attempted to suppress the Hussite heretics, he found himself faced with masses of carts on which ribaulds were mounted.* His cavalry could not break through the ring of carts and suffered heavily from the ribaulds. There are references to the use of a very small ribauld carried by individual soldiers—the ancestor of the musket of the sixteenth century. It seems very doubtful, however, that they could compete in effectiveness with either the crossbow or the longbow as a missile weapon. They were very slow-firing and magnificently inaccurate.

It has frequently been claimed that the development of firearms resulted in the abandonment of armor, but actually there seems to have been little connection between the two processes. During the fourteenth century the increased effectiveness of the crossbow and longbow led the knights to increase the thickness and weight of their armor. By the time of Agincourt, a fully armed cavalryman was completely encased in heavy plate armor, and his horse was similarly equipped. As result, the knight was helpless on foot and when mounted could only move with ponderous dignity over the most favorable

* See p. 427.

ground. In short, the heavy cavalry became useful only for charges under ideal conditions. By the end of the century most troops were using lighter armor to increase their mobility. The officers continued to wear the massive plate armor, but even in the heavy cavalry the ordinary soldier began to reduce the weight of his equipment. Certainly throughout the sixteenth century armor was an effective protection against the handguns of the day. Only a lucky shot that hit a weak spot could pierce heavy plate armor.

The fifteenth century saw one interesting development in tactics. The son and successor of Duke Philip of Burgundy, Charles, called the "Bold" or the "Reckless," was an ambitious prince who hoped to build an independent state between France and Germany—to reconstruct the ancient state of Lothaire.* This involved conquering Lorraine, which lay between his possessions in the Low Countries and Burgundy, and Switzerland, through which ran the passes leading to Italy. This scheme led him into a series of wars with the Swiss. Like the northern Welsh and the Highland Scots, the Swiss were essentially spearmen who fought on foot in massive formation. But they had learned something that other mediaeval spearmen had not—to move in close formation without breaking their ranks. The Welsh and the Highlanders massed on the defensive could repulse heavy cavalry, but once they tried to move, their ranks opened and gave the horsemen a chance to break in. The Swiss were drilled so that they could march and charge in solid columns. When Duke Charles led his Burgundian cavalry up the narrow Swiss valleys, the Swiss came charging down with a solid mass of pikes and completely routed the horsemen. During the last decades of the fifteenth and the first of the sixteenth centuries the Swiss spearmen were the most valued soldiers of Europe and were hired by all belligerents to aid in their wars.

The reign of Charles VII saw the establishment of the first regular army that Western Europe had known since the collapse of the Roman Empire. As the Hundred Years' War drew toward its close, the unemployed companies once more became the scourge of France. All sorts of devices were used in the attempt to get rid of them. Several times they were rented to German princes and led off to new and distant wars, but they preferred France and always wandered back again. Charles conceived the idea of taking some of these companies into his service on a permanent basis and using them to fight his wars and sup-

* See p. 91.

press the other companies. In a decree of May 26, 1445, the king announced that he was establishing fifteen *compagnies d'ordonnance.* Each company was to consist of a hundred "lances." A "lance" was the usual fifteenth-century term for a fully armed horseman and his attendants. Each lance in the new companies was to contain a fully armed cavalryman, a knife-wielder whose chief purpose was to kill or capture men knocked down by the knight or squire, two archers, a *valet d'armes,* and a page. The last two were noncombatant servants who cared for the man-at-arms. All these were mounted so that they could move together on the march. Thus Charles had a standing army of 6,000 men. These companies were commanded by great nobles and were named after these commanders. They were the ancestors of the ancient regiments that formed the nucleus of the later French army.

In order to obtain infantry armed with missile weapons who had some training in their use Charles organized a body of militia called Free Archers. Every parish in the royal demesne was to supply a number of men determined by the king's agents. These men were to be equipped by the king, paid a small salary, and exempted from most taxes. In return they were expected to practice regularly and meet at times for drill and instruction. The king's idea was not received with any great enthusiasm among a peasant population unused to arms, and very few men actually became free archers. There are said to have been 8,000 under Charles and 16,000 under his son Louis XI. It seems most unlikely that their drilling was adequate to make them very effective troops. One contemporary suggests that the exemption from taxation tempted the older and more influential villagers, and that when the free archers were mustered they turned out to be mostly aged and portly. Certainly this militia never became an important part of the French military system.

CHAPTER XII

From Feudal to National Monarchy

36. England in the Late Middle Ages
37. France under the House of Valois
38. The Remnants of the Empire

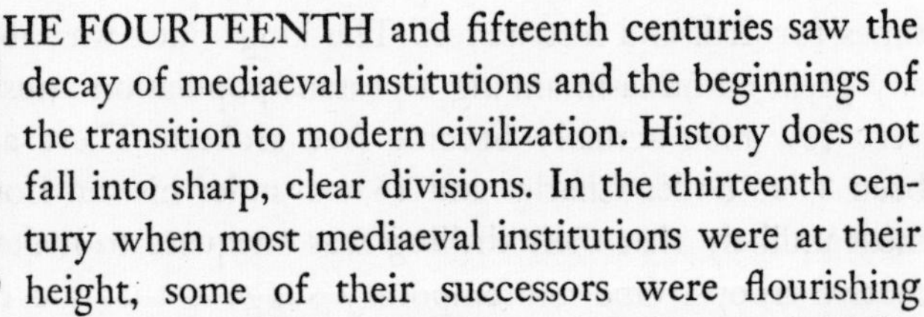

THE FOURTEENTH and fifteenth centuries saw the decay of mediaeval institutions and the beginnings of the transition to modern civilization. History does not fall into sharp, clear divisions. In the thirteenth century when most mediaeval institutions were at their height, some of their successors were flourishing young plants. The basically feudal monarchies of John and Philip Augustus were served by incipient nonfeudal bureaucracies. The noble knight following his liege lord into battle was in danger of being hurt by a crossbow bolt fired by a mercenary soldier. The most powerful of popes was defied by heretics not essentially different from those who eventually brought on the Reformation. But on the whole the thirteenth century was overwhelmingly mediaeval. Henry III, St. Louis, Frederick II, and even Edward I and Philip the Handsome were primarily feudal monarchs in the tradition of Hugh Capet and William the Conqueror. Pope Innocent triumphed over the foes of the Church. The purposes of Albertus Magnus and Thomas Aquinas were the same as those of Abelard, Gratian, and Peter Lombard, and their ways of thought differed but little from those of their predecessors.

In the fourteenth and fifteenth centuries the balance shifted rapidly.

Among the declining mediaeval institutions new ones were taking firm root and growing rapidly. Although some of these new institutions were purely transitional and would disappear in the sixteenth and seventeenth centuries, others became the bases of modern society. The next two chapters will attempt to delineate the broad lines of this process in some of the important phases of Western European civilization.

The political history of the states of Western Europe during the last two centuries of the mediaeval period had a number of interesting aspects. While the authority of princely governments increased very greatly, the power of the princes themselves was not proportionately enlarged. The authority of the feudal state was extremely limited, but it could be exercised without restraint by its rulers. As time went on, the bureaucracies developed strong customs and traditions that tended to restrain the will of the prince. In fact, the officials who composed these bureaucracies began to think of themselves as the servants of the crown as an institution rather than of an individual king. Thus, in the fourteenth century it was not uncommon to see a monarch prevented from doing what he wished because his servants felt that it was against the interest of the crown.

Meanwhile the decay of feudal ideas had vitally changed the relationship between the prince and his people and the institutions that gave it effect. The conception of a primarily tenurial relationship running through the feudal hierarchy gradually disappeared. No longer was the prince's concern limited largely to the interests and desires of his tenants-in-chief; he was the ruler of all the people who lived in his lands and was expected to consider their common welfare. By the fourteenth century the people of a country were no longer thought of as holders of various positions on the feudal ladder, but rather as members of classes or estates. When the prince wanted to exercise authority that was not within his competence, he did not consult his tenants-in-chief, his feudal curia, but the estates of his realm. The system of estates spread throughout Europe and became a vital feature of government. Before long these bodies had grasped the idea that the power to grant was also the power to refuse, and they so became a restraint on both the princes and their bureaucracies.

This change in the relationship between the prince and the inhabitants of his lands brought the beginnings of what the historian calls nationalism. The subjects of each prince began to feel that they had common interests and were bound together through their ruler. They developed a feeling that this was the way God had intended things to be and would not lightly transfer their allegiance to another ruler. This was very apparent when attempts were made to carry out the treaty of Brétigny: the French inhabitants of the lands added to English Gascony stubbornly resisted the transfer of their allegiance. It was seen later in fierce peasant risings against the English in northern France after the treaty of Troyes. Except perhaps in England where a realm isolated from others was inhabited by people with a common language, culture, and tradition, this nationalism was not popular. The French did not think of themselves as the French people, but rather as the subjects of the king of France. This strong traditional feeling for a dynasty could, however, be a very potent patriotic force. As it developed in the various states of Western Europe, the map of the region became more stabilized and lasting conquests by force much more difficult.

36. England in the Late Middle Ages

THE MONARCHY of the Plantagenet kings of England founded by Henry II reached it height under Edward I (1272–1307).* Edward made the most of the ancient feudal sources of royal revenue as well as property taxes and customs duties. In war he used the feudal levy as well as drafts of infantry and paid companies. His government was conducted by a highly efficient bureaucracy of royal servants who were completely subject to his will. The great office of justiciar disappeared, to be replaced by that of chief justice, which was purely legal in its functions. No officer of state was in a position to hamper the king's personal authority. The most important institution in the bureaucracy was the body of sworn councilors who advised the king and conducted the routine business of government. This group of royal servants decided major questions of policy and drew up legislation. It was the dominant force in Parliament. This body, whether composed of the magnates alone or of magnates with the representatives of shires and towns, was summoned to grant money and to confirm legislation drawn by the council. It was used to extend the king's authority but was never allowed to limit it. The barons were ruled

* See pp. 271–5.

with an iron hand. By highly dubious methods, in complete defiance of feudal custom and ordinary decency, several of the greatest baronies were brought into the hands of members of the royal house. In short, Edward was a strong, efficient, and high-handed ruler, whose death was certain to bring a reaction against his methods of government.

Edward II (1307–27) was a striking contrast to his father. Ineffective, weak, and vacillating, he was always under the thumb of some stronger character—his queen, Isabelle of France, his Gascon favorite Peter Gaveston, or the English Dispenser family. In the early years of his reign he was obliged to accept the tutelage of a coalition of barons led by his cousin Thomas, earl of Lancaster. The primary object of these barons, commonly called the Lords Ordainers, was to limit the king's control over the royal administration. Appointments to the great offices of state such as those of chancellor and treasurer were to be approved by the magnates in Parliament—that is, by the Great Council. Although the Lords Ordainers claimed that they acted in the common interest, they were in fact greedy and self-seeking. Like earlier coalitions of the same sort, this alliance eventually fell to pieces. Thomas of Lancaster murdered Peter Gaveston and was in turn defeated and executed by Edward. The realm was then governed in the king's name by the haughty and incredibly rapacious Dispensers, until Queen Isabelle and her lover Roger Mortimer overthrew them and forced the feeble king to abdicate in favor of his son. Edward II was soon brutally murdered by his custodians. For a few years the young king watched the disgraceful spectacle of his mother and Mortimer plundering England, but when they executed his favorite uncle, Edward lost patience. Gathering a band of knights he seized the queen and her lover. Mortimer was executed, and Isabelle was confined to a royal manor.

The long reign of Edward III (1327–77)—only three monarchs in England's history occupied the throne for so many years—was a period of immense importance in the development of English political institutions. There were two basic questions at issue. By far the more important of these was whether the royal government should be conducted by men who were simply the king's servants, bound to accept his will without question, or whether its more vital functions should be performed by officers of state responsible to the realm as a whole. Edward was inclined to set up an administration of royal servants like that of his grandfather. The barons wanted the great officers of state to be answerable to the magnates in Parliament and insisted that there should be a strong baronial element in the king's council. Once, in a moment when he desperately needed funds, Edward agreed to permit baronial control of his ministers, but he promptly revoked his promise. Throughout his reign he appointed his own officials as he saw fit, but he did accept the fact that the great officers of state had a responsibility beyond the mere execution of his will. Late in his reign, when advancing years had enfeebled him, the barons were able to enforce this conception of ministerial responsibility. Several royal servants were convicted of improper acts by the magnates in Parliament. Thus the principle was advanced that while it was extremely difficult to force the king to obey the law, his ministers could be punished for carrying out illegal commands. This was the beginning of the practice known as impeachment—trial of an officer of state by the lords in Parliament at the request of the commons.

Although to the people of the fourteenth century the all-important issue was the control of the royal government that ruled England from day to day, week to week, month to month, and year to year, historians are inclined to be more interested in the development of Parliament because of its later importance. The reign of Edward III was peculiarly propitious for the growth of Parliamentary institutions and functions. Although the king was unwilling to have the barons control his administration, Edward was not basically much interested in the internal government of England. He was essentially a soldier who was chiefly preoccupied with his wars in France. In general, he was willing to make almost any concession in return for the vast sums of money needed for his military operations. At the same time his military success made him a national hero and his open, genial, easy manners brought him the affection of his people. Hence the process of Parliamentary development that might have led to bitter quarrels under another monarch was essentially amiable.

During Edward's reign the composition and organization of Parliament began to assume the form that was to last until today. One of the most significant developments was in the nature of the Great Council, soon to become the House of Lords. The Magna Carta had defined this body as an assembly of tenants-in-chief. Although the minor tenants-in-chief were never actually summoned, the Great Council continued for some time to be in theory at least a body of barons—that is, major tenants-in-chief. But by the middle of the thirteenth century feudalism was little more than a series of forms. Tenure had no real meaning, and power was no longer determined by the number of knightly vassals a man had. Importance in the realm was largely the result of a combination of personal qualities and money income. Henry III summoned men who were not tenurial barons to the Great Council, and Edward I paid little attention to tenurial qualifications. He summoned the men who seemed to him to be important. In the reign of Edward III it began to be customary to summon the son of a man who had sat in the Great Council. Although the right of the heir to succeed to a seat in the Council was not firmly established in custom until the fifteenth century, it became the usual practice during Edward's reign. Thus the parliamentary peerage of England began to take definite form in the fourteenth century. This peerage was personal. Once a man had been summoned to a Parliament, his heirs were presumed to be entitled to be summoned whether or not they possessed any particular estates.

This same period saw a gradual reduction in the ecclesiastical element in Parliament. Abbots and priors found attendance burdensome and did their best to avoid it. During the reigns of Edward II and Edward III individual prelates were continually claiming exemption on the ground that they did not hold by barony. While some of these requests were refused, many more were granted, and the crown accepted the doctrine that only prelates holding by barony were subject to summons. Actually, however, the tenurial system was too obsolete to be seen clearly. A limited list of abbots and priors liable to summons was established, but its composition had little to do with tenure. It seems to have been based primarily on the wealth and importance of the house. The only definite principle that seems to have been in operation was the exemption of orders like the Cistercian that clearly held their possessions in free alms. The representatives of the lower clergy also disappeared from Parliament. Although they are still solemnly summoned today, they ceased to attend in the fourteenth century. When the king wanted money from the clergy, he negotiated with ecclesiastical assemblies, and hence the presence of the clergy in Parliament was unnecessary and might involve them unduly in secular affairs. By the end of Edward's reign the ecclesiastics sitting in Parliament were reduced to twenty-one bishops and twenty-seven abbots and priors. Usually this was enough to provide an ecclesiastical majority in the House of Lords.

As we have seen, throughout the reign of Edward I the term "Parliament" could be applied to a meeting of the king's council with the magnates; but under his son and grandson the presence of the representatives of the shires and towns became more and more frequent. When such a full Parliament met in solemn conclave the whole body sat together—king, council, magnates, and representatives. But the lords of the Great Council dealt with many affairs that were beyond the competence of the representatives and hence held many sessions by themselves. The knights of the shires and the burghers also met separately, to debate issues in advance of the general meetings. As these two groups had one thing in common, that of being outside the Great Council, they frequently met together to decide their policy. Soon one finds them referred to collectively as "the commons." Gradually in this way the two houses of Parliament came into being. The magnates of the Great Council became the House of Lords, and the representatives of the shires and towns, the House of Commons.

Before the reign of Edward III the Commons had little actual share in the work of Parliament. At first they even received a differently worded summons that made clear that their function was limited to hearing and approving the decisions of their betters. The abandonment of this special form did not, however, change their actual position. They did little beyond confirming and approving the actions of the magnates. Thus, under Edward II they approved the ordinances made by the Lords Ordainers and participated in accepting the abdication of the king, but all initiative lay in the hands of the council and the magnates. There was, however, one means by which the Commons could take the initiative—they could draw up petitions and present them to the Lords. If the Lords approved them, they would be transmitted to the king and council. This device was used rarely under Edward II, but in the reign of Edward III it became the usual way of creating new legislation. When the Commons felt there was a need for a new law, they would draw up a petition and send it to the Lords. If passed by them and accepted by the king, it became a statute. But the Commons had in this period no way of controlling the eventual form of legislation. Lords, council, and king could change it much as they pleased before issuing it. Nevertheless it became customary for most legislation to be initiated in the Commons and for all grants of money to have their origin there.

King Edward's continual need of money to wage his war in France gave Parliament many opportunities to increase its authority. On only a few occasions was it expressly stated that grants would be made in return for concessions, but it was generally understood that this would be the case. Edward promised to levy no direct taxes without the approval of Parliament. Later he admitted that body's right to control customs duties. He even permitted Parliamentary committees to supervise the expenditure of the money granted, by auditing accounts. Moreover, he frequently consulted Parliament about important questions of policy, such as the making of truces. In short, in his reign Parliament as a whole, Lords and Commons, became an integral part of the English government. When in Edward's old age his administration fell into disorder, everyone assumed that it was the business of Parliament to bring about a reform. The result was the impeachment of corrupt and inefficient officials.

The reign of Edward III saw important developments in the administration of justice. The House of Lords emerged clearly as the supreme court of the realm. In the case of a peer accused of felony or treason, it was the court of original jurisdiction. It also heard appeals from the decisions of the courts of common law. Meanwhile a new court, that of the chancellor, had taken definite form. According to the accepted theory it was the king's duty to see that justice was done. If injustice was found that had no remedy in the law, the king should devise some means of remedying it. The chancellor, as the custodian of the king's conscience, was expected to perform this function. A few examples must suffice. If a man failed to carry out a contract, he could be sued at common law and compelled to pay a penalty, but he could not be forced to carry out the contract. The chancellor's court could oblige him to do this. The common law covered only written agreements and took no notice of oral arrangements, but the chancellor would enforce oral agreements if they were properly established. The chancellor also protected a useful social device conceived by the nobles. If the holder of a great estate wanted to safeguard it, he gave it as a fief to a commission usually composed of high ecclesiastics and family friends. The commission promised to hold the estate intact and allow the former owner and his heirs full use of it. This scheme had important advantages. If the lord engaged in rebellion and was convicted of treason, his property was safe, since it was not legally his. Only by a bill of attainder, a statute passed by Parliament declaring a man and his heirs unable to hold office or property, could his estate be forfeited. Moreover, a spendthrift heir could not dissipate the estate. But these agreements were not recognized by the common law. They could be enforced only through chancery.

Perhaps the most important judicial development of Edward's reign was the establishment of the justices of the peace. As early as the time of Edward I officials called keepers of the peace had been established in every county to supervise the sheriff and coroners in the performance of their duties. Soon they were given the authority to receive indictments and order the arrest of the persons indicted. In 1329 they were given the power to try those accused of felony, and so became justices of the peace. In 1388 it was provided that all the justices of a county should meet in the county seat four times a year to try cases and transact other business. Thus were established the Quarter Sessions that have been so important a part of the English judicial system. The justices were appointed by the king from the ranks of the nobles and lesser landholders. They were expected to be men of substance. As they were drawn from the same social classes that produced the lords and knights of the shires, they were the darlings of Parliament. Whenever Parliament passed an act requiring local enforcement, the task was likely to be given to the justices. Under the Statute of Laborers they set the wages for laborers. They licensed alehouses. As individuals or in groups of two, they were empowered to enforce innumerable statutes. Bit by bit they gathered into their hands the police court jurisdiction that had once belonged to the popular and franchise courts. Soon the hundred courts disappeared, and the county court became merely a tribunal for insignificant civil cases. The justices of the peace became the chief power in local government. Although they were appointed by the crown and were royal officials, they were unpaid, and their primary loyalty was to their class in society.

The establishment of the justices of the peace marked the rise to political importance of the class known as the gentry. The fourteenth century saw considerable changes in the social structure of England. At the head of society stood some fifty great families whose position was based on large money incomes. For the most part these incomes were drawn from ancient franchises, feudal dues, and the rents from extensive landed estates, but some—especially the members of the royal family—had generous annuities from the exchequer. The heads of these houses possessed strong stone castles and could quickly raise small private armies. These armies were procured by what was known as "livery and maintenance." "Livery" was a retaining fee paid to a man on condition that he serve the employer in arms when called upon. "Maintenance" was general support of the lesser man by the greater, especially before the courts. As many of these great men were captains in the French wars, their followers were likely to be experienced soldiers. Livery and maintenance were a perpetual source of disorder. The great men overawed judges and juries, at times by actual threats of violence, to protect their followers. Moreover, the possessor of a private army was always tempted to use it against his neighbors, or even against the government. These great men were either peers or the heads of rising families that would soon attain the peerage. They are the men referred to when one speaks of nobles or barons.

Below this group of peers and rich knights who would soon become peers were the gentry. In theory, the mark of a gentleman was the rightful possession of a coat of arms; but arms were not too difficult to procure for those whose position made them suitable for them. Perhaps the best definition of a gentleman is one who owned enough land so that he could live in reasonable style on the rents without taking any active part in agricultural production. The gentleman would live in a manor house lightly fortified with moat and stone walls. He would probably be the lord of at least one manor with the right of presentation to a church or two and perhaps the patronage over a small monastic house. He might be a knight, but knighthood had by the fourteenth century become a rather rare dignity, and few gentlemen achieved it. Mostly they were called *armigers* or squires; Chaucer preferred the older term of franklin. The knights of the shire—who, incidentally, were rarely knights—were chosen from among the more substantial gentry. As a matter of fact, the representatives of the boroughs were likely to be gentlemen from the surrounding countryside. A small rural borough felt that it could best be represented by gentlemen who could hold their own with the knights and even with the lords. Then the justices of the peace were by statute required to be gentlemen. Thus, although no individual gentleman could compete in political authority with a peer, as a class they were extremely powerful. In most respects their economic and social interests coincided with those of the peers, and the two classes cooperated effectively. There was, however, one matter on which they were inclined to differ. The peer could afford civil war and disorder if it seemed likely to gain him something, but the gentleman as a rule wanted peace and order.

It is important to notice that in England the line between burgher and gentleman was not very rigid. The cadets of gentle houses frequently became apprenticed to merchants and themselves eventually acquired mercantile fortunes. Then if a prosperous merchant bought a landed estate, it took only a generation or so for his family to be fully accepted among the gentry. In the vicinity of the woolen manufacturing towns that arose during the fifteenth century it was difficult to distinguish between gentleman and merchant. The wool merchant bought sheep pasture and the wool-growing gentleman or his sons entered the wool trade. In short, the laws and ideas that kept the French lesser nobility, the group that corresponded to the English gentry, from any connection with trade did not exist in England. The gentry and merchants in reality formed one middle class between the peers and the mass of the people.

One other class deserves mention—the yeomen. The yeoman was either a small freeholder or the tenant of a large farm. He worked himself, but he frequently employed hired labor as well. This class rose rapidly in numbers and importance during the fourteenth and fifteenth centuries. When the manorial lords ceased to cultivate their demesnes, they either divided them into small freeholds or into large tenant farms. Added to the small freeholds that already existed, this created a large yeoman class. Like other English classes, it was far from static. An energetic and successful peasant family could gradually increase its holdings until it attained yeoman status, and prosperous yeomen merged easily into the gentry. In practice, to become a gentleman the yeoman simply had to obtain enough property so that he could live off the rents and acquire legally or by pure usurpation a coat of arms. The yeoman freeholder differed from the tenant in only one important particular; he could vote for the knights of the shire. Legislation of the reign of Henry VI limited the franchise to freeholders with an income of forty shillings a year from their freeholds. As forty shillings was a very small sum—many peasant holdings were worth that much—this statute gave the vote to all freeholders. The fact that they supplied the pikemen and archers who served England in her wars was enough to give the yeoman class a position of importance.

When Edward III died, in 1377, his eldest son, Edward the Black Prince, was already dead. The heir to the throne was the latter's young son Richard. By far the most powerful figure in England was the third son of the late king, John of Ghent, duke of Lancaster. John had married the great-granddaughter of Edmund of Lancaster, younger brother of Edward I. With her he had acquired the ancient earldoms of Lancaster, Leicester, Derby, and Lincoln, the great barony of Pontefract, and extensive lands in South Wales. John was an energetic and ambitious but not very successful soldier. He had used English money and troops in a futile effort to obtain the crown of Castile in the name of his second wife and was a master of expensive and utterly useless marches through France. Although he was the head of a strong faction among the English nobles, he was detested by the country at large. The war in France was going in favor of the French, and John was the most obvious person to blame for it. Nevertheless, in the early years of his nephew's reign John dominated the English government.

Young Richard II (1377–99) came to the throne in a time of widespread discontent. In 1348 and 1349 the terrible bubonic plague called the Black Death had ravaged England and reduced the population by as much as one third. The most serious immediate effect was an acute shortage of labor to till the fields and hence a sharp rise in food prices. The laborers who were left immediately demanded higher wages or, if they were tenants, more favorable terms. Parliament promptly passed the Statute of Laborers that froze both wages and prices. Although this statute was practically impossible to enforce with the almost nonexistent police organization of the day, it annoyed the laboring classes. High wages and an improved standard of living had seemed within their grasp, only to be snatched away by the government, in intention even if not in fact. Then, the costs of the long French war began to bear heavily on the English exchequer, and Parliament was driven to every possible means to raise money. The upper classes believed that the property taxes weighed unduly on them while the peasants escaped paying their share. In order to spread the burden, Parliament imposed a poll or head tax. The first such tax was moderate in amount and was collected successfully, but a second effort in 1381 led to trouble. The tax was heavy and the assessment poorly distributed, so that an unusually heavy burden fell on the poor. As a result there was wholesale evasion. When the exchequer officials found on examining the returns that the English population had apparently decreased enormously since the levy of a few years before, they sent out special commissions to investigate. These commissions were attacked by the irate populace, and many of their members slain. Soon the peasants of eastern England were in open revolt.

The peasants of Kent, under the command of a rather disreputable ex-soldier named Wat Tyler, took Rochester castle by surprise; seized the town of Canterbury, opening the local jail and murdering some high ecclesiastics; and then appeared before London. By themselves they would have had no chance of taking this great walled town, but the lower classes in the city sympathized with them, and opened the gates. For some days London was in the grip of a reign of terror, while the peasants roamed about burning the houses of such dignitaries as John of Ghent and murdering anyone they disliked. Eventually the young king held a conference with the rebel leaders and promised them all they wanted—abolition of unfree tenure, a fixed rent per acre for land, and numerous other privileges. All the following night the royal clerks labored drawing up charters granting these rights. But at a second conference, on the following day, Wat Tyler was suddenly slain by one of the king's escort. Meanwhile the London upper classes who composed the town militia were arming and mustering. Deprived of their leader, the peasants were helpless before the pikes of the burghers. Soon the lords of the countryside arrived with their troops, and the rebels were dispersed. A series of local risings in Essex, Norfolk, and Suffolk were successful for a while, but were crushed as soon as the lords mustered their troops.

Actually the revolt was not a very savage affair. The peasants hated two groups, government officials and high ecclesiastics, and slew all they laid hands on. The London lower classes hated the Flemish weavers brought in by Edward III and murdered a large number of them. During the reign of terror in London any creditor was likely to have his throat cut. But attacks on members of the upper classes in general were rare. The peasants did, however, burn the manor houses, apparently in the naïve belief that by destroying the records of their obligations to their lords the obligations would end. For the time, the repression of the revolt was equally gentle. Some three hundred peasants were hanged, but the rest were granted amnesty. Like most violent risings, the revolt did more harm than good to the peasants' cause. Parliament passed various restrictive statutes, including one making it a felony to insult a magnate. Moreover, the manorial lords with the support of the government revived long-forgotten obligations and generally tightened up their control of their tenants. While the gradual process of emancipating the villeins that had been going on for a century or more was not stopped, it was slowed down for the time being.

When Richard II became old enough to take the government of the realm into his own hands, he set about making himself the master of England. While it is not certain that he embraced the theory of absolute monarchy in the modern sense, he was determined to remove the limitations on the royal power. He filled the bureaucracy with servants completely obedient to him. He also created peerages for many of his favorites and appointed some of them members of his council. Thus he secured firm control of the council and a strong party in the House of Lords. As the sheriffs conducted the elections for knights of the shire and a majority of the boroughs were royal, a king could always pack the House of Commons if he took sufficient trouble; but the English kings had as a rule been either too conscientious or too lazy to do so. Richard went at it with energy and produced a well-packed Parliament. Early in his reign a baronial coalition calling itself the Lords Appellant had attempted to dominate Richard's government, much as the Lords Ordainers had that of Edward II. In 1397 those who had participated in this coalition were arrested, convicted by the packed House of Lords, and either executed or exiled. Parliament was persuaded to delegate its powers to a committee chosen by the King. This maneuvre practically made him absolute in power. But Richard was most anxious to have his full power sanctioned by law. He summoned the royal judges to Nottingham and placed before them a series of questions relating to the royal power. As the judges were his appointees and removable by him, they gave him the answers he wanted.

If the interpretation of the law of England made by the judges at Nottingham was allowed to stand, the English king would have practically absolute power. In doing this Richard went too far. The English barons and people were used to quarreling more or less amiably with their monarchs as to what limits should be set to the royal authority, but they had no intention of even considering the doctrine that there should be no such limits. Moreover, Richard showed all too clearly how he intended to use his power. All the shires of England were declared guilty of offences against the crown and were heavily fined. Some years before this Richard had exiled Henry of Lancaster, son of John of Ghent, but had promised that he should receive his great inheritance when his father died. Instead, when John died, Richard seized all his vast lands. In short, Richard made it clear that he intended to be absolute in practice as well as in theory. The result was a baronial revolt led by Henry of Lancaster. Richard's favorites whom he had created peers could vote his way in council and Parliament, but they lacked the resources to be of much use in a civil war. Soon the King found himself deserted and was obliged to surrender to his adversary.

Parliament met and solemnly declared Richard deposed for violating the law that governed both king and people. While Parliament had accepted and approved the abdication of Edward II, it had never before deposed a king. Richard was deprived of the throne for unlawful conduct, and thus an important precedent was established. As soon as the throne was declared vacant, Henry of Lancaster claimed it by hereditary right. His argument was little short of fantastic—that Edmund of Lancaster, his mother's great grandfather, was in reality the eldest son of Henry III, and that Edward I had been a usurper. Henry actually had no claim to the throne by hereditary right. The true heir was Edmund Mortimer, earl of March, great-grandson of John of Ghent's elder brother Lionel, duke of Clarence. Parliament brushed Henry's claim away as casually as it deserved. But Edmund was an infant, and Henry the head of a victorious baronial coalition with an army in possession of the kingdom. Hence Parliament elected Henry king without any reference to hereditary right. Another precedent had been established. Parliament had chosen a king who was not the legal heir to the throne.

Henry IV (1399–1413) was a competent captain and a conscientious and able ruler, but the circumstances surrounding his accession made it almost inevitable that his reign would be a troubled one. He owed the throne primarily to the support of a group of great barons headed by Henry Percy, earl of Northumberland, the master of northeastern England. These lords expected grants and favors in return for their support. When these were not forthcoming with satisfactory speed, they were ready for another rising. Henry was barely seated on the throne, when a group of barons revolted to restore King Richard. Henry promptly arranged the murder of the deposed monarch, but this did not halt the trouble. Throughout his reign he was faced with a series of baronial revolts. Meanwhile the Welsh, who had long pined for freedom from the English yoke, had found a leader in Owen Glendower. Owen raised the standard of rebellion in Wales and formed alliances with the disaffected barons. The revolts all failed, and the Welsh were suppressed; but these victories required all Henry's limited resources.

Parliament did not neglect to take advantage of Henry's troubles. As it had made him king, it could presumably depose him and give the crown to another. Moreover, the continual rebellions kept Henry in need of money, and he had to make frequent requests for grants. Parliament secured the right to approve the appointment of royal officials and members of the council. While this power disappeared after the accession of Edward IV, it was an interesting precursor of later Parliamentary government. King Henry was also obliged to confirm the privileges claimed by Parliament—that no action could be taken against a member for remarks made in Parliament, and that no member could be arrested while on the way to a session, during the session, or while going home afterwards. Finally, Henry accepted as a matter of course the control over taxation and legislation that Parliament had acquired under Edward III. A statute of the Lancastrian period forbade the king or council to alter the wording of legislation after it was passed by Parliament.

Henry IV died in 1413 and was succeeded by his son, Henry V (1413–22). As this monarch devoted most of his time and energy to the renewal of the war with France, there is little to say about his reign in England.* Baronial plots continued, but there was no serious open revolt. The most dangerous of these conspiracies centered about the person of young Edmund Mortimer, earl of March, rightful heir to the throne. Edmund himself would not have been a serious menace, but his sister Anne had married a prince of the royal house: Richard, earl of Cambridge, second son of Edmund, duke of York, fourth son of Edward III. This marriage brought about an alliance between two of the most powerful families in England. In 1415 Richard of Cambridge was executed for participation in a conspiracy, and his elder brother, Edward, duke of York, died at Agincourt a few months later. In 1424 Edmund Mortimer died childless. This made Richard, duke of York—the son and heir of Richard of Cambridge and Anne Mortimer—not only the possessor of the enormous estates of the families of Mortimer and York, but also the rightful king by laws of inheritance.

When Henry V died, in 1422, his son Henry VI (1422–61) was but a few months old. The government was taken over by the young king's uncles. John, duke of Bedford, became regent of France and Humphrey, duke of Gloucester, lord protector of England. We have discussed Humphrey in the chapter on the Hundred Years' War.† His adventurous and turbulent nature kept England in a state of confusion until he was finally replaced by members of the house of Beaufort. Late

* See pp. 349–52. † See pp. 358–9.

in life John of Ghent had married a lady by whom he had already had several children. They took the name of Beaufort and were legitimized by Parliament but specifically denied any right of succession to the throne. A strong and domineering clan, the Beauforts dominated the government of young Henry VI. Eventually they were joined by an equally strong character, Margaret, daughter of René the Good, duke of Anjou, who became Henry's queen. Margaret's life was filled with frustration. She was able, ambitious, determined, and a lover of power. Her father was a lazy, amiable lover of wine, women, and song, who allowed his nephew, King Louis XI of France, to wheedle him out of most of his extensive lands. Henry VI was a gentle, kindly man who was never very bright and who went completely insane when he was about thirty.

Even before he went insane Henry VI was utterly unable to rule his realm. Constitutionally unable to say "no," Henry gave everyone whatever they asked for, even if he had given it to someone else the day before. Not only were the royal revenues dissipated, but there were lines of men waiting for every office and pension. The King never had any money, and as a result never paid his officials or troops. Such important posts as governor of Calais were held by great lords who paid the garrisons out of their own pockets and ruled as they saw fit, completely ignoring the weak and penniless king. At home the nobles and their armed retainers carried on continual private wars and plundered the country at will. There was only one man in England of any real stature—Richard, duke of York. When Henry went insane, he was made regent and acknowledged as the heir to the throne if Henry had no son. Unfortunately for the peace of the realm the poor mad king produced a son and heir. While there is no evidence that Richard of York had any disloyal intentions or planned any harm to Henry or his son, Queen Margaret suspected him of such plans. With the support of the Beauforts and other nobles, she attacked the Duke's lands and drove him from England. But Richard was soon back in England with an army, and the fierce civil war known as the Wars of the Roses began. The name was derived from the badges assumed by the two parties—red roses for Lancaster, white roses for York.

For five years the fortunes of war wavered, but in 1460 the royal forces defeated the Yorkists at the battle of Wakefield. Richard of York was killed in battle and one of his sons was murdered in cold blood after he was captured. Ironically enough the death of Richard was a crushing blow to his Lancastrian foes. He had been a conscientious, amiable man who had only risen in revolt in self defense. His son and successor, Edward, was very different. He was for one thing by far the ablest captain of his day, with a keen eye for strategy as well as tactics. He was also ambitious, selfish, cruel, and extremely able as an administrator. Within a year of his father's death he had routed the Lancastrians and assumed the crown as Edward IV (1461–83). But Queen Margaret refused to give up, and the civil war continued. In 1471 she won the alliance of Edward's most powerful supporter, Richard Neville, earl of Warwick, and for a while gravely threatened Edward's position, but the King finally crushed all his foes in a series of overwhelming victories. Margaret was driven into exile, and her son Edward slain. Poor King Henry had not played a very glamorous part in the war. Whichever side had him led him on to the field of battle, and he stood there in a daze until someone captured him. Eventually Edward imprisoned him in the Tower of London, where he died.

Edward IV died in 1483, leaving two young sons and several daughters. The obvious candidate for regent was his brother Duke Richard of Gloucester. Richard had served Edward loyally and ably throughout the civil wars and was fully competent to handle the realm until his young nephew came of age. The two years following Edward's death are the most mysterious in English history. The accounts of the period that have survived were written under the Tudors and were intended to please those highly opinionated monarchs. As the first Tudor won the crown by overthrowing Richard III, their historians looked with little favor on the last of the Plantagenet kings. In fact they have painted him as a monster of perfidy and cruelty. The clear facts are few. Richard assumed the office of Protector of the realm upon his brother's death and apparently began to make arrangements for his nephew's coronation. Then suddenly Parliament declared the two young princes illegitimate, and Duke Richard assumed the crown. The princes were lodged in the Tower of London, but one must remember that it was a royal residence as well as a prison. Both of them disappeared shortly after Richard's coronation.

The new king was not destined for a long reign. In a castle high in the Breton hills overlooking the Bay of Biscay there languished in prison a young Englishman—Henry Tudor, earl of Richmond. Henry was the grandson of a petty Welsh gentleman, Owen Tudor, who had won the heart and hand of Catherine of France, widow of Henry V.

His mother, Margaret Beaufort, was the last of that mighty house and the wife of a powerful English baron, Lord Stanley, ancestor of the earls of Derby. As the Beauforts had been specifically denied any right of succession, Henry's claim to the throne was at best slim; but he was the only possible candidate of the house of Lancaster. And Louis XI of France was heartily tired of the rule of the house of York, which had favored his bitter foe, the Duke of Burgundy. Louis got Henry out of prison, aided him to raise a few troops, and sent him off to England. On August 21, 1485 three armies met on Bosworth field. One was commanded by young Henry Tudor, and one by King Richard III, but the largest of the three was composed of nobles headed by Lord Stanley, who were trying to decide which party to join. Lord Stanley finally moved to his stepson's aid, and most of Richard's army promptly changed sides. King Richard III died fighting fiercely on the field of battle. The victorious Henry Tudor was declared king by Parliament and made a bow to hereditary right by marrying Elizabeth, daughter of Edward IV.

According to the Tudor historians, Richard of Gloucester concocted the story that his nephews were illegitimate, persuaded Parliament to accept it, and had the two boys murdered. In fact, they assert that some twenty years later one of Richard's former officials confessed that he had committed the crime at his master's command. Richard's modern defenders point out that it is most unusual for a man who had for years been loyal to his brother to suddenly betray his trust and murder his nephews. They also indicate that the evidence is weak and comes from biased sources. To them it seems clear that Henry Tudor found the young princes in the Tower and promptly got them out of the way. Some day perhaps the problem will be solved. In the meantime, one can only say that if Henry found the princes alive, he would most undoubtedly have disposed of them.

The Wars of the Roses had little effect on England. They were fought by nobles at the head of their bands of armed retainers. In general, the participants were careful not to annoy the population more than was necessary: the site of one skirmish was moved so that it would not injure a wheat field. London and the other great towns calmly ignored the war and closed their gates to the contending forces. While many nobles were killed in battle and others were executed after capture, most of them left heirs to carry on their lines. As the barons had been turbulent and disorderly before the wars started, they could hardly become much worse. It does seem likely, however, that the wars finally ended the patience of the middle class—the country gentlemen and the townsmen. When Henry VII ascended the throne they were heartily tired of noble anarchy and were ready to support a strong king who could check it.

The reign of Edward IV had been in some ways a preparation for the reigns of his Tudor successors. When he came to the throne, Edward was by far the richest baron of England. He had promptly confiscated the vast estates of the house of Lancaster and of all the lords of the Lancastrian party. He had fought only one foreign war, and that war was highly profitable. He crossed to Calais with an army, invaded France, and allowed himself to be bought off with a generous lump sum and an annual pension. Hence Edward did not need to ask Parliament for money and rarely bothered to call it into session. Moreover, while he was an able ruler and an excellent soldier, Edward was incredibly lazy and given to the pursuit of pleasure. As a result he did nothing and so annoyed few people. His rule was arbitrary, but he did nothing that would move men to oppose so dangerous a monarch. Thus Parliament fell once more into the background, and England was given a brief foretaste of the high-handed rule of the house of Tudor. But under the Plantagenet and Lancastrian kings, Parliament had become deeply rooted in English political tradition and had established precedents that were to be remembered by the foes of Stuart absolutism. And England had never developed the institutions that encouraged such absolutism. The English paid bureaucracy was very small—twelve judges, a few great officers of state, and a small group of royal servants. There was no standing army, not even a royal bodyguard. If an English king were to rule as an absolute monarch, he had to do it by the consent of his people.

37. France under the House of Valois

The French government in the reign of Philip IV (1285–1314) was in many ways similar to that of England under Edward I (1272–1307). Philip had a council much like Edward's. His *chambre des comptes* exercised the functions of the English exchequer and his parlement those of the three central courts. The estates general contained the same basic elements as the English Parliament and was used by the crown in much the same way. Philip's baillis and seneschals were not very different from Edward's sheriffs. Both kings drew their revenues from a mixture of feudal and manorial dues and general taxes. Both employed the feudal levy but usually paid the members for their services. There were, however, important differences between the two realms. The French bureaucracy was very much larger than the English. Then, France was far less unified than England. The king's government ruled the royal demesne and had little to do with the lands of the princes. But even within the demesne the provinces had different customs and interests, and there was a good deal of local patriotism. Under Philip's sons, many of these provinces secured charters guaranteeing them special privileges.* The king of France could not rule his demesne as a unit, to say nothing of his whole kingdom.

These differences become more obvious if one compares the France of Philip VI (1328–50) with the England of Edward III (1327–77). The French bureaucracy was growing at a terrifying rate and had become immense. One example must suffice. In 1340 the Parlement of Paris had 167 members as against the twelve judges of the English central courts. Moreover, provincial particularism was even stronger than before. The Estates General rarely represented the whole realm but only the north, or Languedoil, while the southern provinces acted through the estates of Languedoc. In addition, there were provincial estates. When the king needed money, he sought it as he saw fit from the Estates General, the estates of Languedoc, or the provincial estates. Often he made a series of bargains with the various provinces. The same procedure was used for the lands of the princes. They were asked to allow the taxes to be collected in their lands and usually received a share—often as much as a third—for their cooperation. In short, in the period when the English Parliament was becoming an established part of English government through active cooperation with Edward III, the Estates General was simply one of many bodies the French king could consult when he needed money.

The regular revenues of King Philip VI from his royal demesne just about covered the peacetime cost of the government. Whenever he contemplated waging war, he had to seek additional funds. The chief reliance of the French government in the form of a general tax was a levy on sales, which varied in amount from time to time and from province to province. Then in 1343 appeared the *gabelle* or salt tax. Un-

* See pp. 257–8.

der this system the royal government established a monopoly on the sale of salt and took its profit as the tax. At first the gabelle was introduced as a local and temporary device, but it was soon used throughout the realm whenever the crown received a grant of money. Finally there was a hearth tax that was originally called a *fouage*, and later a *taille*. Despite frequent levies of these various taxes, the government never had enough money to cover its military expenses and was obliged to resort to all sorts of special devices. The most obvious was to borrow money; and this was done on a large scale. Far more serious in its effect on the economy of the country was the crown's proclivity for changing the metal content of the money. The system was both ingenious and tempting. The coinage would be depreciated so that the king could pay his obligations in cheap money. Then when he was about to collect a tax, he would reform the money so that his income would be in good coins. Between 1337 and 1350 the money was changed twenty-four times. Although there seems to be no way to determine how much the government actually profited from these maneuvers, there is no question about their harmful effect on the country. When a merchant made a contract, he never could be sure in what sort of coin payment would be made.

Throughout the reign of Philip VI and the first years of John the Good (1350–64) the bourgeoisie grew more and more restive. The sales taxes bore heavily on them, and they were the source of most of the loans procured by the crown. They also suffered severely from the frequent alterations of the money; in fact, that was probably their chief grievance. As the armies of France met defeat after defeat, the bourgeoisie had less and less enthusiasm for paying to support the war. They felt that the nobles, who were entirely exempt from the hearth tax, were running the war at their expense and running it very badly. This discontent was brought to a climax by the battle of Poitiers. The king had conducted the battle with magnificent incompetence and then had followed his chivalric ideas with no regard for his obligations to his people in staying on the field after all hope of victory was gone. He had been captured, and enormous sums would be needed to ransom him. The nobility as a whole had not even shown chivalrous bravery. The entire second division under the Duke of Orleans had fled from the field without striking a blow.* The good people of the towns, especially the inhabitants of Paris, were thoroughly exasperated. More-

* See pp. 338–40.

over they had a leader, Etienne Marcel, provost of the merchants of Paris. The office of provost of the merchants was essentially that of mayor of the merchant settlement on the right bank of the Seine, and its holder was a powerful figure, with all the powers of government except high justice. Etienne Marcel belonged to one of the great merchant families of Paris that had supplied many officials to the royal government. Marcel was an able, honest man with genuine sympathy for the plight of the lower classes as well as the bourgeoisie. His chief fault was a lack of good judgment in choosing allies.

As the Dauphin Charles needed money desperately to pay his troops and prepare to ransom his father, he was obliged to summon a meeting of the Estates General immediately after the battle of Poitiers. Under the leadership of Marcel and a few others, the members of the third estate insisted on imposing conditions on the government. The Estates granted a sales tax of eight pennies on the pound and a gabelle, but they were to name officials to collect the money and pay it to the troops. Moreover, the Dauphin was forced to promise that when he needed funds, he would seek them from the Estates General. But this was only the beginning. When the Estates General met again in February, 1357, Marcel and his friends were well organized and determined to carry through a general program of governmental reform. Their first step was to demand the suspension from office of twenty-two of the highest officials of the government. Then they declared that the Estates should meet frequently—if necessary more than once a year. No important political move such as the conclusion of a truce or peace should be made without their consent. The money could not be altered without their approval. The expenses of the government were to be greatly reduced, and all grants made from the royal demesne since the time of Philip IV were to be revoked. This last was a point very dear to the middle classes. The royal demesne was the crown's natural source of revenue, and it was wrong for the king to diminish it by making gifts to nobles from it.

Marcel and his friends in the Estates General made one serious mistake: they demanded the release from prison of Charles the Bad, king of Navarre and count of Evreux. Charles was undoubtedly the victim of arbitrary action on the part of King John, and Marcel may have been genuinely sorry for him as well as feeling that an enemy of the King would be an ally of the reformers. But Charles was a powerful figure in the Paris region because of his lands and castles along the border between the Ile de France and Normandy. Moreover, he was greedy, ambitious, and had all the prejudices and beliefs of the noble in an unusually violent form. As soon as he was free, he went to war with the Dauphin and increased the general confusion. Meanwhile the people of Paris grew more and more impatient. Paper reforms were all very well, but they wanted some sort of definite action, and they slowly pressed Marcel toward open violence. One day a mob headed by Marcel broke into the Dauphin's house and murdered two high government officials in his presence. Up to that time the Dauphin had hoped to come to terms with the rebels, but this assault on his household moved him to leave Paris. Charles the Bad tried to occupy the city, but Marcel was beginning to distrust him and refused to allow his troops to enter. This led to a weird situation. While the Parisian militia manned the walls, Charles the Bad and the Dauphin both laid siege to the city from different sides. Thus Paris was besieged by two armies each fiercely hostile to the other.

The bourgeoisie was not the only class that had suffered from the war. The peasants had seen their fields laid waste and their homes burned again and again. They were heavily taxed by the royal government. Moreover, when their lord was captured, they had to contribute to his ransom. Then, the English had discovered a very convenient device for raising money. They would capture a castle and sell it back to its owner at a high price. To the noble it seemed far less trouble to collect from his peasants the money to buy back the castle than to defend it adequately in the first place. Obviously the war weighed most heavily on the people of certain particularly exposed regions, and one of the worst of these was the northern district adjoining the English base at Calais. Hence in 1358 a savage peasant rising broke out in the country around Beauvais and spread rapidly to neighboring districts. The peasants seized the castles of the nobles and murdered the nobles and their families. Actually we have little idea how many nobles were killed. The chronicles tell of castles captured and horrible atrocities committed, but a very small number of cases could have furnished them with their material. It seems likely on the whole that the victims were few.

When Marcel learned of the peasant revolt, he committed another error of judgment by sending messengers to seek their alliance. While he was very likely moved by genuine sympathy for the peasants as well as by a desire for any help he could get, he should have realized that negotiations with them would alienate both nobles and bourgeoisie. The peasants promptly sent a large force into the vicinity of Paris. This army, or rather mob, attacked the town of Meaux where the Dauphin's wife and a number of other noble ladies were living and besieged the ladies and their slender escort of troops in the market place. There they were found by the famous Gascon captain, John de Grailly, captal of Buch, as he returned home from an expedition to Prussia. The captal rescued the ladies and massacred all the peasants he could find. Meanwhile, Charles the Bad and the Dauphin had both come to the defense of their class and turned their troops against the rebels. The peasants could not face the soldiers and were quickly crushed. Contemporary chronicles estimate that 20,000 were slain by the angry and frightened lords. While this is probably an exaggeration, it seems clear that the revolt was savagely punished. Marcel's relations with the peasants had deeply disturbed the conservative elements among his supporters in Paris. One night as he made the rounds of the guard posts on the walls he was murdered, and the city was delivered to the Dauphin.

Etienne Marcel and his supporters were responsible for the only serious attempt to make the Estates General an integral and effective part of the French government. Although the rapidity of their failure was largely the result of Marcel's inability to control his Parisian followers, it seems unlikely that their effort could have had any permanent result. For one thing the Estates General represented only the Languedoïl. Then, the nobles were the dominant political and military force in the country, and they had little or no interest in the reform program; in fact some of its provisions were aimed at them. It was essentially a movement conducted by the third estate, which was by far the weakest of the elements that made up the Estates General. Finally, the period of confusion that gave Marcel his opportunity was followed by the reign of an able and strong monarch, Charles V. It seems most unlikely that Charles would have allowed the Estates to retain an authority that seemed to limit the royal power.

Just as Charles V (1364–80) found effective captains to recover the lands conquered by the English, he appointed able men of middle-class origin to head his civil government. The country as a whole was so well pleased to be under a strong government that kept order at home and conducted the war successfully that there was little inclination on anyone's part to question the king's authority. Charles strengthened the royal power in several ways. The long period of war had seriously affected the prosperity of the great towns of northern France, where the communal movement had been strongest, and many of them were facing bankruptcy. Charles used their difficulties as an opportunity to suppress the communal governments and place the towns more directly under royal control. Charles also succeeded in establishing taxation on a regular and semipermanent basis. As his entire reign was devoted to war against the English and the free companies, he was always in need of money. He persuaded the Estates General to vote him taxes without setting a fixed time limit to the grant. Then he simply continued to collect them without bothering to ask the Estates' approval. While Charles clearly doubted the propriety of this policy and on his death-bed asked his son to discontinue it, he did make the country accustomed to regular taxation levied at the king's will.

During the early years of the reign of Charles VI (1380–1422), the government was carried on by the officials who had served his father so well. But these tried civil servants were thoroughly detested by the princes of the royal house and their noble friends, who objected to seeing men of low birth controlling the government. When Charles went insane, the princes took over, and dismissed their opponents. For the rest of Charles' reign the parties led by the dukes of Orleans and Burgundy struggled for power while the less powerful dukes of Berry and Bourbon tried to keep some sort of peace. Until the assassination of Louis of Orleans, the contest between the two parties was nonviolent and depended largely on the king's state. When Charles was sane, Orleans ruled. When he was insane, Burgundy was the master.* Both princes used their periods of power for their own benefit, by such measures as exempting their own lands from royal taxes. Although the routine functions of government were carried on as always by the professional civil servants, all was confusion at the top.

The years just before the battle of Agincourt saw a series of events much like those that followed the battle of Poitiers. The Duke of Burgundy was in actual control of Paris, but the Dauphin and his entourage favored the Armagnac party. The lower classes of Paris, led by a certain Simon Caboche, made a series of attacks on members of the Armagnac party, including some in the Dauphin's household. While the Duke of Burgundy saved some of those threatened and kept the rising from getting too far out of hand, a number of noblemen and

* See pp. 348–9.

high officials were assassinated by the mob. Eventually the Duke of Burgundy left the city and it was seized by the Armagnacs who suppressed the revolt. Meanwhile a group of civil servants who were for the most part Burgundian in sympathy had been planning a reform of the government. Although they had no actual connection with Caboche or his followers, their scheme is known as the Cabochian Ordinance. It is an extremely interesting document. Its authors took it for granted that the government should be conducted by a bureaucracy of royal servants. Although they could conceive of this bureaucracy controlling the king if he did something harmful to the crown, such as alienating too much of the royal demesne, they had no thought of giving anybody else any control over the government. Their only interest was to try to make that government honest and effective. Their method was to have all important decisions made not by one man but by a committee or council. Practically every officer was supplied with a council to advise him. The members of these councils, as well as the officials, were to be elected by the traditional governing bodies of the bureaucracy, the Parlement and the chambre des comptes. It was, of course, a grandly impractical plan that fortunately was never tried, but it shows how far apart the political ideas of France and England had grown.

Charles VII (1422–61) is commonly known as the "Well-served," and rarely has an appellation been more appropriate. Jeanne d'Arc won him his crown, and Richmont and his fellow captains expelled the English from France.* His finances were managed by a great merchant, Jacques Coeur, who both augmented the royal revenue and spread the commercial influence of France into the eastern Mediterranean. The wisdom of Charles' ministers brought about the military reforms already mentioned, primarily the establishment of a standing army, and complete royal control of taxation. After Charles' reign the king no longer felt any need to consult the Estates General before levying taxes. Charles himself was a feeble monarch with little will or force of character. His very weakness made him an innovator. During the years when Paris was English and Burgundian, he had grown accustomed to living in the Loire country. Perhaps, also, he could not forgive the Parisians for their support of his foes. At any rate he continued to reside at his castle of Chinon and other residences in that region. He became deeply enamoured of a beautiful, gentle girl named Agnes Sorel who became the first mistress *en titre* of a French king. Many if

* See pp. 352–60.

not most of the monarchs of France had had mistresses, but they were kept out of the public eye. With Charles the office of royal mistress became a well-recognized dignity and remained such until the Revolution.

Although Charles' ministers succeeded in increasing the royal authority in his demesne, his lack of any effective control over the princes kept him from being a powerful monarch. The treaty of Arras gave the Duke of Burgundy almost complete independence.* Duke Philip ruled the duchy of Burgundy and the county of Flanders in France; and the Free County of Burgundy, the county of Holland, and the duchies of Hainault and Brabant in the Holy Roman Empire. Brittany was almost equally independent. While the royal princes whose lands lay in the interior of the kingdom were not quite so autonomous as Philip the Good, they were pretty much the masters of their own lands. René the Good, duke of Anjou, held the county of Provence and the duchy of Lorraine in the Empire. Charles, duke of Orleans, ruled the scattered but vast estates of his house. The duke of Bourbon had a small but well-integrated domain in the center of France. Important lands in Normandy belonged to the duke of Alençon. In addition to the royal princes, a few great lords had almost equal power and independence. The most dangerous of these were the great barons of the south: the count of Foix, who was also king of Navarre; the lord of Albret; and the count of Armagnac. Each of these princes had his own court, his petty bureaucracy, and his private army. They were continually forming alliances for their mutual benefit to plague Charles and his government. One of the most pleasant features of the period was the fact that most of these leagues against Charles were headed by his son, the Dauphin Louis. Occasionally one of the weaker princes would go too far. Thus the duke of Alençon and the count of Armagnac lost their lands for making the error of revolting without adequate support from the greater lords.

While the princes who either had sufficient autonomy to levy their own taxes or could at least oblige the king to give them a good share of the royal levies taken from their estates flourished, the lesser nobles were in a difficult position. In the thirteenth and fourteenth centuries most of them had leased their productive lands at fixed rents. Hence any inflation seriously reduced their real income. And the fourteenth and fifteenth centuries were a period of fairly steady inflation in France.

* See p. 359.

During the Hundred Years' War this was largely the result of depreciation of the coinage, but once the war was over France rapidly recovered its prosperity, and prices rose rapidly as in any boom period. Thus, only the greatest of the nobles could live in noble style on the revenues of their estates, and they were forced to seek other sources of income. The most natural course was to enter the service of the king or a prince. The king and the duke of Burgundy employed many nobles as soldiers and officials and granted pensions to many others whose support they wanted. Indeed the idea of a pension from the royal treasury was far from repugnant to the lesser princes. Most of the coalitions against the crown were dissolved by the simple expedient of giving generous annuities to the leaders. In short, if the nobles were to live like nobles, they had to do so at the expense of the general taxpayer.

When Charles VII died in 1461, the Dauphin Louis was in exile at the court of his father's bitter enemy Philip the Good. Louis had fled from France after the collapse of one of his conspiracies against the king. From his refuge in Burgundy he had bribed his father's physician to notify him promptly of any good news about the king's failing health, if not actually to hasten the process. Louis (1461–83) was the most unpleasant and unkingly man ever to occupy the throne of France. He was extremely homely and dressed meanly. When he first entered his realm as king, he noticed some people smiling at his costume and promptly inflicted a crushing fine on the town he was passing through. While he was very religious, his religion was largely a matter of superstition, leading him to cover his clothes with religious insignia and to bribe all the saints before undertaking an important operation. He had no sense of ordinary decency. When he learned that his daughter was so hopeless a cripple that she could never bear children, he promptly married her to Louis, the heir of the house of Orleans, in order to extinguish that princely line. King Louis loved low company. His favorite pastime was sitting in a public tavern drinking and telling dirty stories. He surrounded himself with low-born men, many of whom had criminal records, and made them his most trusted servants and officials. His only noble taste was for hunting, and he spent enormous sums on horses and hunting dogs. He was, however, an effective king. The middle classes who were becoming more and more important admired his simple if crude tastes. His officials, although cruel and unprincipled, served him well—or went quickly to the gallows. Louis was highly intelligent, completely lacking in scruples, and a master of intrigue. All these qualities were of help in dealing with the princes. He had no use whatever for war. Bad luck could bring a disastrous defeat. It was just as cheap and far more effective to get one's way by intrigue, well enforced with bribes.

The chief task facing Louis if he wanted to solidify the royal authority was to reduce the power of the princes. Shortly after he ascended the throne, a great coalition calling itself the League of the Public Weal rose in revolt under the leadership of his own brother the Duke of Berry and the dukes of Burgundy, Bourbon, and Anjou. A great battle was fought, in which both sides retreated as soon as they came together, and victory was claimed by the one that retired the shortest distance. Then the two armies faced each other quietly for some months across a river. Eventually the "Public Weal" was safeguarded by generous grants of lands and pensions to the princes and their chief followers. Louis was obliged to give Normandy to his brother, thus cutting the royal demesne off from the channel and connecting the princely estates of Burgundy with those of the duke of Brittany through the lands of their ally. The princes believed that they had won the struggle and had reduced Louis to complete impotence. In this they were very sadly mistaken. The King soon succeeded in sowing seeds of dissension between his brother and the duke of Brittany and before long made the former's position in Normandy so uncomfortable that he gladly accepted Gascony instead and thus became separated from his princely associates. There, in the pleasant lands of the south, he rapidly drank himself to death.

By far the most dangerous of the princes was the Duke of Burgundy. The revenues from the prosperous towns of the Low Countries made him the richest prince of Western Europe; only the Republic of Venice could compete with him in this respect. His court was unrivaled for splendor and luxury, and in it were developing the etiquette and complicated ceremonial procedures that were to mark the royal courts of later years. Philip the Good was a patron of arts and letters. Italian craftsmen embellished the Burgundian capital at Dijon, and the best Flemish artists painted the Duke and his courtiers. While Philip's personal taste in literature ran chiefly to salacious stories, he was a generous patron of a wide variety of writers. Throughout his life the Duke dreamed of leading the forces of Christendom in a grand crusade to crush the Turkish power, but he never did anything about it except to inaugurate the magnificent chivalric order of the Golden Fleece. Philip had a large and effective army and was served by many of the greatest nobles of France. Fortunately for the French monarchy he preferred dreaming about crusades to nourishing practical political designs. As long as he was left alone in his estates, he was content to be the most powerful and magnificent of French princes.

In 1467 Duke Philip died and was succeeded by his son Charles, known as the Rash. The new duke was determined to make the most of the political opportunities that his father had ignored. If he could add Alsace and Lorraine to his domains, he would have the northern part of the ancient kingdom of Lothaire.* Once that was accomplished, the conquest of either the valley of the Rhone or Switzerland would place him at the gates to Italy, and that peninsula was in no state to resist so powerful a prince. But even without Italy he could have a great state between France and Germany, and diligent diplomacy backed by might should persuade the emperor to grant him the royal title he craved. In short, Charles was not content to remain a French prince but wanted to be king of Lotharingia. Shortly after his succession Charles strengthened his position by an alliance with the house of York sealed by the Duke's marriage to Margaret, sister of Edward IV. If the French state was not to be gravely weakened, Louis had to defeat the plans of the Burgundian duke.

King Louis promptly put his skill at intrigue and bribery to work against his formidable foe. His agents stirred up discontent in the lands of Charles and his allies, while generous subsidies flowed to all the Duke's enemies. Soon Louis had so many different schemes on foot that he could not keep track of them all. In 1468 he paid a visit to Charles at Péronne, apparently forgetting that his agents were stirring up a revolt against the Duke's ally, the bishop of Liége. When the impetuous duke heard that the people of Liége had rebelled with Louis' encouragement, he imprisoned his royal guest. By skillful bribery of Charles' ministers, Louis secured his freedom, but he was obliged to suffer the humiliation of helping Charles to punish Liége. The Duke's plans went well. Within a few years he had conquered all Alsace and Lorraine except for a few towns. While the Emperor Frederick III showed no enthusiasm for granting him the royal dignity, he recognized Charles' conquest of the two duchies. In 1476 Charles turned his arms against the Swiss, but there he met defeat. In two great battles

* See p. 91.

the Swiss spearmen routed the chivalry of Burgundy. Then Swiss troops paid by Louis entered the service of the duke of Lorraine and marched to relieve the town of Nancy, which was being besieged by Charles. Louis had also thoughtfully bribed one of Charles' mercenary captains to betray him. As a result the Burgundians were defeated and the Duke slain.

The death of Charles gave Louis a magnificent opportunity, but one that he did not know how to exploit. The heir to the vast Burgundian lands was the Duke's daughter Mary, who was in the custody of the stubborn burghers of Flanders. Whoever married Mary would acquire her lands, but he would have to be acceptable to both Mary and the burghers. As the latter were French in their sympathy, Louis seemed in a strong position. Unfortunately Louis' son Charles, the obvious candidate, was a mere baby, and despite the King's urging Mary refused to consider him. Although there were several French princes who would have been acceptable, Louis hesitated to let one of them take the place of Charles the Rash. While he pondered his problem, the Emperor acted. Maximilian of Hapsburg, son and heir of Frederick III, married Mary and became lord of her lands. All Louis could do was declare the marriage illegal because it lacked his consent and seize the duchy of Burgundy. As Flanders was too strong to occupy, it passed to Maximilian and was lost to France forever. This marriage was one of the chief bases for the long and bitter struggle between the kings of France and the house of Hapsburg, as each one claimed all the lands of Charles the Rash. If Louis had been really farsighted, he would have married Mary to a French prince.

Although the defeat of Charles the Rash was probably Louis' greatest triumph, he was equally successful with other princes. By a skillful combination of bribes and threats he persuaded the amiable and weak-willed René the Good to make a will leaving to Louis the duchy of Anjou and the county of Provence. The death of the duke of Berry brought the duchies of Berry and Gascony into the royal demesne. Louis secured the friendship of the house of Bourbon by marrying his daughter Anne to Peter, lord of Beaujeu, brother and eventual heir of the duke of Bourbon. When Louis died in 1483, the duke of Brittany was the only major prince in a position of real independence. Anne de Beaujeu, acting as regent for her brother Charles VIII, was to bring this great fief into the hands of the crown by arranging the marriage of Charles with Anne, duchess of Brittany.

At the close of the reign of Louis XI the French monarchy was well on the way to becoming absolute. The government was conducted by a bureaucracy almost completely dependent on the king's will. The king could levy taxes as he saw fit. With this revenue he maintained a standing army to support his authority. Only two princely houses of importance remained in existence, Orleans and Bourbon, and both were allied by marriage to the royal family. While there were a number of secondary houses, such as the dukes of Lorraine and Montpensier and the lords of Albret, who could give trouble if they formed an effective coalition, their diverse interests made a dangerous combination unlikely. The nobles of France were to make attempts in the future to dominate the royal government, but their efforts to rival it were at an end.

38. The Remnants of the Empire

DURING the fourteenth and fifteenth centuries the Holy Roman Empire was a conglomeration of practically independent states. In Germany there were some 1,600 such units, ranging in size and importance from the duchies of Austria, Bavaria and Saxony, the margravate of Brandenburg, and the County Palatine of the Rhine, to small free cities and the territories of petty imperial knights. No German state was powerful enough to exercise even temporary hegemony over the others. If the emperor was to have any real authority, he had to draw it from outside Germany. Throughout this period the imperial power usually rested on the possession of either Bohemia or Hungary, or both. The ancient kingdom of Burgundy was gradually being absorbed by France. The last Capetian kings of the senior line had gained possession of Lyons and its environs. The Free County of Burgundy passed into the hands of French princes. In 1343 Humbert II, dauphin of Viennois, bequeathed that important state to the French royal house as a permanent appanage for the heir to the throne. Provence went to Louis XI at the death of René the Good. Although the counts of Savoy remained independent vassals of the empire, they were under French influence.

Italy was composed of a number of independent states. Throughout the whole period the kingdom of Sicily was ruled by princes of the house of Aragon—a cadet line until 1409, when the king of Aragon inherited Sicily. The kingdom of Naples continued in the possession of the descendants of Charles of Anjou until the death of Joanna II, in 1435. Before Joanna's death, Louis III, duke of Anjou, had attempted to seize Naples, and another unsuccessful effort was made by his brother René the Good. But Alfonso V (1416–58), king of Aragon and Sicily, took possession of the kingdom, and René was left to nurse the empty title of king of Naples. To the north of Naples lay the Papal States. Tuscany was divided between Florence and Siena. In the north, Venice, Genoa, and Milan were the dominant powers, but there were a number of other important city-states such as Mantua, Ferrara, and Modena. Politically these states showed a wide variation. Venice and Genoa were aristocratic republics. Milan was ruled in turn by two ducal families, the Visconti and the Sforza, who were in theory deputies of the emperor but in practice independent princes. Florence was in theory a democratic republic, but early in the fifteenth century it came under the domination of the house of Medici. Although the Medici rulers took no title and conducted the government primarily as political bosses, their authority was complete. Ferrara was throughout the period in the possession of a well-established hereditary ducal dynasty. All these states waged war upon one another in the hope of extending their boundaries. Moreover, outside powers, France, Aragon, and occasionally the emperor, were continually intriguing in Italy and trying to play a part in its politics. Soon Italy was to be a battlefield between France and Spain, but in our period France was too well occupied with England and Burgundy to exert any effective force in Italy, and Spain's ability to intervene came only after her unification under Ferdinand and Isabella.

Except for the reign of Louis of Wittelsbach, duke of Bavaria, from 1314–47, and the reigns of two minor princes who were kings of Germany but never achieved the imperial crown, the Holy Roman Empire during the fourteenth and fifteenth centuries was ruled by either the house of Hapsburg or that of Luxembourg. In 1273 the princes elected as king Rudolf of Hapsburg, a petty Swabian baron. Rudolf (1273–91) began the series of marriages that was to make the fortune of his house. His eldest son, Albert (1298–1308), who succeeded him as emperor, married the heiress of the duchy of Austria, while a second son, Rudolf, married the heiress of Bohemia. Unfortunately Bohemia did not remain in the hands of the Hapsburgs. In 1308 Henry of Luxembourg was chosen emperor, and he secured the heiress of Bohemia for his son John, the blind king of Bohemia who fell at Crécy. Then in 1347, John's son, Charles, king of Bohemia, defeated and deposed Louis of Wittelsbach and became emperor. He was succeeded in turn by his sons Wenceslas (1378–1400) and Sigismund (1410–37). Sigismund married the heiress of Hungary and left all his lands to his son-in-law Albert V (1438–39) of Hapsburg, who assumed the imperial title but died before he could be crowned at Rome. On Albert's death the crowns of Bohemia and Hungary passed to his son, but his distant cousin Frederick was elected emperor. Frederick III (1440–93) was the last emperor to be crowned at Rome and also the feeblest prince who ever sat on the imperial throne. The only territory he ruled directly was the duchy of Austria, and he lost that for a considerable period. But he had the family skill in one respect; he married his son Maximilian to Mary of Burgundy and thus laid a firm foundation for the future power of his house.

In general, the emperors took little interest in the welfare of either Germany or Italy and devoted their attention to building up their own princely estates. The only imperial power that they really valued was the right to bestow a vacant fief on whomever they pleased. Perhaps the most important step of this variety was the grant by the Emperor Sigismund of the Margravate of Brandenburg to Frederick of Hohenzollern, thus inaugurating the rise of that famous house. The form that the Holy Roman Empire had taken of its own accord was formalized by the Emperor Charles IV in 1356 by the publication of the famous Golden Bull. Seven princes, the archbishops of Mainz, Treves, and Cologne, the count palatine of the Rhine, the duke of Saxony, the margrave of Brandenburg, and the king of Bohemia, were designated as electors who had the legal power to choose the emperor. When an emperor died, they were to meet at once in the city of Frankfort on the Main and elect a new emperor by majority vote. Any elector who did not attend or send a proxy, forfeited his right to participate in that election. The electoral dignity was to be hereditary in the male line, except in Bohemia, where the crown was elective; and no electoral state could be divided among heirs. The electors were given almost all the rights of sovereign princes. Moreover, the Bull suggested that they should serve as a supervisory committee over Germany as a whole. The Golden Bull made disputed imperial elections less likely and protected at least some German states from the fragmentation that had been proceeding at an alarming rate. It also settled the legal form of the Empire for the rest of its existence.

One more event of this period deserves notice here—the creation of the Swiss Confederation. Northern Switzerland was originally a part of the duchy of Swabia, and in the fourteenth century the Hapsburgs, who were the most powerful house in Swabia, attempted to extend their authority over that region. In 1291 three cantons called the Forest Cantons formed a league for defense against Hapsburg ambitions, and in 1315 they inflicted a crushing defeat on Leopold II, duke of Austria. Other cantons, including those of Lucerne, Zürich, and Bern joined the three Forest Cantons, and in 1386 the confederation again defeated the Hapsburg forces. The confederation then took the offensive and began to expand its territory at the expense of various petty lords, the counts of Savoy, and the Hapsburgs. In 1477, as we have seen, the Swiss defeated the forces of Charles the Rash and became recognized throughout Europe as a formidable military power. The confederation was ruled by a federal diet, but the cantons retained almost complete independence. While they would usually combine effectively against an outside enemy, they frequently quarreled among themselves and at times resorted to civil war. The strength of the Confederation lay not in the effectiveness of its government, but in its topography and the military qualities of its inhabitants.

CHAPTER XIII

The Decline of the Mediaeval Church

39. The Babylonian Captivity
40. Schism and Councils
41. Heresies

HE FOURTEENTH and fifteenth centuries saw the disintegration of Western European Christendom as it had been established in the early Middle Ages. The magnificent ecclesiastical structure created by the popes of the eleventh, twelfth, and thirteenth centuries was not destroyed, but it was shaken to its very foundations and gravely weakened. Although the heresies that challenged the established theological system were successfully suppressed, they laid the foundations for the Reformation. To some extent the afflictions that fell upon the Church were the result of internal conditions. As the church was manned by human beings, there was a strong tendency to worldliness and the sins that tempt all mankind. Moreover, although the church produced isolated enthusiasts who labored for reform, none of them had the widespread influence of the early abbots of Cluny, St. Bernard of Clairvaux, St. Dominic, or St. Francis. For a time the church seems to have lost the inner reservoir of spiritual power that had in the past enabled it to reform itself.

Even more dangerous than the deficiencies of the church and the clergy was the gradual secularization of society as a whole. The secular spirit that had long been strong in literature increased its hold in that realm and began to affect the fine arts. Commercial activities were playing an increasingly important part in the world. Most important of all was the rapid development of the secular point of view in politics. This has frequently been cited as the result of the spreading knowledge of Roman law that pictured the dominance of the secular state, but while the influence of civil lawyers was certainly important, it seems doubtful that they were the chief factor. Far more significant was the development of what one might call statism. The general appearance of estates show clearly that princes and peoples were beginning to think of themselves as political units with definite interests. The common welfare of the state gradually became far more important in their eyes than the interests of Christendom as a whole. Philip Augustus would have been aghast at the suggestion that he would be justified in destroying the papacy if the interests of France demanded such a step, but such an idea would not have seriously disturbed Philip IV and would have seemed quite natural to Charles VII. This feeling that the welfare of the secular state was man's first concern had profound effects within the church organization. Many, perhaps most, prelates of the fourteenth and fifteenth centuries believed that their primary duty was to their prince. Thus secular politics became a vital and extremely dangerous element in ecclesiastical polity.

39. The Babylonian Captivity

WE HAVE seen in a previous chapter how the papacy in a long and bitter struggle defeated the Emperor Frederick II, destroyed the house of Hohenstaufen, and broke the power of the Holy Roman Empire.* During this contest the kings of France had been in general allies of the popes. Although King Louis IX had declined to give material aid to the papacy in its war against Frederick II, he had permitted his brother Charles of Anjou to conquer the kingdom of Naples and Sicily. St. Louis' son, Philip III, had supported his uncle vigorously. He met his death on a "crusade" against the king of Aragon, who had deprived Charles of Sicily—a crusade preached by the papacy for Charles' benefit. While both these French monarchs had had disputes with the papacy over the question of taxation of the clergy, they had been settled amicably on the basis of each party taking a share

* See pp. 285–6.

of the proceeds. When the year 1285 saw the death of both King Philip III and Pope Martin IV, the French monarchy was considered one of the chief bulwarks of the papal authority.

As young Philip IV (1285–1314) strove to extricate the remnants of his father's crusading army from its unfortunate invasion of Catalonia, he may well have felt some resentment toward the papacy for having encouraged the expedition. Philip was a man of virtuous life and deep personal piety, but he was cold, calculating, and ruthless, and imbued with determination to increase the royal power. He surrounded himself with men trained in the civil law who believed in the supremacy of the secular state. Although the ideas of Peter Dubois, who advocated the seizure by the secular princes of all the property and temporal authority of the church and the support of the clergy by regular salaries from the secular government, were probably more advanced than those of most of Philip's entourage, they show clearly the general trend of thought at his court. Moreover, the men who served King Philip had no shadow of a scruple in regard to the means by which they achieved their ends. They believed that sufficiently outrageous and numerous false accusations made with overwhelming energy and confidence could destroy any opponent. And judicious use of torture could always produce witnesses to support the most fantastic charges.

Philip IV quarreled mildly with Pope Honorius IV (1285–87) and Pope Nicholas IV (1288–92), but as they were amiable pontiffs no serious crisis arose. Then, in July 1294, the ten cardinals who composed the College met to elect a successor to Nicholas IV. Two mighty Roman noble families dominated the College of Cardinals—the Orsini and the Colonna. While the representatives of these two houses struggled for victory in the conclave, their adherents waged bloody battles in the streets of Rome. Finally one of the cardinals thought of a brilliant and novel compromise. A revered hermit who dwelt on a mountain in the kingdom of Naples was elected pope and in a state of decided bemusement took the name of Celestine V. Before the worthy but completely innocent pontiff escaped from the clutches of his natural lord, Charles II of Anjou, king of Naples, he had created twelve new cardinals, of whom eight were Frenchmen and four Neapolitans. Both pope and cardinals soon discovered that a saint was out of place on St. Peter's throne, and before a year was out Celestine had resigned. Celestine had been encouraged if not forced into this decision by the most vigorous of the cardinals, Benedict Gaetani, and in December 1294 Benedict became pope as Boniface VIII (1294–1303).

Scion of a minor noble family, the aged Boniface was haughty, overbearing, vain, and incredibly ambitious. While it seems most improbable that he had any large percentage of the vices credited to him by his enemies, his personal morals were clearly not above reproach. He was determined to exalt his own position and that of his great office, but he was almost equally interested in expanding the fortune of his family. His vanity led him to distribute statuettes of himself, and under the influence of his overbearing bad temper he once kicked an envoy to his court. Far more serious, however, were his efforts to provide for his family at the expense of other noble houses—particularly the Colonna. Early in his reign he gave his nephew money from the papal treasury to buy a valuable estate. The Colonna, who had wanted the estate themselves, raided the convoy carrying the purchase money and stored the treasure in one of their strongholds. Boniface promptly preached a crusade against the Colonna, captured their castles, gave their lands to his relatives, and exiled or imprisoned the members of the house. By these means he supplied himself with many bitter enemies among the Roman nobility; and thus weakened at home, he gaily plunged into conflict with the two dominant monarchs of Western Europe.

In 1295 Philip IV (1285–1314) of France and Edward I (1272–1307) of England were preparing for war over the duchy of Gascony, and both of them wanted to raise funds by taxing their clergy. In 1296 Boniface issued the bull *Clericis Laicos*, which forbade the clergy of any state to pay taxes to the prince without the consent of the pope. King Philip promptly placed a ban on the export of gold and silver from his realm, thus cutting off the flow of money to the papal court. This first time Boniface soon became reasonable. He declared that the king could tax the clergy when the need was great, and that he should be the judge of the need. To demonstrate even more completely his affection for the French monarchy, Boniface canonized Louis IX. But soon this accord between the two men disappeared.

A bishop of southern France had incurred Philip's enmity, and he set his lawyers to work to destroy him. They drew up a magnificent list of charges, and Philip asked the pope to degrade the bishop so that he could punish him. Although the bishop was accused of heresy and a fine set of vices, it was clear that the real difficulty was purely political, and Boniface declined to act. After a vigorous exchange of recriminations with King Philip, Boniface issued a bull reasserting the doctrine of *Clericis Laicos*. It was on this occasion that Philip sought the support of his people by summoning the estates of his realm.* Boniface on his part issued another bull, *Unam Sanctam*, which expressed in its most extreme form the doctrine of the papal supremacy over kings. In 1303 he threatened Philip with excommunication. Despite his support from his people, Philip was unwilling to face this most terrible of ecclesiastical weapons. He resolved to strike first.

One of Philip's servitors was a peculiarly fascinating personage named William de Nogaret, who was a past master at the art of drawing up accusations and then providing witnesses to support them. When the King suspected that the bishop of Troyes, who was in charge of the revenues of the county of Champagne, was a thief, he sent Nogaret into action. Nogaret charged and proved to his own and the King's satisfaction that the bishop had conspired with a witch to kill the queen by sticking pins in an image of her and had committed various other horrible crimes. When one of Nogaret's agents was asked if a witness was testifying entirely voluntarily, he assured the court that he was. All the agent had done to encourage him was to strip him naked, daub honey on him, and hang him over a beehive. It was to this ingenious and devoted servant that Philip entrusted the task of suppressing Pope Boniface. Nogaret started with his usual list of accusations. Boniface was a heretic and a sorcerer deeply steeped in black magic. He had poisoned a number of high ecclesiastics. Perhaps the most delightful item in the long list of charges was the statement that Boniface kept mistresses to conceal the fact that he was a sodomite. Then, having built up his justification, Nogaret set off for Italy in company with one of Boniface's most implacable foes, Sciara Colonna. In the vicinity of Rome they gathered a band consisting of partisans of the Colonna family, well mixed with ordinary brigands, and marched to Anagni, where Boniface was staying with his relatives. On September 7, 1303, the desperadoes attacked the town and captured the aged pontiff. Although the nobles of the countryside soon forced Nogaret to release the Pope, the shock and humiliation were too much for Boniface, and he died soon after.

The new pope, Benedict XI (1303–1304) found himself in a most

* See p. 260.

embarrassing position. He had been a servant and friend of Boniface, and no pope worthy of the name could allow the crime committed at Anagni to go completely unpunished. Yet Benedict was a cautious man and had no desire to cross swords with King Philip. Hence he attempted an ingenious solution. All the censures heaped on the French king by Boniface were revoked, but he was directed to punish Nogaret. Pope Benedict died before he found out whether or not this pusillanimous maneuver was going to be effective.

In June, 1305, the College of Cardinals elected to the papal office Bertrand de Got, archbishop of Bordeaux. While there is no definite evidence that Philip was responsible for Bertrand's election, it seems very likely that he was. The French cardinals formed a powerful minority in the College. Although they were not numerous enough to choose one of their own number, they could strongly influence the election. The archbishop of Bordeaux was a subject of Philip's foe Edward I and so was not branded as a Frenchman in the eyes of the Italian cardinals. A contemporary chronicle asserts that Philip and Bertrand met, and that the archbishop made various promises in return for Philip's support. While it seems clear from the royal itinerary that this meeting never took place, it is fairly certain that a similar agreement was reached by negotiation through envoys. There can be little doubt that when Bertrand ascended the papal throne as Clement V (1305–13), he was the man of the French king.

When he learned of his election, Clement summoned the cardinals to meet him at Lyons, and there he was consecrated and enthroned. He then took up his residence in the city of Avignon on the east bank of the Rhone. Avignon was the seat of the county of Venaissin, a part of the kingdom of Burgundy belonging to the counts of Provence. It was thus in the territory of the Empire, but it depended on the princes of the house of Anjou, and Philip's lands lay just across the Rhone. Without actually being in France, the pope was completely subject to French influence. He soon showed that this was no accident. Of the twenty-eight cardinals created by Clement, twenty-five were Frenchmen. The papacy had conquered the Hohenstaufens, but it had itself been captured by the Capetians. A French pope, surrounded by French cardinals, lived in a French-speaking city on the French frontier.

No sooner was Clement seated on the papal throne than Nogaret began to insist that his conduct toward Boniface should be declared justified. The Pope pleaded to be spared this supreme humiliation and managed to defer action for some six years, but eventually he was obliged to open an inquest into Boniface's behavior and allow Nogaret to present his case. As one would expect, the case was a good one and well supported by witnesses. The fact that only a few points here and there were true did not trouble Nogaret. He cheerfully demanded that Boniface's bones should be disinterred and publicly burned. Finally a compromise was reached. The Pope withdrew all ecclesiastical censures leveled against Philip or any of his servants in connection with the affair and declared that the king had acted in a praiseworthy and just manner. Thus Clement was spared the actual formal condemnation of his predecessor.

While the affair of Pope Boniface was hanging fire at the papal court, Philip IV and his servants were engaged in an equally honorable enterprise. When Acre fell to the Moslems in 1291, most of the Templars in Palestine perished in its defense.* The remnants of the order, those who had not been in the Holy Land and a few who had escaped from other Palestinian strongholds, retired to live on their extensive estates scattered over Western Europe. The order had been created to defend the Holy Land, and once they were expelled from Palestine the Templars had no useful function. As they were for the most part rude, unlettered soldiers; they simply lived well and drank well from the revenues of their lands. Naturally the impecunious princes of the day cast greedy eyes on the rich properties no longer serving the purpose for which they had been given. But King Philip was not the man to admit that his motive was pure greed; he had to find a better reason. It has been argued that he considered the Templars a danger to his state. Although one can see some possible danger in a well-disciplined military order, it is hard to believe that the Templars were numerous enough to worry Philip much.

Whether his motive was fear mixed with greed or pure greed, the king decided to crush the Templars. Once more his experts went to work. They declared that the order had abandoned its old rule and adopted one full of blasphemous heresies. When a knight was initiated, he was obliged to deny Christ and to perform obscene rites before statues of the devil. The order reeked with the most horrible vices. King Philip was profoundly shocked. Every Templar in France was arrested, and the houses of the order were thoroughly searched. Edward I and other princes were informed of the crimes of which the

* See p. 218.

Templars were suspected and were urged to take action against them. Edward arrested the leaders of the order in England and waited to see what would come next.

The search of the houses of the Templars was not very fruitful. The searchers found a few copies of the ancient rule supposed to have been written by St. Bernard and one figurine of a woman's head. But Philip's agents were not discouraged. They went to work with their instruments of torture on the imprisoned Templars and soon obtained ample confirmation of all their charges. Then, bursting with pride, they notified Pope Clement of the horrible scandal they had uncovered. The Pope promptly sent commissioners to hear the evidence and report their findings to a council. But once the Templars found themselves before a reasonably impartial body, they immediately repudiated their confessions. This gravely alarmed Philip. Some Templars had already denied the truth of their earlier evidence. If all were to do so, his case would be ruined. The situation required drastic action.

Although the case against the order of the Temple was before the papal commissioners, the Templars themselves were under the jurisdiction of the local prelates. At Philip's command, the archbishop of Sens condemned some fifty Templars to be burned, and the sentence was immediately carried out. This removed some troublesome witnesses and dissuaded others from changing their testimony. Finally the affair was brought before a council assembled at Vienne. Once more poor Clement was forced to issue a strange decision. The order was not condemned, but it was ordered dissolved, and Philip was congratulated for his zeal. The French king held the property of the Templars for some years and then turned it over to the Hospitalers with a generous bill for the expenses he had incurred in seizing and managing it. Edward I seized the Temple's property, milked it, and handed it over to the Hospital, but he did not bother the Templars themselves.

For seventy-two years the seat of the papacy was at Avignon. While the successors of Clement V tried hard to be true spiritual heads of all Christendom, they could not escape very far from the dominance of the French kings. And so obvious was their dependence on France that even when they were in fact being impartial, no one would believe it. Moreover, although the Avignon popes were neither wicked nor corrupt, they had no great spiritual enthusiasm and lived in extreme luxury in their pleasant city. They built the magnificent palace that still stands on the bank of the Rhone and enclosed the city with great walls. Many of the cardinals lived in the luxurious suburb of Villeneuve on the French side of the river. As the absence of the pope from Rome deprived him almost entirely of the revenues of the Patrimony of St. Peter, he was obliged to seek other income to support his court, and the great expansion of the papal revenues from Christendom as a whole came in the time of the Avignon popes. These taxes were resented everywhere, but they were particularly objectionable in England, where the pope was regarded as an ally of the king of France. This period saw the growth of strong antipapal tendencies in the English realm. In 1351 the Statute of Provisors abolished the pope's right to appoint to ecclesiastical offices in England, and two years later the Statute of Praemunire forbade the appeal of any case from an English to a foreign court. Some twenty years later John Wyclif was to develop a political campaign against papal authority into a full-blown heresy. Thus the period of papal residence in Avignon, which is commonly called the Babylonian Captivity, did the prestige and influence of the pope grave harm.

40. Schism and Councils

THE AVIGNON popes were fully aware of the disadvantages of their position, and each one played with the idea of returning to Rome. Unfortunately Italy was in a state of continuous political confusion, and the propitious time for the return never seemed to come. Finally, in 1377, Pope Gregory XI (1370–78) landed in Italy and proceeded to Rome. It is likely that he thought of the trip as a visit rather than a permanent change of residence, but he died in March 1378 in the Eternal City. This gave the Romans their opportunity, and they were determined to see that the French cardinals who were in a majority in the College were obliged to elect an Italian pope. From the whole countryside armed bands converged on the city, and the cardinals were subjected to pressure and even threats. On April 8, 1378 the conclave finally chose an Italian prelate who took the name of Urban VI (1378–89), and a few days later he was enthroned in the presence of twelve of the sixteen cardinals.

But the French cardinals were dissatisfied with the election, and on August 9 thirteen of them met at Fondi. After long consultations, they declared that the election of Urban was invalid, as it had been brought about by outside pressure, and they elected as pope a Frenchman, Robert of Geneva, who took the name of Clement VII (1378–94). Thus began the Great Schism, with popes at both Rome and Avignon. Today the church accepts Urban as the rightful pope, but this decision is based on faith rather than historical evidence. The historian can only say he does not know who was the true pope. If the cardinals were really forced by threats to elect Urban against their will, Clement was the rightful pope. If, on the other hand, they simply changed their minds later, Urban's election was valid.

Only by conscious effort of the imagination can a modern Protestant comprehend the consternation created in Western Europe by the Great Schism. The pope was far more than the administrative head of the Church: as the successor to St. Peter, he was in a sense the church's very foundation and the chosen custodian of the Christian way of life. In his hands were the symbolic keys to Heaven and Hell, the terrible power to bind and loose. Moreover, as each pope claimed to be the only true pope, each one was inclined to appoint to every ecclesiastical office under papal control. Not only did men not know who was the rightful pope, but they could not even be sure who was the rightful bishop of a diocese. This was especially true in regions where war was raging. When the English occupied a French diocese, a bishop acknowledging the Roman pope was likely to replace the one recognizing the pope at Avignon. Although the division of territory between the two popes did not absolutely follow political lines, there was a strong inclination in that direction. The friends of France were likely to accept the Avignon pope, and her foes the Roman. England was one of the Roman pope's firmest adherents, while Scotland stood equally fervently for his rival. Thus the church and Christendom itself was rent asunder. The dignity and prestige of both the papacy and the Church it headed sank very low in the minds of men.

This impasse—two popes neither of whom would yield to the other—naturally turned many men's minds to a consideration of the status of the papacy. The foundations for novel ideas in regard to this question had been firmly laid in the early fourteenth century by a number of scholars. By far the greatest of these as a political philosopher was Marsilio of Padua, who early in the second decade of the century was rector of the university of Paris. Some years later Marsilio wrote his *Defensor Pacis,* in which he examined the bases of political authority. Marsilio stated that all political power came from the people as a whole. The prince should be elected by the people, should be subject to the laws made by them, and should be their servant rather than their master. This does not mean that Marsilio was a democrat in the modern sense; he would have given far more weight to the voice of people of importance than to the masses. In all probability he thought of some body such as an estates of the realm as the proper vehicle for the expression of the people's will. But he clearly did not believe in hereditary monarchy by divine right. To him the true church was the entire mass of believers. The ecclesiastical organization headed by the pope was created by men to serve their spiritual needs. Like the princes, the clergy from the pope to the parish priest were the servants of the people. The clergy had no business interfering in any way in secular affairs. The supreme authority in all matters spiritual as well as temporal was the people as a whole. The people expressed their will in spiritual matters through a general council which was the supreme power in Christendom. As the prince was the elected head of the people, it was his duty to convoke a council when it was needed.

Marsilio's doctrines appealed strongly to Emperor Louis of Bavaria. As the Avignon papacy supported the Francophile house of Luxembourg against him, Louis was bitterly hostile to the pope and welcomed Marsilio's attacks on the validity of his authority. Two other scholars whose ideas were very similar to Marsilio's, John of Jardun and William of Ockham, also served Louis. While Ockham's system was rather less completely developed than Marsilio's, he believed firmly in the separation of temporal and spiritual power, the complete independence of the secular authority in its own sphere, and the superiority of a general council over the pope. These three scholars were extremely radical, and comparatively few men of their day were willing to accept all or even a large part of their views. Faced with the situation of a divided papacy, however, many men began to consider the possibility of having a general council to restore the church's unity and attempt to prevent similar scandals in the future. Moreover, as we have seen, the financial demands of the Avignon popes had created widespread discontent and revived the ancient cry that the clergy were luxurious and corrupt. From many men, but especially from the scholars in the universities, came the demand that the schism be ended and the church reformed.

In the last years of the fourteenth century, after the schism had lasted some twenty years, the two popes made rather feeble attempts to come to an agreement. The plan was for the two pontiffs to resign simultaneously and allow the combined cardinals to elect a new pope, but for one reason or another nothing was actually accomplished. Finally a fair number of cardinals of both parties grew discouraged and summoned a council to meet at Pisa in 1409. This move was clearly illegal. By the tradition and law of the Roman Catholic Church, only a pope could call a general council. The reformers argued that the secular power could do so, but no one believed the cardinals had this authority. Nevertheless, the council met and promptly made the situation worse. The council as a whole declared the two popes deposed and ordered the twenty-four cardinals present to elect a new one. Their first choice lived only a short time. They then elected Baldassare Cossa, who took the name of John XXIII (1410–15). The new pope was a soldier of very disreputable life who was haughty, intolerant, and violent. Moreover, as neither the pope at Avignon nor the one at Rome would recognize the actions of the council and accept the decree of deposition, Christendom had three popes instead of two.

In 1410 the Holy Roman Emperor and king of Bohemia, Wenceslas of Luxembourg, an amiable monarch whose chief defect was that he was usually drunk, relinquished the imperial crown, and the electors chose as his successor his younger brother, Sigismund, king of Hungary. Sigismund was the most enthusiastic lover and most incompetent soldier of his age, but he had a high conception of the imperial office and strove hard to fill it adequately. He listened with sympathy to those who argued that the only solution to the woes of the church was a council summoned by the emperor. By that time more than the Great Schism and the general confusion in the church was at stake: John Hus and his followers were rapidly leading Bohemia from the Catholic fold.* In the year 1413 Sigismund issued the summons for a council to meet at Constance in the autumn of the following year. Unwillingly, but unable to resist the pressure that was applied to him, Pope John issued bulls authorizing the meeting. The Roman pope, Gregory XII (1406–15), agreed to send envoys to the session without recognizing its authority. The Avignon pope, Benedict XIII (1394–1422), held aloof.

The Council of Constance was a magnificent ecclesiastical assembly. There were present three patriarchs, twenty-nine cardinals, thirty-

* See pp. 425–7.

three archbishops, 150 bishops, one hundred abbots, and some 300 doctors of theology. Its first business was the Hussite heresy, which we shall discuss later. Not until early in 1415 did the council embark seriously on the problem of the schism. Pope John had come to the meeting, but he soon grew alarmed at the tone of the council and hastily departed. The assembled delegates then declared that a general council obtained its authority directly from Christ, and that even a pope had to obey and furthermore, that it was the duty of a pope to abdicate if a council declared such action was necessary for the well-being of the church. On May 14, 1415, Pope John was suspended under charges of fornication, adultery, incest, sodomy, and poisoning his predecessor. He was probably guilty of a moderate percentage of these offences, and on May 29 he was solemnly deposed. On July 4 Gregory XII resigned. This left but one pope—the Avignon pontiff Benedict XIII. Now that his rivals were removed, this very stubborn gentleman was inclined to stick to his office, claiming to be the one true pope. While the French king and the prelates of northern France had deserted his cause, southern France, Castile, Aragon, Navarre, and Scotland remained loyal.

In the summer of 1415, Sigismund himself conducted negotiations with Benedict and his supporters. He could not move the Pope, but he persuaded all the kings to desert his cause and send delegates to Constance. The affair dragged on, and it was not until 1417 that the council deposed Benedict. Even that did not shake him. He retired to a strong castle and maintained his claim until his death in 1422. He was succeeded by Clement VIII (1423–29), who held his position until 1429, when he resigned. Thus, despite rivals and councils the Avignon popes held their own for fifty years; but after the deposition of Benedict by the Council of Constance few if any princes recognized them.

The Council of Constance was organized so as to give full sway to the political interest of the princes. The delegates were divided into nations, and each nation voted separately. At first there were four nations—French, German, Italian, and English—but when the Spanish princes abandoned the cause of Benedict XIII, their delegates were formed into a fifth nation. Many members of the council were in no hurry to elect a new pope. They wanted to conduct a reform of the structure and laws of the church while there was no pope to object. But the most vigorous of the secular princes of Europe, King Henry V of England, clamored for an immediate election. He wanted a pope favorable to the English cause to support his activities in France. To secure a quick election he sent to Constance his uncle Henry Beaufort, bishop of Winchester. Under Beaufort's pressure, the council finally decided on a procedure for electing a pope. The cardinals and six representatives from each nation were to vote in six separate groups. Two thirds of the votes of each group were required for an election. By this method the council chose the Cardinal Odo Colonna, who took office as Martin V (1417–31).

One of the chief purposes of the Council of Constance was to reform the church. During the course of its deliberations two large committees were established to draw up recommendations to this end. But while there were zealous reformers who wanted to make extensive changes in the organization and law of the church, most of the delegates did not regard reform with any great enthusiasm. The recommendations drawn up by the commissions and put into the form of decrees by the council were for the most part mere reaffirmations of well-established canon law. The only really radical provisions had to do with the function of councils. It was decreed that a council was to be held in five years, another seven years later, a third ten years after that, and then one every ten years. In case of a schism, a council was to meet within a year to heal it. In addition to considering the schism, heresy, and reform, the council spent a great deal of time on miscellaneous matters. All the ordinary routine business of the papal curia was carried on by it during the session. Then, there were various disputes to settle. The prelates of the Orleanist party in France complained about the Burgundian clerk Jean Petit, who had preached the virtue of tyrannicide after the murder of Louis of Orleans. They wanted the council to declare the doctrine heretical, and to condemn Jean and his ducal master. After long and fierce debate the council gently hedged. It announced that tyrannicide was unjustifiable, but carefully mentioned no names.

The Council of Constance had healed the Great Schism and had made some rather ineffective gestures toward church reform. It had also announced in unmistakable terms the supremacy of a general council over the pope and had provided for the summoning of councils at regular intervals. This question of the proper relationship between pope and council was highly controversial and extremely complicated. Although Pope Martin V owed his election to the Council of Constance, he had no intention of accepting the doctrine of concili-

supremacy. With him stood a strong group of conservative ecclesiastics who believed firmly in the traditional organization of the church. The supporters of conciliar supremacy were moved by varied motives and advanced several different theories to justify their position. Some were earnest churchmen who had been horrified by the Great Schism and believed that such scandals could be avoided only by conciliar action in case of need. Others were enthusiasts for reform who were convinced that the papacy was not a suitable instrument for the purpose. As the pope had a vested interest in many of the worst abuses, such as the indiscriminate use of indulgences, he was unlikely to lead a reform. The church could be saved only by its whole membership acting through a council.

A powerful group of prelates were moved by a more mundane motive. If a council of the whole church was supreme in Christendom, would not a national council be supreme within the limits of a state? The papacy was the only ecclesiastical authority that limited the princes' control over their churches. If the pope was made a servant rather than a master, princely power could be greatly increased. This point of view was advanced by prelates who wanted to free their own national churches from outside interference. It also received the support of most princes when they were thinking in long-range terms. But unfortunately for the conciliar party, the princes often gave primary concern to immediate problems. Whatever the papacy might become in the future, it had been in the past and was still a potent political power. Although a prince might realize that in the long run it was to the interest of his dynasty to reduce the papal power, he might at the moment be desperately anxious to win the support of the reigning pope. Hence, throughout the controversy the policy of the princes was inconsistent and vacillating.

Three chief theories of the basis of ecclesiastical authority were advanced by the conciliar party. One group, following in general the ideas of Marsilio of Padua, maintained that ultimate authority rested in he whole community of believers and that it should exert its power rough a council. These men were inclined to argue that laymen as l as clerks should have a voice in the council. Then another group, ably the largest, believed that the church consisted of all the clergy hat they through their representatives in the council held the e power. Finally, some argued that the church was essentially ic of bishops. Christ gave his powers to all his disciples, and through apostolic succession these powers had passed to the bishops.

The first council provided for in the decrees of the Council of Constance met at Pavia in 1423. It argued mildly with the pope and accomplished little. The next council scheduled for seven years later opened at Basel in July 1431. Its first business was to attempt to bring back into the fold the Hussite heretics of Bohemia. The chief demand of the Hussites was that everyone be given both the bread and the wine at communion. When the council showed an inclination to accept this demand, it was dissolved by Pope Eugenius IV (1431–47). The council refused to recognize this decree, announced that a council could not be dissolved without its consent, and summoned the pope to attend its sessions. It then voted a series of reforms that were aimed primarily at the papacy. One of these measures would have practically wiped out the revenues of the pope; no payment was to be made for appointment to ecclesiastical office or for the issuance of papal bulls or letters. Another decree returned episcopal elections to the chapters. In September 1437, Pope Eugenius once more declared the council dissolved and summoned a council to meet at Ferrara. Although obviously the chief reason for this move was to weaken the Council of Basel by drawing off all but the most determined foes of papal power, the official reason for the meeting at Ferrara, which was later moved to Florence, was to heal the schism with the Greek church. Faced with the rapidly growing power of the Turks, the Byzantine emperor felt that his only hope lay in union with Western Europe.* After a long debate, the Greek representatives at Florence accepted the pope's terms, and a decree of union was issued; but as it was never recognized by the Greek church as a whole it had no real effect. The Council of Ferrara did, however, draw many churchmen from Basel, and in September 1439 it solemnly decreed that a council was not superior to a pope.

Although many ecclesiastics had deserted Basel for Ferrara, others remained in session. In January, 1438, the council suspended Pope Eugenius and in the following year solemnly deposed him. They then elected as pope a secular prince, Amadeus of Savoy, who took office as Felix V (1439–49). For ten years more the Council of Basel maintained itself and its pope. Only in 1449 did its members finally give up and come to terms with Pope Nicholas V (1447–55). Pope Felix resigned and was made a cardinal, while the Council of Basel was dissolved. This eighteen-year struggle by the churchmen assembled at

* See p. 55.

Basel marked the end of the conciliar movement, and the victory rested with the papacy. A council was not superior to the pope, it could only be summoned by the pope, and the pope could dissolve it at will. Perhaps even more important was the fact that the church had most decidedly not been reformed. In fact, the pope who finally triumphed over the Council of Basel, Nicholas V, was a scholarly sceptic most noted as a patron of arts and letters—the first Renaissance pope. At his court lived as his librarian Lorenzo Valla, who had proved the Donation of Constantine to be a forgery and who was to advocate such novel ideas as turning all nunneries into what a less broad-minded age would call houses of ill fame. If the work of reform that was carried out a century later at the Council of Trent could have been done at Constance and Basel, it is quite possible that the Reformation would never have taken place.

When all pretense of cooperation between the Council of Basel and Pope Eugenius came to an end, a number of princes took independent action to make the decrees of the council effective in their lands. In 1438 a council of the French church adopted the Pragmatic Sanction of Bourges. This proclaimed the supremacy of a council over a pope and declared that councils should meet every ten years. It forbade the payment of annates and ended all papal rights to appoint men to benefices in France. Bishops and abbots were to be elected by the chapters. The king and princes would "use benign and well-intentioned solicitation in favor of persons of merit who were zealous for the good of the church and the realm." This passage shows clearly the difference in interests between princes and reformers. The Council of Basel had simply decreed the right of chapters to elect without interference from the papacy, but the reformers had no desire to give the pope's former power to the prince. The Pragmatic Sanction of Bourges made the king the master of the French church. Although the Pragmatic Sanction was repealed by Louis XI, its essential provisions are found in the concordats that later governed the relations between the French kings and the popes. Although councils and their supremacy were soon forgotten, the king's control of the church remained firm. In 1439 the German princes issued the Pragmatic Sanction of Mainz, which applied the decrees of the Council of Basel in Germany, but in 1448 an agreement between the princes and the pope restored most of the papal powers. The princes of Germany had to wait until the Reformation to achieve mastery over their churches.

41. *Heresies*

WHILE the internal organization and general prestige of the church was being shaken by the Babylonian Captivity of the papacy, the Great Schism, and the Conciliar movements, its open foes, the heretics, were steadily increasing in numbers. This development of heresy has been obscured for both contemporary and later historians by two facts. The most powerful and dangerous of the early mediaeval heresies, that of the Cathari, was successfully destroyed in Western Europe. By the early years of the fourteenth century the Cathari had disappeared from their former strongholds, Italy and southern France. They continued to flourish east of the Adriatic Sea until the Balkans were conquered by the Turks. For considerable periods their religion was the official faith of Bosnia. Then, the heretics of Western Europe in the fourteenth century were very widely scattered and, except for a few remote districts, were not numerous enough in any one region to dominate it. Although they occasionally found noble sympathizers, and once in a great while a noble joined their ranks, they were in general drawn from the humble classes of society and so received comparatively little attention from historians.

Throughout the fourteenth century the most important of the heretical sects was that of the Waldensians. The Albigensian crusade and the Inquisition wiped out pretty completely the Waldensians of Languedoc, but they continued to flourish and even increased in the country to the east of the Rhone and Saône. They were strong in their original center, the city of Lyons and its vicinity. Their chief refuge lay, however, in the mountain valleys of eastern Dauphigny and Provence, where they frequently comprised the entire population. They were also numerous in the mountains of Savoy and Piedmont. From this strategic base in the very center of Western Europe their influence spread in all directions. Although they found it difficult to maintain themselves in the more populous parts of Italy, they survived in many remote, hilly regions. They spread rapidly throughout Germany and Bohemia.

Although the center of Waldensian power lay in the mountain valleys of eastern France and northern Italy, Germany and the Netherlands were the chief homes of heresy during the fourteenth century. To some extent this was the result of the failure of the papal efforts to establish the Inquisition in the region, as a result of the indifference if not actual hostility of the princes. Perhaps more important was the fact that most of the heresies of the period were based on mysticism, to which the people of Germany seem to have been particularly susceptible. Probably the most widespread and dangerous of these heresies was that of the Brethren of the Free Spirit. They were essentially pantheists who believed that God was in everything and that all living things reverted to God at death. Hence there could be neither Hell nor Purgatory, and the conception of sin was impossible. All man did was inspired by God. They believed that all property should be held in common and that work was unnecessary. While the more elevated members of this sect led an extremely austere life, avoiding all worldly interests and passions, the doctrine of the nonexistence of sin was an encouragement to looser behavior on the part of the less devout. Obviously the beliefs of the Brethren were dangerous to both the church and the Christian faith. They were regarded correctly as peculiarly obnoxious heretics and were vigorously persecuted by whatever machinery was available.

In their efforts to suppress the Brethren of the Free Spirit, the ecclesiastical authorities were gravely hampered by the difficulty of distinguishing between them and various orthodox groups that lived similar lives. In the thirteenth century the Low Countries had been the nursery of many informal religious communities, especially of women. A group of women would gather together, lead a common life, and support themselves by work or begging. While they promised chastity and obedience while they lived in the community, they retained their private property and could leave the community at will. Such women were commonly called Beguines. They were greatly favored by the counts of Flanders and other great lords of the region, and in the fourteenth century the idea spread through Germany. Soon there were similar communities of men known as Beghards. While most of the Beguines and Beghards lived in these settled communities, many began wandering about as beggars. The Brethren of the Free Spirit and other heretical sects were inclined to call themselves Beghards and to be so known by the people in general. This caused endless confusion. Several popes drew the line clearly between those living in settled communities and those wandering about. The former were to be protected; the latter suppressed.

Yet the papacy itself aided in the confusion. When the Inquisition was temporarily established in Germany in 1369 with the support of the Emperor Charles IV, it had no buildings to use as courts and prisons. To supply these the houses of the Beguines and Beghards were confiscated. Despite all the efforts of the church the heretical sects flourished. In the fifteenth century the appearance of the still more dangerous Hussites diverted the church's attention from them. There can be no question that they played a vital part in preparing the ground for the Reformation.

Probably the most bizarre movement that bedeviled the church in the fourteenth and fifteenth centuries was that of the Flagellants. This movement had its origin in the universal terror resulting from the Black Death. People believed that the plague was a judgment of God on sinful mankind and that only extraordinary measures could save men from its ravages. Bands of men and women gathered together and travelled about the country flogging one another. They preached the belief that anyone who subjected himself to this for thirty-three days would be completely cleansed from all his sins. At first, everyone looked on the Flagellants with sympathy. The feeling that inspired them was generally shared, and their method seemed in conformity with the basic asceticism that formed an important element in Christianity. But soon both secular and lay authorities grew alarmed at the wandering mobs. This alarm was increased when the marchers developed inclinations toward killing Jews and even members of the clergy who opposed them. Moreover, the pope saw clearly the danger in their doctrine. If man could achieve salvation by flagellation, what room was there for the church and its rites? In October, 1349, the Flagellants were solemnly condemned, and all authorities were ordered to suppress them. As in the case of other heretics, the intention outstripped the means, and the Flagellants remained a continual if sporadic problem well into the fifteenth century.

The profound mysticism that produced the Brethren of the Free Spirit and appeared in a much cruder form in the beliefs of the Flagellants was also responsible for several movements that remained within the limits of orthodoxy. Mysticism had, of course, always been an important element in Christianity. The Neoplatonic doctrines that formed the basis of Christian theology contained strong mystical elements, and Christians had always sought to know God through their emotions as well as through their intellects. The basic impulses of such enthusiastic Christians as Bernard of Clairvaux and Francis of Assisi were essentially mystic, and from at least the eleventh century on there was a continuous tradition of mystical ideas and teachings.

The most famous of the pure mystics of the early Middle Ages was Joachim of Flora, who lived in the second half of the twelfth century. He believed that he had received a revelation prophesying the early coming of the kingdom of God and the complete spiritual rejuvenation of mankind. Rather over-optimistically, he placed this event in the year 1260. Even more than St. Francis himself he was the inspiration of the Spiritual Franciscans, whose mystic doctrines and stubborn defence of their founder's ideas led them into conflict with their own order and the papacy.* Mysticism was always a serious problem for the mediaeval church. On the one hand, religion was essentially a matter of emotion as well as of reason, and all truly great churchmen were moved by emotion to some extent. The men who could move the masses, the enthusiastic reformers and successful preachers, were almost certain to be essentially mystical in their approach. On the other hand, mysticism could easily slip across the line into heresy. The man who thought in terms of direct union with God through emotional contemplation was all too likely to forget the established intermediary, the church.

The most noted of the orthodox mystics of the fourteenth century were two Dominicans: Eckehart, who lived 1260–1327, and his disciple Tauler, whose life spanned the period 1290–1361. Both found their inspiration in Neoplatonism, and both taught ideas that verged on heresy. In fact, a number of Eckehart's teachings were condemned as heretical in the year of his death. These elements of heresy grew out of the pantheistic tendencies in Neoplatonism, where divinity was thought of as all pervasive. In fact the basic ideas of Eckehart and Tauler were not very different from those of the Brethren of the Free Spirit—the conviction of the essential unity of man and God. But the two Dominicans did not draw from this belief the heretical conclusion that there was no need for the church and its sacraments. Instead the sacraments played an important part in their thought, and they were violent opponents of the Brethren. Tauler became the leader of a group called the "Friends of God," composed of laymen and ecclesiastics who hoped to reform the church from within by enthusiastically living and preaching the Christian life. Nevertheless, despite their orthodoxy,

* See p. 318.

the followers of Eckehart and Tauler played a part in paving the way for Martin Luther.

Although all these people, Waldensians and orthodox and heretical mystics, did much to prepare the minds of men especially in Germany for the easy acceptance of the doctrines of Luther and Calvin, the most important mediaeval precursors of the Reformation were the Englishman John Wyclif, and the Czech John Hus. There is no question about Wyclif's influence on Hus and his followers, and the connection between Hus and Luther is fairly clear. Certainly Luther made use of Wyclif's translation of the Bible in making his own.

John Wyclif took his name from Wiclif in Yorkshire, which formed part of the honor of Richmond which belonged to the house of Lancaster. In 1360 he was master of Balliol College in Oxford. In 1368 he received his B.D. degree, and four years later he became a doctor of divinity. In 1374 he was given the rich living of Lutterworth, probably as a sort of retaining fee from the crown. Wyclif had won considerable fame as a theologian and may well have expressed views about clerical property that had attracted the attention of Edward III. At any rate, in July, 1374, he was appointed a member of a royal commission being sent to Bruges to negotiate with papal envoys in regard to a number of questions in dispute between the pope and the English king.

One of the most acute of these was Edward's refusal to pay the tribute promised by John when he became a papal vassal. The Commission made little or no progress, and Wyclif returned to Oxford. There he began to compose a series of works on the relations between civil and ecclesiastical authority.

The center of Wyclif's argument was his doctrine of dominion, which he took largely from works of earlier writers. True dominion belongs only to God; man acts as his deputy on earth. All righteous men have an equal right to dominion, that is, to the goods of the earth. Before Adam's fall all property was common, but the introduction of sin brought private property into existence. The church, however, should not take advantage of this fact. It should adhere to the higher law that banned private property. This application of the doctrine of dominion to church property was Wyclif's addition to his predecessor's works. Actually, he did not advocate depriving the church of all its possessions. If it used its property righteously, it should keep it. The prince had the right and duty to decide what part of its property the church should be allowed to retain.

At this time a group of English nobles headed by John of Ghent were looking with greedy eyes on the possessions of the church. The idea of a partial seizure of church property had already occurred to them, and they were delighted to find an ecclesiastical supporter. In 1376 Wyclif was summoned to London to explain his views to the council, and during his visit he was encouraged to expound his opinions in the churches of the capital. This aroused the young and energetic bishop of London, William Courtenay. The bishop summoned Wyclif to appear before him to give an account of his unorthodox behavior. Wyclif answered the summons accompanied by John of Ghent, and the hearing degenerated into a bitter quarrel between the Duke of Lancaster and the bishop; but someone sent an account of Wyclif's teachings to Rome. Pope Gregory XI, who had recently returned to Rome from Avignon, found eighteen grave errors in Wyclif's teachings and promptly despatched a series of bulls to England. The bishops were to investigate as to whether or not he had really expressed these views, and if he had they were to arrest and imprison him. Edward was ordered to assist the bishops. By the time the bulls reached England, Edward III had died. The mother of the young Richard II, the Princess of Wales, forbade the bishops to condemn Wyclif, but they ordered him not to preach or teach the condemned doctrines.

The teachings of Wyclif condemned by Gregory XI had been concerned with political relations between church and state, and they had the firm support of John of Ghent and his party. Had his speculations remained confined to this field, the church could have done little against him. But soon he began to express novel theological opinions, especially in regard to the eucharist. He maintained that the bread and wine retained its substance—that is, it remained bread and wine—after its consecration by the priest. Christ was present spiritually, but not in substance. This teaching immediately lost him many of his supporters. The friars who held little property had looked on with considerable pleasure while he attacked the wealth of the clergy, but they promptly condemned his views on the mass. Many of his former friends at Oxford were alienated, and John of Ghent was profoundly shocked. Although it is clear that the powerful Duke of Lancaster continued to protect Wyclif's person from arrest and punishment, he no longer defended his theories. Courtenay was able to obtain the condemnation of Wyclif's works and his expulsion from Oxford. Wyclif's friends were also dismissed from the university. He himself retired to Lutterworth, where he lived in peace for the few years left to him.

Wyclif's theological views were largely based on the works of St. Augustine. Like Luther and Calvin after him, he found there the emphasis on the absolute power and dominance of God's will. To him it was inconceivable that anything could happen that was not actively willed by God. Hence, he believed in the doctrine of predestination. Some men were predestined to salvation and others to damnation. The pope might well be one of the latter. While the sacraments were useful and harmless, they were obviously completely unnecessary. The whole church and its rites had little place in a belief founded on the doctrine of predestination. Wyclif maintained that the Christian way of life should be sought in the Bible itself rather than in the teachings of the church. Hench it was necessary that the Bible should be available to everyone. Under his direction, certain of his followers produced two English translations that were to play an important part in the background of the Reformation. In short, Wyclif was clearly an extremely dangerous heretic. His political teachings endangered the property and revenues of the church. His theological views destroyed its spiritual authority. The clergy became a mere convenience unnecessary to salvation.

Even before Wyclif's death his followers began preaching his doctrines in the English countryside. Some of these men were Oxford scholars, but more were poor priests. Later, laymen began to wander about spreading Wyclif's teachings throughout the land. The followers of Wyclif were called Lollards, probably after a rather obscure German heretical sect. The teachings of Wyclif appealed particularly to three groups: radical scholars, poor country people, and great lords who hoped to seize the property of the church. While open Lollardy at Oxford was soon suppressed, it remained for many years as a secret belief among the scholars. The preachers who wandered about the countryside were, of course, violating ecclesiastical law by preaching condemned views and doing so without license, but during the reign of Richard II the church could do little but arrest and imprison them. They usually cheerfully recanted and equally cheerfully returned to their preaching. When Henry IV came to the throne, Parliament passed a new statute called *De Haeretico Comburendo.* Under this, all who preached Lollardy were to be handed over to the church for trial, and if condemned, were to be burned by the secular authority. To Henry IV this statute was more or less of a formality. Although some Lollards were burned, the statute was not enforced with any great enthusiasm. Henry V, however, persecuted the sect with ruthlessness and vigor. By the end of his reign open Lollardy had almost completely disappeared. There is some evidence that in various country districts it survived in secret until the Reformation.

Despite the statute providing for the burning of heretics, a fair number of nobles, including members of the House of Lords, remained open Lollards throughout the reign of Henry IV. They had a definite program for confiscating church lands and hoped to get it passed by Parliament. Early in the reign of Henry V their leader, John Oldcastle, Lord Cobham, stirred up several Lollard revolts and engineered a number of plots one of which seems to have had as its purpose the kidnapping of the king. There seems to have been some connection between the Lollard lords and the Mortimer party. After the failure of his plots, Oldcastle fled to Wales and remained in hiding until 1417, when he was arrested and executed. His death ended the political phase of Lollardy. Oldcastle is particularly interesting because Shakespeare's Sir John Falstaff seems to have been a combination of John Oldcastle and John Fastolf, a noted soldier of the day.

Although Wyclif's followers never had any great influence in England and were fairly quickly suppressed, his ideas were extremely potent in the affairs of a distant land. From 1378 to 1419 Wenceslas, eldest son of the Emperor Charles IV, ruled the kingdom of Bohemia. His sister Anne was the first wife of King Richard II of England. Many Bohemians followed Anne to England, and some were scholars who studied at the universities. There they soon learned of the teachings of Wyclif, and as early as 1380 some of his works were known in Bohemia. In 1401–02 a noted Bohemian scholar, Jerome of Prague, brought Wyclif's theological writings over from England to add to the political works that had already arrived. Jerome was an enthusiastic supporter of Wyclif's ideas and soon found allies among other Bohemian scholars.

Charles IV, Holy Roman Emperor and king of Bohemia, had been primarly devoted to the interests of his kingdom of Bohemia and hoped to make it the chief state of the empire. In 1347 he founded the university of Prague. It soon became a great international center of learning, with its faculty divided into the four traditional "nations." Thus, although it was the only university in Bohemia, it was essentially controlled by foreign scholars, as the Czechs formed but one of the four nations. It was among the Czech scholars at the university of Prague that Jerome of Prague found the most enthusiastic support for Wyclif's ideas. By 1403 the clergy became alarmed at the rapid spread of the new doctrines, and the archepiscopal chapter submitted forty-five articles drawn from Wyclif's works to the university for an opinion as to their orthodoxy. After a fierce debate, they were duly condemned as heretical, but a minority of the Czech scholars opposed this action. Among these dissidents was Master John Hus.

John Hus, who had been born in 1370, received his B.A. in 1393 and his M.A. in 1396. He never proceeded to the doctorate. Hus was an eloquent preacher, a writer of hymns, and an enthusiast for religious reform. He was extremely popular as a preacher among all classes of society and was very strong in his attacks on the evils of the church and the corrupt life of part of the clergy. A group of men interested in church reform had endowed a church, Bethlehem Chapel in Prague, to serve as a center for the preaching of Christian life. In 1402 Hus was appointed as the preacher in this church. Any enthusiastic foe of clerical vice was likely to slip into heresy, and this was particularly true in an enviroment where Wyclif's ideas were current. As early as 1401, Hus is said to have remarked in private conversation that he believed the elements remained unchanged when the bread and wine were consecrated in the mass and that a sinful priest could not perform a valid sacrament. In 1403, as we have seen, Hus was one of the Czech masters who opposed the condemnation of Wyclif's works. Although he was clearly sympathetic to much of Wyclif's teaching and certainly accepted some of it early in his career, as late as 1411 he solemnly denied that he believed in the chief points of Wyclif's doctrines. Hus was a preacher and reformer rather than a theologian and scholar. He used the ideas he needed and apparently did not bother too much about the rest of Wyclif's teaching. Although Hus was friendly with the followers of Wyclif in the university during the years 1403–11, he does not seem to have been regarded as one of their party by his fellow Czechs.

The national feeling of the Czechs had long chafed at the control of their university by the three foreign nations. The controversy over Wyclif's works made this issue more acute. While the majority of the Czech masters did not accept Wyclif's teachings and even forbade their students to read his works, they had no desire to take any action against those who did accept them—especially men like Hus who only adopted a few of Wyclif's ideas. It was the German scholars who pressed for active suppression of the heretical ideas. In 1409 an opportunity came for the Czech masters to gain control. The cardinals who had summoned the Council of Pisa in the hope of ending the Great Schism asked all Christians to maintain a position of neutrality between the two popes until the question was settled. The Czech masters, led by Hus, wanted tc follow this policy, but the three other nations voted against it. The archbishop of Prague also refused to be neutral. As King Wenceslas favored neutrality and wanted the support of the university, he was easily persuaded to change the laws of the university so that the Czech nation should have three votes. The Czech masters then voted for neutrality and elected Hus their rector. The archbishop had been troubled for some years by Hus's attacks on the clergy, and his promotion to the rectorship was too much for his patience. The scholars were forbidden to preach, and Prague was placed under interdict.

The crisis in Hus's career came in 1412. The disreputable Pope John XXIII created by the Council of Pisa quarreled with the king of Naples and preached a crusade against him.* Indulgences were promised to all who would join the expedition or contribute money to it. The giving of indulgences in exchange for money to benefit such a pontiff and such a cause was fiercely resented by all the reformers. Hus in particular preached against indulgences in general and this one in particular. He advanced the radical theory that papal commands were invalid if they controverted the law of Christ. This was far too revolutionary a step for most of Hus's supporters. The university renewed its condemnation of Wyclif's works with particular emphasis on certain of his arguments against indulgences that had been used by Hus. This action was vigorously supported by the shocked King Wenceslas. The Pope excommunicated Hus, and ordered Bethlehem Chapel to be razed. King Wenceslas expelled Hus's friends and supporters from the university and from Prague itself. Hus retired to the Bohemian countryside, where he continued his preaching and wrote a number of works. Although he never accepted all of Wyclif's views

* See p. 411.

and remained in a more conservative position than the English heretic, these works show profound influence of Wyclif's ideas.

One of the primary purposes of the Council of Constance was to bring the Hussite heresy to an end. The Emperor Sigismund offered Hus a safe-conduct to attend the council and to return home afterward. On November 3, 1414 Hus arrived at Constance, but despite the imperial safe-conduct the prelates soon cast him into prison. Sigismund made genuine though not overenergetic attempts to obtain his release. The council, however, insisted that Sigismund's safe-conduct to a heretic was invalid. It is interesting to note that in later years a more determined emperor forced the acceptance of a safe-conduct granted Martin Luther. Hus was ordered to state his position on forty-five articles drawn from Wyclif's works and forty-two from his own. He stated that he agreed with some of Wyclif's beliefs and refused to disown his own teachings. On July 6, 1415, Hus was degraded from the priesthood and turned over to the secular power. Sigismund, to his everlasting shame, had him burned. A year later Jerome of Prague, who had come to Constance to support Hus, was also burned.

To many Bohemians of all classes John Hus was a beloved preacher who was being persecuted by the clergy he sought to reform. He was also to a considerable degree a symbol of Czech nationalism. It seems clear that Hus had many friends and supporters, especially among the nobles who had little interest in his religious doctrines. In May, 1415, while Hus was in prison awaiting trial, a large assembly of Bohemian nobles wrote to the council in his favor. His death roused them to fury, and in September 500 nobles swore that they would not recognize any action of the council. For a while the pot simply seethed, but in 1419 a Hussite mob seized Prague and massacred the town council. Sigismund, who had just succeeded his brother Wenceslas as king of Bohemia, marched on Prague and was utterly routed by the rebels. There followed a series of crusades against the Hussites led by the Emperor Sigismund. Each time the proud chivalry of the empire marching in the holy cause were thoroughly routed by the wild peasant armies entrenched behind their gun-laden wagons.

Even while Hus was alive he and his supporters had had rather divergent doctrines. Thus, Hus never accepted the teachings of Wyclif as completely as had Jerome of Prague. Once their leader was dead, the Hussites split into a wide variety of different sects. Almost every known heresy and a few new ones soon appeared under the Hussite cloak, and the members of the party ranged from conservative nobles who wanted only the right to have laymen share the wine with the clergy at communion to wild radicals who wanted complete communism. In 1420 the groups managed to concoct a statement of principles that all agreed on, known as the "Four Articles of Prague"; but it represented little more than the demands they had in common. Men were to preach freely as they wished, the laity were to have the wine, large church estates were to be confiscated, and all sins severely punished. So firm a reputation for moral ardor did the Hussites develop that when the Council of Basel expected a delegation from them it ordered all the prostitutes off the streets of the city.

For well over ten years the Hussites were able to cooperate in war, even though they disagreed in religion. Crusade after crusade was repulsed, and Hussite bands wrought havoc in neighboring states of the empire. But the more conservative wing was alarmed by the radicals and yearned for peace. In 1434, Hussite and Catholic nobles combined to crush the forces of the radicals, and two years later peace was made with Sigismund. Sigismund was duly accepted as king of Bohemia, but he was forced to recognize the beliefs of the conservative Hussites. During the rest of the fifteenth century Bohemia had a confused and violent political history, involving the election of at least one Hussite king. It remained essentially a heretic state until after the Counter Reformation in the sixteenth century. Thus, from the point of view of the church, Bohemia was a cancer of heresy that might easily spread to other parts of Christendom.

At the end of the fifteenth century the magnificent political and spiritual structure of the thirteenth-century church was sadly dilapidated. The popes were cultured, luxury-loving skeptics whose chief interest in the church as a whole was to keep their revenues adequate for their expensive tastes and who looked upon the Patrimony of St. Peter as a source of states for their relatives. The Babylonian Captivity and the Great Schism had gravely lessened the prestige of both the papacy and the church. Despite the earnest efforts of many devoted churchmen no effective general reform had been achieved. Moreover, the secular princes had succeeded to a great extent in setting up national churches largely under their own control and were watching eagerly for any opportunity to make that control more complete. Heresy was rampant in secret in many lands, and openly in Bohemia. The essential foundations for the Reformation were solidly laid.

CHAPTER XIV

Mediaeval Civilization

IN DISCUSSING the culture of a period, historians often employ the German term *Zeitgeist*, the spirit of the age. The culture of each epoch is likely to have a dominant trend that manifests itself to a greater or lesser degree in every one of its phases, such as philosophy, literature, art, and architecture. In a period like the Middle Ages, where the dominant trend is strong and clear, an understanding of the zeitgeist is necessary for any adequate comprehension of the culture of the age. But it is important to remember that every culture contains elements that do not conform to the zeitgeist. Some of these elements have no future and are but dying remnants of earlier civilizations. Others are seeds that will grow and flower in a later period. Too often the impressive grandeur of the central theme of mediaeval culture has tempted historians either to neglect these inconsistent elements, or to try by some *tour de force* to fit them into the general pattern. In this chapter we shall attempt to keep the dominant trend clearly in sight but at the same time give adequate notice to all important contradictory elements, especially those that were to flourish in the future.

42. *Philosophy*

THE CENTRAL theme of mediaeval culture was the Christian faith. The men of the Middle Ages were both deeply religious and intensely practical. Religion was their chief preoccupation because they desired salvation. Although the love of knowledge for its own sake was far from uncommon, the scholars of the age sought knowledge primarily because they hoped it would aid them in achieving salvation. The subtle philosophical mind that rejoiced in close and precise reasoning chose subjects that were relevant to this all-absorbing aim. The scholar who found rare delight in the flowing phrases of Cicero was usually convinced that he sought only a knowledge of the literary art, that he might the better expound the precepts of religion. The sculptor who let his fancy run free in decorating the capitals in a Romanesque church was working to please God by glorifying him. Even when a talent seemed extremely remote from religion, attempts were made to draw it into the religious orbit. God and his Son could hardly be expected to appreciate a good tumbler, but the gentle Virgin Mary was grateful for all harmless activities pursued for her glory.

Historians frequently speak of "mediaeval syntheses"—works of art that incorporate in an orderly relationship all the elements of mediaeval culture. While a complete synthesis is obviously impossible, since not even religion can dominate all phases of civilization, a large proportion of human activities bear some relation to the Christian faith and, as we shall see, the Middle Ages were able to find relationships that would never occur to us. The *Summa Theologica* of Thomas Aquinas is often cited as such a synthesis. In it one finds the accepted ideas about the spiritual and physical world and the virtues and vices of mankind. Everything that could conceivably be related to religion is fitted into its proper place.* Dante's *Divine Comedy* is a similar work of art. There, in Heaven, Purgatory, or Hell, are found the people who represent every phase of human life, each in his or her proper place according to the tenets of the faith. Actually Dante's synthesis is far more complete than that of St. Thomas. The complexities of human

* See p. 289.

thoughts and behavior are seen more clearly and fully through individual men and women than in abstract discussions of virtues and vices.

Thus one might study the *Summa Theologica* long and hard before learning the church's opinion of courtly literature; but when Francesca tells Dante how reading about Lancelot brought her and Paolo to sin, this relationship stands forth clear and precise.* And the warrior baron and gay troubadour Bertran de Born suffers in hell not for robbing merchants or devastating the countryside, but for alienating young Prince Henry from his father King Henry II of England. Some enthusiasts have sought to find syntheses in the great Gothic cathedrals, but their efforts have not been very convincing. While many elements of contemporary culture found their place in the cathedrals, they are most incomplete as syntheses of mediaeval culture.

According to mediaeval theory, philosophy comprised all knowledge that was not relevant to attaining salvation. The study of God and of all else in relation to God was the field of theology. In that field divine revelation was the supreme source of knowledge, and reason could but support it. In the realm of philosophy, reason could reign unchallenged. Actually no such clear delineation of the two subjects was possible. Most philosophical conceptions had some relevance to theological problems. Those that did not were of secondary interest to men who believed that the primary purpose of knowledge was to assist man to achieve salvation. Hence the fields in which reason could operate without consideration for revelation were small and in general neglected. Throughout the Middle Ages philosophy was essentially the handmaiden of theology.

The most absorbing philosophical subject to mediaeval scholars was the question of universals—the controversy between Realists and Nominalists. The Realists were disciples of the Patristic Fathers, the Neoplatonists, and Plato himself. Plato taught that reality was a world of ideal models. The real man was an ideal man; reality lay in the species rather than in the individual. The Patristic Fathers, especially St. Augustine, fully accepted this point of view. Our senses supply us with knowledge about individuals, and our mind comprehends the ideal. The ideal is reality, and the characteristics of individuals are but "accidents." To the extreme Realist only the ideal, the species, was of importance and the individual was of no significance. The extreme

* See p. 454.

Nominalists took the opposite position. To them only the individual was real. General conceptions, universals, and species were mere names.

From one point of view this question of universals was a purely philosophical one concerning the nature of knowledge and how it is acquired. Does all knowledge of reality come from the senses or does the mind play a significant part in the process? But extreme nominalism was dangerous to accepted dogma. If only the individual was real, how could one believe in the Trinity? Moreover, the miracle of the mass involved the transformation of the essence, the reality, of the bread and wine without affecting the accidents of taste and texture. How could this be true if there were no such reality? Christian dogma had been constructed on a foundation of Neoplatonic thought, and a belief in the reality of universals was necessary to its acceptance.

We cannot follow in any detail the long controversy over this question. The extreme realist views of St. Augustine were generally accepted until the early twelfth century. Then Roscelin of Compiègne advanced the extreme nominalist doctrine. His teachings were declared to be heretical, and he was obliged to renounce them; but he had made a strong impression on his ablest student, Peter Abelard. Although Abelard rose to fame as an opponent and critic of the extreme realist William of Champeaux, he did not adopt the nominalist position of Roscelin. To put a long and complicated exposition in brief, rather crude form, Abelard argued that both species and individuals were real. Individuals were fully real, because they could be perceived completely. Universals were partially real, in the sense that they were the common elements of many individuals. This position of Abelard's is usually described as moderate realism. St. Thomas Aquinas arrived at a similar solution to the problem—a compromise between the extremes of realism and nominalism. The individual is reality that can be fully and concretely perceived by the senses. The universal, the common nature of things, can be comprehended partially by the mind. In philosophy as in theology, St. Thomas dominated the thought of the later Middle Ages, but his views were not accepted by all scholars. Nominalism in its extreme form was revived in the fourteenth century by William of Ockham, who as we have seen played an important part in the history of heresy.

The mediaeval scholar was inclined to limit his interests to subjects having a direct relation to the achievement of salvation. His treatment of every question, moreover, was dominated by some accepted authority. This was the natural result of his intellectual environment. The Bible and the works of the Fathers were divinely inspired sources of truth and could not be questioned. They had to be accepted as a matter of faith. Reason could be used to comment on and interpret these inspired works. Men who were accustomed to follow authority in the most important of intellectual activities were bound to search for similar authority in other fields. This was easily found in the works of ancient writers, particularly Aristotle. He was the master of those who know—the Philosopher. On every subject treated by him he was accepted as the supreme authority. But even if authority had played a less important part in the intellectual life of the Middle Ages, it is most doubtful whether the men of the day could have quickly passed beyond the limits of ancient knowledge. It took several centuries to absorb and comprehend the heritage left by Greece and Rome. With that great storehouse still unexhausted, men were little inclined to launch out for themselves in the search for new knowledge.

43. Science

THE EARLY Middle Ages was inevitably a dark age in respect to the physical and natural sciences. As they were only remotely related to salvation, they aroused little interest. When they were discussed, the primary motive was to draw from them religious inspiration. Fanciful life cycles of real or mythical animals were used to demonstrate principles of dogma. Thus the lion has three characteristics. As he moves along, he erases his footprints with his tail. This symbolizes the secrecy of the Incarnation. Then, the lion sleeps with his eyes open. That is the way the body of Christ slept on the cross. Finally, the lioness bears her cub dead and on the third day the father roars in its face and brings it to life. This signifies Christ's resurrection on the third day. Arithmetic was largely a discussion of the religious significance of such numbers as twelve and three. But even without this overwhelming absorption with religion, little progress could have been made until the scientific works of the Greek and Arab worlds became available in the twelfth century. Before that there was little scientific knowledge available, and devotees of extreme realism were unlikely to carry observation very far. What was observed by the senses was the accidents that marked individuals and hence was of little importance.

By the middle of the thirteenth century the scientific works of the Greeks and Arabs had been thoroughly absorbed, and the knowledge they contained had become an integral part of the culture of Western Europe. Scholars began to take an interest in the possibilities of observation and experiment. Aristotle had realized the importance of these methods of obtaining knowledge, and they were emphasized by the great commentator on Aristotle, Albertus Magnus. Although science as such was of little interest to Thomas Aquinas, he too pointed out the value of observation and experiment. But the chief figure in thirteenth-century scientific thought was the English Franciscan, Roger Bacon, who was a contemporary of St. Thomas. Bacon's basic point of view was thoroughly traditional. He accepted without question the divine inspiration of the Bible and the works of the Church Fathers. He insisted that knowledge was of value only in so far as it contributed to man's struggle for salvation. At the same time he had an eager, inquiring mind that was completely devoted to the enlargement of his knowledge. He attempted to extend the fields in which reason should have full play by limiting that of theology. He argued that many subjects covered by the great *summa* of the theologians were properly the concern of philosophy rather than theology. He also believed that new techniques, especially the study of languages, would be a great aid to both philosophy and theology. In support of this view, he pointed out some of the deficiencies of the Vulgate as a translation of the Bible. Then, in the field of philosophy he maintained that authorities should not be regarded with too great respect. Although the inspired writings could not err, Aristotle could. Finally, he advocated the confirmation of knowledge by means of observation and experiment.

Bacon's independence of mind endeared him neither to other scholars nor to his superiors in the Franciscan order. If he had not received the special protection of the pope, he might never have been able to write his learned works. As it was, he spent many years in confinement in the houses of the order. He did little toward making use of the methods of inquiry that he advocated so vigorously, and even if he had done so his conventional basic point of view would have seriously limited the usefulness of his observations and experiments. But his wide range of interests and independent, active mind made him an important figure in mediaeval intellectual history.

Although experimentation never became important in the Middle Ages, the use of observation to confirm or refute hypotheses and the reliance on reason rather than blind adherence to authority became relatively common in the fourteenth century. As an example one can take a subject of primary significance for the physical sciences—the nature and cause of motion. Aristotle believed that all material bodies had a natural motion toward the center of the universe. Motion in any other direction required a violent impetus. Observation soon raised doubts about this theory. If it were correct, an arrow should fall to the ground as soon as it left the bow. And how account for the increasing speed of falling bodies? Soon a theory was developed that once a body was put in motion the commotion caused by it in the air kept it moving. This same force increased the speed of falling bodies. Unfortunately the view was open to a serious objection; if it were correct, an arrow would never fall. Then, in the fourteenth century a group of scholars at the university of Paris arrived at a more satisfactory explanation: once started, the impetus of the motion itself kept the body moving. The problem of the perpetual motion of celestial bodies was neatly solved in true mediaeval fashion; they received their impetus from God. Thus observation was used to refute accepted hypotheses, and reason was called upon to provide more satisfactory ones.

The men of the Middle Ages accepted the classical theory that the earth was composed of four elements: earth, water, air, and fire. The scholars of the early Middle Ages believed that the earth was flat, with the land mass occupying the center and the water flowing around the edge. Although this crude idea probably continued throughout the period in the minds of the uneducated, it did not survive among scholars after the absorption of Greek and Arab learning. Later scholars thought of the earth as a sphere. The basest matter, earth, formed the center, then there was a layer of water, then one of air, and finally came the finest element, fire. In the northern hemisphere, the force of the stars drew the earth above the water in some places. Beyond the earth, the universe consisted of a series of spheres. All these spheres except the outermost revolved about the earth under the impulsion of spirits. The topmost sphere, Heaven, remained still. As time went on, observation obliged scholars to make some modifications in this scheme. Thus the eighth sphere carried the stars, but it was clear that not all stars moved in the same direction. Hence they produced the hypothesis that subsidiary spheres revolving independently were attached to the eighth sphere.

In assaying the progress made in the development of human knowledge during the Middle Ages, it is important to distinguish between the theoretical and the purely pragmatic. Thus in medicine little or no advance was made in theory over the classical and Arab physicians. Hippocrates and Galen remained the accepted authorities. But decided progress was made in the use of herbs and other practical remedies, and the physicians were continually concocting new and ingenious therapeutic devices. Some of these brought them into difficulty with the ecclesiastical authorities. Thus, in the twelfth century there was a general belief that a man could be cured of certain ills by having intercourse with a virgin; but the church could not be expected to approve this remedy. Nevertheless, in the course of their experiments the mediaeval physicians invented some methods of treatment that have since found support in modern medical theory. Increase of knowledge by observation and experience was particularly great in agricultural and industrial techniques. The invention of the horse collar was a development of enormous importance. By the thirteenth century the best agriculturists had discovered that crops were improved if the seed came from other land. In building, working metals, making colored glass, and many other fields, mediaeval technologists made important discoveries. Finally, the alchemists who devoted their efforts to attempts to turn base metals into gold observed many chemical reactions and were the ancestors of the chemists of today. In short, experience guided men with considerable accuracy in many things that we consider to lie within the domain of science. Workmen with no exact knowledge of the laws of physics, of comparative stresses and strains and of strength of materials, built magnificent Gothic cathedrals, which only occasionally fell down.

44. Political and Legal Thought

THE BASIC political ideas of the Middle Ages have already been discussed in connection with political history. The Roman conception of an emperor as secular head of Christendom survived throughout the Middle Ages, despite its lack of relevance to political reality. Only occasionally did princes outside the bounds of the Holy Roman Empire acknowledge the existence of this theory. French twelfth-century writers often described their ruler as *Imperator in Francia*, Emperor in France, to combat any claim that he was subordinate to the Holy Roman Emperor; and Richard of Cornwall, king of the Romans, was obliged to promise not to attempt to exercise imperial authority in England. During the Hundred Years' War, when the kings of France and England played with the pleasant conceit that they would settle their controversy by single combat, the court of the emperor was always chosen as the site of the duel that everyone knew would never take place. But even though the princes of Europe insisted on their sovereignty and within the empire itself the emperor became more and more powerless, Dante in his *De Monarchia* continued the idea of a Christendom ruled by an emperor.

In general, mediaeval political theorists thought of the king in terms of the Hellenistic basileus. He was appointed by God to rule and was consecrated in a religious ceremony that gave him priestly attributes. He was the source of the law and the fountain of justice. But he was not conceived of as a despot responsible only to God. He was appointed to rule for the benefit of his people and was expected to observe his own law. Usually at his coronation he took an oath to govern for the common good and to obey the traditional laws. In short, the royal authority was thought of as limited, but it was also God-given and not to be questioned. One might argue endlessly as to what the royal powers were, but it was agreed by everyone that there were such powers and that they were sacred and inalienable. Most writers emphasized that the chief function of the king was to render justice—to give every man his due. No matter what machinery such as courts and laws might be set up to administer justice, the king retained in men's minds a personal obligation to see that justice was done. Hence, when a mediaeval monarch ignored the established processes of law to order the execution of a rebel, many argued that he was within his rights as the supreme custodian of justice.

The men of the Middle Ages fully realized that law was necessary to justice and hence formed the basis of government. We have already traced the development of canon law and of the English common law. On the continent, each feudal unit had its own customary law, and during the thirteenth and fourteenth centuries many of these were organized into orderly written codes. There was thus a large mass of legal literature intended for the use of judges and lawyers. In addition, scholars continued to comment on the great legal works produced by Justinian's jurists. Although no courts administered this Roman law in its pure state, and hence its study was from one point of view useless, it gave excellent training in legal thought and supplied ideas that slowly took their place in the legal systems of Western Europe. Not even in the regions where customary law was based on Roman law were the two exactly the same, but all European law was influenced to some extent by Roman law. It was particularly influential in systems of law that were to apply to many lands, such as the codes of maritime law. In so far as Western Europe had a secular "common law," this was the Roman law.

One or two general comments on mediaeval law seem in order. The criminal law of the period has been frequently characterized as cruel and barbarous. In the early Middle Ages the Germanic customary law that prevailed over a large part of Western Europe regarded criminal offences as wrongs done to the victims or their families, and amends could be made by money payments. The idea that crimes were offences against society and should be punished by the government developed rather slowly. It was probably derived chiefly from ecclesiastical writings on justice and the duty of princes to enforce it. In their desire to keep public order, the princes introduced corporal punishments. At first these were comparatively simple. Serious crimes were punished by hanging. In many regions it was considered indecent to hang women, and they were drowned or burned instead. Minor offences were punished by mutilation, sometimes on the principle of an eye for an eye.

As time went on, and crimes were classified more carefully, new penalties were devised for various offences. Thus the murder of a master by a servant, or a husband by his wife, became petty treason and was punished by burning alive. Boiling in oil was conceived as a pleasant end for counterfeiters. Soon extremely savage punishments such as drawing and quartering and breaking on the wheel were being used for particularly heinous crimes such as treason. The men of the Middle Ages were not much concerned with the value of human life and had no squeamishness about inflicting pain. Especially in the fourteenth and fifteenth centuries many of their punishments were horribly cruel. But it is unfair to criticize them for relying on corporal punishment. The maintenance of prisons would have been far beyond the resources of the time. Only the church used imprisonment as a means of punishment.

The Germanic peoples thought of law as personal rather than territorial. When the Franks occupied Gaul, they continued to be governed by their customary law, but they did not apply it to the Gallo-Roman population. The same was true of the Visigoths and Ostrogoths. In their view, a man was subject to his own law wherever he might be. Although the gradual development of orderly states brought with it the conception of territorial law, the older idea survived to a considerable extent. Thus, in most mediaeval states Jews were governed by their own law, enforced by themselves. When foreign merchants were granted privileges, the right to trial by their own law was commonly included. And there was a different law for the various classes of society. As we have seen, the Latin kingdom of Jerusalem had different laws and courts for nobles, bourgeoisie, and the natives. While the distinction was not usually quite so clear-cut, in all states different laws applied to the various classes of society. The idea that the same law should apply to everyone who lived in a certain territory was essentially foreign to the mediaeval mind.

45. Social and Economic Ideas

WHEN mediaeval scholars examined the society in which they lived, they saw three classes characterized by different functions. The highest class, the clergy, served God and labored for the salvation of their fellow men. The second class, the nobles, defended the church and society as a whole from its foes. The third class supplied the material needs of the other two. Although the rise of towns and the growing importance of the townsmen tended to divide the third class into two subdivisions, bourgeoisie and peasants, the general conception of a three class society remained intact and was reflected in the idea of the three estates. Actually, of course, these classes bore little relation to the realities of social life. The higher clergy thought and lived like nobles, the lower clergy like peasants. The patterns of thought and ways of life of the bourgeoisie differed strikingly from that of the peasants. In short, mediaeval scholars classified social groups by function rather than by their social and economic characteristics.

Contemporary commentators on mediaeval society were convinced that the three basic classes had been ordained by God and that it was the duty of everyone to be content with his appointed place. God gave every man the qualifications for the place he was destined to fill. Hence a man endowed with the qualities of a peasant could not become a noble. But the idea of nobility by inheritance developed rather slowly. As late as the middle of the twelfth century it was considered conceivable that the son of peasant parents might be given the qualities of a noble and aspire to become one. As long as society consisted essentially of nobles and peasants this theory was tenable from the noble point of view: few peasants were going to be able to rival the nobles and seek admission to their ranks. But the rise of the townsmen changed this situation. They could and did achieve economic equality with the nobles. The doctrine of nobility by birth was clearly developed to keep the bourgeoisie in their place.

The social ideas of the Middle Ages were a mixture of the teachings of the church, ancient custom, and man's natural inclinations. In one area, the attitude toward the poor and the sick, the Christian element was dominant. It seems doubtful that any civilization has accorded the unfortunate more respect and given them better care in relation to the available resources than did that of the Middle Ages. The poor and sick were regarded as a blessing rather than a curse, for they gave men an opportunity to practice the pleasantest and easiest of Christian virtues—charity. Every person of means expected to give alms to the poor. Princes and nobles had almoners and dispensed alms in generous fashion. Lords both lay and ecclesiastical, and even rich merchants, founded hospitals for the care of the sick. All ecclesiastical establishments devoted part of their revenues to charity, and these establishments were numerous and their revenues large. There was a certain amount of feeling that the church did not follow its own teachings with enough enthusiasm and gave too little in alms. The popular legendary hero Robin Hood robbed rich churchmen and gave the money to the poor. Similar tales were very common throughout Western Europe. Even William Marshal, a noble knight, cheerfully robbed a monk and divided the booty among three poor knights—himself and two friends. Although William would have described this as chivalric *largesse* rather than as charity, the two ideas were closely related. Generous contributions to those in need were an essential part of mediaeval ethics.

As has been the case in many societies, a large proportion of the ethical thought and discussion engaged in during the Middle Ages was devoted to the relations between the sexes. While we know very little about the sexual ethics of the primitive Celts and Germans, it is clear that they differed decidedly from those of Christianity. It took several centuries for the church to get its doctrine of marriage accepted, to say nothing of persuading men to observe it. The Germanic warriors were easily persuaded to enter the bonds of matrimony, but it was almost impossible to convince them that the relationship should be permanent and impossible to discourage their liking for concubines. In the Carolingian period divorce could be arranged by mutual declarations of renunciation, and in the twelfth century noblemen were still repudiating their wives with little or no compunction. Only in the thirteenth century was the church's view of marriage fairly generally accepted in the upper classes.

One might say that there were two closely related conceptions of the functions of marriage. To the church it was the lawful means of producing progeny. To the feudal class it was a way of getting legitimate heirs and also a method of forming alliances between families. In the twelfth century this picture was confused to some extent by the appearance of the doctrine of courtly love. As love had no place in marriage, the proponents of the new cult thought of it as extramarital. Actually, courtly or romantic love seems to have had little effect on the institution of marriage during the Middle Ages and simply served to embellish extramarital relations. Little is known about the sexual ethics of the lower classes. There is some evidence that premarital relations were common and that marriage was only entered into when pregnancy occurred, but not enough is known to advance this as a valid generalization.

The ideas of courtly love were among the most important of mediaeval contributions to Western European civilization. In the Middle Ages they were definitely a divergent trend and formed no part of the dominant Christian culture. They were, in fact, frankly heretical. For centuries they remained essentially unrelated to marriage and found their place chiefly in romantic literature. But in the nineteenth century they were embodied in a new and vigorous romantic movement that was strong enough, at least in England and the United States, to make them a serious element in marriage. As the people of the Middle Ages had fully realized, romantic love and Christian marriage were basically incompatible. Their combination has had grave effects on the institution of marriage.

The ethical teachings of the Church were, of course, based primarily on the authority of the Scripture and the Patristic Fathers. In the early Middle Ages there was no serious effort to supply them with any other justification. One of the most interesting and all too little noticed contributions of St. Thomas Aquinas to ethical theory was his effort to justify the moral precepts of the church on the grounds of social desirability. In the case of most sins this was not too difficult; they were manifestly antisocial to the people of the day. Fornication gave him some trouble, as it seemed essentially harmless socially. His final solution was that this sin was likely to lead to a child that had but one parent to bring him up. This work of St. Thomas in developing a system of ethics based on reason as well as authority was a very important step in the history of social thought.

Mediaeval writing on economics was to all practical purposes confined to discussions of economic ethics. This consisted largely in defining the two basic concepts of usury and "just price." In the early Middle Ages any profit from money itself was considered usury. As time went on the range of usury was narrowed. In the thirteenth century it was considered proper to "adventure" money. One could give a merchant a sum of money with the understanding that the investor would share in either the profits or the losses, whichever might occur. Only the lending of money at interest to be paid under all circumstances was usury. The theory of just price involved primarily the circumstances that could be taken into consideration when setting the price for something. In the early Middle Ages the church was inclined to deny that one could charge for transportation from one place to another, but this doctrine that would have made commerce impossible was soon abandoned. In general, transportation of a product and any work done on it could be reflected in the price. The chief question was what expenses of the merchant or artisan could be taken into account in setting a price. St. Thomas believed that any expenditure for a worthy purpose, such as giving alms or aiding to build the walls of one's city, could be reflected in the price of one's products. In fact, he argued that a just price was one determined without greed. This obviously could give merchants all reasonable leeway. Speculation of all sorts was universally condemned. Buying a product and keeping it in the hope of selling later at a higher price was an offence in both secular and ecclesiastical law.

Although the men of the Middle Ages did not express their ideas on what we call economic theory, it is clear that they made certain assumptions that governed their actions in economic matters. The most important of these was the belief that God had created the world as he wanted it to be and that it was essentially stable and unchanging. The possibility that a certain sum of money would purchase less sometime in the future or that prices would rise and hence the same produce would be worth more does not seem to have occurred to them. Kings and nobles blithely rented lands and rights in perpetuity for a fixed money rent. Even when they were caught by inflation they appear not to have had any clear idea as to what had happened. This belief in economic stability led to the doctrine in the field of public finance that a king should be able to support his government and court on his ancient traditional revenues, and that any increase in his sources of income except to meet some immediate emergency was essentially immoral. This theory is found firmly entrenched in the minds of the writers of works on politics throughout the period.

46. Mediaeval Historians

ALL the subjects we have considered up to this point were considered to be in the realm of philosophy, but history was recognized as a separate field of intellectual activity. A large proportion of mediaeval historical writing was in the form of annals. From a very early period, many monasteries kept a record of events of interest to the house. Before the twelfth century almost all of these were narrow in range and slight in bulk. They would record the death of an abbot and the election of his successor, changes in important abbey officers, gifts to the house, important events in the lives of neighboring lords—especially if they had been donors of the house—and occasionally some more remote event such as the death of a king or pope. They are historical sources but hardly history in themselves. Although most of the monastic annals continued throughout the Middle Ages to follow this rather primitive model, at times real historians were entrusted with their composition, and they became true histories. Early in the twelfth century a Norman monk named Orderic Vitalis wrote a *Historia Ecclesiastica*. Basically it was the annals of his own monastery, but Orderic had a genuine historical enthusiasm and no objection to diverging from his theme. Whenever he mentioned a Norman noble house, he was inclined to give an account of its history. He devoted a great deal of space to the activities of the Norman dukes. The result was a vast if rather confused history of Normandy in the eleventh and early twelfth centuries. Unfortunately few continental monastic chroniclers followed Orderic's example. Only an occasional writer made the annals of his monastery of more than local interest. England was the seat of the great monastic historians. Alfred the Great directed a number of monasteries to keep annals and these are now known as the Anglo-Saxon chronicles. They furnish a fairly effective history of England up to the late years of the eleventh century. Their tradition was carried on by Latin writers. Up to the middle of the thirteenth century English history was covered by a series of excellent monastic chroniclers who retained the form of the annals but expanded them into true historical works. The best known of these chroniclers were two monks of St. Albans who wrote the annals of that monastery in the thirteenth century—Roger of Wendover and Matthew Paris. Both had great enthusiasm for collecting materials and a wide range of interests. Both wrote with color and vigor, if not with too great accuracy.

Monastic annals in general had certain distinct characteristics. As cloistered monks, their authors were rarely eyewitnesses of the scenes they depicted and were obliged as a rule to rely on information supplied by visitors to the abbey. Hence from the point of view of accuracy they are not over reliable. Since they were servants of God and were writing for his glory, they could rarely resist a miracle or the opportunity to point a moral. Nevertheless, they were numerous and industrious, and we owe to them much of our knowledge of the Middle Ages.

The early Middle Ages produced comparatively few important historical works. Early in the sixth century Bishop Gregory of Tours composed a *History of the Franks* that recounted the deeds of Clovis and his sons. Gregory was a product of the late Roman schools who wrote with vigor and color. As he is practically the sole source for the period he covered, we cannot estimate his accuracy. Einhard, one of the scholars at Charlemagne's court, wrote a biography of his master based closely on Roman models. Perhaps the greatest historian in Western Europe during this period was the Venerable Bede, who produced an *Ecclesiastical History of the English People*. Bede was the most learned scholar of his day and possessed a genuine historical sense that enabled him to distinguish between what he knew and what he had heard from others. His work is our chief source for early Anglo-Saxon history.*

* See pp. 87–8.

The late eleventh century saw the beginning of a great era of historical writing by secular clerks. William, archbishop of Tyre, composed a detailed account of the First Crusade. Clerks who served in the courts of Henry II and Richard I of England wrote histories of those periods. In France a royal clerk named Rigord began what was to become an official history of the French monarchy. It was carried on with enthusiasm by his successors. In the courts of most monarchs and many prelates clerks turned their hands to history. The secular clerk had both advantages and disadvantages over the monastic chronicler. Since he was actively involved in the affairs of the world, his sources of information were better than those of the monks; but his involvement in politics was likely to make him less impartial.

Before the thirteenth century it was extremely rare for a layman to be literate and hence nearly all historical writing was the work of ecclesiastics. A notable exception was Alfred the Great, who translated the world history of Orosius and may have written parts of the Winchester edition of the Anglo-Saxon chronicle. But from the time of Alfred to the thirteenth century there were no laymen writing history in Western Europe. The earliest important work by a lay hand was produced by a mercenary soldier who served in the wars between England and France in the early thirteenth century. He wrote a detailed, careful, and generally accurate account of the campaigns he served in, especially the invasion of England by Prince Louis of France. A little later, about 1225, a professional writer who was almost certainly a layman wrote a biography of William Marshal, the great English baron. This anonymous historian was far more sophisticated than most of his contemporaries. He distinguishes carefully between what he knows and what he feels is uncertain. Often he cites his sources. Several times he admits that his informants differ and that he does not know just what happened. In everything directly relevant to the career of his hero, he is extremely accurate.

Another lay historian of the early thirteenth century was Geoffrey de Villehardouin, a noble of Champagne, who dictated an account of the Fourth Crusade and the capture of Constantinople. Toward the end of the century John, lord of Joinville, in his old age dictated his *History of St. Louis*, which was primarily an account of the crusades of his royal master. Joinville was old and his memory faulty, so that his work is not too sound as factual history, but his eye for homely detail and his lively style make his book interesting reading today, as it was in his own time.

The thirteenth century saw the last of the important monastic chronicles. While secular clerks continued to write history, the most important works of the later Middle Ages were produced by laymen. Jean Froissart wrote a famous account of a fair part of the Hundred Years' War. Froissart was devoted to chivalric ideas, and his interest centered in brave deeds of arms. While he tells a colorful story, it is hardly well-rounded history. Philippe de Comines started his career as a servant of Charles the Rash, duke of Burgundy, but allowed himself to be seduced into the service of the wily King Louis XI. His history of the times he lived in is sometimes called the first modern historical work. While Comines was more sophisticated than most of his predecessors and his history has a more modern tone, there seems no sound reason to separate him from other lay historians of his age. An admiration for the unscrupulous political methods of Louis XI does not make a writer "modern."

In general, one can say that most mediaeval writers of history lacked a critical point of view. Any information they could obtain was used without much consideration of its possible bias or its accuracy. Like men of all ages, each writer had his prejudices and his own peculiar bias. Each was interested in some things and not in others. But most of them had a sound historical inspiration—the desire to tell what happened to the best of their ability. While their unsophistication made them credulous and uncritical, it also kept them as a rule from writing conscious propaganda. In short, mediaeval historical writing contains a good deal of naïveté but comparatively little downright dishonesty.

In addition to the conventional historical works there were several kinds of writings that are of use to the historian of the Middle Ages. The saints played an extremely important part in popular religion, and accounts of their lives were of wide interest to the people of the day. As a rule the life of a saint was written and rewritten many times and grew fuller and more detailed each time. These accounts are, of course, filled with miraculous events. They are of great value to the student of mediaeval beliefs and religious ideas. Then there were treatises on various subjects. In the thirteenth century an Englishman named Walter of Henley wrote a treatise on agriculture. The treasurer of England, Richard fitz Neal, wrote a work describing the procedures of the English exchequer. A number of scholars wrote works on the proper training of the young. These were usually intended to guide the education of princes and nobles. Books were also produced on the chief noble sports—hunting and tourneying. Finally, the Middle Ages were well supplied with anecdotists. John of Salisbury, one of the great scholars of his day, who died bishop of Chartres, composed a long work that was a combination of a treatise on political science and a book of anecdotes. Walter Map told a series of stories mostly dealing with the court of Henry II. On the continent a century later, Stephen of Bourbon composed a similar work. These are simply random examples chosen from a large number of such books. They are of great value to the historian who wants to add life and color to his work and is prepared to view the precise anecdotes with a sceptical eye. A fair proportion of these tales started in ancient Babylonia and are still going strong today.

47. *Belles-lettres*

EXCEPT for the histories written by laymen, the works we have been discussing were in Latin. Latin was the language of the church and of scholars. It was the only language for serious subjects like theology and philosophy. Moreover, as the clergy were for a long time the only literate class, the clerical work at the courts of kings and nobles was done by men in at least minor orders and was in Latin. Thus most official documents were in that language. As most ecclesiastics centered their attention on serious subjects, *belles-lettres* in Latin did not become extensive until the Renaissance. Great prelates such as Hildebert of Lavardin, bishop of Le Mans and later archbishop of Tours, occasionally turned their hands to Latin verse, and once in a while a lesser clerk would follow their example, but in general the Latin literature was slight in quantity and unexciting in nature. There was, however, one fascinating body of writing in Latin—the so-called Goliardic songs. These were apparently the work of wandering minor clerks, probably university students. They take their name from Golias, a probably legendary person who played a prominent part in the poems. For the most part these were gay poems about drinking and making love. Modeled on the classical poets like Catullus, they were irreverent always, slightly blasphemous sometimes, and basically pagan in thought and expression.

The Goliardic poems were an integral part of a short-lived revival of interest in Latin literature that marked the twelfth century. During the early Middle Ages the church had in general frowned on the reading of works by pagan authors. But the churchmen fully realized that these pagan writers like Cicero supplied the best possible models of Latin prose. Hence in its schools the church used these authors as examples of sound grammar if not as works of literature. In the twelfth century, eager scholars began to be fascinated by the sheer beauty of the style used by the classical Latinists and read them with new interest. At the cathedral school in Chartres a group of able teachers expounded the literary quality as well as the grammatical perfection of the classics, and a number of their students were moved to active study of the pagan authors. It seems likely that the writers of the Goliardic poems were inspired by this movement, as was the more conventional Hildebert of Lavardin. Abelard developed a deep interest in classical times and became so enamored of the Greek philosophers that he decided they had been Christians before Christ, like the Hebrew prophets. By far the most distinguished of these twelfth-century humanists was John of Salisbury, who had studied at Chartres and under Abelard at Paris. He had a genuine enthusiasm for classical style and read all the Latin literary works he could find. Unfortunately the revival of classical literature lasted at most for three generations. The successors of John of Salisbury, like Robert Grosseteste, bishop of Lincoln, and Roger Bacon, carried their interest in classical times so far that they learned Greek, but their attention was entirely devoted to theology and philosophy rather than literature.

The most important mediaeval literature from the point of view of both quantity and interest was in the vernacular languages. The earliest of these works that have survived were written in Germanic tongues. It seems likely that the early Germans were accustomed to composing songs celebrating the deeds of heroic warriors to be sung at feasts and other festive occasions. Charlemagne is said to have ordered a collection of such songs to be made, but if his order was carried out, the collection has been lost. We have only a few fragments of what may have been an extensive literature. By far the most important of these early works is the Anglo-Saxon epic poem *Beowulf*. This seems to be a combination of several songs composed in the Danish peninsula in heathen times, told and retold, and finally reduced to writing after the conversion of the Anglo-Saxons. The central theme of the story is the heroic deeds of Beowulf, who slays two savage monsters and a fire-breathing dragon but is slain himself in the last adventure. This poem is a masterpiece of literature and gives the reader a feeling that in it he has the true spirit of the early German culture. Except for one or two fragments, *Beowulf* is our only surviving example of the Anglo-Saxon epic. It is also in its present form the oldest extant piece of Germanic vernacular literature.

There is, however, a considerable amount of early German literature that survives in comparatively late manuscripts. The oldest of these is the *Hildebrandslied,* a tale of the times of Attila the Hun, which may well have been one of the songs of Charlemagne's time and has come down to us in an eleventh-century manuscript. The cycle of the *Nibelungenlied* is composed of stories that originated in the early German times, but the form in which it has survived dates from the thirteenth century. These entrancing mixtures of heroism and magic form an important part of the literary heritage of Western Europe. Then the Vikings who plundered the coasts of Europe and colonized the wild islands of the North Atlantic and even the American coast composed long *sagas* about their adventures. Here again our earliest manuscripts come from the twelfth century, but many of the stories deal with earlier times. No one who has not read some of this literature can understand the great achievements of these wild adventurers. In fact, it is in the sagas that we can best see the Germanic characteristics —love of freedom, impatience with restraint, reckless bravery, lavish generosity—that formed so important a part of upper-class ethics in the Middle Ages. The military chivalry of later times can only be comprehended through a knowledge of the Germanic warriors.

Beowulf was but a small part of Anglo-Saxon literature. There were two great religious poets, Caedmon and Cynewulf, and many lesser masters of that craft. Alfred the Great translated into Anglo-Saxon a varied series of works—the *Pastoral Care* of Gregory the Great, the history of Orosius, Bede's *Ecclesiastical History*, and Boethius's *De Consolatione Philosophiae*. In Anglo-Saxon England, Latin was reserved for the works of high ecclesiastics writing on purely religious subjects. The chronicles, official documents, royal decrees, tales of battles and noble deeds, and even popular religious works were in the vernacular. Thus England had a written language and flourishing literature of its own at a time when Latin ruled supreme in the rest of Western Europe. Only after the Norman conquest did Anglo-Saxon slowly wither away, to reappear in the fourteenth century as Middle English.

Towards the close of the eleventh century, vernacular literature began to appear in France. The people of this kingdom spoke two different Romance languages—the langue d'oïl in the north, and the langue d'oc in the south, which took their names from the different pronunciation of the word "yes." The earliest literature in the langue d'oc was lyric poetry that had love as its chief theme. The origins of this poetry are obscure. It seems clear that a certain amount of popular poetry had survived in southern France from Roman times, and this may well have served as the original model. Then, across the Pyrenees in Spain there flourished lyrical love poetry among the Arabs. There is some evidence that verse forms, if not ideas, came from this source. At any rate, in the last years of the eleventh century, poets in southern France began composing love poetry in the langue d'oc.

This idea caught the interest of the greatest feudal prince of the region, William IX, count of Poitou and duke of Aquitaine. Duke William began to write poetry, and his patronage was enough to make the new art popular. Soon there were many poets between the Alps and the Pyrenees. They were called troubadours. Some troubadours were men of high rank like Duke William, and many were of knightly birth, but others were simply talented poets who wanted to make a living. The basic idea of troubadour poetry was the beneficial effects of admiration for a worthy woman. Although the troubadours sang of love, this love could be quite distant and yet yield its benefits. By loving a worthy woman a man became a better knight and a better poet. The first troubadours were imaginative artists, but soon this poetry became extremely conventional. All ladies were blond with pure white skin. Their lovers had no interest in food and drink; they did not notice either hot or cold. Their minds were wholly absorbed in love for their ladies. If a lover served his lady long and faithfully and wrote many poems in her honor, she might reward him with a smile, a kiss, or even a more intimate favor. As these ladies were always married, scholars have wondered whether this poetry was an adjunct to adultery. The answer seems fairly simple. When the poet was a great lord, he undoubtedly expected and often obtained the ultimate reward. Certainly Duke William of Aquitaine was no distant admirer of fair ladies. But when the poet was a humble knight praising the wife of a great baron, he confined his love to admiration, if he had any normal discretion. And as the dignity of the lady gave prestige to her lovers, great noblewomen were the usual subjects of the troubadour poems. Troubadour poetry reached its height in imagery, freshness, and vigor about the middle of the twelfth century. While it survived another hundred years, it grew steadily more conventional and less spontaneous. The fearful Albigensian Crusade ravaged the troubadour country, and destroyed much of the gay spirit that had animated its poets.*

The fashion for writing poetry and the interest in love was carried into northern France by Eleanor, duchess of Aquitaine, when she became the wife of King Louis VII. Eleanor was the granddaughter of the earliest troubadour, Duke William IX, and also the patroness of many poets. When Eleanor's marriage to Louis was annulled and she became queen of England, her court remained for some years a center of literature and courtly love. Her imprisonment in Winchester castle for encouraging the revolt of her sons was mourned by many troubadours. Eleanor's place as chief patroness of courtly love was taken by her two daughters, Marie, countess of Champagne, and Alix, countess of Blois. Marie's court at Troyes became the literary capital of France, and her grandson, Thibaut IV, count of Champagne, was the most prolific and one of the most talented lyric poets of the thirteenth century. Writing poetry became as fashionable in the north as it had been in the south. Eleanor's son, King Richard I of England, was an enthusiastic though not very adept poet. During the first half of the thirteenth century northern France produced a dozen or so noble devotees of lyric love poetry. Moreover, the fashion spread to Germany and Italy. While the *Minnesingers* of Germany flourished for a comparatively short time, the troubadour tradition continued in Italy until the Renaissance. Meanwhile, in both France and Germany the writing of poetry had been taken over by the burghers of the great towns and continued among them into the fourteenth century.

When the troubadour ideas were transplanted to the north, the word "love" took on a rather different meaning. To the troubadours distant admiration and faithful service to a lady could bring the benefits bestowed by love, but when the northern writers spoke of love they meant sexual relations. While the noble lady might be put on a pedestal, this was purely as a matter of form, and there was never any doubt what the poet expected from her. This change may have been a result of the fact that the men of the north were less civilized and

* See pp. 311–14.

cruder than those of the south, but it may also have come from the source to which they turned for new ideas about love. When the men of the twelfth century wanted information, they turned naturally to some ancient authority. The devotees of courtly love soon found such a work—Ovid's *Ars Amoris.*

Ovid wrote about a society in which very few women were bound in permanent matrimony—the wives of the most exalted senators with religious duties in the Roman cult. Most husbands and wives could separate by mutual consent, and many couples never bothered with any formal legal connection. The women of Ovid were either lightly bound wives or completely unfettered adventuresses. And there was nothing courtly or romantic about love in Ovid; it was purely and completely sensual. But the courtly lovers managed to ignore his cruder ideas and draw from his book ideas and conceits about the nature of love. Chrétien de Troyes, who served the Countess Marie of Champagne, translated the *Ars Amoris.* Another member of Marie's household, Andrew the Chaplain, drew freely on it in composing a handbook of courtly love that he called *De Amore.* Andrew thought of his work as a guide to all who might want to engage in courtly love. He carefully defined love, showed who was eligible to practice it, invented a code of the laws of love, and supplied sample conversations as aids to efficient seduction. Then, in case his reader didn't believe in courtly love, his last section was a bitter diatribe against women. No more fascinating book was produced by the Middle Ages.

While lyric poetry was developing in southern France, another type of French literature appeared—the *chanson de geste.* The earliest known manuscript of a chanson de geste is the Oxford copy of the *Chanson de Roland* that dates from about 1100. There has been extensive debate among scholars over the origins of the chanson de geste. In the nineteenth century it was generally believed that the Frankish warriors of Carolingian times had composed songs to celebrate their deeds and that these had been passed down from generation to generation and finally combined into long narrative poems. This theory led to the belief that the chansons were of value as historical sources. Later scholars examined the chansons more carefully and compared them with what is known of Carolingian history. They proved that the authors of the chansons knew very little about this history. They came to the conclusion that the chansons de geste were products of the late eleventh and twelfth centuries, and that the authors drew largely on their imagination for their material. The truth probably lies somewhere between these two views. Every people has its legends, its stories passed on from father to son. Such legends were almost certainly used by the authors of the chansons along with anything else they could lay their hands on, such as inscriptions on tombstones and the lives of saints. The bare outline furnished by such sources was generously filled out from the poet's imagination. While there are incidents in the chansons that are historic, they have been modified so much that the songs are of no use to the historian. Thus, after one of Charlemagne's campaigns in Spain, his rear guard was attacked and severely mauled by the Basques in a narrow mountain pass in the Pyrenees. In the Song of Roland the rear guard is attacked by Saracens in a broad valley.

The chansons de geste were clearly composed primarily for the entertainment of the feudal male. Their chief elements were the two subjects in which he was most interested—fighting and feudal politics. The first part of the finest of these poems, the *Chanson de Roland*, consists of the political contest at Charlemagne's court between Roland and Ganelon. Then there came the great battle in which Roland and his companions slew untold thousands of Saracens. Although in some of the chansons feudal warfare between Christians replaced the fighting against Saracens, the general ingredients were the same. Women had little place in these poems. Occasionally we see a mother sending her sons to war or a wife being brutally beaten by her husband. Then here and there appear charming princesses, Christian or Moslem, burning with enthusiasm to join some knight in his bed. Moslem princesses had one great advantage—they had to be converted and baptized, and the latter ceremony involved undressing them and describing their charms in detail. Only in a few late chansons are there feeble glimmerings of the ideas of courtly love. The lyric poems were written to please women, but the chansons de geste were definitely for men's taste.

By the middle of the twelfth century there was an active demand for stories. The nobles and their courts wanted to be entertained during the long evenings, and the wandering minstrel who had good tales to recite could be sure of a generous reward. The *trouvères*, as the composers of these stories were called, used any material they could find. Legends from Roman literature were popular. Thus a trouvère based a romance on the story of Aeneas. With all the formalities of courtly love Aeneas loved and left Dido and finally won Lavinia. But the chief source of tales for the writers of twelfth-century France was the folklore of Wales.

Toward the middle of the twelfth century an English clerk named Geoffrey of Monmouth wrote a *History of the Kings of Britain.* Geoffrey told how the Trojan Brutus came to Britain and became its king. He then recited a history of the kingdom to the reign of Henry I. Among his kings was a heroic warrior named Arthur, who vigorously fought the foes of his realm. Geoffrey's contemporaries had no hesitation in saying that his work was wholly imaginary, and many modern scholars share this view. Geoffrey himself said that he got his material from an old Welsh book. Now there was undoubtedly a large mass of Welsh folklore—tales of giants and fairies, or brave heroes and fair ladies. King Arthur and his knights eventually played an important part in this folklore. But there is no absolutely conclusive evidence that the Welsh knew about King Arthur before Geoffrey wrote. The controversy as to whether Geoffrey invented King Arthur or found him in Welsh tales is too complicated to go into at length. On the whole there seems to be adequate evidence that the Welsh did have such a hero and that Geoffrey got his ideas from them. Be that as it may, Geoffrey's book was immensely popular and was soon carried to France. King Arthur and his knights were seized upon as a marvelous subject for stories. Moreover, the trouvères dipped deeply into Welsh folklore and came up with many tales not used by Geoffrey.

Perhaps the most noted user of this new material was Marie of Champagne's favorite writer, Chrétien de Troyes. He took Welsh stories and wrote into them the ideas of courtly love. When he needed a little variety, he had no objection to using classical material. One of his stories, "Cliges," is laid half at Arthur's court and half in Constantinople. All the chief Arthurian heroes received attention from Chrétien. He wrote a "Tristram" that is lost, a "Lancelot," and a "Percival." The "Lancelot" is a pure work of courtly love. Lancelot, the best of Arthur's knights, gave up everything a knight should hold dear for love. He committed the serious feudal crime of committing adultery with his lord's wife, Queen Guinevere. He allowed himself to be carried in a hangman's cart. He resisted the wiles of all other ladies. He was the perfect courtly lover. Actually Chrétien had his doubts about Lancelot and is careful to say that the Countess Marie gave him the material and told him how to use it. Later he wrote of Percival, the Christian knight, who resisted all ladies. Chrétien de Troyes was a master storyteller, and his tales still make excellent reading. A contemporary of Chrétien, Marie de France, wrote short narrative poems or lays that were an adroit mixture of Welsh legend, courtly love, and the life she saw about her. Her verve and charm make her works also acceptable to the modern reader.

The Arthurian material was immensely popular and was used by many writers. By the thirteenth century the stories about King Arthur and his knights had been developed into an extensive series culminating in the finding of the Holy Grail by Galahad. As time went on the tales grew longer and more numerous. In the fifteenth century an English knight, Sir Thomas Malory, drew from them the material for his *Morte d'Arthur*. This magnificent collection of Arthurian tales, written with great verve and enthusiasm, has inspired English writers ever since that time—notably Alfred, Lord Tennyson; Howard Pyle; and John Erskine. It is an important part of our literary heritage.

Another interesting type of French literature were the *fabliaux*—short stories often based on Aesop's fables. These tales were likely to be coarse in their wit and were clearly intended to amuse not too delicate audiences. While some scholars have assumed that they were intended primarily for the bourgeois taste, there is little doubt that they were fully appreciated in castle halls. Marie de France, whose *Lais* depicted the noble life, was the author of a famous collection of fabliaux that cannot be said to be notable for their delicacy.

During the second half of the thirteenth, the fourteenth, and the fifteenth centuries, the various types of French literature we have already mentioned continued in favor. A few new chansons de geste were produced and old ones remade, usually by lengthening them. Four knights composed the *Cent Ballades* in the conventional themes of courtly love. Christine de Pisan, next to Marie de France the greatest female writer of the Middle Ages, composed the *Book of the Duke of True Lovers*. Christine followed the usual conventions to a certain point and then stopped; her ladies kept their virtue. Duke Philip the Good of Burgundy was fascinated by chivalric ideas. His court produced remodeled chansons de geste and two biographies of perfect knights. Late chivalry in its more exaggerated form can be seen to perfection in these two works—*The Book of the Deeds of Jacques de*

Lalaing and *Le Petit Jehan de Saintré*. In general, one can say that during this period the ideas of chivalry developed in the twelfth and early thirteenth centuries were carried to completely ridiculous lengths.*

There were, however, writers who were thoroughly tired of the conventional ideas. As early as the latter part of the thirteenth century Jean de Meung in his *Roman de la Rose* satirized the ideas of courtly love and many other traditional conceptions. Another famous satirical work, the *Fifteen Joys of Marriage* was a fierce if amusing diatribe against women in general. Another work that is hard to classify tended in the same general direction—*Les Cent Nouvelles*. This was a collection of stories, usually of amorous adventures, supposed to have been told at the court of Duke Philip the Good. They can be taken as a reaction against courtly love or as a new sort of fabliaux. They certainly showed clearly that by the fifteenth century love could be dealt with in literature without using the courtly conventions.

The lyric tradition had never disappeared in France. Throughout this period there were lyric poets, but none of them could be called very distinguished. The fifteenth century saw a revival of the French lyric in three poets—Alan Chartier; Charles, duke of Orleans; and François Villon. Chartier was a writer of fairly conventional love poetry, but he is even better known for his patriotic verse stirring up the French against their English foes. He can be said to share with Jeanne d'Arc the credit for arousing the spirit of France. Charles of Orleans wrote charming love poems. Villon was one of the great poets of the world, and his fame is still strong. Few men have put their personal problems into verse with such feeling, skill, and originality.

Although France was the chief center of literature in Western Europe from the eleventh to the fifteenth centuries, with the exception of Chrétien de Troyes and François Villon, she produced no individual writers that could compare with the best found in other lands. In Italy, the thirteenth and fourteenth centuries saw three truly great literary figures—Dante, Petrarch, and Boccaccio. We have already mentioned Dante in discussing mediaeval ideas.† He was one of the world's greatest poets. Equipped with true poetic insight and rare skill in effective expression, he saw the mediaeval world as a unity, and so depicted it in his *Divine Comedy*. Petrarch was a very different genius. He was brought up in the troubadour tradition, and much of his poetry followed its conventions; but it did so with rare freshness and delicate

* See p. 346. † See pp. 430–1.

vigor. He was also fascinated by classical literature and has been called the first of the humanists.

Boccaccio illustrated even more thoroughly the transition from the Middle Ages to the Renaissance. He too began his career in the tradition of courtly love, but he soon left it behind. The work of which he was most proud was a vast *Genealogy of the Gods*, a rather ponderous Latin monument of classical erudition. But his fame rests on his *Decameron.* This is a collection of short stories of many types and drawn from a wide variety of sources. A large proportion of them deal with the pleasant sins of adultery and fornication. In a good many of the tales the participants in these forbidden delights are members of the regular or secular clergy. Boccaccio was a master storyteller and has been called the father of the modern short story. He was also singularly untroubled by the ethics and moral precepts of the church.

The Norman Conquest stifled for two centuries the development of English literature. While the Anglo-Norman nobles who ruled the land were for the most part bilingual, their taste favored French literature. The earliest major piece of writing in Middle English was Layamon's *Brut*. Layamon was an English priest who early in the thirteenth century composed this history of Britain in narrative verse. Layamon used as his chief source an earlier French poem by the same title that was written by Wace at the court of Henry II. Although Wace drew his original inspiration from Geoffrey of Monmouth, both he and Layamon modified and expanded Geoffrey's work. The thirteenth century also saw the first of a long series of English romances. During the next 300 years English writers produced romances using a wide variety of subjects. These were tales of Anglo-Saxon and Viking heroes, of Arthurian knights, of Richard the Lionhearted, of Roland, of Alexander the Great, and of the siege of Troy. Some of these were little more than translations of earlier works, but others were independent romances. In the fourteenth century the flow of romances continued and in addition there were other interesting works. *Sir Gawayne and the Grene Knight* was a true gem combining Arthurian material and courtly love. Then, there were two major literary figures—Chaucer and Gower. John Gower is known primarily for his *Confessio Amantis*, a rather conventional work on the theme of courtly love that was extremely popular in his day and is still of some interest to students of that cult. Geoffrey Chaucer was one of the world's great poets.

Geoffrey Chaucer stands with Dante far ahead of all other mediaeval writers. While his purpose was less ambitious and less elevated than Dante's, he was his peer in poetic insight and in literary skill. Chaucer is chiefly known for his *Canterbury Tales*. The pilgrims as described in the prologue give us a marvelous survey of the society of the age, from the noble knight to the rude miller and from the gentle abbess to the poor parish priest. Then the tales illustrate almost every mediaeval *genre* and satisfy every taste. There is knightly romance and courtly love. There are sophisticated stories like Boccaccio's. There are crude coarse tales. The weaknesses, vices, and foibles of the various social groups are clearly brought forth. The "Parson's Tale" is essentially a guide to confessors. In short, the *Canterbury Tales* are a marvelous medley of all the threads of late mediaeval literature and the society that produced it. More important throughout the whole is Chaucer's genius for haunting beauty of expression and precise, clear, forceful exposition. Then, Chaucer had an imaginative, original mind. No tale is quite what you would expect it to be. No character is simple, and no story is treated purely conventionally. Chaucer wrote many other works, some of which are of considerable interest. All show in varying degree his supreme genius. He could take an essentially silly tale like that of *Troilus and Crisyde* and turn it into a moving if not entirely credible love story. No one who hopes to understand the Middle Ages should fail to read Chaucer, but one must always beware of Chaucer's genius. A truly great writer is never typical.

48. Art and Architecture

ANY attempt to describe works of art in words is bound to be essentially unsuccessful. Hence, in dealing with mediaeval architecture and art we shall simply mention the major developments, and leave the reader to study the details in the excellent illustrated works that are available. In the early Middle Ages the two dominant groups in society that controlled most of its resources were ecclesiastics and knights. Churches and fortresses were the chief buildings. In the late years of the Roman Empire the Christian churches of Italy were usually simple basilicas—rectangular buildings with wooden roofs. Often they consisted of a nave and one or more aisles separated by rows of columns. The decoration consisted largely in the use of beautiful marble. This style continued dominant in Italy well into the Middle

Ages. Its only serious rival was the Byzantine domed architecture, decorated with mosaics, that appeared in Ravenna and other centers of Byzantine power.

Little is known of the churches of northern Europe before the tenth century. As some were probably made entirely of wood and nearly all had wooden roofs, they were easily destroyed by fire, and those that escaped the flames were later torn down and replaced by new buildings. These churches were probably modeled on the basilicas of Italy. Charlemagne imported workmen from Italy to build a round stone church with a dome at his capital, Aachen. This church was decorated with columns brought from Italy. At one of his favorite manors Charlemagne had a church decorated with mosaics. But these foreign styles did not affect the general architecture of the region. The first important development was the introduction of the barrel vault. This gave the churches a stone roof and made them essentially fireproof, but the great weight of the stone vaults required massive walls to support them. As the builders knew nothing of how to estimate stresses and strains, they took no chances and made their walls heavy enough to hold any conceivable weight. The result was dark, gloomy buildings with few and small windows. This was the style known as Romanesque.

The Romanesque churches give the impression of magnificent solidity. To lighten the total effect they were copiously decorated with carvings. The capitals of the massive columns that separated the nave and aisles were carved with scenes from the Bible or from Holy Legend. Often the façade of the church was a solid mass of sculpture. The tympanum over the doorway usually contained a major effort; the last judgment was a favorite subject for this place. These sculptures had another use beside that of decoration. They taught the sacred stories to the illiterate worshippers. The Romanesque was the dominant style of church architecture in northern Europe during the eleventh and twelfth centuries. In this period the great monasteries had greater resources than the bishops. They had immense lands, plenty of labor, and the patronage of the powerful feudal lords. Hence the greatest Romanesque churches were attached to monastic establishments. The most magnificent of all, the church of Cluny, has been destroyed, but many lesser Romanesque churches still exist.

Towards the end of the twelfth century came the next great stage in the history of architecture—the invention of the Gothic style. The basic discovery that made Gothic possible was extremely simple. By building a vault with ribs, the entire weight could be concentrated on certain points. If these places were made strong enough the rest of the wall could be weak, and thus windows could be increased in size and number. The ribbed vault also made possible the achievement of greater height and daintiness by using a pointed arch; but the pointed arch greatly increased the outward thrust against the walls, and great buttresses were needed at the points of stress. Then someone discovered that the buttress need not actually touch the wall. Flying buttresses could be made to carry the thrust to masses of masonry placed at some distance from the arch. This series of discoveries made possible the Gothic church.

Immediately churches grew loftier, and their walls were almost replaced by great windows which brought in light to expose the beauty of the interior. Soon craftsmen in glass were making the marvelous colored glass that was to turn these windows into things of beauty and through them supply the stories that had been told by the sculpture in the Romanesque. The pure Gothic church was a thing of soaring beauty. The building itself, however, gave little place for sculpture, as the windows occupied most of the wall space. The façade could be decorated with statues, and the tympanums of the doorways continued to contain masterpieces of the sculptors' art; but the mass sculptures of the Romanesque were things of the past. As the Gothic style developed, its forms grew more complicated. In the early churches all the lines were severely structural, but soon many were essentially decorative. Various names are given to the later Gothic styles, such as "Flamboyant," to describe the flamelike appearance of the pointed arches. The vaults became incredibly complicated with false ribs that served no structural purpose and even hanging decorative designs. At its best the late Gothic could be delicately beautiful, but all too often it gave an impression of fussiness. With some few exceptions, the later churches cannot match those of the thirteenth century for majestic beauty.

Although each country, even each region, showed local variations, the two chief styles of mediaeval architecture were international. England, France, Germany, and Spain had their Romanesque and Gothic churches. Italy copied the Gothic as a decorative style, but did not as a rule bother with Gothic structure. It was easier to tie a building together with chains than to build buttresses. Except for the cathedral of Milan, which was built under German influence, Italy had no great Gothic churches.

The great Gothic churches of Europe were for the most part cathedrals. As the towns grew in wealth, the resources of the bishops increased. Then, the cathedral was a source of pride to the citizens, and they were willing to contribute both labor and money to make it as magnificent as possible. The beautiful windows of Chartres cathedral were given by the guilds of the city. Thus religious enthusiasm and municipal pride combined to produce lovely churches.

While abbots and bishops were building their churches, the nobles were constructing military strongholds. In the eleventh century stone castles began to replace the motte and bailey fortresses we have examined earlier.* The earliest form was the simple *tour*. This was a stone tower of two or three stories with enormously massive walls and tiny windows. Usually the door was high above the ground and was reached by wooden steps that could be cut away in time of danger. The walls of a tour were so thick that battering-rams and stone-hurling siege engines made no impression on it. The only effective mode of attacking it was by mining under the walls, and if they were built on rock or surrounded by a moat filled with water this was impossible. The White Tower in the Tower of London is an excellent example of a fortress of this type.

By the latter part of the eleventh century, stone buildings were being added to motte and bailey castles. Usually the first step was to build a stone structure as a place of last resort. These buildings, known as keeps or donjons, were simple rectangular affairs one or two stories high. Later keeps were often massive towers that could be square, octagonal, or round. If the motte was a natural mound, the keep might be built on it. In most cases, however, the motte was artificial and would not carry the weight of the stonework. Hence the keep had to be erected in the bailey. The twelfth century was the great period of keep-building. Soon the wooden palisades that fringed the ditch or moat were replaced by stone walls. By the thirteenth century these walls were likely to be reinforced by towers set to allow flanking fire along the walls. As siege engines were made more effective, the walls were built higher and the towers stronger. In the second half of the

* See pp. 107–08.

THE CATHEDRAL OF NOTRE DAME IN PARIS

The construction of this magnificent Gothic cathedral was begun shortly after 1160 by Maurice de Sully, bishop of Paris. It replaced two older churches that occupied its site. By Maurice's death in 1196 the choir (at extreme right) was finished. His successor built the transept. The lower part of the façade (at extreme left) and part of the nave were begun in 1218. The upper parts of the towers were completed about 1235. Thus the building as shown here was a product of the years 1160–1235.

This illustration shows very clearly the chief exterior features of Gothic construction. Along the choir and nave the flying buttresses carry the stress to the massive main buttresses. The southern portal is embellished by two rose windows. The upper parts of the towers show the delicacy of Gothic ornament at its best. Courtesy of Philip Gendreau.

THE CATHEDRAL OF AMIENS, FRANCE

The cathedral of Amiens is the largest and one of the most impressive of French cathedrals. This is a view of the nave and choir looking toward the apse. An earlier cathedral was completely destroyed by fire in 1218, and two years later the foundations for the nave of the present building were laid. It was finished about 1240. The choir was built between 1250 and 1270.

In Amiens the concentration of stresses which is the chief feature of Gothic architecture was highly developed, with the result that most of the wall space was available for windows. This effect can be seen clearly at the extreme end of the picture. It also accounts for the large amount of light in the nave. The careful design of columns and columnetts accentuates the great height of the nave—some 240 feet. At the end of the nave is a sixteenth-century stone screen separating nave and choir, while to the extreme left of the picture there is a glimpse of a chapel. Courtesy of Clarence Ward.

thirteenth century the keep was abandoned in new castles. There would be an inner enclosure, or *enceinte*, with high walls and great towers. Then there would be an outer enceinte that was less formidable but still strong. The gates were protected by particularly massive towers, and strong stone outworks covered the entrance to the drawbridge that spanned the moat. This line of development took place chiefly in the great fortresses of princes and great lords. Lesser nobles continued to be content with a stone tower and a single stone enceinte, or even with an enceinte alone.

In the early period the lord of the castle and his family lived in the keep. But these thick-walled structures made exceedingly gloomy and cramped homes. By the thirteenth century most great nobles had built pleasant stone houses within the enceinte to serve as residences. Moreover, many lords began to live in their castles only in time of danger. In peacetime they lived in houses protected only by a moat and low wall. Such manor houses were the regular residences of those who could not afford a castle. Whether inside a castle or not, these noble residences had handsome halls where the lord and his retinue could feast and private rooms for the lord and his family. Whether castle or manor house, it was likely to have a chapel.

We know little of what town houses were like before the twelfth century. They were in general humble affairs built of wood. By the twelfth century rich burghers were building stone houses with Romanesque or Gothic windows. The fourteenth and fifteenth centuries saw the erection of very handsome stone houses by rich merchants. The house built by Jacques Coeur at Bourges was as large and magnificent as a royal palace and was of pure Gothic design. The fifteenth century also saw the half-timbered houses that are so familiar in pictures of old towns. The most ambitious buildings in a town were likely to be the guild halls. These were large stone buildings, usually highly decorated. Practically all buildings were decorated in the style fashionable when they were constructed. Thus, very early ones would have round-arched windows often flanked by little pillars with carved capitals or with the arches carved in designs. Later, there would be pointed arches and Gothic decoration.

The artistic spirit of the Middle Ages found expression through a variety of media. There was sculpture in stone, wood, ivory, and bone. Painting was done on parchment, wood, and stone. Then there were embroideries and tapestries of rare beauty. Finally, there were enamels, inlay work, and colored glass. This intense artistic activity was partly the result of genuine love of beauty, but it also grew out of the fact that in an age when few could read pictorial representation was of peculiar importance. The unlettered devotee of the Arthurian legends could enjoy his favorite stories in the carved ivory of a favorite box, or in the murals that decorated the walls of his castle. The descendants of the companions of William the Conqueror could relive the adventure of their ancestors in the marvelous series of embroideries that we call the Bayeux Tapestry.

As we have seen, stone carving occupied an important place in Romanesque architecture. Statuary figures decorated doors and porches. The capitals of the columns were intricately carved with scenes from the Bible or the lives of saints. The carving was essentially crude. The figures were not intended to be lifelike. They had two essential purposes: to fit into the architectural design and to indicate what they were intended to represent. Although the clear, pure architectural lines of some of the figures, such as the statues of the apostles that decorated many doorways, give an impression of charming simplicity and dignity, Romanesque sculpture cannot be called beautiful. It is, however, utterly fascinating as both decorative and didactic art. As the Gothic style developed, the sculptured scenes grew fewer, but statues continued to embellish doorways and porches. The sculptors grew more skillful and less bound to strict architectural lines. Although at times this license was carried to extremes, and the statues came to seem out of place in their architectural setting, they became more attractive to the eye. But the general basic purpose did not change. No mediaeval sculptor worried about anatomy or naturalness. He was decorating a church and teaching a lesson. The effectiveness of sculpture in ivory and bone also depended on the fineness and intricacy of the carving and the general design. The whole work may be quite beautiful, but the individual figures are rarely so.

During the early Middle Ages in Western Europe painting was confined to the illumination of manuscripts, which was a highly developed art. In the eighth century beautiful work was being produced in England, and the ninth and tenth centuries saw the spread of the art through France and Germany. All sorts of books were decorated with pictures, but a favorite vehicle for illustration was the book of hours. A book of hours contained prayers for the different days of the year. It was often illustrated with pictures showing the various seasons and the occupations peculiar to them. Every noble house of any importance wanted to own a beautifully illustrated book of hours. One of the most famous was made for the Duke of Berry, brother of Charles V of France. It was so incredibly costly that when the Duke died, his heirs stopped the work on it, and it was only finished some years later. Although Bibles and other religious books were illuminated, the most extensive illustrations were likely to be found in romances and histories.

The illuminator depended for his artistic effect largely on the richness, depth, and magnificence of his colors. He made no attempt to paint realistic figures, and he knew nothing of perspective. He was satisfied if the drawing showed clearly what was intended. Thus, a man wearing a crown and having the *fleur-de-lys* embroidered on his coat was the king of France. If he was to be shown standing in front of a castle, the castle would be behind him, but it might only reach his knee in height. Moreover, the painters had little knowledge of the costumes of different ages. Alexander the Great wore mediaeval armor and lived in a mediaeval castle. To the modern eye the figures in these illustrations are curious rather than beautiful, but the colors make the pictures highly effective, and they tell us a great deal about the costumes and articles of the time.

In the twelfth, thirteenth, and fourteenth centuries, and perhaps earlier, the interiors of churches and castles were often decorated with mural paintings. Some regions seem to have adopted this idea with more enthusiasm than others. Murals were common in churches in Catalonia and in west-central France, especially in Poitou. They seem to have been more rare in most other regions. Few early examples of murals in castles have survived, but they are frequently described in literary works. Thus we hear of a lady who had her bedroom decorated with scenes from Ovid's *Ars Amoris*. The Arthurian legends were a very popular subject for murals in castle halls. Large embroideries like the Bayeux Tapestry were probably also designed to decorate rooms. By the fourteenth century, mural-painting began to give way to tapestry as wall decoration. Tapestry not only supplied pictures to look at, but also to some extent at least cut down the drafts. Our word "arras" comes from the town of Arras, which was an important center of tapestry manufacture.

49. Education

THE DOMINANT characteristic of education during the Middle Ages was its essentially practical purpose. While there were scholars who loved learning for its own sake, they were exceptional and frequently felt called upon to find excuses for their intellectual curiosity. When John of Salisbury and his fellow humanists of the late twelfth century found pleasure in the beauties of pagan Latin prose, they were careful to point out that their basic purpose was to improve their Latin style for the more effective expression of the church's teachings. The general idea was that a man should have the knowledge required for his occupation; other knowledge was certainly useless and might well be dangerous. Thus Philippe de Novarre advocated teaching noble girls to read so that they could better perform their devotions, but he was vigorously opposed to having them learn to write. If they knew that art, how could one be sure that they would not write love letters? Even the extreme radical, Peter Dubois, when he suggested the foundation of an academy to give advanced education to women, intended that its alumnae should fulfill the very practical function of winning over Moslem princes by becoming their wives. Everyone had his or her proper place in society and should have the education suited to it.

Mediaeval education, therefore, cannot be described solely in terms of academic institutions such as schools and universities. Every baronial household was a school for young nobles. The baron saw that the sons of his vassals and relatives who had been entrusted to him were given the training required to make them good knights.* When a young man was formally dubbed a knight, he graduated from school and was ready to take his place in society. The baron's wife supervised the education of the girls and prepared them for marriage. In the towns the apprentice system of the guilds performed a similar function. The apprentices lived in the master's house and learned the trade under his supervision. The apprentice passed his final examinations when he completed his "masterpiece" and his formal admission to the guild as a master marked his graduation from school.

Throughout the Middle Ages "book learning" in Western Europe, outside of Italy, was largely limited to those in clerical orders. Before

* See p. 118.

the twelfth century, literate laymen were extremely rare. After 1100 they became steadily more numerous. Many princes and nobles were able to read, and both reading and writing must have been common among merchants. But it is easy to exaggerate the real extent of this literacy. All nobles and probably most important merchants were served by clerks who wrote their letters and frequently read to them those that they received. Truly learned laymen were almost unknown. Although one is inclined to doubt the accuracy of the common statement that Thomas More was the first learned layman to appear in England, it is difficult to cite an earlier one. In Italy the situation was quite different. There the Roman tradition survived into the Middle Ages, and there were always well-educated laymen and learned professions staffed by laymen.

The higher schools of the Roman Empire were open to anyone who could pay the fees, and they were heavily subsidized by the state. Their function was to train lawyers and public servants. Hence their emphasis was laid on training in effective public speaking, and they are usually called rhetorical schools. Their curriculum consisted of the seven liberal arts: grammar, rhetoric, dialectic, geometry, arithmetic, astronomy, and music. Boethius divided these subjects into two groups, the first three forming the *trivium*, and the last four the *quadrivium*. The Roman schools must have disappeared in Britain soon after the departure of the legions, and in Gaul they did not survive the fifth century; but they continued to flourish in Italy. There the Roman law remained in force, and the lawyers continued to receive their training in the rhetorical schools. These schools also produced professional letter writers who served the illiterate population. The curricula of these Italian lay schools served as models for the ecclesiastical schools that eventually developed in the rest of Western Europe.

From the sixth century to the twelfth, almost all the schools of Western Europe outside Italy were devoted primarily to training clerks and were closely connected with cathedrals or monasteries. Every abbot was responsible for seeing that the novices of his house received the minimum education required for the proper performance of his religious duties. All monks should be able to read their devotional books and the church services, and it was highly desirable that some at least should be able to write well enough to produce the books needed by the monastery. In some monasteries education was carried much farther. In the sixth century the Irish monasteries were centers of learning where the classics were read and taught. A mixture of Irish and Italian influences produced the famous monastic schools of northern England that were wiped out by the Viking raiders. While the so-called Carolingian Renaissance centered in Charlemagne's palace school, its work was carried on in various monasteries such as St. Martin of Tours, Fulda, and Fleury. The last of these great monastic schools was conducted at Bec in Normandy by Lanfranc and Anselm, who became the first two Norman archbishops of Canterbury. In short, before the eleventh century the schools giving really advanced education were monastic, if one excepts the palace school of Charlemagne, and nearly all truly learned men were monks or prelates who had been trained as monks.

In the sixth and seventh centuries secular clerks received what education they had in the households of bishops. Every bishop had in his service a number of young men in minor orders whose education he supervised. In some cases the bishop himself was the teacher; in others he employed a *magister scholarum.* As the clergy attached to the cathedrals grew more highly organized and the chapters took definite form, the magister scholarum was often an official of the chapter who ran a regular school. Charlemagne directed his bishops to establish schools at their cathedrals, but we do not know how well he was obeyed, and most of the schools founded in his day disappeared during the Viking invasions. In the eleventh and twelfth centuries, church councils regularly called for the establishment of schools at every cathedral; but it took a long time to enforce obedience to these decrees. The chief difficulty seems to have been the unwillingness of the chapters to assign a prebend to support the master. Only in the thirteenth century did the cathedral school system become virtually complete. But before that time several cathedral schools had reached eminence as centers of learning. In the late eleventh and twelfth centuries the school of Chartres was noted for its teaching of the seven liberal arts, especially grammar and rhetoric. It produced such enthusiastic lovers of the Latin classics as John of Salisbury and Hildebert of Le Mans. The schools attached to the cathedrals of Laon and Paris were famous for the study of theology.

The curricula of these cathedral and monastic schools consisted of the trivium or both the trivium and quadrivium. Priscian and Donatus were used as textbooks in teaching grammar. In 1199 Alexander of Villa Dei composed a textbook called the *doctrinale* that remained standard throughout the Middle Ages. It was particularly useful because it was in verse and hence easy to memorize. In addition, the students read fragments of Vergil, Ovid, and Horace. Rhetoric was taught according to traditional formulas as the art of effective expression. Dialectic was essentially the study of logic. Geometry included what geography was known. Before the introduction of Arabic learning, arithmetic was little more than the study of tables giving the dates of movable feasts and some practice in the use of the abacus. Although these early schools produced some men of considerable learning, they were essentially grammar schools devoted to supplying the church with literate clerks. What higher education they gave was more or less accidental and the result of the initiative of individual masters rather than part of the system.

After the appearance of the universities, the cathedral and monastic schools definitely became grammar schools with no ambition to deal with the higher studies. At the same time, many other grammar schools appeared. Even in the early Middle Ages some towns had schools, and by the thirteenth century town grammar schools were common. Then, various members of the clergy engaged in teaching. Collegiate churches that were not cathedrals frequently established schools. In the later Middle Ages it became usual for a noble or rich merchant to establish an endowment for the perpetual support of a priest to say masses for his soul. As such a task was hardly a full-time job, the priest was frequently required to run a school. In the fourteenth century William of Wykeham, bishop of Winchester, conceived the idea of founding a grammar school for the definite purpose of preparing students for the university. He established Winchester College as a grammar school to supply students to his other foundation, New College at Oxford. Eton was later founded in connection with King's College at Cambridge. Thus by the fourteenth century all cathedrals, monasteries, and towns had grammar schools, and there were a fair number of other schools of that grade.

By far the most important educational institutions of the Middle Ages were the universities. The word *universitas* meant basically "all," in a collective sense, and could be used for any group of people cooperating for a common end. It was freely used for the members of a guild. One finds it applied to the barons of England and even the English people as a whole. The universities were essentially educational guilds. In northern Europe they were guilds of masters, while in Italy and southern Europe they were student guilds. In both cases they were formed to protect their members and to further their common educational interests. As masters or students could form such cooperative organizations without specific permission from a prince and without attracting the attention of contemporary chroniclers, no foundation date can be set for the three oldest universities, Bologna, Paris, and Oxford, and the date of the establishment of Cambridge is most uncertain. As a rule one can only say when they received some form of official recognition. Later universities were established by princes, and hence their foundation dates can be easily determined.

As we have seen, masters of rhetoric taught continuously in Italy during the early Middle Ages. These were, naturally, most numerous in the more important towns. Bologna was particularly noted for the effective teaching of the art of expression, and a number of important works on rhetoric were produced by its masters. Then, in the eleventh century, Italian lawyers began to become discontented with the simple manuals of Roman law that they were using and sought a deeper knowledge of their subject. This enthusiasm was increased with the rediscovery of the most important part of the *Corpus Juris Civilis* of Justinian—the Digest. Soon Italian students were exploring the entire body of Roman law, and the chief center of these studies was Bologna. Late in the eleventh century there are references to a master named Pepo who was famous as a teacher at Bologna. But the real founder of Bologna's reputation as a center of legal studies was Irnerius, who was apparently the first to use a comprehensive knowledge of the Roman law in commentaries on the legal codes actually in use. Gratian, whom we have already discussed as the organizer and codifier of the canon law, worked at Bologna in the middle of the twelfth century. As medical studies had already spread through Italy from the famous medical school at Salerno, Bologna in the late twelfth century had at least four curricula: rhetoric, civil law, canon law, and medicine.

The fame of the schools of Bologna drew students from all Western Europe, who flocked there to study under the various masters. As individuals, these students could not protect themselves from being overcharged by landlords and shopkeepers as well as by the masters, and they soon founded two guilds for mutual protection. The students from outside Italy formed the Ultramontane guild or "nation," while the Italians composed the Cismontane. Each nation was headed by an elected *rector*. Soon the masters teaching the different subjects formed guilds of their own, but the student guilds were dominant in all questions except the requirements for degrees. The masters or professors were obliged to swear obedience to the rectors, had to get their permission to leave town, and were fined for beginning a lecture late or for continuing it too long. At first the masters subsisted entirely on student fees. Later, salaried chairs were established in the various subjects.

By the late eleventh century the cathedral school of Paris had become an important center of learning. The chancellor, who was the official of the chapter entrusted with the supervision of the school and with the authority to issue licenses to teach, permitted qualified masters to conduct lectures in houses near the cathedral of Notre Dame on the Ile de la Cité. Actually the only connection between these masters and the cathedral school proper was that they obtained their licenses from the chancellor and could be deprived of them by him. Each master rented a suitable room, gave his lectures, and collected fees from his students, but the chancellor gave the students their licenses to teach and their degrees. When William of Champeaux and Peter Abelard held their famous controversy on the nature of universals, they were both masters teaching under the shelter of Notre Dame. Abelard lived in the house of a canon of Notre Dame and the fair Eloise who diverted his attention from the realms of pure scholarship was the canon's niece.

There was bound to be friction between the chancellor and the masters, especially when the latter included such independent spirits as Abelard. On a hill on the left bank of the Seine directly opposite the Ile de la Cité stood the monastery of St. Geneviève. Its site is now occupied by the Pantheon, which is decorated with murals depicting St. Geneviève's life and good works. Masters who quarreled with the chancellor often moved over the river to teach under the protection of the abbot. As time went on, the land about this monastery and the slope leading down to the Seine became the site of the schools of Paris, and the Ile de la Cité was largely deserted by the masters. There today the University of Paris still stands, in the midst of the Latin quarter.

By the close of the twelfth century the masters teaching at Paris had formed a guild or university. In 1200 a charter of Philip Augustus granting privileges to the masters and students of Paris mentions the university, and within ten years a university official called a "proctor" is referred to. By 1219 the masters of arts had divided themselves into four "nations," each headed by a proctor: France, Normandy, Picardy, and England. About the middle of the thirteenth century there appeared an elected head of all the masters of arts called the rector. The masters of theology, canon law, and medicine formed separate faculties headed by deans. The rector was in theory simply the head of the faculty of arts, but since this was much the largest, he claimed to be the chief officer of the university and after a long and bitter struggle with the dean of the faculty of theology was recognized as such.

In England the town of Oxford was centrally located geographically, and during the first half of the twelfth century wandering masters from Paris and even Bologna occasionally lectured there. The more or less continuous hostilities between King Henry II and Louis VII of France made the position of the English scholars at Paris rather difficult, and in 1167 Henry ordered them all to come home. This may well have marked the establishment of Oxford as a large-scale center of schools. Certainly by 1185 Giraldus Cambrensis read one of his works before a large assembly of masters and students, and by 1209 a perhaps overenthusiastic chronicler estimated the number of students in Oxford at 3000. In 1214 one first hears of the head of the university called the chancellor. For a time the masters were divided into two nations, a northern and a southern, headed by proctors; but before the end of the thirteenth century the nations were abolished, although the two proctors remained as university officials. Unlike Paris the superior faculties at Oxford had no deans and little separate organization. The chancellor and proctors were the officials of the university as a whole, and most of the functions of government were carried out in general assemblies of all the masters.

The origins of Cambridge are extremely obscure, but it seems clear that it was founded by migrants from Oxford and Paris. As the early universities had no buildings but simply rented the facilities they needed, it was easy for the masters and students to move. Several times emigrations from Oxford resulted from quarrels with the town or with the royal government, and some of the migrants seem to have settled at Cambridge. In 1230 the students of Paris had a truly magnificent quarrel with the Queen Regent, Blanche of Castile, and the papal legate who was assisting her in governing the realm for her infant son. Spouting scurrilous poems about the relations between the queen and the legate, the members of the university left Paris *en masse*. Many went to Angers, then held by Blanche's bitter baronial foe, Peter of Dreux, duke of Brittany, but others went to Cambridge.

The thirteenth, fourteenth, and fifteenth centuries saw the foundation of many universities. In 1222 a migration from Bologna started a university at Padua. In 1224 Frederick II established at Naples the first university to be created by princely command. Six years later the pope founded one at Toulouse to aid in the suppression of the Albigensian heretics. The end of the thirteenth century also saw universities established in Spain and Portugal. During the fourteenth century seven were founded in Italy, four in France, and five in Germany. The fifteenth century saw seven new establishments in France and a number of others in Italy and Germany.

Although the universities of Paris, Oxford, and Cambridge differed in many ways, their major characteristics were essentially the same and can be discussed in general terms. Each of the universities conducted a long struggle to become independent of both ecclesiastical and lay authorities. As all the masters and students wore the clerical tonsure and were in orders, they were theoretically exempt from arrest or punishment by the secular government. Actually the heads of the universities obtained for themselves extensive secular authority. The ways in which they attained this end were much the same. A student would commit some offense—tear a wine shop to pieces or rape a woman. The townsmen and their officials would try to arrest the students. Then there would be a riot, sometimes on a grand scale. On one occasion the students of Oxford were besieged for several days by an armed mob. Since the students were also armed, the contest was bitter and was only brought to an end by the arrival of royal troops. After a riot the university officials would appeal to the king, and he nearly always solved the dispute by giving the head of the university increased secular power. If the king hesitated, the university could usually rely on papal support. In the end it always won. The chancellor of Oxford won full jurisdiction over the masters, the students, and their servants. All quarrels over the price of food and lodging between students and townfolk came before him. The rector of the university of Paris also had jurisdiction over all who depended on him. In addition, he had supervision of the guilds that supplied things specially needed by the university, such as booksellers, ink makers, and paper sellers.

When the university of Paris first appeared, the granting of degrees and licenses to teach was in the hands of the chancellor of the chapter of Notre Dame, and the bishop of Paris had ecclesiastical jurisdiction over the masters and students. After a long, fierce struggle involving many appeals to the pope, the powers of bishop and chancellor were reduced to pure formalities. The bishop delegated his jurisdiction to the rector, and although the chancellor continued to give licenses, he was forbidden to refuse them to men presented to him by the faculties. Oxford was even more successful. The bishop of Lincoln lived a long way from Oxford and his local representative, the archdeacon of Oxford, was no match for the chancellor of the university. Soon the chancellor not only had complete ecclesiastical jurisdiction over the masters and students, but he also had the same authority over the town of Oxford. An Oxford citizen charged with a spiritual offense found himself haled before the chancellor.

In order to be admitted to a university a student was expected to prove his ability to read and write Latin, but the examinations were very casual, and many students were poorly prepared. It was to improve this situation that William of Wykeham founded Winchester College as a preparatory school for New College in Oxford. Once admitted, the student started work on grammar, rhetoric, and logic. The master would take a textbook such as the *Doctrinale* of Alexander of Villa Dei, read the text, read the comments made on the text by his more noted predecessors, and then add his own comments. This process was described as "hearing" a book. At Paris, when a student had heard two books on grammar and five on logic, he became a bachelor of arts. He was then a sort of apprentice teacher and could instruct others aspiring for that degree. After hearing five books of Aristotle and some mathematical works, he was entitled to his license to teach. Five or six years of such work led to a master of arts degree. In addition to hearing books, the student was expected to read a few. At Oxford a candidate for a degree had to provide a certain number of masters to swear that he had heard and read the required works.

Although a student could embark on the curricula leading to the doctor's degree in canon or civil law without first obtaining the degree of master of arts, this degree was a prerequisite for work in medicine and theology. Law was taught by the method described above—the reading of texts and commentaries by the master, who added his own comments, which he hoped would in time be used by his successors. In medicine the students heard two types of works, those on theory and those on practice. There was no actual practice in our sense and, of course, no laboratories. The most esteemed and most popular curriculum was theology, and to obtain the doctor's degree was a real achievement. A master of arts spent four years listening to lectures on the Bible and two more hearing discourses on Peter Lombard's *Sentences* to become a bachelor of divinity. He then studied six more years, which were also chiefly devoted to the Bible and the *Sentences,* to receive his license to teach theology. It usually required another year to be formally accepted as a doctor and installed in the doctor's chair. During most of these years of study the student took part in many "disputations" or public debates on points of theology. Participation in a certain number of these was required for the degree. He also as a rule had to preach a number of sermons.

Many students found it extremely difficult to meet the requirements for the degrees and asked for "graces," the waiving of certain requirements. The faculties were inclined to be cooperative for a consideration such as a magnificent banquet with plenty of food and drink. Soon practically no one was meeting the requirements, and all were receiving their degrees through graces. All that was needed was residence for the proper time and money to defray the cost of the graces. This system had a serious effect on the university. No one bothered to attend lectures; and as the masters were paid by student fees, there were soon no more lectures. Thus one could obtain a degree by living in a university for a certain length of time and paying the costs. If you wanted to study and could find someone to teach you, you might learn something.

In the second half of the thirteenth century a number of pious and benevolent men and women began to be troubled by the plight of the poor student. Lodgings and meals were expensive, and many could not afford them. These benefactors founded houses where poor students could be fed and lodged either for nothing or for very low fees. In order to insure some degree of good behavior in these houses there was usually a provision for the support of one or more masters to live with the students. When a student wanted to learn, he sought the aid of one of these masters resident in his house. Thus came into being the colleges that play so important a part in the history of these three universities. The first college at Paris was founded by a rich merchant named Robert de Sorbon in 1258, and the Sorbonne is still famous. By 1500 there were some sixty colleges at Paris. In 1264 Walter of Merton, bishop of Rochester, founded Merton College at Oxford, and at about the same time John Balliol, a great lord of northern England, established Balliol College. The colleges were well endowed with lands and rents. Often the endowment included the right of presentation to a number of churches, which could be bestowed on masters who had taken priestly orders. Thus, when university lectures ceased to be given, the colleges took over the work of instruction. Some of them set examinations that had to be passed before they would allow their students to take degrees.

The students of the Middle Ages were not unlike those of today Some studied and some did not. Many drank and wenched. Most were in perpetual need of money. We have some of the handbooks containing model letters for the use of students. Many of these letters are examples of different excuses for obtaining money from parents, relatives, or patrons, but others show how to invite a girl to supper. As the Middle Ages was a time of violence, both masters and students were inclined to be turbulent. A German master who had slain several of his colleagues was finally dismissed for stabbing one to death in a faculty meeting. A professor at Oxford was charged with getting his students to kill a priest who had offended him. The Oxford rules forbade students to bring bows and arrows to class. Bloody riots between students and townsmen were fairly frequent. Robberies and burglaries by students were all too common. It is important to notice, however, that it was not too difficult to acquire the status of a student and that it was a tempting cloak for men who were essentially criminals. The students were exempt from the secular authorities, and the ecclesiastical courts were notoriously mild. In Paris of the fifteenth century the worst criminal section of the city lay just behind the university, and many of its inhabitants masqueraded as students.

Despite its many and obvious defects, the university performed signal services for mediaeval civilization. It supported scholars and supplied an environment conducive to learning. Most of the eminent scholars of the latter part of the Middle Ages were attached to a university. Then, the various faculties served as authorities on their respective subjects: a pope once apologized for deciding a theological point without consulting the faculty of theology at Paris. The graduates of the universities staffed the learned professions. The masters of arts who did not continue to teach in the universities became the masters of schools. The doctors of civil law either practiced in the lands where Roman law was used or became the servants of secular princes. The canon lawyers carried on the enormous business of the ecclesiastical courts. The doctorate of theology led either to a professorship or to preferment in the church. In short, it seems most unlikely that the general development of civilization that marked the later Middle Ages could have taken place without the universities.

Epilogue

IN FOURTEEN chapters we have surveyed the rise, apogee, and decline of mediaeval civilization. In doing this we have brought the history of European civilization up to the last quarter of the fifteenth century. As the various threads that compose history never change their natures at the same time, the borders between historical periods are never clear cut, but the line between the Middle Ages and the modern period is unusually definite. On the political side, Richard III of England died on Bosworth field in 1485, Louis XI ended his reign in 1483, and the Emperor Frederick III died in 1493. Richard was clearly the last mediaeval monarch of England, and Frederick was the last Holy Roman Emperor to be crowned in Rome. Although some historians call Louis XI a modern king, and they have sound arguments, his deep piety and the nature of the problems he faced were essentially mediaeval. The year 1479 saw the birth of modern Spain, with the accession of Ferdinand and Isabella to the thrones of Aragon and Castile. The son of Louis XI, Charles VIII, was soon to start the bitter wars that changed Italian politics by making the peninsula a pawn in the race for power of her great neighboring states. In the east, Constantinople had fallen to the Turks in 1453, and Ivan III, grand duke of Moscow, whose marriage to the niece of the last Byzantine Emperor gave the masters of Russia a claim to be called Caesar, died in 1505.

Then, these twenty-five years saw the first great strokes toward the expansion of European interests across the seas. In 1487 Bartolomeu Dias rounded the Cape of Good Hope, and in 1492 Columbus reached the West Indies. In 1497 Vasco da Gama made the first direct sea voyage to the East Indies, and in the same year John Cabot first explored the shores of North America.

In the fields of religion and culture, equally vital changes were in the air. The printing press, which had been reasonably perfected about 1450, was beginning to have its overwhelming effect on the distribution of knowledge and ideas. Erasmus was born in 1467, Thomas More in 1478, and Martin Luther in 1483. Copernicus, who is often called the father of modern science, was born in 1473. In Italy the Renaissance was in full bloom—Leonardo da Vinci born in 1452, Pico della Mirandola in 1463, Machiavelli in 1469, Michelangelo in 1475, and Castiglione in 1478.

All this does not mean that there was any sudden break in the threads of history. There was simply a slightly accelerated pace of change. Except for his Italian ambitions Charles VIII had views little different from his father's, and the coronation of emperors at Rome had become a mere formality long before it ceased. Dias and da Gama were the successors of a long line of explorers who sailed down the African coast. Erasmus and More were influenced by earlier humanists, and Luther got many of his ideas from Hus. But the seeds that had been steadily growing during the fourteenth and fifteenth centuries bloomed rather suddenly to produce a very different world.

Before leaving the Middle Ages and passing on into modern history it seems well to pause a moment to consider the accomplishments of the era. Obviously this can be done from two very different points of view, with quite divergent results. One can consider the contributions made by the men of the Middle Ages to later civilizations, or one can estimate the importance of this achievement in terms of their own times. Certain elements of the civilization of the High Middle Ages have had great influence on the modern era. The doctrines of the Roman Catholic Church have been little changed since the *Summa* of Thomas Aquinas, and they are today a very vital element in our culture. The ideas of individual freedom that marked the members of the feudal class became a strong element in later conceptions of the rights of man. The cult of courtly love has lived on in romantic literature and has, at least in Anglo-Saxon lands, been generally accepted as a sound basis for the relations between the sexes. Gothic architecture has stirred the imaginations of the people of the nineteenth and twentieth centuries enough to bring a revival of its use. Many of the stories invented by mediaeval writers are still a part of our literary heritage.

Thus, in the realm of ideas at least, the High Middle Ages has contributed much to later civilizations.

As one might expect, some of the most striking contributions of the Middle Ages to modern times come from the period of transition—the fourteenth and fifteenth centuries. In those years were developed the ideas that form the basis of Protestantism. Then, the parliamentary institutions that have played so important a part in Europe grew out of the ruins of the feudal political system. The beginnings of modern capitalistic enterprise marked the end of mediaeval economic ethics. In short, many important contributions of the period called the Middle Ages to later times cannot properly be called the products of mediaeval civilization. They were institutions that replaced those of the High Middle Ages.

When one views the achievements of the men of the Middle Ages in terms of their own times, one realizes that it was one of the great eras of human history. A vast region was reclaimed from bog, forest, and waste, and turned into fertile farmland. Methods of agriculture were devised that made this region highly productive and enabled it to support a large population. This clearing and placing in cultivation of the waste lands of Europe was a tremendous achievement. On this foundation the men of the Middle Ages built a distinctive civilization.

The feudal, seignorial, and guild systems were essentially novel and were products of great creative imagination. While the complicated hierarchy of the church had been originally modeled on that of the Roman Empire, it was modified by mediaeval ecclesiastics to suit their needs. The monastic system was almost entirely a creation of the Middle Ages. In the realm of ideas the period was equally fertile. The basis of Christian theology had been constructed by the Church Fathers under the Late Roman Empire, but the system was completed by the mediaeval theologians and was supplemented by the canon law. Other fields of thought were woven into the fringes of theology so that a consistent whole was produced. It was a magnificent structure created by men of rare ability. When we criticize these great mediaeval institutions we must remember that the values of the time were different from ours. The nobles who formed the feudal system considered their personal liberties far more important than orderly government. The theologians were convinced that knowledge was only useful if it aided man's chief aim—the attainment of salvation. In the field of literature the Middle Ages produced works that have never been surpassed.

Dante's *Divine Comedy* and Chaucer's *Canterbury Tales* rank among the great literary productions of all time, and *Beowulf*, the *Chanson de Roland*, and the best of the troubadour lyrics are not far behind them. Finally, the men of the Middle Ages demonstrated astounding creative imagination in the realm of architecture. Despite its name, the Romanesque style was their own, and the Gothic was entirely novel, completely unlike anything that had been seen before. The mere erection of the stone churches of mediaeval Europe was a stupendous achievement for men with little engineering knowledge and slight reserves of manpower. And one must remember that the cathedral or abbey church we see in Europe today was usually simply the latest of a series built on the same site. Thus in every broad field of human activity the men of the Middle Ages worked vigorously, effectively, and with creative imagination.

TABLE I

The Descendants of Charlemagne

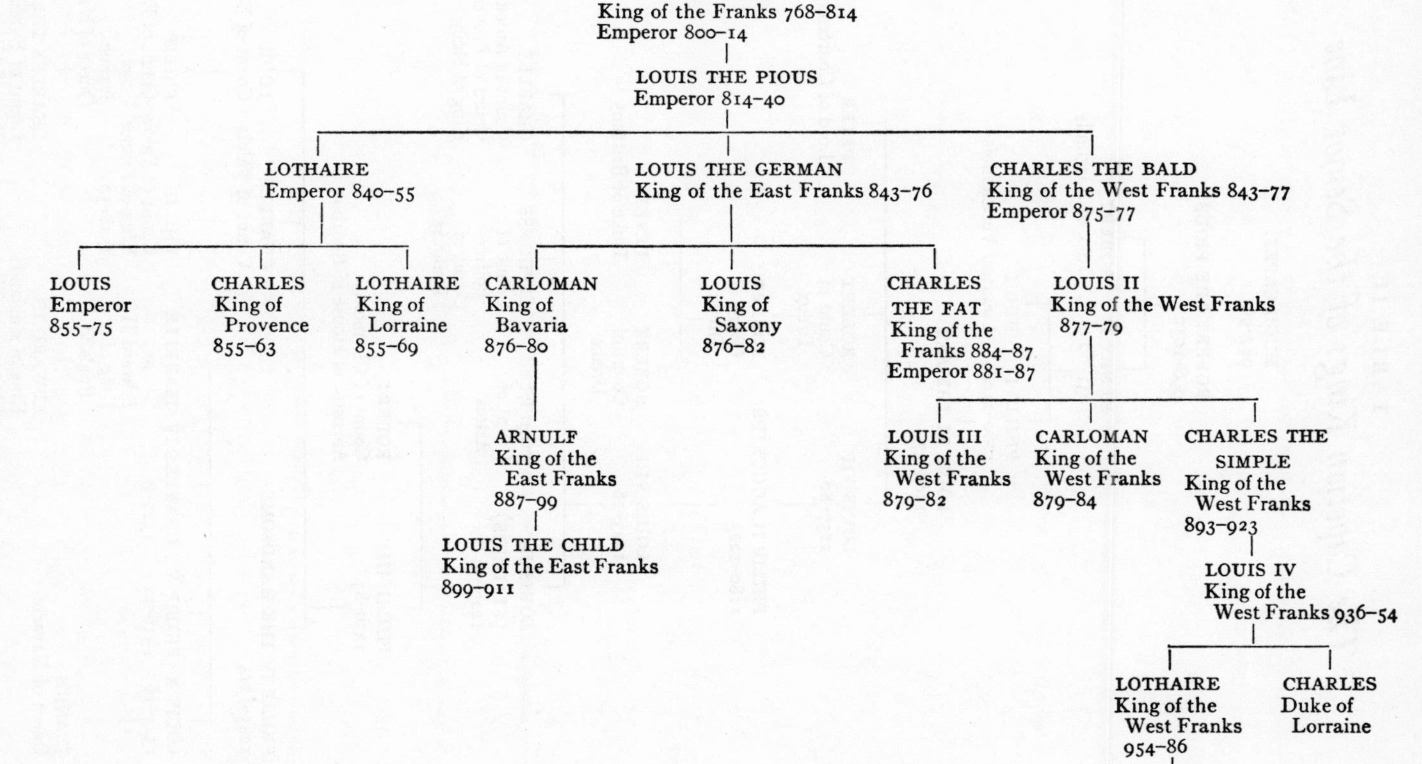

TABLE II

The Capetian Kings of the Senior Line

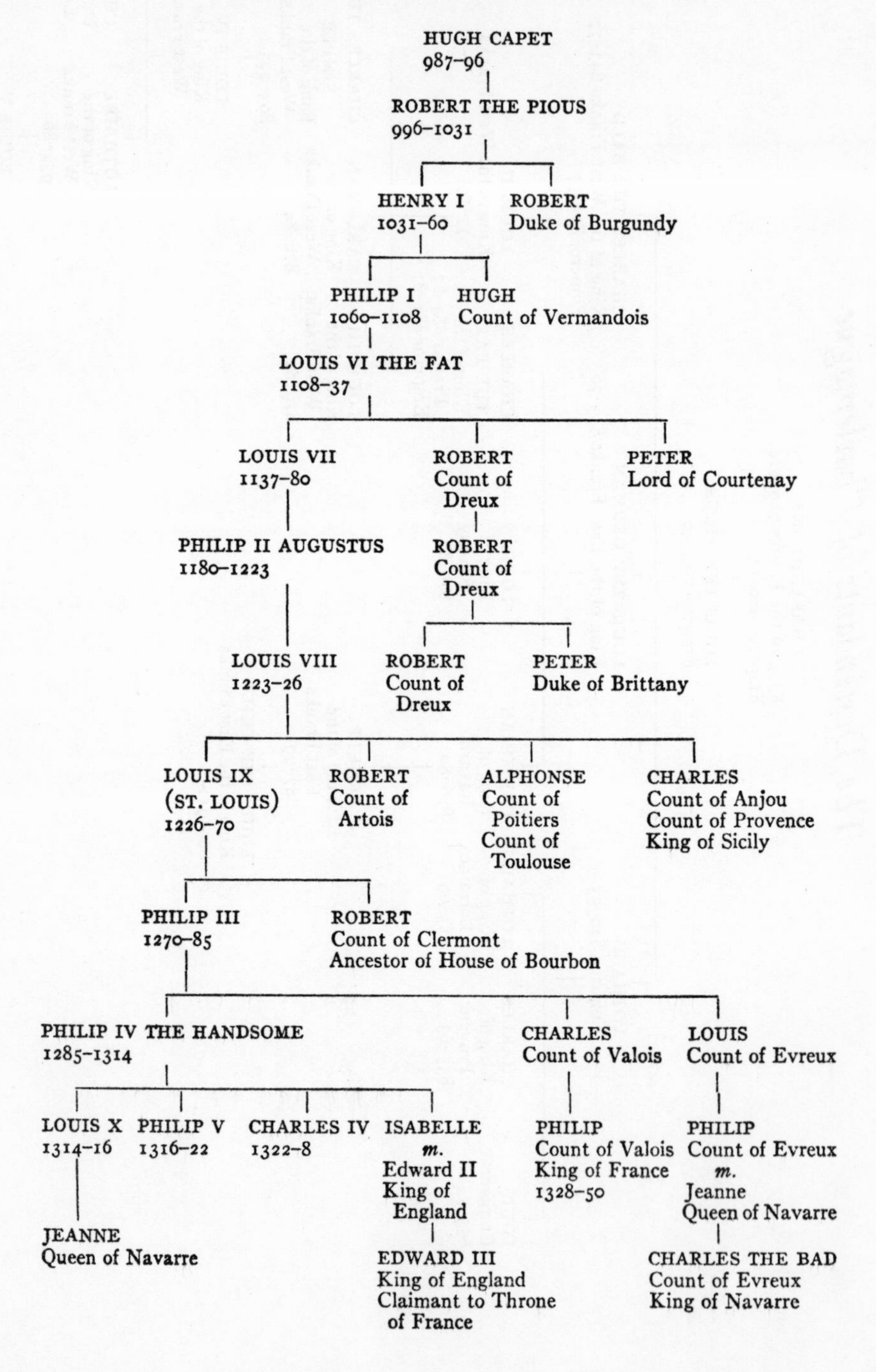
HUGH CAPET
987–96
ROBERT THE PIOUS
996–1031
HENRY I
1031–60
ROBERT
Duke of Burgundy
PHILIP I
1060–1108
HUGH
Count of Vermandois
LOUIS VI THE FAT
1108–37
LOUIS VII
1137–80
ROBERT
Count of
Dreux
PETER
Lord of Courtenay
PHILIP II AUGUSTUS
1180–1223
ROBERT
Count of
Dreux
LOUIS VIII
1223–26
ROBERT
Count of
Dreux
PETER
Duke of Brittany
LOUIS IX
(ST. LOUIS)
1226–70
ROBERT
Count of
Artois
ALPHONSE
Count of
Poitiers
Count of
Toulouse
CHARLES
Count of Anjou
Count of Provence
King of Sicily
PHILIP III
1270–85
ROBERT
Count of Clermont
Ancestor of House of Bourbon
PHILIP IV THE HANDSOME
1285–1314
CHARLES
Count of Valois
LOUIS
Count of Evreux
LOUIS X
1314–16
PHILIP V
1316–22
CHARLES IV
1322–8
ISABELLE
m.
Edward II
King of
England
PHILIP
Count of Valois
King of France
1328–50
PHILIP
Count of Evreux
m.
Jeanne
Queen of Navarre
JEANNE
Queen of Navarre
EDWARD III
King of England
Claimant to Throne
of France
CHARLES THE BAD
Count of Evreux
King of Navarre

TABLE III

The Saxon and Salian Kings of Germany

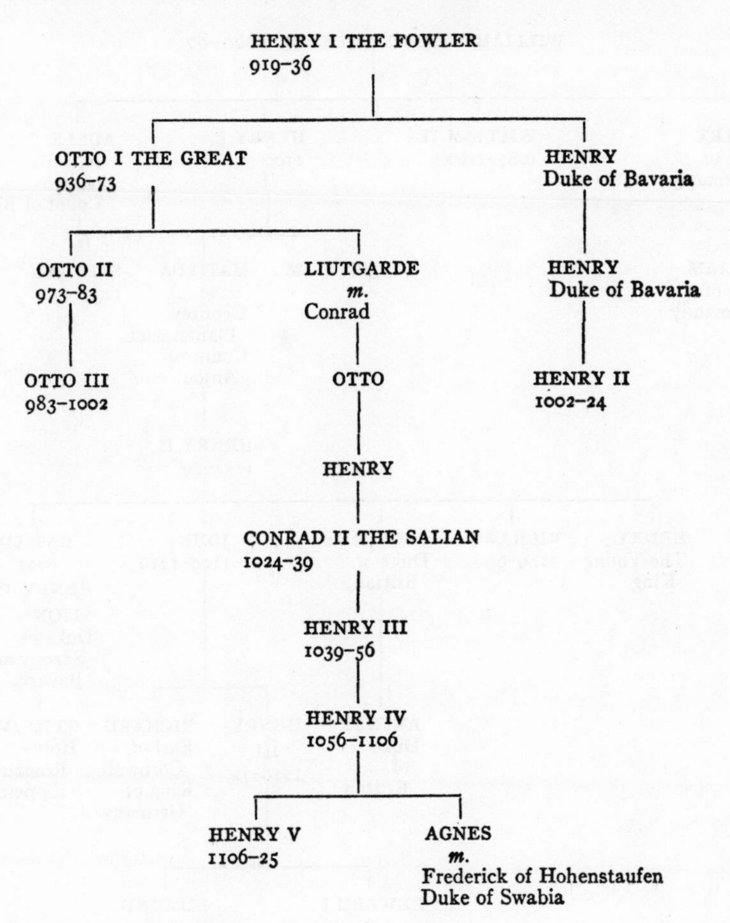

TABLE IV

The Norman and Early Plantagenet Kings of England

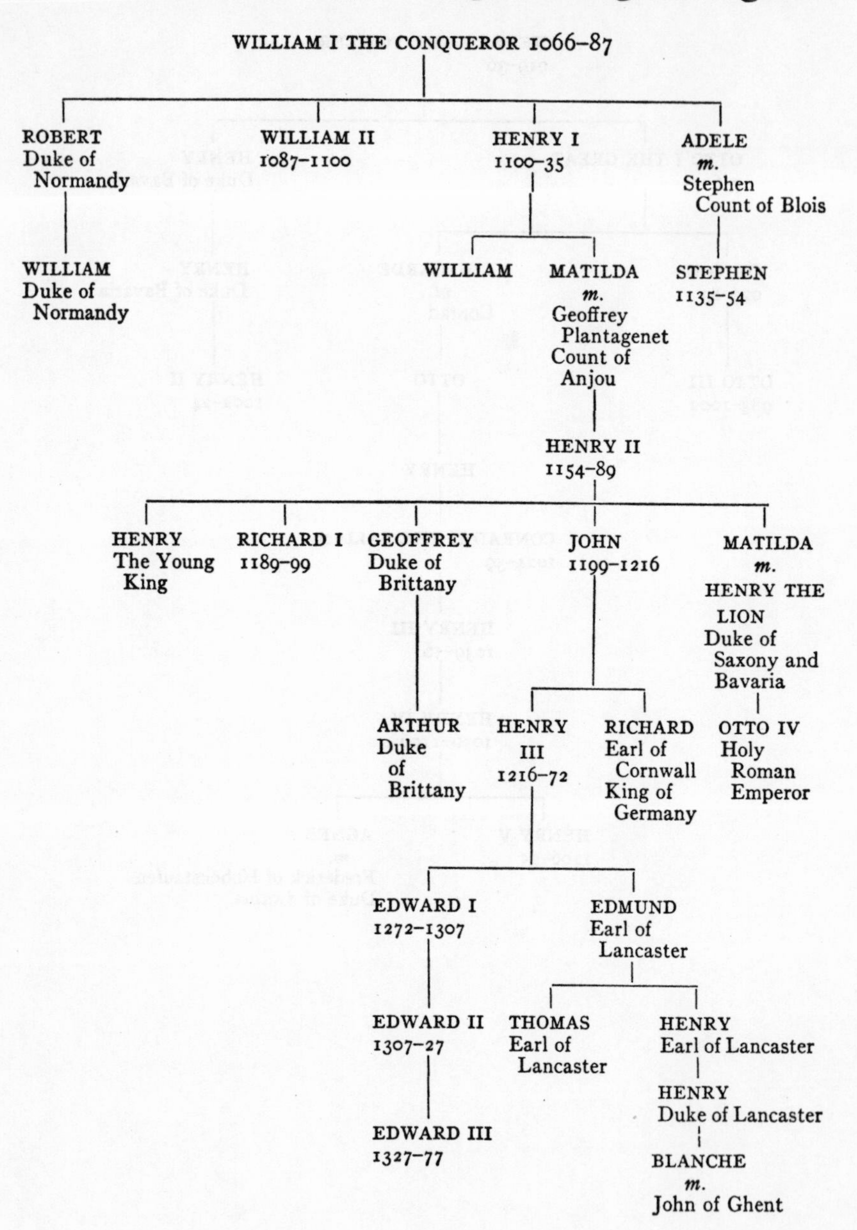

TABLE V

The Hohenstaufens and Their Rivals

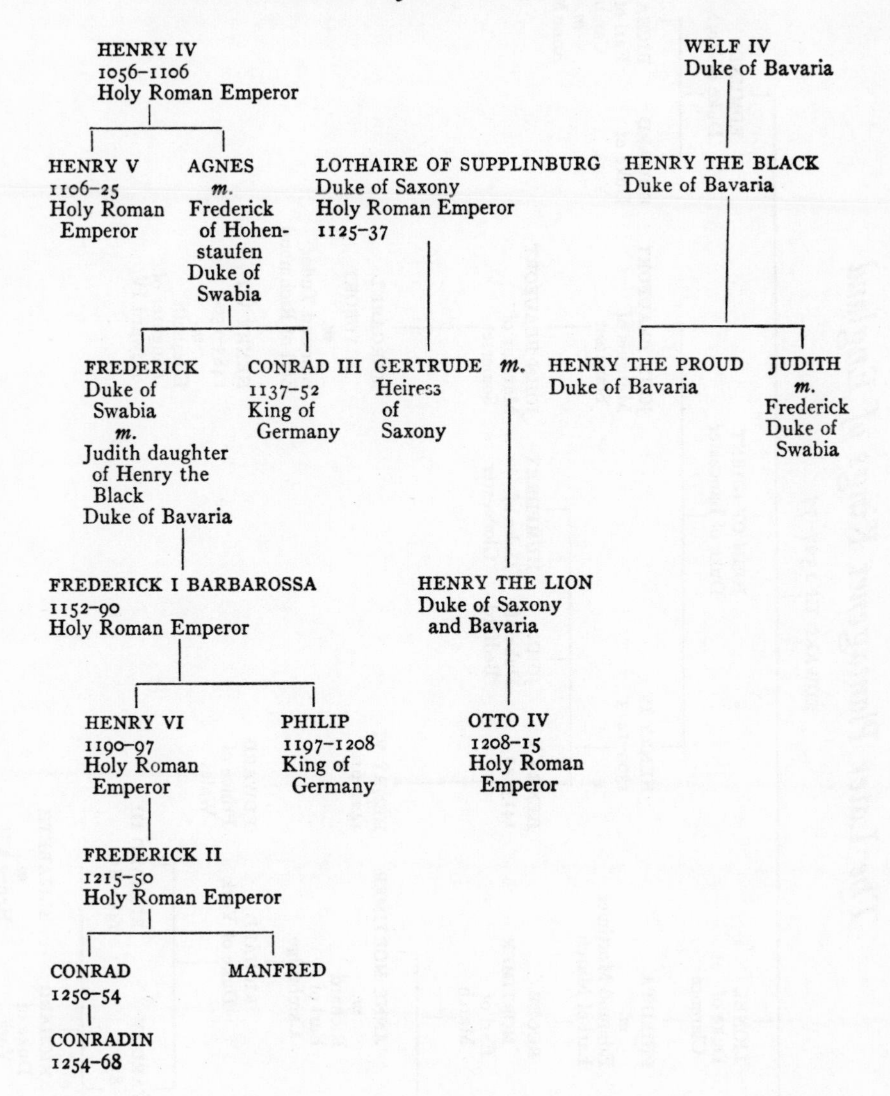

HENRY IV
1056–1106
Holy Roman Emperor
WELF IV
Duke of Bavaria
HENRY V
1106–25
Holy Roman Emperor
AGNES
m.
Frederick of Hohenstaufen
Duke of Swabia
LOTHAIRE OF SUPPLINBURG
Duke of Saxony
Holy Roman Emperor
1125–37
HENRY THE BLACK
Duke of Bavaria
FREDERICK
Duke of Swabia
m.
Judith daughter of Henry the Black
Duke of Bavaria
CONRAD III
1137–52
King of Germany
GERTRUDE
Heiress of Saxony
m.
HENRY THE PROUD
Duke of Bavaria
JUDITH
m.
Frederick
Duke of Swabia
FREDERICK I BARBAROSSA
1152–90
Holy Roman Emperor
HENRY THE LION
Duke of Saxony
and Bavaria
HENRY VI
1190–97
Holy Roman Emperor
PHILIP
1197–1208
King of Germany
OTTO IV
1208–15
Holy Roman Emperor
FREDERICK II
1215–50
Holy Roman Emperor
CONRAD
1250–54
MANFRED
CONRADIN
1254–68

TABLE VI

The Later Plantagenet Kings of England

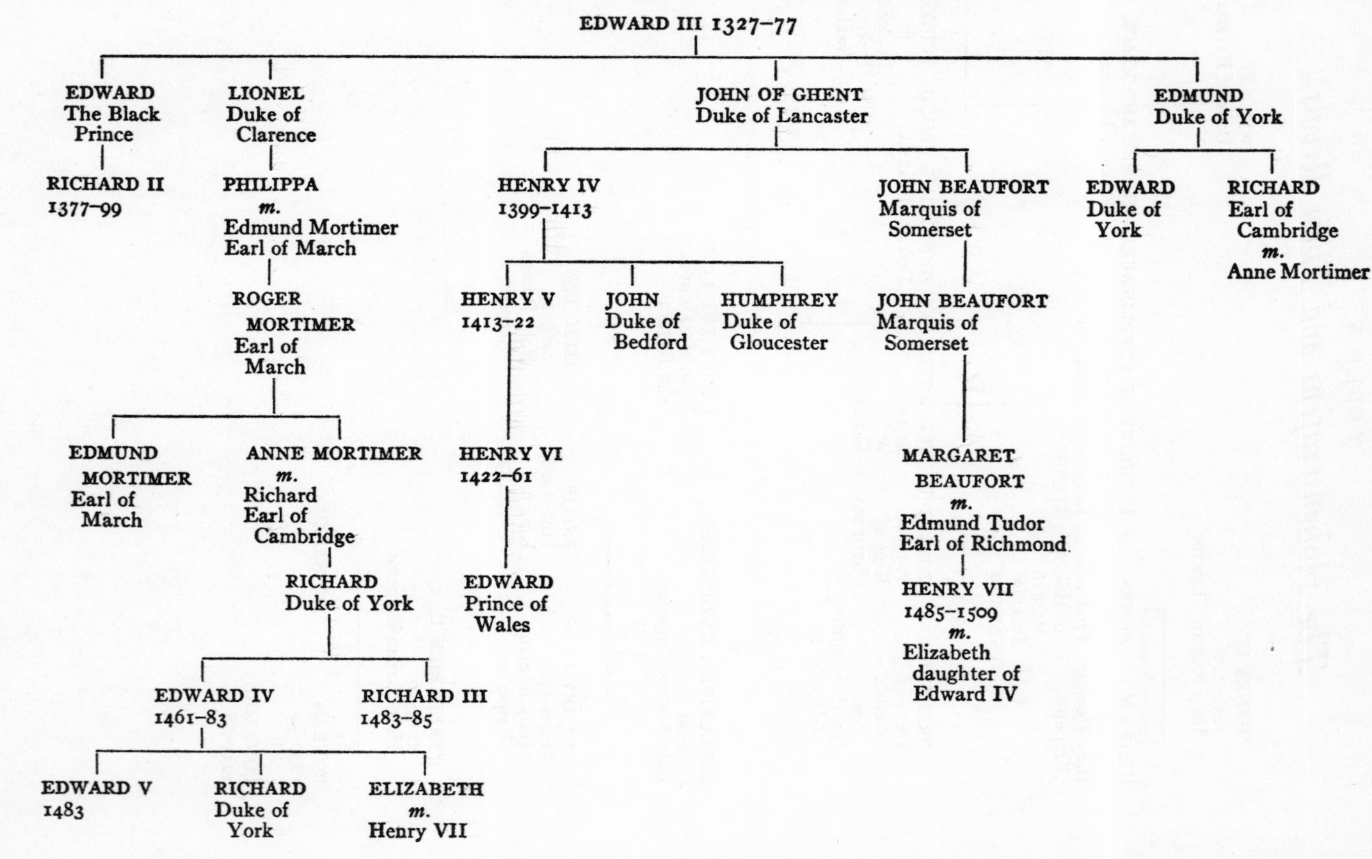
EDWARD III 1327–77
EDWARD
The Black
Prince
RICHARD II
1377–99
LIONEL
Duke of
Clarence
PHILIPPA
m.
Edmund Mortimer
Earl of March
ROGER
MORTIMER
Earl of
March
EDMUND
MORTIMER
Earl of
March
ANNE MORTIMER
m.
Richard
Earl of
Cambridge
RICHARD
Duke of York
EDWARD IV
1461–83
RICHARD III
1483–85
EDWARD V
1483
RICHARD
Duke of
York
ELIZABETH
m.
Henry VII
JOHN OF GHENT
Duke of Lancaster
HENRY IV
1399–1413
HENRY V
1413–22
JOHN
Duke of
Bedford
HUMPHREY
Duke of
Gloucester
HENRY VI
1422–61
EDWARD
Prince of
Wales
JOHN BEAUFORT
Marquis of
Somerset
JOHN BEAUFORT
Marquis of
Somerset
MARGARET
BEAUFORT
m.
Edmund Tudor
Earl of Richmond
HENRY VII
1485–1509
m.
Elizabeth
daughter of
Edward IV
EDMUND
Duke of York
EDWARD
Duke of
York
RICHARD
Earl of
Cambridge
m.
Anne Mortimer

TABLE VII

The Valois Kings of France

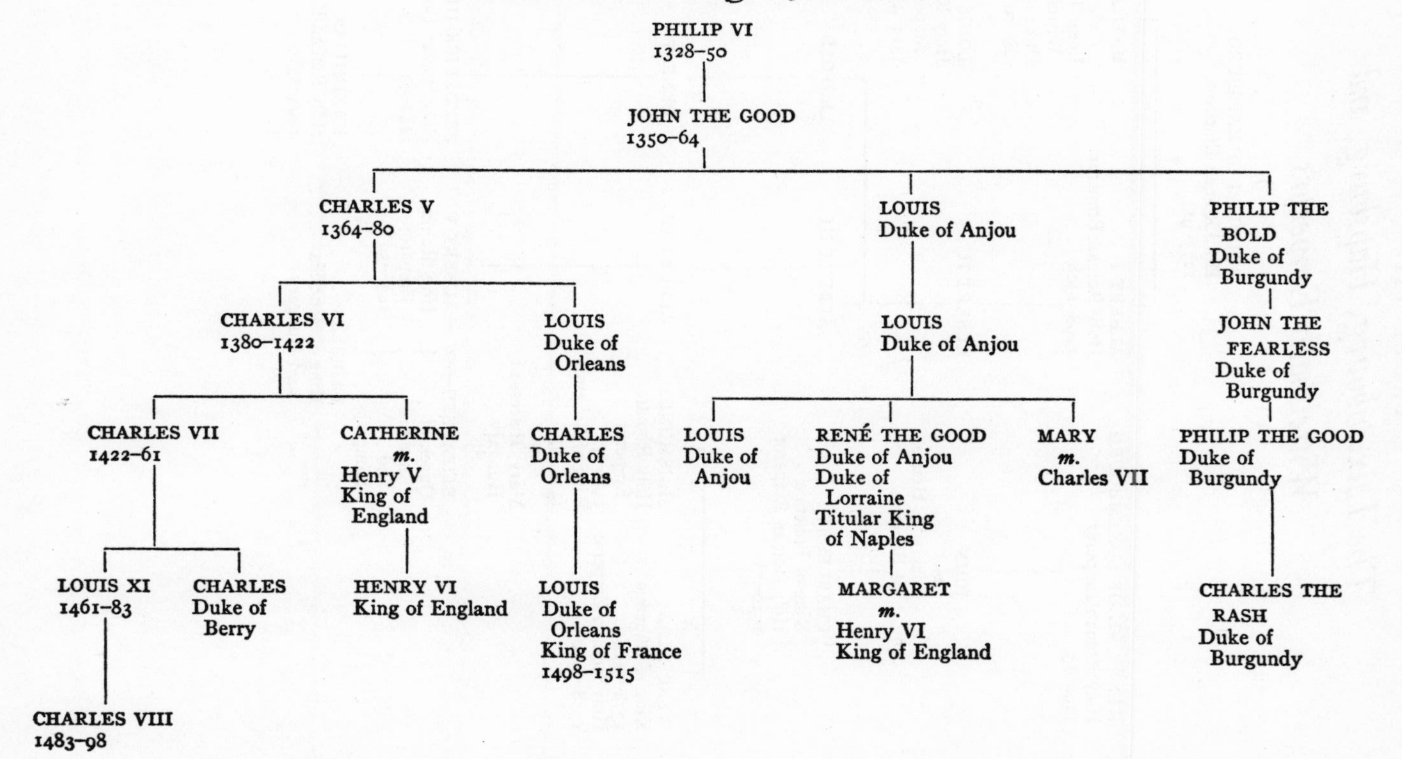

TABLE VIII

The Luxembourg, Hapsburg, and Wittelsbach Emperors

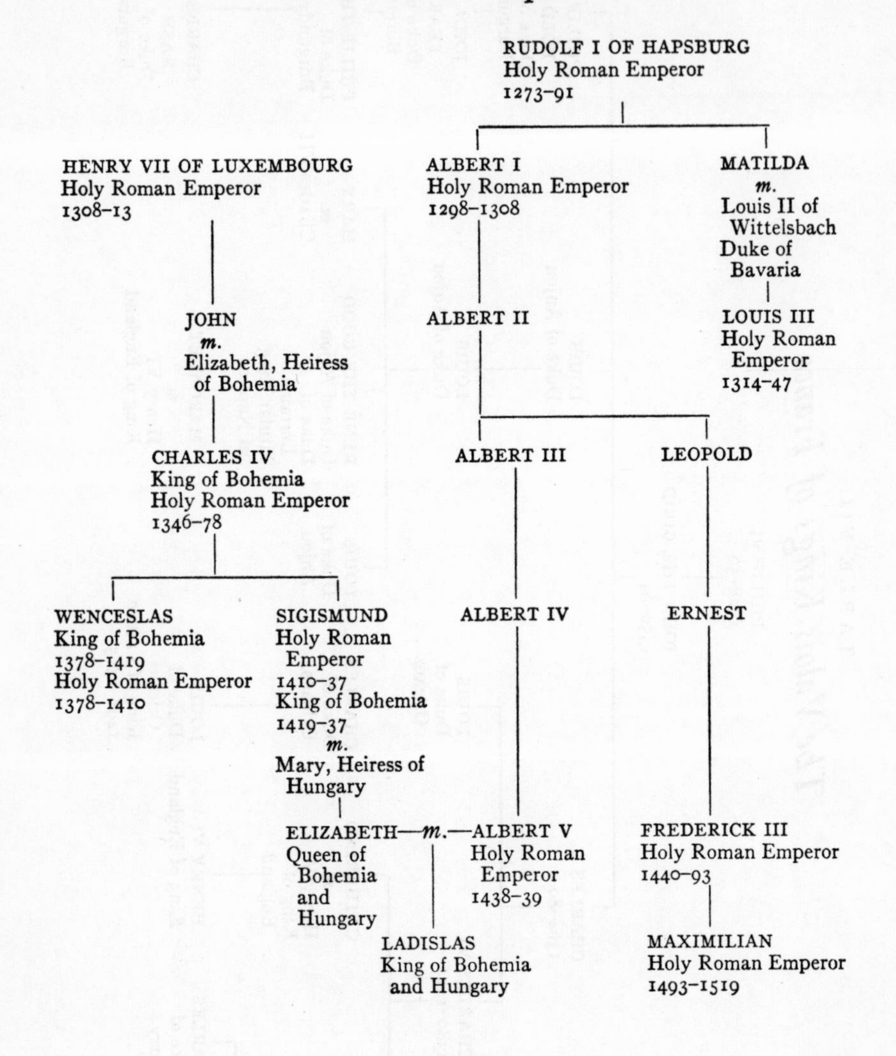
RUDOLF I OF HAPSBURG
Holy Roman Emperor
1273–91
HENRY VII OF LUXEMBOURG
Holy Roman Emperor
1308–13
ALBERT I
Holy Roman Emperor
1298–1308
MATILDA
m.
Louis II of Wittelsbach
Duke of Bavaria
JOHN
m.
Elizabeth, Heiress of Bohemia
ALBERT II
LOUIS III
Holy Roman Emperor
1314–47
CHARLES IV
King of Bohemia
Holy Roman Emperor
1346–78
ALBERT III
LEOPOLD
WENCESLAS
King of Bohemia
1378–1419
Holy Roman Emperor
1378–1410
SIGISMUND
Holy Roman Emperor
1410–37
King of Bohemia
1419–37
m.
Mary, Heiress of Hungary
ALBERT IV
ERNEST
ELIZABETH—m.—ALBERT V
Queen of Bohemia and Hungary
Holy Roman Emperor
1438–39
FREDERICK III
Holy Roman Emperor
1440–93
LADISLAS
King of Bohemia and Hungary
MAXIMILIAN
Holy Roman Emperor
1493–1519

TABLE IX

The Spanish Kings from the Tenth to the Thirteenth Century

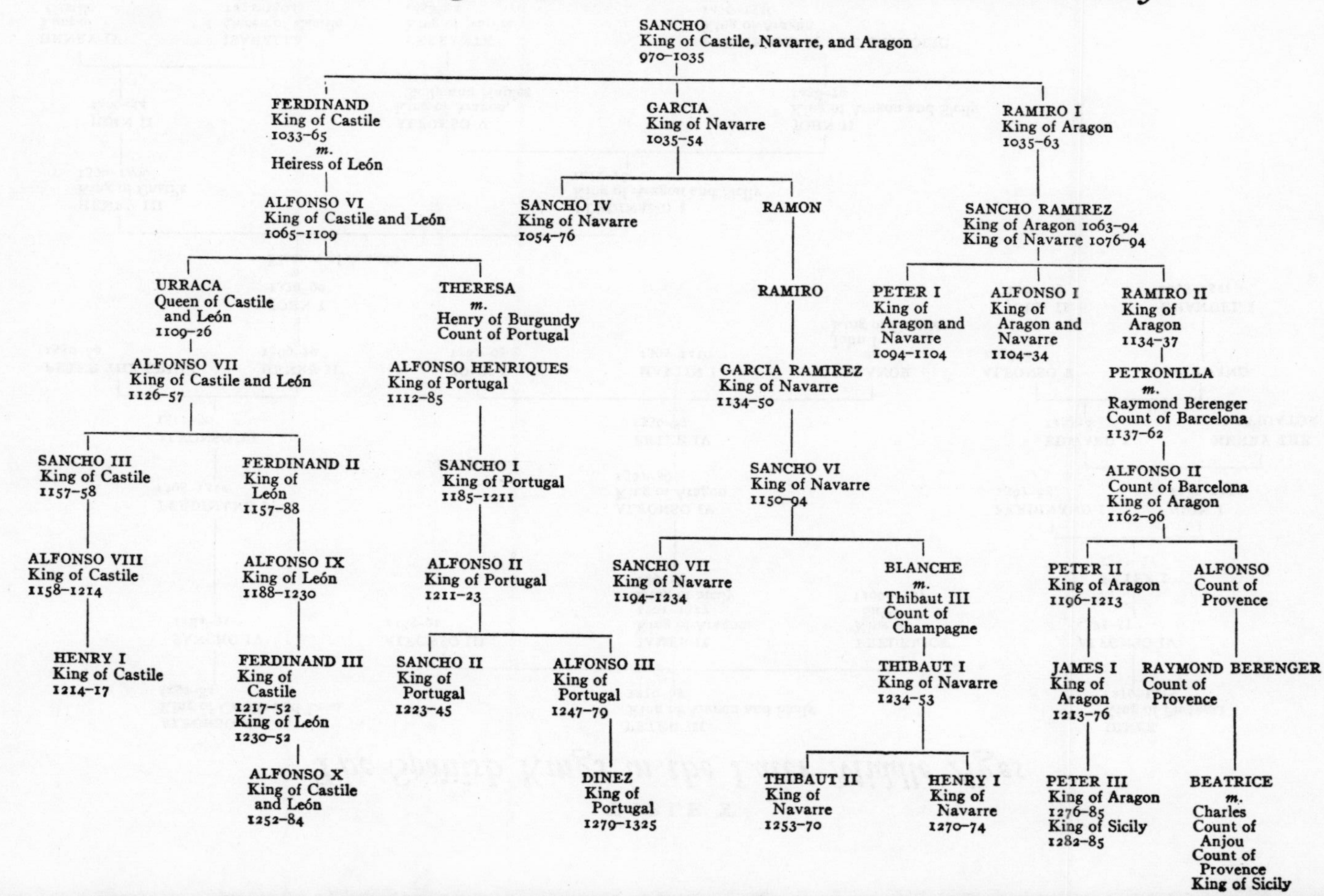

TABLE X

The Spanish Kings in the Later Middle Ages

Castile

- ALFONSO X, King of Castile and León, 1252–84
  - SANCHO IV, 1284–95
    - FERDINAND IV, 1295–1312
      - ALFONSO XI, 1312–50
        - PETER THE CRUEL, 1350–69
        - HENRY II, 1369–79
          - JOHN I, 1379–90, *m.* Eleanor of Aragon
            - HENRY III, King of Castile, 1390–1406
              - JOHN II, 1406–54
                - HENRY IV, King of Castile, 1454–74
                - ISABELLA, Queen of Castile, 1474–1504, *m.* Ferdinand, King of Aragon
            - FERDINAND I, King of Aragon and Sicily, 1412–16
              - ALFONSO V, King of Aragon, Sicily and Naples, 1416–58
                - FERRANTE, King of Naples, 1458–94
              - JOHN II, King of Aragon and Sicily, 1458–79
                - FERDINAND II THE CATHOLIC, King of Aragon, 1479–1516, *m.* Isabella, Queen of Castile

Aragon

- PETER III, King of Aragon and Sicily, 1276–85
  - ALFONSO III, 1285–91
  - JAMES II, King of Aragon, 1291–1327, King of Sicily, 1291–6
    - ALFONSO IV, King of Aragon, 1327–36
      - PETER IV, 1336–87
        - JOHN I, 1387–95
        - MARTIN I, 1395–1410
        - ELEANOR, *m.* John I, King of Castile
  - FREDERICK, King of Sicily, 1296–1337

Portugal

- DINEZ, King of Portugal, 1279–1325
  - ALFONSO IV, 1325–57
    - PETER I, 1357–67
      - FERDINAND I, 1367–83
      - JOHN I, 1385–1433
        - EDWARD I, 1433–8
          - ALFONSO V, 1438–81
            - JOHN II, 1481–95
          - FERDINAND
            - EMANUEL I, 1495–1521
        - HENRY THE NAVIGATOR

Bibliography

General

THE STANDARD large-scale scholarly account of the Middle Ages as a whole is the *Cambridge medieval history* (1911–36), 8 vols. This contains a detailed and authoritative account of almost every conceivable pertinent subject. The best one-volume history of the period is J. W. Thompson and E. M. Johnson, *An introduction to medieval Europe* (1937). Although often classed as a textbook, this work is beyond the ordinary textbook level in size and scope. The reader in search of works on special subjects should consult bibliographies. The standard work is L. J. Paetow, *Guide to the study of medieval history* (rev. ed., 1931). Gray C. Boyce, who played a large part in preparing the 1931 edition, is at work on a new revision of this study. John L. La Monte, in his *The world of the middle ages* (1949), has made a highly successful attempt to list the important books that have appeared since 1931, and his bibliography should be used until the new edition of Paetow appears. As Paetow's *Guide* does not deal with English history, a reader seeking books in that field should consult W. E. Lunt, *History of England* (1945), which contains full and well-selected bibliographies. Anyone interested in reading the works of mediaeval writers in English translations should consult C. P. Farrer and A. P. Evans, *Bibliography of English translations from medieval sources* (1946). The best historical atlas is William R. Shepherd, *Historical atlas* (1921). Excellent maps may also be found in the *Cambridge medieval history*.

CHAPTER I: *Roman and German*

The standard works on Roman history in general are the *Cambridge ancient history* (1939), Vol. XII; M. Rostovtzeff, *History of the ancient world: Rome* (1931); Tenney Frank, *History of Rome* (1923); and A. E. R. Boak, *History of Rome to 565 A.D.* An important part of the period covered in this chapter is dealt with in detail in J. B. Bury, *History of the later Roman empire from the death of Theodosius to the death of Justinian* (1923). A very useful work is S. Dill, *Roman society in the last century of the western empire* (1898). E. R. Goodenough, *The church in the Roman empire* (1931), is an excellent account of the early development of the Church. The whole process of transition from ancient to mediaeval civilization is well described in H. S. B. Moss, *The birth of the middle ages* (1935); E. Emerton, *Introduction to the middle ages* (1888); F. Lot, *The end of the ancient world and the beginning of the middle ages* (1931); and R. F. Arragon, *The transition from the ancient to the medieval world* (1936). The best general work on the invasions is J. B. Bury, *The invasions of Europe by the barbarians* (1928).

T. Hodgkin, *Italy and her invaders* (1880–99), 8 vols.; and R. H. Hodgkin, *History of the Anglo-Saxons*, give detailed accounts of the invasions into Italy and England.

CHAPTER II: *Eastern Orthodox Civilization*

The most detailed and authoritative account of the Byzantine Empire available in English is A. A. Vasiliev, *History of the Byzantine empire* (1928–29), 2 vols. Two shorter but good treatments of the subject are C. Diehl, *History of the Byzantine empire* (1925), and S. Runciman, *Byzantine civilization* (1933). Two recent specialized studies, P. Charanis, *Church and state in the later Roman empire* (1939), and J. M. Hussey, *Church and learning in the Byzantine empire* (1937), deal with important subjects. Robert Byron, *The Byzantine achievement* (1929), is an excellent work on Byzantine culture. The best work on the Moslems is P. K. Hitti, *History of the Arabs* (1946). H. A. Gibbons, *Foundation of the Ottoman empire* (1916), is the standard work on this subject. The most recent detailed accounts of the early history of Russia are G. Vernadsky, *Ancient Russia* (1944), and *Kievan Russia* (1948). Kluchevsky, *History of Russia* (1911–12), is still useful. F. Nowak, *Medieval Slavdom and the rise of Russia* (1930), approaches the subject from a somewhat different point of view.

CHAPTER III: *The Germanic Kingdoms*

H. S. B. Moss, *The birth of the middle ages* (1935), and E. Emerton, *Introduction to the middle ages* (1888), supply good surveys of the Merovingian and Carolingian periods. The best special book on the Merovingians is S. Dill, *Roman society in Gaul in the Merovingian age* (1926). There is no adequate book in English on the Carolingian empire. The standard work in French is A. Kleinclausz, *L'empire carolingien* (1902). T. Hodgkin, *Charles the Great* (1897), and H. W. C. Davis, *Charlemagne* (1899), are biographies of Charlemagne by distinguished scholars. The most recent and authoritative work on Anglo-Saxon England is Sir Frank Stenton, *Anglo-Saxon England* (1947). More detailed, but covering only part of the Anglo-Saxon period, is R. H. Hodgkin, *History of the Anglo-Saxons* (1935), 2 vols. The feudal institutions of the Carolingian period are well described in C. E. Odegaard, *Vassi and fidèles in the Carolingian empire* (1945). The Vikings and the civilization from which they came are thoroughly treated in T. D. Kendrick, *A history of the Vikings* (1930). A useful older work is A. Mawer, *The Vikings* (1913).

CHAPTER IV: *Knights and Peasants*

By far the most thorough and scholarly account of the settlement of Western Europe and the mediaeval agrarian systems is the *Cambridge economic history* (1941), Vol. I, edited by J. H. Clapham and Eileen Power. It is, however, rather heavy going for the ordinary reader. E. Lipson, *Economic history of England* (1937), Vol. I; M. M. Knight, *Economic history of Europe to the end of the middle ages* (1926); and P. Boissonade, *Life and work in medieval Europe* (1927), give briefer and more readable accounts. N. Neilson, *Medieval agrarian economy* (1936), is an excellent monograph devoted to this subject. The best description of the techniques of mediaeval agriculture is found in R. E. Prothero, *English farming past and present* (1912). Cecil Curwen, *Plough and pasture* (1946), is an extremely stimulating brief discussion of the broad lines of agricultural development. Anyone who reads French with ease should consult M. Bloch, *Les caractères originaux de l'histoire rurale française* (1931). This is a basic work that paved the way for most modern research in the field. There are two good books on village life: H. S. Bennett, *Life on the English manor* (1937), and G. C. Homans, *English villagers of the thirteenth century* (1940).

The best discussion of the feudal system in English is Carl Stephenson, *Mediaeval feudalism* (1942). F. S. Ganshof, *Feudalism* (1952), is another valuable brief study of the subject, from a somewhat different point of view. The standard modern work on feudalism is M. Bloch, *La société féodale* (1939–40), 2 vols. It is far more detailed than the books by Stephenson and Ganshof, but it is rather hard reading even for one who has a good mastery of French. Anyone interested in seeing how feudalism worked in a particular country should read Sir Frank Stenton, *The first century of English feudalism* (1932). The connection between the feudal system and the agrarian economy is shown in S. Painter, *Studies in the history of the English feudal barony* (1943), and in Edward Miller, *The abbey and bishopric of Ely* (1951). There is one book that gives an excellent picture of mediaeval rural life as a whole: W. S. Davis, *Life on a mediaeval barony* (1926). Unfortunately it was written for boys, and the tone is condescending and hence rather annoying.

CHAPTER V: *The Unification of Western Christendom*

J. A. Foakes-Jackson, *Introduction to the history of Christianity* (1921); and D. S. Schaff, *History of the Christian Church* (1907), Vol. V; are general church histories including this period. The best single volume on the subject is S. Baldwin, *The organization of medieval Christianity* (1929). Z. N. Brooke, *The English church and the papacy from the Conquest to the reign of John* (1933), shows the effects of the development of papal power on England. The standard work on the reform movement is A. Fliche, *La réforme grégorienne* (1924–37), 3 vols. A. J. MacDonald, *Hildebrand, a life of Gregory VII* (1932), and J. P. Whitney, *Hildebrandine essays* (1932), are useful books in English on the subject. By far the best book on monasticism is Dom David Knowles, *The monastic order in England* (1941). An older but still useful work is Cardinal Gasquet's *Monastic life in the middle ages* (1922). Particular phases of monasticism are excellently treated in Eileen Power, *Medieval English nunneries* (1922), and Joan Evans, *Monastic life at Cluny* (1931). J. McCann, *St. Benedict* (1937), and W. Williams, *St. Bernard of Clairvaux* (1935), are good biographies of these two monastic leaders. G. G. Coulton, *Five centuries of religion* (1923), Vol. I, is a mine of information about monasticism in this period.

CHAPTER VI: *The Development of Feudal Monarchy*

The development of feudal monarchy in both France and England is brilliantly discussed by a great scholar in C. Petit-Dutaillis, *Feudal monarchy in France and England from the tenth to the thirteenth century* (1936). F. Funck-Brentano, *The middle ages* (1923), gives a brief account of the early Capetian kings. A. Luchaire, *Les premiers Capétiens*, in Lavisse, *Histoire de France* (1911), is by far the best detailed treatment of the early Capetian period and will well repay the efforts of anyone who can read easy French. Two recent French surveys, F. Lot, *La France des origines à la guerre de cent ans* (1941), and R. Fawtier, *Les Capétiens et la France* (1942), also cover this period.

For the late Anglo-Saxon period in England Sir Frank Stenton, *Anglo-Saxon England* (1947), is the standard work. The Norman period is brilliantly covered in A. L. Poole, *From Domesday Book to Magna Carta* (1951). There are two excellent older books: G. B. Adams, *England from the Norman Conquest to the death of John* (1905), and H. W. C. Davis, *England under the Normans and Angevins* (1905). Sir Frank Stenton, *William the Conqueror* (1908), is a good biography.

The best book on the history of mediaeval Germany is G. Barraclough, *The origins of modern Germany* (1946). His *Medieval Germany* (1938), 2 vols., is a more detailed work. J. W. Thompson, *Feudal Germany* (1927), is still very useful especially for the controversy between popes and emperors and the eastward expansion of Germany.

CHAPTER VII: *The Expansion of Europe*

At present the only satisfactory detailed history of the Crusades is René Grousset, *Histoire des croisades* (1934–36), 3 vols. S. Runciman is writing a multivolume *History of the Crusades,* of which several volumes have appeared. A large-scale cooperative history of the Crusades is being written under the direction of a committee of editors headed by Kenneth Setton, and two volumes should appear during 1953. As this is the work of scholars from many nations, it should be the standard authoritative treatment of the subject. R. A. Newhall, *The crusades* (1927), is a useful brief account. A. C. Krey, *The first crusade* (1921), is the work of an expert in the field. There are a number of good biographies of leaders of the First Crusade: J. C. Andressohn, *Ancestry and life of Godfrey de Bouillon* (1947); Marshall Baldwin, *Raymond III of Tripolis* (1936); R. B. Yewdale, *Bohemond I of Antioch* (1924); and R. Nicholson, *Tancred* (1940). On the Latin kingdom one should consult D. C. Munro, *The kingdom of the crusaders* (1935), and John L. La Monte, *Feudal monarchy in the Latin kingdom of Jerusalem.*

For Spain the best work is still R. Merriman, *Rise of the Spanish empire* (1918). A more recent book on part of the region is H. J. Chaytor, *History of Aragon and Catalonia* (1933). A brilliant brief account of the Norman conquest of Sicily will be found in C. H. Haskins, *The Normans in European history* (1915). Fuller treatments are J. W. Osborne, *The greatest Norman conquest* (1937), and E. Curtis, *Roger of Sicily and the Normans in lower Italy* (1912).

CHAPTER VIII: *The Revival of Urban Life*

The standard authoritative work on commerce and industry in the Middle Ages is the *Cambridge economic history*, Vol. II, which was published at the end of 1953. The general works on economic history have sections devoted to these subjects: H. Pirenne, *Economic and social history of Europe* (1936); H. Heaton, *Economic history of Europe* (1936); M. M. Knight, *Economic history of Europe to the end of the middle ages* (1926); E. Lipson, *Economic history of England* (1937), Vol. I; and P. Boissonade, *Life and work in medieval Europe* (1927). H. Pirenne, *Mediaeval cities* (1925), is a brilliant brief account of urban development. Although Carl Stephenson, *Borough and town* (1933), is chiefly concerned with England, it has a valuable chapter on continental towns. F. Schevill, *History of Florence* (1936), and W. F. Butler, *The Lombard communes* (1906), are valuable for the Italian towns. F. W. Hill, *Medieval Lincoln* (1948), is an excellent descriptive account of a mediaeval town. R. A. De Roover, *The Medici bank, its organization, management, operations, and decline* (1948), is a brilliant study of early banking; and Eileen Power, *The wool trade in English medieval history* (1942), is an equally effective discussion of an important phase of mediaeval commerce.

CHAPTER IX: *The Feudal Monarchies*

C. Petit-Dutaillis, *Feudal monarchy in France and England from the tenth to the thirteenth century* (1936), covers this period as well as the earlier one. An outstanding work on France is A. Luchaire, *Social France in the time of Philip Augustus* (1912). This is one of the great books on mediaeval history and a model account of a king's reign. S. Painter, *The scourge of the clergy, Peter of Dreux, duke of Brittany* (1937), gives a picture of French feudal politics. F. Funck-Brentano, *The middle ages* (1923), supplies a brief but excellent account of this period. In addition most of the books on England contain a good deal of information about France as well.

The general histories mentioned under Chapter VI cover this period of English history: A. L. Poole, *From Domesday Book to Magna Carta* (2nd ed., 1955); G. B. Adams, *History of England from the Norman Conquest to the death of John* (1905); and H. W. C. Davis, *England under the Normans and Angevins* (1905). T. F. Tout, *History of England from the accession of Henry III to the death of Edward III* (1905), follows G. B. Adams in the same series and covers the period indicated. Sir Maurice Powicke, *The thirteenth century* (2nd ed., 1962), in the "Oxford Series", is the authoritative work on the reigns of Henry III and Edward I. Kate Norgate has written a series of books on this period: *England under the Angevin kings* (1887), 2 vols.; *Richard the Lion Heart* (1924); and *John Lackland*. Although lacking imagination and interpretation, they are useful factual accounts. The reigns of John and Henry III are covered by two recent works: S. Painter, *The reign of King John* (1949), and Sir Maurice Powicke, *Henry III and the Lord Edward* (1947). Useful biographies are L. F. Salzman, *Henry II* (1914); S. Painter, *William Marshal, knight-errant, baron, and regent of England* (1933); Sir Maurice Powicke, *Stephen Langton* (1928); and C. Bemont, *Simon de Montfort*, translated and revised by E. F. Jacob (1930). R. F. Treharne, *The baronial plan of reform, 1256-1263* (1932), is a valuable work on that significant subject.

For the Holy Roman Empire, G. Barraclough, *The origins of modern Germany* (1946), is much the best work. J. W. Thompson, *Feudal Germany* (1927), covers this period, but his interpretation of it is not generally accepted today. There are two good biographies in English: A. L. Poole, *Henry the Lion* (1912), and E. Kantorowicz, *Frederick II* (1931).

CHAPTER X: *Mediaeval Theocracy at its Height*

D. S. Schaff, *History of the Christian church* (1907), Vol. V, covers this period as well as the earlier one. The best work on the specific period is S. Packard, *Europe and the church under Innocent III* (1927). W. E. Lunt, *Papal revenues in the middle ages* (1934), 2 vols., is an extremely valuable work on papal finances and financial machinery. Sir Maurice Powicke, *Stephen Langton* (1928), supplies a valuable insight into ecclesiastical politics and policies. H. D. Sedgwick, *Italy in the thirteenth century* (1928), is useful for Innocent III. An extremely illuminating book on the early heresies is E. S. Davison, *Forerunners of St. Francis* (1927). The second volume of G. G. Coulton, *Five centuries of religion* (1927), tells a great deal about contemporary monasticism and the friars. A. Jessop, *The coming of the friars* (1928), is a useful book on the early friars, as is R. F. Bennet, *The early Dominicans* (1927). Lives of the founders of the two orders of friars are B. Jarrett, *Life of Saint Dominic* (1924), and Paul Sabatier, *Life of St. Francis of Assisi,* translated by Louise S. Houghton (1922).

CHAPTER XI: *The Hundred Years' War*

The only satisfactory book on the Hundred Years' War as a whole is Edouard Perroy, *The Hundred Years War*, translated by W. B. Wells with an introduction by David C. Douglas (1951). There are several useful works on military history. The most recent and authoritative is F. Lot, *L'art militaire et les armées au moyen âge* (1946). C. Oman, *A history of the art of war in the middle ages* (1923), 2 vols., is still very useful, but many of Oman's ideas are no longer generally accepted. For a detailed study of the development of the English army and tactics that won so many battles in the Hundred Years' War the reader should consult John E. Morris, *The Welsh wars of Edward I* (1901). Richard A. Newhall, *The English conquest of Normandy, 1416–1424* (1924), is an excellent account of that phase of the war.

CHAPTER XII: *From Feudal to National Monarchy*

The volumes of the "Oxford Series" covering the later Middle Ages have not yet been announced. The standard books are C. Oman, *History of England from the accession of Richard II to the death of Richard III* (1906), and K. H. Vickers, *England in the later middle ages* (1914). G. M. Trevelyan, *England in the age of Wycliffe* (1909), is a brilliant summary of English society in the late fourteenth century. C. L. Kingsford, *Henry V* (1901), is a good biography, as is K. H. Vickers, *Humphrey, duke of Gloucester* (1907). R. B. Mowat, *Wars of the Roses* (1914), is a good brief account of the civil wars.

F. Funck-Brentano, *The middle ages* (1923), continues to be a convenient brief account. Edouard Perroy, *The Hundred Years War* (1951), gives a good summary of French history during the period. The years after the close of the war are ably treated in P. Champion, *Louis XI,* translated by Winifred S. Whale (1929). A. Cartellieri, *The court of Burgundy* (1929), gives an excellent account of the environment of the Burgundian dukes. A. B. Kerr, *Jacques Coeur* (1928), is a good biography. For all the various phases of the history of this period one should consult J. Huizinga, *The waning of the middle ages* (1924).

CHAPTER XIII: *The Decline of the Mediaeval Church*

Here too, D. S. Schaff, *History of the Christian church* (1907), Vol. V, gives a general account. More concentrated on this period are L. E. Binns, *The decline and fall of the medieval papacy* (1934), and A. Flick, *The decline of the medieval church* (1930), 2 vols. T. S. R. Boase, *Boniface VIII* (1933), is a good account of that papal reign. M. Spinka, *John Hus and the Czech reform* (1933), and H. B. Workman, *John Wyclif* (1926), describe the careers of the two chief heretics of the age. E. F. Jacob, *Essays on the conciliar epoch* (1943), and J. H. Wylie, *The Council of Constance* (1900), are valuable for the conciliar movement. W. E. Lunt, *Papal revenues in the middle ages* (1934), 2 vols., is particularly important for an understanding of the problems facing the Avignon popes.

CHAPTER XIV: *Mediaeval Civilization*

The standard book on the intellectual history of the Middle Ages is H. O. Taylor, *The medieval mind* (1927), 2 vols. Frederick B. Artz, *The mind of the middle ages* (1952), is the best recent book on mediaeval ideas. Other valuable works on intellectual history are E. K. Rand, *The founders of the middle ages* (1928), C. H. Haskins, *The Renaissance of the twelfth century* (1927), G. C. Crump and E. F. Jacob, *The legacy of the middle ages* (1926); and F. J. C. Hearnshaw, *Medieval contributions to modern civilization* (1921). The fullest and best treatment of mediaeval philosophy is found in M. de Wulf, *History of medieval philosophy*, English translation by E. C. Messenger (1925–26), 2 vols. The subject is treated more briefly in A. C. McGiffert, *History of Christian thought* (1932), 2 vols. E. Gilson has written two valuable books, *The spirit of medieval philosophy* (1930), and *Reason and revelation in the middle ages* (1938). A very useful and stimulating brief work on an important subject is Meyrick H. Carré, *Realists and nominalists* (1942). The basic book on mediaeval political theory is R. W. Carlyle and A. J. Carlyle, *A history of medieval political theory in the west* (1903–36), 8 vols. C. H. McIlwain, *Growth of political thought in the west* (1932), has important and stimulating chapters on the Middle Ages. The best, in fact the only thorough, book on historical literature is J. W. Thompson, *History of historical writing* (1942), 2 vols. The standard work on mediaeval science is L. Thorndike, *History of magic and experimental science* (1923–40), 6 vols. C. H. Haskins, *Studies in mediaeval science* (1924), is a useful collection of essays. L. C. MacKinney, *Early medieval medicine* (1937), is a valuable brief treatment of this subject.

The *Cambridge history of English literature* (1903), vol. I, supplies the best general account of mediaeval literature in England. Gaston Paris, *Medieval French literature* (1903), and Urban T. Holmes, Jr., *A history of old French literature from the origins to 1300* (1948), cover French literature. W. A. Craigie, *The Icelandic sagas* (1913), is the standard English work on that subject. W. P. Ker, *Epic and romance* (1908), is a general summary of mediaeval romantic literature. There are two excellent books on mediaeval Latin poetry: Helen Waddell, *Medieval Latin lyrics* (1929), and J. A. Symonds, *Wine, women, and song* (1884). Chivalric literature is dealt with in C. S. Lewis, *The allegory of love* (1936); R. L. Kilgour, *The decline of chivalry* (1937); and S. Painter, *French chivalry* (1940).

The standard history of mediaeval architecture is A. K. Porter, *Medieval architecture: its origins and development* (rev. ed., 1912), 2 vols. K. J. Conant, *Early mediaeval church architecture* (1942), is a stimulating brief treatment of this subject. C. R. Morey has written two valuable books on art: *Christian art* (1935), and *Medieval art* (1942).

The standard history of mediaeval universities is H. Rashdall, *The universities of Europe in the middle ages*, rev. ed. by Sir Maurice Powicke and A. B. Emden (1936), 3 vols. C. H. Haskins, *The rise of the universities* (1923), is an excellent brief study.

CHAPTER XXV Medieval Civilization

The standard book on the intellectual history of the Middle Ages is H. O. Taylor, *The mediaeval mind* (1925), 2 vols. Frederick B. Artz, *The mind of the middle ages* (1953), is the best recent book on medieval ideas. Other valuable works on intellectual history are E. K. Rand, *The founders of the middle ages* (1928), C. H. Haskins, *The Renaissance of the twelfth century* (1927), and C. G. Crump and E. F. Jacob, *The legacy of the middle ages* (1926), and F. J. C. Hearnshaw, *Mediaeval contributions to modern civilisation* (1921). The fullest and best treatment of medieval philosophy is found in Maurice de Wulf, *History of mediaeval philosophy*, English translation by E. C. Messenger (1926–38), 3 vols. The subject is treated more briefly in A. C. McGiffert, *History of Christian thought* (1932–33), 2 vols. É. Gilson has written two valuable books, *The spirit of mediaeval philosophy* (1936), and *Reason and revelation in the middle ages* (1938). A very fresh and stimulating brief work on an important subject is Meyrick H. Carré, *Realists and nominalists* (1946). The basic book on medieval political theory is R. W. Carlyle and A. J. Carlyle, *A history of mediaeval political theory in the west* (1903–36), 6 vols. C. H. McIlwain, *Growth of political thought in the west* (1932), has an important and stimulating chapter on the Middle Ages. The best, in fact the only thorough, book on historical literature is J. W. Thompson, *History of historical writing* (1942), 2 vols. The standard work on medieval science is L. Thorndike, *History of magic and experimental science* (1923–58), 8 vols. C. H. Haskins, *Studies in mediaeval science* (1924), is a useful collection of essays. L. C. MacKinney, *Early medieval medicine* (1937), is a valuable brief treatment of this subject.

The *Cambridge history of English literature* (1907), vol. I, supplies the best general account of medieval literature in England. Gaston Paris, *Mediaeval French literature* (1903), and Urban T. Holmes, Jr., *A history of old French literature from the origins to 1300* (1937), cover French literature. W. A. Craigie, *The Icelandic sagas* (1913), is the standard English work on that subject. W. P. Ker, *Epic and romance* (1908), is a general summary of medieval romantic literature. There are two excellent works on medieval Latin poetry—Helen Waddell, *Mediaeval Latin lyrics* (1929), and J. A. Symonds, *Wine, women, and song* (1884). Chivalric literature is dealt with in C. S. Lewis, *The allegory of love* (1936), R. L. Kilgour, *The decline of chivalry* (1937), and Sidney Painter, *French chivalry* (1940).

The standard history of medieval architecture is A. K. Porter, *Medieval architecture, its origins and development* (1909), 2 vols. K. J. Conant, *Early medieval church architecture* (1942), is a stimulating brief treatment of the subject. C. R. Morey has written two valuable books on art: *Christian art* (1935), and *Medieval art* (1942).

The standard history of medieval universities is H. Rashdall, *The universities of Europe in the middle ages*, revised by F. M. Powicke and A. B. Emden (1936), 3 vols. C. H. Haskins, *The rise of the universities* (1923), is an excellent brief essay.

Index

A Note

ON THE TYPE IN WHICH THIS BOOK IS SET

This book was set on the Linotype in Janson, a recutting made direct from the type cast from matrices (now in possession of the Stempel foundry, Frankfurt am Main) made by Anton Janson some time between 1660 and 1687.

Of Janson's origin nothing is known. He may have been a relative of Justus Janson, a printer of Danish birth who practised in Leipzig from 1614 to 1635. Some time between 1657 and 1668 Anton Janson, a punch-cutter and type-founder, bought from the Leipzig printer Johann Erich Hahn the type-foundry which had formerly been a part of the printing house of M. Friedrich Lankisch. Janson's types were first shown in a specimen sheet issued at Leipzig about 1675. Janson's successor, and perhaps his son-in-law, Johann Karl Edling, issued a specimen sheet of Janson types in 1689. His heirs sold the Janson matrices in Holland to Wolffgang Dietrich Erhardt.

The book was [illegible], printed, and bound by KINGSPORT PRESS, INC., Kingsport, Tennessee, and has been reproduced in Great Britain by photolithography by LOWE AND BRYDONE (PRINTERS) LTD. LONDON.

A Note

ON THE TYPE IN WHICH THIS BOOK IS SET

This book was set on the Linotype in JANSON, *a recutting made direct from the type cast from matrices (now in possession of the Stempel foundry, Frankfurt am Main) made by Anton Janson some time between 1660 and 1687.*

Of Janson's origin nothing is known. He may have been a relative of Justus Janson, a printer of Danish birth who practised in Leipzig from 1614 to 1635. Some time between 1657 and 1668 Anton Janson, a punch-cutter and type-founder, bought from the Leipzig printer Johann Erich Hahn the type-foundry which had formerly been a part of the printing house of M. Friedrich Lankisch. Janson's types were first shown in a specimen sheet issued at Leipzig about 1675. Janson's successor, and perhaps his son-in-law, Johann Karl Edling, issued a specimen sheet of Janson types in 1689. His heirs sold the Janson matrices in Holland to Wolffgang Dietrich Erhardt.

The book was first composed, printed, and bound by KINGSPORT PRESS, INC., *Kingsport, Tennessee, and has been reprinted in Great Britain by photolithography by* LOWE AND BRYDONE (PRINTERS) LTD, *London.*
